# PLAY...
# CRICKET...
# 1981

## 34th edition

### EDITED BY GORDON ROSS

*Statistics by Michael Fordham and Barry McCaully*

*Front cover: Geoffrey Boycott. Photo: Colorsport*

# Twin blade winner.

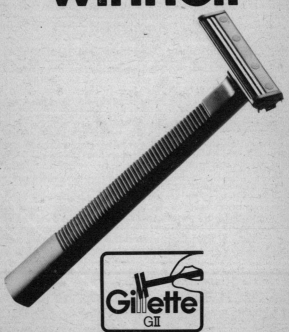

# WHERE FROM HERE?

## by Gordon Ross

During the last year, the game of cricket has presented a less attractive face to the world at large. Once, it was thought to be the very model of the way sport should be played – hard on the field, but a camaraderie off it which continued long after the stumps had been drawn. Spectators, too, had a code of behaviour symptomatic with the environment. Admittedly, there has been a radical change in social behaviour world-wide, and it is difficult for sport to divorce itself from that change. But, having said that, the new situation throws an immense responsibility on the shoulders of the governing bodies to do all in their power to preserve some sort of decorum in the conduct of sport and sportsmen. When the situation has reached the point where a cricketer throws a brick at a spectator, then firm control becomes absolutely vital. Equally disturbing and distasteful were the scenes at Lord's during the Centenary Test against Australia when the captains and umpires were assaulted in what has always been regarded as a sanctuary – the Members' Pavilion. MCC were swift to set up an enquiry and in due course issued a statement that appropriate action had been taken against the proven offenders, though they did not stipulate what that appropriate action was. We can only assume that the punishment fitted the crime.

The Centenary Test was a huge success as a meeting ground for generations of English and Australian cricketers. Purely as a cricket match it was ruined by the weather – a great shame for so many enthusiasts who had come from far and wide, and, of course, for Cornhill, who have given such a fillip to Test cricket with their generous sponsorship. This rain-ruined game, which ended in an honourable draw, did at least provide a distinguished milestone for Geoff Boycott. His 128 not out in the second innings (his 19th Test century) took his Test runs beyond 7,000, a figure only previously exceeded by Hammond, Cowdrey and Sobers. Only Cowdrey, who played in 114 Tests, has played in more than Boycott, whose Centenary Test match was his 94th.

The weather also cut deep inroads into the five-match Test series between England and West Indies. After West Indies had won the first Test at Trent Bridge by the narrow margin of two

3

wickets, rain disrupted the other four and prevented a decisive finish being achieved in any of them, leaving West Indies winners of the series by the only game completed. The series was still not without it's share of brilliant cricket and excitement, not least the dramatic climax to the Fourth Test at The Oval when West Indies were poised for victory on the last day to be thwarted in the end by cricket's greatest attraction—a last-wicket partnership. Willey (100 not out) and Willis (24 not out) added 117 when England were 92 for nine. For once the battery of West Indies fast bowlers was held at bay. This was only the third 10th-wicket century stand for England – Foster and Rhodes in 1903-04, and Higgs and Snow in 1966. Botham took his 150th Test wicket in this, his 29th Test, exactly three years since his debut, a truly remarkable performance.

Although it has always been said that the three-day County Championship is the one that really counts (except in the number of spectators), there was more than ever interest in the Gillette Cup in 1980, for it was to be the last. Cricket is indeed fortunate to find such a successor to Gillette as National Westminster Bank, whose sponsorship over a five-year period is index-linked, and in the first year is worth £250,000. As if to show that a good team is indifferent to whether it is playing one-day or three-day cricket, Middlesex won both the Schweppes County Championship and the Gillette Cup. Rarely, at any time, did Middlesex look like not winning the Gillette Cup, except, ironically, for about ten minutes in a match at Lord's against Ireland, competing in the competition for the first time. In 1981, Ireland will be making cricket history when they play Gloucestershire in Dublin in a first-round game in the National Westminster Bank Trophy on 11 July. The cricket world may give them precious little chance, but then they gave Durham little chance against Yorkshire, Lincolnshire little chance against Glamorgan and Hertfordshire little chance against Essex.

The Schweppes County Championship (now limited to a total of twenty-two matches per county, whereas there was a time when some counties played over thirty) turned out to be an all-London affair, as with the Gillette Cup. Middlesex and Surrey ran away from the rest of the field to such an extent that Surrey led Notts, who were in third place, by 67 points. Some counties will argue that they spent just about as much time in the pavilion watching rain as they did on the field of play, and this may well be true, but then cricket always has been swings and roundabouts when plagued, as it is so often, by weather. Middlesex were indebted to some fine performances by their South African pace bowler, Van der Bijl, and will certainly miss him this summer as he is not planning to return to this country. The irrepressible Robin Jackman scaled new heights with Surrey, aided by Sylvester Clarke from Barbados.

The connoisseurs, at the beginning, had every reason for believing that Essex would figure prominently in the season's honours. They had won both the Schweppes County Championship and the Benson and Hedges Cup in 1979, after years of trials and tribulations had brought them many disappointing failures. But 1980 was to be failure again, though their players may still be asking themselves how on earth they were beaten in the final of the Benson and Hedges, or by Surrey at Chelmsford in the Gillette Cup. It seemed totally out of keeping to find Hampshire at the foot of the Championship table though they were without their two West Indian Test players. They managed only one Championship victory. There must be better times ahead, especially if Hampshire take Warwickshire as their inspiration. In 1979 Warwickshire were at the bottom of the John Player League. They lost thirteen matches out of sixteen, and won only two. When in the early part of the 1980 season they were at the top of the table, few took this position seriously, and fully expected them to falter as the bigger guns began to overhaul them. But they never did. Warwickshire remained at the top to the bitter end and were John Player League champions – and deservedly so.

As we look towards this summer of 1981 we have the question of floodlit cricket in our minds. The match on Chelsea's football ground on 15 August between Essex (originally this was Surrey's idea, but they were involved elsewhere when it came to it) and West Indies attracted a useful crowd, but watching endless sixes being banged on a short boundary is no night out for genuine lovers of the game. It is just fascinating that association football is seeking the help of cricket, when so many of us were told years ago that cricket was dead. It has turned out to be an interesting corpse!

## EVENTS IN THE WEST INDIES

As this Annual went to press at the beginning of March, it was not going to be possible to report fully on the ill-fated tour, so rather than record events in two years of *Playfair* it was decided to leave reporting of the whole until 1982.

# Pakistan v Australia 1979-80

## FIRST TEST MATCH

**PLAYED AT KARACHI, 27, 28, 29 FEBRUARY, 2 MARCH**

**PAKISTAN WON BY 7 WICKETS**

### AUSTRALIA

| | | | |
|---|---:|---|---:|
| B.M. Laird lbw b Imran | 6 | c Miandad b Qasim | 23 |
| G.N. Yallop c Taslim b Tausif | 12 | c Majid b Qasim | 16 |
| K.J. Hughes c Majid b Tausif | 85 | st Taslim b Tausif | 8 |
| *G.S. Chappell st Taslim b Qasim | 20 | c Taslim b Tausif | 13 |
| D.W. Hookes c Majid b Qasim | 0 | lbw b Qasim | 0 |
| A.R. Border lbw b Qasim | 30 | not out | 58 |
| †R.W. Marsh c Haroon b Tausif | 13 | c Mudassar b Qasim | 1 |
| G.R. Beard b Imran | 9 | b Qasim | 4 |
| R.J. Bright c Majid b Qasim | 15 | c Majid b Qasim | 0 |
| D.K. Lillee not out | 12 | lbw b Qasim | 5 |
| G. Dymock c Wasim b Tausif | 3 | b Tausif | 0 |
| Extras (B8, LB9, NB3) | 20 | (B4, LB5, W1, NB2) | 12 |
| **Total** | **225** | | **140** |

### PAKISTAN

| | | | |
|---|---:|---|---:|
| †Taslim Arif c Marsh b Bright | 58 | b Bright | 8 |
| Haroon Rashid b Bright | 6 | b Bright | 10 |
| Zaheer Abbas c Lillee b Bright | 8 | not out | 18 |
| *Javed Miandad c Border b Chappell | 40 | b Bright | 21 |
| Wasim Raja c sub (Lawson) b Chappell | 0 | not out | 12 |
| Majid Khan c Border b Bright | 89 | | |
| Mudassar Nazar c Border b Bright | 29 | | |
| Imran Khan c Border b Chappell | 9 | | |
| Sarfraz Nawaz c Chappell b Bright | 17 | | |
| Iqbal Qasim not out | 14 | | |
| Tausif Ahmed b Bright | 0 | | |
| Extras (LB12, NB10) | 22 | (LB3, NB4) | 7 |
| **Total** | **292** | **(3 wkts)** | **76** |

### BOWLING

| PAKISTAN | O | M | R | W | | O | M | R | W | FALL OF WICKETS | | | |
|---|---|---|---|---|---|---|---|---|---|---|---|---|---|
| | | | | | | | | | | | A | P | A | P |
| Imran | 16 | 4 | 28 | 2 | — | | | | | | 1st | 1st | 2nd | 2nd |
| Sarfraz | 13 | 4 | 20 | 0 | — | 7 | 2 | 7 | 0 | 1st | 8 | 34 | 38 | 17 |
| Mudassar | 2 | 0 | 6 | 0 | — | 2 | 0 | 4 | 0 | 2nd | 39 | 44 | 51 | 26 |
| Qasim | 30 | 12 | 69 | 4 | —42 | 22 | 49 | 7 | 3rd | 93 | 120 | 52 | 60 |
| Tausif | 30.2 | 9 | 64 | 4 | —34 | 11 | 62 | 3 | 4th | 93 | 121 | 59 | — |
| Wasim | 2 | 0 | 5 | 0 | — | 4 | 1 | 6 | 0 | 5th | 161 | 134 | 89 | — |
| Majid | 2 | 0 | 13 | 0 | — | 1 | 1 | 0 | 0 | 6th | 177 | 210 | 90 | — |
| **AUSTRALIA** | | | | | | | | | | 7th | 181 | 238 | 106 | — |
| Lillee | 28 | 4 | 76 | 0 | —11 | 2 | 22 | 0 | 8th | 199 | 266 | 108 | — |
| Dymock | 5 | 2 | 5 | 0 | — | 2 | 0 | 9 | 0 | 9th | 216 | 292 | 139 | — |
| Bright | 46.5 | 17 | 87 | 7 | —11 | 5 | 24 | 3 | 10th | 225 | 292 | 140 | — |
| Beard | 17 | 8 | 39 | 0 | — 1.1 | 0 | 14 | 0 | | | | | |
| Chappell | 20 | 3 | 49 | 3 | | | | | | | | | | |
| Yallop | 2 | 0 | 14 | 0 | | | | | | | | | | |

# SECOND TEST MATCH

## PLAYED AT FAISALABAD, 6, 7, 8, 10, 11, MARCH
### MATCH DRAWN
#### AUSTRALIA

| | |
|---|---|
| J.M. Wiener b Ehteshamuddin | 5 |
| B.M. Laird c Tasim b Sarfraz | 0 |
| K.J. Hughes c Ehteshamuddin b Tausif | 88 |
| *G.S. Chappell lbw b Sarfraz | 235 |
| G.N. Yallop b Wasim | 172 |
| A.R. Border run out | 4 |
| †R.W. Marsh lbw b Tausif | 71 |
| G.R. Beard c Sarfraz b Tausif | 13 |
| R.J. Bright b Wasim | 5 |
| D.K. Lillee lbw b Wasim | 0 |
| G. Dymock not out | 0 |
| Extras (B11, LB10, NB3) | 24 |
| **Total** | **617** |

#### PAKISTAN

| | |
|---|---|
| †Taslim Arif not out | 210 |
| Haroon Rashid lbw b Dymock | 21 |
| Zaheer Abbas run out | 19 |
| *Javed Miandad not out | 106 |
| Wasim Raja | |
| Majid Khan | |
| Mudassar Nazar | |
| Sarfraz Nawaz | |
| Iqbal Qasim | |
| Ehteshamuddin | |
| Tausif Ahmed | |
| Extras (B7, LB4, NB15) | 26 |
| **Total (2 wkts)** | **382** |

## BOWLING

| PAKISTAN | O | M | R | W | | FALL OF WICKETS | | |
|---|---|---|---|---|---|---|---|---|
| | | | | | | | A | P |
| Sarfraz | 49 | 13 | 119 | 2 | — | | 1st | 1st |
| Ehteshamuddin | 18 | 2 | 59 | 1 | — | | | |
| Qasim | 56 | 11 | 156 | 0 | — | 1st | 1 | 87 |
| Tausif | 33 | 3 | 77 | 3 | — | 2nd | 21 | 159 |
| Wasim | 30 | 5 | 100 | 3 | — | 3rd | 200 | — |
| Majid | 22 | 2 | 66 | 0 | — | 4th | 417 | — |
| Miandad | 3 | 0 | 16 | 0 | — | 5th | 434 | — |
| **AUSTRALIA** | | | | | | 6th | 561 | — |
| Lillee | 21 | 4 | 91 | 0 | — | 7th | 585 | — |
| Dymock | 20 | 5 | 49 | 1 | — | 8th | 592 | — |
| Bright | 33 | 9 | 71 | 0 | — | 9th | 612 | — |
| Border | 3 | 2 | 3 | 0 | — | 10th | 617 | — |
| Beard | 15 | 4 | 30 | 0 | — | | | |
| Hughes | 8 | 1 | 19 | 0 | — | | | |
| Laird | 2 | 1 | 3 | 0 | — | | | |
| Chappell | 6 | 3 | 5 | 0 | — | | | |
| Wiener | 5 | 1 | 19 | 0 | — | | | |
| Marsh | 10 | 1 | 51 | 0 | — | Note: Chappell kept wicket after tea |
| Yallop | 3 | 0 | 15 | 0 | — | on the last day while Marsh bowled. |

7

# THIRD TEST MATCH

### PLAYED AT LAHORE, 18, 19, 21, 22, 23, MARCH
### MATCH DRAWN
### AUSTRALIA

| | | | | |
|---|---|--:|---|--:|
| J.M. Wiener | b Qasim | 93 | c Mudassar b Imran | 4 |
| B.M. Laird | b Tausif | 17 | c Taslim b Tausif | 63 |
| K.J. Hughes | b Qasim | 1 | c Qasim b Imran | 0 |
| *G.S. Chappell | lbw b Imran | 56 | b Qasim | 57 |
| G.N. Yallop | lbw b Qasim | 3 | c & b Wasim | 34 |
| A.R. Border | not out | 150 | st Miandad b Azhar | 153 |
| †R.W. Marsh | b Qasim | 8 | run out | 13 |
| G.R. Beard | lbw b Imran | 39 | c sub (Sultan Rana) b Taslim | 49 |
| R.J. Bright | not out | 26 | not out | 10 |
| D.K. Lillee | | | not out | 1 |
| G. Dymock | | | | |
| Extras | (B4, LB6, NB4) | 14 | (LB4, NB3) | 7 |
| **Total** | (7 wkts dec) | 407 | (8 wkts) | 391 |

### PAKISTAN

| | | |
|---|---|--:|
| Mudassar Nazar | c Yallop b Lillee | 59 |
| †Taslim Arif | c Marsh b Bright | 31 |
| Iqbal Qasim | c Marsh b Lillee | 5 |
| Azmat Rana | c Chappell b Beard | 49 |
| *Javed Miandad | c Marsh b Bright | 14 |
| Wasim Raja | c Border b Lillee | 55 |
| Majid Khan | not out | 110 |
| Azhar Khan | b Bright | 14 |
| Imran Khan | c Chappell b Bright | 56 |
| Sarfraz Nawaz | st Marsh b Bright | 5 |
| Tausif Ahmed | | |
| Extras | (LB4, W1, NB17) | 22 |
| **Total** | (9 wkts dec) | 420 |

## BOWLING

| PAKISTAN | O | M | R | W | | O | M | R | W | FALL OF WICKETS | | | |
|---|--:|--:|--:|--:|---|--:|--:|--:|--:|---|--:|--:|--:|
| | | | | | | | | | | | *A* | *P* | *A* |
| Imran | 28 | 7 | 86 | 2 | — | 12 | 3 | 30 | 2 | | *1st* | *1st* | *2nd* |
| Sarfraz | 28 | 6 | 67 | 0 | — | 14 | 5 | 42 | 0 | 1st | 50 | 37 | 4 |
| Mudassar | 6 | 1 | 16 | 0 | — | 2 | 0 | 20 | 0 | 2nd | 53 | 53 | 7 |
| Qasim | 39 | 10 | 90 | 4 | — | 34 | 8 | 111 | 1 | 3rd | 136 | 133 | 115 |
| Tausif | 21 | 3 | 81 | 1 | — | 26 | 3 | 72 | 1 | 4th | 153 | 161 | 149 |
| Wasim | 14 | 3 | 45 | 0 | — | 9 | 1 | 42 | 1 | 5th | 204 | 177 | 192 |
| Azhar | 2 | 1 | 1 | 0 | — | 1 | 0 | 1 | 1 | 6th | 218 | 270 | 223 |
| Miandad | 2 | 0 | 5 | 0 | — | 4 | 0 | 14 | 0 | 7th | 298 | 299 | 357 |
| Majid | 2 | 0 | 2 | 0 | — | 9 | 3 | 24 | 0 | 8th | — | 410 | 390 |
| Taslim | | | | | — | 5 | 0 | 28 | 1 | 9th | — | 420 | — |
| **AUSTRALIA** | | | | | | | | | | 10th | — | — | — |
| Lillee | 42 | 9 | 114 | 3 | — | | | | | | | | |
| Dymock | 24 | 6 | 66 | 0 | — | | | | | | | | |
| Bright | 56 | 14 | 172 | 5 | — | | | | | | | | |
| Beard | 10 | 5 | 26 | 1 | — | | | | | | | | |

In Australia's 2nd innings Miandad kept wicket when Taslim bowled.

# New Zealand v West Indies 1979-80

## FIRST TEST MATCH

**PLAYED AT DUNEDIN, 8, 9, 10, 12, 13, FEBRUARY**
**NEW ZEALAND WON BY 1 WICKET**

### WEST INDIES

| | | | | |
|---|---|--:|---|--:|
| C.G. Greenidge | c Cairns b Hadlee | 2 | lbw b Hadlee | 3 |
| D.L. Haynes | c & b Cairns | 55 | c Webb b Troup | 105 |
| L.G. Rowe | lbw b Hadlee | 1 | lbw b Hadlee | 12 |
| A.I Kallicharran | lbw b Hadlee | 0 | c Cairns b Troup | 0 |
| *C.H. Lloyd | lbw b Hadlee | 24 | c Lees b Hadlee | 5 |
| C.L. King | c Coney b Troup | 14 | c Broock b Cairns | 41 |
| †D.L. Murray | c Edgar b Troup | 6 | lbw b Hadlee | 30 |
| D.R. Parry | b Broock | 17 | c & b Hadlee | 1 |
| J. Garner | c Howarth b Cairns | 0 | b Hadlee | 2 |
| M.A. Holding | lbw b Hadlee | 4 | c Cairns b Troup | 3 |
| C.E.H. Croft | not out | 0 | not out | 1 |
| Extras | (LB8, NB9) | 17 | (LB4, NB5) | 9 |
| **Total** | | **140** | | **212** |

### NEW ZEALAND

| | | | | |
|---|---|--:|---|--:|
| J.G. Wright | b Holding | 21 | b Holding | 11 |
| B.A. Edgar | lbw b Parry | 65 | c Greenidge b Holding | 6 |
| *G.P. Howarth | c Murray b Croft | 33 | c Greenidge b Croft | 11 |
| J.M. Parker | b Croft | 0 | c Murray b Garner | 5 |
| P.N. Webb | lbw b Parry | 5 | lbw b Garner | 5 |
| J.V. Coney | b Holding | 8 | lbw b Croft | 2 |
| †W.K. Lees | run out | 18 | lbw b Garner | 0 |
| R.J. Hadlee | c Lloyd b Garner | 51 | b Garner | 17 |
| B.L. Cairns | b Croft | 30 | c Murray b Holding | 19 |
| G.B. Troup | c Greenidge b Croft | 0 | not out | 7 |
| S.L. Boock | not out | 0 | not out | 2 |
| Extras | (B5, LB2, NB11) | 18 | (B7, LB5, NB7) | 19 |
| **Total** | | **249** | **(9 wkts)** | **104** |

### BOWLING

| NEW ZEALAND | O | M | R | W | | O | M | R | W |
|---|--:|--:|--:|--:|---|--:|--:|--:|--:|
| Hadlee | 20 | 9 | 34 | 5 | — 36 | 13 | 68 | 6 |
| Troup | 17 | 6 | 26 | 2 | — 36.4 | 13 | 57 | 3 |
| Cairns | 15 | 5 | 32 | 2 | — 25 | 10 | 63 | 1 |
| Boock | 13 | 4 | 31 | 1 | — 11 | 4 | 15 | 0 |
| **WEST INDIES** | | | | | | | | |
| Holding | 22 | 5 | 50 | 2 | — 16 | 7 | 24 | 3 |
| Croft | 25 | 3 | 64 | 4 | — 11 | 2 | 25 | 2 |
| Garner | 25.5 | 8 | 51 | 1 | — 23 | 6 | 36 | 4 |
| King | 1 | 0 | 3 | 0 | | | | |
| Parry | 22 | 6 | 63 | 2 | | | | |

### FALL OF WICKETS

| | WI 1st | NZ 1st | WI 2nd | NZ 2nd |
|---|--:|--:|--:|--:|
| 1st | 3 | 42 | 4 | 15 |
| 2nd | 4 | 109 | 21 | 28 |
| 3rd | 4 | 110 | 24 | 40 |
| 4th | 72 | 133 | 29 | 44 |
| 5th | 91 | 145 | 116 | 44 |
| 6th | 105 | 159 | 180 | 44 |
| 7th | 124 | 168 | 186 | 54 |
| 8th | 125 | 222 | 188 | 73 |
| 9th | 136 | 236 | 209 | 100 |
| 10th | 140 | 249 | 212 | — |

# SECOND TEST MATCH

## WEST INDIES

| | | | |
|---|---:|---|---:|
| C.G. Greenidge c Boock b Troup | 91 | c Lees b Troup | 97 |
| D.L. Haynes c Parker b Hadlee | 0 | c Cairns b Coney | 122 |
| L.G. Rowe lbw b Cairns | 11 | c Boock b Howarth | 100 |
| C.L. King b Cairns | 0 | not out | 100 |
| A.I. Kallicharran c Wright b Cairns | 75 | c Lees b Troup | 0 |
| *C.H. Lloyd c Howarth b Cairns | 14 | b Boock | 7 |
| †D.L. Murray c Webb b Cairns | 6 | not out | 1 |
| J. Garner c sub (McEwan) b Cairns | 0 | | |
| C.E.H. Croft b Hadlee | 0 | | |
| A.M.E. Roberts not out | 17 | | |
| M.A. Holding lbw b Hadlee | 0 | | |
| Extras (B1, LB9, NB4) | 14 | (B5, LB8, W1, NB6) | 20 |
| **Total** | **228** | | **447** |

## NEW ZEALAND

| | |
|---|---:|
| J.G. Wright b Croft | 5 |
| B.A. Edgar c Murray b Holding | 21 |
| P.N. Webb b Roberts | 1 |
| *G.P. Howarth b Holding | 147 |
| J.M. Parker b Garner | 42 |
| J.V. Coney c King b Roberts | 80 |
| †W.K. Lees c Rowe b Garner | 3 |
| R.J. Hadlee b Kallicharran | 103 |
| B.L. Cairns run out | 1 |
| G.B. Troup not out | 13 |
| S.L. Boock c & b Kallicharran | 6 |
| Extras (B18, LB6, NB14) | 38 |
| **Total** | **460** |

## BOWLING

| NEW ZEALAND | O | M | R | W | | O | M | R | W | FALL OF WICKETS | | | |
|---|---:|---:|---:|---:|---|---:|---:|---:|---:|---|---:|---:|---:|
| | | | | | | | | | | | *WI* | *NZ* | *WI* |
| Hadlee | 23.3 | 5 | 58 | 3 | — | 22 | 7 | 64 | 0 | | *1st* | *1st* | *2nd* |
| Troup | 21 | 7 | 38 | 1 | — | 27 | 7 | 84 | 2 | 1st | 1 | 15 | 225 |
| Cairns | 32 | 8 | 85 | 6 | — | 28 | 8 | 107 | 0 | 2nd | 28 | 18 | 233 |
| Coney | 13 | 2 | 33 | 0 | — | 19 | 2 | 71 | 1 | 3rd | 28 | 53 | 234 |
| Boock | | | | | — | 18 | 3 | 69 | 1 | 4th | 190 | 175 | 268 |
| Howarth | | | | | — | 5 | 0 | 32 | 1 | 5th | 190 | 267 | 436 |
| **WEST INDIES** | | | | | | | | | | 6th | 210 | 292 | — |
| Roberts | 29 | 6 | 82 | 2 | — | | | | | 7th | 210 | 390 | — |
| Holding | 29 | 5 | 97 | 2 | — | | | | | 8th | 214 | 404 | — |
| Garner | 28 | 4 | 75 | 2 | — | | | | | 9th | 224 | 448 | — |
| Croft | 24 | 3 | 78 | 1 | — | | | | | 10th | 228 | 460 | — |
| King | 9 | 0 | 70 | 0 | — | | | | | | | | |
| Kallicharran | 6.4 | 1 | 16 | 2 | — | | | | | | | | |
| Rowe | 5 | 2 | 4 | 0 | — | | | | | | | | |

# THIRD TEST MATCH
## PLAYED AT AUCKLAND, 1, 2, 3, 4, 5, MARCH
## MATCH DRAWN

### WEST INDIES

| | | | |
|---|---|---|---|
| C.G. Greenidge c McEwan b Hadlee | 7 | c Lees b Cairns | 74 |
| D.L. Haynes c Edgar b Cairns | 9 | b Troup | 48 |
| L.G. Rowe run out | 50 | c Lees b Troup | 5 |
| A.I. Kallicharran c Cairns b Troup | 46 | lbw b Troup | 25 |
| *C.H. Lloyd c Wright b Troup | 11 | c Lees b Troup | 42 |
| C.L. King c Troup b Hadlee | 23 | c Howarth b Troup | 9 |
| †D.L. Murray c Lees b Hadlee | 16 | lbw b Cairns | 7 |
| A.M.E. Roberts not out | 35 | c McEwan b Troup | 26 |
| J. Garner b Troup | 3 | b Hadlee | 7 |
| M.A. Holding lbw b Hadlee | 5 | not out | 16 |
| C.E.H. Croft b Troup | 6 | | |
| Extras (B1, LB7, NB1) | 9 | (B1, LB2, NB2) | 5 |
| **Total** | **220** | **(9 wkts dec)** | **264** |

### NEW ZEALAND

| | | | |
|---|---|---|---|
| J.G. Wright c Greenidge b Croft | 23 | c Haynes b Kallicharran | 23 |
| B.A. Edgar b Roberts | 127 | not out | 22 |
| *G.P. Howarth c Haynes b Croft | 47 | run out | 1 |
| P.E. McEwan b Croft | 5 | b Garner | 21 |
| J.M. Parker lbw b Garner | 0 | run out | 1 |
| J.V. Coney not out | 49 | not out | 1 |
| †W.K. Lees b Garner | 23 | | |
| R.J. Hadlee c Murray b Garner | 7 | | |
| B.L. Cairns c Murray b Garner | 1 | | |
| G.B. Troup b Garner | 0 | | |
| S.L. Boock lbw b Garner | 0 | | |
| Extras (B4, LB8, NB11) | 23 | (LB3, NB1) | 4 |
| **Total** | **305** | **(4 wkts)** | **73** |

### BOWLING

| NEW ZEALAND | O | M | R | W | | O | M | R | W | FALL OF WICKETS | | | |
|---|---|---|---|---|---|---|---|---|---|---|---|---|---|
| | | | | | | | | | | | WI | NZ | WI | NZ |
| Hadlee | 31 | 8 | 75 | 4 | — | 29 | 8 | 62 | 1 | | 1st | 1st | 2nd | 2nd |
| Troup | 31.2 | 11 | 71 | 4 | — | 29.1 | 5 | 95 | 6 | 1st | 10 | 75 | 86 | 4 |
| Cairns | 20 | 9 | 56 | 1 | — | 30 | 7 | 76 | 2 | 2nd | 36 | 171 | 92 | 30 |
| Boock | 2 | 0 | 9 | 0 | — | 6 | 1 | 26 | 0 | 3rd | 116 | 185 | 137 | 32 |
| WEST INDIES | | | | | | | | | | 4th | 116 | 186 | 147 | 71 |
| Roberts | 34 | 6 | 90 | 1 | — | 9 | 2 | 24 | 0 | 5th | 146 | 241 | 169 | — |
| Holding | 33 | 3 | 54 | 0 | — | 4 | 1 | 11 | 0 | 6th | 167 | 277 | 193 | — |
| Croft | 33 | 6 | 81 | 3 | — | 10 | 4 | 17 | 0 | 7th | 169 | 299 | 228 | — |
| Garner | 36.2 | 15 | 56 | 6 | — | 9 | 1 | 17 | 1 | 8th | 178 | 303 | 239 | — |
| King | 2 | 1 | 1 | 0 | | | | | | | | | | |
| Kallicharran | | | | | — | 4 | 4 | 0 | 1 | | | | | |

11

# England v West Indies 1980

## FIRST CORNHILL TEST MATCH

### PLAYED AT TRENT BRIDGE, 5, 6, 7, 9, 10, JUNE
### WEST INDIES WON BY 2 WICKETS

#### ENGLAND

| | | | | |
|---|---|--:|---|--:|
| G.A. Gooch | c Murray b Roberts | 17 | run out | 27 |
| G. Boycott | c Murray b Garner | 36 | b Roberts | 75 |
| C.J. Tavaré | b Garner | 13 | c Richards b Garner | 4 |
| R.A. Woolmer | c Murray b Roberts | 46 | c Murray b Roberts | 29 |
| D.I. Gower | c Greenidge b Roberts | 20 | lbw b Garner | 1 |
| *I.T. Botham | c Richards b Garner | 57 | c Richards b Roberts | 4 |
| P. Willey | b Marshall | 13 | b Marshall | 38 |
| †A.P.E. Knott | lbw b Roberts | 6 | lbw b Marshall | 7 |
| J.K. Lever | c Richards b Holding | 15 | c Murray b Garner | 4 |
| R.G.D. Willis | b Roberts | 8 | b Garner | 9 |
| M. Hendrick | not out | 7 | not out | 2 |
| Extras | (B7, LB11, NB4, W3) | 25 | (B20, LB12, NB10, W10) | 52 |
| **Total** | | **263** | | **252** |

#### WEST INDIES

| | | | | |
|---|---|--:|---|--:|
| C.G. Greenidge | c Knott b Hendrick | 53 | c Knott b Willis | 6 |
| D.L. Haynes | c Gower b Willis | 12 | run out | 62 |
| I.V.A. Richards | c Knott b Willis | 64 | lbw b Botham | 48 |
| S.F.A. Bacchus | b Willis | 30 | c Knott b Hendrick | 19 |
| A.I. Kallicharran | b Botham | 17 | c Knott b Willis | 9 |
| †D.L. Murray | b Willis | 64 | c Hendrick b Willis | 16 |
| *C.H. Lloyd | c Knott b Lever | 9 | lbw b Willis | 3 |
| M.D. Marshall | c Tavaré b Gooch | 20 | b Willis | 7 |
| A.M.E. Roberts | lbw b Botham | 21 | not out | 22 |
| J. Garner | c Lever b Botham | 2 | | |
| M.A. Holding | not out | 0 | not out | 0 |
| Extras | (B1, LB9, NB4, W2) | 16 | (LB8, NB9) | 17 |
| **Total** | | **308** | (8 wkts) | **209** |

### BOWLING

| WEST INDIES | O | M | R | W | | O | M | R | W | FALL OF WICKETS | | | |
|---|--:|--:|--:|--:|---|--:|--:|--:|--:|---|--:|--:|--:|
| | | | | | | | | | | | E | WI | E | WI |
| Roberts | 25 | 7 | 72 | 5 | — | 24 | 6 | 57 | 3 | | | | | |
| Holding | 23.5 | 7 | 61 | 1 | — | 26 | 5 | 65 | 0 | | *1st* | *1st* | *2nd* | *2nd* |
| Marshall | 19 | 3 | 52 | 1 | — | 24 | 8 | 44 | 2 | 1st | 27 | 19 | 46 | 11 |
| Richards | 1 | 0 | 9 | 0 | — | | | | | 2nd | 72 | 107 | 68 | 69 |
| Garner | 23 | 9 | 44 | 3 | — | 34.1 | 20 | 30 | 4 | 3rd | 74 | 151 | 174 | 109 |
| Greenidge | | | | | — | 3 | 2 | 4 | 0 | 4th | 114 | 165 | 175 | 125 |
| **ENGLAND** | | | | | | | | | | 5th | 204 | 186 | 180 | 129 |
| Willis | 20.1 | 5 | 82 | 4. | — | 26 | 4 | 65 | 5 | 6th | 208 | 227 | 183 | 165 |
| Lever | 20 | 5 | 76 | 1 | — | 8 | 2 | 25 | 0 | 7th | 228 | 265 | 218 | 180 |
| Hendrick | 19 | 4 | 69 | 1 | — | 14 | 5 | 40 | 1 | 8th | 246 | 306 | 237 | 205 |
| Willey | 5 | 3 | 4 | 0 | — | 2 | 0 | 12 | 0 | 9th | 254 | 308 | 248 | — |
| Botham | 20 | 6 | 50 | 3 | — | 16.4 | 6 | 48 | 1 | 10th | 263 | 308 | 252 | — |
| Gooch | 7 | 2 | 11 | 1 | — | 2 | 1 | 20 | 0 | | | | | |

# SECOND CORNHILL TEST MATCH

## PLAYED AT LORD'S, 19, 20, 21, 23, 24 JUNE

### MATCH DRAWN

#### ENGLAND

| | | | | |
|---|---|---:|---|---:|
| G.A. Gooch | lbw b Holding | 123 | b Garner | 47 |
| G. Boycott | c Murray b Holding | 8 | not out | 49 |
| C.J. Tavaré | c Greenidge b Holding | 42 | lbw b Garner | 6 |
| R.A. Woolmer | c Kallicharran b Garner | 15 | not out | 19 |
| M.W. Gatting | b Holding | 18 | | |
| *I.T. Botham | lbw b Garner | 8 | | |
| D.L. Underwood | lbw b Garner | 3 | | |
| P. Willey | b Holding | 4 | | |
| †A.P.E. Knott | c Garner b Holding | 9 | | |
| R.G.D. Willis | b Garner | 14 | | |
| M. Hendrick | not out | 10 | | |
| Extras | (B4, LB1, NB6, W4) | 15 | (B1, NB11) | 12 |
| **Total** | | **269** | (2 wkts) | **133** |

#### WEST INDIES

| | | |
|---|---|---:|
| C.G. Greenidge | lbw b Botham | 25 |
| D.L. Haynes | lbw b Botham | 184 |
| I.V.A. Richards | c sub (Dilley) b Willey | 145 |
| C.E.H. Croft | run out | 0 |
| A.I. Kallicharran | c Knott b Willis | 15 |
| S.F.A. Bacchus | c Gooch b Willis | 0 |
| *C.H. Lloyd | b Willey | 56 |
| †D.L. Murray | c Tavaré b Botham | 34 |
| A.M.E. Roberts | b Underwood | 24 |
| J. Garner | c Gooch b Willis | 15 |
| M.A. Holding | not out | 0 |
| Extras | (B1, LB9, NB9, W1) | 20 |
| **Total** | | **518** |

### BOWLING

| WEST INDIES | O | M | R | W | | O | M | R | W |
|---|---:|---:|---:|---:|---|---:|---:|---:|---:|
| Roberts | 18 | 3 | 50 | 0 | — | 13 | 3 | 24 | 0 |
| Holding | 28 | 11 | 67 | 6 | — | 15 | 5 | 51 | 0 |
| Garner | 24.3 | 8 | 36 | 4 | — | 15 | 6 | 21 | 2 |
| Croft | 20 | 3 | 77 | 0 | — | 8 | 2 | 24 | 0 |
| Richards | 5 | 1 | 24 | 0 | — | 1 | 0 | 1 | 0 |
| **ENGLAND** | | | | | | | | | |
| Willis | 31 | 12 | 103 | 3 | — | | | | |
| Botham | 37 | 7 | 145 | 3 | — | | | | |
| Underwood | 29.2 | 4 | 108 | 1 | — | | | | |
| Hendrick | 11 | 2 | 32 | 0 | — | | | | |
| Gooch | 7 | 1 | 26 | 0 | — | | | | |
| Willey | 25 | 8 | 73 | 2 | — | | | | |
| Boycott | 7 | 2 | 11 | 0 | — | | | | |

#### FALL OF WICKETS

| | E | WI | E |
|---|---:|---:|---:|
| | 1st | 1st | 2nd |
| 1st | 20 | 37 | 71 |
| 2nd | 165 | 260 | 96 |
| 3rd | 190 | 275 | — |
| 4th | 219 | 326 | — |
| 5th | 220 | 330 | — |
| 6th | 231 | 437 | — |
| 7th | 232 | 469 | — |
| 8th | 244 | 486 | — |
| 9th | 245 | 518 | — |
| 10th | 269 | 518 | — |

# THIRD CORNHILL TEST MATCH

## PLAYED AT OLD TRAFFORD, 10, 11, 12, 14, 15 JULY
### MATCH DRAWN

### ENGLAND

| | | | | |
|---|---|---|---|---|
| G. Boycott c Garner b Roberts | 5 | lbw b Holding | 86 |
| G.A. Gooch lbw b Roberts | 2 | c Murray b Marshall | 26 |
| B.C. Rose b Marshall | 70 | c Kallicharran b Holding | 32 |
| W. Larkins lbw b Garner | 11 | c Murray b Marshall | 33 |
| M.W. Gatting c Richards b Marshall | 33 | c Kallicharran b Garner | 56 |
| *I.T. Botham c Murray b Garner | 8 | lbw b Holding | 35 |
| P. Willey b Marshall | 0 | not out | 62 |
| †A.P.E. Knott run out | 2 | c & b Garner | 6 |
| J.E. Emburey c Murray b Roberts | 3 | not out | 28 |
| G.R. Dilley b Garner | 0 | | |
| R.G.D. Willis not out | 5 | | |
| Extras (LB4, NB4, W3) | 11 | (B5, LB8, NB13, W1) | 27 |
| **Total** | **150** | (7 wkts) | **391** |

### WEST INDIES

| | |
|---|---|
| C.G. Greenidge c Larkins b Dilley | 0 |
| D.L. Haynes c Knott b Willis | 1 |
| I.V.A. Richards b Botham | 65 |
| S.F.A. Bacchus c Botham b Dilley | 0 |
| A.I. Kallicharran c Knott b Botham | 13 |
| *C.H. Lloyd c Gooch b Emburey | 101 |
| †D.L. Murray b Botham | 17 |
| M.D. Marshall c Gooch b Dilley | 18 |
| A.M.E. Roberts c Knott b Emburey | 11 |
| J. Garner lbw b Emburey | 0 |
| M.A. Holding not out | 4 |
| Extras (B2, LB13, NB12, W3) | 30 |
| **Total** | **260** |

### BOWLING

| WEST INDIES | O | M | R | W | | O | M | R | W | FALL OF WICKETS | | | |
|---|---|---|---|---|---|---|---|---|---|---|---|---|---|
| | | | | | | | | | | | E | WI | E |
| Roberts | 11.2 | 3 | 23 | 3 | — | 14 | 2 | 36 | 0 | | 1st | 1st | 2nd |
| Holding | 14 | 2 | 46 | 0 | — | 34 | 8 | 100 | 3 | 1st | 3 | 4 | 32 |
| Garner | 11 | 4 | 34 | 3 | — | 40 | 11 | 73 | 2 | 2nd | 18 | 25 | 86 |
| Marshall | 12 | 5 | 36 | 3 | — | 35 | 5 | 116 | 2 | 3rd | 35 | 25 | 181 |
| Richards | | | | | — | 16 | 6 | 31 | 0 | 4th | 126 | 67 | 217 |
| Lloyd | | | | | — | 1 | 0 | 1 | 0 | 5th | 130 | 100 | 290 |
| Bacchus | | | | | — | 1 | 0 | 3 | 0 | 6th | 132 | 154 | 290 |
| Haynes | | | | | — | 1 | 0 | 2 | 0 | 7th | 142 | 209 | 309 |
| Kallicharran | | | | | — | 1 | 0 | 2 | 0 | 8th | 142 | 250 | — |
| ENGLAND | | | | | | | | | | 9th | 142 | 250 | — |
| Willis | 14 | 1 | 99 | 1 | — | | | | | 10th | 150 | 260 | — |
| Dilley | 28 | 7 | 47 | 3 | — | | | | | | | | |
| Botham | 20 | 6 | 64 | 3 | — | | | | | | | | |
| Emburey | 10.3 | 1 | 20 | 3 | — | | | | | | | | |

# FOURTH CORNHILL TEST MATCH

### PLAYED AT THE OVAL, 24, 25, 26, 28, 29 JULY
### MATCH DRAWN

## ENGLAND

| | | | |
|---|---|---|---|
| G.A. Gooch lbw b Holding | 83 | lbw b Holding | 0 |
| G. Boycott run out | 53 | c Murray b Croft | 5 |
| B.C. Rose b Croft | 50 | lbw b Garner | 41 |
| W. Larkins lbw b Garner | 7 | b Holding | 0 |
| M.W. Gatting b Croft | 48 | c Murray b Garner | 15 |
| P. Willey c Lloyd b Holding | 34 | not out | 100 |
| †A.P.E. Knott c Lloyd b Marshall | 3 | lbw b Holding | 3 |
| *I.T. Botham lbw b Croft | 9 | c Greenidge b Garner | 4 |
| J.E. Emburey b Holding b Marshall | 24 | c Bacchus b Croft | 2 |
| G.R. Dilley b Garner | 1 | c sub b Holding | 1 |
| R.G.D. Willis not out | 1 | not out | 24 |
| Extras (B7, LB21, NB19, W10) | 57 | (LB6, NB7, W1) | 14 |
| **Total** | 370 | (9 wkts, dec) | 209 |

## WEST INDIES

| | |
|---|---|
| C.G. Greenidge lbw b Willis | 6 |
| D.L. Haynes c Gooch b Dilley | 7 |
| I.V.A. Richards c Willey b Botham | 26 |
| S.F.A. Bacchus c Knott b Emburey | 61 |
| A.I. Kallicharran c Rose b Dilley | 11 |
| †D.L. Murray hit wkt b Dilley | 0 |
| M.D. Marshall c Rose b Emburey | 45 |
| J. Garner c Gatting b Botham | 46 |
| M.A. Holding lbw b Dilley | 22 |
| C.E.H. Croft not out | 0 |
| *C.H. Lloyd absent hurt | 0 |
| Extras (LB12, NB28, W1) | 41 |
| **Total** | 265 |

## BOWLING

| WEST INDIES | O | M | R | W | | O | M | R | W | FALL OF WICKETS | | | |
|---|---|---|---|---|---|---|---|---|---|---|---|---|---|
| | | | | | | | | | | | E | WI | E |
| Holding | 28 | 5 | 67 | 2 | — | 29 | 7 | 79 | 4 | | 1st | 1st | 2nd |
| Croft | 35 | 9 | 97 | 3 | — | 10 | 6 | 8 | 2 | 1st | 155 | 15 | 2 |
| Marshall | 29.3 | 6 | 77 | 2 | — | 23 | 7 | 47 | 0 | 2nd | 157 | 34 | 10 |
| Garner | 33 | 8 | 67 | 2 | — | 17 | 5 | 24 | 3 | 3rd | 182 | 72 | 13 |
| Richards | 3 | 1 | 5 | 0 | — | 9 | 3 | 15 | 0 | 4th | 269 | 99 | 18 |
| Kallicharran | | | | | — | 6 | 1 | 22 | 0 | 5th | 303 | 105 | 63 |
| ENGLAND | | | | | | | | | | 6th | 312 | 187 | 67 |
| Willis | 19 | 5 | 58 | 1 | — | | | | | 7th | 336 | 197 | 73 |
| Dilley | 23 | 6 | 57 | 4 | — | | | | | 8th | 343 | 261 | 84 |
| Botham | 18.2 | 8 | 47 | 2 | — | | | | | 9th | 368 | 265 | 92 |
| Emburey | 23 | 12 | 38 | 2 | — | | | | | 10th | 370 | — | — |
| Gooch | 1 | 0 | 2 | 0 | — | | | | | | | | |
| Willey | 11 | 5 | 22 | 0 | — | | | | | | | | |

# FIFTH CORNHILL TEST MATCH

## PLAYED AT HEADINGLEY, 7, 8, 9, 11, 12 AUGUST

### MATCH DRAWN

### ENGLAND

| | | | |
|---|---|---|---|
| G.A. Gooch c Marshall b Garner | 14 | lbw b Marshall | 55 |
| G. Boycott c Kallicharran b Holding | 4 | c Kallicharran b Croft | 47 |
| B.C. Rose b Croft | 7 | not out | 43 |
| W. Larkins c Kallicharran b Garner | 9 | lbw b Marshall | 30 |
| M.W. Gatting c Marshall b Croft | 1 | lbw b Holding | 1 |
| *I.T. Botham c Richards b Holding | 37 | lbw b Marshall | 7 |
| P. Willey c Murray b Croft | 1 | c Murray b Holding | 10 |
| †D.L. Bairstow lbw b Marshall | 40 | not out | 9 |
| J.E. Emburey not out | 13 | | |
| C.M. Old c Garner b Marshall | 6 | | |
| G.R. Dilley b Garner | 0 | | |
| Extras (B3, LB3, NB4, W1) | 11 | (B5, LB11, NB7, W2) | 25 |
| **Total** | **143** | **(6 wkts)** | **227** |

### WEST INDIES

| | |
|---|---|
| C.G. Greenidge lbw b Botham | 34 |
| D.L. Haynes b Emburey | 42 |
| *I.V.A. Richards b Old | 31 |
| S.F.A. Bacchus c & b Dilley | 11 |
| A.I. Kallicharran c Larkins b Dilley | 37 |
| C.L. King c Bairstow b Gooch | 12 |
| †D.L. Murray c Emburey b Dilley | 14 |
| M.D. Marshall c Bairstow b Dilley | 0 |
| J. Garner c Emburey b Gooch | 0 |
| M.A. Holding b Old | 35 |
| C.E.H. Croft not out | 1 |
| Extras (B2, LB9, NB14, W3) | 28 |
| **Total** | **245** |

### BOWLING

| WEST INDIES | O | M | R | W | | O | M | R | W | FALL OF WICKETS | | | |
|---|---|---|---|---|---|---|---|---|---|---|---|---|---|
| | | | | | | | | | | | E | WI | E |
| Holding | 10 | 4 | 34 | 2 | — | 23 | 2 | 62 | 2 | | *1st* | *1st* | *2nd* |
| Croft | 12 | 3 | 35 | 3 | — | 19 | 2 | 65 | 1 | 1st | 9 | 83 | 95 |
| Garner | 14 | 4 | 41 | 3 | — | 1 | 0 | 1 | 0 | 2nd | 27 | 105 | 126 |
| Marshall | 11 | 3 | 22 | 2 | — | 19 | 5 | 42 | 3 | 3rd | 28 | 133 | 129 |
| King | | | | | — | 12 | 3 | 32 | 0 | 4th | 34 | 142 | 162 |
| Richards | | | | | — | 1 | 1 | 0 | 0 | 5th | 52 | 170 | 174 |
| **ENGLAND** | | | | | | | | | | 6th | 59 | 196 | 203 |
| Dilley | 23 | 6 | 79 | 4 | — | | | | | 7th | 89 | 198 | — |
| Old | 28.5 | 9 | 64 | 2 | — | | | | | 8th | 131 | 207 | — |
| Botham | 19 | 8 | 31 | 1 | — | | | | | 9th | 140 | 207 | — |
| Emburey | 6 | 0 | 25 | 1 | — | | | | | 10th | 143 | 245 | — |
| Gooch | 8 | 3 | 18 | 2 | — | | | | | | | | |

# TEST MATCH AVERAGES

## ENGLAND–BATTING AND FIELDING

| | M | I | NO | Runs | HS | Avge | 100 | 50 | Ct | St |
|---|---|---|---|---|---|---|---|---|---|---|
| B.C. Rose | 3 | 6 | 1 | 243 | 70 | 48.60 | — | 2 | 2 | — |
| G. Boycott | 5 | 10 | 1 | 368 | 86 | 40.88 | — | 3 | — | — |
| G.A. Gooch | 5 | 10 | 0 | 394 | 123 | 39.40 | 1 | 2 | 5 | — |
| P. Willey | 5 | 9 | 2 | 262 | 100* | 37.42 | 1 | 1 | 1 | — |
| R.A. Woolmer | 2 | 4 | 1 | 109 | 46 | 36.33 | — | — | — | — |
| M.W. Gatting | 4 | 7 | 0 | 172 | 56 | 24.57 | — | 1 | 1 | — |
| J.E. Embury | 3 | 5 | 2 | 70 | 28* | 23.33 | — | — | 2 | — |
| R.G.D. Willis | 4 | 6 | 3 | 61 | 24* | 20.33 | — | — | — | — |
| I.T. Botham | 5 | 9 | 0 | 169 | 57 | 18.77 | — | 1 | 2 | — |
| C.J. Tavare | 2 | 4 | 0 | 65 | 42 | 16.25 | — | — | 2 | — |
| W. Larkins | 3 | 6 | 0 | 90 | 33 | 15.00 | — | — | 2 | — |
| A.P.E. Knott | 4 | 7 | 0 | 36 | 9 | 5.14 | — | — | 11 | — |
| G.R. Dilley | 4 | 5 | 1 | 2 | 1 | 0.50 | — | — | 1 | — |
| M. Hendrick | 2 | 3 | 3 | 19 | 10* | — | — | — | 1 | — |

*Played in one Test:* D.L. Bairstow 40, 9* (2 ct); D.I. Gower 20, 1 (1 ct); J.K. Lever 15, 4 (1 ct); C.M. Old 6; D.L. Underwood 3.

## ENGLAND–BOWLING

| | Overs | Mdns | Runs | Wkts | Avge | Best | 5 wI | 10 wM |
|---|---|---|---|---|---|---|---|---|
| J.E. Embury | 39.3 | 13 | 83 | 6 | 13.83 | 3-20 | — | — |
| G.R. Dilley | 74 | 19 | 183 | 11 | 16.63 | 4-57 | — | — |
| R.G.D. Willis | 110.1 | 27 | 407 | 14 | 29.07 | 5-65 | 1 | — |
| I.T. Botham | 131 | 41 | 385 | 13 | 29.61 | 3-50 | — | — |

*Also bowled:* G. Boycott 7-2-11-0; G.A. Gooch 25-7-59-3; M. Hendrick 44-11-141-2; J.K. Lever 28-4-101-1; C.M. Old 28.5-9-64-2; D.L. Underwood 29.2-7-108-1; P. Willey 43-16-111-2.

## WEST INDIES–BATTING AND FIELDING

| | M | I | NO | Runs | HS | Avge | 100 | 50 | Ct | St |
|---|---|---|---|---|---|---|---|---|---|---|
| I.V.A. Richards | 5 | 6 | 0 | 379 | 145 | 63.16 | 1 | 2 | 6 | — |
| D.L. Haynes | 5 | 6 | 0 | 308 | 184 | 51.33 | 1 | 1 | — | — |
| C.H. Lloyd | 4 | 4 | 0 | 169 | 101 | 42.25 | 1 | — | 2 | — |
| M.A. Holding | 5 | 6 | 4 | 61 | 35 | 30.50 | — | — | 1 | — |
| A.M.E. Roberts | 3 | 4 | 1 | 78 | 24 | 26.00 | — | — | — | — |
| D.L. Murray | 5 | 6 | 0 | 145 | 64 | 24.16 | — | 1 | 14 | — |
| C.G. Greenidge | 5 | 6 | 0 | 124 | 53 | 20.66 | — | 1 | 3 | — |
| S.F.A.F. Bacchus | 5 | 6 | 0 | 121 | 61 | 20.16 | — | 1 | 1 | — |
| M.D. Marshall | 4 | 5 | 0 | 90 | 45 | 18.00 | — | — | 2 | — |
| A.I. Kallicharran | 5 | 6 | 0 | 102 | 37 | 17.00 | — | — | 6 | — |
| J. Garner | 5 | 5 | 0 | 63 | 46 | 12.60 | — | — | 4 | — |
| C.E.H. Croft | 3 | 3 | 2 | 4 | 1* | 1.00 | — | — | — | — |

*Played in one Test:* C.L. King 12.

## WEST INDIES–BOWLING

| | Overs | Mdns | Runs | Wkts | Avge | Best | 5 wI | 10 wM |
|---|---|---|---|---|---|---|---|---|
| J. Garner | 212.4 | 73 | 371 | 26 | 14.26 | 4-30 | — | — |
| A.M.E. Roberts | 105.2 | 24 | 262 | 11 | 23.81 | 5-72 | 1 | — |
| M.D. Marshall | 172.3 | 42 | 436 | 15 | 29.06 | 3-36 | — | — |
| M.A. Holding | 230.5 | 56 | 632 | 20 | 31.60 | 6-67 | 1 | — |
| C.E.H. Croft | 104 | 25 | 306 | 9 | 34.00 | 3-35 | — | — |

*Also bowled:* S.F.A.F. Bacchus 1-0-3-0; C.G. Greenidge 3-2-4-0; D.L. Haynes 1-0-2-0; A.I. Kallicharran 7-1-24-0; C.L. King 12-3-32-0; C.H. Lloyd 1-0-1-0; I.V.A. Richards 36-12-85-0.

# FIRST-CLASS TOUR AVERAGES

| WEST INDIES | M | I | NO | Runs | HS | Avge | 100 | 50 | Ct | St |
|---|---|---|---|---|---|---|---|---|---|---|
| I.V.A. Richards | 13 | 17 | 1 | 911 | 145 | 56.93 | 4 | 4 | 13 | — |
| C.H. Lloyd | 12 | 12 | 2 | 487 | 116 | 48.70 | 3 | 1 | 6 | — |
| D.L. Haynes | 14 | 22 | 3 | 874 | 184 | 46.00 | 1 | 6 | 2 | — |
| A.I. Kallicharran | 15 | 19 | 1 | 653 | 90 | 36.27 | — | 5 | 14 | — |
| C.G. Greenidge | 13 | 18 | 2 | 577 | 165 | 36.06 | 1 | 2 | 7 | — |
| S.F.A.F. Bacchus | 15 | 23 | 2 | 710 | 164* | 33.80 | 1 | 4 | 14 | — |
| D.A. Murray | 6 | 8 | 2 | 161 | 49 | 26.83 | — | — | 16 | 1 |
| D.L. Murray | 12 | 14 | 2 | 315 | 64 | 26.25 | — | 2 | 33 | 2 |
| M.D. Marshall | 12 | 12 | 2 | 211 | 52 | 21.10 | — | 1 | 2 | — |
| J. Garner | 11 | 10 | 0 | 206 | 104 | 20.60 | 1 | — | 8 | — |
| D.R. Parry | 11 | 13 | 8 | 103 | 26* | 20.60 | — | — | 2 | — |
| M.A. Holding | 11 | 11 | 6 | 99 | 35 | 19.80 | — | — | 2 | — |
| A.M.E. Roberts | 9 | 10 | 1 | 114 | 31 | 12.66 | — | — | — | — |
| C.L. King | 9 | 11 | 2 | 86 | 26 | 9.55 | — | — | 4 | — |
| C.E.H. Croft | 9 | 4 | 3 | 8 | 7* | 8.00 | — | — | — | — |
| L.G. Rowe | 3 | 2 | 0 | 13 | 13 | 6.50 | — | — | — | — |

*Played in one match:* T. Mohamed 2, 45.

| | Overs | Mdns | Runs | Wkts | Avge | Best | 5 wI | 10 wM |
|---|---|---|---|---|---|---|---|---|
| J. Garner | 351 | 123 | 683 | 49 | 13.93 | 5-22 | 1 | — |
| M.D. Marshall | 336.3 | 86 | 864 | 49 | 17.63 | 7-56 | 2 | — |
| D.R. Parry | 303.1 | 93 | 800 | 40 | 20.00 | 5-83 | 1 | — |
| A.M.E. Roberts | 234.2 | 57 | 657 | 27 | 24.33 | 5-72 | 1 | — |
| M.A. Holding | 392.1 | 96 | 1096 | 44 | 24.90 | 6-67 | 2 | — |
| C.E.H. Croft | 230.3 | 54 | 690 | 25 | 27.60 | 6-80 | 1 | — |
| C.L. King | 98 | 24 | 301 | 7 | 43.00 | 4-46 | — | — |

Also bowled: S.F.A.F. Bacchus 2-0-11-0; C.G. Greenidge 6-3-6-0; D.L. Haynes 1-0-2-0; A.I. Kallicharran 15-3-55-2; C.H. Lloyd 1-0-1-0; D.A. Murray 1-0-1-0; I.V.A. Richards 68-21-177-1.

| AUSTRALIA | M | I | NO | Runs | HS | Avge | 100 | 50 | Ct | St |
|---|---|---|---|---|---|---|---|---|---|---|
| A.R. Border | 4 | 7 | 3 | 321 | 95 | 80.25 | — | 3 | 3 | — |
| R.W. Marsh | 5 | 7 | 4 | 172 | 56 | 57.33 | — | 2 | 11 | — |
| G.S. Chappell | 4 | 6 | 0 | 303 | 101 | 50.50 | 1 | 2 | 4 | — |
| G.M. Wood | 4 | 7 | 1 | 282 | 112 | 47.00 | 1 | 1 | 4 | — |
| K.J. Hughes | 5 | 9 | 1 | 249 | 117 | 31.12 | 1 | 1 | 3 | — |
| B.M. Laird | 5 | 9 | 1 | 240 | 85 | 30.00 | — | 3 | 3 | — |
| D.K. Lillee | 4 | 4 | 1 | 81 | 33 | 27.00 | — | — | — | — |
| A.A. Mallett | 4 | 3 | 1 | 49 | 30* | 24.50 | — | — | 4 | — |
| G.N. Yallop | 3 | 5 | 1 | 108 | 45 | 18.00 | — | — | 5 | — |
| J. Dyson | 3 | 6 | 1 | 66 | 33 | 13.20 | — | — | — | — |
| J.R. Thomson | 3 | 4 | 0 | 42 | 33 | 10.50 | — | — | 3 | — |
| L.S. Pascoe | 4 | 3 | 1 | 8 | 6 | 4.00 | — | — | 1 | — |

*Also batted:* R.J. Bright (3 matches) 21 (1 ct); G. Dymock (2 matches) 37.

| | Overs | Mdns | Runs | Wkts | Avge | Best | 5 wI | 10 wM |
|---|---|---|---|---|---|---|---|---|
| D.K. Lillee | 116.2 | 25 | 391 | 20 | 19.55 | 6-133 | 1 | — |
| L.S. Pascoe | 114.1 | 14 | 445 | 17 | 26.17 | 5-59 | 2 | — |
| R.J. Bright | 105.1 | 40 | 292 | 7 | 41.71 | 3-20 | — | — |
| J.R. Thomson | 68 | 15 | 265 | 6 | 44.16 | 2-45 | — | — |
| A.A. Mallett | 77.2 | 16 | 282 | 5 | 56.40 | 2-69 | — | — |

Also bowled: G.S. Chappell 16-4-51-2; G. Dymock 42-6-184-2.
Results: Played 5. Won 1 (Hampshire). Lost 2 (Surrey, Nottinghamshire). Drawn 2 (Lancashire, England).

# England v Australia 1980

## CORNHILL CENTENARY TEST MATCH

**PLAYED AT LORD'S, 28, 29, 30 AUGUST, 1, 2 SEPTEMBER**

**MATCH DRAWN**

### AUSTRALIA

| | | | | |
|---|---|---:|---|---:|
| B.M. Laird c Bairstow b Old | | 24 | c Bairstow b Old | 6 |
| G.M. Wood st Bairstow b Emburey | | 112 | lbw b Old | 8 |
| *G.S. Chappell c Gatting b Old | | 47 | b Old | 59 |
| K.J. Hughes c Athey b Old | | 117 | lbw b Botham | 84 |
| G.N. Yallop lbw b Hendrick | | 2 | | |
| A.R. Border not out | | 56 | not out | 21 |
| †R.W. Marshall not out | | 16 | | |
| D.K. Lillee | | | | |
| A.A. Mallett | | | | |
| R.J. Bright | | | | |
| L.S. Pascoe | | | | |
| Extras (B1, LB8, NB2) | | 11 | (B1, LB8, NB2) | 11 |
| **Total** (5 wkts, dec) | | 385 | (4 wkts, dec) | 189 |

### ENGLAND

| | | | | |
|---|---|---:|---|---:|
| G.A. Gooch c Bright b Lillee | | 8 | lbw b Lillee | 16 |
| G. Boycott c Marsh b Lillee | | 62 | not out | 128 |
| C.W.J. Athey b Lillee | | 9 | c Laird b Pascoe | 1 |
| D.I. Gower b Lillee | | 45 | b Mallett | 35 |
| M.W. Gatting lbw b Pascoe | | 12 | not out | 51 |
| *I.T. Botham c Wood b Pascoe | | 0 | | |
| P. Willey lbw b Pascoe | | 5 | | |
| †D.L. Bairstow lbw b Pascoe | | 6 | | |
| J.E. Emburey lbw b Pascoe | | 3 | | |
| C.M. Old not out | | 24 | | |
| M. Hendrick c Border b Mallett | | 5 | | |
| Extras (B6, LB8, NB12) | | 26 | (B3, LB2, NB8) | 13 |
| **Total** | | 205 | (3 wkts) | 244 |

### BOWLING

| ENGLAND | O | M | R | W | | O | M | R | W | FALL OF WICKETS | | | | |
|---|---|---|---|---|---|---|---|---|---|---|---|---|---|---|
| Old | 35 | 9 | 91 | 3 | — | 20 | 6 | 47 | 3 | | *A* | *E* | *A* | *E* |
| Hendrick | 30 | 6 | 67 | 1 | — | 15 | 4 | 53 | 0 | | *1st* | *1st* | *2nd* | *2nd* |
| Botham | 22 | 2 | 89 | 0 | — | 9.2 | 1 | 43 | 1 | 1st | 64 | 10 | 15 | 19 |
| Emburey | 38 | 9 | 104 | 1 | — | 9 | 2 | 35 | 0 | 2nd | 150 | 41 | 28 | 43 |
| Gooch | 8 | 3 | 16 | 0 | — | | | | | 3rd | 260 | 137 | 139 | 124 |
| Willey | 1 | 0 | 7 | 0 | — | | | | | 4th | 267 | 151 | 189 | — |
| AUSTRALIA | | | | | | | | | | 5th | 320 | 158 | — | — |
| Lillee | 15 | 4 | 43 | 4 | — | 19 | 5 | 53 | 1 | 6th | — | 163 | — | — |
| Pascoe | 18 | 5 | 59 | 5 | — | 17 | 1 | 73 | 1 | 7th | — | 164 | — | — |
| Chappell | 2 | .0 | 2 | 0 | — | | | | | 8th | — | 173 | — | — |
| Bright | 21 | 6 | 50 | 0 | — | 25 | 9 | 44 | 0 | 9th | — | 200 | — | — |
| Mallett | 7.2 | 3 | 25 | 1 | — | 21 | 2 | 61 | 1 | 10th | — | 205 | — | — |

# Pakistan v West Indies 1980-81

## FIRST TEST MATCH

**PLAYED AT LAHORE, 24, 25, 27, 28, 29 NOVEMBER**

**MATCH DRAWN**

**PAKISTAN**

| | | | |
|---|---|---|---|
| †Taslim Arif c Murray b Garner | 32 | retired hurt | 8 |
| Sadiq Mohammad c Murray b Marshall | 19 | lbw b Croft | 28 |
| Mansur Akhtar c Murray b Croft | 13 | b Clarke | 0 |
| *Javed Miandad c Richards b Croft | 6 | run out | 30 |
| Majid Khan c Bacchus b Garner | 4 | not out | 62 |
| Wasim Raja c Kallicharran b Richards | 76 | lbw b Clarke | 3 |
| Imran Khan lbw b Marshall | 123 | c Marshall b Richards | 9 |
| Abdul Qadir retired hurt | 18 | c Haynes b Richards | 1 |
| Sarfraz Nawaz c Richards b Croft | 55 | c Garner b Haynes | 4 |
| Iqbal Qasim b Marshall | 3 | | |
| Mohammed Nazir (Jun) not out | 1 | | |
| Extras (B1, LB4, NB13, W1) | 19 | (B2, LB2, NB7) | 11 |
| | | | |
| **Total** | **369** | (7 wkts) | **156** |

### WEST INDIES

| | |
|---|---|
| D.L. Haynes c Qasim b Nazir | 40 |
| S.F.A.F. Bacchus lbw b Imran | 0 |
| I.V.A. Richards b Nazir | 75 |
| A. I. Kallicharran c Sadiq b Qadir | 11 |
| *C.H. Lloyd c Miandad b Qasim | 22 |
| H.A. Gomes b Raja | 43 |
| †D.A. Murray c Majid b Qadir | 50 |
| M.D. Marshall b Sarfraz | 9 |
| J. Garner c Taslim b Quadir | 15 |
| C.E.H. Croft not out | 7 |
| S.T. Clarke st Taslim b Qadir | 15 |
| Extras (B3, LB6, NB1) | 10 |
| | |
| **Total** | **297** |

### BOWLING

| WEST INDIES | O | M | R | W | | O | M | R | W | FALL OF WICKETS | | | |
|---|---|---|---|---|---|---|---|---|---|---|---|---|---|
| | | | | | | | | | | | P | WI | P |
| Clarke | 23 | 3 | 69 | 0 | — | 12 | 3 | 26 | 2 | | 1st | 1st | 2nd |
| Croft | 28 | 7 | 91 | 3 | — | 20 | 7 | 37 | 1 | 1st | 31 | 1 | 15 |
| Marshall | 21.5 | 5 | 88 | 3 | — | 15 | 4 | 30 | 0 | 2nd | 65 | 118 | 57 |
| Garner | 27 | 6 | 71 | 2 | — | 9 | 3 | 17 | 0 | 3rd | 67 | 119 | 101 |
| Richards | 7 | 0 | 31 | 1 | — | 11 | 3 | 20 | 2 | 4th | 72 | 143 | 112 |
| Gomes | — | — | — | — | — | 4 | 0 | 9 | 0 | 5th | 95 | 158 | 125 |
| Kallicharran | — | — | — | — | — | 1 | 0 | 4 | 0 | 6th | 188 | 225 | 133 |
| Haynes | — | — | — | — | — | 1 | 0 | 2 | 1 | 7th | 356 | 255 | 156 |
| **PAKISTAN** | | | | | | | | | | 8th | 368 | 275 | — |
| Imran | 16 | 2 | 39 | 1 | — | | | | | 9th | 369 | 276 | — |
| Sarfraz | 13 | 3 | 40 | 1 | — | | | | | 10th | — | 297 | — |
| Qadir | 40.4 | 4 | 132 | 4 | — | | | | | | | | |
| Qasim | 12 | 4 | 18 | 1 | — | | | | | | | | |
| Wasim | 10 | 3 | 21 | 1 | — | | | | | | | | |
| Nazir | 17 | 4 | 37 | 2 | — | | | | | | | | |

# SECOND TEST MATCH
## PLAYED AT FAISALABAD, 8, 9, 11, 12 DECEMBER
### WEST INDIES WON BY 156 RUNS

## WEST INDIES

| | | | |
|---|---|---|---|
| D.I. Haynes lbw b Iqbal Qasim | 15 | lbw b Abdul Qadir | 12 |
| S.F.A.F. Bacchus c Sikander b Abdul Qadir | 45 | b Iqbal Qasim | 17 |
| I.V.A. Richards b Nazir | 72 | c Sub (Sikander) b Qasim | 67 |
| A.I. Kallicharran lbw b Abdul Qadir | 8 | lbw b Nazir | 27 |
| *C.H. Lloyd c Mansur b Nazir | 20 | lbw b Iqbal Qasim | 37 |
| H.A. Gomes c Iqbal Qasim b Nazir | 8 | c Mansur b Iqbal Qasim | 1 |
| †D.A. Murray c Majid b Abdul Qadir | 31 | b Nazir | 19 |
| M.D. Marshall b Nazir | 0 | c Miandad b Nazir | 1 |
| R. Nanan lbw b Nazir | 8 | c Raja b Iqbal Qasim | 8 |
| C.E.H. Croft b Taslim b Iqbal Qasim | 2 | lbw b Iqbal Qasim | 1 |
| S.T. Clarke not out | 8 | not out | 35 |
| Extras (B12, LB5, NB1) | 18 | (B9, LB7, NB1) | 17 |
| **Total** | **235** | | **242** |

## PAKISTAN

| | | | |
|---|---|---|---|
| †Taslim Arif lbw b Clarke | 0 | c Richards b Croft | 18 |
| Mansur Akhtar c Lloyd b Marshall | 16 | c Nanan b Marshall | 7 |
| Zaheer Abbas b Clarke | 2 | lbw b Marshall | 33 |
| *Javed Miandad c & b Clarke | 50 | c Lloyd b Croft | 22 |
| Majid Khan c Murray b Marshall | 26 | b Clarke | 3 |
| Wasim Raja st Murray b Nanan | 21 | not out | 38 |
| Imran Khan c Richards b Croft | 29 | c Richards b Nanan | 0 |
| Abdul Qadir b Nanan | 4 | b Croft | 0 |
| Iqbal Qasim b Croft | 0 | c Richards b Nanan | 5 |
| Sikander Bakht c Lloyd b Richards | 6 | c Lloyd b Marshall | 1 |
| Mohammed Nazir Jr. not out | 2 | c Nanan b Marshall | 0 |
| Extras (B4, LB7, NB9) | 20 | (B4, LB4, NB10) | 18 |
| **Total** | **176** | | **145** |

## BOWLING

| PAKISTAN | O | M | R | W | | O | M | R | W | | FALL OF WICKETS | | | |
|---|---|---|---|---|---|---|---|---|---|---|---|---|---|---|
| | | | | | | | | | | | WI | P | WI | P |
| Imran | 10 | 6 | 36 | 0 | — | 3 | 0 | 6 | 0 | | 1st | 1st | 2nd | 2nd |
| Sikander | 7 | 2 | 22 | 0 | — | 4 | 0 | 9 | 0 | 1st | 39 | 0 | 22 | 14 |
| Iqbal Qasim | 19 | 3 | 54 | 2 | — | 32.2 | 5 | 89 | 6 | 2nd | 99 | 2 | 47 | 43 |
| Abdul Qadir | 15.3 | 1 | 48 | 3 | — | 17 | 4 | 45 | 1 | 3rd | 127 | 32 | 129 | 60 |
| Nazir | 22 | 7 | 44 | 5 | — | 33 | 13 | 76 | 3 | 4th | 150 | 73 | 150 | 71 |
| Wasim | 4 | 0 | 13 | 0 | — | — | — | — | — | 5th | 176 | 122 | 153 | 77 |
| **WEST INDIES** | | | | | | | | | | 6th | 187 | 132 | 171 | 122 |
| Clarke | 13 | 2 | 28 | 3 | — | 12 | 2 | 36 | 1 | 7th | 187 | 149 | 186 | 122 |
| Croft | 16 | 4 | 35 | 2 | — | 13 | 0 | 29 | 3 | 8th | 207 | 150 | 189 | 124 |
| Marshall | 9 | 1 | 39 | 2 | — | 9.4 | 0 | 25 | 4 | 9th | 223 | 167 | 198 | 132 |
| Nanan | 20 | 1 | 54 | 2 | — | 16 | 6 | 37 | 2 | 10th | 235 | 176 | 242 | 145 |
| Richards | 0.2 | 0 | 0 | 1 | | | | | | | | | | |

# THIRD TEST MATCH
## PLAYED AT KARACHI 22, 23, 24, 26, 27 DECEMBER
## MATCH DRAWN

### PAKISTAN

| | | | |
|---|---:|---|---:|
| Shafiq Ahmed lbw b Clarke | 0 | lbw b Garner | 17 |
| Sadiq Mohammad lbw b Croft | 0 | c Bacchus b Clarke | 36 |
| Zaheer Abbas not out | 13 | lbw b Croft | 1 |
| *Javed Miandad c Lloyd b Clarke | 60 | c Haynes b Clarke | 5 |
| Majid Khan c Bacchus b Croft | 0 | c Murray b Croft | 18 |
| Wasim Raja c Bacchus b Croft | 2 | not out | 77 |
| Imran Khan lbw b Garner | 21 | c Murray b Marshall | 12 |
| Ejaz Faqih b Marshall | 0 | c Murray b Marshall | 8 |
| †Wasim Bari c Murray b Clarke | 23 | b Garner | 3 |
| Iqbal Qasim c Richards b Clarke | 0 | b Croft | 2 |
| Mohammed Nazir Jr. b Garner | 0 | not out | 2 |
| Extras (LB1, NB7, W1) | 9 | (B4, LB3, NB16) | 23 |
| **Total** | **128** | **(9 wkts)** | **204** |

### WEST INDIES

| | |
|---|---:|
| D.L. Haynes lbw b Quasim | 1 |
| S.F.A.F. Baachus b Imran | 16 |
| I.V.A. Richards c Zaheer b Quasim | 18 |
| A.I. Kallicharran b Imran | 4 |
| *C.H. Lloyd c Miandad b Imran | 1 |
| †D.A. Murray c Miandad b Quasim | 42 |
| H.A. Gomes c Miandad b Nazir | 61 |
| M.D. Marshall b Nazir | 0 |
| S.T. Clarke b Quasim | 17 |
| J. Garner lbw b Imran | 1 |
| C.E.H. Croft not out | 3 |
| Extras (LB1, W4) | 5 |
| **Total** | **169** |

### BOWLING

| WEST INDIES | O | M | R | W | | O | M | R | W | FALL OF WICKETS | | | |
|---|---|---|---|---|---|---|---|---|---|---|---|---|---|
| Clarke | 15 | 7 | 27 | 4 | — | 11 | 3 | 14 | 2 | | *P* | *WI* | *P* |
| Croft | 14 | 5 | 27 | 3 | — | 23 | 6 | 50 | 3 | | *1st* | *1st* | *2nd* |
| Garner | 18.1 | 8 | 27 | 2 | — | 19 | 4 | 39 | 2 | 1st | 0 | 19 | 30 |
| Marshall | 14 | 0 | 38 | 1 | — | 17 | 1 | 54 | 2 | 2nd | 0 | 21 | 76 |
| Richards | — | — | — | — | | 8 | 2 | 10 | 0 | 3rd | 5 | 43 | 78 |
| Gomes | — | — | — | — | | 6 | 0 | 14 | 0 | 4th | 14 | 43 | 82 |
| **PAKISTAN** | | | | | | | | | | 5th | 53 | 44 | 85 |
| Imran | 29 | 5 | 66 | 4 | | | | | | 6th | 57 | 143 | 122 |
| Quasim | 34.1 | 11 | 48 | 4 | | | | | | 7th | 111 | 143 | 146 |
| Nazir | 9 | 2 | 21 | 2 | | | | | | 8th | 112 | 160 | 150 |
| Ejaz | 4 | 1 | 9 | 0 | | | | | | 9th | 112 | 161 | 178 |
| Wasim Raja | 1 | 0 | 8 | 0 | | | | | | 10th | 128 | 169 | — |
| Majid | 8 | 3 | 12 | 0 | | | | | | | | | |

# FOURTH TEST MATCH

## PLAYED AT MULTAN, 30, 31 DECEMBER
## 2, 3, 4 JANUARY
## MATCH DRAWN

### WEST INDIES

| | | | |
|---|---|---|---|
| D.L. Haynes b Imran | 5 | st Wasim Bari b Iqbal | 31 |
| S.F.A.F. Bacchus lbw b Imran | 2 | c Zaheer b Iqbal | 39 |
| I.V.A. Richards not out | 120 | c Sadiq b Nazir | 12 |
| A.I. Kallicharran lbw Imran | 18 | not out | 12 |
| H.A. Gomes lbw b Iqbal | 32 | | |
| *C.H. Lloyd run out | 9 | not out | 17 |
| †D.A. Murray c Wasim Bari b Iqbal | 0 | lbw b Nazir | 0 |
| S.T. Clarke c Miandad b Imran | 28 | | |
| M.D. Marshall c Miandad b Nazir | 3 | | |
| J. Garner c Nazir b Imran | 2 | | |
| C.E.H. Croft lbw b Sarfraz | 3 | lbw b Nazir | 1 |
| Extras (B15, LB6, NB3, W3) | 27 | (LB3, W1) | 4 |
| **Total** | **249** | | **116** |

### PAKISTAN

| | |
|---|---|
| Shafiq Ahmed c Garner b Clarke | 0 |
| Sadiq Mohammed b Clarke | 3 |
| Majid Khan c Richards b Garner | 41 |
| *Javed Miandad c Haynes b Croft | 57 |
| †Wasim Bari run out | 8 |
| Zaheer Abbas c Murray b Marshall | 8 |
| Wasim Raja not out | 29 |
| Imran Khan c Haynes b Croft | 10 |
| Sarfraz Nawaz b Garner | 1 |
| Iqbal Qasim c Richards b Garner | 1 |
| Mohammed Nazir (Jun) lbw b Garner | 0 |
| Extras (NB8) | 8 |
| **Total** | **166** |

### BOWLING

| PAKISTAN | O | M | R | W | | O | M | R | W |
|---|---|---|---|---|---|---|---|---|---|
| Imran | 22 | 6 | 62 | 5 | — | 11 | 0 | 27 | 0 |
| Sarfraz | 15.2 | 6 | 24 | 1 | — | 5 | 1 | 15 | 0 |
| Iqbal | 28 | 9 | 61 | 2 | — | 12 | 2 | 35 | 2 |
| Nazir | 26 | 8 | 69 | 1 | — | 15 | 3 | 35 | 3 |
| Wasim Raja | 2 | 0 | 6 | 0 | — | | | | |
| **WEST INDIES** | | | | | | | | | |
| Clarke | 12 | 1 | 43 | 2 | — | | | | |
| Croft | 16 | 3 | 33 | 2 | — | | | | |
| Marshall | 12 | 1 | 44 | 1 | — | | | | |
| Garner | 17.2 | 4 | 38 | 4 | — | | | | |

### FALL OF WICKETS

| | WI | P | WI |
|---|---|---|---|
| | 1st | 1st | 2nd |
| 1st | 9 | 2 | 57 |
| 2nd | 22 | 4 | 84 |
| 3rd | 58 | 104 | 84 |
| 4th | 134 | 104 | 85 |
| 5th | 146 | 120 | 85 |
| 6th | 153 | 137 | — |
| 7th | 198 | 163 | — |
| 8th | 201 | 164 | — |
| 9th | 208 | 166 | — |
| 10th | 249 | 166 | — |

# Australia v New Zealand 1980-81

## FIRST TEST MATCH

**PLAYED AT BRISBANE, 28, 29, 30 NOVEMBER**

**AUSTRALIA WON BY 10 WICKETS**

### NEW ZEALAND

| | | | | |
|---|---|---:|---|---:|
| J.G. Wright | c Marsh b Pascoe | 29 | c Walters b Lillee | 1 |
| B.A. Edgar | c Marsh b Lawson | 20 | c Hughes b Lillee | 51 |
| P.E. McEwan | c Border b Lillee | 6 | c Hughes b Lillee | 0 |
| *G.P. Howarth | c & b Higgs | 65 | c Wood b Lillee | 4 |
| J.M. Parker | b Pascoe | 52 | c Dyson b Lawson | 4 |
| M.G. Burgess | c Chappell b Pascoe | 0 | c Wood b Lillee | 2 |
| †I.D.S. Smith | c Hughes b Lillee | 7 | c Hughes b Pascoe | 7 |
| R.J. Hadlee | c Marsh b Higgs | 10 | not out | 51 |
| B.L. Cairns | c Border b Higgs | 0 | c Border b Lillee | 0 |
| J.G. Bracewell | not out | 6 | c Border b Lawson | 0 |
| B.P. Bracewell | b Higgs | 0 | b Pascoe | 8 |
| Extras | (LB18, NB7, W5) | 30 | (B4, LB4, NB5, W1) | 14 |
| **Total** | | **225** | | **142** |

### AUSTRALIA

| | | | | |
|---|---|---:|---|---:|
| G.M. Wood | c Parker b J. Bracewell | 111 | not out | 32 |
| J. Dyson | lbw b Cairns | 30 | not out | 24 |
| *G.S. Chappell | c McEwan b Cairns | 35 | | |
| K.J. Hughes | c Wright b Hadlee | 9 | | |
| A.R. Border | run out | 36 | | |
| K.D. Walters | b Cairns | 17 | | |
| †R.W. Marsh | b Hadlee | 8 | | |
| D.K. Lillee | c Parker b Cairns | 24 | | |
| G.F. Lawson | c sub (Boock) b Hadlee | 16 | | |
| L.S. Pascoe | b Cairns | 5 | | |
| J.D. Higgs | not out | 1 | | |
| Extras | (B1, LB7, NB5) | 13 | (B2, LB2, NB3) | 7 |
| **Total** | | **305** | (0 wkts) | **63** |

### BOWLING

| AUSTRALIA | O | M | R | W | | O | M | R | W | FALL OF WICKETS | | | |
|---|---|---|---|---|---|---|---|---|---|---|---|---|---|
| Lillee | 18 | 7 | 36 | 2 | — | 15 | 1 | 53 | 6 | | *NZ* | *A* | *NZ* |
| Pascoe | 19 | 4 | 41 | 3 | — | 13.1 | 2 | 30 | 2 | | *1st* | *1st* | *2nd* |
| Lawson | 12 | 2 | 39 | 1 | — | 8 | 0 | 26 | 2 | 1st | 64 | 80 | 6 |
| Chappell | 4 | 1 | 18 | 0 | — | — | — | — | — | 2nd | 71 | 145 | 9 |
| Higgs | 16.1 | 3 | 59 | 4 | — | 5 | 1 | 19 | 0 | 3rd | 76 | 160 | 14 |
| Walters | 1 | 0 | 2 | 0 | — | — | — | — | — | 4th | 193 | 225 | 30 |
| **NEW** | | | | | | | | | | 5th | 193 | 235 | 34 |
| **ZEALAND** | | | | | | | | | | 6th | 209 | 250 | 58 |
| Hadlee | 37 | 8 | 83 | 3 | — | 6 | 0 | 28 | 0 | 7th | 209 | 268 | 61 |
| B. Bracewell | 22 | 8 | 71 | 0 | — | 3 | 3 | 0 | 0 | 8th | 209 | 299 | 114 |
| Cairns | 38.5 | 11 | 87 | 5 | — | 7.3 | 3 | 16 | 0 | 9th | 221 | 299 | 114 |
| J. Bracewell | 18 | 5 | 51 | 1 | — | 5 | 0 | 12 | 0 | 10th | 225 | 305 | 142 |

# SECOND TEST MATCH
## PLAYED AT PERTH 12, 13, 14 DECEMBER
## AUSTRALIA WON BY 8 WICKETS

### NEW ZEALAND

| | | | |
|---|---|---|---|
| J.G. Wright b Pascoe | 10 | c Marsh b Hogg | 3 |
| B.A. Edgar c Border b Lillee | 0 | c Hughes b Pascoe | 0 |
| J.M. Parker c Chappell b Hogg | 3 | c Hughes b Hogg | 18 |
| P.E. McEwan c Marsh b Lillee | 8 | c Marsh b Lillee | 16 |
| J.V. Coney b Hogg | 71 | c Marsh b Higgs | 0 |
| *M.G. Burgess c Hughes b Lillee | 43 | lbw b Higgs | 18 |
| †W.K. Lees c Marsh b Pascoe | 5 | not out | 25 |
| R.J. Hadlee c Hughes b Pascoe | 23 | c Chappell b Higgs | 0 |
| J.G. Bracewell lbw b Lillee | 6 | run out | 16 |
| B.L. Cairns c Pascoe b Lillee | 13 | c Border b Higgs | 6 |
| G.B. Troup not out | 0 | c Marsh b Lillee | 0 |
| Extras (LB3, NB9, W2) | 14 | (LB12, NB5, W2) | 19 |
| **Total** | **196** | | **121** |

### AUSTRALIA

| | | | |
|---|---|---|---|
| G.M. Wood c Bracewell b Hadlee | 0 | c Lees b Hadlee | 0 |
| J. Dyson c Bracewell b Cairns | 28 | not out | 25 |
| *G.S. Chappell c Cairns b Troup | 12 | c Lees b Hadlee | 13 |
| K.J. Hughes c Lees b Hadlee | 3 | not out | 16 |
| A.R. Border b Cairns | 10 | | |
| K.D. Walters c Coney b Hadlee | 55 | | |
| †R.W. Marsh c Coney b Hadlee | 91 | | |
| D.K. Lillee c & b Hadlee | 8 | | |
| R.M. Hogg b Cairns | 3 | | |
| L.S. Pascoe not out | 30 | | |
| J.D. Higgs c Coney b Cairns | 7 | | |
| Extras (B3, LB4, NB10, W1) | 18 | (LB1) | 1 |
| **Total** | **265** | **(2 wkts)** | **55** |

### BOWLING

| AUSTRALIA | O | M | R | W | | O | M | R | W | FALL OF WICKETS | | | |
|---|---|---|---|---|---|---|---|---|---|---|---|---|---|
| | | | | | | | | | | | NZ | A | NZ | A |
| Lillee | 23.5 | 5 | 63 | 5 | — | 15.1 | 7 | 14 | 2 | | 1st | 1st | 2nd | 2nd |
| Hogg | 16 | 5 | 29 | 2 | — | 10 | 2 | 25 | 2 | 1st | 6 | 0 | 0 | 3 |
| Pascoe | 20 | 3 | 61 | 3 | — | 10 | 1 | 30 | 1 | 2nd | 13 | 22 | 27 | 31 |
| Chappell | 7 | 3 | 5 | 0 | — | 3 | 1 | 7 | 0 | 3rd | 24 | 25 | 38 | — |
| Higgs | 5 | 1 | 13 | 0 | — | 8 | 2 | 25 | 4 | 4th | 28 | 50 | 63 | — |
| Walters | 2 | 0 | 11 | 0 | — | 2 | 1 | 1 | 0 | 5th | 116 | 68 | 64 | — |
| NEW | | | | | | | | | | 6th | 133 | 156 | 73 | — |
| ZEALAND | | | | | | | | | | 7th | 171 | 156 | 115 | — |
| Hadlee | 27 | 8 | 87 | 5 | — | 11.1 | 4 | 20 | 2 | 8th | 177 | 187 | 115 | — |
| Troup | 22 | 5 | 57 | 1 | — | 1 | 0 | 1 | 0 | 9th | 196 | 244 | 121 | — |
| Cairns | 28.1 | 7 | 88 | 4 | — | 5 | 2 | 17 | 0 | 10th | 196 | 265 | 121 | — |
| Bracewell | 4 | 1 | 15 | 0 | — | 5 | 0 | 16 | 0 | | | | | |

# THIRD TEST MATCH

**PLAYED AT MELBOURNE, 26, 27, 28, 29, 30 DECEMBER**
**MATCH DRAWN**

## AUSTRALIA

| | | | | |
|---|---|---:|---|---:|
| G.M. Wood c Lees b Hadlee | | 0 | c Lees b Hadlee | 21 |
| J. Dyson b Troup | | 13 | lbw b Cairns | 16 |
| *G.S. Chappell c Coney b Hadlee | | 42 | b Hadlee | 78 |
| K.J. Hughes c Parker b Hadlee | | 51 | b Hadlee | 30 |
| A.R. Border c Cairns b Coney | | 45 | c Lees b Hadlee | 9 |
| K.D. Walters b Coney | | 107 | run out | 2 |
| †R.W. Marsh c Parker b Coney | | 1 | lbw b Cairns | 0 |
| D.K. Lillee b Cairns | | 27 | c Coney b Bracewell | 8 |
| R.M. Hogg run out | | 0 | b Hadlee | 12 |
| L.S. Pascoe b Cairns | | 0 | not out | 0 |
| J.D. Higgs not out | | 6 | b Hadlee | 0 |
| Extras (B7, LB13, NB6, W3) | | 29 | (B6, LB4, NB2) | 12 |
| **Total** | | **321** | | **188** |

## NEW ZEALAND

| | | | | |
|---|---|---:|---|---:|
| J.G. Wright c Chappell b Higgs | | 4 | c Wood b Hogg | 44 |
| R.A. Edgar lbw b Higgs | | 21 | run out | 25 |
| *G.P. Howarth b Hogg | | 65 | lbw b Chappell | 20 |
| J.M. Parker c Marsh b Pascoe | | 56 | lbw b Chappell | 1 |
| M.G. Burgess lbw b Pascoe | | 49 | not out | 10 |
| J.V. Coney not out | | 55 | lbw b Hogg | 3 |
| J.G. Bracewell c Chappell b Pascoe | | 0 | | |
| †W.K. Lees lbw b Hogg | | 4 | b Lillee | 7 |
| R.J. Hadlee c Border b Hogg | | 9 | not out | 5 |
| B.L. Cairns lbw b Higgs | | 18 | | |
| G.B. Troup c Hughes b Hogg | | 1 | | |
| Extras (B13, LB12, NB10) | | 35 | (B2, LB8, NB2, W1) | 13 |
| **Total** | | **317** | **(6 wkts)** | **128** |

## BOWLING

| NEW ZEALAND | O | M | R | W | | O | M | R | W | FALL OF WICKETS | | | |
|---|---:|---:|---:|---:|---|---:|---:|---:|---:|---|---:|---:|---:|
| | | | | | | | | | | | *A* | *NZ* | *A* *NZ* |
| Hadlee | 39 | 8 | 89 | 3 | — | 27.2 | 7 | 57 | 6 | | *A* | *NZ* | *A* *NZ* |
| Troup | 26 | 5 | 54 | 1 | — | 11 | 1 | 31 | 0 | | *1st* | *1st* | *2nd* *2nd* |
| Cairns | 35 | 6 | 83 | 2 | — | 33 | 13 | 65 | 2 | 1st | 0 | 27 | 25 50 |
| Bracewell | 9 | 0 | 38 | 0 | — | 15 | 2 | 22 | 1 | 2nd | 32 | 32 | 64 95 |
| Coney | 12.3 | 6 | 28 | 3 | — | 1 | 0 | 1 | 0 | 3rd | 75 | 157 | 111 97 |
| **AUSTRALIA** | | | | | | | | | | 4th | 159 | 163 | 128 101 |
| Lillee | 21 | 4 | 49 | 0 | — | 13 | 3 | 30 | 1 | 5th | 190 | 247 | 131 101 |
| Hogg | 26.2 | 9 | 60 | 4 | — | 8 | 1 | 14 | 2 | 6th | 192 | 247 | 131 121 |
| Higgs | 29 | 6 | 87 | 3 | — | 12 | 4 | 24 | 0 | 7th | 261 | 264 | 149 — |
| Pascoe | 26 | 6 | 75 | 3 | — | 11 | 1 | 35 | 0 | 8th | 261 | 280 | 185 — |
| Border | 4 | 1 | 6 | 0 | — | 2 | 1 | 5 | 0 | 9th | 261 | 316 | 188 — |
| Chappell | 1 | 0 | 5 | 0 | — | 7 | 4 | 7 | 2 | 10th | 321 | 317 | 188 — |
| Hughes | | | | | — | 1 | 1 | 0 | 0 | | | | |

# Australia v India 1980-81

## FIRST TEST MATCH

**PLAYED AT SYDNEY, 2, 3, 4 JANUARY**
**AUSTRALIA WON BY AN INNINGS AND 4 RUNS**

### INDIA

| | | | | |
|---|---|---:|---|---:|
| *S.M. Gavaskar | c Marsh b Lillee | 0 | c Marsh b Hogg | 10 |
| C.P.S Chauhan | c Border b Pascoe | 20 | c Walters b Pascoe | 36 |
| D.B. Vengsarkar | c Marsh b Lillee | 22 | c Marsh b Pascoe | 34 |
| G.R. Viswanath | b Hogg | 26 | st Marsh b Higgs | 24 |
| Yashpal Sharma | c Marsh b Pascoe | 6 | c Walters b Lillee | 4 |
| S. Patil | retired hurt | 65 | c Wood b Lillee | 4 |
| Kapil Dev | c Marsh b Pascoe | 22 | c sub b Higgs | 19 |
| †S.M.H. Kirmani | c Walters b Lillee | 27 | not out | 43 |
| R.M.H. Binny | c Marsh b Pascoe | 3 | lbw b Lillee | 0 |
| K.D. Ghavri | c Wood b Lillee | 7 | c Hogg b Higgs | 21 |
| D.R. Doshi | not out | 0 | c Lillee b Higgs | 0 |
| Extras | (LB1, NB2) | 3 | (B2, LB3, W1) | 6 |
| **Total** | | **201** | | **201** |

### AUSTRALIA

| | | |
|---|---|---:|
| G.M. Wood | c Kirmani b Kapil Dev | 9 |
| J. Dyson | c Gavaskar b Kapil Dev | 0 |
| *G.S. Chappell | c Kapil Dev b Ghavri | 204 |
| K.J. Hughes | c Kirmani b Kapil Dev | 24 |
| A.R. Border | c Kirmani b Kapil Dev | 31 |
| K.D. Walters | c Viswanath b Ghavri | 67 |
| †R.W. Marsh | c Binny b Ghavri | 12 |
| D.K. Lillee | c Doshi b Ghavri | 5 |
| R.M. Hogg | not out | 26 |
| L. Pascoe | c Doshi b Ghavri | 7 |
| J.D. Higgs | b Kapil Dev | 2 |
| Extras | (B4, LB3, NB9, W3) | 19 |
| **Total** | | **406** |

### BOWLING

| AUSTRALIA | O | M | R | W | | O | M | R | W |
|---|---:|---:|---:|---:|---|---:|---:|---:|---:|
| Lillee | 20.2 | 3 | 86 | 4 | — | 18 | 2 | 79 | 3 |
| Hogg | 14 | 1 | 51 | 1 | — | 9 | 1 | 24 | 1 |
| Pascoe | 19 | 6 | 61 | 4 | — | 11 | 2 | 35 | 2 |
| Higgs | — | — | — | — | — | 18 | 8 | 45 | 4 |
| Walters | — | — | — | — | — | 6 | 3 | 12 | 0 |
| **INDIA** | | | | | | | | | |
| Kapil Dev | 36.1 | 7 | 97 | 5 | — | | | | |
| Ghavri | 30 | 7 | 107 | 5 | — | | | | |
| Binny | 15 | 1 | 70 | 0 | — | | | | |
| Doshi | 27 | 0 | 103 | 0 | — | | | | |
| Chauhan | 1 | 0 | 10 | 0 | — | | | | |

### FALL OF WICKETS

| | I | A | I |
|---|---:|---:|---:|
| | 1st | 1st | 2nd |
| 1st | 0 | 3 | 21 |
| 2nd | 36 | 14 | 74 |
| 3rd | 62 | 95 | 92 |
| 4th | 70 | 169 | 110 |
| 5th | 78 | 341 | 120 |
| 6th | 145 | 355 | 140 |
| 7th | 183 | 363 | 144 |
| 8th | 186 | 365 | 144 |
| 9th | 201 | 376 | 201 |
| 10th | 201 | 406 | 201 |

# SECOND TEST MATCH

**MATCH DRAWN**

## AUSTRALIA

| | | | | |
|---|---|---|---|---|
| J. Dyson c Gavaskar b Kapil Dev | 30 | lbw b Ghavri | | 28 |
| G.M. Wood c Doshi b Yadav | 125 | c Patil b Doshi | | 3 |
| *G.S. Chappell c Chauhan b Doshi | 36 | st Kirmani b Doshi | | 52 |
| K.J. Hughes c Yashpal b Yadav | 213 | b Kapil Dev | | 53 |
| A.R. Border c Gavaskar b Kapil Dev | 57 | b Doshi | | 7 |
| K.D. Walters c Viswanath b Yadav | 20 | not out | | 33 |
| †R.W. Marsh run out | 0 | c Kirmani b Yadav | | 23 |
| B. Yardley c Viswanath b Doshi | 12 | c Vengsarkar b Yadav | | 2 |
| D.K. Lillee c Kapil Dev b Doshi | 2 | not out | | 10 |
| R.M. Hogg c & b Yadav | 11 | | | |
| L.S. Pascoe not out | 1 | | | |
| Extras (LB13, NB7, W1) | 21 | (B2, LB5, NB3) | | 10 |
| | —— | | | —— |
| **Total** | 528 | (7 wkts dec) | | 221 |

## INDIA

| | | | | |
|---|---|---|---|---|
| *S.M. Gavaskar b Pascoe | 23 | c Chappell b Pascoe | | 5 |
| S. Yadav c Chappell b Yardley | 16 | not out | | 0 |
| G.R. Viswanath lbw b Hogg | 3 | b Pascoe | | 16 |
| D.B. Vengsarkar lbw b Lillee | 2 | c Chappell b Border | | 37 |
| C.P.S. Chauhan c Marsh b Lillee | 97 | c Marsh b Pascoe | | 11 |
| S.M. Patil lbw b Hogg | 174 | lbw b Lillee | | 9 |
| Yashpal Sharma c Marsh b Lillee | 47 | lbw b Yardley | | 13 |
| Kapil Dev c Border b Lillee | 2 | c Marsh b Lillee | | 7 |
| †S.M.H. Kirmani b Pascoe | 6 | c Marsh b Chappell | | 14 |
| K.D. Ghavri c Wood b Yardley | 3 | not out | | 7 |
| D.R. Doshi not out | 6 | | | |
| Extras (B11, LB10, NB17, W2) | 40 | (B7, LB1, NB8) | | 16 |
| | —— | | | —— |
| **Total** | 419 | (8 wkts) | | 135 |

### BOWLING

| INDIA | O | M | R | W | | O | M | R | W | FALL OF WICKETS | | | |
|---|---|---|---|---|---|---|---|---|---|---|---|---|---|
| | | | | | | | | | | | *A* | *I* | *A* | *I* |
| Kapil Dev | 32 | 5 | 112 | 2 | — | 17 | 3 | 55 | 1 | | *1st* | *1st* | *2nd* | *2nd* |
| Ghavri | 27 | 3 | 106 | 0 | — | 11 | 2 | 37 | 1 | 1st | 84 | 77 | 5 | 13 |
| Doshi | 48 | 6 | 146 | 3 | — | 33 | 11 | 49 | 3 | 2nd | 152 | 112 | 74 | 16 |
| Yadav | 42.4 | 6 | 143 | 4 | — | 29 | 6 | 70 | 2 | 3rd | 234 | 115 | 118 | 44 |
| **AUSTRALIA** | | | | | | | | | | 4th | 363 | 130 | 138 | 57 |
| Lillee | 34 | 10 | 80 | 4 | — | 19 | 7 | 38 | 2 | 5th | 393 | 238 | 165 | 90 |
| Hogg | 28 | 6 | 100 | 2 | — | 3 | 0 | 11 | 0 | 6th | 399 | 385 | 204 | 103 |
| Pascoe | 17 | 2 | 62 | 2 | — | 11 | 2 | 32 | 3 | 7th | 435 | 393 | 208 | 126 |
| Yardley | 44.4 | 16 | 90 | 2 | — | 24 | 13 | 25 | 1 | 8th | 461 | 399 | — | 128 |
| Chappell | 6 | 2 | 14 | 0 | — | 9 | 6 | 4 | 1 | 9th | 505 | 409 | — | — |
| Walters | 3 | 0 | 21 | 0 | — | | | | | 10th | 528 | 419 | — | — |
| Border | 4 | 1 | 11 | 0 | — | 9 | 5 | 9 | 1 | | | | | |
| Hughes | 1 | 0 | 1 | 0 | — | | | | | | | | | |

## PLAYED AT MELBOURNE 7, 8, 9, 10, 11 FEBRUARY
### INDIA WON BY 59 RUNS

### INDIA

| Batsman | 1st innings | | 2nd innings | |
|---|---|---|---|---|
| *S.M. Gavaskar | c Hughes b Pascoe | 10 | lbw b Lillee | 70 |
| C.P.S. Chauhan | c Yardley b Pascoe | 0 | c Yardley b Lillee | 85 |
| D.B. Vengsarkar | c Border b Lillee | 12 | c Marsh b Pascoe | 41 |
| G.R. Viswanath | c Chappell b Yardley | 114 | b Lillee | 30 |
| S.M. Patil | c Hughes b Lillee | 23 | c Chappell b Yardley | 36 |
| Yashpal Sharma | c Marsh b Lillee | 4 | b Pascoe | 9 |
| Kapil Dev | c Hughes b Pascoe | 5 | b Yardley | 0 |
| †S.M.H. Kirmani | c Marsh b Lillee | 25 | run out | 9 |
| K.D. Ghavri | run out | 0 | run out | 11 |
| N.S. Yadav | not out | 20 | absent hurt | 0 |
| D.R. Doshi | c Walters b Yardley | 0 | b Lillee | 7 |
| Extras | (B1, LB8, NB9, W6) | 24 | (B11, LB8, NB7) | 26 |
| **Total** | | **237** | | **324** |

### AUSTRALIA

| Batsman | 1st innings | | 2nd innings | |
|---|---|---|---|---|
| J. Dyson | c Kirmani b Kapil Dev | 16 | c Kirmani b Ghavri | 3 |
| G.M. Wood | c Doshi b Ghavri | 10 | st Kirmani b Doshi | 10 |
| *G.S. Chappell | c & b Ghavri | 76 | b Ghavri | 0 |
| K.J. Hughes | c Chauhan b Yadav | 24 | b Doshi | 16 |
| A.R. Border | b Yadav | 124 | c Kirmani b Kapil Dev | 9 |
| K.D. Walters | st Kirmani b Doshi | 78 | not out | 18 |
| †R.W. Marsh | c sub b Doshi | 45 | b Kapil Dev | 3 |
| B. Yardley | lbw b Doshi | 0 | b Kapil Dev | 7 |
| D.K. Lillee | c & b Patil | 19 | b Kapil Dev | 4 |
| L.S. Pascoe | lbw b Patil | 3 | run out | 6 |
| J.D. Higgs | not out | 1 | b Kapil Dev | 0 |
| Extras | (B12, LB6, NB5) | 23 | (LB5, NB2) | 7 |
| **Total** | | **419** | | **83** |

### BOWLING

| AUSTRALIA | O | M | R | W | | O | M | R | W |
|---|---|---|---|---|---|---|---|---|---|
| Lillee | 25 | 6 | 65 | 4 | — | 32.1 | 5 | 104 | 4 |
| Pascoe | 22 | 11 | 29 | 3 | — | 29 | 4 | 80 | 2 |
| Chappell | 5 | 2 | 9 | 0 | — | — | — | — | — |
| Yardley | 13 | 3 | 45 | 2 | — | 31 | 11 | 65 | 2 |
| Higgs | 19 | 2 | 65 | 0 | — | 15 | 3 | 41 | 0 |
| Border | — | — | — | — | — | 2 | 0 | 8 | 0 |
| **INDIA** | | | | | | | | | |
| Kapil Dev | 19 | 7 | 41 | 1 | — | 16.4 | 4 | 28 | 5 |
| Doshi | 52 | 14 | 109 | 3 | — | 22 | 9 | 33 | 2 |
| Ghavri | 39 | 4 | 110 | 2 | — | 8 | 4 | 10 | 2 |
| Yadav | 32 | 6 | 100 | 2 | — | — | — | — | — |
| Chauhan | 2 | 0 | 8 | 0 | — | — | — | — | — |
| Patil | 12.3 | 4 | 28 | 2 | — | 0 | 0 | 5 | 0 |

FALL OF WICKETS

| | I | I | A | A |
|---|---|---|---|---|
| | 1st | 1st | 2nd | 2nd |
| 1st | 0 | 30 | 165 | 11 |
| 2nd | 22 | 32 | 176 | 11 |
| 3rd | 43 | 81 | 243 | 18 |
| 4th | 91 | 189 | 245 | 40 |
| 5th | 99 | 320 | 260 | 50 |
| 6th | 115 | 356 | 296 | 55 |
| 7th | 164 | 356 | 296 | 61 |
| 8th | 190 | 413 | 308 | 69 |
| 9th | 230 | 413 | 324 | 79 |
| 10th | 237 | 419 | — | 83 |

# Prudential Trophy
## ENGLAND v WEST INDIES
### PLAYED AT HEADINGLEY, 28, 29 MAY
### WEST INDIES WON BY 24 RUNS

### WEST INDIES

| | | |
|---|---|---:|
| C.G. Greenidge | b Botham | 78 |
| D.L. Haynes | c Tavare b Old | 19 |
| I.V.A. Richards | c Gower b Gooch | 7 |
| S.F.A.F. Bacchus | c Lever b Gooch | 2 |
| A.I. Kallicharran | c Botham b Old | 10 |
| *C.H. Lloyd | c & b Lever | 21 |
| M.D. Marshall | b Botham | 6 |
| †D.L. Murray | run out | 9 |
| A.M.E. Roberts | c Botham b Dilley | 10 |
| J. Garner | run out | 14 |
| M.A. Holding | not out | 0 |
| Extras (B5, LB15, W2) | | 22 |
| **Total (55 overs)** | | 198 |

### ENGLAND

| | | |
|---|---|---:|
| G. Boycott | c Kallicharran b Garner | 5 |
| P. Willey | c Richards b Marshall | 7 |
| C.J. Tavare | not out | 82 |
| G.A. Gooch | c Murray b Richards | 2 |
| D.I. Gower | c Murray b Holding | 12 |
| *I.T. Botham | c Murray b Marshall | 30 |
| D. Lloyd | b Greenidge | 1 |
| †D.L. Bairstow | c Garner b Holding | 16 |
| C.M. Old | b Marshall | 4 |
| G.R. Dilley | c Haynes b Roberts | 0 |
| J.K. Lever | run out | 6 |
| Extras (B3, LB4, W2) | | 9 |
| **Total (51.2 overs)** | | 174 |

**Man of the Match:** C.J. Tavare

## BOWLING

| ENGLAND | O | M | R | W | | FALL OF WICKETS | |
|---|---|---|---|---|---|---|---|
| | | | | | | WI | E |
| Dilley | 11 | 3 | 41 | 1 | | | |
| Lever | 11 | 4 | 36 | 1 | 1st | 36 | 11 |
| Botham | 11 | 1 | 45 | 2 | 2nd | 49 | 15 |
| Old | 11 | 4 | 12 | 2 | 3rd | 51 | 23 |
| Gooch | 7 | 2 | 30 | 2 | 4th | 110 | 38 |
| Willey | 4 | 0 | 12 | 0 | 5th | 151 | 81 |
| **WEST INDIES** | | | | | 6th | 161 | 86 |
| Holding | 9 | 3 | 16 | 2 | 7th | 163 | 130 |
| Roberts | 11 | 4 | 30 | 1 | 8th | 178 | 149 |
| Garner | 9.2 | 0 | 20 | 1 | 9th | 197 | 150 |
| Marshall | 11 | 2 | 28 | 3 | 10th | 198 | 174 |
| Richards | 7 | 0 | 50 | 1 | | | |
| Greenidge | 4 | 0 | 21 | 1 | | | |

# ENGLAND v WEST INDIES
## PLAYED AT LORD'S 30 MAY
## ENGLAND WON BY 3 WICKETS

### WEST INDIES

| | | |
|---|---|---:|
| C.G. Greenidge | c Lever b Marks | 39 |
| D.L. Haynes | c Willis b Marks | 50 |
| S.F.A.F. Bacchus | run out | 40 |
| *I.V.A. Richards | c Lever b Botham | 26 |
| A.I. Kallicharran | c Willis b Old | 11 |
| C.L. King | run out | 33 |
| A.M.E. Roberts | not out | 25 |
| J. Garner | run out | 0 |
| M.D. Marshall | b Willis | 0 |
| M.A. Holding | b Willis | 0 |
| †D.A. Murray | did not bat | |
| Extras (LB9, NB2) | | 11 |
| **Total** (55 overs) (9 wkts) | | 235 |

### ENGLAND

| | | |
|---|---|---:|
| P. Willey | c & b Holding | 56 |
| G. Boycott | run out | 70 |
| C.J. Tavare | c Murray b Holding | 5 |
| G.A. Gooch | c Bacchus b Marshall | 12 |
| D.I. Gower | c Bacchus b Roberts | 12 |
| *I.T. Botham | not out | 42 |
| V.J. Marks | b Holding | 9 |
| †D.L. Bairstow | run out | 2 |
| J.K. Lever | not out | 0 |
| C.M. Old | did not bat | |
| R.G.D. Willis | did not bat | |
| Extras (LB22, NB2, W4) | | 28 |
| **Total** (54.3 overs) (7 wkts) | | 236 |

**Man of the Match:** G. Boycott

### BOWLING

| ENGLAND | O | M | R | W |
|---|---|---|---|---|
| Willis | 10 | 1 | 25 | 2 |
| Lever | 7 | 1 | 23 | 0 |
| Botham | 11 | 2 | 71 | 1 |
| Old | 11 | 1 | 43 | 1 |
| Marks | 11 | 1 | 44 | 2 |
| Willey | 5 | 0 | 18 | 0 |
| **WEST INDIES** | | | | |
| Roberts | 11 | 3 | 42 | 1 |
| Holding | 11 | 0 | 28 | 3 |
| Garner | 10.3 | 0 | 41 | 0 |
| Marshall | 11 | 1 | 45 | 1 |
| Richards | 5 | 0 | 28 | 0 |
| Greenidge | 6 | 0 | 24 | 0 |

| FALL OF WICKETS | WI | E |
|---|---|---|
| 1st | 86 | 135 |
| 2nd | 113 | 143 |
| 3rd | 147 | 156 |
| 4th | 169 | 160 |
| 5th | 186 | 178 |
| 6th | 231 | 212 |
| 7th | 233 | 231 |
| 8th | 233 | — |
| 9th | 235 | — |
| 10th | 235 | — |

# ENGLAND v AUSTRALIA

### PLAYED AT THE OVAL 20 AUGUST
### ENGLAND WON BY 23 RUNS

## ENGLAND

| | | |
|---|---|---|
| G.A. Gooch | b Border | 54 |
| G. Boycott | c Hughes b Lillee | 99 |
| A.R. Butcher | lbw b Dymock | 14 |
| C.W.J. Athey | c Chappell b Lillee | 32 |
| M.W. Gatting | not out | 17 |
| *I.T. Botham | c Yallop b Lillee | 4 |
| P. Willey | c Yallop b Lillee | 2 |
| †D.L. Bairstow | not out | 9 |
| R.D. Jackman | did not bat | |
| C.M. Old | did not bat | |
| M. Hendrick | did not bat | |
| Extras (B2, LB8, NB4, W3) | | 17 |
| **Total** (55 overs) (6 wkts) | | 248 |

## AUSTRALIA

| | | |
|---|---|---|
| B.M. Laird | lbw b Gooch | 15 |
| G.M. Wood | c Athey b Jackman | 4 |
| *G.S. Chappell | c Bairstow b Hendrick | 36 |
| A.R. Border | b Hendrick | 13 |
| K.J. Hughes | not out | 73 |
| G.N. Yallop | b Hendrick | 0 |
| †R.W. Marsh | c Bairstow b Hendrick | 41 |
| D.K. Lillee | c Willey b Hendrick | 0 |
| J.R. Thomson | run out | 15 |
| G. Dymock | not out | 14 |
| L.S. Pascoe | did not bat | |
| Extras (B3, LB10, W1) | | 14 |
| **Total** (55 overs) (8 wkts) | | 225 |

**Man of the Match:** M. Hendrick

## BOWLING

| AUSTRALIA | O | M | R | W | FALL OF WICKETS | | |
|---|---|---|---|---|---|---|---|
| | | | | | | E | A |
| Lillee | 11 | 1 | 35 | 4 | | | |
| Thomson | 11 | 3 | 25 | 0 | 1st | 108 | 11 |
| Dymock | 9 | 0 | 50 | 1 | 2nd | 140 | 36 |
| Pascoe | 11 | 1 | 50 | 0 | 3rd | 212 | 68 |
| Border | 11 | 2 | 61 | 1 | 4th | 221 | 71 |
| Chappell | 2 | 0 | 10 | 0 | 5th | 225 | 75 |
| **ENGLAND** | | | | | 6th | 232 | 161 |
| Old | 9 | 0 | 43 | 0 | 7th | — | 161 |
| Jackman | 11 | 0 | 46 | 1 | 8th | — | 192 |
| Botham | 9 | 1 | 28 | 0 | 9th | — | — |
| Gooch | 7 | 0 | 29 | 1 | 10th | — | — |
| Hendrick | 11 | 3 | 31 | 5 | | | |
| Willey | 8 | 0 | 34 | 0 | | | |

# ENGLAND v AUSTRALIA
## PLAYED AT BIRMINGHAM 22 AUGUST
## ENGLAND WON BY 47 RUNS

### ENGLAND

| | | |
|---|---|---:|
| G.A. Gooch | b Thomson | 108 |
| G. Boycott | c Marsh b Border | 78 |
| C.W.J. Athey | b Pascoe | 51 |
| R.O. Butcher | c Dyson b Pascoe | 52 |
| M.W. Gatting | run out | 2 |
| *I.T. Botham | b Pascoe | 2 |
| †D.L. Bairstow | b Lillee | 6 |
| R.D. Jackman | c Marsh b Pascoe | 6 |
| J.E. Emburey | not out | 1 |
| C.M. Old | not out | 2 |
| M. Hendrick | did not bat | |
| Extras (B4, LB3, NB4, W1) | | 12 |
| **Total** (55 overs) (8 wkts) | | 320 |

### AUSTRALIA

| | | |
|---|---|---:|
| B.M. Laird | c Emburey b Hendrick | 36 |
| J. Dyson | b Hendrick | 24 |
| K.J. Hughes | c & b Gooch | 98 |
| A.R. Border | run out | 26 |
| G.N. Yallop | not out | 52 |
| D.K. Lillee | b Hendrick | 21 |
| R.J. Bright | not out | 5 |
| *G.S. Chappell | did not bat | |
| †R.W. Marsh | did not bat | |
| J.R. Thomson | did not bat | |
| L.S. Pascoe | did not bat | |
| Extras (B1, LB9, W1) | | 11 |
| **Total** (55 overs) (5 wkts) | | 273 |

**Man of the Match:** G.A. Gooch

## BOWLING

| AUSTRALIA | O | M | R | W | | FALL OF WICKETS | |
|---|---|---|---|---|---|---|---|
| | | | | | | *E* | *A* |
| Thomson | 11 | 1 | 69 | 1 | 1st | 154 | 53 |
| Lillee | 11 | 0 | 43 | 1 | 2nd | 215 | 80 |
| Pascoe | 11 | 0 | 69 | 4 | 3rd | 292 | 119 |
| Bright | 8 | 0 | 48 | 0 | 4th | 298 | 222 |
| Chappell | 11 | 0 | 65 | 0 | 5th | 302 | 259 |
| Border | 3 | 0 | 14 | 1 | 6th | 311 | — |
| **ENGLAND** | | | | | 7th | 313 | — |
| Old | 11 | 2 | 44 | 0 | 8th | 318 | — |
| Jackman | 11 | 1 | 45 | 0 | 9th | — | — |
| Botham | 11 | 1 | 41 | 0 | 10th | — | — |
| Hendrick | 10 | 0 | 54 | 3 | | | |
| Emburey | 8 | 0 | 51 | 0 | | | |
| Gooch | 3 | 0 | 16 | 1 | | | |
| Boycott | 1 | 0 | 11 | 0 | | | |

# ENGLAND v AUSTRALIA
# 1876-77 to 1980
## SERIES BY SERIES

| Season | | Visiting Captain | P | E W | A W | D |
|--------|---|------------------|---|-----|-----|---|
| 1876-77 | In Australia | J. Lillywhite (E) | 2 | 1 | 1 | 0 |
| 1878-79 | In Australia | Lord Harris (E) | 1 | 0 | 1 | 0 |
| 1880 | In England | W.L. Murdoch (A) | 1 | 1 | 0 | 0 |
| 1881-82 | In Australia | A. Shaw (E) | 4 | 0 | 2 | 2 |
| 1882 | In England | W.L. Murdoch (A) | 1 | 0 | 1 | 0 |
| | | **The Ashes** | | | | |
| 1882-83 | In Australia | Hon. I.F.W. Bligh (E) | 4† | 2 | 2 | 0 |
| 1884 | In England | W.L. Murdoch (A) | 3 | 1 | 0 | 2 |
| 1884-85 | In Australia | A. Shrewsbury (E) | 5 | 3 | 2 | 0 |
| 1886 | In England | H.J.H. Scott (A) | 3 | 3 | 0 | 0 |
| 1886-87 | In Australia | A. Shrewsbury (E) | 2 | 2 | 0 | 0 |
| 1887-88 | In Australia | W.W. Read (E) | 1 | 1 | 0 | 0 |
| 1888 | In England | P.S. McDonnell (A) | 3 | 2 | 1 | 0 |
| 1890 | In England | W.L. Murdoch (A) | 2* | 2 | 0 | 0 |
| 1891-92 | In Australia | W.G. Grace (E) | 3 | 1 | 2 | 0 |
| 1893 | In England | J.McC. Blackham (A) | 3 | 1 | 0 | 2 |
| 1894-95 | In Australia | A.E. Stoddart (E) | 5 | 3 | 2 | 0 |
| 1896 | In England | G.H.S. Trott (A) | 3 | 2 | 1 | 0 |
| 1897-98 | In Australia | A.E. Stoddart (E) | 5 | 1 | 4 | 0 |
| 1899 | In England | J. Darling (A) | 5 | 0 | 1 | 4 |
| 1901-02 | In Australia | A.C. MacLaren (E) | 5 | 1 | 4 | 0 |
| 1902 | In England | J. Darling (A) | 5 | 1 | 2 | 2 |
| 1903-04 | In Australia | P.F. Warner (E) | 5 | 3 | 2 | 0 |
| 1905 | In England | J. Darling (A) | 5 | 2 | 0 | 3 |
| 1907-08 | In Australia | A.O. Jones (E) | 5 | 1 | 4 | 0 |
| 1909 | In England | M.A. Noble (A) | 5 | 1 | 2 | 2 |
| 1911-12 | In Australia | J.W.H.T. Douglas (E) | 5 | 4 | 1 | 0 |
| 1912 | In England | S.E. Gregory (A) | 3 | 1 | 0 | 2 |
| 1920-21 | In Australia | J.W.H.T. Douglas (E) | 5 | 0 | 5 | 0 |
| 1921 | In England | W.W. Armstrong (A) | 5 | 0 | 3 | 2 |
| 1924-25 | In Australia | A.E.R. Gilligan (E) | 5 | 1 | 4 | 0 |
| 1926 | In England | H.L. Collins (A) | 5 | 1 | 0 | 4 |
| 1928-29 | In Australia | A.P.F. Chapman (E) | 5 | 4 | 1 | 0 |
| 1930 | In England | W.M. Woodfull (A) | 5 | 1 | 2 | 2 |
| 1932-33 | In Australia | D.R. Jardine (E) | 5 | 4 | 1 | 0 |
| 1934 | In England | W.M. Woodfull (A) | 5 | 1 | 2 | 2 |
| 1936-37 | In Australia | G.O.B. Allen (E) | 5 | 2 | 3 | 0 |
| 1938 | In England | D.G. Bradman (A) | 4* | 1 | 1 | 2 |
| 1946-47 | In Australia | W.R. Hammond (E) | 5 | 0 | 3 | 2 |
| 1948 | In England | D.G. Bradman (A) | 5 | 0 | 4 | 1 |
| 1950-51 | In Australia | F.R. Brown (E) | 5 | 1 | 4 | 0 |
| 1953 | In England | A.L. Hassett (A) | 5 | 1 | 0 | 4 |
| 1954-55 | In Australia | L. Hutton (E) | 5 | 3 | 1 | 1 |
| 1956 | In England | I.W. Johnson (A) | 5 | 2 | 1 | 2 |
| 1958-59 | In Australia | P.B.H. May (E) | 5 | 0 | 4 | 1 |
| 1961 | In England | R. Benaud (A) | 5 | 1 | 2 | 2 |
| 1962-63 | In Australia | E.R. Dexter (E) | 5 | 1 | 1 | 3 |
| 1964 | In England | R.B. Simpson (A) | 5 | 0 | 1 | 4 |
| 1965-66 | In Australia | M.J.K. Smith (E) | 5 | 1 | 1 | 3 |

34

| Season | | Visiting Captain | P | E W | A W | D |
|--------|--|------------------|---|-----|-----|---|
| 1968 | In England | W.M. Lawry (A) | 5 | 1 | 1 | 3 |
| 1970-71 | In Australia | R. Illingworth (E) | 6* | 2 | 0 | 4 |
| 1972 | In England | I.M. Chappell (A) | 5 | 2 | 2 | 1 |
| 1974-75 | In Australia | M.H. Denness(E) | 6 | 1 | 4 | 1 |
| 1975 | In England | I.M. Chappell (A) | 4 | 0 | 1 | 3 |
| 1976-77 | In Australia | A.W. Greig (E) | 1 | 0 | 1 | 0 |
| 1977 | In England | G.S. Chappell (A) | 5 | 3 | 0 | 2 |
| 1978-79 | In Australia | J.M. Brearley (E) | 6 | 5 | 1 | 0 |
| 1979-80 | In Australia | J.M. Brearley (E) | 3 | 0 | 3 | 0 |
| 1980 | In England | G.S. Chappell (A) | 1 | 0 | 0 | 1 |
| | | At Lord's | 26 | 5 | 9 | 12 |
| | | At The Oval | 27 | 12 | 5 | 10 |
| | | At Manchester | 22 | 6 | 4 | 12 |
| | | At Leeds | 17 | 4 | 5 | 8 |
| | | At Nottingham | 13 | 3 | 3 | 7 |
| | | At Birmingham | 5 | 1 | 1 | 3 |
| | | At Sheffield | 1 | 0 | 1 | 0 |
| | | At Melbourne | 46 | 16 | 23 | 7 |
| | | At Sydney | 45 | 20 | 22 | 3 |
| | | At Adelaide | 22 | 7 | 12 | 3 |
| | | At Brisbane | 12 | 4 | 5 | 3 |
| | | At Perth | 4 | 1 | 2 | 1 |
| | | In England | 111 | 31 | 28 | 52 |
| | | In Australia | 129 | 48 | 64 | 17 |
| | | | 240 | 79 | 92 | 69 |

* The Test matches at Manchester in 1890 and 1938 and the third Test match at Melbourne in 1970-71 were abandoned without a ball being bowled and are excluded from this schedule.
† The Ashes were awarded to England after a series of three matches which England won 2-1. A fourth unofficial match was played which was won by Australia, each innings being played on a different pitch.
N.B. The Ashes were not at stake in 1976-77, 1979-80 and 1980.

## HIGHEST INNINGS TOTALS
### England

| | | |
|--|--|--|
| 903-7d | The Oval | 1938 |
| 658-8d | Nottingham | 1938 |
| 636 | Sydney | 1928-29 |
| 627-9d | Manchester | 1934 |
| 611 | Manchester | 1964 |

### Australia

| | | |
|--|--|--|
| 729-6d | Lord's | 1930 |
| 701 | The Oval | 1934 |
| 695 | The Oval | 1930 |
| 659-8d | Sydney | 1946-47 |
| 656-8d | Manchester | 1964 |
| 645 | Brisbane | 1946-47 |
| 604 | Melbourne | 1936-37 |
| 601-8d | Brisbane | 1954-55 |
| 600 | Melbourne | 1924-25 |

## LOWEST INNINGS TOTALS
### England

| | | |
|--|--|--|
| 45 | Sydney | 1886-87 |
| 52 | The Oval | 1948 |
| 53 | Lord's | 1888 |
| 61 | Melbourne | 1901-02 |
| 61 | Melbourne | 1903-04 |

### Australia

| | | |
|--|--|--|
| 36 | Birmingham | 1902 |
| 42 | Sydney | 1887-88 |
| 44 | The Oval | 1896 |
| 53 | Lord's | 1896 |
| 58 | Brisbane | 1936-37 |
| 60 | Lord's | 1888 |
| 63 | The Oval | 1882 |
| 65 | The Oval | 1912 |
| 66 | Brisbane | 1928-29 |

## HIGHEST INDIVIDUAL INNINGS FOR ENGLAND

| | | | |
|---|---|---|---|
| 364 | L. Hutton | at The Oval | 1938 |
| 281 | R.E. Foster | at Sydney | 1903-04 |
| 256 | K.F. Barrington | at Manchester | 1964 |
| 251 | W.R. Hammond | at Sydney | 1928-29 |
| 240 | W.R. Hammond | at Lord's | 1938 |
| 231* | W.R. Hammond | at Sydney | 1936-37 |
| 216* | E. Paynter | at Nottingham | 1938 |
| 200 | W.R. Hammond | at Melbourne | 1928-29 |

*A total of 166 centuries have been scored for England.*

## HIGHEST INDIVIDUAL INNINGS FOR AUSTRALIA

| | | | |
|---|---|---|---|
| 334 | D.G. Bradman | at Leeds | 1930 |
| 311 | R.B. Simpson | at Manchester | 1964 |
| 307 | R.M. Cowper | at Melbourne | 1965-66 |
| 304 | D.G. Bradman | at Leeds | 1934 |
| 270 | D.G. Bradman | at Melbourne | 1936-37 |
| 266 | W.H. Ponsford | at The Oval | 1934 |
| 254 | D.G. Bradman | at Lord's | 1930 |
| 244 | D.G. Bradman | at The Oval | 1934 |
| 234 | S.G. Barnes | at Sydney | 1946-47 |
| 234 | D.G. Bradman | at Sydney | 1946-47 |
| 232 | D.G. Bradman | at The Oval | 1930 |
| 232 | S.J. McCabe | at Nottingham | 1938 |
| 225 | R.B. Simpson | at Adelaide | 1965-66 |
| 212 | D.G. Bradman | at Adelaide | 1936-37 |
| 211 | W.L. Murdoch | at The Oval | 1884 |
| 207 | K.R. Stackpole | at Brisbane | 1970-71 |
| 206* | W.A. Brown | at Lord's | 1938 |
| 206 | A.R. Morris | at Adelaide | 1950-51 |
| 201* | J. Ryder | at Sydney | 1924-25 |
| 201 | S.E. Gregory | at Sydney | 1894-95 |

*A total of 184 centuries have been scored for Australia.*

## A CENTURY IN EACH INNINGS OF A MATCH
### FOR ENGLAND

| | | | | |
|---|---|---|---|---|
| 176 | & 127 | H. Sutcliffe | at Melbourne | 1924-25 |
| 119* | & 177 | W.R. Hammond | at Adelaide | 1928-29 |
| 147 | & 103* | D.C.S. Compton | at Adelaide | 1946-47 |

### FOR AUSTRALIA

| | | | | |
|---|---|---|---|---|
| 136 | & 130 | W. Bardsley | at The Oval | 1909 |
| 122 | & 124* | A.R. Morris | at Adelaide | 1946-47 |

## A CENTURY ON DEBUT IN SERIES
### FOR ENGLAND

| | | | |
|---|---|---|---|
| 152 | W.G. Grace (on Test debut) | at The Oval | 1880 |
| 154* | K.S. Ranjitsinhji (on Test debut) | at Manchester | 1896 |
| 287 | R.E. Foster (on Test debut) | at Sydney | 1903-04 |
| 119 | G. Gunn (on Test debut) | at Sydney | 1907-08 |
| 115 | H. Sutcliffe | at Sydney | 1924-25 |
| 137 | M. Leyland | at Melbourne | 1928-29 |
| 173 | K.S. Duleepsinhji | at Lord's | 1930 |
| 102 | Nawab of Pataudi (on Test debut) | at Sydney | 1932-33 |
| 100 | L. Hutton | at Nottingham | 1938 |
| 102 | D.C.S. Compton | at Nottingham | 1938 |
| 109 | W. Watson | at Lord's | 1953 |
| 112 | R. Subba Row | at Birmingham | 1961 |
| 120 | J.H. Edrich | at Lords | 1964 |
| 174 | D.W. Randall | at Melbourne | 1976-77 |

## FOR AUSTRALIA

| | | | |
|---|---|---|---|
| 165* | C. Bannerman (on Test debut) | at Melbourne | 1876-77 |
| 107 | H. Graham (on Test debut) | at Lord's | 1893 |
| 104 | R.A. Duff (on Test debut) | at Melbourne | 1903-04 |
| 116 | R.J. Hartigan (on Test debut) | at Adelaide | 1907-08 |
| 104 | H.L. Collins (on Test debut) | at Sydney | 1920-21 |
| 110 | W.H. Ponsford (on Test debut) | at Sydney | 1924-25 |
| 164 | A. Jackson (on Test debut) | at Adelaide | 1928-29 |
| 112 | R.N. Harvey | at Leeds | 1948 |
| 101* | J.W. Burke (on Test debut) | at Adelaide | 1950-51 |
| 155 | K.D. Walters (on Test debut) | at Brisbane | 1965-66 |
| 108 | G.S. Chappell (on Test debut) | at Perth | 1970-71 |
| 102 | G.N. Yallop | at Brisbane | 1978-79 |

## RECORD WICKET PARTNERSHIPS FOR ENGLAND

| | | | |
|---|---|---|---|
| 1st | 323 | J.B. Hobbs & W. Rhodes at Melbourne | 1911-12 |
| 2nd | 382 | L. Hutton & M. Leyland at The Oval | 1938 |
| 3rd | 262 | W.R. Hammond & D.R. Jardine at Adelaide | 1928-29 |
| 4th | 222 | W.R. Hammond & E. Paynter at Lord's | 1938 |
| 5th | 206 | E. Paynter & D.C.S. Compton at Nottingham | 1938 |
| 6th | 215 { | L. Hutton & J. Hardstaff at The Oval | 1938 |
| | | G. Boycott & A.P.E. Knott at Nottingham | 1977 |
| 7th | 143 | F.E. Woolley & J. Vine at Sydney | 1911-12 |
| 8th | 124 | E.H. Hendren & H. Larwood at Brisbane | 1928-29 |
| 9th | 151 | W.H. Scotton & W.W. Read at The Oval | 1884 |
| 10th | 130 | R.E. Foster & W. Rhodes at Sydney | 1903-04 |

## RECORD WICKET PARTNERSHIPS FOR AUSTRALIA

| | | | |
|---|---|---|---|
| 1st | 244 | R.B. Simpson & W.M. Lawry at Adelaide | 1965-66 |
| 2nd | 451 | W.H. Ponsford & D.G. Bradman at The Oval | 1934 |
| 3rd | 276 | D.G. Bradman & A.L. Hassett at Brisbane | 1946-47 |
| 4th | 388 | W.H. Ponsford & D.G. Bradman at Leeds | 1934 |
| 5th | 405 | S.G. Barnes & D.G. Bradman at Sydney | 1946-47 |
| 6th | 346 | J.H.W. Fingleton & D.G. Bradman at Melbourne | 1936-37 |
| 7th | 165 | C. Hill & H. Trumble at Melbourne | 1897-98 |
| 8th | 243 | C. Hill & R.J. Hartigan at Adelaide | 1907-08 |
| 9th | 154 | S.E. Gregory & J. McC. Blackham at Sydney | 1894-95 |
| 10th | 127 | J.M. Taylor & A.A. Mailey at Sydney | 1924-25 |

## HIGHEST RUN AGGREGATE IN A TEST RUBBER FOR:

| | | | |
|---|---|---|---|
| England in England | 562 (Av. 62.44) | D.C.S. Compton | 1948 |
| England in Australia | 905 (Av. 113.12) | W.R. Hammond | 1928-29 |
| Australia in England | 974 (Av. 139.14) | D.G. Bradman | 1930 |
| Australia in Australia | 810 (Av. 90.00) | D.G. Bradman | 1936-37 |

## BEST INNINGS BOWLING FIGURES FOR:

| | | | |
|---|---|---|---|
| England in England | 10-53 | J.C. Laker at Manchester | 1956 |
| England in Australia | 8-35 | G.A. Lohmann at Sydney | 1886-87 |
| Australia in England | 8-31 | F. Laver at Manchester | 1909 |
| Australia in Australia | 9-121 | A.A. Mailey at Melbourne | 1920-21 |

## TEN WICKETS OR MORE IN A MATCH

35 occurrences for England (the last by I.T. Botham at Perth in 1979-80) and 33 occurrences for Australia (the last by D.K. Lillee at Melbourne in 1979-80).

## HIGHEST WICKET AGGREGATE IN A TEST RUBBER FOR:

| | | | |
|---|---|---|---|
| England in England | 46 (Av. 9.60) | J.C. Laker | 1956 |
| England in Australia | 38 (Av. 23.18) | M.W. Tate | 1924-25 |
| Australia in England | 31 (Av. 17.67) | D.K. Lillee | 1972 |
| Australia in Australia | 41 (Av. 12.85) | R.M. Hogg | 1978-79 |

| | | |
|---|---|---|
| **HIGHEST MATCH AGGREGATE** | 1753-40 wkts Adelaide | 1920-21 |
| **LOWEST MATCH AGGREGATE** | 291-40 wkts Lord's | 1888 |

# THE WISDEN BOOK OF COUNTY CRICKET 1873 to 1980

## Christopher Martin-Jenkins and Frank Warwick

The first truly comprehensive book on county cricket. Christopher Martin-Jenkins recaptures the fever of competition between the counties in the early years, the golden age of the inter-war period and reviews the changes made since the war in various attempts to help county cricket through successive financial crises.

Frank Warwick provides the most complete collection of statistical information ever gathered on county cricket, paying tribute to the real stalwarts of the county game.

A WISDEN CRICKET LIBRARY title
Illustrated with photographs
416 pp   £11.95
Available from May 14

# THE GILLETTE CUP 1963 to 1980

Gordon Ross

The Gillette Cup began at Old Trafford in May 1963. By the time of the last final in 1980 there had been 374 Gillette Cup ties, producing some of the greatest cricket the game has ever known.

This book is the official history of the Cup and it provides a comprehensive coverage of the games played, an insight into cricket's first sponsor, and full statistics of the ties. Above all it captures the carnival spirit with which the Gillette Cup will always be associated.

Illustrated
192pp    £6.95

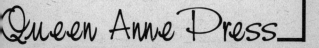
Queen Anne Press

# Swivel head winner.

Gillette
CONTOUR

# MIDDLESEX WIN THE
# LAST GILLETTE FINAL

It was perhaps fitting that London staged a 'Derby' game between Middlesex and Surrey in this last ever Gillette Cup final, although there had seemed a possibility at one time during the season that Sussex might meet Worcestershire to restage the first final played in 1963. In being able to play the last final on the Saturday without any interference from the weather in a particularly bad summer, Gillette completed a remarkable spell of good fortune on cup final day. In the eighteen years, seventeen of the finals have begun and been completed on the Saturday. The odd one, in 1974, turned out to be a day of sunshine, but the ground had taken a relentless soaking on the Thursday, and any reasonable hope that there might be play was dispelled with a very heavy downpour about nine o'clock on the Saturday morning.

Sussex were strongly fancied for most of the season, especially as they were favoured with four consecutive matches at Hove, where they have always been difficult to beat. They beat Suffolk by eight wickets; Glamorgan by 104 runs; Warwickshire by nine wickets–and then came Middlesex and a hurricane named 'Daniel'. In a devastating spell of fast-bowling, Wayne Daniel totally destroyed Sussex after Middlesex had made only 179, which many thought would not be enough. Then came Daniel. When he bowled Barclay for nought, bowled Mendis for three, and had Parker caught for one, Daniel had taken three wickets for six runs in twenty-six balls–and that was only the start of it. He was to take three more wickets to conclude with the remarkable analysis of 10-2-15-6. Middlesex won comfortably by 64 runs. In fact most of what Middlesex had done in the Gillette Cup they had done comfortably, except for a very minor hiccup against Ireland when they were 67 for five. They beat Notts by four wickets and then Worcestershire by ten wickets at Worcester.

Surrey had had a different sort of journey to the final, yet by far the most impressive on paper. They had beaten Northants, Gloucestershire, Essex and Yorkshire, but by far the most hair-raising encounter was at Chelmsford. Surrey scored 195 for seven in their 60 overs. With three overs left and three wickets standing, Essex wanted only five runs–the result surely was a foregone conclusion. But history has proved that there is no such thing in Gillette Cup cricket. At the dramatic conclusion the scores were level, but Surrey won through having lost the least number of wickets. Essex have never appeared—and never will—in a Gillette final. It is unlikely, however, that they have ever been as close as on this day, and against Somerset at Taunton in the 1978 semi-final: in both cases the scores were level; in both cases Essex lost. Surrey were rarely in trouble against Yorkshire at The Oval in a two-day game (both semi-finals were), although Yorkshire's players may say in their defence that the ball was moving about a good deal more when they batted on the first day than when Surrey's turn came.

The final—the last—did not produce a cliff-hanging finish—nor did it ever seem likely to, for Middlesex were just that bit too good all along. It was a placid final except for a flourish of aggression towards the end when Roland Butcher rattled up a quick fifty, apparently on the instructions of his captain Mike Brearley, who had one eye on the fading light and wanted to finish the game before the light deteriorated to such an extent that it made batting conditions hazardous. Butcher's hustle cost Brearley his century. He was 96 not out at the close and thus just missed scoring what would have been only the fourth century in a Gillette Cup final, and only the second by an Englishman. The distinguished triumvirate of cup final centurians are Geoff Boycott, 146 not out for Yorkshire against Surrey in 1965; Clive Lloyd, 126 for Lancashire against Warwickshire in 1972; and Viv Richards, 117 for Somerset against Northants in 1979.

If there was a moment when Surrey supporters cherished a genuine hope that they may be able to win it was at tea. Surrey had scored 201. Middlesex were 57 for two. A quick wicket after tea and the result could have been wide open. Mike Brearley and Mike Gatting made certain that this didn't happen. Brearley, who towards the end of this season was probably batting better than at any time in his career, played a masterly innings; he was in no hurry to score runs when he was seeing off Clarke and Jackman, and then paced the innings just right. When he asked Butcher to have a go he still had plenty of wickets in hand, so there was no risk at all even if Butcher had got out by taking chances. So Mike Brearley received the Gillette Cup from Denis Sanan, Managing Director of Gillette UK. Middlesex had won it for the second and last time.

42

*Total Man of the Match awards are given in brackets where relevant.*

# 1980 RESULTS

### FIRST ROUND – 2 JULY
### Devon v Cornwall at Exeter
Devon 229-5 in 60 overs (Wallen 104, Green 54)
Cornwall 84 in 37.1 overs (Goulding 5-21)
**Result:** Devon won by 145 runs
**Man of the Match:** G. Wallen
**Adjudicator:** C.J. Barnett

### Middlesex v Ireland at Lord's
Ireland 102 in 51.4 overs (Van der Bijl 5-12)
Middlesex 103-5 in 38.3 overs
**Result:** Middlesex won by 5 wickets
**Man of the Match:** V.A.P. Van der Bijl
**Adjudicator:** J.C. Laker

### Somerset v Worcestershire at Taunton
Somerset 165 in 49.1 overs
Worcestershire 168-8 in 59.2 overs (Humphries 51)
**Result:** Worcestershire won by 2 wickets
**Man of the Match:** D.J. Humphries
**Adjudicator:** W.J. Edrich

### Surrey v Northamptonshire at The Oval
Northamptonshire 141 in 59.5 overs (Jackman 6-32)
Surrey 143-3 in 43 overs (Smith 59*)
**Result:** Surrey won by 7 wickets
**Man of the Match:** R.D. Jackman (2)
**Adjudicator:** J.T. Murray

### Sussex v Suffolk at Hove
Suffolk 185-8 in 60 overs (Timur Mohammad 85, Done 53)
Sussex 186-2 in 49.1 overs (Phillipson 70*, Imran Khan 63*)
**Result:** Sussex won by 8 wickets
**Man of the Match:** Imran Khan (3)
**Adjudicator:** K.F. Barrington

### Warwickshire v Oxfordshire at Edgbaston
Warwickshire 314-6 in 60 overs (Amiss 82, Lloyd 63)
Oxfordshire 180-8 in 60 overs (Nurton 67*)
**Result:** Warwickshire won by 134 runs
**Man of the Match:** D.L. Amiss (3)
**Adjudicator:** R.T. Simpson

### 2 – 3 JULY
### Nottinghamshire v Durham at Trent Bridge
Durham 186 in 59.1 overs (Wasim Raja 53, Hacker 4-30)
Nottinghamshire 187-6 in 58.5 overs
**Result:** Nottinghamshire won by 4 wickets
**Man of the Match:** Wasim Raja
**Adjudicator:** C. Washbrook

43

## SECOND ROUND 16 JULY

### Derbyshire v Hampshire at Derby

Derbyshire 215-8 in 60 overs (Miller 58)
Hampshire 216-6 in 57.5 overs (Jesty 118, Pocock 73*)
**Result:** Hampshire won by 4 wickets
**Man of the Match:** T.E. Jesty (3)
**Adjudicator:** R.T. Simpson

### Leicestershire v Essex at Leicester

Essex 310-7 in 60 overs (McEwan 119, Hardie 65)
Leicestershire 197 in 52.2 overs
**Result:** Essex won by 113 runs
**Man of the Match:** K.S. McEwan
**Adjudicator:** J.T. Murray

### Nottinghamshire v Middlesex at Trent Bridge

Nottinghamshire 190-7 in 60 overs
Middlesex 194-6 in 57.4 overs (Gatting 95*)
**Result:** Middlesex won by 4 wickets
**Man of the Match:** M.W. Gatting
**Adjudicator:** J.H. Edrich

### Surrey v Gloucestershire at The Oval

Surrey 200 in 60 overs (Knight 59)
Gloucestershire 192-9 in 60 overs (Procter 52)
**Result:** Surrey won by 8 runs
**Man of the Match:** R.D.V. Knight (4) (3 with Gloucestershire)
**Adjudicator:** W.J. Edrich

### Sussex v Glamorgan at Hove

Sussex 258-7 in 60 overs (Mendis 119, Parker 67)
Glamorgan 154 in 48.3 overs
**Result:** Sussex won by 104 runs
**Man of the Match:** G.D. Mendis
**Adjudicator:** J.D. Robertson

### Warwickshire v Devon at Edgbaston

Devon 143-8 in 60 overs (Green 59)
Warwickshire 147-3 in 43.2 overs (Lloyd 81)
**Result:** Warwickshire won by 7 wickets
**Man of the Match:** B.C. Green
**Adjudicator:** C.J. Barnett

### Worcestershire v Lancashire at Worcester

Worcestershire 265-9 in 60 overs (Turner 115, Neale 51)
Lancashire 226-9 in 60 overs (Hayes 63)
**Result:** Worcestershire won by 39 runs
**Man of the Match:** G.M. Turner
**Adjudicator:** K.F. Barrington

### Yorkshire v Kent at Headingley

Yorkshire 279-6 in 60 overs (Athey 115, Boycott 87)
Kent 233 in 56 overs (Woolmer 91)
**Result:** Yorkshire won by 46 runs
**Man of the Match:** C.W.J. Athey
**Adjudicator:** C. Washbrook

44

## QUARTER FINALS – 30 JULY
### Worcestershire v Middlesex at Worcester
Worcestershire 126 in 54.2 overs
Middlesex 127-0 in 44.5 overs (Radley 64*)
**Result:** Middlesex won by 10 wickets
**Man of the Match:** S.P. Hughes
**Adjudicator:** C. Washbrook

### Essex v Surrey at Chelmsford
Surrey 195-7 in 60 overs (Clinton 58)
Essex 195 in 59.5 overs (Hardie 70, Jackman 5-22)
**Result:** Surrey won on least wickets lost
**Man of the Match:** R.D. Jackman (3)
**Adjudicator:** W.J. Edrich

### Sussex v Warwickshire at Hove
Warwickshire 210-8 in 60 overs (Smith 64)
Sussex 214-1 in 49.1 overs (Mendis 141*)
**Result:** Sussex won by 9 wickets
**Man of the Match:** G.D. Mendis (2)
**Adjudicator:** J.H. Edrich

### Hampshire v Yorkshire at Southampton
Hampshire 196 in 58 overs (Turner 53)
Yorkshire 197-3 in 54.5 overs (Athey 93*, Love 61*)
**Result:** Yorkshire won by 7 wickets
**Man of the Match:** C.W.J. Athey (2)
**Adjudicator:** K.F. Barrington

## SEMI-FINALS – 13-14 AUGUST
### Surrey v Yorkshire at The Oval
Yorkshire 135 in 53.5 overs (Clarke 4-38)
Surrey 136-6 in 47.5 overs
**Result:** Surrey won by 4 wickets
**Man of the Match:** R.D.V. Knight (5) (3 with Gloucestershire)
**Adjudicator:** W.J. Edrich

### Sussex v Middlesex at Hove
Middlesex 179 in 60 overs
Sussex 115 in 49.2 overs (Daniel 6-15)
**Result:** Middlesex won by 64 runs
**Man of the Match:** W.W. Daniel (2)
**Adjudicator:** K.F. Barrington

---

### GILLETTE CUP WINNERS

| | | | |
|---|---|---|---|
| 1963 | Sussex | 1972 | Lancashire |
| 1964 | Sussex | 1973 | Gloucestershire |
| 1965 | Yorkshire | 1974 | Kent |
| 1966 | Warwickshire | 1975 | Lancashire |
| 1967 | Kent | 1976 | Northamptonshire |
| 1968 | Warwickshire | 1977 | Middlesex |
| 1969 | Yorkshire | 1978 | Sussex |
| 1970 | Lancashire | 1979 | Somerset |
| 1971 | Lancashire | 1980 | Middlesex |

# THE GILLETTE CUP FINAL

## PLAYED AT LORD'S 6 SEPTEMBER
## MIDDLESEX WON BY 7 WICKETS

### SURREY

| | | |
|---|---|---|
| A.R. Butcher | b Selvey | 29 |
| G.S. Clinton | c Radley b Selvey | 13 |
| *R.D.V. Knight | c & b Embury | 11 |
| D.M. Smith | c Van der Bijl b Daniel | 50 |
| G.R.J. Roope | b Hughes | 35 |
| M.A. Lynch | c Gatting b Hughes | 3 |
| Intikhab Alam | c Butcher b Van der Bijl | 34 |
| D.J. Thomas | b Hughes | 4 |
| R.D. Jackman | b Daniel | 5 |
| S.T. Clarke | not out | 3 |
| †C.J. Richards | run out | 0 |
| Extras (B1, LB5, W1, NB7) | | 14 |
| | | |
| **Total** (60 overs) | | 201 |

### MIDDLESEX

| | | |
|---|---|---|
| *J.M. Brearley | not out | 96 |
| †P.R. Downton | c Clarke b Knight | 13 |
| C.T. Radley | c & b Thomas | 5 |
| M.W. Gatting | b Jackman | 24 |
| R.O. Butcher | not out | 50 |
| Extras (B3, LB11) | | 14 |
| | | |
| **Total** (53.5 overs) (3 wkts) | | 202 |

Did not bat: G.D. Barlow, J. Emburey, V.A.P. Van der Bijl,
S. Hughes, M.W.W. Selvey, W.W. Daniel
**Man of the Match:** J.M. Brearley (4)
**Adjudicator:** I.T. Botham

### BOWLING

| MIDDLESEX | O | M | R | W | | FALL OF WICKETS | | |
|---|---|---|---|---|---|---|---|---|
| | | | | | | | *S* | *M* |
| Daniel | 12 | 3 | 33 | 2 | | 1st | 26 | 44 |
| Selvey | 12 | 5 | 17 | 2 | | 2nd | 52 | 57 |
| Hughes | 11 | 0 | 60 | 3 | | 3rd | 59 | 121 |
| Emburey | 12 | 2 | 34 | 1 | | 4th | 109 | |
| Gatting | 1 | 0 | 11 | 0 | | 5th | 123 | |
| Van der Bijl | 12 | 0 | 32 | 1 | | 6th | 185 | |
| **SURREY** | | | | | | 7th | 186 | |
| Jackman | 11 | 1 | 31 | 1 | | 8th | 195 | |
| Clarke | 8.5 | 1 | 29 | 0 | | 9th | 201 | |
| Knight | 10 | 2 | 38 | 1 | | 10th | 201 | |
| Thomas | 12 | 0 | 38 | 1 | | | | |
| Intikhab | 12 | 0 | 52 | 0 | | | | |

# GILLETTE CUP
## PRINCIPAL RECORDS

**Highest innings total:** 371-4 off 60 overs, Hampshire v Glamorgan (Southampton) 1975.

**Highest innings total by a Minor County:** 229-5 off 60 overs, Devon v Cornwall (Exeter) 1980.

**Highest innings total by a side batting second:** 297-4 off 57.1 overs, Somerset v Warwickshire (Taunton) 1978.

**Highest innings total by a side batting first and losing:** 292-5 off 60 overs, Warwickshire v Somerset (Taunton) 1978.

**Lowest innings total:** 41 off 20 overs, Cambridgeshire v Buckinghamshire (Cambridge) 1972; 41 off 19.4 overs, Middlesex v Essex (Westcliff) 1972; 41 off 36.1 overs, Shropshire v Essex (Wellington) 1974.

**Lowest innings total by a side batting first and winning:** 98 off 56.2 overs, Worcestershire v Durham (Chester-le-Street) 1968.

**Highest individual innings:** 177 C.G. Greenidge, Hampshire v Glamorgan (Southampton) 1975.

**Highest individual innings by a Minor County player:** 132 G. Robinson, Lincolnshire v Northumberland (Jesmond) 1971.

93 centuries have been scored in the competition.

**Record Wicket Partnerships**

| | | | |
|---|---|---|---|
| 1st | 227 | R.E. Marshall & B.L. Reed, Hampshire v Bedfordshire (Goldington) | 1968 |
| 2nd | 223 | M.J. Smith & C.T. Radley, Middlesex v Hampshire (Lord's) | 1977 |
| 3rd | 160 | B. Wood & F.C. Hayes, Lancashire v Warwickshire (Birmingham) | 1976 |
| 4th | 234* | D. Lloyd & C.H. Lloyd, Lancashire v Gloucestershire (Manchester) | 1978 |
| 5th | 141 | T.E. Jesty & N.E.J. Pocock, Hampshire v Derbyshire (Derby) | 1980 |
| 6th | 105 | G.S. Sobers & R.A. White, Nottinghamshire v Worcestershire (Worcester) | 1974 |
| 7th | 107 | D.R. Shepherd & D.A. Graveney, Gloucestershire v Surrey (Bristol) | 1973 |
| 8th | 69 | S.J. Rouse & D.J. Brown, Warwickshire v Middlesex (Lord's) | 1977 |
| 9th | 87 | M.A. Nash & A.E. Cordle, Glamorgan v Lincolnshire (Swansea) | 1974 |
| 10th | 45 | A.T. Castell & D.W. White, Hampshire v Lancashire (Manchester) | 1970 |
| **Hat-tricks:** | | J.D.F. Larter, Northamptonshire v Sussex (Northampton) | 1963 |
| | | D.A.D. Sydenham, Surrey v Cheshire (Hoylake) | 1964 |
| | | R.N.S. Hobbs, Essex v Middlesex (Lord's) | 1968 |
| | | N.M. McVicker, Warwickshire v Lincolnshire (Birmingham) | 1971 |

**Seven wickets in an innings:** 7-15 A.L. Dixon, Kent v Surrey (The Oval) 1968. P.J. Sainsbury (Hampshire) 7-30 in 1965 and R.D. Jackman (Surrey) 7-33 in 1970 have also achieved this feat.

**Most 'Man of the Match' awards:** 6 B.L. D'Oliveira (Worcestershire), C.H. Lloyd (Lancashire) and B. Wood (Lancashire); 5 M.C. Cowdrey (Kent), A.W. Greig (Sussex) and R.D.V. Knight (Gloucestershire and Surrey).

# NORTHAMPTONSHIRE WIN
# THE BENSON & HEDGES

By the narrowest margin of six runs, Northants prevented Essex from taking the Benson and Hedges Cup for the second year in succession. Had Essex won, they would have been the first county to win successively. The players of Essex (and their disappointed supporters) have every reason for saying 'We should have won'. Essex were 112 for one needing 210 to win, with Graham Gooch and Ken McEwan in full flow – and there are few faster scorers in county cricket than this pair. Before this partnership was broken Northants must have felt that the game was about to slip away from them. But in a flash, 112 for one became 129 for five. Essex had one last genuine hope in Norbert Phillip, their fast bowler from Bioche, Dominica, who had also been known to slash quick runs when they were needed. (In fact he once scored 160 runs and took ten wickets for 130 in a two-innings match for Combined Islands against Guyana at Georgetown in 1977-78.) Phillip nearly swung this game round and was still not out when Essex ran out of overs with two wickets still standing and just six runs needed for victory. If they had still had a wicket in hand, it could have been an absorbing situation had there been just one more over. The innings of the match was that played by Allan Lamb for Northants; his 72 was the major contribution to a total of 209, one which won him the Man of the Match award.

Northants, who were top of the Group B table, had had a close call, too, in the semi-final against Middlesex. This time they won by 11 runs in a fascinating game at Lord's. Northants were 136 for one – and all out 206. Middlesex were 16 for three – but then 114 for three as Mike Gatting assumed full responsibility for the Middlesex batting. He needed some support which was never forthcoming, and, apart from his score of 91 and Slack's 42, no other batsman reached 20. The Man of the Match, deservedly, despite Gatting's magnificent innings, was Richard Williams; he scored 73 not out and in five overs of tantalising off-spin took two wickets for 24. Middlesex, who went on to win both the Schweppes County Championship and the Gillette Cup, headed their group table in this competition and were third in the John Player League – to prove overwhelmingly that they were the best side in the country in 1980.

*Total Gold Awards are given in brackets where relevant.*

# 1980 RESULTS

### Start due 10 May

Lord's. **Middlesex** 215-2 beat **Surrey** 211-8 by 8 wickets. **Gold Award: J.M. Brearley (3).**

Titwood. **Leicestershire** 148-2 beat **Scotland** 146-7 by 8 wickets. **Gold Award: R.G. Swan.**

Leeds. **Warwickshire** 269-9 beat **Yorkshire** 268-4 by 1 wicket. **Gold Award: J.H. Hampshire (2).**

Nottingham. **Nottinghamshire** 269-5 beat **Derbyshire** 166 by 103 runs. **Gold Award: N. Nanan.**

Bristol. **Glamorgan** 228-8 beat **Gloucestershire** 227-8 by 1 run. **Gold Award: A.A. Jones (4 – 2 for Middlesex, 1 for Somerset).**

Chelmsford. **Essex** 220-6 beat **Sussex** 217-6 by 4 wickets. **Gold Award: K.W.R. Fletcher (4).**

Canterbury. **Somerset** 245-1 beat **Kent** 242-7 by 9 wickets. **Gold Award: B.C. Rose.**

Northampton. **Northamptonshire** 203-8 beat **Combined Universities** 134-9 by 69 runs. **Gold Award: N. Russom.**

### Start due 14 May

Southampton. **Middlesex** 202-3 beat **Hampshire** 199 by 7 wickets. **Gold Award: G.D. Barlow (2).**

Titwood. **Derbyshire** 121-0 beat **Scotland** 116 by 10 wickets. **Gold Award: J.G. Wright (3).**

Watford. **Essex** 158-1 beat **Minor Counties** 157 by 9 wickets. **Gold Award: G.A. Gooch (5).**

Hove. **Sussex** 238-5 beat **Gloucestershire** 229-7 by 5 runs. **Gold Award: G.D. Mendis.**

The Oval. **Surrey** 201-7 beat **Kent** 199 by 3 wickets. **Gold Award: S.T. Clarke.**

Cambridge. **Worcestershire** 152-3 beat **Combined Universities** 150-7 by 7 wickets. **Gold Award: J.D. Inchmore (2).**

Birmingham. **Northamptonshire** 206-4 beat **Warwickshire** 202-9 by 6 wickets. **Gold Award: W. Larkins (2).**

Manchester. **Lancashire** 232-5 beat **Nottinghamshire** 119 by 113 runs. **Gold Award: D. Lloyd.**

### Start due 17 May

Taunton. **Middlesex** 282-6 beat **Somerset** 281-8 by 1 run. **Gold Award: P.H. Edmonds.**

Chesterfield. **Lancashire** 249-3 beat **Derbyshire** 216 by 33 runs. **Gold Award: B.W. Reidy (2).**

Bristol. **Gloucestershire** 225-5 beat **Essex** 224 by 5 wickets. **Gold Award: A.W. Stovold (5).**

The Oval. **Surrey** 168-8 beat **Hampshire** 167 by 2 wickets. **Gold Award: D.M. Smith.**

Leicester. **Nottinghamshire** 255-6 beat **Leicestershire** 192 by 63 runs. **Gold Award: M.K. Bore.**

Birmingham. **Warwickshire** 167-3 beat **Combined Universities** 166-6 by 7 wickets. **Gold Award: A. Odendaal.**

Worcester. **Worcestershire** 270-6 beat **Yorkshire** 269-6 by 4 wickets. **Gold Award: Younis Ahmed (3 – 1 for Surrey).**

Swansea. **Glamorgan** 176-0 beat **Minor Counties** 175-9 by 10 wickets. **Gold Award: J.A. Hopkins (3).**

Nottingham. **Nottinghamshire** 143-4 beat **Scotland** 141-8 by 6 wickets. **Gold Award: R.J. Hadlee.**

Chelmsford. **Essex** 149-5 beat **Glamorgan** 147 by 5 wickets. **Gold Award: K.W.R. Fletcher (5).**

Leicester. **Lancashire** 184 beat **Leicestershire** 181 by 3 runs. **Gold Award: B.W. Reidy (3).**

Northampton. **Northamptonshire** 169-9 beat **Worcestershire** 164 by 5 runs. **Gold Award: G.M. Turner (4).**

Hove. **Sussex** 237-9 beat **Minor Counties** 207-7 by 30 runs. **Gold Award: Imran Khan (6** – 1 for Worcestershire, 1 for Combined Universities).

Canterbury. **Kent** 212-9 beat **Hampshire** 211-8 by 1 run. **Gold Award: T.E. Jesty (6).**

Taunton. **Surrey** 216-6 beat **Somerset** 215-7 by 4 wickets. **Gold Award: R.D. Jackman.**

Oxford. **Yorkshire** 151-1 beat **Combined Universities** by 9 wickets. **Gold Award: C.W.J. Athey.**

Lord's. **Middlesex** 213-8 beat **Kent** 133 by 80 runs. **Gold Award: V.A.P. Van der Bijl.**

Bournemouth. **Somerset** 204 beat **Hampshire** 149 by 55 runs. **Gold Award: V.J. Marks (2).**

Derby. **Leicestershire** 202-6 beat **Derbyshire** 188 by 14 runs. **Gold Award: D.I. Gower.**

Manchester. **Lancashire** 213-3 beat **Scotland** 152-8 by 61 runs. **Gold Award: D. Lloyd (2).**

Chippenham. **Minor Counties** 212-8 beat **Gloucestershire** 209 by 3 runs. **Gold Award: B.L. Cairns.**

Worcester. **Worcestershire** 228-5 beat **Warwickshire** 227-9 by 5 wickets. **Gold Award: E.J.O. Hemsley (3).**

Bradford. **Northamptonshire** 205-9 beat **Yorkshire** 203-8 by 2 runs. **Gold Award: R.G. Williams.**

Cardiff. **Sussex** 189-2 beat Glamorgan 185-9 by 8 wickets. **Gold Award: G.D. Mendis (2).**

## QUARTER FINALS

Lord's. **Middlesex** 195 beat **Sussex** 166 by 29 runs. **Gold Award: J.E. Emburey.**

Chelmsford. **Essex** 270-5 beat **Surrey** 184 by 86 runs. **Gold Award: K.S. McEwan (5).**

Northampton. **Northamptonshire** 149-3 beat **Nottinghamshire** 143 by 7 wickets. **Gold Award: T.M. Lamb.**

Manchester. **Worcestershire** 314-5 beat **Lancashire** 269 by 45 runs. **Gold Award: G.M. Turner (5).**

## SEMI FINALS

Northampton. **Northamptonshire** 206 beat **Middlesex** 195 by 11 runs. **Gold Award: R.G. Williams (2).**

Worcester. **Essex** 240-2 beat **Worcestershire** 236-9 by 8 wickets. **Gold Award: G.A. Gooch (6).**

## GROUP TABLES

| Group A | P | W | L | Pts |
|---|---|---|---|---|
| Lancashire | 4 | 4 | 0 | 8 |
| Nottinghamshire | 4 | 3 | 1 | 6 |
| Leicestershire | 4 | 2 | 2 | 4 |
| Derbyshire | 4 | 1 | 3 | 2 |
| Scotland | 4 | 0 | 4 | 0 |
| *Group B* | | | | |
| Northamptonshire | 4 | 4 | 0 | 8 |
| Worcestershire | 4 | 3 | 1 | 6 |
| Warwickshire | 4 | 2 | 2 | 4 |
| Yorkshire | 4 | 1 | 3 | 2 |
| Combined Universities | 4 | 0 | 4 | 0 |
| *Group C* | | | | |
| Essex | 4 | 3 | 1 | 6 |
| Sussex | 4 | 3 | 1 | 6 |
| Glamorgan | 4 | 2 | 2 | 4 |
| Gloucestershire | 4 | 1 | 3 | 2 |
| Minor Counties | 4 | 1 | 3 | 2 |
| *Group D* | | | | |
| Middlesex | 4 | 4 | 0 | 8 |
| Surrey | 4 | 3 | 1 | 6 |
| Somerset | 4 | 2 | 2 | 4 |
| Kent | 4 | 1 | 3 | 2 |
| Hampshire | 4 | 0 | 4 | 0 |

# THE BENSON & HEDGES CUP FINAL

### PLAYED AT LORD'S 19, 21 JULY
### NORTHAMPTONSHIRE WON BY 6 RUNS

## NORTHAMPTONSHIRE

| | | |
|---|---|--:|
| G. Cook | c Gooch b Pont | 29 |
| W. Larkins | c Denness b Pont | 18 |
| R.G. Williams | c McEwan b Pont | 15 |
| A.J. Lamb | c Hardie b Phillip | 72 |
| P. Willey | c McEwan b Turner | 15 |
| T.J. Yardley | c Smith b Gooch | 0 |
| †G. Sharp | c Fletcher b Pont | 8 |
| *P.J. Watts | run out | 22 |
| Sarfraz Nawaz | not out | 10 |
| T.M. Lamb | lbw b Turner | 4 |
| B.J. Griffiths | b Turner | 0 |
| Extras (B1, LB8, W4) | | 16 |
| **Total** (54.5 overs) | | 209 |

## ESSEX

| | | |
|---|---|--:|
| M.H. Denness | b Willey | 14 |
| G.A. Gooch | c A.J. Lamb b T.M. Lamb | 60 |
| K.S. McEwan | b Willey | 38 |
| *K.W.R. Fletcher | b Sarfraz | 29 |
| B.R. Hardie | b Watts | 0 |
| K.R. Pont | b Williams | 2 |
| S. Turner | c Watts b Sarfraz | 16 |
| N. Phillip | not out | 32 |
| †N. Smith | b Sarfraz | 2 |
| R.E. East | not out | 2 |
| J.K. Lever | did not bat | |
| Extras (B1, LB5, W3) | | 9 |
| **Total** (55 overs) (8 wkts) | | 203 |

## BOWLING

| ESSEX | O | M | R | W | FALL OF WICKETS | | |
|---|--:|--:|--:|--:|---|--:|--:|
| | | | | | | N | E |
| Lever | 11 | 3 | 38 | 0 | 1st | 36 | 52 |
| Phillip | 11 | 1 | 38 | 1 | 2nd | 61 | 112 |
| Turner | 10.5 | 2 | 33 | 3 | 3rd | 78 | 118 |
| Pont | 11 | 1 | 60 | 4 | 4th | 110 | 121 |
| Gooch | 11 | 0 | 24 | 1 | 5th | 110 | 129 |
| **NORTHANTS** | | | | | 6th | 131 | 160 |
| Sarfraz | 11 | 3 | 23 | 3 | 7th | 190 | 180 |
| Griffiths | 7 | 0 | 46 | 0 | 8th | 193 | 198 |
| Watts | 8 | 1 | 30 | 1 | 9th | 209 | — |
| T.M. Lamb | 11 | 0 | 42 | 1 | 10th | 209 | — |
| Willey | 11 | 1 | 34 | 2 | | | |
| Williams | 7 | 0 | 19 | 1 | | | |

**Man of the Match:** A.J. Lamb

# BENSON & HEDGES CUP
## PRINCIPAL RECORDS

**Highest innings total:** 350-3 off 55 overs, Essex v Combined Universities (Chelmsford) 1979.
**Highest innings total by a side batting second:** 282 off 50.5 overs, Gloucestershire v Hampshire (Bristol) 1974.
**Highest innings total by a side batting first and losing:** 268-5 off 55 overs, Leicestershire v Worcestershire (Worcester) 1976.
**Lowest completed innings total:** 61 off 26 overs, Sussex v Middlesex (Hove) 1978.
**Highest individual innings:** 173* C.G. Greenidge, Hampshire v Minor Counties (South) (Amersham) 1973.
76 centuries have been scored in the competition.

**Record Wicket Partnerships**

| | | | |
|---|---|---|---|
| 1st | 241 | S.M. Gavaskar & B.C. Rose, Somerset v Kent (Canterbury) | 1980 |
| 2nd | 285* | C.G. Greenidge & D.R. Turner, Hampshire v Minor Counties (South) (Amersham) | 1973 |
| 3rd | 227 | M.E.J.C. Norman & B.F. Davison, Leicestershire v Warwickshire (Coventry) | 1972 |
| | 227 | D. Lloyd & F.C. Hayes, Lancashire v Minor Counties (North) (Manchester) | 1973 |
| 4th | 184* | D. Lloyd & B.W. Reidy, Lancashire v Derbyshire (Chesterfield) | 1980 |
| 5th | 134 | M. Maslin & D.N.F. Slade, Minor Counties (East) v Nottinghamshire (Nottingham) | 1976 |
| 6th | 114 | M.J. Khan & G.P. Ellis, Glamorgan v Gloucestershire (Bristol) | 1975 |
| 7th | 102 | E.W. Jones & M.A. Nash, Glamorgan v Hampshire (Swansea) | 1976 |
| 8th | 109 | R.E. East & N. Smith, Essex v Northamptonshire (Chelmsford) | 1977 |
| 9th | 81 | J.N. Shepherd & D.L. Underwood, Kent v Middlesex (Lord's) | 1975 |
| 10th | 61 | J.M. Rice & A.M.E. Roberts, Hampshire v Gloucestershire (Bristol) | 1975 |

**Hat-tricks:** G.D. McKenzie, Leicestershire v Worcestershire (Worcester) 1972. K. Higgs, Leicestershire v Surrey (Lord's) 1974. A.A. Jones, Middlesex v Essex (Lord's) 1977. M.J. Procter, Gloucestershire v Hampshire (Southampton) 1977. W. Larkins, Northamptonshire v Combined Universities (Northampton) 1980.
**Seven wickets in an innings:** 7-12 W.W. Daniel, Middlesex v Minor Counties (East) (Ipswich) 1978.
**Most 'Gold' awards:** 10 B. Wood (all for Lancashire), 9 J.H. Edrich (Surrey).

---

### BENSON & HEDGES CUP WINNERS

| | | | |
|---|---|---|---|
| 1972 | Leicestershire | 1977 | Gloucestershire |
| 1973 | Kent | 1978 | Kent |
| 1974 | Surrey | 1979 | Essex |
| 1975 | Leicestershire | 1980 | Northamptonshire |
| 1976 | Kent | | |

# WARWICKSHIRE WIN
# THE JOHN PLAYER

There can never have been a more surprising winner of the John Player League than in this summer of 1980 when Warwickshire won. In 1979, Warwickshire were seventeenth and last in the table; in 1978 they had fared very little better, finishing sixteenth. As a result, when they were out in front in the early part of the 1980 season, no one took their challenge seriously, fully expecting them to fade as the pressure came from the more likely contenders. But hang on they did – and every credit to them – to beat Somerset narrowly, by 2 points, with Middlesex a further 2 points behind Somerset. As with all cricket, the weather in a bad summer plays a dominant part and Sussex, for example, can justifiably say that they were harshly treated, having had four no-result matches whereas both Warwickshire and Somerset did not have one. But this situation has been part and parcel of cricket since the game was invented. Warwickshire's success means that a different county has won the competition for the last five years, and that in the twelve years of its existence only seven counties have won – Lancashire, Leicestershire and Hampshire have each won on two occasions, with Kent having the principal honour of winning three times. Worcestershire, Somerset and Warwickshire are individual winners, so that ten counties still have this as an achievement in mind but never accomplished.

## JOHN PLAYER LEAGUE FINAL TABLE

|    |                      | P  | W  | L  | NR | Tie | Pts |
|----|----------------------|----|----|----|----|-----|-----|
| 1  | Warwickshire (17)    | 16 | 11 | 4  | 0  | 1   | 46  |
| 2  | Somerset (1)         | 16 | 11 | 5  | 0  | 0   | 44  |
| 3  | Middlesex (4)        | 16 | 10 | 5  | 1  | 0   | 42  |
| 4  | Leicestershire (6)   | 16 | 9  | 6  | 1  | 0   | 38  |
| 5  | Surrey (12)          | 16 | 8  | 6  | 2  | 0   | 36  |
| 6  | Derbyshire (16)      | 16 | 8  | 7  | 1  | 0   | 34  |
|    | Northamptonshire (12)| 16 | 8  | 7  | 1  | 0   | 34  |
|    | Worcestershire (3)   | 16 | 8  | 7  | 1  | 0   | 34  |
| 9  | Sussex (12)          | 16 | 6  | 6  | 4  | 0   | 32  |
| 10 | Gloucestershire (8)  | 16 | 7  | 8  | 1  | 0   | 30  |
| 11 | Hampshire (10)       | 16 | 6  | 8  | 2  | 0   | 28  |
|    | Kent (2)             | 16 | 6  | 8  | 1  | 1   | 28  |
| 13 | Lancashire (10)      | 16 | 6  | 9  | 1  | 0   | 26  |
| 14 | Essex (6)            | 16 | 6  | 10 | 0  | 0   | 24  |
|    | Nottinghamshire (8)  | 16 | 6  | 10 | 0  | 0   | 24  |
|    | Yorkshire (4)        | 16 | 6  | 10 | 0  | 0   | 24  |
| 17 | Glamorgan (12)       | 16 | 4  | 10 | 2  | 0   | 20  |

1979 positions in brackets

# JOHN PLAYER LEAGUE
## PRINCIPAL RECORDS

**Highest innings total:** 307-4 off 38 overs. Worcs v Derbyshire (Worcester) 1975.

**Highest innings total by a side batting second:** 261-8 off 39.1 overs, Warwickshire v Nottinghamshire (Birmingham) 1976; 261 off 36.2 overs, Worcestershire v Sussex (Horsham) 1980.

**Highest innings total by a side batting first and losing:** 260-5 off 40 overs, Nottinghamshire v Warwickshire (Birmingham) 1976.

**Lowest completed innings total:** 23 off 19.4 overs, Middlesex v Yorkshire (Leeds) 1974.

**Highest individual innings:** 163* C.G. Greenidge, Hampshire v Warwickshire (Birmingham) 1979.

150 centuries have been scored in the League.

**Record Wicket Partnerships**

| | | | |
|---|---|---|---|
| 1st | 218 | A.R. Butcher & G.P. Howarth, Surrey v Glos (Oval) | 1976 |
| 2nd | 179 | B.W. Luckhurst & M.H. Denness, Kent v Somerset (Canterbury) | 1973 |
| 3rd | 182 | H. Pilling & C.H. Lloyd, Lancashire v Somerset (Manchester) | 1970 |
| 4th | 175* | M.J.K. Smith & D.L. Amiss, Warwickshire v Yorkshire (Birmingham) | 1970 |
| 5th | 163 | A.G.E. Ealham & B.D. Julien, Kent v Leicestershire (Leicester) | 1977 |
| 6th | 121 | C.P. Wilkins & A.J. Borrington, Derbyshire v Warwickshire (Chesterfield) | 1972 |
| 7th | 96* | R. Illingworth & J. Birkenshaw, Leicestershire v Somerset (Leicester) | 1971 |
| 8th | 95* | D. Breakwell & K.F. Jennings, Somerset v Nottinghamshire (Nottingham) | 1976 |
| 9th | 86 | D.P. Hughes & P. Lever, Lancashire v Essex (Leyton) | 1973 |
| 10th | 57 | D.A. Graveney & J.B. Mortimore, Gloucestershire v Lancashire (Tewkesbury) | 1973 |

**Four wickets in four balls:** A. Ward, Derbyshire v Sussex (Derby) 1970.

**Hat-tricks** (excluding above): R. Palmer, Somerset v Gloucestershire (Bristol) 1970. K.D. Boyce, Essex v Somerset (Westcliff) 1971. G.D. McKenzie, Leicestershire v Essex (Leicester) 1972. R.G.D. Willis, Warwickshire v Yorkshire (Birmingham) 1973. W. Blenkiron, Warwickshire v Derbyshire (Buxton) 1974. A. Buss, Sussex v Worcestershire (Hastings) 1974. J.M. Rice, Hampshire v Northamptonshire (Southampton) 1975. M.A. Nash, Glamorgan v Worcestershire (Worcester) 1975. A. Hodgson, Northamptonshire v Sussex (Northampton) 1976. A.E. Cordle, Glamorgan v Hampshire (Portsmouth) 1979. C.J. Tunnicliffe, Derbyshire v Worcestershire (Derby) 1979.

**Eight wickets in an innings:** 8-26 K.D. Boyce, Essex v Lancashire (Manchester) 1971.

---

### JOHN PLAYER LEAGUE CHAMPIONS

| | |
|---|---|
| 1969 Lancashire | 1975 Hampshire |
| 1970 Lancashire | 1976 Kent |
| 1971 Worcestershire | 1977 Leicestershire |
| 1972 Kent | 1978 Hampshire |
| 1973 Kent | 1979 Somerset |
| 1974 Leicestershire | 1980 Warwickshire |

# MIDDLESEX ARE THE COUNTY CHAMPIONS

Middlesex won the Schweppes County Championship as they had threatened to do for most of the season in what became finally a two-horse race with Surrey. Nottinghamshire, in third place, a highly commendable improvement on the previous year when they finished ninth, were never likely to catch either of the two sides ahead of them, and finished as many as 67 points behind. Surrey fell short of Middlesex by only 13 points, both sides having won ten matches. After them, Notts won six matches and Sussex, in fourth place, won four – although the dreadful weather which cut deep inroads into cricket of all denominations had a considerable effect on the results of almost every county. The allocation of bonus points does make an enormous difference to the final position in the table. Sussex who were fourth in the table had exactly the same playing record as Lancashire who were fifteenth – won 4, lost 3, drawn 15. It was the difference in bonus points won which enabled one side to finish fourth and the other fifteenth. It was a sad season for Hampshire who won only one game out of their twenty-two, and understandably fell from twelfth in the previous season, to seventeenth at the foot of the table. Without Barry Richards, Andy Roberts and Gordon Greenidge, this was a young side going through a period of transition and, if not winning, hopefully learning all the time. It was a wretched season for Kent, too. It must be a very long time since they finished sixteenth (fifth the previous season) and managed to win only two County Championship games.

Stuart Surridge, when he was captain of Surrey during their golden Championship years in the fifties, always said that it is bowlers who win matches. His view seems to have been confirmed by Surrey and Middlesex. Successful bowling places much less of a burden upon a team's batsmen and, although obviously not as potent, the Middlesex attack in its variation is reminiscent of the Surrey attack during their famous Championship years. With Wayne Daniel and Vintcent van der Bijl to open, and Mike Selvey as the back-up; John Emburey with spin, and even without Phil Edmonds who missed much of the season because of an operation on his knee; Simon Hughes introduced late in the season with good effect; Bill Merry and Mike Gatting; there was certainly no shortage of bowlers, and the batting was sound enough usually to get whatever runs the bowlers set them as a target. Mike Brearley was batting probably better than ever before.

Surrey had two decisive wicket-takers in the irrepressible Robin Jackman, who has sailed so close to the England team for so long he almost deserves half a cap, and Sylvester Clarke, who, like so many Barbadian fast bowlers before him, bowls very fast, although he is sometimes wayward in his length and direction until he gets his sights set properly – he can still be a very difficult customer. Both these counties confirmed their ability by winning top places in the two major competitions – the County Championship and the Gillette Cup. Middlesex proved that they were just that much better each time. But Surrey, who have had lean years for too long now, did commendably well and gave the impression that they must be very close to winning something again. There was a time when winning was taken for granted in Kennington; those decisive days will surely never come back, but better times will.

# SCHWEPPES COUNTY CHAMPIONSHIP
# FINAL TABLE

|  |  | P | W | D | L | Bonus Pts Bt | Bonus Pts Bw | Pts |
|---|---|---|---|---|---|---|---|---|
| 1 | Middlesex (13) | 22 | 10 | 10 | 2 | 58 | 80 | 258 |
| 2 | Surrey (5) | 22 | 10 | 8 | 4 | 51 | 74 | 245 |
| 3 | Nottinghamshire (9) | 22 | 6 | 11 | 5 | 42 | 64 | 178 |
| 4 | Sussex (4) | 22 | 4 | 15 | 3 | 60 | 60 | 168 |
|  | Somerset (8) | 22 | 3 | 14 | 5 | 56 | 70 | 168 |
| 6 | Yorkshire (7) | 22 | 4 | 15 | 3 | 51 | 64 | 163 |
| 7 | Gloucestershire (10) | 22 | 4 | 13 | 5 | 39 | 74 | 161 |
| 8 | Essex (1) | 22 | 4 | 15 | 3 | 48 | 64 | 160 |
| 9 | Derbyshire (16) | 22 | 4 | 15 | 3 | 47 | 62 | 157 |
|  | Leicestershire (6) | 22 | 4 | 16 | 2 | 45 | 58 | 157 |
| 11 | Worcestershire (2) | 22 | 3 | 12 | 7 | 54 | 61 | 151 |
| 12 | Northamptonshire (11) | 22 | 5 | 13 | 4 | 41 | 47 | 148 |
|  | Glamorgan (17) | 22 | 4 | 14 | 4 | 43 | 57 | 148 |
| 14 | Warwickshire (15) | 22 | 4 | 15 | 4 | 55 | 54 | 145 |
| 15 | Lancashire (13) | 22 | 4 | 15 | 3 | 26 | 58 | 132 |
| 16 | Kent (5) | 22 | 2 | 12 | 8 | 36 | 59 | 119 |
| 17 | Hampshire (12) | 22 | 1 | 11 | 10 | 34 | 56 | 102 |

1979 positions in brackets
Leicestershire's and Somerset's totals include 6pts in drawn matches when scores were level.
Draws column includes matches where no play was possible.

# COUNTY CHAMPIONS

The earliest winners of the title were decided usually by the least matches lost. In 1888 an unofficial points table was introduced and in 1890 the Championship was constituted officially. Since 1977 it has been sponsored by Schweppes.

| | | | | | |
|---|---|---|---|---|---|
| 1864 | Surrey | 1897 | Lancashire | 1946 | Yorkshire |
| 1865 | Nottinghamshire | 1898 | Yorkshire | 1947 | Middlesex |
| 1866 | Middlesex | 1899 | Surrey | 1948 | Glamorgan |
| 1867 | Yorkshire | 1900 | Yorkshire | 1949 { | Middlesex |
| 1868 | Nottinghamshire | 1901 | Yorkshire | | Yorkshire |
| 1869 { | Nottinghamshire | 1902 | Yorkshire | 1950 { | Lancashire |
| | Yorkshire | 1903 | Middlesex | | Surrey |
| 1870 | Yorkshire | 1904 | Lancashire | 1951 | Warwickshire |
| 1871 | Nottinghamshire | 1905 | Yorkshire | 1952 | Surrey |
| 1872 | Nottinghamshire | 1906 | Kent | 1953 | Surrey |
| 1873 { | Gloucestershire | 1907 | Nottinghamshire | 1954 | Surrey |
| | Nottinghamshire | 1908 | Yorkshire | 1955 | Surrey |
| 1874 | Gloucestershire | 1909 | Kent | 1956 | Surrey |
| 1875 | Nottinghamshire | 1910 | Kent | 1957 | Surrey |
| 1876 | Gloucestershire | 1911 | Warwickshire | 1958 | Surrey |
| 1877 | Gloucestershire | 1912 | Yorkshire | 1959 | Yorkshire |
| 1878 | Undecided | 1913 | Kent | 1960 | Yorkshire |
| 1879 { | Nottinghamshire | 1914 | Surrey | 1961 | Hampshire |
| | Lancashire | 1919 | Yorkshire | 1962 | Yorkshire |
| 1880 | Nottinghamshire | 1920 | Middlesex | 1963 | Yorkshire |
| 1881 | Lancashire | 1921 | Middlesex | 1964 | Worcestershire |
| 1882 { | Nottinghamshire | 1922 | Yorkshire | 1965 | Worcestershire |
| | Lancashire | 1923 | Yorkshire | 1966 | Yorkshire |
| 1883 | Nottinghamshire | 1924 | Yorkshire | 1967 | Yorkshire |
| 1884 | Nottinghamshire | 1925 | Yorkshire | 1968 | Yorkshire |
| 1885 | Nottinghamshire | 1926 | Lancashire | 1969 | Glamorgan |
| 1886 | Nottinghamshire | 1927 | Lancashire | 1970 | Kent |
| 1887 | Surrey | 1928 | Lancashire | 1971 | Surrey |
| 1888 | Surrey | 1929 | Nottinghamshire | 1972 | Warwickshire |
| 1889 { | Surrey | 1930 | Lancashire | 1973 | Hampshire |
| | Lancashire | 1931 | Yorkshire | 1974 | Worcestershire |
| | Nottinghamshire | 1932 | Yorkshire | 1975 | Leicestershire |
| 1890 | Surrey | 1933 | Yorkshire | 1976 | Middlesex |
| 1891 | Surrey | 1934 | Lancashire | 1977 { | Kent |
| 1892 | Surrey | 1935 | Yorkshire | | Middlesex |
| 1893 | Yorkshire | 1936 | Derbyshire | 1978 | Kent |
| 1894 | Surrey | 1937 | Yorkshire | 1979 | Essex |
| 1895 | Surrey | 1938 | Yorkshire | 1980 | Middlesex |
| 1896 | Yorkshire | 1939 | Yorkshire | | |

# THE COUNTIES AND
# THEIR PLAYERS
## Compiled by Michael Fordham

### Abbreviations

| | | | |
|---|---|---|---|
| B | Born | HSC | Highest score for County if different from highest first-class score |
| RHB | Right-hand bat | | |
| LHB | Left-hand bat | | |
| RF | Right-arm fast | HSGC | Highest score Gillette Cup |
| RFM | Right-arm fast medium | HSJPL | Highest score John Player League |
| RM | Right-arm medium | | |
| LF | Left-arm fast | HSBH | Highest score Benson & Hedges Cup |
| LFM | Left-arm fast medium | | |
| LM | Left-arm medium | BB | Best bowling figures |
| OB | Off-break | BBUK | Best bowling figures in this country |
| LB | Leg-break | | |
| LBG | Leg-break and googly | BBTC | Best bowling figures in Test cricket if different from above |
| SLA | Slow left-arm orthodox | | |
| SLC | Slow left-arm 'chinaman' | | |
| WK | Wicket-keeper | BBC | Best bowling figures for County if different from above |
| * | Not out or unfinished stand | | |
| HS | Highest score | | |
| HSUK | Highest score in this country | BBGC | Best bowling figures Gillette Cup |
| | | BBJPL | Best bowling figures John Player League |
| HSTC | Highest score in Test cricket if different from above | | |
| | | BBBH | Best bowling figures Benson & Hedges Cup |

When a player is known by a name other than his first name, the name in question has been underlined.

All Test appearances are complete to 4th September 1980.

'Debut' denotes 'first-class debut' and 'Cap' means '1st XI county cap'.

*Wisden 1980* indicates that a player was selected as one of *Wisden's* Five Cricketers of the Year for his achievements in 1980.

Owing to the increasing number of privately arranged overseas tours of short duration, only those which may be regarded as major tours have been included.

# DERBYSHIRE

**Formation of present club:** 1870.
**Colours:** Chocolate, amber, and pale blue.
**Badge:** Rose and crown.
**County Champions:** 1936.
**Gillette Cup Finalists:** 1969.
**Best final position in John Player League:** 3rd in 1970.
**Benson & Hedges Cup Finalists:** 1978.
**Gillette Man of the Match Awards:** 15.
**Benson & Hedges Gold Awards:** 25.

**Secretary:** D.A. Harrison, County Cricket Ground, Nottingham Road, Derby DE2 6DA.
**Captain:** G. Miller.
**Prospects of Play Telephone No:** Derby (0332) 44849.

# DERBYSHIRE

**Iain Stuart ANDERSON** (Dovecliff GS and Wulfric School, Burton-on-Trent) B Derby 24/4/1960. RHB, OB. Debut 1978. HS: 75 v Worcs (Worcester) 1978. HSJPL: 21 v Middlesex (Lord's) 1978.

**Kim John BARNETT** (Leek HS) B Stoke-on-Trent 17/7/1960. RHB, LB. Played for county and Northants 2nd XIs and Staffordshire in 1976 and for Warwickshire 2nd XI in 1977 and 1978. Toured Australia with England under-19 team in 1978-79. Debut 1979. HS: 96 v Lancs (Chesterfield) 1979. HSGC: 22 v Somerset (Taunton) 1979. HSJPL: 48* v Lancs (Buxton) 1980. HSBH: 34 v Notts (Nottingham) 1980. BB: 4-76 v Warwickshire (Birmingham) 1980. BBJPL: 3-39 v Yorks (Chesterfield) 1979.

**Anthony John (Tony) BORRINGTON** (Spondon Park GS) B Derby 8/12/1948. RHB, LB. Played for MCC Schools at Lord's in 1967. Played in one John Player League match in 1970. Debut 1971. Cap 1977. Benson & Hedges Gold awards: 4. HS: 137 v Yorks (Sheffield) 1978. HSGC: 29 v Somerset (Taunton) 1979. HSJPL: 101 v Somerset (Taunton) 1977. HSBH: 81 v Notts (Nottingham) 1974. Trained as a teacher at Loughborough College of Education.

**Kevin Graham BROOKS** (Clarks GS, Bristol, Monkseaton GS, Whitley Bay) B Reading 15/10/1959. RHB, RM. Played for Hants 2nd XI 1979. Debut 1980. One match v Warwickshire (Birmingham). Also played in Benson & Hedges Cup (two matches) and John Player League (three matches). HS: 8 v Warwickshire (Birmingham) 1980. HSBH: 10 v Notts (Nottingham) 1980.

**Michael (Mike) HENDRICK** B Darley Dale (Derbyshire) 22/10/1948. RHB, RFM. Debut 1969. Cap 1972. Elected Best Young Cricketer of the Year in 1973 by the Cricket Writers Club. *Wisden* 1977. Benefit in 1980. Tests 28 between 1974 and 1980. Tours: West Indies 1973-74, Australia and New Zealand 1974-75, Pakistan and New Zealand 1977-78, Australia 1978-79, Australia (returned home early through injury) 1979-80. Hat-trick v West Indians (Derby) 1980. Gillette Man of the Match awards: 1. Benson & Hedges Gold awards: 2. HS: 46 v Essex (Chelmsford) 1973. HSTC: 15 v Australia (Oval) 1977. HSGC: 17 v Middlesex (Derby) 1978. HSJPL: 21 v Warwickshire (Buxton) 1974. HSBH: 32 v Notts (Chesterfield) 1973. BB: 8-45 v Warwickshire (Chesterfield) 1973. BBTC: 4-28 v India (Birmingham) 1974. BBGC: 4-16 v Middlesex (Chesterfield) 1975. BBJPL: 6-7 v Notts (Nottingham) 1972. BBBH: 5-30 v Notts (Chesterfield) 1975 and 5-30 v Lancs (Southport) 1976.

**Alan HILL** (New Mills GS) B Buxworth (Derbyshire) 29/6/1950. RHB, OB. Joined staff 1970. Debut 1972. Cap 1976. Played for Orange Free State in 1976-77 Currie Cup competition. Gillette Man of the Match awards: 1. Benson & Hedges Gold awards: 1. 1,000 runs (2)—1,303 runs (av. 34.28) in 1976 best. HS: 160* v Warwickshire (Coventry) 1976. HSGC: 72 v Middlesex (Derby) 1978. HSJPL: 120 v Northants (Buxton) 1976. HSBH: 102* v Warwickshire (Ilkeston) 1978. BB: 3-5 Orange Free State v Northern Transvaal (Pretoria) 1976-77.

**Peter Noel KIRSTEN** (South African College School, Cape Town) B Pietermaritzburg, Natal, South Africa 14/5/1955. RHB, OB. Debut for Western Province in Currie Cup 1973-74. Played for Sussex v Australians 1975 as well as playing for County 2nd XI. Played for Derbyshire 2nd XI in 1977 and made debut for County in 1978. Cap 1978. Scored 4 centuries in 4 consecutive innings and 6 in 7 innings including 2 in match—173* and 103 Western Province v Eastern Province (Cape Town) 1976-77. 1,000 runs (3)—1,895 runs (av. 63.16) in 1980 best. Also scored 1,074 runs (av. 76.71) in 1976-77. Scored 6 centuries (including 3 double centuries) in 1980 to equal County record. Benson & Hedges Gold awards: 1. HS: 213* v Glamorgan (Derby) 1980. HSGC: 29 v Hants (Derby) 1980. HSJPL: 102 v Glamorgan (Swansea) 1979. HSBH: 70 v Surrey (Derby) 1979. BB: 4-44 v Middlesex (Derby) 1979. BBJPL: 5-34 v Northants (Long Eaton) 1979.

**Geoffrey (Geoff) MILLER** (Chesterfield GS) B Chesterfield 8/9/1952. RHB, OB. Toured India 1970-71 and West Indies 1972 with England Young Cricketers. Won Sir Frank Worrell Trophy as Outstanding Boy Cricketer of 1972. Debut 1973. Cap 1976. Elected Best Young Cricketer of the Year in 1976 by the Cricket Writers Club. Appointed county captain in 1979. Tests: 24 between 1976 and 1979-80. Tours: India, Sri Lanka and Australia 1976-77, Pakistan and New Zealand 1977-78, Australia 1978-79, Australia (returned home early through injury) 1979-80, West Indies 1980-81. Benson & Hedges Gold awards: 2. HS: 98* England v Pakistan (Lahore) 1977-78. HSUK: 95 v Lancs (Manchester) 1978. HSGC: 59* v Worcs (Worcester) 1978. HSJPL: 84 v Somerset (Chesterfield) 1980. HSBH: 75 v Warwickshire (Derby) 1977. BB: 7-54 v Sussex (Hove) 1977. BBTC: 5-44 v Australia (Sydney) 1978-79. BBJPL: 4-22 v Yorks (Huddersfield) 1978. BBBH: 3-23 v Surrey (Derby) 1979.

**Paul Geoffrey NEWMAN** (Alderman Newton's GS, Leicester) B Leicester 10/1/1959. RHB, RFM. Played for Leics 2nd XI in 1978 and 1979. Debut 1980. HS: 29* v Sussex (Derby) 1980. BBJPL: 4-30 v Sussex (Derby) 1980.

**Stephen (Steve) OLDHAM** B High Green, Sheffield 26/7/1948. RHB, RFM. Debut for Yorkshire 1974. Left county after 1979 season and made debut for Derbyshire in 1980. Cap 1980. Benson & Hedges Gold awards: 1 (for Yorks). HS: 50 Yorks v Sussex (Hove) 1979. HSJPL: 38* Yorks v Glamorgan (Cardiff) 1977. BB: 5-40 Yorks v Surrey (Oval) 1978. BBC: 4-41 v Surrey (Derby) 1980. BBGC: 3-45 Yorks v Lancs (Leeds) 1974. BBJPL: 4-21 Yorks v Notts (Scarborough) 1974. BBBH: 5-32 Yorks v Minor Counties (North) (Scunthorpe) 1978.

**Philip Edgar (Phil) RUSSELL** (Ilkeston GS) B Ilkeston 9/5/1944. RHB, RM/OB. Debut 1965. Not re-engaged after 1972 season, but rejoined staff in 1974 and is now County coach. Cap 1975. Played in one Benson & Hedges Cup match and one John Player League match in 1980. HS: 72 v Glamorgan (Swansea) 1970. HSGC: 27* v Middlesex (Derby) 1978. HSJPL: 47* v Glamorgan (Buxton) 1975. HSBH: 22* v Lancs (Southport) 1976. BB: 7-46 v Yorks (Sheffield) 1975. BBGC: 3-44 v Somerset (Taunton) 1975. BBJPL: 6-10 v Northants (Buxton) 1976. BBBH: 3-28 v Kent (Lord's) 1978.

**David Stanley STEELE** B Stoke-on-Trent 29/9/1941. Elder brother of J.F. Steele of Leics and cousin of B.S. Crump, former Northants player. Wears glasses. RHB, SLA. Played for Staffordshire from 1958 to 1962. Debut for Northants 1963. Cap 1965. Benefit (£25,500) in 1975. *Wisden* 1975. Transferred to Derbyshire in 1979 as county captain. Relinquished post during season. Cap 1979. Tests: 8 in 1975 and 1976. 1,000 runs (10)—1,756 runs (av. 48.77) in 1975 best. Hat-trick v Glamorgan (Derby) 1980. Had match double of 100 runs and 10 wkts (130, 6-36 and 5-39) v Derbyshire (Northampton) 1978. Gillette Man of the Match Awards: 1 (for Northants). HS: 140* Northants v Worcs (Worcester) 1971. HSC: 127* v Indians (Derby) 1979. HSTC: 106 v West Indies (Nottingham) 1976. HSGC: 109 Northants v Cambs (March) 1975. HSJPL: 76 Northants v Sussex (Hove) 1974. HSBH: 69 Northants v Warwickshire (Northampton) 1974. BB: 8-29 Northants v Lancs (Northampton) 1966. BBC: 7-133 v Notts (Worksop) 1980. BBJPL: 4-21 v Notts (Derby) 1979.

# DERBYSHIRE

**Robert William (Bob) TAYLOR** B Stoke 17/7/1941. RHB, WK. Played for Bignall End (N. Staffs and S. Cheshire League) when only 15 and for Staffordshire from 1958 to 1960. Debut 1960 for Minor Counties v South Africans (Stoke-on-Trent). Debut for county 1961. Cap 1962. Testimonial (£6,672) in 1973. Appointed county captain during 1975 season. Relinquished post during 1976 season. *Wisden* 1976. 2nd testimonial in 1981. Tests: 26 between 1970-71 and 1979-80. Tours: Australia and New Zealand 1970-71, 1974-75, Australia with Rest of the World team 1971-72, West Indies 1973-74, Pakistan and New Zealand 1977-78, Australia 1978-79. Australia and India 1979-80. Withdrew from India, Sri Lanka and Pakistan tour 1972-73. Dismissed 80 batsmen (77 ct 3 st) in 1962, 83 batsmen (81 ct 2 st) in 1963, and 86 batsmen (79 ct 7 st) in 1965. Dismissed 7 batsmen in innings (equals Test record) and 10 batsmen in match (all caught) for Test record v India (Bombay) 1979-80. Dismissed 10 batsmen in match, all caught v Hants (Chesterfield) 1963 and 7 in innings, all caught v Glamorgan (Derby) 1966. Gillette Man of the Match Awards: 1. Benson & Hedges Gold awards: 1. HS: 97 International Wanderers v South African Invitation XI (Johannesburg) 1975-76 and 97 v Australia (Adelaide) 1978-79. HSUK: 75 v Yorks (Chesterfield) 1980. HSGC: 53* v Middlesex (Lord's) 1965. HSJPL: 43* v Glos (Burton-on-Trent) 1969. HSBH: 31* v Hants (Southampton) 1976.

**Colin John TUNNICLIFFE** B Derby 11/8/1951. RHB, LFM. Debut 1973. Left staff after 1974 season. Re-appeared in 1976. Cap 1977. Hat-trick in John Player League v Worcs (Derby) 1979. HS: 82* v Middlesex (Ilkeston) 1977. HSGC: 13 v Somerset (Ilkeston) 1977. HSJPL: 42 v Yorks (Huddersfield) 1978. HSBH: 28 v Warwickshire (Birmingham) 1979. BB: 7-36 v Essex (Chesterfield) 1980. BBJPL: 3-12 v Essex (Chesterfield) 1974. BBBH: 3-16 v Lancs (Manchester) 1978.

**John WALTERS** B Brampton (Yorks) 7/8/1949. LHB, RFM. Has played in Huddersfield League. Debut 1977. HS: 90 v Yorks (Chesterfield) 1978. HSGC: 21* v Hants (Derby) 1980. HSJPL: 55* v Worcs (Worcester) 1978. HSBH: 12 v Warwickshire (Birmingham) 1979. BB: 4-100 v Worcs (Derby) 1979. BBJPL: 4-14 v Glamorgan (Swansea) 1979.

**Barry WOOD** B Ossett (Yorks) 26/12/1942. RHB, RM. Brother of R. Wood who played occasionally for Yorkshire some years ago. Debut for Yorks 1964. Joined Lancs by special registration, making debut for County in 1966. Cap 1968. Played for Eastern Province in Currie Cup in 1971-72 and 1973-74. Testimonial (£62,429) in 1979. Left County after 1979 season and made debut for Derbyshire in 1980. Cap 1980. Tests: 12 between 1972 and 1978. Tours: India, Pakistan and Sri Lanka 1972-73, New Zealand 1974-75 (flown out as reinforcement). 1,000 runs (6)—1,492 runs (av. 38.25) in 1971 best. Gillette Man of the Match Awards: 6 (for Lancs). Benson & Hedges Gold Awards: 8 (for Lancs). HS: 198 Lancs v Glamorgan (Liverpool) 1976. HSC: 113 v Warwickshire (Birmingham) 1980. HSTC: 90 v Australia (Oval) 1972. HSGC: 116 Lancs v Kent (Canterbury) 1979. HSJPL: 90* Lancs v Notts (Manchester) 1977 and 90* v Hants (Southampton) 1980. HSBH: 79 Lancs v Minor Counties (North) (Longton) 1975. BB: 7-52 Lancs v Middlesex (Manchester) 1968. BBC: 3-22 v Sussex (Derby) 1980. BBGC: 4-17 Lancs v Hants (Manchester) 1975. BBJPL: 5-19 Lancs v Kent (Manchester) 1971. BBBH: 5-12 Lancs v Derbyshire (Stockport) 1976.

**John Geoffrey WRIGHT** (Christ's College, Christchurch and Otago University) B Darfield, New Zealand 5/7/1954. LHB, RM. Debut for Northern Districts in Shell Cup in 1975-76. Debut for county 1977. Cap 1977. Tests: 11 for New Zealand between 1977-78 and 1979-80. Tours: New Zealand to England 1978, Australia 1980-81. 1,000 runs (3) – 1,504 runs (av. 48.51) in 1980 best. Benson & Hedges

Gold Awards: 3. HS: 166* v Lancs (Manchester) 1980. HSTC: 88 New Zealand v Pakistan (Napier) 1978-79. HSGC: 87* v Sussex (Hove) 1977. HSJPL: 92* v Worcs (Worcester) 1980. HSBH: 102 v Worcs (Chesterfield) 1977.

**NB.** The following players whose particulars appeared in the 1980 Annual have been omitted: H. Cartwright, J.W. Lister (not re-engaged), R.J. McCurdy, A.J. McLellan (not re-engaged), A.J. Mellor (not re-engaged), R.C. Wincer (not re-engaged). The career records of Mellor and Wincer will be found elsewhere in this Annual.

# County Averages

**Schweppes Championship: Played 20, won 4, drawn 13, lost 3, abandoned 2**
**All first-class matches: Played 21, won 4, drawn 13, lost 4, abandoned 2**

### BATTING AND FIELDING

| Cap | | M | I | NO | Runs | HS | Avge | 100 | 50 | Ct | St |
|---|---|---|---|---|---|---|---|---|---|---|---|
| 1978 | P.N. Kirsten | 21 | 36 | 6 | 1895 | 213* | 63.16 | 6 | 8 | 12 | — |
| 1977 | J.G. Wright | 20 | 36 | 5 | 1504 | 166* | 48.51 | 3 | 10 | 9 | — |
| 1980 | B. Wood | 17 | 30 | 3 | 880 | 113 | 32.59 | 2 | 2 | 24 | — |
| 1976 | G. Miller | 20 | 27 | 5 | 662 | 78* | 30.09 | — | 6 | 20 | — |
| 1979 | D.S. Steele | 20 | 31 | 7 | 698 | 86* | 29.08 | — | 3 | 19 | — |
| — | J. Walters | 17 | 26 | 4 | 460 | 72 | 20.90 | — | 2 | 16 | — |
| — | K.J. Barnett | 16 | 21 | — | 362 | 69 | 17.23 | — | 2 | 10 | — |
| — | I.S. Anderson | 13 | 15 | 4 | 187 | 36 | 17.00 | — | — | 8 | — |
| 1977 | C.J. Tunnicliffe | 20 | 24 | 7 | 264 | 56* | 15.52 | — | 1 | 14 | — |
| 1962 | R.W. Taylor | 21 | 23 | 6 | 241 | 75 | 14.17 | — | 1 | 35 | 5 |
| 1972 | M. Hendrick | 12 | 13 | 5 | 98 | 33 | 12.25 | — | — | 8 | — |
| 1977 | A.J. Borrington | 6 | 10 | 1 | 93 | 36 | 10.33 | — | — | — | — |
| 1980 | S. Oldham | 19 | 10 | 4 | 41 | 7 | 1.83 | — | — | 7 | — |

Played in three matches: P.G. Newman 8, 6*, 17*, 29* (1 ct).
Played in two matches: A. Hill 2, 5, 0, 7 (1 ct); R.C. Wincer did not bat.
Played in one match: K.G. Brooks 3, 8 (2ct); A.J. Mellor 0, 0.

### BOWLING

| | Type | O | M | R | W | Avge | Best | 5 wI | 10 wM |
|---|---|---|---|---|---|---|---|---|---|
| M. Hendrick | RFM | 355.5 | 107 | 719 | 52 | 13.82 | 7-19 | 4 | — |
| D.S. Steele | SLA | 430 | 123 | 1221 | 54 | 22.61 | 7-133 | 4 | 1 |
| G. Miller | OB | 563.4 | 177 | 1422 | 55 | 25.85 | 5-52 | 2 | — |
| C.J. Tunnicliffe | LFM | 427.5 | 89 | 1244 | 47 | 26.46 | 7-36 | 2 | — |
| K.J. Barnett | LB | 55.3 | 13 | 230 | 7 | 32.85 | 4-76 | — | — |
| S. Oldham | RFM | 460.2 | 102 | 1381 | 41 | 33.68 | 4-41 | — | — |
| B. Wood | RM | 142 | 29 | 364 | 10 | 36.40 | 3-22 | — | — |

Also bowled: I.S. Anderson 23-2-94-0; P.N. Kirsten 28.5-8-90-1; A.J. Mellor 6-1-37-0; P.G. Newman 40.2-7-143-4; R.C. Wincer 27-5-109-3; J.G. Wright 0.4-0-4-1; J. Walters 35.4-1-130-1.

# County Records

### First-class cricket

| | | | |
|---|---|---|---|
| Highest innings | For | 645 v Hampshire (Derby) | 1898 |
| totals: | Agst | 662 by Yorkshire (Chesterfield) | 1898 |
| Lowest innings | For | 16 v Nottinghamshire (Nottingham) | 1879 |
| totals: | Agst | 23 by Hampshire (Burton-on-Trent) | 1958 |
| Highest indi- | For | 274 G. Davidson v Lancashire (Manchester) | 1896 |
| vidual innings: | Agst | 343* P.A. Perrin for Essex (Chesterfield) | 1904 |
| Best bowling | For | 10-40 W. Bestwick v Glamorgan (Cardiff) | 1921 |
| in an innings: | Agst | 10-74 T.F. Smailes for Yorkshire (Sheffield) | 1939 |
| Best bowling | For | 16-84 C. Gladwin v Worcs (Stourbridge) | 1952 |
| in a match: | Agst | 16-101 G. Giffen for Australians (Derby) | 1886 |
| Most runs in a season: | | 2165 (av. 48.1) D.B. Carr | 1959 |
| runs in a career: | | 20516 (av. 31.41) D. Smith | 1927-1952 |
| 100s in a season: | | 6 by L.F. Townsend | 1933 |
| | | 6 by P.N. Kirsten | 1980 |
| 100s in a career: | | 30 by D. Smith | 1927-1952 |
| wickets in a season: | | 168 (av. 19.55) T.B. Mitchell | 1935 |
| wickets in a career: | | 1670 (av. 17.11) H.L. Jackson | 1947-1963 |

## RECORD WICKET STANDS

| | | | |
|---|---|---|---|
| 1st | 322 | H. Storer & J. Bowden v Essex (Derby) | 1929 |
| 2nd | 349 | C.S. Elliot & J.D. Eggar v Notts (Nottingham) | 1947 |
| 3rd | 246 | J. Kelly & D.B. Carr v Leicestershire (Chesterfield) | 1957 |
| 4th | 328 | P. Vaulkhard & D. Smith v Notts (Nottingham) | 1946 |
| 5th | 203 | C.P. Wilkins & I.R. Buxton v Lancashire (Manchester) | 1971 |
| 6th | 212 | G.M. Lee & T.S. Worthington v Essex (Chesterfield) | 1932 |
| 7th | 241* | G.H. Pope & A.E.G. Rhodes v Hampshire (Portsmouth) | 1948 |
| 8th | 182 | A.H.M. Jackson & W. Carter v Leicestershire (Leicester) | 1922 |
| 9th | 283 | A.R. Warren & J. Chapman v Warwickshire (Blackwell) | 1910 |
| 10th | 93 | J. Humphries & J. Horsley v Lancashire (Derby) | 1914 |

### One-day cricket

| | | | |
|---|---|---|---|
| Highest innings | Gillette Cup | 250-9 v Hants (Bournemouth) | 1963 |
| totals: | John Player League | 260-6 v Glos (Derby) | 1972 |
| | Benson & Hedges Cup | 225-6 v Notts (Nottingham) | 1974 |
| Lowest innings | Gillette Cup | 79 v Surrey (Oval) | 1967 |
| totals: | John Player League | 70 v Surrey (Derby) | 1972 |
| | Benson & Hedges Cup | 102 v Yorks (Bradford) | 1975 |
| Highest indi- | Gillette Cup | 87* J.G. Wright v Sussex (Hove) | 1977 |
| vidual innings: | John Player League | 120 A. Hill v Northants (Buxton) | 1976 |
| | Benson & Hedges Cup | 111* P.J. Sharpe v Glamorgan (Chesterfield) | 1976 |
| Best bowling | Gillette Cup | 6-18 T.J.P. Eyre v Sussex (Chesterfield) | 1969 |
| figures: | John Player League | 6-7 M. Hendrick v Notts (Nottingham) | 1972 |
| | Benson & Hedges Cup | 6-33 E.J. Barlow v Glos (Bristol) | 1978 |

# ESSEX

**Formation of present club:** 1876.
**Colours:** Blue, gold and red.
**Badge:** Three seaxes with word 'Essex' underneath.
**County Champions:** 1979.
**Gillette Cup semi-finalists:** 1978.
**John Player League runners-up:** (3): 1971, 1976
and 1977
**Benson & Hedges Cup winners:** 1979.
**Benson & Hedges Cup Finalists:** 1980.
**Gillette Man of the Match Awards:** 14.
**Benson & Hedges Gold Awards:** 28
**Secretary:** P.J. Edwards, The county Ground, New Writtle Street,
Chelmsford CM2 0PG.
**Captain:** K.W.R. Fletcher.
**Prospects of Play Telephone No:** Chelmsford matches only. Chelmsford (0245)
66794.

**David Laurence ACFIELD** (Brentwood School & Cambridge) B Chelmsford
24/7/1947. RHB, OB. Debut 1966. Blue 1967-68. Cap 1970. Benefit in 1981. HS:
42 Cambridge U v Leics (Leicester) 1967. BB: 7-36 v Sussex (Ilford) 1973. BBJPL:
5-14 v Northants (Northampton) 1970. Also obtained Blue for fencing (sabre). Has
appeared in internationals in this sport and represented Great Britain in Olympic
Games at Mexico City and Munich. Obtained degree in History.

**Raymond Eric (Ray) EAST** B Manningtree (Essex) 20/6/1947. RHB, SLA.
Debut 1965. Cap 1967. Benefit (£29,000) in 1978. Hat-trick: The Rest v MCC Tour
XI (Hove) 1973. Benson & Hedges Gold Awards: 3. HS: 113 v Hants (Chelmsford)
1976. HSGC: 38* v Glos (Chelmsford) 1973. HSJPL: 25* v Glamorgan (Colchester) 1976. HSBH: 54 v Northants (Chelmsford) 1977. BB: 8-30 v Notts (Ilford)
1977. BBGC: 4-28 v Herts (Hitchin) 1976. BBJPL: 6-18 v Yorks (Hull) 1969.
BBBH: 5-33 v Kent (Chelmsford) 1975.

**Keith William Robert FLETCHER** B Worcester 20/5/1944. RHB, LB. Debut
1962. Cap 1963. Appointed county vice-captain in 1971 and county captain in 1974.
Benefit (£13,000) in 1973. *Wisden* 1973. Tests: 52 between 1968 and 1976-77. Also
played in 4 matches v Rest of the World in 1970. Tours: Pakistan 1966-67, Ceylon
and Pakistan 1968-69, Australia and New Zealand, 1970-71, 1974-75, India, Sri
Lanka and Pakistan 1972-73, West Indies 1973-74, India, Sri Lanka and Australia
1976-77. 1,000 runs (16)—1,890 runs (av. 41.08) in 1968 best. Scored two centuries
in match (111 and 102*) v Notts (Nottingham) 1976. Gillette Man of the Match
Awards: 1. Benson & Hedges Gold Awards: 5. HS: 228* v Sussex (Hastings) 1968.
HSTC: 216 v New Zealand (Auckland) 1974-75. HSGC: 74 v Notts (Nottingham)
1969. HSJPL: 99* v Notts (Ilford) 1974. HSBH: 90 v Surrey (Oval) 1974. BB: 5-41
v Middlesex (Colchester) 1979.

**Neil Alan FOSTER** (Philip Morant School, Colchester) B Colchester 6/5/1962.
6ft. 3in. tall. RHB, RM. Played for 2nd XI in 1979. Toured West Indies with England
Young Cricketers in 1980. Debut 1980. One match v Kent (Ilford) 1980. HS: 8* v Kent
(Ilford) 1980. BB: 3-51 v Kent (Ilford) 1980.

**Christopher GLADWIN** (Langdon Comprehensive School, Newham) B East

## ESSEX

Ham 10/5/1962. LHB, RM. Played for 2nd XI since 1979. Has not yet appeared in first-class cricket.

**Graham Alan GOOCH** (Norlington Junior HS, Leyton) B Leytonstone 23/7/1953. Cousin of G.J. Saville, former Essex player and assistant secretary of club. RHB, RM. Toured West Indies with England Young Cricketers 1972. Debut 1973. Cap 1975. *Wisden* 1979. Tests: 26 between 1975 and 1980. Tours: Australia 1978-79, Australia and India 1979-80, West Indies 1980-81. 1,000 runs (4) – 1,437 runs (av. 47.90) in 1980 best. Shared 2nd wicket partnership record for county, 321 with K.S. McEwan v Northants (Ilford) 1978. Scored record aggregate of runs in limited overs competitions in 1979 – 1,137 runs (av. 54.14). Benson & Hedges Gold Awards: 6. HS: 205 v Cambridge U (Cambridge) 1980. HSTC: 123 v West Indies (Lord's) 1980. HSGC: 61 v Somerset (Taunton) 1978. HSJPL: 90* v Middlesex (Lord's) 1978. HSBH: 138 v Warwickshire (Chelmsford) 1979. BB: 5-40 v West Indians (Chelmsford) 1976. BBJPL: 3-14 v Derbyshire (Derby) 1978.

**Brian Ross HARDIE** (Larbert HS) B Stenhousemuir 14/1/1950. RHB, RM. Has played for Stenhousemuir in East of Scotland League. Debut for Scotland 1970. His father and elder brother K.M. Hardie have also played for Scotland. Debut for Essex by special registration in 1973. Cap 1974. 1,000 runs (5)—1,522 runs (av. 43.48) in 1975 best. Scored two centuries in match for Scotland v MCC, Aberdeen 1971, a match not regarded as first-class. HS: 162 v Warwickshire (Birmingham) 1975. HSGC: 83 v Staffs (Stone) 1976. HSJPL: 94 v Northants (Northampton) 1971. HSBH: 53 v Glos (Bristol) 1980.

**Reuben HERBERT** (Barstaple Comprehensive School, Basildon) B Cape Town 1/12/1957. RHB, OB. Debut 1976. Did not play in 1978 or 1979. Re-appeared in 1980. HS: 14* v Lancs (Blackpool) 1980. BB: 3-64 v Lancs (Blackpool) 1980.

**Robert James LEIPER** (Chigwell School) B Woodford Green (Essex) 30/8/1961. LHB. Played for 2nd XI since 1977. Has not yet appeared in first-class cricket.

**John Kenneth LEVER** B Stepney 24/2/1949. RHB, LFM. Debut 1967. Cap 1970. *Wisden* 1978. Benefit in 1980. Tests: 18 between 1976-77 and 1980. Tours: India, Sri Lanka and Australia 1976-77, Pakistan and New Zealand 1977-78, Australia 1978-79, Australia and India 1979-80. 100 wkts (2)—106 wkts (av. 15.18) in 1978 and 106 wkts (av. 17.30) in 1979. Gillette Man of the Match Awards: 3. Benson & Hedges Gold Awards: 1 HS: 91 v Glamorgan (Cardiff) 1970. HSTC: 53 v India (Delhi) 1976-77 (on debut). HSJPL: 23 v Worcs (Worcester) 1974. HSBH: 12* v Warwickshire (Birmingham) 1975. BB: 8-49 (13-87 match) v Warwickshire (Birmingham) 1979. BBTC: 7-46 v India (Delhi) 1976-77 (on debut). BBGC: 5-8 v Middlesex (Westcliff) 1972. BBJPL: 5-13 v Glamorgan (Ebbw Vale) 1975. BBBH: 5-16 v Middlesex (Chelmsford) 1976.

**Alan William LILLEY** (Caterham Secondary High School, Ilford) B Ilford 8/5/1959. RHB, WK. Debut 1978. Scored century in second innings of debut match v Notts (Nottingham) 1978. Benson & Hedges Gold Awards: 1 HS: 100* v Notts (Nottingham) 1978. HJPL: 60 v Northants (Chelmsford) 1980. HSBH: 119 v Combined Universities (Chelmsford) 1979.

**Michael Stephen Anthony McEVOY** (Colchester RGS) B Jorhat Assam, India 25/1/1956. RHB, RM. Debut 1976. HS: 67* v Yorks (Middlesborough) 1977. HSJPL: 15 v Leics (Chelmsford) 1980. Trained as a teacher at Borough Road College of Education.

**Kenneth Scott (Ken) McEWAN** (Queen's College, Queenstown) B Bedford, Cape Province, South Africa 16/7/1952. RHB, OB. Debut for Eastern Province in 1972-73 Currie Cup competition. Played for T.N. Pearce's XI v West Indians (Scarborough) 1973. Debut for county and cap 1974. *Wisden* 1977. Played for Western Australia in 1979-80 and 1980-81. 1,000 runs (7)—1,821 runs (av. 49.21) in 1976 best. Scored 4 consecutive centuries in 1977 including two centuries in match (102 and 116) v Warwickshire (Birmingham). Shared 2nd wicket partnership record for county, 321 with G.A. Gooch v Northants (Ilford) 1978. Gillette Man of the Match Awards: 1. Benson & Hedges Gold Awards: 5. HS: 218 v Sussex (Chelmsford) 1977. HSGC: 119 v Leics (Leicester) 1980. HSJPL: 136 v Sussex (Hastings) 1980. HSBH: 133 v Notts (Chelmsford) 1978.

**Norbert PHILLIP** (Dominica GS, Roseau) B Bioche, Dominica 12/6/1948. RHB, RFM. Debut 1969-70 for Windward Islands v Glamorgan and has played subsequently for Combined Islands in Shell Shield competition. Debut for county and cap 1978. Tests: 9 for West Indies between 1977-78 and 1978-79. Tour: West Indies to India and Sri Lanka 1978-79. Had match double of 100 runs and 10 wickets (160 and 10-131), Combined Islands v Guyana (Georgetown) 1977-78. HS: 134 v Glos (Gloucester) 1978. HSTC: 47 West Indies v India (Calcutta) 1978-79. HSGC: 45 v Surrey (Chelmsford) 1980. HSJPL: 36 v Worcs (Colchester) and 36 v Northants (Chelmsford) 1980. HSBH: 32* v Northants (Lord's) 1980. BB: 6-33 v Pakistanis (Chelmsford) 1978. BBTC: 4-48 West Indies v India (Madras) 1978-79. BBJPL: 4-19 v Northants (Chelmsford) 1980. BBBH: 4-32 v Glamorgan (Chelmsford) 1980.

**Keith Rupert PONT** B Wanstead 16/1/1953. RHB, RM. Debut 1970. Cap 1976. Benson & Hedges Gold Awards: 2. HS: 113 v Warwickshire (Birmingham) 1973. HSGC: 39 v Somerset (Taunton) 1978. HSJPL: 52 v Glamorgan (Chelmsford) 1979. HSBH: v Notts (Ilford) 1976. BB: 5-33 v Middlesex (Southend) 1980. BBJPL: 4-24 v Derbyshire (Chelmsford) 1979. BBBH: 4-60 v Northants (Lord's) 1980.

**Derek Raymond PRINGLE** (Felsted School and Cambridge) B Nairobi, Kenya 18/9/1958. 6ft. 4½in. tall. Son of late Donald Pringle who played for East Africa in 1975 Prudential Cup. RHB, RM. Toured India with England Schools C.A. 1977-78. Debut 1978. Did not play for county in 1979, re-appeared in 1980. Blue 1979-80. HS: 123 Camb U v Notts (Cambridge) 1980. HSC: 50* v Cambridge U (Cambridge) 1978. HSJPL: 19* v Sussex (Hastings) 1980. HSBH: 58 Combined Universities v Essex (Chelmsford) 1979. BB: 6-90 Cambridge v Warwickshire (Cambridge) 1980. BBC: 3-34 v Glos (Gloucester) 1980.

**Gary Edward SAINSBURY** (Beal HS, Ilford) B Wanstead 17/1/1958. RHB, LM. Played for 2nd XI since 1977. Debut 1979. BB: 4-85 v Surrey (Oval) 1980. Obtained degree in Statistics at University of Bath.

**Neil SMITH** (Ossett GS) B Dewsbury 1/4/1949. RHB, WK. Debut for Yorks 1970. Debut for county by special registration in 1973. Cap 1975. HS: 126 v Somerset (Leyton) 1976. HSGC: 12 v Leics (Southend) 1977. HSJPL: 60 v Middlesex (Lord's) 1980. HSBH: 61 v Northants (Chelmsford) 1977.

**Stuart TURNER** B Chester 18/7/1943. RHB, RFM. Debut 1965. Cap 1970. Played for Natal in 1976-77 and 1977-78 Currie Cup competition. Benefit (£37,288) in 1979. Hat-trick: v Surrey (Oval) 1971. HS: 121 v Somerset (Taunton) 1970. HSGC: 50 v Lancs (Chelmsford) 1971. HSJPL: 87 v Worcs (Chelmsford)

## ESSEX

1975. HSBH: 41* v Minor Counties (East) (Chelmsford) 1977. BB: 6-26 v Northants (Northampton) 1977. BBGC: 3-16 v Glamorgan (Ilford) 1971. BBJPL: 5-35 v Hants (Chelmsford) 1978. BBBH: 4-22 v Minor Counties (South) (Bedford) 1975.

**NB.** The following player whose particulars appeared in the 1980 Annual has been omitted: M.H. Denness (appointed 2nd XI captain). His career record will be found elsewhere in this Annual.

# County Averages

**Schweppes Championship: Played 22, won 4, drawn 15, lost 3**
**All first-class matches: Played 24, won 4, drawn 17, lost 3**

## BATTING AND FIELDING

| Cap | | M | I | NO | Runs | HS | Avge | 100 | 50 | Ct | St |
|---|---|---|---|---|---|---|---|---|---|---|---|
| 1975 | G.A. Gooch | 13 | 23 | 5 | 1019 | 205 | 56.61 | 5 | — | 12 | — |
| 1963 | K.W.R. Fletcher | 24 | 38 | 4 | 1349 | 122* | 39.67 | 1 | 9 | 23 | — |
| 1974 | K.S. McEwan | 23 | 38 | 6 | 1217 | 140* | 38.03 | 2 | 8 | 16 | — |
| 1974 | B.R. Hardie | 24 | 36 | 4 | 1084 | 95 | 33.87 | — | 6 | 21 | — |
| 1970 | S. Turner | 18 | 28 | 7 | 662 | 83* | 31.52 | — | 4 | 7 | — |
| 1977 | M.H. Denness | 18 | 30 | 4 | 805 | 87 | 30.96 | — | 8 | 7 | — |
| — | M.S.A. McEvoy | 16 | 29 | 0 | 600 | 65 | 20.68 | — | 2 | 14 | — |
| 1978 | N. Phillip | 20 | 24 | 4 | 376 | 77* | 18.80 | — | 2 | 5 | — |
| 1967 | R.E. East | 20 | 25 | 4 | 361 | 47 | 17.19 | — | — | 7 | — |
| 1975 | N. Smith | 21 | 25 | 5 | 290 | 63* | 14.50 | — | 1 | 39 | 2 |
| 1976 | K.R. Pont | 12 | 17 | 2 | 210 | 36 | 14.00 | — | — | 5 | — |
| — | D.R. Pringle | 8 | 10 | 1 | 109 | 40* | 12.11 | — | — | 4 | — |
| 1970 | J.K. Lever | 20 | 19 | 10 | 104 | 18* | 11.55 | — | — | 5 | — |
| — | R. Herbert | 3 | 4 | 1 | 29 | 14* | 9.66 | — | — | 3 | — |
| 1970 | D.L. Acfield | 20 | 19 | 8 | 83 | 26 | 7.54 | — | — | 4 | — |

*Played in two matches: G.E. Sainsbury 2*, 0*.*
*Played in one match: N. Foster 8*; A.W. Lilley 9, 6.*

## BOWLING

| | Type | O | M | R | W | Avge | Best | 5 wI | 10 wM |
|---|---|---|---|---|---|---|---|---|---|
| G.A. Gooch | RM | 111 | 28 | 292 | 12 | 24.33 | 3-57 | — | — |
| R.E. East | SLA | 530.2 | 135 | 1494 | 61 | 24.49 | 6-56 | 5 | 2 |
| D.L. Acfield | OB | 553.5 | 171 | 1210 | 47 | 25.74 | 6-37 | 2 | — |
| G.E. Sainsbury | LM | 57 | 10 | 189 | 7 | 27.00 | 4-85 | — | — |
| J.K. Lever | LFM | 563 | 119 | 1602 | 59 | 27.15 | 6-121 | 3 | — |
| K.R. Pont | RM | 124.4 | 28 | 306 | 11 | 27.81 | 5-33 | 1 | — |
| S. Turner | RFM | 481.4 | 94 | 1343 | 45 | 29.84 | 6-69 | 2 | — |
| D.R. Pringle | RM | 111.1 | 25 | 324 | 10 | 32.40 | 3-34 | — | — |
| N. Phillip | RFM | 412.2 | 59 | 1412 | 40 | 35.30 | 6-47 | 1 | — |
| K.W.R. Fletcher | LB | 33.2 | 2 | 246 | 5 | 49.20 | 1-13 | — | — |

*Also bowled: N. Foster 25-5-80-3; R. Herbert 36.4-3-148-3.*

# County Records

### First-Class Cricket

| | | | |
|---|---|---|---|
| Highest innings | For | 692 v Somerset (Taunton) | 1895 |
| totals: | Agst | 803-4 by Kent (Brentwood) | 1934 |
| Lowest innings | For | 30 v Yorkshire (Leyton) | 1901 |
| totals: | Agst | 31 by Derbyshire (Derby) and by Yorkshire (Huddersfield) | 1914 & 1935 |
| Highest indi- | For | 343* P.A. Perrin v Derbyshire (Chesterfield) | 1904 |
| vidual innings: | Agst | 332 W.H. Ashdown for Kent (Brentwood) | 1934 |
| Best bowling | For | 10-32 H. Pickett v Leicestershire (Leyton) | 1895 |
| in an innings: | Agst | 10-40 E.G. Dennett for Gloucestershire (Bristol) | 1906 |
| Best bowling | For | 17-119 W. Mead v Hampshire (Southampton) | 1895 |
| in a match: | Agst | 17-56 C.W.L. Parker for Glos (Gloucester) | 1925 |
| Most runs in a season: | | 2308 (av. 56.29) J. O'Connor | 1934 |
| runs in a career: | | 29162 (av. 36.18) P.A. Perrin | 1896-1928 |
| 100s in a season: | | 9 by J. O'Connor and D.J. Insole | 1934 & 1955 |
| 100s in a career: | | 71 by J. O'Connor | 1921-1939 |
| wickets in a season: | | 172 (av. 27.13) T.P.B. Smith | 1947 |
| wickets in a career: | | 1611 (av. 26.26) T.P.B. Smith | 1929-1951 |

### RECORD WICKET STANDS

| | | | |
|---|---|---|---|
| 1st | 270 | A.V. Avery & T.C. Dodds v Surrey (Oval) | 1946 |
| 2nd | 321 | G.A. Gooch & K.S. McEwan v Northamptonshire (Ilford) | 1978 |
| 3rd | 343 | P.A. Gibb & R. Horsfall v Kent (Blackheath) | 1951 |
| 4th | 298 | A.V. Avery & R. Horsfall v Worcestershire (Clacton) | 1948 |
| 5th | 287 | C.T. Ashton & J. O'Connor v Surrey (Brentwood) | 1934 |
| 6th | 206 | J.W.H.T. Douglas & J. O'Connor v Glos (Cheltenham) | 1923 |
| | | B.R. Knight & R.A.G. Luckin v Middlesex (Brentwood) | 1962 |
| 7th | 261 | J.W.H.T. Douglas & J. Freeman v Lancashire (Leyton) | 1914 |
| 8th | 263 | D.R. Wilcox & R.M. Taylor v Warwickshire (Southend) | 1946 |
| 9th | 251 | J.W.H.T. Douglas & S.N. Hare v Derbyshire (Leyton) | 1921 |
| 10th | 218 | F.H. Vigar & T.P.B. Smith v Derbyshire (Chesterfield) | 1947 |

### One-day cricket

| | | | |
|---|---|---|---|
| Highest innings | Gillette Cup | 316-6 v Staffordshire (Stone) | 1976 |
| totals: | John Player League | 283-6 v Gloucestershire (Cheltenham) | 1975 |
| | Benson & Hedges Cup | 350-3 v Combined Universities (Chelmsford) | 1979 |
| Lowest innings | Gillette Cup | 100 v Derbyshire (Brentwood) | 1965 |
| totals: | John Player League | 69 v Derbyshire (Chesterfield) | 1974 |
| | Benson & Hedges Cup | 123 v Kent (Canterbury) | 1973 |
| Highest indi- | Gillette Cup | 119 K.S. McEwan v Leicestershire (Leicester) | 1980 |
| vidual innings: | John Player League | 136 K.S. McEwan v Sussex (Hastings) | 1980 |
| | Benson & Hedges Cup | 138 G.A. Gooch v Warwickshire (Chelmsford) | 1979 |
| Best bowling | Gillette Cup | 5-8 J.K Lever v Middlesex (Westcliff) | 1972 |
| figures: | John Player League | 8-26 K.D. Boyce v Lancs (Manchester) | 1971 |
| | Benson & Hedges Cup | 5-16 J.K. Lever v Middlesex (Chelmsford) | 1976 |

# GLAMORGAN

**Formation of present club:** 1888.
**Colours:** Blue and gold.
**Badge:** Gold daffodil.
**County Champions (2):** 1948 and 1969.
**Gillette Cup finalists:**
**Best final position in John Player League:** 8th in 1977.
**Benson & Hedges Cup quarter-finalists (5):** 1972, 1973, 1977, 1978 and 1979.
**Gillette Man of the Match Awards:** 13.
**Benson & Hedges Gold Awards:** 20.
**Secretary:** P.B. Clift, 6 High Street, Cardiff CF1 2PW.
**Cricket Manager:** T.W. Cartwright.
**Captain:** M.A. Nash.
**Prospects of Play Telephone Nos:** Cardiff (0222) 29956 or 387367
Swansea (0792) 466321

**Terry DAVIES** B St Albans (Herts) 25/10/1960. 5ft 4ins tall. RHB. WK. Played for 2nd XI in 1978. Debut 1979. One match v Sri Lankans (Swansea). Did not play in 1980.

**Norman George FEATHERSTONE** (King Edward VII High School, Johannesburg) B Que Que, Rhodesia 20/8/1949. RHB, OB. Debut for Transvaal B 1967-68 and for Middlesex 1968. Cap 1971. Benefit (£30,000) in 1979. Left county after 1979 season and made debut for Glamorgan 1980. Cap 1980. 1,000 runs in season (3) – 1,156 runs (av. 35.03) in 1975 best. Scored two centuries in match (127* and 100*) Middlesex v Kent (Canterbury) 1975. Gillette Man of the Match Awards: 1 (for Middlesex). Benson & Hedges Gold Awards: 1 (for Middlesex). HS: 147 Middlesex v Yorks (Scarborough) 1975. HSC: 107 v Glos (Swansea) 1980. HSGC: 72* Middlesex v Worcs (Worcester) 1975. HSJPL: 82* Middlesex v Notts (Lord's) 1976. HSBH: 56* Middlesex v Sussex (Hove) 1975 and 56 Middlesex v Kent (Lord's) 1975. BB: 5-32 Middlesex v Notts (Nottingham) 1978. BBC: 5-90 v Somerset (Taunton) 1980. BBGC: 3-17 Middlesex v Glamorgan (Lord's) 1977. BBJPL: 4-10 Middlesex v Worcs (Worcester) 1978. BBBH: 4-33 Middlesex v Minor Counties (East) (Lord's) 1976.

**David Arthur FRANCIS** (Cwmtawe Comprehensive School, Pontardawe) B Clydach (Glamorgan) 29/11/1953. RHB, OB. Debut 1973 after playing for 2nd XI in 1971 and 1972. HS: 110 v Warwickshire (Nuneaton) 1977. HSGC: 62* v Worcs (Worcester) 1977. HSJPL: 101* v Warwickshire (Birmingham) 1980. HSBH: 59 v Warwickshire (Birmingham) 1977.

**Robin Nicholas Stuart HOBBS** (Raine's Foundation School, Stepney) B Chippenham (Wilts) 8/5/1942. RHB, LBG. Debut for Essex 1961. Cap 1964. Benefit: (£13,500) in 1974. Retired at end of 1975 season. Played for Suffolk from 1976 to 1978. Debut for county in 1979 having been appointed as County Captain. Cap 1979. Relinquished captaincy after 1979 season. Tests: 7 between 1967 and 1971. Tours: South Africa 1964-65, Pakistan 1966-67, West Indies 1967-68, Ceylon and Pakistan 1968-69. 100 wkts (2) – 102 wkts (av. 21.40) in 1970 best. Hat-trick: Essex v Middlesex (Lord's) 1968 in Gillette Cup. Benson & Hedges Gold Awards: 1 (for Essex). HS: 100 Essex v Glamorgan (Ilford) 1968 and 100 Essex v Australians (Chelmsford) 1975 in 44 minutes. HSC: 29 v Leics (Leicester) 1979. HSTC: 15* v India (Birmingham) 1967. HSGC: 34 Essex v Lancs (Chelmsford) 1971. HSJPL:

54* Essex v Yorks (Colchester) 1970. HSBH: 40 Essex v Middlesex (Lord's) 1972. BB: 8-63 (13-164 match) Essex v Glamorgan (Swansea) 1966. BBC: 3-21 v Oxford U. (Oxford) 1979. BBTC: 3-25 v India (Birmingham) 1967. BBGC: 4-55 Essex v Wilts (Chelmsford) 1969. BBJPL: 6-22 Essex v Hants (Harlow) 1973. BBBH: 3-41 v Derbyshire (Cardiff) 1979.

**Geoffrey Clark HOLMES** (West Denton HS, Newcastle-upon-Tyne) B Newcastle-upon-Tyne 16/9/1958. RHB, RM. Debut 1978. HS: 100* v Glos (Bristol) 1979. HSJPL: 43* v Hants (Portsmouth) 1979. HSBH: 30 v Glos (Bristol) 1980. BB: 5-86 v Surrey (Oval) 1980. BBJPL: 3-17 v Notts (Swansea) 1980.

**John Anthony HOPKINS** B Maesteg 16/6/1953. Younger brother of J.D. Hopkins, formerly on staff and who appeared for Middlesex. RHB, WK. Debut 1970. Cap 1977. 1,000 runs (4) – 1,371 runs (av. 33.43) in 1978 best. Gillette Man of the Match Awards: 1. Benson & Hedges Gold Awards: 3. HS: 230 v Worcs (Worcester) 1977 – the fourth highest score for the county. HSGC: 63 v Leics (Swansea) 1977. HSJPL: 65 v Essex (Swansea) 1980. HSBH: 103* v Minor Counties (Swansea) 1980. Trained as a teacher at Trinity College of Education, Carmarthen.

**JAVED MIANDAD KHAN** B Karachi 12/6/1957. RHB, LBG. Debut 1973-74 for Karachi Whites in Patron Trophy tournament aged 16 years 5 months. Has subsequently played for various Karachi, Sind and Habib Bank sides. Vice-captain of Pakistan Under-19 side in England in 1974 and Captain of Under-19 side in Sri Lanka 1974-75. Scored 227 for Sussex 2nd XI v Hants (Hove) 1975 whilst qualifying for county. Debut for Sussex 1976. Cap 1977. Left county after end of 1979 season and made debut for Glamorgan in 1980. Cap 1980. Tests: 30 for Pakistan between 1976-77 and 1979-80, captaining Pakistan in 3 tests. Tours: Pakistan to Australia and West Indies 1976-77, England 1978, New Zealand and Australia 1978-79, India 1979-80. 1,000 runs (2) – 1,460 runs (av. 54.07) in 1980 best. Scored 163 for Pakistan v New Zealand (Lahore) 1976-77 on Test debut and 206 v New Zealand (Karachi) in third Test becoming youngest double-century maker in Test cricket at age of 19 years 141 days. Scored two centuries in match (107 and 123) Habib Bank v National Bank (Lahore) 1980-81. Gillette Man of the Match Awards: 1 (for Sussex). HS: 311 Karachi Whites v National Bank (Karachi) 1974-75. HSUK: 181 v Warwickshire (Birmingham) 1980. HSTC: 206 Pakistan v New Zealand (Karachi) 1976-77. HSGC: 75 Sussex v Lancs (Hove) 1978. HSJPL: 98* Sussex v Lancs (Hastings) 1979. HSBH: 76 Sussex v Surrey (Oval) 1977. BB: 7-39 Habib Bank v Industrial Development Bank of Pakistan (Lahore) 1980-81. BBUK: 4-10 Sussex v Northants (Northampton) 1977. BBTC: 3-74 Pakistan v New Zealand (Hyderabad) 1976-77.

**Alan JONES** B Velindre, Swansea 4/11/1938. LHB, OB. Joined staff in 1955. Debut 1957. Cap 1962. Played for Western Australia in 1963-64, for Northern Transvaal in 1975-76 and for Natal in 1976-77. Benefit (£10,000) in 1972. County captain from 1976 to 1978. *Wisden* 1977. Testimonial in 1980. Played one match v Rest of World in 1970. 1,000 runs (20) – 1,865 runs (av. 34.53) in 1966 and 1,862 runs (av. 38.00) in 1968 best. Scored two centuries in match (187* and 105*) v Somerset (Glastonbury) 1963, (132 and 156*) v Yorks (Middlesbrough) 1976 and (147 and 100) v Hants (Swansea) 1978. Shared in record partnership for any wicket for county, 330 for 1st wkt with R.C. Fredericks v Northants (Swansea) 1972. Shared in 2nd wkt partnership record for county, 238 with A.R. Lewis v Sussex (Hastings) 1962. Completed 30,000 runs in 1979. Has scored more runs and centuries for county than any other player. Gillette Man of the Match Awards: 2. Benson & Hedges Gold Awards: 1. HS: 204* v Hants (Basingstoke) 1980. HSGC: 124* v Warwickshire (Birmingham) 1976. HSJPL: 110* v Glos (Cardiff) 1978. HSBH: 89 v Worcs (Cardiff) 1979. BBJPL: 3-21 v Northants (Wellingborough) 1975.

# GLAMORGAN

**Allan Arthur JONES** (St. John's College, Horsham) B Horley, Surrey 9/12/1947. RHB, RFM. 6ft 4ins tall. Debut for Sussex 1966. Left staff in 1969 and made debut for Somerset in 1970. Cap 1972. Played for Northern Transvaal in 1972-73 Currie Cup Competition and for Orange Free State in 1976-77. Left Somerset after 1975 season and made debut for Middlesex in 1976. Cap 1976. Not re-engaged after 1979 season and made debut for Glamorgan in 1980. Took 3 wkts in 4 balls, Somerset v Notts (Nottingham) 1972. Hat-trick in Benson & Hedges Cup, Middlesex v Essex (Lord's) 1977. Benson & Hedges Gold Awards: 4 (2 for Middlesex, 1 for Somerset). HS: 33 Middlesex v Kent (Canterbury) 1978. HSC: 12 v Sussex (Swansea) 1980. HSJPL: 18* Somerset v Sussex (Hove) 1973. HSBH: 14 v Essex (Chelmsford) 1980. BB: 9-51 Somerset v Sussex (Hove) 1972. BBC: 5-51 v Warwickshire (Cardiff) 1980. BBGC: 5-23 Middlesex v Kent (Canterbury) 1977. BBJPL: 6-34 Somerset v Essex / (Westcliff) 1971. BBBH: 5-16 Middlesex v Minor Counties (East) (Lakenham) 1977.

**Alan Lewis JONES** (Ystalyfera GS and Cwmtawe Comprehensive School) B Alltwen, Glamorgan 1/6/1957. No relation to A. and E.W. Jones. LHB. Played for 2nd XI in 1972. Debut 1973 at age of 16 years 99 days. Toured West Indies with England Young Cricketers 1976. HS: 83 v Worcs (Worcester) 1979. HSGC: 11 v Hants (Southampton) 1975. HSJPL: 62 v Hants (Cardiff) 1975. HSBH: 36 v Worcs (Cardiff) 1979. Trained as a teacher at Cardiff College of Education.

**Eifion Wyn JONES** B Velindre, Swansea 25/6/1942. Brother of A. Jones. RHB, WK. Debut 1961. Cap 1967. Benefit (£17,000) in 1975. Dismissed 94 batsmen (85 ct 9 st) in 1970. Dismissed 7 batsmen (6 ct 1 st) in innings v Cambridge U (Cambridge) 1970. Benson & Hedges Gold Awards: 1. HS: 146* v Sussex (Hove) 1968. HSGC: 67* v Herts (Swansea) 1969. HSJPL: 48 v Hants (Cardiff) 1971. HSBH: 39* v Minor Counties (West) (Amersham) 1977.

**Michael John (Mike) LLEWELLYN** B Clydach, Glamorgan 27/11/1953. LHB, OB. Debut 1970 at age of 16 years 202 days. Cap 1977. Gillette Man of the Match Awards: 1. Benson & Hedges Gold Awards: 2. HS: 129* v Oxford U (Oxford) 1977. HSGC: 62 v Middlesex (Lord's) 1977. HSJPL: 79* v Glos (Bristol) 1977. HSBH: 63 v Hants (Swansea) 1973. BB: 4-35 v Oxford U (Oxford) 1970.

**Barry John LLOYD** B Neath 6/9/1953. RHB, OB. Formerly on MCC groundstaff. Debut 1972. HS: 45* v Hants (Portsmouth) 1973. HSJPL: 14 v Worcs (Worcester) 1980. BB: 4-49 v Hants (Portsmouth) 1973. BBJPL: 3-22 v Derbyshire (Derby) 1980. Trained as a teacher at Bangor Normal College.

**Ezra Alphonsa MOSELEY** (Christ Church High School) B Christ Church, Barbados 5/1/1958. RHB, RFM. Debut 1980 taking 6-102 v Essex (Swansea) in debut match. HS: 70* v Kent (Canterbury) 1980. BB: 6-41 v Middlesex (Cardiff) 1980.

**Malcolm Andrew NASH** (Wells Cathedral School) B Abergavenny, Monmouthshire 9/5/1945. LHB, LM. Debut 1966. Cap 1969. Benefit (£18,000) in 1978. Appointed County Captain in 1980. Benson & Hedges Gold Awards: 3. Hat-trick in John Player League v Worcs (Worcester) 1975. HS: 130 v Surrey (Oval) 1976. HSGC: 51 v Lincs (Swansea) 1974. HSJPL: 68 v Essex (Purfleet) 1972. HSBH: 103* v Hants (Swansea) 1976. BB: 9-56 (14-137 match) v Hants (Basingstoke) 1975. BBGC: 3-14 v Staffs (Stoke) 1971. BBJPL: 6-29 v Worcs (Worcester) 1975. BBBH 4-12 v Surrey (Cardiff) 1975.

**Rodney Craig ONTONG** (Selborne College, East London) B Johannesburg, South Africa 9/9/1955. RHB, RFM. Debut 1972-73 for Border in Currie Cup competition. Debut for county 1975 after being on MCC staff. Transferred to Transvaal for 1976-77 season. Cap 1979. Scored 1,157 runs (av. 34.02) in 1979. Benson and Hedges Gold Awards: 1. HS: 135* v Warwickshire (Birmingham) 1979. HSGC: 64 v Somerset (Cardiff) 1978. HSJPL: 55 v Lancs (Cardiff) 1979. HSBH: 50* v Glos (Swansea) 1979. BB: 7-60 Border v Northern Transvaal (Pretoria) 1975-76. BBUK: 5-40 v Glos (Cardiff) 1979. BBJPL: 4-31 v Middlesex (Lord's) 1979. BBBH: 4-28 v Worcs (Cardiff) 1979.

**Neil James PERRY** B Sutton, Surrey 27/5/1958. RHB, SLA. On Surrey staff 1977. Joined county 1978. Debut 1979. BB: 3-51 v Indians (Swansea) 1979.

**John Gregory THOMAS** (Cwmtawe School, Swansea) B Garnswllt (Glamorgan) 12/8/1960. 6ft 3ins tall. RHB, RM. Debut 1979. One match v Sri Lankans (Swansea). Did not play in 1980. HS: 34 v Sri Lankans (Swansea) 1979. Training as a teacher at Cardiff College of Education.

NB. The following players whose particulars appeared in the 1980 annual have been omitted: A.E. Cordle (not re-engaged), A.J. Mack (not re-engaged), Parvez Mir and G. Richards. In addition A.H. Wilkins joined Gloucestershire and his particulars will be found under that county.

The career records of Cordle, Mack and Wilkins will be found elsewhere in this annual.

# County Averages

**Schweppes County Championship: Played 21, won 4, drawn 13, lost 4, abandoned 1.**
**All first-class matches: Played 22, won 4, drawn 14, lost 4, abandoned 1.**

## BATTING AND FIELDING

| Cap | | M | I | NO | Runs | HS | Avge | 100 | 50 | Ct | St |
|---|---|---|---|---|---|---|---|---|---|---|---|
| 1980 | Javed Miandad | 20 | 32 | 5 | 1460 | 181 | 54.07 | 3 | 6 | 7 | — |
| 1962 | A. Jones | 21 | 37 | 4 | 1393 | 204* | 42.21 | 2 | 7 | 5 | — |
| 1980 | N.G. Featherstone | 22 | 34 | 6 | 1015 | 107 | 36.25 | 1 | 8 | 10 | — |
| 1977 | J.A. Hopkins | 22 | 39 | 1 | 1123 | 112 | 29.55 | 2 | 5 | 22 | — |
| — | E.A. Moseley | 14 | 16 | 6 | 294 | 70* | 29.40 | — | 2 | 2 | — |
| 1977 | M.J. Llewellyn | 14 | 19 | 5 | 395 | 69 | 28.21 | — | 2 | 4 | — |
| — | D.A. Francis | 9 | 14 | 3 | 276 | 78* | 25.09 | — | 2 | 2 | — |
| — | B.J. Lloyd | 12 | 14 | 7 | 140 | 30 | 20.00 | — | 5 | — |
| 1967 | E.W. Jones | 22 | 29 | 5 | 465 | 67 | 19.37 | — | 3 | 43 | 2 |
| 1979 | R.C. Ontong | 5 | 7 | 1 | 110 | 52 | 18.33 | — | 1 | 1 | — |
| — | G.C. Holmes | 18 | 28 | 6 | 393 | 40 | 17.86 | — | — | 8 | — |
| 1969 | M.A. Nash | 18 | 24 | 2 | 342 | 49* | 15.54 | — | — | 9 | — |
| — | A.L. Jones | 3 | 5 | 0 | 47 | 22 | 9.40 | — | — | 3 | — |
| — | A.J. Mack | 8 | 7 | 4 | 17 | 6 | 5.66 | — | — | — | — |
| 1967 | A.E. Cordle | 5 | 4 | 1 | 17 | 6* | 5.66 | — | — | 2 | — |
| 1979 | R.N.S. Hobbs | 7 | 8 | 2 | 34 | 14 | 5.66 | — | — | 1 | — |
| — | A.A. Jones | 16 | 14 | 3 | 50 | 12 | 4.54 | — | — | 4 | — |
| — | N.J. Perry | 6 | 5 | 1 | 11 | 6 | 2.75 | — | — | 7 | — |

## GLAMORGAN

### BOWLING

| | Type | O | M | R | W | Avge | Best | 5 wI | 10 wM |
|---|---|---|---|---|---|---|---|---|---|
| M.A. Nash | LM | 611.4 | 196 | 1723 | 74 | 23.28 | 7-79 | 4 | 2 |
| E.A. Moseley | RFM | 430 | 94 | 1340 | 51 | 26.27 | 6-41 | 2 | — |
| A.A. Jones | RFM | 445 | 76 | 1604 | 41 | 39.12 | 5-51 | 1 | — |
| G.C. Holmes | RM | 149 | 29 | 522 | 12 | 43.50 | 5-86 | 1 | — |
| N.G. Featherstone | OB | 154 | 40 | 487 | 11 | 44.27 | 5-90 | 1 | — |
| N.J. Perry | SLA | 88.5 | 33 | 268 | 6 | 44.66 | 2-13 | — | — |
| A.E. Cordle | RFM | 162 | 56 | 370 | 8 | 46.25 | 3-84 | — | — |
| A.J. Mack | LM | 98 | 17 | 362 | 7 | 51.71 | 3-32 | — | — |
| R.N.S. Hobbs | LBG | 113.3 | 27 | 414 | 8 | 51.75 | 2-58 | — | — |
| B.J. Lloyd | OB | 208.1 | 57 | 679 | 11 | 61.72 | 4-95 | — | — |

*Also bowled:* Javed Miandad 34-8-132-2; R.C. Ontong 73-12-289-4.

# County Records

### First-class cricket

| | | | |
|---|---|---|---|
| Highest innings totals: | For – 587-8d v Derbyshire (Cardiff) | | 1951 |
| | Agst – 653-6d by Gloucestershire (Bristol) | | 1928 |
| Lowest innings totals: | For – 22 v Lancashire (Liverpool) | | 1924 |
| | Agst – 33 by Leicestershire (Ebbw Vale) | | 1965 |
| Highest individual innings: | For – 287* D.E. Davies v Gloucestershire (Newport) | | 1939 |
| | Agst – 302* W.R. Hammond for Glos (Bristol) | | 1934 |
| | 302 W.R. Hammond for Glos (Newport) | | 1939 |
| Best bowling in an innings: | For – 10-51 J. Mercer v Worcester (Worcester) | | 1936 |
| | Agst – 10-18 G. Geary for Leics (Pontypridd) | | 1929 |
| Best bowling in a match: | For – 17-212 J.C. Clay v Worcs (Swansea) | | 1937 |
| | Agst – 16-96 G. Geary for Leics (Pontypridd) | | 1929 |
| Most runs in a season: | 2,071 (av. 49.30) W.G.A. Parkhouse | | 1959 |
| runs in a career: | 30,314 (av. 33.13) A. Jones | | 1957-1980 |
| 100s in a season: | 7 by W.G.A. Parkhouse | | 1950 |
| 100s in a career: | 46 by A. Jones | | 1957-1980 |
| wickets in a season: | 176 (av. 17.34) J.C. Clay | | 1937 |
| wickets in a career: | 2,174 (av. 20.95) D.J. Shepherd | | 1950-1972 |

### RECORD WICKET STANDS

| | | | |
|---|---|---|---|
| 1st | 330 | A. Jones & R.C. Fredericks v Northamptonshire (Swansea) | 1972 |
| 2nd | 238 | A. Jones & A.R. Lewis v Sussex (Hastings) | 1962 |
| 3rd | 313 | D.E. Davies & W.E. Jones v Essex (Brentwood) | 1948 |
| 4th | 263 | G. Lavis & C. Smart v Worcestershire (Cardiff) | 1934 |
| 5th | 264 | M. Robinson & S.W. Montgomery v Hampshire (Bournemouth) | 1949 |
| 6th | 230 | W.E. Jones & B.L. Muncer v Worcestershire (Worcester) | 1953 |
| 7th | 195* | W. Wooller & W.E. Jones v Lancashire (Liverpool) | 1947 |
| 8th | 202 | D. Davies & J.J. Hills v Sussex (Eastbourne) | 1928 |
| 9th | 203* | J.J. Hills & J.C. Clay v Worcestershire (Swansea) | 1929 |
| 10th | 131* | C. Smart & W.D. Hughes v South Africans (Cardiff) | 1935 |

**One-day cricket**

| | | | |
|---|---|---|---|
| Highest innings totals: | Gillette Cup | 283-3 v Warwickshire (Birmingham) | 1976 |
| | John Player League | 266-6 v Northants (Wellingborough) | 1975 |
| | Benson & Hedges Cup | 245-7 v Hampshire (Swansea) | 1976 |
| Lowest innings totals: | Gillette Cup | 76 v Northants (Northampton) | 1968 |
| | John Player League | 42 v Derbyshire (Swansea) | 1979 |
| | Benson & Hedges Cup | 68 v Lancs (Manchester) | 1973 |
| Highest individual innings: | Gillette Cup | 124* A. Jones v Warwickshire (Birmingham) | 1976 |
| | John Player League | 110* A. Jones v Glos (Cardiff) | 1978 |
| | Benson & Hedges Cup | 103* M.A. Nash v Hants (Swansea) | 1976 |
| | | 103* J.A. Hopkins v Minor Counties (Swansea) | 1980 |
| Best bowling figures: | Gillette Cup | 5-21 P.M. Walker v Cornwall (Truro) | 1970 |
| | John Player League | 6-29 M.A. Nash v Worcs (Worcester) | 1975 |
| | Benson & Hedges Cup | 5-17 A.H. Wilkins v Worcs (Worcester) | 1978 |

# GLOUCESTERSHIRE

**Formation of present club:** 1871.
**Colours:** Blue, gold, brown silver, green and red.
**Badge:** Coat of Arms of the City and County of Bristol.
**County Champions (3):** 1874, 1876 and 1877.
**Joint Champions:** 1873.
**Gillette Cup Winners:** 1973.
**Best Position in John Player League:** 6th in 1969, 1973 and 1977.
**Benson & Hedges Cup winners:** 1977.
**Gillette Man of the Match Awards:** 17.
**Benson & Hedges Gold Awards:** 20
**Secretary:** A.S. Brown, County Ground, Nevil Road, Bristol BS7 9EJ.
**Captain:** M.J. Procter.
**Prospects of Play Telephone Nos:** Bristol (0272) 48461
Cheltenham (0242) 22000
Gloucester (0452) 24621.

**Philip BAINBRIDGE** (Hanley HS and Stoke-on-Trent Sixth Form College) B Stoke-on-Trent 16/4/1958. RHB, RM. Played for four 2nd XIs in 1976 – Derbyshire, Glos, Northants and Warwickshire. Debut 1977. HS: 81* v Indians (Bristol) 1979. HSGC: 20 v Surrey (Oval) 1980. HSJPL: 35 v Sussex (Moreton-in-Marsh) 1980. HSBH: 16* v Essex (Bristol) 1980. BB: 4-48 v Warwickshire (Birmingham) 1980. BBJPL: 4-27 v Middlesex (Cheltenham) 1980. Trained as a teacher at Borough Road College of Education.

**Brian Maurice BRAIN** (King's School, Worcester) B Worcester 13/9/1940. RHB, RFM. Debut for Worcs 1959. Left staff in 1960. Rejoined staff in 1963 and reappeared in 1964. Cap 1966. Left staff in 1971, but rejoined in 1973. Not re-engaged after 1975 season and joined Glos in 1976. Cap 1977. Testimonial in 1981. Gillette Man of the Match Awards: 1 (for Worcs). HS: 57 v Essex (Cheltenham) 1976. HSGC: 21* Worcs v Sussex (Worcester) 1967. HSJPL: 33 v Kent (Canterbury) 1978. HSBH: 16 v Warwickshire (Bristol) 1978. BB: 8-55 Worcs v Essex (Worcester) 1975. BBC: 7-51 v Australians (Bristol) 1977. BBGC: 4-13 Worcs v Durham (Chester-le-Street) 1968. BBJPL: 4-27 Worcs v Somerset (Taunton) 1970. BBBH: 4-30 v Somerset (Bristol) 1977.

**Andrew James (Andy) BRASSINGTON** B Bagnall, Staffordshire 9/8/1954. RHB, WK. Debut 1974. Cap 1978. HS: 28 v Glamorgan (Cardiff) 1975. HSGC: 20 v Hants (Bristol) 1979. Plays soccer as a goalkeeper.

**Brian Christopher (Chris) BROAD** (Colston's School, Bristol) B Bristol 29/9/1957. 6ft 4ins tall. LHB, RM. Played for 2nd XI since 1976. Debut 1979. Shared in first wkt partnerships of 126 and 89 with S.J. Windaybank in their debut match v Cambridge U (Cambridge). Scored century before lunch against Oxford U (Oxford) on opening day of 1980 season. HS: 129 v Northants (Bristol) 1979. HSJPL: 54 v Somerset (Bristol) 1980. HSBH: 40 v Sussex (Hove) 1980. Trained as a teacher at St Paul's College, Cheltenham.

**Ian BROOME** B Bradenstoke, Wilts 6/5/1960. RHB, RM. Played for 2nd XI since 1979. Played one John Player League in 1980 v Kent (Canterbury). Has yet to appear in first-class cricket.

**John Henry CHILDS** B Plymouth 15/8/1951. LHB, SLA. Played for Devon 1973-74. Debut 1975. Cap 1977. HS: 12 v Derbyshire (Ilkeston) 1977. HSJPL: 11* v Essex (Cheltenham) 1975. HSBH: 10 v Somerset (Bristol) 1979. BB: 8-34 v Hants (Basingstoke) 1978. BBJPL: 4-15 v Northants (Northampton) 1976.

**David Anthony GRAVENEY** (Millfield School) B Bristol 2/1/1953. Son of J.K.R. Graveney. 6ft 4ins tall. RHB, SLA. Debut 1972. Cap 1976. HS: 119 v Oxford U (Oxford) 1980. HSGC: 44 v Surrey (Bristol) 1973. HSJPL: 44 v Essex (Cheltenham) 1975. HSBH: 21 v Somerset (Street) 1975. BB: 8-85 v Notts (Cheltenham) 1974. BBGC: 3-67 v Leics (Leicester) 1975. BBJPL: 4-22 v Hants (Lydney) 1974. BBBH: 3-32 v Middlesex (Bristol) 1977.

**Alastair James HIGNELL** (Denstone College and Cambridge) B Cambridge 4/9/1955. RHB, LB. Scored 117* and 78* for England Schools v All India Schools (Birmingham) 1973 and 133 for England Young Cricketers v West Indies Young Cricketers (Arundel) 1974. Debut 1974. Cap 1977. Blue 1975-76-77-78. Captain in last two years. 1,000 runs (2) – 1,140 runs (av. 30.81) in 1976 best. Scored two centuries in match (108 and 145) for Cambridge U v Surrey (Cambridge) 1978. Benson & Hedges Gold Awards: 1 (for Combined Universities). HS: 149 Cambridge U v Glamorgan (Cambridge) 1977 and 149* v Northants (Bristol) 1979. HSGC: 85* v Northants (Bristol) 1977. HSJPL: 51 v Northants (Northampton) 1976. HSBH: 63 Combined Universities v Worcs (Worcester) 1978. Blue for rugby 1974-75 (captain) -76-77 (captain). Plays for Bristol. Toured Australia with England Rugby team 1975. 14 caps for England between 1975 and 1978-79.

**Martin <u>David</u> PARTRIDGE** (Marling School, Stroud) B Birdlip, Glos 25/10/1954. LHB, RM. Debut 1976. HS: 90 v Notts (Nottingham) 1979. HSGC: 20 v Surrey (Oval) 1980. HSJPL: 33 v Warwickshire (Moreton-in-Marsh) 1979. HSBH: 27 v Warwickshire (Bristol) 1978. BB: 5-29 v Worcs (Worcester) 1979. BBJPL: 5-47 v Kent (Cheltenham) 1977. Studied civil engineering at Bradford University.

**Michael John (Mike) PROCTER** (Hilton College, Natal) B Durban 15/9/1946. RHB, RF/OB. Vice-captain of South African Schools team to England 1963. Debut for county 1965 in one match v South Africans. Returned home to make debut for Natal in 1965-66 Currie Cup competition. Joined staff in 1968. Cap 1968. *Wisden* 1969. Transferred to Western Province for 1969-70 Currie Cup competition, Rhodesia in 1970-71 and Natal 1976-77. Appointed county captain in 1977. Benefit (£15,500) in 1976. Is now regarded as an English player for qualification purposes. Tests: 7 for South Africa v Australia 1966-67 and 1969-70. Played in 5 matches for Rest of World v England in 1970. 1,000 runs (2) – 1,786 runs (av. 45.79) in 1971 best. 100 wkts (2) – 109 wkts (av. 18.04) in 1977 best. Scored 6 centuries in 6 consecutive innings for Rhodesia 1970-71 to equal world record. Scored two centuries in match (114 and 131) for Rhodesia v International Wanderers (Salisbury) 1972-73. Hat-tricks (4): v Essex (Westcliff) 1972 – all lbw – and also scored a century in the match, v Essex (Southend) 1977, v Leics (Bristol) 1979 and also scored a century, and in next match v Yorks (Cheltenham) 1979 – all lbw. Also v Hants (Southampton) in Benson & Hedges Cup 1977. Had match double of 100 runs and 10 wkts (108 and 13-73) v Worcs (Cheltenham) 1977 and (108 and 14-76) v Worcs (Cheltenham) 1980. Gillette Man of the Match awards: 2. Benson & Hedges Gold Awards: 6. HS: 254 Rhodesia v Western Province (Salisbury) 1970-71. HSUK: 203 v Essex (Gloucester) 1978. HSTC: 48 South Africa v Australia (Cape Town) 1969-70. HSGC: 107 v Sussex (Hove) 1971. HSJPL: 109 v Warwickshire (Cheltenham) 1972. HSBH: 154* v Somerset (Taunton) 1972. BB: 9-71 Rhodesia v Transvaal (Bulawayo) 1972-73. BBUK: 8-30 v Worcs (Worcester) 1979. BBTC:

# GLOUCESTERSHIRE

6-73 South Africa v Australia (Port Elizabeth) 1969-70. BBGC: 4-21 v Yorks (Leeds) 1976. BBJPL: 5-8 v Middlesex (Gloucester) 1977. BBBH: 6-13 v Hants (Southampton) 1977.

**SADIQ MOHAMMAD** B Junagadh, India 3/5/1945. LHB, LBG. Youngest of family of five cricket-playing brothers which includes Hanif and Mushtaq Mohammad. Debut in Pakistan 1959-60 at age of 14 years 9 months and has played subsequently for various Karachi sides, Pakistan International Airways and United Bank. Played for Northants 2nd XI in 1967 and 1968, for Nelson in Lancs League in 1968, and subsequently for Poloc, Glasgow in Scottish Western Union. Played for D.H. Robins' XI v Oxford U 1969 and for Essex v Jamaica XI in 1970. Debut for county 1972. Cap 1973. Played for Tasmania against MCC in 1974-75. Tests: 38 for Pakistan between 1969-70 and 1979-80. Tours: Pakistan to England 1971, 1974 and 1978, Australia and New Zealand 1972-73, Australia and West Indies 1976-77, India 1979-80. 1,000 runs (7) – 1,759 runs (av. 47.54) in 1976 best. Scored 1,169 runs (av. 41.75) in Australia and New Zealand 1972-73. Scored 4 centuries in 4 consecutive innings in 1976 including two centuries in match (163* and 150) v Derbyshire (Bristol). Also scored two centuries in match (171 and 103) v Glamorgan (Bristol) 1979. Gillette Man of the Match Awards: 1. Benson & Hedges Gold Awards: 3. HS: 184* v New Zealanders (Bristol) 1973. HSTC: 166 Pakistan v New Zealand (Wellington) 1972-73. HSGC: 122 v Lancs (Manchester) 1975. HSJPL: 131 v Somerset (Imperial Ground, Bristol) 1975. HSBH: 128 v Minor Counties (South) (Bristol) 1974. BB: 7-34 United Bank v Universities (Peshawar) 1978-79. BBUK: 5-37 v Kent (Bristol) 1973. BBGC: 3-19 v Oxfordshire (Bristol) 1975. BBJPL: 3-27 v Hants (Bristol) 1972. BBBH: 3-20 v Minor Counties (South) (Bristol) 1972.

**Andrew Willis STOVOLD** (Filton HS) B Bristol 19/3/1953. RHB, WK. Toured West Indies with England Young Cricketers 1972. Played for 2nd XI since 1971. Debut 1973. Cap 1976. Played for Orange Free State in 1974-75 and 1975-76 Currie Cup competition. 1,000 runs (3) – 1,388 runs (av. 36.52) in 1979 best. Benson & Hedges Gold Awards: 5. HS: 196 v Notts (Nottingham) 1977. HSGC: 45 v Lancs (Manchester) 1978. HSJPL: 98* v Kent (Cheltenham) 1977. HSBH: 104 v Leics (Leicester) 1977.

**Martin Willis STOVOLD** (Thornbury GS) B Bristol 28/12/1955. Younger brother of A.W. Stovold. LHB. Played in one John Player League match v Essex (Gloucester) 1978. Debut 1979. HS: 75* v Oxford U (Oxford) 1980. HSJPL: 27 v Somerset (Bristol) 1980. HSBH: 32 v Essex (Bristol) 1980. Trained as a teacher at Loughborough College.

**David SURRIDGE** (Richard Hale School, Hertford, Southampton and Cambridge Universities) B Bishops Stortford, Herts 6/1/1956. RHB, RFM. Played for Hertfordshire from 1976 to 1979. Debut for Cambridge U and Blue 1979. Debut for county 1980. Played one match v Oxford U (Oxford) and in 5 one-day matches before incurring back injury which prevented him from playing again. HS: 14 Cambridge U v Yorks (Cambridge) 1979. HSBH: 11* Combined Universities v Northants (Cambridge) 1979. BB: 4-22 Cambridge U v Oxford U (Lord's) 1979. BBC: 3-24 v Oxford U (Oxford) 1980.

**Alan Haydn WILKINS** (Whitchurch HS, Cardiff) B Cardiff 22/8/1953. RHB, LM. Played in two John Player League matches for Glamorgan in 1975. Debut for county 1976. Left county after 1979 season and made debut for Glos in 1980. HS: 70 Glamorgan v Notts (Worksop) 1977. HSC: 44 v West Indians (Bristol) 1980. HSGC: 18* Glamorgan v Somerset (Cardiff) 1978. HSBH: 27 v Minor Counties

(Chippenham) 1980. BB: 6-79 Glamorgan v Hants (Southampton) 1979. BBC: 5-50 v Hants (Cheltenham) 1980. BBJPL: 5-23 Glamorgan v Warwickshire (Birmingham) 1978. BBBH: 5-17 Glamorgan v Worcs (Worcester) 1978. Trained as a teacher at Loughborough College of Education.

**Stephen James WINDAYBANK** (Cotham GS) B Pinner, Middlesex 20/10/1956. RHB. Played for 2nd XI in 1978. Debut 1979. Played one match v Oxford U (Oxford), one Benson & Hedges and two John Player League matches in 1980. Shared in first wkt partnership of 126 and 89 with B.C. Broad in their debut match v Cambridge U (Cambridge). HS: 53 v Cambridge U (Cambridge) 1979. HSJPL: 13 v Leics (Leicester) 1980.

**Anthony John WRIGHT** (Alleyne's GS, Stevenage) B Stevenage, Herts 27/6/1962. RHB, RM. Played for 2nd XI since 1979. Played in two John Player League matches in 1980. Has yet to appear in first-class cricket.

**Syed ZAHEER ABBAS** B Sialkot, Pakistan 24/7/1947. RHB, OB. Wears glasses. Debut for Karachi Whites 1965-66, subsequently playing for Pakistan International Airways. *Wisden* 1971. Debut for county 1972. Cap 1975. Tests: 40 for Pakistan between 1969-70 and 1979-80. Played in 5 matches for Rest of the World v Australia 1971-72. Tours: Pakistan to England 1971 and 1974, Australia and New Zealand 1972-73, Australia and West Indies 1976-77, New Zealand and Australia 1978-79, India 1979-80. Rest of World to Australia 1971-72. 1,000 runs (9) – 2,554 runs (av 75.11) in 1976 best. Scored 1,597 runs (av. 84.05) in Pakistan 1973-74 – the record aggregate for a Pakistan season. Scored 4 centuries in 4 consecutive innings in 1970-71. Scored two centuries in a match twice in 1976 – 216* and 156* v Surrey (Oval) and 230* and 104* v Kent (Canterbury) and once in 1977 – 205* and 108* v Sussex (Cheltenham) to create record of being only player ever to score a double-century and a century in a match on three occasions. Was dismissed, hit the ball twice, for Pakistan International Airways v Karachi Blues (Karachi) 1969-70. Gillette Man of the Match Awards: 4. HS: 274 Pakistan v England (Birmingham) 1971. HSC: 230* v Kent (Canterbury) 1977. HSGC: 131* v Leics (Leicester) 1975. HSJPL: 114* v Hants (Bristol) 1976. HSBH: 98 v Surrey (Oval) 1975. BB: 5-15 Dawood Club v Railways (Lahore) 1975-76.

**Barry DUDDLESTON** (Stockport School) B Bebington (Cheshire) 16/7/1945. RHB, SLA. Debut for Leics 1966. Cap 1969. Played for Rhodesia from 1976-77 to 1979-80 in Currie Cup competitions. Benefit in 1980. Not re-engaged after 1980 season and has joined Glos for 1981 as coach and 2nd XI captain. 1,000 runs (8) – 1,374 runs (av. 31.22) in 1970 best. Shared in 1st wkt partnership record for Leics, 390 with J.F. Steele v Derbyshire (Leicester) 1979. Also shared in 7th wkt partnership record for county, 206 with J. Birkenshaw v Kent (Canterbury) 1969. Gillette Man of the Match Awards: 2. Benson & Hedges Gold Awards: 4. HS: 202 Leics v Derbyshire (Leicester) 1979. HSGC: 125 Leics v Worcs (Leicester) 1979. HSJPL: 152 Leics v Lancs (Manchester) 1975. HSBH: 90 Leics v Warwickshire (Leicester) 1973. BB: 4-6 Leics v Surrey (Leicester) 1972.

NB. The following player whose particulars appeared in the 1980 annual has been omitted: B.K. Shantry.

# County Averages

**Schweppes County Championship: Played 21, Won 4, Drawn 12, Lost 5, Abandoned 1.**
**All first-class matches: Played 23, Won 5, Drawn 12, Lost 6, Abandoned 1.**

## BATTING AND FIELDING

| Cap | | M | I | NO | Runs | HS | Avge | 100 | 50 | Ct | St |
|-----|---|---|---|----|------|----|------|-----|----|----|----|
| 1975 | Zaheer Abbas | 20 | 35 | 1 | 1296 | 173 | 38.11 | 2 | 7 | 4 | |
| 1977 | A.J. Hignell | 15 | 23 | 5 | 630 | 100* | 35.00 | 1 | 3 | 11 | |
| 1968 | M.J. Procter | 19 | 33 | 2 | 1081 | 134* | 34.87 | 1 | 7 | 17 | |
| 1973 | Sadiq Mohammad | 22 | 40 | 4 | 1172 | 92 | 32.55 | — | 10 | 27 | |
| — | B.C. Broad | 20 | 35 | 1 | 961 | 120 | 28.26 | 3 | 3 | 7 | — |
| 1976 | A.W. Stovold | 22 | 39 | 2 | 958 | 89 | 25.89 | — | 6 | 10 | — |
| — | M.D. Partridge | 11 | 18 | 6 | 286 | 48 | 23.83 | — | — | 4 | |
| — | M.W. Stovold | 5 | 8 | 2 | 137 | 75* | 22.83 | — | 1 | — | — |
| 1976 | D.A. Graveney | 21 | 31 | 7 | 513 | 119 | 21.37 | 1 | 2 | 8 | — |
| — | P. Bainbridge | 17 | 29 | 2 | 422 | 71 | 15.62 | — | 1 | 12 | — |
| — | A.H. Wilkins | 19 | 24 | 3 | 262 | 44 | 12.47 | — | — | 8 | — |
| 1977 | B.M. Brain | 22 | 26 | 5 | 185 | 37* | 8.80 | — | — | 3 | — |
| 1978 | A.J. Brassington | 23 | 30 | 8 | 113 | 14* | 5.13 | — | — | 45 | 14 |
| 1977 | J.H. Childs | 15 | 19 | 10 | 44 | 8* | 4.40 | — | — | 6 | — |

*Played in one match:* D. Surridge did not bat; S.J. Windaybank 20, 43 (1 ct).

## BOWLING

| | Type | O | M | R | W | Avge | Best | 5 wI | 10 wM |
|---|------|---|---|---|---|------|------|------|-------|
| M.J. Procter | RF/OB | 372.1 | 102 | 931 | 51 | 18.25 | 7-16 | 3 | 1 |
| A.H. Wilkins | LM | 393.5 | 86 | 1245 | 52 | 23.94 | 5-50 | 2 | — |
| J.H. Childs | SLA | 373.4 | 98 | 1034 | 43 | 24.04 | 6-90 | 2 | — |
| B.M. Brain | RFM | 525.5 | 104 | 1609 | 57 | 28.22 | 6-68 | 3 | — |
| D.A. Graveney | SLA | 554.4 | 152 | 1598 | 55 | 29.05 | 6-49 | 4 | — |
| P. Bainbridge | RM | 144.4 | 23 | 504 | 15 | 33.60 | 4-48 | — | — |
| M.D. Partridge | RM | 161.5 | 36 | 572 | 11 | 52.00 | 3-18 | — | — |

*Also bowled:* B.C. Broad 28-8-109-3; A.J. Hignell 2-1-3-1; Sadiq Mohammad 54.5-3-252-1; A.W. Stovold 4.4-0-24-0; D. Surridge 21-11-33-4; Zaheer Abbas 11-3-46-2.

# County Records

### First-class cricket

| | | | |
|---|---|---|---|
| Highest innings totals: | For | – 653-6d v Glamorgan (Bristol) | 1928 |
| | Agst | – 774-7d by Australians (Bristol) | 1948 |
| Lowest innings totals: | For | – 17 v Australians (Cheltenham) | 1896 |
| | Agst | – 12 by Northamptonshire (Gloucester) | 1907 |
| Highest individual innings: | For | – 318* W.G. Grace v Yorkshire (Cheltenham) | 1876 |
| | Agst | – 296 A.O. Jones for Notts (Nottingham) | 1903 |
| Best bowling in an innings: | For | – 10-40 E.G. Dennett v Essex (Bristol) | 1906 |
| | Agst | – 10-66 A.A. Mailey for Aust (Cheltenham) | 1921 |
| | | and K. Smales for Notts (Stroud) | 1956 |
| Best bowling in a match: | For | – 17-56 C.W.L. Parker v Essex (Gloucester) | 1925 |
| | Agst | – 15-87 A.J. Conway for Worcestershire (Moreton-in-Marsh) | 1914 |

| | | |
|---|---|---|
| Most runs in a season: | 2,860 (av. 69.75) W.R. Hammond | 1933 |
| runs in a career: | 33,664 (av. 57.05) W.R. Hammond | 1920-1951 |
| 100s in a season: | 13 by W.R. Hammond | 1938 |
| 100s in a career: | 113 by W.R. Hammond | 1920-1951 |
| wickets in a season: | 222 (av. 16.80 & 16.37) T.W.J. Goddard | 1937 & 1947 |
| wickets in a career: | 3,170 (av. 19.44) C.W.L. Parker | 1903-1935 |

## RECORD WICKET STANDS

| | | | |
|---|---|---|---|
| 1st | 395 | D.M. Young & R.B. Nicholls v Oxford U (Oxford) | 1962 |
| 2nd | 256 | C.T.M. Pugh & T.W. Graveney v Derbyshire (Chesterfield) | 1960 |
| 3rd | 336 | W.R. Hammond & B.H. Lyon v Leicestershire (Leicester) | 1933 |
| 4th | 321 | W.R. Hammond & W.L. Neale v Leicestershire (Gloucester) | 1937 |
| 5th | 261 | W.G. Grace & W.O. Moberley v Yorkshire (Cheltenham) | 1876 |
| 6th | 320 | G.L. Jessop & J.H. Board v Sussex (Hove) | 1902 |
| 7th | 248 | W.G. Grace & E.L. Thomas v Sussex (Hove) | 1896 |
| 8th | 239 | W.R. Hammond & A.E. Wilson v Lancashire (Bristol) | 1938 |
| 9th | 193 | W.G. Grace & S.A. Kitcat v Sussex (Bristol) | 1896 |
| 10th | 131 | W.R. Gouldsworthy & J.G. Bessant v Somerset (Bristol) | 1923 |

### One-day cricket

| | | | |
|---|---|---|---|
| Highest innings totals: | Gillette Cup | 327-7 v Berkshire (Reading) | 1966 |
| | John Player League | 255 v Somerset (Imperial Ground, Bristol) | 1975 |
| | Benson & Hedges Cup | 282 v Hants (Bristol) | 1974 |
| Lowest innings totals: | Gillette Cup | 86 v Sussex (Hove) | 1969 |
| | John Player League | 49 v Middlesex (Bristol) | 1978 |
| | Benson & Hedges Cup | 62 v Hants (Bristol) | 1975 |
| Highest individual innings: | Gillette Cup | 131* Zaheer Abbas v Leics (Leicester) | 1975 |
| | John Player League | 131 Sadiq Mohammad v Somerset (Imperial Ground, Bristol) | 1975 |
| | Benson & Hedges Cup | 154* M.J. Procter v Somerset (Taunton) | 1972 |
| Best bowling figures: | Gillette Cup | 5-39 R.D.V. Knight v Surrey (Bristol) | 1971 |
| | John Player League | 5-8 M.J. Procter v Middlesex (Gloucester) | 1977 |
| | Benson & Hedges Cup | 6-13 M.J. Procter v Hampshire (Southampton) | 1977 |

# HAMPSHIRE

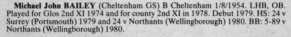

**Formation of present club:** 1863.
**Colours:** Blue, gold and white.
**Badge:** Tudor rose and crown.
**County Champions (2):** 1961 and 1973.
**Gillette Cup Semi-Finalists (2):** 1966 and 1976.
**John Player League Champions (2):** 1975 and 1978.
**Benson & Hedges Cup Semi-Finalists (2):** 1975 and 1977.
**Fenner Trophy Winners (3):** 1975, 1976 and 1977.
**Gillette Man of the Match Awards:** 25.
**Benson & Hedges Gold Awards:** 23.
**Secretary:** A.K. James, County Cricket Ground,
  Northlands Road, Southampton SO9 2TY.
**Captain:** N.E.J. Pocock.
**Prospects of Play Telephone Nos:** Southampton (0703) 24155
  Bournemouth (0202) 25872
  Basingstoke (0256) 3646

  **Michael John BAILEY** (Cheltenham GS) B Cheltenham 1/8/1954. LHB, OB. Played for Glos 2nd XI 1974 and for county 2nd XI in 1978. Debut 1979. HS: 24 v Surrey (Portsmouth) 1979 and 24 v Northants (Wellingborough) 1980. BB: 5-89 v Northants (Wellingborough) 1980.

  **Nigel Geoffrey COWLEY** B Shaftesbury, Dorset 1/3/1953. RHB, OB. Debut 1974. Cap 1978. HS: 109* v Somerset (Taunton) 1977. HSGC: 63* v Glos (Bristol) 1979. HSJPL: 49* v Warwickshire (Southampton) 1980. HSBH: 59 v Glos (Southampton) 1977. BB: 5-44 v Derbyshire (Basingstoke) 1979. BBGC: 4-20 v Middlesex (Lord's) 1979. BBJPL: 4-46 v Sussex (Hove) 1980.

  **Christopher Colin CURZON** B Lenton, Nottingham 22/12/1958. RHB, WK. Debut for Notts 1978. Not re-engaged by county after 1980 season and has joined Hants for 1981. HS: 45 Notts v Glamorgan (Swansea) 1980. HSJPL: 28* Notts v Kent (Nottingham) 1980. HSBH: 15 Notts v Northants (Northampton) 1980.

  **Shaun Francis GRAF** (St. Bede's College, Mentone, Melbourne) B Melbourne, Australia 19/5/1957. LHB, RFM. Played for Glamorgan and Glos 2nd XIs and Wiltshire in 1979. Debut for Victoria 1979-80. Debut for county 1980. HS: 58* Victoria v Western Australia (Perth) 1979-80. HSC: 57* v Essex (Chelmsford) 1980. HSBH: 25* v Surrey (Oval) 1980. BB: 4-71 Victoria v South Australia (Adelaide) 1979-80. BBGC: 3-44 v Derbyshire (Derby) 1980. BBJPL: 3-24 v Leics (Leicester) 1980.

  **Cuthbert Gordon GREENIDGE** B St. Peter, Barbados 1/5/1951. RHB, RM. Debut 1970. Cap 1972. Has subsequently played for Barbados. *Wisden* 1976. Tests: 30 for West Indies between 1974-75 and 1980. Tours: West Indies to India, Sri Lanka and Pakistan 1974-75, Australia 1975-76, England 1976 and 1980, Australia and New Zealand 1979-80, Pakistan 1980-81. 1,000 runs (9) – 1,952 runs (av. 55.77) in 1976 best. Scored two centuries in match (134 and 101) West Indies v England (Manchester) 1976, and (136 and 120) v Kent (Bournemouth) 1978. Gillette Man of the Match Awards: 3. Benson & Hedges Gold Awards: 4. HS: 273* D.H. Robins' XI v Pakistan (Eastbourne) 1974. HSC: 259 v Sussex (Southampton)

82

1975. HSTC: 134 West Indies v England (Manchester) 1976. HSGC: 177 v Glamorgan (Southampton) 1975 – record for all one-day competitions. HSJPL: 163* v Warwickshire (Birmingham) 1979 – record for competition. HSBH: 173* v Minor Counties (South) (Amersham) 1973 – record for competition – and shared in partnership of 285* for second wicket with D.R. Turner – the record partnership for all one-day competitions. BB: 5-49 v Surrey (Southampton) 1971.

**Trevor Edward JESTY** B Gosport 2/6/1948. RHB, RM. Debut 1966. Cap 1971. Played for Border in 1973-74 and Griqualand West in 1974-75 and 1975-76 Currie Cup competitions. Played for Canterbury in Shell Trophy in 1979-80. 1,000 runs (4) – 1,288 runs (av. 35.77) in 1976 best. Gillette Man of the Match Awards: 3. Benson & Hedges Gold Awards: 6. Took 3 wkts in 4 balls v Somerset (Portsmouth) 1969. HS: 159* v Somerset (Bournemouth) 1976. HSGC: 118 v Derbyshire (Derby) 1980. HSJPL: 107 v Surrey (Southampton) 1977. HSBH: 105 v Glamorgan (Swansea) 1977. BB: 7-75 v Worcs (Southampton) 1976. BBGC: 6-46 v Glos (Bristol) 1979. BBJPL: 6-20 v Glamorgan (Cardiff) 1975. BBBH: 4-28 v Somerset (Taunton) 1974.

**Steven John MALONE** (King's School, Ely) B Chelmsford 19/10/1953. RHB, RM. Debut for Essex 1975 playing in one match v Cambridge U (Cambridge). Re-appeared in corresponding match in 1978. Did not play in 1979 and made debut for Hants in 1980. HS: 20 v Notts (Nottingham) 1980. BB: 3-56 v Lancs (Portsmouth) 1980. BBJPL: 4-39 v Yorks (Basingstoke) 1980.

**Malcolm Denzil MARSHALL** (Parkinson Comprehensive School, Barbados) B St. Michael, Barbados 18/4/1958. RHB, RFM. Debut for Barbados 1977-78 in last match of Shell Shield competition. Debut for county 1979. Tests: 7 between 1978-79 and 1980. Tours: West Indies to India and Sri Lanka 1978-79, Australia and New Zealand 1979-80, England 1980, Pakistan 1980-81. HS: 72* v Northants (Welling-borough) 1980. HSTC: 45 West Indies v England (Oval) 1980. HSGC: 21* v Middlesex (Lord's) 1979. HSJPL: 20 v Middlesex (Lord's) 1979. HSBH: 15 v Derbyshire (Derby) 1979. BB: 7-56 West Indians v Worcs (Worcester) 1980. BBC: 5-39 v Worcs (Bournemouth) 1980. BBTC: 4-25 West Indies v Pakistan (Faisalabad) 1980-81. BBJPL: 5-13 v Glamorgan (Portsmouth) 1979.

**Mark Charles Jefford NICHOLAS** (Bradfield College) B London 29/9/1957. RHB, RFM. Debut 1978. HS: 112 v Somerset (Bournemouth) 1980. HSGC: 28 v Yorks (Southampton) 1980. HSJPL: 62 v Derbyshire (Southampton) 1980. BBBH: 3-29 v Surrey (Oval) 1980.

**Robert James (Bobby) PARKS** (Eastbourne GS) B Cuckfield, Sussex 15/6/1959. Son of J.M. Parks and grandson of J.H. Parks. RHB, WK. Played for 2nd XI since 1976. Debut 1980. HS: 64* v Essex (Chelmsford) 1980.

**Nicholas Edward Julian (Nick) POCOCK** (Shrewsbury School) B Maracaibo, Venezuela 15/12/1951. RHB, LM. Debut 1976. Appointed county captain in 1980. Cap 1980. HS: 143* v Middlesex (Portsmouth) 1979. HSGC: 73* v Derbyshire (Derby) 1980. HSJPL: 53* v Northants (Northampton) 1978. HSBH: 41 v Somerset (Bournemouth) 1980.

**John Michael RICE** (Brockley CGS, London) B Chandler's Ford, Hants 23/10/1949. 6ft 3ins tall. RHB, RM. On Surrey staff 1970, but not re-engaged. Debut 1971. Cap 1975. Hat-trick in John Player League v Northants (Southampton) 1975. Gillette Cup Man of the Match Awards: 1. Benson & Hedges Gold Awards: 1. HS: 96* v Somerset (Weston-super-Mare) 1975. HSGC: 40 v Glos (Bristol) 1979.

83

HSJPL: 91 v Yorks (Leeds) 1979. HSBH: 43 v Lancs (Southampton) 1977. BB: 7-48 v Worcs (Worcester) 1977. BBGC: 5-35 v Yorks (Bournemouth) 1977. BBJPL: 5-14 v Northants (Southampton) 1975. BBBH: 3-20 v Somerset (Bournemouth) 1975.

**Christopher Lyall (Kippy) SMITH** (Northlands HS, Durban) B Durban, South Africa 15/10/1958. RHB, OB. Debut for Natal B 1977-78. One match v Rhodesia B (Pinetown). Debut for Glamorgan 1979. One match v Sri Lankans (Swansea). Debut for Hants 1980. Will be regarded as an English player for qualification purposes in May 1983. Scored 1,048 runs (av. 31.75) in 1980. HS: 130 v Kent (Bournemouth) 1980. HSJPL: 66 v Middlesex (Bournemouth) 1980. HSBH: 48 v Kent (Canterbury) 1980.

**John William SOUTHERN** (The William Ellis School, Highgate) B King's Cross, London 2/9/1952. 6ft 3½ins tall. RHB, SLA. Debut 1975. Cap 1978. HS: 61* v Yorks (Bradford) 1979. HSBH: 14 v Somerset (Bournemouth) 1980. BB: 6-46 v Glos (Bournemouth) 1975. Obtained BSc degree in Chemistry at Southampton University.

**Keith STEVENSON** (Bemrose GS, Derby) B Derby 6/10/1950. RHB, RFM. Debut for Derbyshire 1974. Left county after 1977 season and made debut for Hants in 1978. Cap 1979. HS: 33 Derbyshire v Northants (Chesterfield) 1974. HSC: 25 v Glos (Cheltenham) 1980. HSGC: 14 Derbyshire v Surrey (Ilkeston) 1976. BB: 7-22 v Oxford U (Oxford) 1979. BBGC: 4-21 Derbyshire v Surrey (Ilkeston) 1976. BBJPL: 3-22 v Essex (Chelmsford) 1980. BBBH: 4-38 v Somerset (Bournemouth) 1980.

**Vivian Paul TERRY** (Millfield School) B Osnabruck, West Germany 14/1/1959. RHB, RM. Played for 2nd XI since 1976. Debut 1978. HS: 31 v Worcs (Bournemouth) 1980. HSGC: 11 v Middlesex (Lord's) 1979. HSJPL: 33 v Glos (Basingstoke) 1979.

**Timothy Maurice (Tim) TREMLETT** (Richard Taunton College, Southampton) B Wellington, Somerset 26/7/1956. Son of M.F. Tremlett, former Somerset player. RHB, RM. Debut 1976. HS: 84 v Glamorgan (Basingstoke) 1980. HSJPL: 28 v Glos (Cheltenham) 1980. HSBH: 15* v Derbyshire (Derby) 1979. BB: 5-30 v Notts (Nottingham) 1980. BBJPL: 4-24 v Northants (Wellingborough) 1980. BBBH: 3-21 v Combined Universities (Cambridge) 1978.

**David Roy TURNER** B Chippenham, Wilts 5/2/1949. LHB, RM. Played for Wiltshire in 1965. Debut 1966. Cap 1970. Played for Western Province in 1977-78 Currie Cup competition. Benefit in 1981. 1,000 runs (6) – 1,269 runs (av. 36.25) in 1976 best. Gillette Man of the Match Awards: 1. Benson & Hedges Gold Awards: 3. HS: 181* v Surrey (Oval) 1969. HSGC: 86 v Northants (Southampton) 1976. HSJPL: 109 v Surrey (Oval) 1980. HSBH: 123* v Minor Counties (South) (Amersham) 1973.

NB. The following players whose particulars appeared in the 1980 annual have been omitted: R.E. Hayward, D.J. Rock (left staff), G.R. Stephenson (retired) and M.N.S. Taylor (appointed assistant secretary).
The career records of Stephenson and Taylor will be found elsewhere in this annual.

## County Averages

**Schweppes County Championship: Played 22, Won 1, Drawn 11, Lost 10.**
**All first-class matches: Played 24, Won 2, Drawn 11, Lost 11.**

### BATTING AND FIELDING

| Cap | | M | I | NO | Runs | HS | Avge | 100 | 50 | Ct | St |
|---|---|---|---|---|---|---|---|---|---|---|---|
| — | C.L. Smith | 20 | 35 | 2 | 1048 | 130 | 31.75 | 3 | 3 | 11 | — |
| 1970 | D.R. Turner | 20 | 35 | 3 | 925 | 115* | 28.90 | 1 | 4 | 7 | — |
| — | M.D. Marshall | 5 | 10 | 1 | 251 | 72* | 27.88 | — | 2 | 4 | — |
| 1972 | C.G. Greenidge | 3 | 6 | 0 | 167 | 65 | 27.83 | — | 1 | — | — |
| — | T.M. Tremlett | 17 | 30 | 4 | 717 | 84 | 27.57 | — | 7 | 4 | — |
| — | M.C.J. Nicholas | 18 | 31 | 1 | 783 | 112 | 26.10 | 1 | 3 | 9 | — |
| 1971 | T.E. Jesty | 16 | 25 | 3 | 522 | 114* | 23.72 | 1 | 2 | 6 | — |
| 1980 | N.E.J. Pocock | 24 | 40 | 3 | 874 | 66 | 23.62 | — | 5 | 27 | — |
| — | R.J. Parks | 7 | 13 | 3 | 233 | 64* | 23.30 | — | 2 | 12 | 5 |
| 1978 | N.G. Cowley | 23 | 37 | 3 | 766 | 80* | 22.52 | — | 4 | 12 | — |
| 1973 | M.N.S. Taylor | 10 | 15 | 2 | 279 | 58 | 21.46 | — | 1 | 3 | — |
| — | M.J. Bailey | 5 | 9 | 5 | 82 | 24 | 20.50 | — | — | 1 | — |
| — | S.F. Graf | 15 | 19 | 5 | 284 | 57* | 20.28 | — | 1 | 9 | — |
| 1969 | G.R. Stephenson | 17 | 23 | 5 | 304 | 65 | 16.88 | — | 1 | 19 | 1 |
| 1978 | J.W. Southern | 22 | 25 | 7 | 282 | 46* | 15.66 | — | — | 11 | — |
| — | V.P. Terry | 3 | 6 | 0 | 87 | 31 | 14.50 | — | — | 1 | — |
| — | S.J. Malone | 7 | 11 | 5 | 70 | 20 | 11.66 | — | — | 1 | — |
| 1975 | J.M. Rice | 9 | 16 | 0 | 171 | 30 | 10.68 | — | — | 6 | — |
| 1979 | K. Stevenson | 23 | 26 | 8 | 156 | 25 | 8.66 | — | — | 9 | — |

### BOWLING

| | Type | O | M | R | W | Avge | Best | 5 wI | 10 wM |
|---|---|---|---|---|---|---|---|---|---|
| M.D. Marshall | RFM | 141 | 42 | 306 | 17 | 18.00 | 5-39 | 1 | — |
| M.N.S. Taylor | RM | 89.5 | 17 | 261 | 9 | 29.00 | 4-46 | — | — |
| K. Stevenson | RFM | 493.4 | 105 | 1588 | 53 | 29.96 | 5-66 | 2 | — |
| J.W. Southern | SLA | 556.1 | 143 | 1530 | 51 | 30.00 | 6-109 | 2 | — |
| N.G. Cowley | OB | 458.4 | 125 | 1271 | 40 | 31.77 | 4-47 | — | — |
| T.M. Tremlett | RM | 178.2 | 32 | 579 | 17 | 34.05 | 5-30 | 1 | — |
| S.J. Malone | RM | 140.1 | 27 | 457 | 13 | 35.15 | 3-56 | — | — |
| T.E. Jesty | RM | 205.2 | 56 | 584 | 14 | 41.71 | 3-11 | — | — |
| S.F. Graf | RFM | 313.5 | 72 | 889 | 20 | 44.45 | 2-24 | — | — |
| M.J. Bailey | OB | 83 | 14 | 280 | 5 | 56.00 | 5-89 | 1 | — |

*Also bowled:* M.C.J. Nicholas 16.2-0-67-0; N.E.J. Pocock 1-0-8-0; J.M. Rice 94-20-269-3; C.L. Smith 26-7-61-0; G.R. Stephenson 1-1-0-0; D.R. Turner 7.1-1-33-0.

## County Records

### First-class cricket

| | | |
|---|---|---|
| Highest innings totals: | For – 672-7d v Somerset (Taunton) | 1899 |
| | Agst – 742 by Surrey (The Oval) | 1909 |
| Lowest innings totals: | For – 15 v Warwickshire (Birmingham) | 1922 |
| | Agst – 23 by Yorkshire (Middlesbrough) | 1965 |
| Highest individual innings: | For – 316 R.H. Moore v Warwickshire (Bournemouth) | 1937 |
| | Agst – 302* P. Holmes for Yorkshire (Portsmouth) | 1920 |

## HAMPSHIRE

| | | | |
|---|---|---|---|
| Best bowling in an innings: | For | – 9-25 R.M.H. Cottam v Lancs (Manchester) | 1965 |
| | Agst | – 9-21 L.B. Richmond for Notts (Nottingham) | 1921 |
| Best bowling in a match: | For | – 16-88 J.A. Newman v Somerset (Weston-super-Mare) | 1927 |
| | Agst | – 17-119 W. Mead for Essex (Southampton) | 1895 |
| Most runs in a season: | | 2,854 (av. 79.27) C.P. Mead | 1928 |
| runs in a career: | | 48,892 (av. 48.84) C.P. Mead | 1905-1936 |
| 100s in a season: | | 12 by C.P. Mead | 1928 |
| 100s in a career: | | 138 by C.P. Mead | 1905-1936 |
| wickets in a season: | | 190 (av. 15.61) A.S. Kennedy | 1922 |
| wickets in a career: | | 2,669 (av. 18.22) D. Shackleton | 1948-1969 |

## RECORD WICKET STANDS

| | | | |
|---|---|---|---|
| 1st | 249 | R.E. Marshall & J.R. Gray v Middlesex (Portsmouth) | 1960 |
| 2nd | 321 | G. Brown & E.I.M. Barrett v Gloucestershire (Southampton) | 1920 |
| 3rd | 344 | C.P. Mead & G. Brown v Yorkshire (Portsmouth) | 1927 |
| 4th | 263 | R.E. Marshall & D.A. Livingstone v Middlesex (Lord's) | 1970 |
| 5th | 235 | G. Hill & D.F. Walker v Sussex (Portsmouth) | 1937 |
| 6th | 411 | R.M. Poore & E.G. Wynyard v Somerset (Taunton) | 1899 |
| 7th | 325 | G. Brown & C.H. Abercrombie v Essex (Leyton) | 1913 |
| 8th | 178 | C.P. Mead & C.P. Brutton v Worcestershire (Bournemouth) | 1925 |
| 9th | 230 | D.A. Livingstone & A.T. Castell v Surrey (Southampton) | 1962 |
| 10th | 192 | A. Bowell & W.H. Livsey v Worcestershire (Bournemouth) | 1921 |

NB. A partnership of 334 for the first wicket by B.A. Richards, C.G. Greenidge and D.R. Turner occurred against Kent at Southampton in 1973. Richards retired hurt after 241 runs had been scored and in the absence of any official ruling on the matter, it is a matter of opinion as to whether it should be regarded as the first-wicket record for the county.

### One-day cricket

| | | | |
|---|---|---|---|
| Highest innings totals: | Gillette Cup | 371-4 v Glamorgan (Southampton) | 1975 |
| | John Player League | 288-5 v Somerset (Weston-super-Mare) | 1975 |
| | Benson & Hedges Cup | 321-1 v Minor Counties (South) (Amersham) | 1973 |
| Lowest innings totals: | Gillette Cup | 98 v Lancashire (Manchester) | 1975 |
| | John Player League | 43 v Essex (Basingstoke) | 1972 |
| | Benson & Hedges Cup | 94 v Glamorgan (Swansea) | 1973 |
| Highest individual innings: | Gillette Cup | 177 C.G. Greenidge v Glamorgan (Southampton) | 1975 |
| | John Player League | 163* C.G. Greenidge v Warwickshire (Birmingham) | 1979 |
| | Benson & Hedges Cup | 173* C.G. Greenidge v Minor Counties (South) (Amersham) | 1973 |
| Best bowling figures: | Gillette Cup | 7-30 P.J. Sainsbury v Norfolk (Southampton) | 1965 |
| | John Player League | 6-20 T.E. Jesty v Glamorgan (Cardiff) | 1975 |
| | Benson & Hedges Cup | 5-24 R.S. Herman v Gloucestershire (Bristol) | 1975 |

# KENT

**Formation of present club:** 1859, re-organised 1870.
**Colours:** Red and white.
**Badge:** White horse.
**County Champions (6):** 1906, 1909, 1910, 1913, 1970 and 1978.
**Joint Champions:** 1977.
**Gillette Cup Winners (2):** 1967 and 1974.
**Gillette Cup Finalists:** 1971.
**John Player League Champions (3):** 1972, 1973 and 1976.
**Benson & Hedges Cup Winners (3):** 1973, 1976 and 1978.
**Benson & Hedges Cup Finalists:** 1977.
**Fenner Trophy Winners (2):** 1971 and 1973.
**Gillette Man of the Match Awards:** 23.
**Benson & Hedges Gold Awards:** 29.
**Secretary:** M.D. Fenner, St. Lawrence Ground, Canterbury CT1 3NZ.
**Cricket Manager:** J.C.T. Page.
**Captain:** Asif Iqbal.

ASIF IQBAL RAZVI (Osmania University, Hyderabad, India) B Hyderabad, India 6/6/1943. Nephew of Ghulam Ahmed, former Indian off-break bowler and Test cricketer. RHB, RM. Debut 1959-60 for Hyderabad in Ranji Trophy. Migrated to Pakistan in 1961 and has since appeared for various Karachi teams, Pakistan International Airways and National Bank. Captained Pakistan under-25 v England under-25 in 1966-67. Debut for county and cap 1968. *Wisden* 1967. County Captain in 1977. Benefit in 1981. Re-appointed County Captain for 1981. Tests: 58 for Pakistan between 1964-65 and 1979-80 captaining Pakistan in 6 Tests. Tours: Pakistan to Australia and New Zealand 1964-65, 1972-73 (vice-captain), England 1967, 1971 (vice-captain) and 1974 (vice-captain), Australia and West Indies 1976-77, India 1979-80 (captain), Pakistan Eaglets to England 1963, Pakistan 'A' to Ceylon 1964, Pakistan International Airways to East Africa 1964. 1,000 runs (6) – 1,379 runs (av. 39.40) in 1970 best. Scored 1,029 runs (av. 41.16) in Australia and New Zealand 1972-73. Scored two centuries in match (104 and 110*) Pakistan International Airways v Habib Bank (Lahore) 1976-77. Scored 146 v England (Oval) 1967 sharing in 9th-wkt partnership of 190 with Intikhab Alam after Pakistan were 65-8 – record 9th-wicket stand in Test cricket. Gillette Man of the Match Awards: 3. Benson & Hedges Gold Awards: 4. HS: 196 National Bank v Pakistan International Airways (Lahore) 1976-77. HSTC: 175 Pakistan v New Zealand (Dunedin) 1972-73. HSUK: 171 v Glos (Folkstone) 1978. HSGC: 89 v Lancs (Lord's) 1971. HSJPL: 106 v Glos (Maidstone) 1976. HSBH: 75 v Middlesex (Canterbury) 1978. BB: 6-45 Pakistan Eaglets v Cambridge U (Cambridge) 1963. BBTC: 5-48 Pakistan v New Zealand (Wellington) 1964-65. BBC: 4-11 v Lancs (Canterbury) 1968. BBGC: 4-18 v Lancs (Canterbury) 1979. BBJPL: 3-3 v Northants (Tring) 1977. BBBH: 5-42 v Middlesex (Lord's) 1980.

Mark Richard BENSON (Sutton Valence School) B Shoreham, Sussex 6/7/1958. LHB, OB. Played for 2nd XI since 1978. Debut 1980. HS: 58* v Middlesex (Lord's) 1980. HSJPL: 29 v Worcs (Worcester) 1980.

Christopher Stuart (Chris) COWDREY (Tonbridge School) B Farnborough, Kent 20/10/1957. Eldest son of M.C. Cowdrey. RHB, RM. Played for 2nd XI at age of 15. Captain of England Young Cricketers team to West Indies 1976. Played in one John Player League match in 1976. Debut 1977. Cap 1979. Benson & Hedges Gold

# KENT

Awards: 1. HS: 101* v Glamorgan (Swansea) 1977. HSGC: 23* v Lancs (Canterbury) 1979. HSJPL: 74 v Worcs (Worcester) 1978. HSBH: 114 v Sussex (Canterbury) 1977. BB: 3-17 v Hants (Bournemouth) 1980.

**Graham Roy DILLEY** B Dartford 18/5/1959. 6ft 3ins tall. LHB, RF. Debut 1977. Cap 1980. Tests: 5 in 1979-80 and 1980. Tours: Australia and India 1979-80, West Indies 1980-81. HS: 81 v Northants (Northampton) 1979. HSTC: 38* v Australia (Perth) 1979-80. HSJPL: 17 v Derbyshire (Canterbury) 1980. HSBH: 13* v Hants (Canterbury) 1980. BB: 6-66 v Middlesex (Lord's) 1979. BBTC: 4-57 v West Indies (Oval) 1980. BBJPL: 4-20 v Glos (Canterbury) 1980. BBBH: 3-29 v Hants (Canterbury) 1980.

**Alan George Ernest EALHAM** B Ashford, Kent 30/8/1944. RHB, OB. Debut 1966. Cap 1970. County Captain from 1978 to 1980. Benefit in 1982. 1,000 runs (3) – 1,363 runs (av. 34.94) in 1971 best. Held 5 catches in innings v Glos (Folkstone) 1966, all in outfield off D.L. Underwood, Gillette Man of the Match Awards: 1. Benson & Hedges Gold Awards: 4. HS: 153 v Worcs (Canterbury) 1979. HSGC: 85* v Glamorgan (Swansea) 1979. HSJPL: 83 v Leics (Leicester) 1977. HSBH: 94* v Sussex (Canterbury) 1977.

**Kevin Bertram Sidney JARVIS** (Springhead School, Northfleet) B Dartford 23/4/1953. 6ft 3in tall. RHB, RFM. Debut 1975. Cap 1977. Benson & Hedges Gold Awards: 1. HS: 12* v Cambridge U (Canterbury) 1977 and 12 v Sussex (Hove) 1978. BB: 8-97 v Worcs (Worcester) 1978. BBGC: 3-53 v Sussex (Canterbury) 1976. BBJPL: 4-27 v Surrey (Maidstone) 1977. BBBH: 4-34 v Worcs (Lord's) 1976.

**Graham William JOHNSON** (Shooters Hill GS) B Beckenham 8/11/1946. RHB, OB. Debut 1965. Cap 1970. 1,000 runs (3) – 1,438 runs (av. 31.26) in 1973 and 1,438 runs (av. 35.95) in 1975 best. Gillette Man of the Match Awards: 1. Benson & Hedges Gold Awards: 3. HS: 168 v Surrey (Oval) 1976. HSGC: 120* v Bucks (Canterbury) 1974. HSJPL: 89 v Sussex (Hove) 1976. HSBH: 85* v Minor Counties (South) (Canterbury) 1975. BB: 6-32 v Surrey (Tunbridge Wells) 1978. BBJPL: 5-26 v Surrey (Oval) 1974. Studied at London School of Economics.

**Nicholas John (Nick) KEMP** (Tonbridge School) B Bromley 16/12/1956. RHB, RM. Played for 2nd XI since 1974. Toured West Indies with England Young Cricketers 1976. Debut 1977. HS: 23 v Surrey (Oval) 1980. HSJPL: 11 v Surrey (Oval) 1980. BB: 6-119 v Surrey (Oval) 1980.

**Alan Philip Eric KNOTT** B Belvedere, Kent 9/4/1946. RHB, WK. Can bowl OB. Debut 1964. Cap 1965. Elected Best Young Cricketer of the Year in 1965 by Cricket Writers Club. *Wisden* 1969. Played for Tasmania 1969-70 whilst coaching there. Benefit (£27,037) in 1976. Tests: 93 betweem 1967 and 1980. Played in 5 matches against Rest of World in 1970. Tours: Pakistan 1966-67, West Indies 1967-68 and 1973-74, Ceylon and Pakistan 1968-69, Australia and New Zealand 1970-71, 1974-75, India, Sri Lanka and Pakistan 1972-73, India, Sri Lanka and Australia 1976-77. 1,000 runs (2) – 1,209 runs (av. 41.68) in 1971 best. Scored two centuries in match (127* and 118*) v Surrey (Maidstone) 1972. Gillette Man of the Match Awards: 2. Benson & Hedges Gold Awards: 1. HS: 156 MCC v South Zone (Bangalore) 1972-73. HSUK: 144 v Sussex (Canterbury) 1976. HSTC: 135 v Australia (Nottingham) 1977. HSGC: 46 v Notts (Nottingham) 1975. HSJPL: 60 v Hants (Canterbury) 1969. HSBH: 65 v Combined Universities (Oxford) 1976. Dismissed 84 batsmen (74 ct 10 st) in 1965. 81 batsmen (73 ct 8st) in 1966, and 98 batsmen (90 ct 8 st) in 1967. Dismissed 7 batsmen (7 ct) on debut in Test cricket v Pakistan (Nottingham) 1967. Holds record for most dismissals in Test cricket.

KENT

**Charles James Castell ROWE** (King's School, Canterbury) B Hong Kong 27/11/1951. RHB, OB. Debut 1974. Cap 1977. Scored 1,065 runs (av. 35.50) in 1978. HS: 147* v Sussex (Canterbury) 1979. HSGC: 18* v Somerset (Canterbury) 1978. HSJPL: 81 v Somerset (Canterbury) 1980. HSBH: 40 v Combined Universities (Canterbury) 1977. BB: 6-46 v Derbyshire (Dover) 1976. BBJPL: 5-32 v Worcs (Worcester) 1976.

**John Neil SHEPHERD** (Alleyn's School, Barbados) B St. Andrew, Barbados 9/11/1943. RHB, RM. Debut 1964-65 in one match for Barbados v Cavaliers and has played subsequently for Barbados in Shell Shield competition. Debut for county 1966. Cap 1967. Played for Rhodesia in 1975-76 Currie Cup competition. *Wisden* 1978. Benefit (£58,537) in 1979. Tests: 5 for West Indies in 1969 and 1970-71. Tour: West Indies to England 1969. Scored 1,157 runs (av. 29.66) and took 96 wkts (av. 18.72) in 1968. Gillette Man of the Match Awards: 1. Benson & Hedges Gold Awards: 2. HS: 170 v Northants (Folkestone) 1968. HSTC: 32 West Indies v England (Lord's) 1969. HSGC: 101 v Middlesex (Canterbury) 1977. HSJPL: 94 v Hants (Southampton) 1978. HSBH: 96 v Middlesex (Lord's) 1975. BB: 8-40 West Indians v Glos (Bristol) 1969. BBTC: 5-104 West Indies v England (Manchester) 1969. BBC: 8-83 v Lancs (Tunbridge Wells) 1977. BBGC: 4-23 v Essex (Leyton) 1972. BBJPL: 4-17 v Middlesex (Lord's) 1978. BBBH: 4-25 v Derbyshire (Lord's) 1978.

**Guy Dennis SPELMAN** (Sevenoaks School) B Westminster 18/10/1958. 6ft 3½ins tall. LHB, RM. Played in three John Player League matches in 1978. Debut 1980. BBJPL: 3-30 v Northants (Luton) 1980. Studied at Nottingham University.

**Christopher James (Chris) TAVARE** (Sevenoaks School and Oxford) B Orpington 27/10/1954. RHB, RM. Scored 124* for England Schools v All-India Schools (Birmingham) 1973. Debut 1974. Blue 1975-76-77. Cap 1978. Tests: 2 in 1980. 1,000 runs (4) – 1,534 runs (av. 45.11) in 1978 best. Benson & Hedges Gold Awards: 3 (2 for Combined Universities). HS: 150* v Essex (Tunbridge Wells) 1979. HSTC: 42 v West Indies (Lord's) 1980. HSGC: 87 v Lancs (Canterbury) 1979. HSJPL: 136* v Glos (Canterbury) 1978. HSBH: 95 v Surrey (Oval) 1980.

**Neil Royston TAYLOR** (Cray Technical School) B Orpington 21/7/1959. RHB, OB. Played for 2nd XI since 1977. Debut 1979 scoring 110 v Sri Lankans (Canterbury) in debut match. HS: 110 as above.

**Derek Leslie UNDERWOOD** (Beckenham and Penge GS) B Bromley 8/6/1945. RHB, LM. Debut 1963, taking 100 wkts and being the youngest player ever to do so in debut season. Cap 1964 (second youngest Kent player to have received this award). Elected Best Young Cricketer of the Year in 1966 by the Cricket Writers Club. *Wisden* 1968. Benefit (£24,114) in 1975. Awarded MBE in 1981 New Year's Honours List. Took 1,000th wkt in first-class cricket in New Zealand 1970-71 at age of 25 years 264 days – only H. Rhodes (in 1902) and G.A. Lohmann (in 1890) have achieved the feat at a younger age. Took 200th wkt in Test cricket against Australia in 1975. Tests: 79 between 1966 and 1980. Played in 3 matches against Rest of World in 1970. Tours: Pakistan 1966-67, Ceylon and Pakistan 1968-69, Australia and New Zealand 1970-71, 1974-75, India, Sri Lanka and Pakistan 1972-73, West Indies 1973-74, India, Sri Lanka and Australia 1976-77, Australia and India 1979-80. 100 wkts (9) – 157 wkts (av. 13.80) in 1966 best. Hat-trick v Sussex (Hove) 1977. HS: 80 v Lancs (Manchester) 1969. HSTC: 45* v Australia (Leeds) 1968. HSGC: 28 v Sussex (Tunbridge Wells) 1963. HSJPL: 22 v Worcs (Dudley) 1969. HSBH: 17 v Essex (Canterbury) 1973. BB: 9-28 v Sussex (Hastings) 1964 and 9-32 v Surrey (Oval) 1978. BBTC: 8-51 v Pakistan (Lord's) 1974. BBGC: 4-57 v Leics

89

**KENT**

(Canterbury) 1974. BBJPL: 5-19 v Glos (Maidstone) 1972. BBBH: 5-35 v Surrey (Oval) 1976.

**Stuart Nicholas Varney WATERTON** (Gravesend School for Boys) B Dartford 6/12/1960. RHB, WK. Debut 1980. HS: 40* v Surrey (Maidstone) 1980. Is studying at Loughborough College.

**Robert Andrew (Bob) WOOLMER** (Skinners' School, Tunbridge Wells) B Kanpur, India 14/5/1948. RHB, RM. Debut 1968. Cap 1970. *Wisden* 1975. Played for Natal between 1973-74 and 1975-76 in Currie Cup competition. Tests: 17 between 1975 and 1980. Tour: India, Sri Lanka and Australia 1976-77. 1,000 runs (5) – 1,749 runs (av. 47.27) in 1976 best. Hat-trick for MCC v Australians (Lord's) 1975. Gillette Man of the Match Awards: 2. Benson & Hedges Gold Awards: 3. HS: 171 v Sussex (Hove) 1980. HSTC: 149 England v Australia (Oval) 1975. HSGC: 91 v Yorks (Leeds) 1980. HSJPL: 112* v Notts (Nottingham) 1980. HSBH: 79 v Derbyshire (Lord's) 1978. BB: 7-47 v Sussex (Canterbury) 1969. BBGC: 4-28 v Somerset (Taunton) 1979. BBJPL: 6-9 v Derbyshire (Chesterfield) 1979. BBBH: 4-14 v Sussex (Tunbridge Wells) 1972.

NB. The following players whose particulars appeared in the 1980 annual have been omitted: R.W. Hills (left staff) and D. Nicholls (retired). In addition P.R. Downton joined Middlesex and his particulars will be found under that county.

The career records of Hills and Downton will be found elsewhere in this annual.

# County Averages

**Schweppes County Championship: Played 22, Won 2, Drawn 12, Lost 8.**
**All first-class matches: Played 23, Won 2, Drawn 12, Lost 9.**

### BATTING AND FIELDING

| Cap | | M | I | NO | Runs | HS | Avge | 100 | 50 | Ct | St |
|---|---|---|---|---|---|---|---|---|---|---|---|
| 1978 | C.J. Tavare | 19 | 31 | 5 | 1075 | 144* | 41.34 | 4 | 4 | 20 | — |
| 1970 | R.A. Woolmer | 17 | 28 | 1 | 839 | 171 | 31.07 | 3 | 3 | 12 | 1 |
| — | N.R. Taylor | 10 | 17 | 4 | 396 | 63 | 30.46 | — | 1 | 9 | — |
| 1970 | A.G.E. Ealham | 20 | 29 | 2 | 801 | 145 | 29.66 | 1 | 4 | 5 | — |
| 1965 | A.P.E. Knott | 16 | 21 | 4 | 504 | 85* | 29.64 | — | 1 | 28 | 3 |
| 1967 | J.N. Shepherd | 20 | 23 | 8 | 428 | 100 | 28.53 | 1 | 1 | 9 | — |
| 1979 | C.S. Cowdrey | 21 | 31 | 3 | 768 | 87 | 27.42 | — | 5 | 22 | — |
| 1977 | C.J.C. Rowe | 15 | 24 | 2 | 539 | 109 | 24.50 | 1 | 2 | 8 | — |
| — | M. Benson | 9 | 13 | 2 | 248 | 58* | 22.54 | — | 2 | 2 | — |
| 1970 | G.W. Johnson | 21 | 29 | 5 | 509 | 84 | 21.20 | — | 2 | 10 | — |
| 1968 | Asif Iqbal | 9 | 16 | 2 | 208 | 41 | 14.85 | — | — | — | — |
| — | S.N.V. Waterton | 7 | 9 | 1 | 110 | 40* | 13.75 | — | — | 11 | 1 |
| — | N.J. Kemp | 5 | 5 | 0 | 48 | 23 | 9.60 | — | — | 2 | — |
| 1980 | G.R. Dilley | 9 | 5 | 3 | 16 | 12* | 8.00 | — | — | 4 | — |
| 1977 | R.W. Hills | 11 | 16 | 4 | 82 | 12 | 6.83 | — | — | 11 | — |
| 1964 | D.L. Underwood | 20 | 15 | 6 | 44 | 11* | 4.88 | — | — | 4 | — |
| 1977 | K.B.S. Jarvis | 18 | 11 | 4 | 12 | 4 | 1.71 | — | — | 2 | — |
| — | G.D. Spelman | 6 | 7 | 1 | 9 | 4 | 1.50 | — | — | 2 | — |

## BOWLING

| | Type | O | M | R | W | Avge | Best | 5 wI | 10 wM |
|---|---|---|---|---|---|---|---|---|---|
| D.L. Underwood | **LM** | 555.5 | 201 | 1310 | 60 | 21.83 | 7-75 | 4 | 2 |
| K.B.S. Jarvis | **RFM** | 384.3 | 86 | 1209 | 53 | 22.81 | 6-100 | 2 | — |
| G.W. Johnson | **OB** | 351.1 | 95 | 959 | 42 | 22.83 | 5-41 | 4 | 1 |
| G.R. Dilley | **RF** | 187 | 45 | 562 | 22 | 25.54 | 5-94 | 1 | — |
| J.N. Shepherd | **RM** | 473.1 | 118 | 1220 | 44 | 27.72 | 5-40 | 1 | — |
| R.A. Woolmer | **RM** | 54 | 15 | 154 | 5 | 30.80 | 2-12 | — | — |
| C.S. Cowdrey | **RM** | 53.3 | 8 | 188 | 6 | 31.33 | 3-17 | — | — |
| R.W. Hills | **RM** | 197 | 54 | 524 | 16 | 32.75 | 3-27 | — | — |
| G.D. Spelman | **RM** | 98.1 | 23 | 291 | 7 | 41.57 | 2-27 | — | — |
| N.J. Kemp | **RM** | 80.5 | 5 | 348 | 7 | 49.71 | 6-119 | 1 | — |

*Also bowled:* Asif Iqbal 7-3-13-0; A.G.E. Ealham 5-0-42-0; A.P.E. Knott 1-0-5-1; C.J.C. Rowe 48-12-132-4; C.J. Tavare 14.3-2-71-0; N.R. Taylor 9-2-20-0.

# County Records

### First-class cricket

| | | |
|---|---|---|
| Highest innings totals: | For – 803-4d v Essex (Brentwood) | 1934 |
| | Agst – 676 by Australians (Canterbury) | 1921 |
| Lowest innings totals: | For – 18 v Sussex (Gravesend) | 1867 |
| | Agst – 16 by Warwickshire (Tonbridge) | 1913 |
| Highest individual innings: | For – 332 W.H. Ashdown v Essex (Brentwood) | 1934 |
| | Agst – 344 W.G. Grace for MCC (Canterbury) | 1876 |
| Best bowling in an innings: | For – 10-30 C. Blythe v Northamptonshire (Northampton) | 1907 |
| | Agst – 10-48 C.H.G. Bland for Sussex (Tonbridge) | 1899 |
| Best bowling in a match: | For – 17-48 C. Blythe v Northamptonshire (Northampton) | 1907 |
| | Agst – 17-106 T.W.J. Goddard for Gloucestershire (Bristol) | 1939 |
| Most runs in a season: | 2,894 (av. 59.06) F.E. Woolley | 1928 |
| runs in a career: | 48,483 (av. 42.05) F.E. Woolley | 1906-1938 |
| 100s in a season: | 10 by F.E. Woolley | 1928 & 1934 |
| 100s in a career: | 112 by F.E. Woolley | 1906-1938 |
| wickets in a season: | 262 (av. 14.74) A.P. Freeman | 1933 |
| wickets in a career: | 3,359 (av. 14.45) A.P. Freeman | 1914-1936 |

### RECORD WICKET STANDS

| | | | |
|---|---|---|---|
| 1st | 283 | A.E. Fagg & P.R. Sunnucks v Essex (Colchester) | 1938 |
| 2nd | 352 | W.H. Ashdown & F.E. Woolley v Essex (Brentwood) | 1934 |
| 3rd | 321 | A. Hearne & J.R. Mason v Nottinghamshire (Nottingham) | 1899 |
| 4th | 297 | H.T.W. Hardinge & A.P.F. Chapman v Hampshire (Southampton) | 1926 |
| 5th | 277 | F.E. Woolley & L.E.G. Ames v New Zealanders (Canterbury) | 1931 |
| 6th | 284 | A.P.F. Chapman & G.B. Legge v Lancashire (Maidstone) | 1927 |
| 7th | 248 | A.P. Day & E. Humphreys v Somerset (Taunton) | 1908 |
| 8th | 157 | A.L. Hilder & C. Wright v Essex (Gravesend) | 1924 |
| 9th | 161 | B.R. Edrich & F. Ridgway v Sussex (Tunbridge Wells) | 1949 |
| 10th | 235 | F.E. Woolley & A. Fielder v Worcestershire (Stourbridge) | 1909 |

## KENT

### One-day cricket

| | | | |
|---|---|---|---|
| Highest innings totals: | Gillette Cup | 297-3 v Worcestershire (Canterbury) | 1970 |
| | John Player League | 278-5 v Gloucestershire (Maidstone) | 1976 |
| | Benson & Hedges Cup | 280-3 v Surrey (Oval) | 1976 |
| Lowest innings totals: | Gillette Cup | 60 v Somerset (Taunton) | 1979 |
| | John Player League | 84 v Gloucestershire (Folkestone) | 1969 |
| | Benson & Hedges Cup | 73 v Middlesex (Canterbury) | 1979 |
| Highest individual innings: | Gillette Cup | 129 B.W. Luckhurst v Durham (Canterbury) | 1974 |
| | John Player League | 142 B.W. Luckhurst v Somerset (Weston-super-Mare) | 1970 |
| | Benson & Hedges Cup | 114 C.S. Cowdrey v Sussex (Canterbury) | 1977 |
| Best bowling figures: | Gillette Cup | 7-15 A.L. Dixon v Surrey (Oval) | 1967 |
| | John Player League | 6-9 R.A. Woolmer v Derbyshire (Chesterfield) | 1979 |
| | Benson & Hedges Cup | 5-21 B.D. Julien v Surrey (Oval) | 1973 |

# LANCASHIRE

**Formation of present club:** 1864.
**Colours:** Red, green and blue.
**Badge:** Red rose.
**County Champions (8):** 1881, 1897, 1904, 1926, 1927, 1928, 1930 and 1934.
**Joint Champions (4):** 1879, 1882, 1889 and 1950.
**Gillette Cup Winners (4):** 1970, 1971, 1972 and 1975.
**Gillette Cup Finalists (2):** 1974 and 1976.
**John Player League Champions (2):** 1969 and 1970.
**Benson & Hedges Cup Semi-Finalists (2):** 1973 and 1974.
**Gillette Man of the Match Awards:** 35.
**Benson & Hedges Gold Awards:** 25.

**Secretary:** C.D. Hassell, Old Trafford, Manchester M16 0PX.
**Cricket Manager:** J.D. Bond.
**Captain:** C.H. Lloyd.
**Prospects of Play Telephone No:** 061-872 0261

John **ABRAHAMS** (Heywood GS) B Cape Town, South Africa 21/7/1952. LHB, OB. Son of Cecil J. Abrahams, former professional for Milnrow and Radcliffe in Central Lancashire League. Has lived in this country since 1962. Debut 1973. HS: 126 v Cambridge U (Cambridge) 1978. HSGC: 46 v Northants (Lord's) 1976. HSJPL: 59 v Hants (Manchester) 1979. HSBH: 47 v Leics (Leicester) 1980.

Paul John Walter **ALLOTT** (Altrincham County Grammar School for Boys) B Altrincham (Cheshire) 14/9/1956. 6ft 4ins tall. RHB, RFM. Played for Cheshire in 1976 and for county 2nd XI in 1977. Debut 1978. HS: 30* v Essex (Blackpool) 1980. HSGC: 19* v Worcs (Worcester) 1980. HSJPL: 22* v Middlesex (Manchester) 1979. BB: 5-39 v Worcs (Southport) 1979. BBJPL: 3-15 v Warwickshire (Birmingham) 1979. Studied at Durham University.

Douglas Keith **BECKETT** (Cheadle Hulme School) B Hampton Court, Surrey 29/8/1959. RHB, RM. Played for Cheshire in 1978 and 1979 and for Derbyshire 2nd XI in 1979. Played for county in two John Player League matches and one Gillette Cup match in 1980. Has yet to appear in first-class cricket. HSJPL: 11 v Sussex (Manchester) 1980. Studied at Manchester University.

Ian **COCKBAIN** (Bootle GS) B Bootle 19/4/1958. RHB, SLA. Played for 2nd XI since 1976. Debut 1979. HS: 69* v Middlesex (Lord's) 1980. HSJPL: 34 v Warwickshire (Liverpool) 1980. HSBH: 53 v Worcs (Manchester) 1980.

Graeme **FOWLER** (Accrington GS) B Accrington 20/4/1957. RHB, WK. Played for 2nd XI since 1973. Played in one John Player League match v Derbyshire (Chesterfield) 1978. Debut 1979. HS: 106* v Notts (Manchester) 1980. HSJPL: 34 v Glamorgan (Manchester) 1980. Studied at Durham University.

Frank Charles **HAYES** (De La Salle College, Salford) B Preston 6/12/1946. RHB, RM. Debut 1970 scoring 94 and 99 in first two matches after scoring 203* for 2nd XI v Warwickshire 2nd XI (Birmingham). Cap 1972. County Captain from 1978 to 1980. Tests: 9 between 1973 and 1976. Tour: West Indies 1973-74. 1,000 runs (6) – 1,311 runs (av. 35.43) in 1974 best. Scored 34 in one over (6 4 6 6 6 6) off M.A. Nash v Glamorgan (Swansea) 1977. Gillette Man of the Match Awards: 1. Benson &

93

## LANCASHIRE

Hedges Gold Awards: 2. HS: 187 v Indians (Manchester) 1974. HSTC: 106* v West Indies (Oval) 1973 in second innings on Test debut. HSGC: 93 v Warwickshire (Birmingham) 1976. HSJPL: 84* v Somerset (Bath) 1980. HSBH: 102 v Minor Counties (North) (Manchester) 1973. Amateur soccer player. Studied at Sheffield University.

**Kevin Anthony HAYES** (Queen Elizabeth's GS, Blackburn) B Thurnscoe, Yorks 26/9/1962. No relation to F.C. Hayes. Has lived in Lancs since 1969. RHB, RM. Played for 2nd XI in 1979. Plays for East Lancashire in Lancashire League. Debut 1980. One match v Oxford U (Oxford). HS: 27 v Oxford U (Oxford) 1980. Entered Oxford University in 1980. Soccer Blue 1980-81.

**William (Willie) HOGG** (Ulverston Comprehensive School) B Ulverston 12/7/1955. RHB, RFM. Debut 1976 after playing as professional for Preston in Northern League. HS: 19 v Middlesex (Lord's) 1978. BB: 7-84 v Warwickshire (Manchester) 1978. BBJPL: 4-23 v Essex (Ilford) 1979. BBBH: 4-35 v Hants (Manchester) 1979.

**David Paul HUGHES** (Newton-le-Willows GS) B Newton-le-Willows, Lancs 13/5/1947. RHB, SLA. Debut 1967. Cap 1970. Played for Tasmania in 1975-76 and 1976-77 whilst coaching there. Testimonial in 1981. Gillette Man of the Match Awards: 1. HS: 101 v Cambridge U (Cambridge) 1975. HSGC: 42* v Middlesex (Lord's) 1974. HSJPL: 84 v Essex (Leyton) 1973. HSBH: 42* v Minor Counties (West) (Watford) 1978. BB: 7-24 v Oxford U (Oxford) 1970. BBGC: 4-61 v Somerset (Manchester) 1972. BBJPL: 6-29 v Somerset (Manchester) 1977. BBBH: 5-23 v Minor Counties (West) (Watford) 1978.

**Andrew KENNEDY** (Nelson GS) B Blackburn 4/11/1949. LHB, RM. Debut 1970. Cap 1975. Elected Best Young Cricketer of the Year in 1975 by the Cricket Writers' Club. 1,000 runs (2) – 1,194 runs (av. 34.11) in 1980 best. Gillette Man of the Match Awards: 1. HS: 176* v Leics (Leicester) 1974. HSGC: 131 v Middlesex (Manchester) 1978. HSJPL: 89 v Yorks (Manchester) 1978. HSBH: 91 v Notts (Manchester) 1980. BB: 3-58 v Warwickshire (Liverpool) 1980.

**Peter Granville LEE** B Arthingworth, Northants 27/8/1945. RHB, RFM. Debut for Northants 1967. Joined Lancs in 1972. Cap 1972. Wisden 1975. 100 wkts (2) – 112 wkts (av. 18.45) in 1975 best. HS: 26 Northants v Glos (Northampton) 1969. HSGC: 10* v Middlesex (Lord's) 1974. HSJPL: 27* Northants v Derbyshire (Chesterfield) 1971. BB: 8-34 v Oxford U (Oxford) 1980. BBGC: 4-7 v Cornwall (Truro) 1977. BBJPL: 4-17 v Derbyshire (Chesterfield) 1972. BBBH: 4-32 v Worcs (Manchester) 1973.

**Clive Hubert LLOYD** (Chatham HS, Georgetown) B Georgetown, British Guiana 31/8/1944. 6ft 4½ins tall. Cousin of L.R. Gibbs. LHB, RM. Wears glasses. Debut 1963-64 for Guyana (then British Guiana). Played for Haslingden in Lancashire League in 1967 and also for Rest of World XI in 1967 and 1968. Debut for county v Australians 1968. Cap 1969. Wisden 1970. Testimonial (£27,199) in 1977. Appointed County Captain for 1981. Tests: 74 for West Indies between 1966-67 and 1980, captaining West Indies in 38 Tests. Played in 5 matches for Rest of World 1970 and 2 in 1971-72. Scored 118 on debut v England (Port of Spain) 1967-68, 129 on debut v Australia (Brisbane) 1968-69, and 82 and 78* on debut v India (Bombay) 1966-67. Tours: West Indies to India and Ceylon 1966-67, Australia and New Zealand 1968-69, England 1969, 1973, 1976 (captain), and 1980 (captain), Rest of World to Australia 1971-72 (returning early owing to back injury), India, Sri Lanka and Pakistan 1974-75 (captain), Australia 1975-76 (captain), Australia and New

94

Zealand 1979-80 (captain), Pakistan 1980-81 (captain). 1,000 runs (8) – 1,603 runs (av. 47.14) in 1970 best. Also scored 1,000 runs in Australia and New Zealand 1968-69 and in India, Sri Lanka and Pakistan 1974-75. Scored 201* in 120 minutes for West Indians v Glamorgan (Swansea) 1976 to equal record for fastest double-century in first-class cricket. Gillette Man of the Match Awards: 6. HS: 242* West Indies v India (Bombay) 1974-75. HSUK: 217* v Warwickshire (Manchester) 1971. HSGC: 126 v Warwickshire (Lord's) 1972. HSJPL: 134* v Somerset (Manchester) 1970. HSBH: 73 v Notts (Manchester) 1974. BB: 4-48 v Leics (Manchester) 1970. BBGC: 3-39 v Somerset (Taunton) 1970. BBJPL: 4-33 v Middlesex (Lord's) 1971. BBBH: 3-23 v Derbyshire (Manchester) 1974.

**David LLOYD** (Accrington Secondary TS) B Accrington 18/3/1947. LHB, SLA. Debut 1965. Cap 1968. County Captain from 1973 to 1977. Testimonial (£40,171) in 1978. Tests: 9 in 1974 and 1974-75. Tour: Australia and New Zealand 1974-75. 1,000 runs (9) – 1,510 runs (av. 47.18) in 1972 best. Scored two centuries in match (116 and 104*) v Worcs (Southport) 1979. Gillette Man of the Match Awards: 3. Benson & Hedges Gold Awards: 2. HS: 214* England v India (Birmingham) 1974. HSC: 195 v Glos (Manchester) 1973. HSGC: 121* v Glos (Manchester) 1978. HSJPL: 103* v Northants (Bedford) 1971. HSBH: 113 v Minor Counties (North) (Manchester) 1973 and 113 v Scotland (Manchester) 1980. BB: 7-38 v Glos (Lydney) 1966. BBJPL: 3-23 v Glos (Manchester) 1980. BBBH: 4-17 v Notts (Manchester) 1980.

**Michael Francis (Mick) MALONE** (Scarborough HS, Perth) B Perth, Australia 9/10/1950. RHB, RFM. Debut for Western Australia 1974-75. Played for Haslingden in Lancashire League in 1979. Debut for county 1979. Tests: 1 for Australia in 1977. Tours: Australia to England 1977, Pakistan 1979-80. HS: 46 Australia v England (Oval) 1977. HSC: 38 in both innings v Northants (Southport) 1980. BB: 7-88 v Notts (Blackpool) 1979. BBTC: 5-63 Australia v England (Oval) 1977.

**Steven Joseph O'SHAUGHNESSY** B Bury 9/9/1961. RHB, RM. Debut 1980. HS: 50 v Oxford U (Oxford) 1980. HSJPL: 38 v Hants (Southampton) 1980. BBJPL: 3-23 v Hants (Southampton) 1980.

**Harry PILLING** (Ashton TS) B Ashton-under-Lyne, Lancs 23/2/1943. 5ft 3ins tall. RHB, OB. Debut 1962. Cap 1965. Testimonial (£9,500) in 1974. Played in only one match and one Benson & Hedges match in 1979. 1,000 runs (8) – 1,606 runs (av. 36.50) in 1967 best. Scored two centuries in match (119* and 104*) v Warwickshire (Manchester) 1970. Gillette Man of the Match Awards: 3. Benson & Hedges Gold Awards: 3. HS: 149* v Glamorgan (Liverpool) 1976. HSGC: 90 v Middlesex (Lord's) 1973. HSJPL: 85 v Sussex (Hove) 1970. HSBH: 109* v Glamorgan (Manchester) 1973.

**Neal Victor RADFORD** (Athlone High School, Johannesburg) B Luanshya, Northern Rhodesia (now Zambia) 7/6/1957. RHB, RFM. Played for Glamorgan 2nd XI and for Burnley in Lancashire League in 1978. Played for county 2nd XI in 1979 and as professional for Bacup in Lancashire League in 1979 and 1980. Debut for Transvaal B in President's competition 1978-79. Debut for county 1980. HS: 38* Transvaal v Griqualand West (Kimberley) 1979-80. HSC: 34 v Northants (Southport) 1980. BB: 5-47 Transvaal B v Western Province B (Johannesburg) 1979-80. BBGC: 3-52 v Worcs (Worcester) 1980. BBJPL: 3-28 v Sussex (Manchester) 1980.

**Bernard Wilfrid REIDY** (St. Mary's College, Blackburn) B Bramley Meade, Whalley, Lancs 18/9/1953. LHB, LM. Toured West Indies with England Young Cricketers 1972. Played for 2nd XI since 1971. Debut 1973. Cap 1980. Benson & Hedges Gold Awards: 3. HS: 131* v Derbyshire (Chesterfield) 1979. HSGC: 18 v

## LANCASHIRE

Glos (Manchester) 1975. HSJPL: 74 v Glamorgan (Manchester) 1980. HSBH: 109* v Derbyshire (Chesterfield) 1980. BB: 5-61 v Worcs (Worcester) 1979. BBJPL: 3-33 v Surrey (Manchester) 1978.

**Christopher John SCOTT** (Ellesmere Park HS) B Swinton, Manchester 16/9/1959. LHB, WK. Played for 2nd XI since 1975. Debut 1977 aged 17 years 8 months. HS: 16 v Cambridge U (Cambridge) 1979. HSBH: 18 v Leics (Leicester) 1980.

**Jack SIMMONS** (Accrington Secondary TS) B Clayton-le-Moors, Lancs 28/3/1941. RHB, OB. Debut for 2nd XI 1959. Played for Blackpool in Northern League as professional. Debut 1968. Cap 1971. Played for Tasmania from 1972-73 to 1978-79 whilst coaching there. Testimonial in 1980. Hat-trick v Notts (Liverpool) 1977. Gillette Man of the Match Awards: 1. Benson & Hedges Gold Awards: 2. HS: 112 v Sussex (Hove) 1970. HSGC: 54* v Essex (Manchester) 1979. HSJPL: 65 v Essex (Manchester) 1980. HSBH: 64 v Derbyshire (Manchester) 1978. BB: 7-59 Tasmania v Queensland (Brisbane) 1978-79. BBUK: 7-64 v Hants (Southport) 1973. BBGC: 5-49 v Worcs (Worcester) 1974. BBJPL: 5-28 v Northants (Peterborough) 1972. BBBH: 4-31 v Yorks (Manchester) 1975. Has played soccer in Lancs Combination.

**Mark Andrew WALLWORK** B Salford 14/12/1960. RHB, WK. Plays for Farnworth in Bolton League. Has joined staff for 1981. Has yet to appear in first-class cricket. Is studying dentistry at Newcastle University.

**Roger Graeme WATSON** B Rawtenstall 14/1/1964. LHB, OB. Has joined staff for 1981. Has yet to appear in first-class cricket.

NB. The following players whose particulars appeared in the 1980 annual have been omitted: G.F. Lawson, R.M. Ratcliffe (not re-engaged) and G.E. Trim (not re-engaged).

The career records of Ratcliffe and Trim will be found elsewhere in this annual.

# County Averages

Schweppes County Championship: Played 20, won 4, drawn 13, lost 3, abandoned 2.
All first-class matches: Played 22, won 5, drawn 14, lost 3, abandoned 2.

## BATTING AND FIELDING

| Cap | | M | I | NO | Runs | HS | Avge | 100 | 50 | Ct | St |
|---|---|---|---|---|---|---|---|---|---|---|---|
| 1972 | F.C. Hayes | 21 | 33 | 6 | 1117 | 102* | 41.37 | 1 | 9 | 6 | — |
| 1968 | D. Lloyd | 19 | 30 | 6 | 827 | 112* | 34.45 | 1 | 3 | 11 | — |
| 1975 | A. Kennedy | 22 | 38 | 3 | 1194 | 169* | 34.11 | 1 | 7 | 12 | — |
| 1980 | B.W. Reidy | 16 | 27 | 5 | 671 | 110* | 30.50 | 1 | 4 | 9 | — |
| — | S.J. O'Shaughnessy | 4 | 5 | 2 | 91 | 50* | 30.33 | — | 1 | 2 | — |
| 1971 | J. Simmons | 21 | 30 | 6 | 682 | 96 | 28.41 | — | 5 | 20 | — |
| 1970 | D.P. Hughes | 18 | 21 | 6 | 405 | 66* | 27.00 | — | 2 | 18 | — |
| — | G. Fowler | 10 | 12 | 1 | 262 | 106* | 23.81 | 1 | — | 7 | 2 |
| — | I. Cockbain | 17 | 27 | 6 | 388 | 69* | 18.47 | — | 2 | 10 | — |
| — | M.F. Malone | 16 | 14 | 3 | 181 | 38 | 16.45 | — | — | — | — |
| — | N. Radford | 4 | 7 | — | 115 | 34 | 16.42 | — | — | 2 | — |
| 1965 | H. Pilling | 3 | 6 | 1 | 80 | 56* | 16.00 | — | 1 | 1 | — |
| — | J. Abrahams | 9 | 14 | — | 191 | 59 | 13.64 | — | 2 | 3 | — |
| — | G.E. Trim | 5 | 8 | — | 105 | 31 | 13.12 | — | 1 | 1 | — |
| 1976 | R.M. Ratcliffe | 4 | 3 | — | 38 | 26 | 12.66 | — | — | — | — |
| — | P.J.W. Allott | 11 | 11 | 4 | 72 | 30* | 10.28 | — | — | 1 | — |
| — | C.J. Scott | 17 | 18 | 5 | 75 | 14 | 5.76 | — | — | 41 | 2 |
| — | W. Hogg | 15 | 13 | 5 | 18 | 5* | 2.25 | — | — | 2 | — |
| 1972 | P.G. Lee | 7 | 3 | 1 | 0 | 0* | 0.00 | — | — | 1 | — |

*Played in two matches:* C.H. Lloyd 0, 101; 33 (2 ct).
*Played in one match:* K.A. Hayes 27 (1 ct).

## BOWLING

| | Type | O | M | R | W | Avge | Best | 5 wI | 10 wM |
|---|---|---|---|---|---|---|---|---|---|
| P.J.W. Allott | RFM | 183 | 47 | 473 | 23 | 20.56 | 4-30 | — | — |
| W. Hogg | RFM | 340.1 | 69 | 1114 | 51 | 21.84 | 6-45 | 2 | 1 |
| M.F. Malone | RFM | 466 | 131 | 1191 | 45 | 26.46 | 5-57 | 2 | — |
| P.G. Lee | RFM | 193.1 | 56 | 512 | 18 | 28.44 | 8-34 | 1 | — |
| B.W. Reidy | LM | 188.2 | 46 | 543 | 19 | 28.57 | 4-24 | — | — |
| D. Lloyd | SLA | 167 | 35 | 515 | 16 | 32.18 | 4-39 | — | — |
| D.P. Hughes | SLA | 336.1 | 96 | 861 | 26 | 33.11 | 5-40 | 1 | — |
| J. Simmons | OB | 398.3 | 110 | 988 | 24 | 41.16 | 4-43 | — | — |
| A. Kennedy | RM | 63 | 17 | 209 | 5 | 41.80 | 3-58 | — | — |

*Also bowled:* J. Abrahams 14-5-48-0; S.J. O'Shaughnessy 27-6-70-1; N. Radford
48.5-11-176-2; R.M. Ratcliffe 88.1-30-238-2.

# County Records

### First-class cricket

| | | | |
|---|---|---|---|
| Highest innings<br>totals: | For – 801 v Somerset (Taunton) | | 1895 |
| | Agst – 634 v Surrey (The Oval) | | 1898 |
| Lowest innings<br>totals: | For – 25 v Derbyshire (Manchester) | | 1871 |
| | Agst – 22 by Glamorgan (Liverpool) | | 1924 |
| Highest indi-<br>vidual innings | For – 424 A.C. MacLaren v Somerset (Taunton) | | 1895 |
| | Agst – 315* T.W. Hayward for Surrey (The Oval) | | 1898 |
| Best bowling<br>in innings | For – 10-55 J. Briggs v Worcestershire (Manchester) | | 1900 |
| | Agst – 10-40 G.O.B. Allen for Middlesex (Lord's) | | 1929 |
| Best bowling<br>in a match: | For – 17-91 H. Dean v Yorkshire (Liverpool) | | 1913 |
| | Agst – 16-65 G. Giffen for Australians (Manchester) | | 1886 |
| Most runs in a season: | 2,633 (av. 56.02) J.T. Tyldesley | | 1901 |
| runs in a career: | 34,222 (av. 45.02) G.E. Tyldesley | | 1909-1936 |
| 100s in a season: | 11 by C. Hallows | | 1928 |
| 100s in a career: | 90 by G.E. Tyldesley | | 1909-1936 |
| wickets in a season: | 198 (av. 18.55) E.A. McDonald | | 1925 |
| wickets in a career: | 1,816 (av. 15.12) J.B. Statham | | 1950-1968 |

## RECORD WICKET STANDS

| | | | |
|---|---|---|---|
| 1st | 368 | A.C. MacLaren & R.H. Spooner v Gloucestershire (Liverpool) | 1903 |
| 2nd | 371 | F.B. Watson & G.E. Tyldesley v Surrey (Manchester) | 1928 |
| 3rd | 306 | E. Paynter & N. Oldfield v Hampshire (Southampton) | 1938 |
| 4th | 324 | A.C. MacLaren & J.T. Tyldesley v Notts (Nottingham) | 1904 |
| 5th | 249 | B. Wood & A. Kennedy v Warwickshire (Birmingham) | 1975 |
| 6th | 278 | J. Iddon & H.R.W. Butterworth v Sussex (Manchester) | 1932 |
| 7th | 245 | A.H. Hornby & J. Sharp v Leicestershire (Manchester) | 1912 |
| 8th | 158 | J. Lyon & R.M. Ratcliffe v Warwickshire (Manchester) | 1979 |
| 9th | 142 | L.O.S. Poidevin & A. Kermode v Sussex (Eastbourne) | 1907 |
| 10th | 173 | J. Briggs & R. Pilling v Surrey (Liverpool) | 1885 |

### One-day cricket

| | | | |
|---|---|---|---|
| Highest innings<br>totals: | Gillette Cup | 304-9 v Leics (Manchester) | 1963 |
| | John Player League | 255-5 v Somerset<br>(Manchester) | 1970 |
| | Benson & Hedges Cup | 275-5 v Minor Counties<br>(North) (Manchester) | 1973 |
| Lowest innings<br>totals: | Gillette Cup | 59 v Worcs (Worcester) | 1963 |
| | John Player League | 76 v Somerset (Manchester) | 1972 |
| | Benson & Hedges Cup | 82 v Yorks (Bradford) | 1972 |
| Highest indi-<br>vidual innings: | Gillette Cup | 131 A. Kennedy v Middlesex<br>(Manchester) | 1978 |
| | John Player League | 134* C.H. Lloyd v Somerset<br>(Manchester) | 1970 |
| | Benson & Hedges Cup | 113 D. Lloyd v Minor Counties<br>(North) (Manchester) | 1973 |
| | | 113 D. Lloyd v Scotland<br>(Manchester) | 1980 |
| Best bowling<br>figures: | Gillette Cup | 5-28 J.B. Statham v Leics<br>(Manchester) | 1963 |
| | John Player League | 6-29 D.P. Hughes v Somerset<br>(Manchester) | 1977 |
| | Benson & Hedges Cup | 5-12 B. Wood v Derbyshire<br>(Southport) | 1976 |

# LEICESTERSHIRE

**Formation of present club:** 1879.
**Colours:** Scarlet and dark green.
**Badge:** Running fox (gold) on green background.
**County Champions:** 1975.
**Gillette Cup Semi-Finalists:** 1977.
**John Player League Champions (2):** 1974 and 1977.
**Benson & Hedges Cup Winners (2):** 1972 and 1975.
**Benson & Hedges Cup Finalists:** 1974.
**Fenner Trophy Winners:** 1979.
**Gillette Man of the Match Awards:** 15.
**Benson & Hedges Gold Awards:** 30.
**Secretary:** F.M. Turner, County Ground, Grace Road, Leicester LE2 8AD.
**Captain:** R.W. Tolchard.
**Prospects of Play Telephone No:** Leicester (0533) 832128, 831880

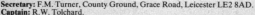

**Jonathan Philip AGNEW** (Uppingham School) B Macclesfield, Cheshire 4/4/1960. 6ft 3½ins tall. RHB, RF. Played for Surrey 2nd XI in 1976 and 1977. Debut 1978. HS: 31 v Glamorgan (Leicester) 1980. BB: 4-36 v Hants (Southampton) 1980.

**John Christopher (Chris) BALDERSTONE** B Huddersfield 16/11/1940. RHB, SLA. Played for Yorks from 1961 to 1970. Specially registered and made debut for Leics in 1971. Cap 1973. Tests: 2 in 1976. 1,000 runs (6) – 1,472 runs (av. 43.29) 1980 best. Hat-trick v Sussex (Eastbourne) 1976. Gillette Man of the Match Awards: 2. Benson & Hedges Gold Awards: 5. HS: 178* v Notts (Nottingham) 1977. HSTC: 35 v West Indies (Leeds) 1976. HSGC: 119* v Somerset (Taunton) 1973. HSJPL: 96 v Northants (Leicester) 1976. HSBH: 101* v Hants (Leicester) 1975. BB: 6-25 v Hants (Southampton) 1978. BBGC: 4-33 v Herts (Leicester) 1977. BBJPL: 3-29 v Worcs (Leicester) 1971. Soccer for Huddersfield Town, Carlisle United, Doncaster Rovers and Queen of the South.

**Timothy James (Tim) BOON** (Edlington Comprehensive School, Doncaster) B Doncaster 1/11/1961. RHB, RM. Played for Yorks 2nd XI in 1978 and 1979. Captained England Young Cricketers in West Indies 1980. Debut 1980. HS: 53 v Northants (Leicester) 1980. HSJPL: 24 v Glos (Leicester) 1980.

**Peter BOOTH** (Whitcliffe Mount GS, Cleckheaton) B Shipley, Yorks 2/11/1952. RHB, RFM. Played for MCC Schools at Lord's 1970 and 1971. Toured West Indies with England Youth Team 1972. Debut 1972. Cap 1976. HS: 58* v Lancs (Leicester) 1976. HSGC: 40* v Glamorgan (Swansea) 1977. HSJPL: 22* v Derbyshire (Leicester) 1976. HSBH: 29* v Derbyshire (Leicester) 1979. BB: 6-93 v Glamorgan (Swansea) 1978. BBGC: 5-33 v Northants (Northampton) 1977. BBJPL: 4-20 v Warwickshire (Leicester) 1977. BBBH: 3-27 v Hants (Leicester) 1975. Trained as a teacher at Loughborough College.

**Nigel Edwin BRIERS** (Lutterworth GS) B Leicester 15/1/1955. RHB. Cousin of N. Briers who once played for county in 1967. Debut 1971 at age of 16 years 103 days. Youngest player ever to appear for county. Shared in 5th wicket partnership record for county, 235 with R.W. Tolchard v Somerset (Leicester) 1979. Benson & Hedges Gold Awards: 1. HS: 119 v Warwickshire (Birmingham) 1979. BSGC: 20 v Worcs (Leicester) 1979. HSJPL: 81 v Worcs (Worcester) 1978. HSBH: 71* v Hants (Southampton) 1979.

## LEICESTERSHIRE

**Ian Paul BUTCHER** (John Ruskin HS, Croydon) B Farnborough, Kent 1/7/1962. RHB, WK. Brother of A.R. Butcher of Surrey. Played in last two John Player League matches of 1979. Debut 1980. One match v Oxford U (Oxford). Also played in one John Player League match in 1980. HSJPL: 16 v Surrey (Leicester) 1979.

**Patrick Bernard (Paddy) CLIFT** (St. George's College, Salisbury) B Salisbury, Rhodesia 14/7/1953. RHB, RM. Debut for Rhodesia 1971-72. Debut for county 1975. Cap 1976. Hat-trick v Yorks (Leicester) 1976. HS: 88* v Oxford U (Oxford) 1979. HSGC: 48* v Worcs (Leicester) 1979. HSJPL: 51* v Somerset (Leicester) 1979. HSBH: 91 v Notts (Leicester) 1980. BB: 8-17 v MCC (Lord's) 1976. BBGC: 3-36 v Worcs (Leicester) 1979. BBJPL: 4-14 v Lancs (Leicester) 1978. BBBH: 4-13 v Minor Counties (East) (Amersham) 1978.

**Russell Alan COBB** (Trent College) B Leicester 18/5/1961. RHB, LM. Played for 2nd XI since 1977. Toured Australia 1979 and West Indies 1980 with England Young Cricketers. Debut 1980. One match v Oxford U (Oxford).

**Nicholas Grant Billson (Nick) COOK** (Lutterworth GS) B Leicester 17/6/1956. RHB, SLA. Played for 2nd XI since 1974. Debut 1978. HS: 75 v Somerset (Taunton) 1980. HSJPL: 13* v Kent (Leicester) 1979. BB: 6-57 v Essex (Leicester) 1979.

**Brian Fettes DAVISON** (Gifford Technical HS, Rhodesia) B Bulawayo, Rhodesia 21/12/1946. RHB, RM. Debut for Rhodesia 1967-68 in Currie Cup competition. Debut for county 1970 after having played for International Cavaliers. Cap 1971. County Captain in 1980. Played for Tasmania in 1979-80 and 1980-81. Is now regarded as an English player for qualification purposes. 1,000 runs (10) – 1,818 runs (av. 56.81) in 1976 best. Gillette Man of the Match Awards: 1. Benson & Hedges Gold Awards: 6. HS: 189 v Australians (Leicester) 1975. HSGC: 99 v Essex (Southend) 1977. HSJPL: 85* v Glamorgan (Cardiff) 1974. HSBH: 158* v Warwickshire (Coventry) 1972. BB: 5-52 Rhodesia v Griqualand West (Bulawayo) 1967-68. BBUK: 4-99 v Northants (Leicester) 1970. BBJPL: 4-29 v Glamorgan (Neath) 1971. Has played hockey for Rhodesia.

**Grant FORSTER** (Seaham Comprehensive School) B Seaham, Co. Durham 27/5/1961. LHB, OB. Played for Northants 2nd XI from 1978 to 1980. Debut for Northants 1980. One match v Cambridge U (Cambridge). Has joined Leics for 1981.

**Michael Anthony (Mike) GARNHAM** (Camberwell GS, Melbourne, Scotch College, Perth, Australia, Park School, Barnstaple) B Johannesburg 20/8/1960. RHB, WK. Played for Devon and Glos 2nd XI in 1976 and 1977. Toured India with English Schools Cricket Association in 1977. Played for Glos in last John Player League match of 1978 v Warwickshire (Birmingham). Debut for Glos 1979 playing in three matches and two John Player League matches. Left county and made debut for Leics in 1980. HS: 21 Glos v Northants (Bristol) 1980. HSC: 14 v Cambridge U (Cambridge) 1980. HSGC: 25 v Essex (Leicester) 1980. HSJPL: 28 v Surrey (Oval) 1980. Is studying at East Anglia University.

**David Ivon GOWER** (King's School, Canterbury) B Tunbridge Wells 1/4/1957. LHB, OB. Toured South Africa with English Schools XI 1974-75 and West Indies with England Young Cricketers 1976. Debut 1975. Cap 1977. *Wisden* 1978. Elected Best Young Cricketer of the Year in 1978 by Cricket Writers' Club. Tests: 22 between 1978 and 1980. Tours: Australia 1978-79, Australia and India 1979-80, West Indies 1980-81. 1,000 runs (2) – 1,142 runs (av. 32.62) in 1980 best. Gillette Man of the Match Awards: 1. Benson & Hedges Gold Awards: 1. HS: 200* England

100

v India (Birmingham) 1979. HSC: 144* v Hants (Leicester) 1977. HSGC: 117* v Herts (Leicester) 1977. HSJPL: 135* v Warwickshire (Leicester) 1977. HSBH: 114* v Derbyshire (Derby) 1980. BB: 3-47 v Essex (Leicester) 1977.

**Kenneth (Ken) HIGGS** B Sandyford, Staffordshire 14/1/1937. LHB, RM. Played for Staffordshire 1957. Debut for Lancs 1958. Cap 1959. *Wisden* 1967. Benefit (£8,390) in 1968. Retired after 1969 season. Re-appeared for Leics in 1972. Cap 1972. Appointed County Vice-Captain in 1973 and County Captain for 1979 relinquishing post at end of season. Is now county coach. Tests: 15 between 1965 and 1968. Shared in 10th wkt partnership of 128 with J.A. Snow v West Indies (Oval) 1966 – 2 runs short of then record 10th wkt partnership in Test cricket. Also shared in 10th wkt partnership record for county, 228 with R. Illingworth v Northants (Leicester) 1977. Tours: Australia and New Zealand 1965-66, West Indies 1967-68. 100 wkts (5) – 132 wkts (av. 19.42) in 1960 best. Hat-tricks (3) – Lancs v Essex (Blackpool) 1960, Lancs v Yorks (Leeds) 1968 and v Hants (Leicester) 1977. Hat-trick also in Benson & Hedges Cup Final v Surrey (Lord's) 1974. Benson & Hedges Gold Awards: 1. HS: 98 v Northants (Leicester) 1977. HSTC: 63 England v West Indies (Oval) 1966. HSGC: 25 Lancs v Somerset (Taunton) 1966. HSJPL: 17* v Notts (Nottingham) 1975. BB: 7-19 Lancs v Leics (Manchester) 1965. BBTC: 6-91 v West Indies (Lord's) 1966. BBC: 7-44 v Middlesex (Lord's) 1978. BBGC: 6-20 v Staffs (Longton) 1975. BBJPL: 6-17 v Glamorgan (Leicester) 1973. BBBH: 4-10 v Surrey (Lord's) 1974. Soccer for Port Vale.

**David John MUNDEN** (Gateway School, Leicester) B Leicester 7/8/1957. Son of V.S. Munden, former Leics player. LHB, LB. Played for 2nd XI since 1975. Has yet to appear in first-class cricket. Trained as a teacher at Borough Road College of Education.

**Gordon James PARSONS** B Slough, Bucks 17/10/1959. LHB, RM. Played for county 2nd XI since 1976 and also for Buckinghamshire in 1977. Debut 1978. HS: 25* v Glamorgan (Leicester) 1980. HSGC: 22 v Essex (Leicester) 1980. BB: 4-38 v Essex (Chelmsford) 1980. BBJPL: 3-27 v Surrey (Oval) 1980.

**John Frederick STEELE** B Stafford 23/7/1946. Younger brother of D.S. Steele of Derbyshire. RHB, SLA. Debut 1970. Was 12th man for England v Rest of World (Lord's) a month after making debut. Cap 1971. Played for Natal in 1973-74 and 1977-78 Currie Cup competition. 1,000 runs (6) – 1,347 runs (av. 31.32) in 1972 best. Shared in 1st wkt partnership record for county, 390 with B. Dudleston v Derbyshire (Leicester) 1979. Gillette Man of the Match Awards: 3. Benson & Hedges Gold Awards: 4. HS: 195 v Derbyshire (Leicester) 1971. HSGC: 108* v Staffs (Longton) 1975. HSJPL: 92 v Essex (Leicester) 1973. HSBH: 91 v Somerset (Leicester) 1974. BB: 7-29 Natal B v Griqualand West (Umzinto) 1973-74 and 7-29 v Glos (Leicester) 1980. BBGC: 5-19 v Essex (Southend) 1977. BBJPL: 5-22 v Glamorgan (Leicester) 1979. BBBH: 3-17 v Cambridge U (Leicester) 1972.

**Leslie Brian TAYLOR** (Heathfield HS, Earl Shilton) B Earl Shilton, Leics 25/10/1953. 6ft 3½ins tall. RHB, RFM. Debut 1977. Hat-trick v Middlesex (Leicester) 1979. HS: 15 v Kent (Canterbury) 1978. HSJPL: 15* v Somerset (Taunton) 1980. BB: 6-61 v Essex (Ilford) 1979. BBGC: 3-11 v Hants (Leicester) 1978. BBJPL: 5-23 v Notts (Nottingham) 1978.

**Roger William TOLCHARD** (Malvern College) B Torquay 15/6/1946. RHB, WK. Played for Devon in 1963 and 1964. Also played for Hants 2nd XI and Public Schools v Combined Services (Lord's) in 1964. Debut 1965. Cap 1966. Appointed Vice-Captain in 1970. Relinquished appointment in 1973. Appointed County Cap-

101

## LEICESTERSHIRE

tain for 1981. Tests: 4 in 1976-77. Tours: India, Pakistan and Sri Lanka 1972-73, India, Sri Lanka and Australia 1976-77, Australia 1978-79. Scored 998 runs (av. 30.24) in 1970. Shared in 5th-wicket partnership record for county, 235 with N.E. Briers v Somerset (Leicester) 1979. Benson & Hedges Gold Awards: 4. HS: 126* v Cambridge U (Cambridge) 1970. HSGC: 86* v Glos (Leicester) 1975. HSJPL: 103 v Middlesex (Lord's) 1972 and was dismissed obstructing the field. HSBH: 92* v Worcs (Worcester) 1976. Had soccer trial for Leicester City.

**David Alan WENLOCK** (Lutterworth GS) B Leicester 16/4/1959. RHB, RM. Played for 2nd XI in 1979. Debut 1980. HS: 13* v Warwickshire (Leicester) 1980. HSJPL: 11 v Sussex (Hove) 1980. HSBH: 15 v Lancs (Leicester) 1980.

NB. The following players whose particulars appeared in the 1980 annual have been omitted: B. Dudleston (left staff), M. Schepens (not re-engaged) and K. Shuttleworth (not re-engaged). In addition J. Birkenshaw has joined Worcestershire and his particulars will be found under that county.
  The career records of all these players will be found elsewhere in this annual.

# County Averages

**Schweppes County Championship: Played 22, Won 4, Drawn 16, Lost 2.**
**All first-class matches: Played 25, Won 4, Drawn 18, Lost 3.**

### BATTING AND FIELDING

| Cap | | M | I | NO | Runs | HS | Avge | 100 | 50 | Ct | St |
|---|---|---|---|---|---|---|---|---|---|---|---|
| 1971 | B.F. Davison | 21 | 32 | 4 | 1310 | 151 | 46.78 | 2 | 8 | 18 | — |
| 1973 | J.C. Balderstone | 24 | 39 | 5 | 1472 | 158* | 43.29 | 2 | 9 | 17 | — |
| 1966 | R.W. Tolchard | 23 | 34 | 8 | 898 | 109 | 34.53 | 1 | 6 | 43 | 6 |
| 1977 | D.I. Gower | 22 | 32 | 1 | 1041 | 138 | 33.58 | 2 | 3 | 15 | — |
| 1971 | J.F. Steele | 22 | 37 | 4 | 979 | 118 | 29.66 | 2 | 4 | 16 | — |
| 1965 | J. Birkenshaw | 14 | 18 | 4 | 412 | 76 | 29.42 | — | 2 | 8 | — |
| 1976 | P. Booth | 4 | 3 | 1 | 49 | 41* | 24.50 | — | — | 1 | — |
| 1976 | P.B. Clift | 22 | 26 | 5 | 512 | 67 | 24.38 | — | 3 | 12 | — |
| | T.J. Boon | 8 | 12 | 1 | 253 | 53 | 23.00 | — | 1 | — | — |
| | N.E. Briers | 19 | 26 | 2 | 444 | 94 | 18.50 | — | 2 | 5 | — |
| 1969 | B. Dudleston | 8 | 14 | 1 | 234 | 83 | 18.00 | — | 2 | 2 | — |
| | D.A. Wenlock | 4 | 5 | 3 | 30 | 13* | 15.00 | — | — | 1 | — |
| | N.G.B. Cook | 25 | 24 | 9 | 180 | 75 | 12.00 | — | 1 | 13 | — |
| | G.J. Parsons | 14 | 13 | 4 | 106 | 25* | 11.77 | — | — | 8 | — |
| | J.P. Agnew | 15 | 13 | 0 | 98 | 31 | 7.53 | — | — | 5 | — |
| | L.B. Taylor | 19 | 14 | 8 | 28 | 8 | 4.66 | — | — | 7 | — |

*Played in three matches:* K. Higgs 7*, 2* (2 ct); K. Shuttleworth 0, 6 (1 ct)
*Played in two matches:* M.A. Garnham 14 (2 ct)
*Played in one match:* I.P. Butcher and R.A. Cobb did not bat; M. Schepens 8, 0.

**BOWLING**

| | Type | O | M | R | W | Avge | Best | 5 wI | 10 wM |
|---|---|---|---|---|---|---|---|---|---|
| J.F. Steele | SLA | 347.5 | 139 | 704 | 40 | 17.60 | 7-29 | 1 | — |
| P.B. Clift | RM | 551.3 | 172 | 1282 | 56 | 22.89 | 5-43 | 2 | — |
| N.G.B. Cook | SLA | 754.1 | 237 | 1856 | 75 | 24.74 | 5-17 | 4 | — |
| J.P. Agnew | RF | 247.4 | 52 | 880 | 31 | 28.38 | 4-36 | — | — |
| G.J. Parsons | RM | 206 | 40 | 722 | 24 | 30.08 | 4-38 | — | — |
| J. Birkenshaw | OB | 135.4 | 35 | 374 | 12 | 31.16 | 4-34 | — | — |
| K. Higgs | RFM | 96.5 | 30 | 222 | 6 | 37.00 | 3-80 | — | — |
| L.B. Taylor | RFM | 385.5 | 83 | 1164 | 30 | 38.80 | 4-59 | — | — |
| P. Booth | RFM | 71 | 19 | 217 | 5 | 43.40 | 3-49 | — | — |
| J.C. Balderstone | SLA | 129.4 | 37 | 368 | 8 | 46.00 | 2-17 | — | — |

*Also bowled:* T.J. Boon 13-5-50-0; N.E. Briers 13-2-36-0; B.F. Davison 13.4-2-56-1; B. Dudleston 9-4-11-2; D.I. Gower 2-1-1-0; K. Shuttleworth 52-9-140-1; D.A. Wenlock 27.5-4-89-2.

# County Records

**First-class cricket**

| Highest innings totals: | For – 701-4d v Worcestershire (Worcester) | 1906 |
|---|---|---|
| | Agst – 739-7d by Nottinghamshire (Nottingham) | 1903 |
| Lowest innings totals: | For – 25 v Kent (Leicester) | 1912 |
| | Agst – 24 by Glamorgan (Leicester) | 1971 |
| Highest individual innings: | For – 252* S. Coe v Northants (Leicester) | 1914 |
| | Agst – 341 G.H. Hirst for Yorkshire (Leicester) | 1905 |
| Best bowling in an innings: | For – 10-18 G. Geary v Glamorgan (Pontypridd) | 1929 |
| | Agst – 10-32 H Pickett for Essex (Leyton) | 1958 |
| Best bowling in a match: | For – 16-96 G. Geary v Glamorgan (Pontypridd) | 1929 |
| | Agst – 16-102 C. Blythe for Kent (Leicester) | 1909 |
| Most runs in a season: | 2,446 (av. 52.04) G.L. Berry | 1937 |
| runs in a career: | 30,143 (av. 30.32) G.L. Berry | 1924-1951 |
| 100s in a season: | 7 by G.L. Berry and W. Watson | 1937 and 1959 |
| 100s in a career: | 45 by G.L. Berry | 1924-1951 |
| wickets in a season: | 170 (av. 18.96) J.E. Walsh | 1948 |
| wickets in a career: | 2,130 (av. 23.19) W.E. Astill | 1906-1939 |

## RECORD WICKET STANDS

| 1st | 390 | B. Dudleston & J.F. Steele v Derbyshire (Leicester) | 1979 |
|---|---|---|---|
| 2nd | 287 | W. Watson & A. Wharton v Lancashire (Leicester) | 1961 |
| 3rd | 316* | W. Watson & A. Wharton v Somerset (Taunton) | 1961 |
| 4th | 270 | C.S. Dempster & G.S. Watson v Yorkshire (Hull) | 1937 |
| 5th | 235 | N.E. Briers & R.W. Tolchard v Somerset (Leicester) | 1979 |
| 6th | 262 | A.T. Sharpe & G.H.S. Fowke v Derbyshire (Chesterfield) | 1911 |
| 7th | 206 | B. Dudleston & J. Birkenshaw v Kent (Canterbury) | 1969 |
| 8th | 164 | M.R. Hallam & C.T. Spencer v Essex (Leicester) | 1964 |
| 9th | 160 | W.W. Odell & R.T. Crawford v Worcestershire (Leicester) | 1902 |
| 10th | 228 | R. Illingworth & K. Higgs v Northamptonshire (Leicester) | 1977 |

## LEICESTERSHIRE

### One-day cricket

| | | | |
|---|---|---|---|
| Highest innings totals: | Gillette Cup | 326-6 v Worcestershire (Leicester) | 1979 |
| | John Player League | 262-6 v Somerset (Frome) | 1970 |
| | Benson & Hedges Cup | 327-4 v Warwickshire (Coventry) | 1972 |
| Lowest innings totals: | Gillete Cup | 56 v Northamptonshire (Leicester) | 1964 |
| | John Player League | 36 v Sussex (Leicester) | 1973 |
| | Benson & Hedges Cup | 82 v Hampshire (Leicester) | 1973 |
| Highest individual innings: | Gillette Cup | 125 B. Dudleston v Worcestershire (Leicester) | 1979 |
| | John Player League | 152 B. Dudleston v Lancs (Manchester) | 1975 |
| | Benson & Hedges Cup | 158* B.F. Davison v Warwickshire (Coventry) | 1972 |
| Best bowling figures: | Gillette Cup | 6-20 K. Higgs v Staffs (Longton) | 1975 |
| | John Player League | 6-17 K. Higgs v Glamorgan (Leicester) | 1973 |
| | Benson & Hedges Cup | 5-20 R. Illingworth v Somerset (Leicester) | 1974 |

# MIDDLESEX

**Formation of present club:** 1863.
**Colours:** Blue.
**Badge:** Three seaxes.
**County Champions (7):** 1866, 1903, 1920, 1921, 1947, 1976 and 1980.
**Joint Champions (2):** 1949 and 1977.
**Gillette Cup Winners (2):** 1977 and 1980.
**Gillette Cup Finalists:** 1975.
**Best Position in John Player League:** 3rd in 1977 and 1980.
**Benson & Hedges Cup Finalists:** 1975.
**Gillette Man of the Match Awards:** 27.
**Benson & Hedges Gold Awards:** 21.

**Secretary:** A.J. Burridge, Lord's Cricket Ground, St. John's Wood Road, London NW8 8QN.
**Captain:** J.M. Brearley, OBE.
**Prospects of Play Telephone No:** 01-286 8011

**Graham Derek BARLOW** (Ealing GS) B Folkestone 26/3/1950. LHB, RM. Played in MCC Schools matches at Lord's 1968. Debut 1969. Cap 1976. Tests: 3 in 1976-77 and 1977. Tour: India, Sri Lanka and Australia 1976-77. 1,000 runs (4) – 1,478 runs (av. 49.26) in 1976 best. Gillette Man of the Match Awards: 1. Benson & Hedges Gold Awards: 2. HS: 160* v Derbyshire (Lord's) 1976. HSTC: 7* v India (Calcutta) 1976-77. HSGC: 76* v Warwickshire (Birmingham) 1975. HSJPL: 114 v Warwickshire (Lord's) 1979. HSBH: 129 v Northants (Northampton) 1977. Studied at Loughborough College for whom he played rugby.

**John Michael (Mike) BREARLEY** (City of London School and Cambridge) B Harrow 28/4/1942. RHB. Occasional WK. Debut 1961 scoring 1,222 runs (av. 35.94) in first season. Blue 1961-62-63-64 (capt 1963-64). Cap 1964. Elected Best Young Cricketer of the Year in 1964 by the Cricket Writers' Club. Did not play in 1966 or 1967, but re-appeared in latter half of each season between 1968 and 1970. Appointed County Captain in 1971. Wisden 1976. Awarded OBE in 1978 New Year Honours List. Benefit (£31,000) in 1978. Tests: 35 between 1976 and 1979-80, captaining England in 27 Tests between 1977 and 1979. Tours: South Africa 1964-65, Pakistan 1966-67 (captain), India, Sri Lanka and Australia (vice-captain) 1976-77, Pakistan and New Zealand 1977-78 (captain), returned home early owing to injury, Australia 1978-79 (captain), Australia and India 1979-80 (captain). 1,000 runs (9) – 2,178 runs (av. 44.44) in 1964 best. Holds record for most runs scored for Cambridge University (4,310 runs, av. 38.48). Gillette Man of the Match Awards: 4. Benson & Hedges Gold Awards: 3. HS: 312* MCC Under-25 v North Zone (Peshawar) 1966-67. HSUK: 173* v Glamorgan (Cardiff) 1974. HSTC: 91 v India (Bombay) 1976-77. HSGC: 124* v Bucks (Lord's) 1975. HSJPL 109* v Somerset (Taunton) 1980. HSBH: 100* v Surrey (Lord's) 1980.*

**Roland Orlando BUTCHER** B East Point, St. Philip, Barbados 14/10/1953. RHB, RM. Debut 1974. Played for Barbados in 1974-75 Shell Shield competition. Cap 1979. Has qualified as an English player and appeared in second Prudential match v Australia 1980. Tour: West Indies 1980-81. HS: 179 v Yorks (Scarborough) 1980. HSGC: 50* v Surrey (Lord's) 1980. HSJPL: 94 v Surrey (Oval) 1979.

**Mark Francis COHEN** (Stratford College, Cork) B Cork, Irish Republic

27/3/1961. RHB. Debut 1980 for Ireland v Scotland (Perth). Has joined county for 1981.

**Norman George COWANS** B Enfield St. Mary, Jamaica 17/4/1961. 6ft 3ins tall. RHB, RFM. Played for 2nd XI since 1978. Debut 1980. One match v Oxford U (Oxford).

**Wayne Wendell DANIEL** B St. Philip, Barbados 16/1/1956. RHB, RF. Toured England with West Indies Schoolboys team 1974. Played for 2nd XI in 1975. Debut for Barbados 1975-76. Debut for county and cap 1977. Tests: 5 for West Indies in 1975-76 and 1976. Tour: West Indies to England 1976. Gillette Man of the Match Awards: 2. Benson & Hedges Gold Awards: 2. Took 51 wickets (av. 13.72) in limited-overs matches in 1980 to equal record of R.J. Clapp of Somerset in 1974. HS: 53* Barbados v Jamaica (Bridgetown) 1979-80. HSC: 30* v Notts (Lord's) 1978. HSTC: 11 West Indies v India (Kingston) 1975-76. HSGC: 14 v Lancs (Manchester) 1978. HSJPL: 14 v Kent (Lord's) 1980. HSBH: 20* v Derbyshire (Derby) 1978. BB: 7-95 Barbados v Guyana (Georgetown) 1979-80. BBC: 6-33 v Sussex (Lord's) 1977. BBTC: 4-53 West Indies v England (Nottingham) 1976. BBGC: 6-15 v Sussex (Hove) 1980. BBJPL: 4-12 v Worcs (Worcester) 1980. BBBH: 7-12 v Minor Counties (East) (Ipswich) 1978 – record for competition.

**Paul Rupert DOWNTON** (Sevenoaks School) B Farnborough, Kent 4/4/1957. Son of G. Downton, former Kent player. RHB, WK. Played for Kent 2nd XI at age of 16. Vice-captain of England Young Cricketers team to West Indies 1976. Debut for Kent 1977. Cap 1979. Left county after 1979 season and made debut for Middlesex in 1980. Tours: Pakistan and New Zealand 1977-78, West Indies 1980-81. HS: 90* v Derbyshire (Uxbridge) 1980. HSGC: 10 v Sussex (Hove) 1980. HSJPL: 19* Kent v Worcs (Canterbury) 1979. Studied Law at Exeter University.

**Phillipe Henri (Phil) EDMONDS** (Gilbert Rennie HS, Lusaka, Skinner's School, Tunbridge Wells, Cranbrook School and Cambridge) B Lusaka, Northern Rhodesia (now Zambia) 8/3/1951. RHB, SLA. Debut for Cambridge U and county 1971. Blue 1971-73 (capt in 1973). Cap 1974. Elected Best Young Cricketer of the Year in 1974 by the Cricket Writers' Club. Played for Eastern Province in 1975-76 Currie Cup competition. Tests: 18 between 1975 and 1979. Tours: Pakistan and New Zealand 1977-78, Australia 1978-79. Benson & Hedges Gold Awards: 1. HS: 141* v Glamorgan (Lord's) 1979. HSTC: 50 v New Zealand (Christchurch) 1977-78. HSGC: 63* v Somerset (Lord's) 1979. HSJPL: 52 v Somerset (Taunton) 1980. HSBH: 44* v Notts (Newark) 1976. BB: 8-132 (14-150 match) v Glos (Lord's) 1977. BBTC: 7-66 v Pakistan (Karachi) 1977-78. BBGC: 3-28 v Yorks (Lord's) 1979. BBJPL: 3-19 v Leics (Lord's) 1973. BBBH: 4-11 v Kent (Lord's) 1975. Also played rugby for University and narrowly missed obtaining Blue.

**Richard Gary ELLIS** B Paddington 20/10/1960. RHB. Joined staff 1979. Has yet to appear in first-class cricket. Is studying at Oxford University.

**John Ernest EMBUREY** B Peckham 20/8/1952. RHB, OB. Played for Surrey Young Cricketers 1969-70. Joined county staff 1972. Debut 1973. Cap 1977. Tests: 10 between 1978 and 1980. Tours: Australia 1978-79, Australia and India 1979-80 (as replacement for G. Miller), West Indies 1980-81. Benson & Hedges Gold Awards: 1. HS: 91* v Surrey (Oval) 1979. HSTC: 42 v Australia (Adelaide) 1978-79. HSGC: 36* v Lancs (Manchester) 1978. HSJPL: 30 v Lancs (Lord's) 1978. HSBH: 34* v Sussex (Lord's) 1980. BB: 7-36 v Cambridge U (Cambridge) 1977. BBTC: 4-46 v Australia (Sydney) 1978-79. BBJPL: 4-43 v Worcs (Worcester) 1976. BBBH: 3-35 v Kent (Lord's) 1980.

**Michael William (Mike) GATTING** (John Kelly Boys HS, Cricklewood) B Kingsbury, Middlesex 6/6/1957. RHB, RM. Represented England Young Cricketers 1974. Debut 1975. Toured West Indies with England Young Cricketers 1976. Cap 1977. Tests: 7 in 1977-78 and 1980. Tours: Pakistan and New Zealand 1977-78, West Indies 1980-81. 1,000 runs (2) – 1,166 runs (av. 33.31) in 1978 best. Gillette Man of the Match Awards: 1. Benson & Hedges Gold Awards: 2. HS: 136 v Surrey (Lord's) 1980. HSTC: 56 v West Indies (Manchester) 1980. HSGC: 95* v Notts (Nottingham) 1980. HSJPL: 85 v Notts (Lord's) 1976. HSBH 95* v Somerset (Taunton) 1980. BB: 5-59 v Leics (Lord's) 1978. BBJPL: 4-32 v Kent (Lord's) 1978. BBBH: 3-19 v Kent (Lord's) 1980.

**Simon Peter HUGHES** (Latymer Upper School, Hammersmith) B Kingston-upon-Thames 20/12/1959. RHB, RFM. Played for 2nd XI in 1979. Debut 1980. Gillette Man of the Match Awards: 1. BB: 4-36 v Glamorgan (Cardiff) 1980. BBGC: 3-23 v Worcs (Worcester) 1980. Is studying geography at Durham University.

**Kevan David JAMES** (Edmonton Comprehensive School) B Lambeth 18/3/1961. LHB, LM. Played for 2nd XI since 1978. Toured Australia in 1979 and West Indies in 1980 with England Young Cricketers. Debut 1980. Played in one match v Oxford U (Oxford), one Benson & Hedges match and one John Player League match. HS: 16 v Oxford U (Oxford) 1980. BB: 3-14 v Oxford U (Oxford) 1980.

**Rajesh Jaman MARU** (Pinner VIth Form College) B Nairobi, Kenya 28/10/1962. RHB, SLA. Played for 2nd XI in 1979. Toured West Indies in 1980 with England Young Cricketers. Debut 1980. HS: 13 v Essex (Lord's) 1980. BB: 3-29 v Warwickshire (Birmingham) 1980.

**William Gerald (Bill) MERRY** B Newbury, Berks 8/8/1955. RHB, RM. Played for Leics 2nd XI in 1976 and for Hertfordshire between 1976 and 1978. Debut 1979. HS: 6* v Cambridge U (Cambridge) 1980. BB: 4-24 v Somerset (Taunton) 1980. BBJPL: 3-29 v Lancs (Manchester) 1979. BBBH: 3-19 Minor Counties (West) v Derbyshire (Derby) 1978.

**Clive Thornton RADLEY** (King Edward VI GS, Norwich) B Hertford 13/5/1944. RHB, LB. Debut 1964. Cap 1967. Benefit (£26,000) in 1977. *Wisden* 1978. Tests: 8 in 1977-78 and 1978. Tours: Pakistan and New Zealand 1977-78 (as replacement for J.M. Brearley), Australia 1978-79. 1,000 runs (13) – 1,491 runs (av. 57.34) in 1980 best. Shared in 6th wicket partnership record for county, 227 with F.J. Titmus v South Africans (Lord's) 1965. Gillette Man of the Match Awards: 2. Benson & Hedges Gold Awards: 2. HS: 171 v Cambridge U (Cambridge) 1976. HSTC: 158 v New Zealand (Auckland) 1977-78. HSGC: 105* v Worcs (Worcester) 1975. HSJPL: 133* v Glamorgan (Lord's) 1969. HSBH: 121* v Minor Counties (East) (Lord's) 1976.

**Michael Walter William (Mike) SELVEY** (Battersea GS and Manchester and Cambridge Universities) B Chiswick 25/4/1948. RHB, RFM. Debut for Surrey 1968. Debut for Cambridge U and Blue 1971. Debut for Middlesex 1972. Cap 1973. Played for Orange Free State in 1973-74 Currie Cup competition. Tests: 3 in 1976 and 1976-77. Tour: India, Sri Lanka and Australia 1976-77. Took 101 wkts (av. 19.09) in 1978. Benson & Hedges Gold Awards: 1. HS: 45 v Essex (Colchester) 1979. HSGC: 14 v Derbyshire (Derby) 1978. HSJPL: 38 v Essex (Southend) 1977 and 38* v Essex (Chelmsford) 1979. HSBH: 27* v Surrey (Lord's) 1973. BB: 7-20 v Glos (Gloucester) 1976. BBTC: 4-41 v West Indies (Manchester) 1976. BBGC: 3-32 v Somerset (Lord's) 1977. BBJPL: 5-18 v Glamorgan (Cardiff) 1975. BBBH: 5-39 v Glos (Lord's) 1972. Played soccer for University.

## MIDDLESEX

**Wilfred Norris SLACK** B Troumaca, St. Vincent 12/12/1954. LHB, RM. Played for Buckinghamshire in 1976. Debut 1977. HS: 66 v Notts (Nottingham) 1979. HSGC: 12 v Ireland (Lord's) 1980. HSJPL: 57 v Kent (Lord's) 1978. HSBH: 42 v Northants (Lord's) 1980.

**Andrew Geoffrey SMITH** B Muswell Hill 10/6/1957. RHB. Joined staff 1980. Has yet to appear in first-class cricket.

**Keith Patrick TOMLINS** (St. Benedict's School, Ealing) B Kingston-upon-Thames 23/10/1957. RHB, RM. Debut 1977. HS: 94 v Worcs (Worcester) 1978. HSJPL: 16 v Glos (Cheltenham) 1980. BBJPL: 4-24 v Notts (Lord's) 1978. Studied at Durham University.

**Vintcent Adriaan Pieter VAN DER BIJL** (Diocesan College, Rondebosch) B Cape Town 19/3/1948. 6ft 7ins tall. Son of P.G.V. Van der Bijl, former South African Test cricketer. RHB, RFM. Debut for South African Universities v Western Province 1967-68. Debut for Natal 1968-69. Toured England with W. Isaacs XI in 1969. Debut for county 1980. Cap 1980. *Wisden* 1980. Gillette Man of the Match Awards: 1. Benson & Hedges Gold Awards: 1. HS: 87 Natal v Zimbabwe-Rhodesia (Durban) 1979-80. HSC: 76 v Notts (Lord's) 1980. HSGC: 25 v Ireland (Lord's) and 25 v Sussex (Hove) 1980. HSJPL: 47 v Kent (Lord's) 1980. HSBH: 30 v Sussex (Lord's) 1980. BB: 8-35 Natal v Western Province (Pietermaritzburg) 1971-72. BBC: 6-47 v Sussex (Hove) 1980. BBGC: 5-12 v Ireland (Lord's) 1980.

NB. The following players whose particulars appeared in the 1980 annual have been omitted: R.P. Moulding and M.J. Smith (retired). In addition P.B. Fisher and I.J. Gould have joined Worcestershire and Sussex respectively and their particulars will be found under these counties. F.J. Titmus who played in five matches has not been included.

The career records of all these players will be found elsewhere in this annual.

# County Averages

**Schweppes County Championship: Played 22, won 10, drawn 10, lost 2.
All first-class matches: Played 24, won 10, drawn 12, lost 2.**

## BATTING AND FIELDING

| Cap | | M | I | NO | Runs | HS | Avge | 100 | 50 | Ct | St |
|------|------------------|----|----|----|------|------|-------|-----|----|----|----|
| 1967 | C.T. Radley | 24 | 34 | 8 | 1491 | 136* | 57.34 | 5 | 5 | 18 | — |
| 1977 | M.W. Gatting | 14 | 16 | 3 | 645 | 136 | 49.61 | 2 | 2 | 15 | — |
| 1964 | J.M. Brearley | 23 | 33 | 5 | 1335 | 134* | 47.67 | 5 | 5 | 18 | — |
| 1976 | G.D. Barlow | 24 | 32 | 8 | 1002 | 128* | 41.75 | 3 | 4 | 11 | — |
| — | P.R. Downton | 9 | 15 | 2 | 521 | 90* | 40.07 | — | 4 | 26 | 3 |
| 1979 | R.O. Butcher | 16 | 22 | 2 | 792 | 179 | 39.60 | 2 | 3 | 16 | — |
| 1977 | I.J. Gould | 15 | 16 | 4 | 388 | 57 | 32.33 | — | 3 | 36 | 7 |
| — | V.A.P. Van der Bijl | 20 | 16 | 3 | 331 | 76 | 25.46 | — | 1 | 5 | — |
| 1973 | M.W.W. Selvey | 21 | 17 | 4 | 322 | 40* | 24.76 | — | 1 | 3 | — |
| — | K.P. Tomlins | 6 | 8 | 1 | 169 | 55 | 24.14 | — | 1 | 2 | — |
| 1977 | J.E. Emburey | 17 | 13 | 3 | 227 | 43* | 22.70 | — | — | 18 | — |
| — | W.N. Slack | 10 | 13 | — | 276 | 47 | 21.23 | — | — | 1 | — |
| 1974 | P.H. Edmonds | 15 | 11 | 1 | 177 | 52 | 17.70 | — | 1 | 6 | — |
| 1967 | M.J. Smith | 5 | 6 | — | 83 | 24 | 13.83 | — | — | 1 | — |
| — | R.J. Maru | 9 | 7 | 1 | 49 | 13 | 8.16 | — | — | 8 | — |
| — | F.J. Titmus | 5 | 6 | 3 | 23 | 10* | 7.66 | — | — | 2 | — |
| 1977 | W.W. Daniel | 19 | 12 | 4 | 56 | 15 | 7.00 | — | — | 3 | — |
| — | S.P. Hughes | 5 | 4 | 2 | 0 | 0* | 0.00 | — | — | 3 | — |
| — | W.G. Merry | 5 | 1 | 1 | 6 | 6* | — | — | — | 1 | — |

*Played in one match:* K.D. James 16; N.G. Cowans 1.

## BOWLING

| | Type | O | M | R | W | Avge | Best | 5 wI | 10 wM |
|---------------------|------|-------|-----|------|----|-------|------|------|-------|
| V.A.P. Van der Bijl | RFM | 642.3 | 217 | 1252 | 85 | 14.72 | 6-47 | 4 | 1 |
| J.E. Emburey | OB | 648.5 | 219 | 1296 | 68 | 19.05 | 6-31 | 5 | 1 |
| S.P. Hughes | RFM | 110.4 | 25 | 352 | 18 | 19.55 | 4-36 | — | — |
| W.G. Merry | RM | 96 | 21 | 300 | 15 | 20.00 | 4-24 | — | — |
| W.W. Daniel | RF | 492.5 | 112 | 1454 | 67 | 21.70 | 5-32 | 1 | — |
| F.J. Titmus | OB | 149.2 | 38 | 313 | 12 | 26.08 | 3-55 | — | — |
| P.H. Edmonds | SLA | 449 | 140 | 1073 | 37 | 29.00 | 5-94 | 1 | — |
| M.W. Gatting | RM | 61.4 | 9 | 192 | 6 | 32.00 | 2-3 | — | — |
| M.W.W. Selvey | RFM | 485.3 | 155 | 1188 | 37 | 32.10 | 5-42 | 2 | — |
| R.J. Maru | SLA | 140.4 | 36 | 412 | 12 | 34.33 | 3-29 | — | — |

*Also bowled:* G.D. Barlow 8-0-31-2; J.M. Brearley 16.4-3-70-0; N.G. Cowans 16-4-42-1; I.J. Gould 2-1-1-0; K.D. James 15-6-29-4; C.T. Radley 8-2-23-3; K.P. Tomlins 31-8-103-0.

# County Records

### First-class cricket

| | | |
|---|---|---|
| Highest innings totals: | For – 642-3d v Hampshire (Southampton) | 1923 |
| | Agst – 665 by West Indians (Lord's) | 1939 |
| Lowest innings totals: | For – 20 v MCC (Lord's) | 1864 |
| | Agst – 31 by Gloucestershire (Bristol) | 1924 |
| Highest individual innings: | For – 331* J.D.B. Robertson v Worcs (Worcester) | 1949 |
| | Agst – 316* J.B. Hobbs for Surrey (Lord's) | 1926 |
| Best bowling in an innings: | For – 10-40 G.O.B. Allen v Lancs (Lord's) | 1929 |
| | Agst – 9-38 R.C. Robertson-Glasgow for Somerset (Lord's) | 1924 |
| Best bowling in a match: | For – 16-114 { G. Burton v Yorks (Sheffield) | 1888 |
| | { J.T. Hearne v Lancs (Manchester) | 1898 |
| | Agst – 16-109 C.W.L. Parker for Glos (Cheltenham) | 1930 |
| Most runs in a season: | 2,650 (av. 85.48) W.J. Edrich | 1947 |
| runs in a career: | 40,302 (av. 49.81) E.H. Hendren | 1907-1937 |
| 100s in a season: | 13 by D.C.S. Compton | 1947 |
| 100s in a career: | 119 by E.H. Hendren | 1907-1937 |
| wickets in a season: | 158 (av. 14.63) F.J. Titmus | 1955 |
| wickets in a career: | 2,358 (av. 21.25) F.J. Titmus | 1949-1980 |

### RECORD WICKET STANDS

| | | | |
|---|---|---|---|
| 1st | 312 | W.E. Russell & M.J. Harris v Pakistanis (Lord's) | 1967 |
| 2nd | 380 | F.A. Tarrant & J.W. Hearne v Lancashire (Lord's) | 1914 |
| 3rd | 424* | W.J. Edrich & D.C.S. Compton v Somerset (Lord's) | 1948 |
| 4th | 325 | J.W. Hearne & E.H. Hendren v Hampshire (Lord's) | 1919 |
| 5th | 338 | R.S. Lucas & T.C. O'Brien v Sussex (Hove) | 1895 |
| 6th | 227 | C.T. Radley & F.J. Titmus v South Africans (Lord's) | 1965 |
| 7th | 271* | E.H. Hendren & F.T. Mann v Nottinghamshire (Nottingham) | 1925 |
| 8th | 182* | M.H.C. Doll & H.R. Murrell v Nottinghamshire (Lord's) | 1913 |
| 9th | 160* | E.H. Hendren & T.J. Durston v Essex (Leyton) | 1927 |
| 10th | 230 | R.W. Nicholls & W. Roche v Kent (Lord's) | 1899 |

### One-day cricket

| | | | |
|---|---|---|---|
| Highest innings totals: | Gillette Cup | 280-8 v Sussex (Lord's) | 1965 |
| | John Player League | 256-9 v Worcs (Worcester) | 1976 |
| | Benson & Hedges Cup | 303-7 v Northants (Northampton) | 1977 |
| Lowest innings totals: | Gillette Cup | 41 v Essex (Westcliff) | 1972 |
| | John Player League | 23 v Yorkshire (Leeds) | 1974 |
| | Benson & Hedges Cup | 97 v Northants (Lord's) | 1976 |
| Highest individual innings: | Gillette Cup | 124* J.M. Brearley v Buckinghamshire (Lord's) | 1975 |
| | John Player League | 133* C.T. Radley v Glamorgan (Lord's) | 1969 |
| | Benson & Hedges Cup | 129 G.D. Barlow v Northants (Northampton) | 1977 |
| Best bowling figures: | Gillette Cup | 6-15 W.W. Daniel v Sussex (Hove) | 1980 |
| | John Player League | 6-6 R.W. Hooker v Surrey (Lord's) | 1969 |
| | Benson & Hedges Cup | 7-12 W.W. Daniel v Minor Counties (East) (Ipswich) | 1978 |

# NORTHAMPTONSHIRE

**Formation of present club:** 1820, reorganised 1878.
**Colours:** Maroon.
**Badge:** Tudor Rose.
**County Championship Runners-up (4):** 1912, 1957, 1965 and 1976.
**Gillette Cup Winners:** 1976.
**Gillette Cup Finalists:** 1979.
**Best final position in John Player League:** 4th in 1974.
**Benson & Hedges Cup Winners:** 1980.
**Fenner Trophy Winners:** 1978.
**Gillette Man of the Match Awards:** 17.
**Benson & Hedges Gold Awards:** 15.

**Secretary:** K.C. Turner, County Ground, Wantage Rd, Northampton, NN1 4TJ.
**Captain:** G. Cook.
**Prospects of Play Telephone No:** Northampton (064) 32697.

**Christopher Derek (Chris) BOODEN** (Ratcliffe Comprehensive School, Wolverton) B Newport Pagnell, Bucks 22/6/1961. RHB, RM. Played for 2nd XI since 1978. Debut 1980 (two matches). HS: 6* v Derbyshire (Derby) 1980.

**Robin James BOYD-MOSS** (Bedford School and Cambridge) B Hatton, Ceylon (now Sri Lanka) 16/12/1959. RHB, SLA. Played for Bedfordshire from 1977 to 1979 and for County 2nd XI in 1979. Debut for Cambridge U and County in 1980. Blue 1980. HS: 71 Cambridge U v Middlesex (Cambridge) 1980. HSC: 56 v Essex (Northampton) 1980. HSJPL: 34 v Yorks (Scarborough) 1980. HSBH: 58 Combined Universities v Northants (Northampton) 1980. Rugby Blue 1980-81.

**Robert Michael CARTER** B King's Lynn 25/5/1960. RHB, RM. Played for 2nd XI since 1976. Debut 1978. HS: 32 v Sussex (Eastbourne) 1980. HSJPL: 21* v Surrey (Oval) 1979. BB: 4-27 v Glos (Bristol) 1980. BBJPL: 3-35 v Worcs (Milton Keynes) 1978. Has played soccer for Norwich City.

**Geoffrey (Geoff) COOK** (Middlesbrough HS) B Middlesbrough 9/10/1951. RHB, SLA. Debut 1971. Cap 1975. Played for Eastern Province in 1978-79 and 1979-80 Currie Cup competition. Appointed County Captain for 1981. 1,000 runs (5) – 1,241 runs (av. 35.45) in 1979 best. Gillette Man of Match Awards: 2. Benson & Hedges Gold Awards: 1. HS: 172 Eastern Province v Northern Transvaal (Port Elizabeth) 1979-80. HSUK: 155 v Derbyshire (Northampton) 1978. HSGC: 114* v Surrey (Northampton) 1979. HSJPL: 85 v Leics (Leicester) 1976. HSBH: 96 v Minor Counties (East) (Northampton) 1978. Has played soccer for Wellingborough Town in Southern League.

**Brian James (Jim) GRIFFITHS** B Wellingborough 13/6/1949. RHB, RFM. Debut 1974. Cap 1978. HS: 11 v Middlesex (Lord's) 1978. BB:7-52 v Yorks (Leeds) 1980. BBGC: 3-39 v Leics (Northampton) 1979. BBJPL: 4-22 v Somerset (Weston-Super-Mare) 1977. BBBH: 5-43 v Sussex (Eastbourne) 1979.

**Allan Joseph LAMB** (Wynberg Boys' High School) B Langebaanweg, Cape Province, South Africa 20/6/1954. RHB, RM. Debut for Western Province in Currie Cup 1972-73. Debut for county and cap 1978. *Wisden* 1980. 1,000 runs (2) – 1,797

111

**NORTHAMPTONSHIRE**

runs (av. 66.55) in 1980 best. Benson & Hedges Gold Awards: 2. HS: 178 v Leics (Leicester) 1979. HSGC: 101 v Sussex (Hove) 1979. HSJPL: 77 v Warwickshire (Northampton) 1979. HSBH: 77 v Essex (Northampton) 1979.

**Hon. Timothy Michael (Tim) LAMB** (Shrewsbury School and Oxford) B Hartford, Cheshire 24/3/1953. Younger son of Lord Rochester. RHB, RM. Debut for Oxford U 1973. Blue 1973-74. Debut for Middlesex 1974. Left county and made debut for Northants in 1978. Cap 1978. Benson & Hedges Gold Awards: 1. HS: 77 Middlesex v Notts (Lord's) 1976. HSC: 33 v Notts (Northampton) 1978. HSGC: 12 v Surrey (Oval) 1980. HSJPL: 27. Middlesex v Hants (Basingstoke) 1976. HSBH: 10* v Combined Universities (Northampton) 1980. BB: 7-56 v Cambridge U (Cambridge) 1980. BBGC: 4-52 v Sussex (Hove) 1979. BBJPL: 5-13 v Notts (Northampton) 1979. BBBH: 5-44 Middlesex v Yorks (Lord's) 1975.

**Wayne LARKINS** B Roxton, Beds 22/11/1953. RHB, RM. Joined staff 1969. Debut 1972. Cap 1976. Tests: 5 in 1979-80 and 1980. Tour: Australia and India 1979-80. 1,000 runs (3) – 1,772 runs (av. 45.43) in 1980 best. Shared in 2nd wkt partnership record for county, 322 with R.G. Williams v Leics (Leicester) 1980. "Hat-trick" in Benson & Hedges Cup v Combined Universities (Northampton) 1980. Benson & Hedges Gold Awards: 2. HS: 170* v Worcs (Northampton) 1978. HSTC: 33 v West Indies (Manchester) 1980. HSGC: 92* v Leics (Northampton) 1979. HSJPL: 111 v Leics (Wellingborough) 1979. HSBH: 108 v Warwickshire (Birmingham) 1980. BB: 3-34 v Somerset (Northampton) 1976. BBJPL: 5-32 v Essex (Ilford) 1978. BBBH: 4-37 v Combined Universities (Northampton) 1980.

**Neil Alan MALLENDER** (Beverley G.S.) B Kirk Sandall, Yorks 13/8/1961. RHB, RFM. Toured West Indies in 1980 with England Young Cricketers. Debut 1980. BB: 3-29 v Essex (Northampton) 1980.

**Ian George PECK** (Bedford School and Cambridge) B Great Staughton, Huntingdonshire 18/10/1957. RHB, WK. Played for Bedfordshire from 1976 to 1979. Debut for Cambridge U 1978. Blue 1980 (Captain). Re-elected captain for 1981. Debut for county 1980. One match v Somerset (Northampton). HS: 34 Cambridge U v Essex (Cambridge) 1980. HSBH: 31 Combined Universities v Worcs (Cambridge) 1980. Blue for Rugby 1979-80. Elected Rugby Captain for 1980-81 but had to relinquish post through injury. Toured Japan, Fiji and Tonga with England team in 1979.

**Sarfraz NAWAZ** (Government College, Lahore) B Lahore, Pakistan 1/12/1948. RHB, RFM. Debut 1967-68 for West Pakistan Governor's XI v Punjab University at Lahore and subsequently played for various Lahore sides and United Bank. Debut for county 1969. Not re-engaged after 1971 season, but rejoined staff in 1974. Cap 1975. Tests: 37 for Pakistan between 1968-69 and 1979-80. Tours: Pakistan to England 1971, 1974 and 1978, Australia and New Zealand 1972-73, Australia and West Indies 1976-77, New Zealand and Australia 1978-79. Took 101 wkts (av. 20.30) in 1975. Gillette Man of Match Awards: 1. Benson & Hedges Gold Awards: 1. HS: 86 v Essex (Chelmsford) 1975. HSTC: 55 Pakistan v West Indies (Lahore) 1980-81. HSGC: 39* v Surrey (Oval) 1980. HSJPL: 59* v Yorks (Scarborough) 1980. HSBH: 50 v Kent (Northampton) 1977. BB: 9-86 Pakistan v Australia (Melbourne) 1978-79. BBUK: 8-27 Pakistanis v Notts (Nottingham) 1974. BBC: 7-37 v Somerset (Weston-super-Mare) 1977. BBGC: 4-17 v Herts (Northampton) 1976. BBJPL: 5-15 v Yorks (Northampton) 1975. BBBH: 5-21 v Middlesex (Lord's) 1980.

**George SHARP** B West Hartlepool 12/3/1950. RHB, WK. Can also bowl SLA.

Debut 1968. Cap 1973. HS: 94 v Lancs (Southport) 1980. HSGC: 35* v Durham (Northampton) 1977. HSJPL: 47 v Sussex (Hove) 1974 and 47* v Worcs (Milton Keynes) 1978. HSBH: 43 v Surrey (Northampton) 1979.

**Robert Michael TINDALL** (Harrow School) B Harrow-on-the-Hill 16/6/1959. Son of M. Tindall of Cambridge U and Middlesex. LHB, SLA. Played for 2nd XI in 1978. Played in last John Player League match of 1979. Debut 1980. HS: 60* v Cambridge U (Cambridge) 1980. HSJPL: 14* v Hants (Bournemouth) 1979.

**Duncan James WILD** (Northampton GS) B Northampton 28/11/1962. Son of J. Wild, former Northants player. LHB, RM. Played for 2nd XI since 1978. Toured West Indies with England Young Cricketers in 1980. Debut 1980. One match v Cambridge U (Cambridge) 1980. HS: 22 v Cambridge U (Cambridge) 1980.

**Peter WILLEY** B Sedgefield, County Durham 6/12/1949. RHB, OB. Debut 1966 aged 16 years 180 days scoring 78 in second innings of first match v Cambridge U (Cambridge). Cap 1971. Benefit in 1981. Tests: 12 between 1976 and 1980. Tours: Australia and India 1979-80, West Indies 1980-81. 1,000 runs (2) – 1,115 runs (av. 41.29) in 1976 best. Shared in 4th wkt partnership record for county, 370 with R.T. Virgin v Somerset (Northampton) 1976. Gillette Man of Match Awards: 4. HS: 227 v Somerset (Northampton) 1976. HSTC: 100* v West Indies (Oval) 1980. HSGC: 89 v Sussex (Hove) 1979. HSJPL: 107 v Warwickshire (Birmingham) 1975 and 107 v Hants (Tring) 1976. HSBH: 66* v Warwickshire (Birmingham) 1980. BB: 7-37 v Oxford U (Oxford) 1975. BBGC: 3-37 v Cambs (March) 1975. BBJPL: 4-38 v Leics (Leicester) 1980. BBBH: 3-12 v Minor Counties (East) (Horton) 1977.

**Richard Grenville WILLIAMS** (Ellesmere Port GS) B Bangor, Caernarvonshire 10/8/1957. RHB, OB. 5ft 6½ins tall. Debut for 2nd XI in 1972, aged 14 years 11 months. Debut 1974 aged 16 years 313 days. Toured West Indies with England Young Cricketers 1976. Cap 1979. 1,000 runs (2) – 1,262 runs (av. 34.10) in 1980 best. Scored two centuries in match (109 and 151*) v Warwickshire (Northampton) 1979. Shared in 2nd-wkt partnership record for county, 322 with W. Larkins v Leics (Leicester) 1980. "Hat-trick" v Glos (Northampton) 1980. Gillette Man of Match Awards: 1. Benson & Hedges Gold Awards: 2. HS: 175* v Leics (Leicester) 1980. HSGC: 51 v Durham (Northampton) 1977. HSJPL: 69 v Warwickshire (Nuneaton) 1980. HSBH: 83 v Yorks (Bradford) 1980. BB: 7-73 v Cambridge U (Cambridge) 1980. BBGC: 3-15 v Leics (Northampton) 1979. BBJPL: 4-22 v Yorks (Scarborough) 1980.

**Thomas James (Jim) YARDLEY** (King Charles I GS Kidderminster) B Chaddesley Corbett, Worcs 27/10/1946. LHB, RM. Occasional WK. Debut for Worcs 1967. Cap 1972. Not re-engaged after 1975 season and made debut for Northants in 1976. Cap 1978. Scored 1,066 runs (av. 30.45) in 1971. HS: 135 Worcs v Notts (Worcester) 1973. HSC: 100* v Glos (Northampton) 1980. HSGC: 52 Worcs v Warwickshire (Birmingham) 1972 and 52* Worcs v Warwickshire (Birmingham) 1973. HSJPL: 66* v Middlesex (Lord's) 1977. HSBH: 75* Worcs v Warwickshire (Worcester) 1972.

NB. The following players whose particulars appeared in the 1980 annual have been omitted: V.A. Flynn, L. McFarlane, I.M. Richards and P.J. Watts (retired). In addition G. Forster who made his debut in one match v Cambridge University has joined Leicestershire and his particulars will be found under that county.

The career records of Watts and Forster will be found elsewhere in this annual.

# County Averages

**Schweppes County Championship: Played 22, Won 5, Drawn 13, Lost 4**
**All first-class matches: Played 24, Won 6, Drawn 13, Lost 5**

## BATTING AND FIELDING

| Cap | | M | I | NO | Runs | HS | Avge | 100 | 50 | Ct | St |
|------|------|----|----|----|------|------|-------|-----|----|----|----|
| 1978 | A.J. Lamb | 23 | 39 | 12 | 1797 | 152 | 66.55 | 5 | 6 | 11 | — |
| 1976 | W. Larkins | 20 | 36 | 3 | 1682 | 156 | 50.96 | 4 | 8 | 7 | — |
| 1979 | R.G. Williams | 24 | 41 | 4 | 1262 | 175* | 34.10 | 2 | 6 | 8 | — |
| 1975 | Sarfraz Nawaz | 17 | 16 | 5 | 324 | 50 | 29.45 | — | 1 | 14 | — |
| 1973 | G. Sharp | 23 | 28 | 8 | 562 | 94 | 28.10 | — | 3 | 39 | 3 |
| 1975 | G. Cook | 22 | 39 | 4 | 976 | 109 | 27.88 | 2 | 3 | 21 | — |
| 1978 | T.J. Yardley | 24 | 31 | 5 | 685 | 100* | 26.34 | 1 | 4 | 21 | — |
| — | R.M. Tindall | 8 | 14 | 3 | 204 | 60* | 18.54 | — | 1 | 3 | — |
| 1962 | P.J. Watts | 14 | 15 | 3 | 220 | 37* | 18.33 | — | — | 11 | — |
| 1971 | P. Willey | 13 | 19 | 2 | 305 | 73 | 17.94 | — | 2 | 2 | — |
| 1978 | T.M. Lamb | 24 | 21 | 12 | 108 | 13* | 12.00 | — | — | 8 | — |
| — | R.M. Carter | 13 | 20 | 2 | 213 | 32 | 11.83 | — | — | 4 | — |
| — | R.J. Boyd-Moss | 7 | 10 | 1 | 106 | 56 | 11.77 | — | 1 | 3 | — |
| 1978 | B.J. Griffiths | 22 | 16 | 1 | 35 | 10 | 2.33 | — | — | 5 | — |
| — | N.A. Mallender | 5 | 6 | 3 | 2 | 2* | 1.33 | — | 1 | 1 | — |

*Played in two matches:* C.D. Booden 6* (1 ct)
*Played in one match:* I.G. Peck 4; G. Forster did not bat (1 ct); D.J. Wild 0, 22 (1 ct).

## BOWLING

| | Type | O | M | R | W | Avge | Best | 5 wI | 10 wM |
|------|------|-------|-----|------|-----|-------|------|----|----|
| T.M. Lamb | RM | 627 | 162 | 1725 | 66 | 26.13 | 7-56 | 2 | — |
| Sarfraz Nawaz | RFM | 408.1 | 114 | 1104 | 36 | 30.66 | 6-49 | 3 | — |
| R.M. Carter | RM | 77.2 | 12 | 312 | 10 | 31.20 | 4-27 | — | — |
| B.J. Griffiths | RFM | 564.3 | 143 | 1612 | 51 | 31.60 | 7-52 | 2 | — |
| R.G. Williams | OB | 535.5 | 100 | 1611 | 48 | 33.56 | 7-73 | 3 | — |
| P. Willey | OB | 405.5 | 107 | 938 | 26 | 36.07 | 5-85 | 1 | — |
| N.A. Mallender | RFM | 114.4 | 21 | 393 | 7 | 56.14 | 3-29 | — | — |

*Also bowled:* C.D. Booden 34-1-111-0; R.J. Boyd-Moss 37-4-130-1; G. Cook 3-0-11-0; G. Forster 30-5-100-3; A.J. Lamb 5-0-27-1; W. Larkins 42-3-181-2; G. Sharp 13-2-47-1; R.M. Tindall 32.4-2-162-2; P.J. Watts 8-0-54-0; T.J. Yardley 3-0-14-0.

# County Records

### First-class cricket

| | | |
|---|---|---|
| Highest innings totals: | For – 557-6d v Sussex (Hove) | 1914 |
| | Agst – 670-9d by Sussex (Hove) | 1921 |
| Lowest innings totals: | For – 12 v Gloucestershire (Gloucester) | 1907 |
| | Agst – 33 by Lancashire (Northampton) | 1977 |
| Highest individual innings | For – 300 R. Subba Row v Surrey (The Oval) | 1958 |
| | Agst – 333 K. S. Duleepsinhji for Sussex (Hove) | 1930 |
| Best bowling in an innings: | For – 10-127 V. W. C. Jupp v Kent (Tunbridge Wells) | 1932 |
| | Agst – 10-30 C. Blythe for Kent (Northampton) | 1907 |
| Best bowling in a match: | For – 15-31 G. E. Tribe v Yorkshire (Northampton) | 1958 |
| | Agst – 17-48 C. Blythe for Kent (Northampton) | 1907 |
| Most runs in a season: | 2198 (av. 51.11) D. Brookes | 1952 |
| runs in a career: | 28980 (av. 36.13) D. Brookes | 1934-1959 |
| 100s in a season: | 8 by R. Haywood | 1921 |
| 100s in a career: | 67 by D. Brookes | 1934-1959 |
| wickets in a season: | 175 (av. 18.70) G. E. Tribe | 1955 |
| wickets in a career: | 1097 (av. 21.31) E. W. Clark | 1922-1947 |

## RECORDS WICKET STANDS

| | | | |
|---|---|---|---|
| 1st | 361 | N. Oldfield & V. Broderick v Scotland (Peterborough) | 1953 |
| 2nd | 322 | W. Larkins & R. G. Williams v Leicestershire (Leicester) | 1980 |
| 3rd | 320 | T. L. Livingston & F. Jakeman v South Africans (Northampton) | 1951 |
| 4th | 370 | R. T. Virgin & P. Willey v Somerset (Northampton) | 1976 |
| 5th | 347 | D. Brookes & D. Barrick v Essex (Northampton) | 1952 |
| 6th | 376 | R. Subba Row & A. Lightfoot v Surrey (The Oval) | 1958 |
| 7th | 229 | W. W. Timms & F. A. Walden v Warwickshire (Northampton) | 1926 |
| 8th | 155 | F. R. Brown & A. E. Nutter v Glamorgan (Northampton) | 1952 |
| 9th | 156 | R. Subba Row & S. Starkie v Lancashire (Northampton) | 1955 |
| 10th | 148 | R. Bellamy & V. Murdin v Glamorgan (Northampton) | 1925 |

### One-day cricket

| | | | |
|---|---|---|---|
| Highest innings totals: | Gillette Cup | 275-5 v Notts (Nottingham) | 1976 |
| | John Player League | 259 v Warwickshire (Northampton) | 1979 |
| | Benson & Hedges Cup | 249-3 v Warwickshire (Northampton) | 1974 |
| Lowest innings totals: | Gillette Cup | 62 v Leics (Leicester) | 1974 |
| | John Player League | 41 v Middlesex (Northampton) | 1972 |
| | Benson & Hedges Cup | 85 v Sussex (Northampton) | 1978 |
| Highest individual innings: | Gillette Cup | 114* G. Cook v Surrey (Northampton) | 1979 |
| | John Player League | 115* H. M. Ackerman v Kent (Dover) | 1970 |
| | Benson & Hedges Cup | 131 Mushtaq Mohammad v Minor Counties (East) (Longton) | 1976 |
| Best bowling figures: | Gillette Cup | 5-24 J. D. F. Larter v Leicestershire (Leicester) | 1964 |
| | John Player League | 7-39 A. Hodgson v Somerset (Northampton) | 1976 |
| | Benson & Hedges Cup | 5-21 Sarfraz Nawaz v Middlesex (Lord's) | 1980 |

# NOTTINGHAMSHIRE

**Formation of present club:** 1841, reorganised 1866.
**Colours:** Green and gold.
**Badge:** County Badge of Nottinghamshire.
**County Champions (12):** 1865, 1868, 1871, 1872, 1875, 1880, 1883, 1884, 1885, 1886, 1907 and 1929.
**Joint Champions (5):** (5) 1869, 1873, 1879, 1882 and 1889.
**Gillette Cup Semi-Finalists:** 1969.
**Best final position in John Player League:** 5th in 1975.
**Benson & Hedges Cup Quarter-Finalists (4):** 1973, 1976, 1978 and 1980.
**Gillette Man of the Match Awards:** 13.
**Benson & Hedges Gold Awards:** 20.

**Chief Executive:** P.G. Carling, County Cricket Ground, Trent Bridge, Nottingham NG2 6AG.
**Cricket Manager:** K. Taylor.
**Captain:** C.E.B. Rice.
**Prospects of Play Telephone No:** Nottingham (0602) 869681.

**John Dennis BIRCH** B Nottingham 18/6/1955. RHB, RM. Debut 1973. Benson & Hedges Gold Awards: 1. HS: 105* v Cambridge U (Cambridge) 1980. HSGC: 32 v Yorks (Bradford) 1978. HSJPL: 71 v Yorks (Scarborough) 1978. HSBH: 85 v Minor Counties (North) (Nottingham) 1979. BB: 6-64 v Hants (Bournemouth) 1975. BBJPL: 3-29 v Glamorgan (Swansea) 1976.

**Michael Kenneth (Mike) BORE** B Hull 2/6/1947. RHB, LM. Debut for Yorks 1969. Left county after 1978 season and made debut for Notts in 1979. Cap 1980. Benson & Hedges Gold Awards: 1. HS: 37* Yorks v Notts (Bradford) 1973. HSC: 24* v Yorks (Nottingham) 1980. HSJPL: 28* v Northants (Northampton) 1979. BB: 8-89 v Kent (Folkestone) 1979. BBGC: 3-35 Yorks v Kent (Canterbury) 1971. BBJPL: 4-21 Yorks v Sussex (Middlesbrough) 1970 and 4-21 Yorks v Worcs (Worcester) 1970. BBBH: 6-22 v Leics (Leicester) 1980.

**Kevin Edward COOPER** B Hucknall, Notts 27/12/1957. LHB, RFM. Debut 1976. Cap 1980. HS: 19 v Cambridge U (Cambridge) 1978. HSJPL: 12 v Northants (Northampton) 1979. BB: 6-32 v Derbyshire (Derby) 1978. BBJPL: 4-25 v Hants (Nottingham) 1976. BBBH: 4-23 v Kent (Canterbury) 1979.

**Roy Evatt DEXTER** (Nottingham High School) B Nottingham 13/4/1955. RHB. Debut 1975. HS: 48 v Derbyshire (Ilkeston) 1977.

**Bruce Nicholas FRENCH** (The Meden Comprehensive School, Warsop) B Warsop, Notts 13/8/1959. RHB, WK. Debut 1976 aged 16 years 287 days. Cap 1980. HS: 70* v Worcs (Cleethorpes) 1980. HSJPL: 25 v Northants (Nottingham) 1978.

**Peter John HACKER** B Lenton Abbey, Notts 16/7/1952. RHB, LFM. Debut 1974. Played for Orange Free State in 1979-80 Castle Bowl competition. Cap 1980. HS: 35 v Kent (Canterbury) 1977. BB: 6-35 v Hants (Nottingham) 1980. BBGC: 4-30 v Durham (Nottingham) 1980. BBJPL: 6-16 v Essex (Chelmsford) 1980.

**Richard John HADLEE** (Christchurch Boys' High School) B Christchurch, New

116

Zealand 3/7/1951. Youngest son of W.A. Hadlee, former New Zealand Test cricketer, and brother of D.R. Hadlee. LHB, RFM. Debut for Canterbury 1971-72 in Plunket Shield Competition. Debut for county and cap 1978. Played for Tasmania in 1979-80. Tests: 29 for New Zealand between 1972-73 and 1979-80. Tours: New Zealand to England 1973 and 1978, Australia 1973-74 and 1980-81, Pakistan and India 1976-77. Benson & Hedges Gold Awards: 1. HS: 103 New Zealand v West Indies (Christchurch) 1979-80. HSUK: 101* v Derbyshire (Nottingham) 1978. HSGC: 25 v Durham (Nottingham) 1980. HSJPL: 42 v Leics (Nottingham) 1980. HSBH: 41 v Kent (Canterbury) 1978. BB: 7-23 New Zealand v India (Wellington) 1975-76 and 7-23 v Sussex (Nottingham) 1979. BBJPL: 6-12 v Lancs (Nottingham) 1980. BBBH: 4-13 v Derbyshire (Nottingham) 1980.

**Michael John (Mike, Pasty) HARRIS** B St. Just-in-Roseland, Cornwall 25/5/1944. RHB, WK. Can bowl LBG. Debut for Middlesex 1964. Cap 1967. Left staff after 1968 season and joined Notts by special registration in 1969. Cap 1970. Played for Eastern Province in 1971-72 Currie Cup competition. Played for Wellington in New Zealand Shell Shield competition in 1975-76. Benefit in 1977. 1,000 runs (11) – 2,238 runs (av 50.86) in 1971 best. Scored 9 centuries in 1971 to equal county record. Scored two centuries in match twice in 1971, 118 and 123 v Leics (Leicester) and 107 and 131* v Essex (Chelmsford) and also in 1979, 133* and 102 v Northants (Nottingham). Shared in 1st wicket partnership record for Middlesex, 312 with W.E. Russell v Pakistanis (Lord's) 1967. Benson & Hedges Gold Awards: 2. HS: 201* v Glamorgan (Nottingham) 1973. HSGC: 101 v Somerset (Nottingham) 1970. HSJPL: 104* v Hants (Nottingham) 1970. HSBH: 101 v Yorks (Hull) 1973. BB: 4-16 v Warwickshire (Nottingham) 1969.

**Sheikh Basharat HASSAN** (City HS, Nairobi) B Nairobi, Kenya 24/3/1944. RHB, RM, occasional WK. Debut for East Africa Invitation XI v MCC 1963-64. Played for Coast Invitation XI v Pakistan International Airways 1964. Also played for Kenya against these and other touring sides. Debut for county 1966. Cap 1970. Benefit in 1978. 1,000 runs (5) – 1,395 runs (av. 32.44) in 1970 best. Scored century with aid of a runner v Kent (Canterbury) 1977 – a rare achievement in first-class cricket. HS: 182* v Glos (Nottingham) 1977. HSGC: 79 v Hants (Southampton) 1977. HSJPL: 111 v Surrey (Oval) 1977. HSBH: 98* v Minor Counties (North) (Nottingham) 1973. BB: 3-33 v Lancs (Manchester) 1976. BBGC: 3-20 v Durham (Chester-le-Street) 1967.

**Edward Ernest (Eddie) HEMMINGS** (Campion School, Leamington Spa) B Leamington Spa 20/2/1949. RHB, OB. Debut for Warwickshire 1966. Cap 1974. Left staff after 1978 season and made debut for Notts in 1979. Cap 1980. Hat-trick Warwickshire v Worcs (Birmingham) 1977. HS: 86 v Worcs (Worcester) 1980. HSGC: 20 Warwickshire v Worcs (Birmingham) 1973. HSJPL: 44* Warwickshire v Kent (Birmingham) 1971. HSBH: 61* Warwickshire v Leics (Birmingham) 1974. BB: 7-33 (12-64 match) Warwickshire v Cambridge U (Cambridge) 1975. BBC: 7-62 v Leics (Leicester) 1980. BBJPL: 5-22 Warwickshire v Northants (Birmingham) 1974. BBBH: 3-18 Warwickshire v Oxford and Cambridge Universities (Coventry) 1975.

**Nirmal NANAN** B Preysal Village, Couva, Trinidad 19/8/1951. RHB, LBG. Toured England with West Indian schoolboy team 1970. Debut 1969-70 for South Trinidad v North Trinidad (Pointe-a-Pierre). Debut for county 1971. Did not play in 1978 or 1979 and played only in first two matches of 1980 season. Is now regarded as an English player for qualification purposes. Scored over 1,000 runs for 2nd XI in 1977 and again in 1978. Benson & Hedges Gold Awards: 1. HS: 72 v Oxford U (Oxford) 1971. HSGC: 16 v Hants (Southampton) 1977. HSJPL: 58 v Somerset

## NOTTINGHAMSHIRE

(Torquay) 1972. HSBH: 93 v Derbyshire (Nottingham) 1980. BB: 3-12 v Oxford U (Oxford) 1971.

**Derek William RANDALL** B Retford 24/2/1951. RHB, RM. Played in one John Player League match in 1971. Debut 1972. Cap 1973. *Wisden* 1979. Tests: 27 between 1976-77 and 1979-80. Tours: India, Sri Lanka and Australia 1976-77, Pakistan and New Zealand 1977-78, Australia 1978-79, Australia and India 1979-80. 1,000 runs (3) – 1,546 runs (av. 42.94) in 1976 best. Scored two centuries in match (209 and 146) v Middlesex (Nottingham) 1979. Gillette Man of Match Awards: 1. Benson & Hedges Gold Awards: 3. HS: 209 v Middlesex (Nottingham) 1979. HSTC: 174 v Australia (Melbourne) 1976-77. HSGC: 75 v Sussex (Hove) 1979. HSJPL: 107* v Middlesex (Lord's) 1976. HSBH: 103* v Minor Counties (North) 1979.

**Clive Edward Butler RICE** (St. John's College, Johannesburg) B Johannesburg 23/7/1949. RHB, RFM. Debut for Transvaal 1969-70. Professional for Ramsbottom in Lancashire League in 1973. Played for D.H. Robins' XI v West Indians 1973 and Pakistanis 1974. Debut for county and cap 1975. Appointed county captain for 1978, but was relieved of appointment when his signing for World Series Cricket was announced. Re-appointed county captain during 1979 season. *Wisden* 1980. 1,000 runs (6) – 1,871 runs (av. 66.82) in 1978 best. Scored two centuries in match (131* and 114*) v Somerset (Nottingham) 1980. Benson & Hedges Gold Awards: 2. HS: 246 v Sussex (Hove) 1976. HSGC: 71 v Yorks (Bradford) 1978. Scored 157 for Transvaal v Orange Free State (Bloemfontein) 1975-76 in South African Gillette Cup competition. HSJPL: 120* v Glamorgan (Swansea) 1978. HSBH: 94 v Middlesex (Newark) 1976. BB: 7-62 Transvaal v Western Province (Johannesburg) 1975-76. BBUK: 6-16 v Worcs (Worcester) 1977. BBGC: 3-29 v Sussex (Nottingham) 1975. BBJPL: 4-15 v Hants (Nottingham) 1980. BBBH: 4-9 v Combined Universities (Nottingham) 1977.

**Robert Timothy (Tim) ROBINSON** (High Pavement College, Nottingham) B Sutton-in-Ashfield, Notts 21/11/1958. RHB, RM. Played for Northants 2nd XI in 1974 and 1975 and for county 2nd XI in 1977. Debut 1978. HS: 138 v Leics (Nottingham) 1980. HSGC: 32 v Middlesex (Nottingham) 1980. HSJPL: 35 v Somerset (Nottingham) 1979. Obtained Degree in Accountancy and Financial Management from Sheffield University.

**Kevin SAXELBY** (Magnus GS, Newark) B Worksop 23/2/1959. RHB, RM. Debut 1978. HS: 15 v Surrey (Oval) 1980.

**Paul Adrian TODD** B Morton, Notts 12/3/1953. RHB, RM. Debut 1972. Cap 1977. Gillette Man of Match Awards: 1. Benson & Hedges Gold Awards: 1. 1,000 runs (3) – 1,181 runs (av. 29.52) in 1978 best. HS: 178 v Glos (Nottingham) 1975. HSGC: 105 v Warwickshire (Birmingham) 1979. HSJPL: 79 v Hants (Nottingham) 1978. HSBH: 59 v Kent (Canterbury) 1979.

**William Kenneth (Ken) WATSON** (Dale College, Kingswilliamtown) B Port Elizabeth 21/5/1955. RHB, RFM. 6ft 3ins tall. Debut for Border 1974-75. Played for Northern Transvaal 1975-76 and for Eastern Province from 1976-77. Debut for county 1976. HS: 44 v Australians (Nottingham) 1980. HSJPL: 17 v Worcs (Nottingham) 1980. BB: 6-51 v Derbyshire (Nottingham) 1979. BBJPL: 3-20 v Hants (Bournemouth) 1977.

**Neil Ivan WEIGHTMAN** (Magnus GS, Newark) B Normanton-on-Trent

5/10/1960. LHB, OB. Played for 2nd XI since 1977. Played in last two John Player League matches of 1980. Has yet to appear in first-class cricket.

**Robert Arthur (Bob) WHITE** (Chiswick GS) B Fulham 6/10/1936. LHB, OB. Debut for Middlesex 1958. Cap 1963. Debut for Notts after special registration in 1966 and developed into useful off-break bowler. Cap 1966. Benefit (£11,000) in 1974. Scored 1,355 runs (av. 33.87) in 1963. HS: 116* v Surrey (Oval) 1967, sharing in 7th wicket partnership record for county, 204 with M.J. Smedley. HSGC: 39 v Worcs (Worcester) 1966. HSJPL: 86* v Surrey (Guildford) 1973. HSBH: 52* v Worcs (Worcester) 1973. BB: 7-41 v Derbyshire (Ilkeston) 1971. BBGC: 3-43 v Worcs (Worcester) 1968. BBJPL: 4-15 v Somerset (Bath) 1975. BBBH: 3-27 v Northants (Northampton) 1976.

NB. The following players whose particulars appeared in the 1980 annual have been omitted: M.E. Allbrook (not re-engaged), K.S. Mackintosh (not re-engaged) and H.T. Tunnicliffe (not re-engaged). In addition C.C. Curzon has joined Hampshire and his particulars will be found under that county.

The career records of all these players will be found elsewhere in this annual.

# County Averages

**Schweppes County Championship: Played 22, won 6, drawn 11, lost 5.**
**All first-class matches: Played 24, won 8, drawn 11, lost 5.**

## BATTING AND FIELDING

| Cap | | M | I | NO | Runs | HS | Avge | 100 | 50 | Ct | St |
|---|---|---|---|---|---|---|---|---|---|---|---|
| 1975 | C.E.B. Rice | 23 | 36 | 9 | 1448 | 131* | 53.62 | 5 | 7 | 16 | — |
| 1973 | D.W. Randall | 22 | 37 | 1 | 1361 | 170 | 37.80 | 2 | 8 | 15 | — |
| — | R.T. Robinson | 15 | 26 | 3 | 765 | 138 | 33.26 | 1 | 3 | 7 | — |
| 1970 | S.B. Hassan | 16 | 27 | 3 | 720 | 91 | 30.00 | — | 5 | 19 | — |
| 1978 | R.J. Hadlee | 8 | 9 | 1 | 231 | 68 | 28.87 | — | 1 | 4 | — |
| — | J.D. Birch | 18 | 27 | 5 | 632 | 105* | 28.72 | 1 | 3 | 20 | — |
| 1977 | P.A. Todd | 19 | 35 | 3 | 874 | 71 | 27.31 | — | 8 | 8 | — |
| — | K.S. Mackintosh | 4 | 5 | 3 | 46 | 16* | 23.00 | — | — | 1 | — |
| — | H.T. Tunnicliffe | 10 | 17 | 3 | 296 | 100* | 21.14 | 1 | 1 | 7 | — |
| 1980 | E.E. Hemmings | 24 | 28 | 4 | 496 | 86 | 20.66 | — | 1 | 11 | — |
| 1980 | B.N. French | 15 | 20 | 4 | 317 | 70* | 19.81 | — | 1 | 38 | 6 |
| 1970 | M.J. Harris | 12 | 20 | 2 | 289 | 65 | 16.05 | — | 2 | 11 | — |
| — | C.C. Curzon | 10 | 13 | 1 | 192 | 45 | 16.00 | — | — | 26 | 1 |
| — | W.K. Watson | 6 | 9 | 3 | 85 | 44 | 14.16 | — | — | — | — |
| — | R.E. Dexter | 5 | 8 | 1 | 83 | 32 | 11.85 | — | — | 7 | — |
| 1980 | K.E. Cooper | 15 | 15 | 4 | 93 | 35 | 8.45 | — | — | 3 | — |
| 1980 | M.K. Bore | 16 | 16 | 7 | 63 | 24* | 7.00 | — | — | 2 | — |
| 1980 | P.J. Hacker | 17 | 18 | 7 | 69 | 12 | 6.27 | — | — | 3 | — |

*Played in two matches:* M.E. Allbrook 0* (1 ct).

*Played in two matches:* N. Nanan 11, 10, 0, 5; K. Saxelby 0, 15 (1 ct); R.A. White 2, 6, 2 (1 ct).

## NOTTINGHAMSHIRE

### BOWLING

| | Type | O | M | R | W | Avge | Best | 5 wI | 10 wM |
|---|---|---|---|---|---|---|---|---|---|
| R.A. White | OB | 48 | 16 | 85 | 11 | 7.72 | 6-24 | 1 | 1 |
| R.J. Hadlee | RFM | 222.1 | 82 | 410 | 29 | 14.13 | 5-32 | 1 | — |
| H.T. Tunnicliffe | RM | 85 | 27 | 187 | 9 | 20.77 | 3-55 | — | — |
| P.J. Hacker | LFM | 379.2 | 99 | 1092 | 52 | 21.00 | 6-35 | 2 | — |
| C.E.B. Rice | RFM | 329.4 | 95 | 859 | 39 | 22.02 | 5-25 | 2 | — |
| E.E. Hemmings | OB | 622.5 | 171 | 1700 | 77 | 22.07 | 7-62 | 4 | 1 |
| W.K. Watson | RFM | 124.3 | 23 | 463 | 17 | 27.23 | 5-57 | 1 | — |
| M.K. Bore | LM | 389.2 | 126 | 970 | 32 | 30.31 | 4-24 | — | — |
| K.E. Cooper | RM | 353.3 | 93 | 985 | 31 | 31.77 | 5-31 | 1 | — |
| K.S. Mackintosh | RM | 78 | 15 | 241 | 7 | 34.42 | 3-36 | — | — |

*Also bowled:* M.E. Allbrook 40-6-131-1; J.D. Birch 4-0-24-1; M.J. Harris 11-4-36-0; D.W. Randall 5-0-23-0; R.T. Robinson 6-0-47-1; K. Saxelby 21-2-79-1.

## County Records

### First-class Cricket

| | | |
|---|---|---|
| Highest innings totals: | For – 739-7d v Leicestershire (Nottingham) | 1903 |
| | Agst – 706-4d by Surrey (Nottingham) | 1947 |
| Lowest innings totals: | For – 13 v Yorkshire (Nottingham) | 1901 |
| | Agst – 16 by Derbyshire (Nottingham) and Surrey (The Oval) | 1879 & 1880 |
| Highest individual innings: | For – 312* W.W. Keeton v Middlesex (The Oval) | 1939 |
| | Agst – 345 C.G. Macartney for Australians (Nottingham) | 1921 |
| Best bowling in an innings: | For – 10-66 K. Smales v Gloucestershire (Stroud) | 1956 |
| | Agst – 10-10 H. Verity for Yorkshire (Leeds) | 1932 |
| Best bowling in a match: | For – 17-89 F.C.L. Matthews v Northants (Nottingham) | 1923 |
| | Agst – 17-89 W.G. Grace for Glos (Cheltenham) | 1877 |
| Most runs in a season: | 2,620 (av. 53.46) W.W. Whysall | 1929 |
| runs in a career: | 31,592 (av. 35.70) G. Gunn | 1902-1932 |
| 100s in a season: | 9 by W.W. Whysall | 1928 |
| | and M.J. Harris | 1971 |
| 100s in a career: | 65 by J. Hardstaff | 1930-1955 |
| wickets in a season: | 181 (av. 14.96) B. Dooland | 1954 |
| wickets in a career: | 1,653 (av. 20.34) T. Wass | 1896-1914 |

### RECORD WICKET STANDS

| | | | |
|---|---|---|---|
| 1st | 391 | A.O. Jones & A. Shrewsbury v Gloucestershire (Bristol) | 1899 |
| 2nd | 398 | W. Gunn & A. Shrewsbury v Sussex (Nottingham) | 1890 |
| 3rd | 369 | J. Gunn & W. Gunn v Leicestershire (Nottingham) | 1903 |
| 4th | 361 | A.O. Jones & J. Gunn v Essex (Leyton) | 1905 |
| 5th | 266 | A. Shrewsbury & W. Gunn v Sussex (Hove) | 1884 |
| 6th | 303* | H. Winrow & P.F. Harvey v Derbyshire (Nottingham) | 1947 |
| 7th | 204 | M.J. Smedley & R.A. White v Surrey (Oval) | 1967 |
| 8th | 220 | G.F.H. Heane & R.T. Winrow v Somerset (Nottingham) | 1933 |
| 9th | 167 | W. McIntyre & G. Wootton v Kent (Nottingham) | 1869 |
| 10th | 152 | E. Alletson & W. Riley v Sussex (Hove) | 1911 |

**One-day Cricket**

| | | | |
|---|---|---|---|
| Highest innings totals: | Gillette Cup | 271 v Gloucestershire (Nottingham) | 1968 |
| | John Player League | 260-5 v Warwickshire (Birmingham) | 1976 |
| | Benson & Hedges Cup | 269-5 v Derbyshire (Nottingham) | 1980 |
| Lowest innings totals: | Gillette Cup | 123 v Yorkshire (Scarborough) | 1969 |
| | John Player League | 66 v Yorks (Bradford) | 1969 |
| | Benson & Hedges Cup | 94 v Lancashire (Nottingham) | 1975 |
| Highest individual innings: | Gillette Cup | 107 M. Hill v Somerset (Taunton) | 1964 |
| | John Player League | 120* C.E.B. Rice v Glamorgan (Swansea) | 1978 |
| | Benson & Hedges Cup | 103* D.W. Randall v Minor Counties (North) (Nottingham) | 1979 |
| Best bowling figures: | Gillette Cup | 5-44 B. Stead v Worcestershire (Worcester) | 1974 |
| | John Player League | 6-12 R.J. Hadlee v Lancashire (Nottingham) | 1980 |
| | Benson & Hedges Cup | 6-22 M.K. Bore v Leicestershire (Leicester) | 1980 |

# SOMERSET

Formation of present club: 1875, reorganised 1885.
Colours: Black, silver and maroon.
Badge: Wessex Wyvern.
Best final position in Championship: Third (4): 1892, 1958, 1963 and 1966.
Gillette Cup Winners: 1979.
Gillette Cup Finalists (2): 1967 and 1978.
John Player League Champions: 1979.
Benson & Hedges Cup Semi-Finalists (2): 1974 and 1978.
Gillette Man of the Match Awards: 26.
Benson & Hedges Gold Awards: 2.

Secretary and Chief Executive: D.G. Seward, County Cricket Ground, St. James's Street, Taunton TA1 1JT.
Captain: B.C. Rose.
Prospects of Play Telephone No: Taunton (0823) 70007.

   Ian Terrence BOTHAM B Heswall, Cheshire 24/11/1955. RHB, RFM. Played for 2nd XI in 1971. On MCC staff 1972-73. Played for county in last two John Player League matches of 1973. Debut 1974. Cap 1976. Elected Best Young Cricketer of the Year in 1977 by the Cricket Writers' Club. *Wisden* 1977. Tests: 31 between 1977 and 1980, captaining England in 6 Tests in 1980. Tours: Pakistan and New Zealand 1977-78, Australia 1978-79, Australia and India 1979-80, West Indies 1980-81 (Captain). 1,000 runs (2) – 1,149 runs (av. 42.55) in 1980 best. Took 100 wkts (av. 16.40) in 1978. Became first player ever to score a century and take 8 wkts in innings in a Test match, v Pakistan (Lord's)1978, and to score a century and take 10 wkts in a match, v India (Bombay) 1979-80. Took 100th wkt in Test cricket in 1979 in record time of 2 years 9 days. Achieved double of 1,000 runs and 100 wkts in Tests in 1979 to create records of fewest Tests (21), shortest time (2 years 33 days) and at youngest age (23 years 279 days). These records, with exception of fewest Tests, were beaten by Kapil Dev for India in 1979-80. Hat-trick for MCC v Middlesex (Lord's) 1978. Gillette Man of Match Awards: 1. Benson & Hedges Gold Awards: 3. HS: 228 v Glos (Taunton) 1980 in 184 minutes with 10 6's and 27 4's, scoring 182 between lunch and tea, and sharing in 4th wkt partnership record for county, 310 with P.W. Denning. HSTC: 137 v India (Leeds) 1979. HSGC: 91* v Northumberland (Taunton) 1977. HSJPL: 69 v Hants (Street) 1977. HSBH: 54 v Sussex (Hove) 1978. BB: 8-34 v Pakistan (Lord's) 1978. BBGC: 7-61 v Glamorgan (Cardiff) 1978. BBGC: 3-15 v Kent (Taunton) 1979. BBJPL: 4-10 v Yorks (Scarborough) 1979. BBBH: 4-16 v Combined Universities (Taunton) 1978. Has played soccer for Scunthorpe United.

   Dennis BREAKWELL (Ounsdale Comprehensive School, Wombourne, Wolverhampton) B Brierley Hill, Staffs 2/7/1948. LHB, SLA. Debut for Northants 1969 after being on staff for some years. Left county after 1972 season and joined Somerset by special registration in 1973. Cap 1976. HS: 100* v New Zealanders (Taunton) 1978. HSGC: 19* v Essex (Westcliff) 1974. HSJPL: 44* v Notts (Nottingham) 1976. HSBH: 36* v Glamorgan (Taunton) 1979. BB: 8-39 Northants v Kent (Dover) 1970. BBC: 6-41 v Glamorgan (Swansea) 1979. BBJPL: 4-10 Northants v Derbyshire (Northampton) 1970.

   Peter William (Pete) DENNING (Millfield School) B Chewton Mendip, Somerset 16/12/1949. LHB, OB. Debut 1969. Cap 1973. 1,000 runs (5) – 1,222 runs (av.

122

42.13) in 1979 best. Scored two centuries in match (122 and 107) v Glos (Taunton) 1977. Shared in 4th wkt partnership record for county, 310 with I.T. Botham v Glos (Taunton) 1980. Gillette Man of Match Awards: 4. Benson & Hedges Gold Awards: 2. HS: 184 v Notts (Nottingham) 1980. HSGC: 145 v Glamorgan (Cardiff) 1978. HSJPL: 100 v Northants (Brackley) 1974. HSBH: 87 v Glos (Taunton) 1974. Trained as a teacher at St. Luke's College, Exeter.

**Colin Herbert DREDGE** B Frome 4/8/1954. LHB, RM. 6ft 5ins tall. Debut 1976. Cap 1978. Gillette Man of Match Awards: 1. HS: 56* v Yorks (Harrogate) 1977. HSJPL: 14 v Essex (Taunton) 1978. HSBH: 10* v Worcs (Taunton) 1978. BB: 6-57 v Northants (Northampton) 1980. BBGC: 4-23 v Kent (Canterbury) 1978. BBJPL: 3-8 v Surrey (Taunton) 1980. BBBH: 4-10 v Hants (Bournemouth) 1980. Played soccer for Bristol City Reserves.

**Trevor GARD** (Huish Episcopi School, Langport) B West Lambrook, near South Petheron, Somerset 2/6/1957. RHB, WK. Played for 2nd XI since 1972. Debut 1976. HS: 51* v Indians (Taunton) 1979.

**Joel GARNER** B Barbados 16/12/1952. RHB, RFM. 6ft 8ins tall. Debut for Barbados in Shell Shield competition 1975-76. Debut for county 1977 playing in mid-week matches whilst playing as a professional for Littleborough in Central Lancashire League. Cap 1979. *Wisden* 1979. Tests: 18 for West Indies between 1976-77 and 1980. Tours: West Indies to Australia and New Zealand 1979-80, England 1980, Pakistan 1980-81. Gillette Man of Match Awards: 1. HS: 104 West Indians v Glos (Bristol) 1980. HSTC: 60 West Indies v Australia (Brisbane) 1979-80. HSC: 53 v Yorks (Harrogate) 1979. HSGC: 38* v Glamorgan (Cardiff) 1978. HSJPL: 32 v Kent (Taunton) 1979. HSBH: 17 v Sussex (Hove) 1978. BB: 8-31 v Glamorgan (Cardiff) 1977. BBTC: 6-56 West Indies v New Zealand (Auckland) 1979-80. BBGC: 6-29 v Northants (Lord's) 1979. BBJPL: 3-16 v Notts (Nottingham) 1979. BBBH: 3-23 v Glamorgan (Taunton) 1979.

**Sunil Manohar GAVASKAR** (St. Xavier's High School, Bombay and Bombay University) B Bombay 10/7/1949. 5ft 4½ins tall. RHB, RM. Debut 1966-67 for Vazir Sultan Colts XI in Moin-Ud-Dowlah tournament at Hyderabad, for Bombay in 1967-68 in Irani Trophy, and in 1969-70 in Ranji Trophy. Debut for county on 1-year contract in 1980. Cap 1980. Tests: 63 for India between 1970-71 and 1979-80, captaining India in 18 Tests. Tours: India to West Indies 1970-71, England 1971, 1974 and 1979, New Zealand and West Indies 1975-76, Australia 1977-78 and 1980-81 (Captain), Pakistan 1978-79. 1,000 runs (2) – 1,141 runs (av. 43.88) in 1971 best. Scored 2,121 runs (av. 88.37) with 10 centuries in India and Pakistan in 1978-79. Only player to have scored two centuries in a Test match on three occasions. HS: 282 Bombay v Bihar (Bombay) 1971-72. HSTC: 221 India v England (Oval) 1979. HSC: 155* v Yorks (Weston-Super-Mare) 1980. HSGC: 15 v Worcs (Taunton) 1980. HSJPL: 57* v Notts (Taunton) 1980. HSBH: 123 v Middlesex (Taunton) 1980. BB: 3-43 President's XI v Ranji XI (Jamnagar) 1972-73.

**Hugh Edmond Ivor GORE** B Antigua 18/6/1953. RHB, LFM. Debut for Leeward Islands v Australians 1972-73. Subsequently played for Combined Islands in Shell Shield. Debut for county on 1-year contract in 1980. HS: 67 Combined Islands v Jamaica (Kingstown, St. Vincent) 1980. HSJPL: 22* v Leics (Taunton) 1980. BB: 5-66 v Surrey (Oval) 1980. BBGC: 3-19 v Worcs (Taunton) 1980.

**Keith Francis JENNINGS** B Wellington, Somerset 5/10/1953. RHB, RM. Formerly on MCC staff. Debut 1975. Cap 1978. Benson & Hedges Gold Awards: 1. HS: 49 v West Indians (Taunton) 1976. HSJPL: 51* v Notts (Nottingham) 1976. BB:

5-18 v Sussex (Hove) 1978. BBGC: 3-31 v Derbyshire (Taunton) 1979. BBJPL: 4-33 v Hants (Portsmouth) 1976. BBBH: 4-11 v Minor Counties (South) (Taunton) 1979.

**Jeremy William LLOYDS** (Blundell's School) B Penang, Malaya 17/11/1954. LHB, RM. Played for 2nd XI from 1973 to 1977. Played for Hants, Middlesex and Worcs 2nd XIs in 1978. Debut 1979. HS: 70 v Warwickshire (Taunton) 1980. HSJPL: 29 v Warwickshire (Taunton) 1980. BB: 6-61 Worcs (Weston-super-Mare) 1980.

**Victor James (Vic) MARKS** (Blundell's School and Oxford) B Middle Chinnock, Somerset 25/6/1955. RHB, OB. Debut for both Oxford U and county 1975. Blue 1975-76-77-78 (Captain in 1976-77). Cap 1979. Benson & Hedges Gold Awards: 2. Scored 215 for Oxford U v Army (Aldershot) in non-first class match. HS: 105 Oxford U v Worcs (Oxford) 1976. HSC: 98 v Essex (Leyton) 1976. HSGC: 33* v Essex (Taunton) 1978. HSJPL: 71* v Surrey (Taunton) 1980. HSBH: 81* v Hants (Bournemouth) 1980. BB: 6-33 v Northants (Taunton) 1979. BBJPL: 3-19 v Derbyshire (Taunton) 1979, and 3-19 v Glos (Taunton) 1980. Half-blue for Rugby Fives.

**Hallam Reynold MOSELEY** B Christ Church, Barbados 28/5/1948. RHB, RFM. Toured England with Barbados team in 1969 and made debut v Notts (Nottingham). Subsequently played for Barbados in Shell Shield. Joined county in 1970 and made debut in 1971. Cap 1972. Testimonial (£24,085) in 1979. Is now regarded as an English player for qualification purposes. HS: 67 v Leics (Taunton) 1972. HSGC: 15 v Lancs (Manchester) 1972. HSJPL: 24 v Notts (Torquay) 1972 and 24 v Hants (Weston-super-Mare) 1975. HSBH: 33 v Hants (Bournemouth) 1973. BB: 6-34 v Derbyshire (Bath) 1975 and 6-35 v Glos (Taunton) 1978. BBGC: 4-31 v Surrey (Taunton) 1974. BBJPL: 5-30 v Middlesex (Lord's) 1973. BBBH: 3-17 v Leics (Taunton) 1977.

**Martin OLIVE** (Millfield School) B Watford, Herts 18/4/1958. RHB, RM. Played for 2nd XI since 1974. Debut 1977. HS: 50 v Yorks (Weston-super-Mare) 1980.

**Nigel Francis Mark POPPLEWELL** (Radley College and Cambridge) B Chislehurst, Kent 8/8/1957. Son of O.B. Popplewell, Q.C., former Cambridge Blue. RHB, RM. Played for Buckinghamshire in 1975 and 1978 and for Hants 2nd XI in 1976 and 1977. Debut for Cambridge U 1977. Blue 1977-78-79 (secretary). Debut for county 1979. HS: 135* v Kent (Taunton) 1980. HSJPL: 55 v Surrey (Taunton) 1980. HSBH: 22* Combined Universities v Sussex (Oxford) 1979. BB: 3-18 Cambridge U v Somerset (Bath) 1979. BBC: 3-43 v Lancs (Manchester) 1979.

**Isaac Vivian Alexander (Viv) RICHARDS** (Antigua Grammar School) B St. John's, Antigua 7/3/1952. RHB, OB. Debut 1971-72 for Leeward Islands v Windward Islands and subsequently played for Combined Islands in Shell Shield tournament. Debut for county and cap 1974. *Wisden* 1976. Played for Queensland in 1976-77 Sheffield Shield competition. Tours: 36 for West Indies between 1974-75 and 1980, captaining West Indies in 1 Test in 1980. Tours: West Indies to India, Sri Lanka and Pakistan 1974-75, Australia 1975-76 and 1979-80, England 1976 and 1980 (Vice-Captain), Pakistan 1980-81 (Vice-Captain). 1,000 runs (7) – 2,161 runs (av. 65.48) in 1977 best. Also scored 1,267 runs (av. 60.33) on 1974-75 tour and 1,107 runs (av. 58.26) on 1975-76 tour. Scored 1,710 in 11 Test matches in 1976 including 829 runs in 4 Tests against England – record aggregate for a year and fourth highest aggregate for a Test Series. Scored 99 and 110 v Leics (Taunton) 1978. Gillette Man of Match Awards: 3. Benson & Hedges Gold Awards: 3. HS: 291 West

Indies v England (Oval) 1976. HSC: 241* v Glos (Bristol) 1977. HSGC: 139* v Warwickshire (Taunton) 1978. HSJPL: 126* v Glos (Bristol, Imperial Ground) 1975. HSBH: 85 v Glamorgan (Cardiff) 1978. BB: 3-12 v Hants (Bournemouth) 1980. BBJPL: 3-32 v Glos (Bristol) 1978.

**Peter Michael ROEBUCK** (Millfield School and Cambridge) B Oxford 6/3/1956. RHB, OB. Played for 2nd XI in 1969 at age of 13. Debut 1974. Blue 1975-76-77. Cap 1978. Scored 1,273 runs (av. 47.14) in 1979. Benson & Hedges Gold Awards: 1. HS: 158 Cambridge U v Oxford U (Lord's) 1975. HSC: 131* v New Zealanders (Taunton) 1978. HSGC: 57 v Essex (Taunton) 1978. HSJPL: 50 v Notts (Nottingham) 1979. HSBH: 48 Combined Universities v Kent (Oxford) 1976. BB: 6-50 Cambridge U v Kent (Canterbury) 1977.

**Brian Charles ROSE** (Weston-super-Mare GS) B Dartford, Kent 4/6/1950. LHB, LM. Played for English Schools CA at Lord's 1968. Debut 1969. Cap 1975. Appointed county captain in 1978. *Wisden* 1979. Tests: 8 between 1977-78 and 1980. Tours: Pakistan and New Zealand 1977-78, West Indies 1980-81. 1,000 runs (6) – 1,624 runs (av. 46.40) in 1976 best. Scored two centuries in match (124 and 150*) v Worcs (Worcester) 1980. Gillette Man of Match Awards: 2. Benson & Hedges Gold Awards: 1. HS: 205 v Northants (Weston-super-Mare) 1977. HSTC: 70 v West Indies (Manchester) 1980. HSGC: 128 v Derbyshire (Ilkeston) 1977. HSJPL: 112* v Essex (Ilford) 1980. HSBH: 137* v Kent (Canterbury) 1980. BB: 3-9 v Glos (Taunton) 1975. BBJPL: 3-25 v Lancs (Manchester) 1975. Trained as a teacher at Borough Road College, Isleworth.

**Neil RUSSOM** (Huish's GS, Taunton and Cambridge) B Finchley, London 3/12/1958. RHB, RM. Played for 2nd XI since 1975. Played in one Fenner Trophy match v Northants (Scarborough) in 1978. Debut for Cambridge U 1979. Blue 1980. Debut for county 1980, one match v Glamorgan (Taunton). Benson & Hedges Gold Awards: 1 (for Combined Universities). HS: 79* Cambridge U v Northants (Cambridge) 1980. HSBH: 16* Combined Universities v Worcs (Cambridge) 1980. BB: 4-84 Cambridge U v Leics (Cambridge) 1980. BBBH: 5-40 Combined Universities v Northants (Northampton) 1980.

**Philip Anthony (Phil) SLOCOMBE** (Weston-super-Mare GS and Millfield School) B Weston-super-Mare 6/9/1954. RHB, RM. Played for 2nd XI in 1969 at age of 14. Joined staff 1974. Debut 1975. Cap 1978. 1,000 runs (2) – 1,221 runs (av. 38.15) in 1978 best. Scored 106* & 98 v Worcs (Worcester) 1978. HS: 132 v Notts (Taunton) 1975. HSGC: 42 v Surrey (Oval) 1975. HSJPL: 39 v Glamorgan (Yeovil) 1977. HSBH: 42 v Middlesex (Taunton) 1980. Plays soccer for Weston-Super-Mare in Western League.

**Derek John Somerset TAYLOR** (Amersham College) B Amersham, Bucks 12/11/1942. Twin brother of M.N.S. Taylor of Hants. RHB, WK. Debut for Surrey 1966. Cap 1969. Left staff after 1969 season and made debut for Somerset in 1970. Cap 1971. Testimonial (£20,764) in 1978. Played for Griqualand West in Currie Cup competition 1970-71 and 1971-72. Scored 1,121 runs (av. 28.02) in 1975. Was dismissed obstructing the field in John Player League match v Warwickshire (Birmingham) 1980. HS: 179 v Glamorgan (Swansea) 1974. HSGC: 49 v Kent (Canterbury) 1974. HSJPL: 93 v Surrey (Guildford) 1975. HSBH: 83* v Glos (Street) 1975. Has played soccer for Corinthian Casuals.

NB. The following player whose particulars appeared in the 1980 annual has been omitted: D.R. Gurr (left staff).

# County Averages

**Schweppes County Championship: Played 21, won 3, drawn 13, lost 5, abandoned 1.
All first-class matches: Played 23, won 4, drawn 14, lost 5, abandoned 1.**

## BATTING AND FIELDING

| Cap | | M | I | NO | Runs | HS | Avge | 100 | 50 | Ct | St |
|------|------------------|----|----|----|------|------|-------|-----|----|----|----|
| 1976 | I.T. Botham | 11 | 15 | 0 | 928 | 228 | 61.86 | 2 | 5 | 21 | — |
| 1975 | B.C. Rose | 14 | 20 | 3 | 841 | 150* | 49.47 | 2 | 3 | 4 | — |
| 1971 | D.J.S. Taylor | 20 | 26 | 9 | 743 | 59 | 43.70 | — | 5 | 33 | 4 |
| 1974 | I.V.A. Richards | 4 | 8 | 0 | 306 | 170 | 38.25 | 1 | 1 | 6 | — |
| 1980 | S.M. Gavaskar | 15 | 23 | 3 | 686 | 155* | 34.30 | 2 | 2 | 5 | — |
| — | N.F.M. Popplewell | 14 | 20 | 6 | 445 | 135* | 31.78 | 1 | 1 | 17 | — |
| 1973 | P.W. Denning | 23 | 34 | 2 | 1012 | 184 | 31.62 | 1 | 5 | 14 | — |
| 1979 | V.J. Marks | 22 | 32 | 7 | 765 | 82 | 30.60 | — | 5 | 11 | — |
| — | J.W. Lloyds | 11 | 16 | 3 | 388 | 70 | 29.84 | — | 4 | 7 | — |
| 1978 | P.M. Roebuck | 22 | 35 | 3 | 866 | 101 | 27.06 | 1 | 3 | 11 | — |
| 1976 | D. Breakwell | 12 | 14 | 3 | 276 | 55* | 25.09 | — | 1 | 2 | — |
| — | M. Olive | 9 | 17 | 1 | 290 | 50 | 18.12 | — | 1 | 4 | — |
| 1978 | K.F. Jennings | 11 | 10 | 4 | 104 | 21* | 17.33 | — | — | 13 | — |
| 1978 | P.A. Slocombe | 13 | 18 | 2 | 256 | 114 | 16.00 | 1 | — | 2 | — |
| 1972 | H.R. Moseley | 17 | 9 | 4 | 55 | 16 | 11.00 | — | — | 5 | — |
| — | H.I.E. Gore | 11 | 11 | 5 | 48 | 22* | 8.00 | — | — | 3 | — |
| 1978 | C.H. Dredge | 20 | 21 | 5 | 113 | 21* | 7.06 | — | — | 6 | — |

*Played in three matches:* T. Gard 22, 19 (4 ct 1 st).
*Played in one match:* N. Russom 9.

## BOWLING

| | Type | O | M | R | W | Avge | Best | 5 wI | 10 wM |
|------------------|------|-------|-----|------|----|-------|------|------|-------|
| C.H. Dredge | RM | 571.2 | 136 | 1600 | 63 | 25.39 | 6-57 | 5 | — |
| H.R. Moseley | RFM | 470.5 | 115 | 1193 | 40 | 29.82 | 6-58 | 2 | — |
| J.W. Lloyds | RM | 264 | 55 | 899 | 28 | 32.10 | 6-61 | 2 | 1 |
| I.T. Botham | RFM | 263.1 | 69 | 810 | 25 | 32.40 | 4-38 | — | — |
| N.F.M. Popplewell | RM | 186.5 | 46 | 587 | 17 | 34.52 | 3-54 | — | — |
| K.F. Jennings | RM | 225.2 | 53 | 615 | 14 | 43.92 | 4-87 | — | — |
| V.J. Marks | OB | 766.1 | 196 | 2157 | 46 | 46.89 | 5-77 | 2 | — |
| H.I.E. Gore | LFM | 253.5 | 66 | 669 | 14 | 47.78 | 5-66 | 1 | — |
| D. Breakwell | SLA | 330 | 101 | 910 | 18 | 50.55 | 4-80 | — | — |

*Also bowled:* P.W. Denning 1.5-0-8-0; S.M. Gavaskar 14.2-2-69-0; I.V.A. Richards 30-2-110-3; P.M. Roebuck 24.2-2-113-2; B.C. Rose 5-0-25-0; N. Russom 19-7-54-0; P.A. Slocombe 3-0-18-2; D.J.S. Taylor 2-1-1-0.

# County Records

### First-class cricket

| | | | |
|---|---|---|---|
| Highest innings | For | – 675-9d v Hampshire (Bath) | 1924 |
| totals: | Agst | – 811 by Surrey (The Oval) | 1899 |
| Lowest innings | For | – 25 v Gloucestershire (Bristol) | 1947 |
| totals: | Agst | – 22 by Gloucestershire (Bristol) | 1920 |
| Highest indi- | For | – 310 H. Gimblett v Sussex (Eastbourne) | 1948 |
| vidual innings: | Agst | – 424 A.C. MacLaren for Lancs (Taunton) | 1895 |
| Best bowling | For | – 10-49 E.J. Tyler v Surrey (Taunton) | 1895 |
| in an innings: | Agst | – 10-35 A. Drake for Yorks (Weston-s-Mare) | 1914 |
| Best bowling | For | – 16-83 J.C. White v Worcestershire (Bath) | 1919 |
| in a match: | Agst | – 17-137 W. Brearley for Lancashire (Manchester) | 1905 |

| | | |
|---|---|---|
| Most runs in a season: | 2,761 (av. 56.82) W.E. Alley | 1961 |
| runs in a career: | 21,142 (av. 36.96) H. Gimblett | 1935-1954 |
| 100s in a season: | 10 by W.E. Alley | 1961 |
| 100s in a career: | 49 by H. Gimblett | 1935-1954 |
| wickets in a season: | 169 (av. 19.24) A.W. Wellard | 1938 |
| wickets in a career: | 2,166 (av. 18.02) J.C. White | 1909-1937 |

### RECORD WICKET STANDS

| | | | |
|---|---|---|---|
| 1st | 346 | H.T. Hewett & L.C.H. Palairet v Yorkshire (Taunton) | 1892 |
| 2nd | 286 | J.C.W. MacBryan & M.D. Lyon v Derbyshire (Buxton) | 1924 |
| 3rd | 300 | G. Atkinson & P.B. Wight v Glamorgan (Bath) | 1960 |
| 4th | 310 | P.W. Denning & I.T. Botham v Gloucestershire (Taunton) | 1980 |
| 5th | 235 | J.C. White & C.C.C. Case v Gloucestershire (Taunton) | 1927 |
| 6th | 265 | W.E. Alley & K.E. Palmer v Northants (Northampton) | 1961 |
| 7th | 240 | S.M.J. Woods & V.T. Hill v Kent (Taunton) | 1898 |
| 8th | 143* | E.F. Longrigg & C.J.P. Barnwell v Glos (Bristol) | 1938 |
| 9th | 183 | C. Greetham & H.W. Stephenson v Leicestershire (Weston-super-Mare) | 1963 |
| 10th | 143 | J.J. Bridges & H. Gibbs v Surrey (Weston-super-Mare) | 1919 |

### One-day cricket

| | | | |
|---|---|---|---|
| Highest innings | Gillette Cup | 330-4 v Glamorgan (Cardiff) | 1978 |
| totals: | John Player League | 270-4 v Gloucestershire (Bristol, Imperial) | 1975 |
| | Benson & Hedges Cup | 281-8 v Middlesex (Taunton) | 1980 |
| Lowest innings | Gillette Cup | 59 v Middlesex (Lord's) | 1977 |
| totals: | John Player League | 58 v Essex (Chelmsford) | 1977 |
| | Benson & Hedges Cup | 105 v Hampshire (Bournemouth) | 1975 |
| Highest indi- | Gillette Cup | 145 P.W. Denning v Glamorgan (Cardiff) | 1978 |
| vidual innings: | John Player League | 131 D.B. Close v Yorkshire (Bath) | 1974 |
| | Benson & Hedges Cup | 137* B.C. Rose v Kent (Canterbury) | 1980 |
| Best bowling | Gillette Cup | 6-29 J. Garner v Northamptonshire (Lord's) | 1979 |
| figures: | John Player League | 6-25 G.I. Burgess v Glamorgan (Glastonbury) | 1972 |
| | Benson & Hedges Cup | 4-10 C.H. Dredge v Hampshire (Bournemouth) | 1980 |

127

# SURREY

**Formation of present club:** 1845.
**Colours:** Chocolate.
**Badge:** Prince of Wales' Feathers.
**County Champions (18):** 1864, 1887, 1888, 1890,
  1891, 1892, 1894, 1895, 1899, 1914, 1952, 1953,
  1954, 1955, 1956, 1957, 1958, and 1971.
**Joint Champions (2):** 1889 and 1950.
**Gillette Cup Finalists (2):** 1965 and 1980.
**Best final position in John Player League:** 5th in
  1969 and 1980.
**Benson & Hedges Cup Winners:** 1974.
**Benson & Hedges Cup Finalists:** 1979.
**Gillette Man of the Match Awards:** 18.
**Benson & Hedges Gold Awards:** 26.

**Secretary:** I. F. B. Scott-Browne, Kennington Oval, London, SE11 5SS.
**Cricket manager:** M. J. Stewart.
**Captain:** R. D. V. Knight.
**Prospects of Play Telephone No:** (01) 735 4911.

   **Alan Raymond BUTCHER** (Heath Clark GS, Croydon) B Croydon 7/1/1954.
LHB, SLA. Played in two John Player League matches in 1971. Debut 1972. Cap
1975. Tests: 1 in 1979. 1,000 runs (2) – 1,713 runs (av 46.29) in 1980 best. Benson &
Hedges Gold Awards: 4. HS: 216* v Cambridge U (Cambridge) 1980. HSTC: 20 v
India (Oval) 1979. HSGC: 51 v Derbyshire (Ilkeston) 1976. HSJPL: 113* v War-
wickshire (Birmingham) 1978. HSBH: 72 v Somerset (Taunton) 1980. BB: 6-48 v
Hants (Guildford) 1972. BBJPL: 5-19 Glos (Bristol) 1975. BBBH:3-11 v Lancs
(Manchester) 1974.

   **Robert Giles Lenthall CHEATLE** (Stowe School) B London 31/7/1953. LHB,
SLA. Debut for Sussex 1974. Left county after 1979 season and made debut for
Surrey in 1980. HS: 49 Sussex v Kent (Tunbridge Wells) 1978. HSC: 13* v Yorks
(Oval) 1980. HSJPL: 18* Sussex v Warwickshire (Hove) 1979. HSBH: 16 Sussex v
Somerset (Hove) 1978. BB: 6-32 Sussex v Yorks (Hove) 1979. BBC: 5-28 v Sussex
(Oval) 1980. BBJPL: 4-33 Sussex v Glamorgan (Eastbourne) 1977. BBBH: 3-26 v
Hants (Oval) 1980.

   **Sylvester Theophilus CLARKE** B Christ Church, Barbados 11/12/1954. RHB,
RFM. Debut for Barbados 1977-78. Debut for county 1979. Cap 1980. Tests: 6 for
West Indies between 1977-78 and 1978-79. Tours: West Indies to India and Sri
Lanka 1978-79, Pakistan 1980-81. Hat-tricks (2): Barbados v Trinidad
(Bridgetown) 1977-78, v Notts (Oval) 1980. Benson & Hedges Gold Awards: 1.
HS: 55 v Derbyshire (Derby) 1980. HSTC: 35* West Indies v Pakistan (Faisalabad)
1980-81. HSGC: 11* v Essex (Chelmsford) 1980. HSJPL: 34* v Hants (Oval) 1980.
HSBH: 29* v Kent (Oval) 1980. BB: 6-39 Barbados v Trinidad (Bridgetown)
1977-78. BBUK: 6-61 v Glamorgan (Cardiff) 1979. BBTC: 5-126 West Indies v
India (Bangalore) 1979-80. BBGC: 4-38 v Yorks (Oval) 1980. BBJPL: 3-26 v
Lancs (Oval) 1979. BBBH: 5-23 v Kent (Oval) 1980.

   **Grahame Selvey CLINTON** (Chislehurst and Sidcup GS) B Sidcup 5/51953.
LHB, RM. Toured West Indies with England Young Cricketers 1972. Debut for
Kent 1974. Left county after 1978 season and made debut for Surrey in 1979. Played

for Zimbabwe/Rhodesia in 1979-80 Currie Cup. Cap 1980. 1,000 runs (2) – 1,240 runs (av. 37.57) in 1980 best. Benson & Hedges Gold Awards: 1 (for Kent). HS: 134 v Kent (Oval) 1979. HSGC: 58 v Essex (Chelmsford) 1980. HSJPL: 79* v Notts (Oval) 1980. HSBH: 66 Kent v Surrey (Canterbury) 1976.

**Geoffrey Philip (Geoff) HOWARTH** (Auckland GS) B Auckland 29/3/1951. Younger brother of H. J. Howarth, New Zealand Test cricketer. RHB, OB. Debut for New Zealand under-23 XI v Auckland (Auckland) 1968-69. Joined Surrey staff 1969. Debut 1971. Cap 1974. Tests: 20 for New Zealand between 1974-75 and 1979-80 captaining New Zealand in 3 tests. Tours: New Zealand to Pakistan and India 1976-77, England 1978, Australia 1980-81 (Captain). 1,000 runs (3) – 1,554 runs (av. 37.90) in 1976 best. Scored two centuries in match (122 and 102) New Zealand v England (Auckland) 1977-78. Benson & Hedges Gold Awards: 1. HS: 183 v Hants (Oval) 1979. HSTC: 147 New Zealand v West Indies (Christchurch) 1979-80. HSGC: 34 v Lancs (Manchester) 1977 and 34 v Northants (Northampton) 1979. HSJPL: 122 v Glos (Oval) 1976. HSBH: 80 v Yorks (Oval) 1974. BB: 5-32 Auckland v Central Districts (Auckland) 1973-74. BBJPL: 3-20 v Northants (Northampton) 1976. BBJPL: 4-16 v Warwickshire (Byfleet) 1979.

**INTIKHAB ALAM** B Hoshiarpur, India 28/12/1941. RHB, LBG. Debut for Karachi 1957-58 aged 16 years 9 months and has played continuously for various Karachi sides and Pakistan International Airways since. Professional for West of Scotland Club in Scottish Western Union for some seasons. Debut for county and cap 1969. Benefit (£20,000) in 1978. Tests: 47 for Pakistan between 1959-60 and 1976-77, captaining country in 17 Tests. Played in 5 matches for Rest of World in 1970 and 5 in 1971-72. Took wkt of C. C. McDonald with first ball he bowled in Test cricket. Tours: Pakistan to India 1960-61, England 1962, 1967, 1971 and 1974 (captain on last two tours), Ceylon 1964, Australia and New Zealand 1964-65, 1972-73 (captain), Australia and West Indies 1976-77, Pakistan Eaglets to England 1963, Pakistan International Airways to East Africa 1964, Rest of World to Australia 1971-72 (vice-captain). Took 104 wkts (av. 28.36) in 1971. Hat-trick v Yorks (Oval) 1972. Benson & Hedges Gold Awards: 1. HS: 182 Karachi Blues v Pakistan International Airways B (Karachi) 1970-71. HSUK: 139 v Glos (Oval) 1973. HSTC: 138 Pakistan v England (Hyderabad) 1972-73. HSGC: 50 v Somerset (Oval) 1975. HSJPL: 62 v Northants (Tolworth) 1973 and 62 v Middlesex (Oval) 1977. HSBH: 32 v Middlesex (Lord's) 1973. BB: 8-54 Pakistanis v Tasmania (Hobart) 1972-73. BBUK: 8-61 Pakist…is v Minor Counties (Swindon) 1967. BBTC: 7-52 Pakistan v New Zealand (Dunedin) 1972-73. BBGC: 8-74 v Middlesex (Oval) 1970. BBJPL: 6-25 v Derbyshire (Oval) 1974. BBBH: 3-42 v Essex (Chelmsford) 1973.

**Robin David JACKMAN** (St Edmund's School, Canterbury) B Simla, India 13/8/1945. RHB, RFM. Debut 1964. Cap 1970. Played for Western Province in 1971-72 and Rhodesia from 1972-73 to 1979-80 in Currie Cup competition. *Wisden* 1980. Benefit in 1981. Took 121 wkts (av. 15.40) in 1980. Hat-tricks (3): v Kent (Canterbury) 1971, Western Province v Natal (Pietermaritzburg) 1971-72 and v Yorks (Leeds) 1973. Gillette Man of Match Awards: 3. Benson & Hedges Gold Awards: 1. HS: 92* v Kent (Oval) 1974. HSGC: 31 v Glos (Oval) 1980. HSJPL: 43 v Kent (Maidstone) 1977. HSBH: 36 v Leics (Lord's) 1974. BB: 8-40 Rhodesia v Natal (Durban) 1972-73. BBUK: 8-58 v Lancs (Manchester) 1980. BBGC: 7-33 v Yorks (Harrogate) 1970. BBJPL: 6-34 v Derbyshire (Derby) 1973. BBBH: 4-31 v Kent (Canterbury) 1973.

**Roger David Verdon KNIGHT** (Dulwich College and Cambridge) B Streatham 6/9/1946. LHB, RM. Debut for Cambridge U 1967. Blue 1967-68-69-70. Debut for

129

## SURREY

Surrey 1968. Left county after 1970 season and made debut for Glos by special registration 1971. Cap 1971. Left county after 1975 season and made debut for Sussex in 1976. Cap 1976. Left county after 1977 season and rejoined Surrey for 1978 as county captain. Cap 1978. 1,000 runs (9) – 1,350 runs (av. 38.57) in 1974 best. Gillette Man of Match Awards: 5 (3 for Glos). Benson & Hedges Gold Awards: 4 (1 for Sussex, 2 for Glos). HS: 165* Sussex v Middlesex (Hove) 1976. HSC: 132 v Lancs (Oval) 1980. HSGC: 75 Glos v Glamorgan (Cardiff) 1973. HSJPL: 127 Sussex v Hants (Hove) 1976. HSBH: 117 Sussex v Surrey (Oval) 1977. BB: 6-44 Glos v Northants (Northampton) 1974. BBC: 5-44 v Glos (Cheltenham) 1979. BBGC: 5-39 Glos v Surrey (Bristol) 1971. BBJPL: 5-42 Sussex v Notts (Nottingham) 1977. BBBH: 3-19 Sussex v Surrey (Oval) 1977.

**Monte Alan LYNCH** (Ryden's School, Walton-on-Thames) B Georgetown, British Guiana 21/5/1958. RHB, RM/OB. Debut 1977. HS: 101 v Pakistanis (Oval) 1978. HSGC: 25* v Yorks (Oval) 1980. HSJPL: 52 v Leics (Leicester) 1979. HSBH: 67 v Worcs (Worcester) 1979.

**Andrew NEEDHAM** (Paisley GS and Watford GS) B Calow, Derbyshire 23/3/1957. RHB, OB. Debut 1977. Did not play in 1980. HS: 21 v Sussex (Hove) 1978. HSJPL: 18 v Lancs (Oval) 1979. BB: 3-25 v Oxford U (Oxford) 1977.

**Duncan Brian PAULINE** (Bishop Fox School, Molesey) B Aberdeen 15/12/1960. RHB, RM. Played for 2nd XI since 1977. Toured Australia with England under-19 side in 1978-79. Debut 1979. HS: 46 v Leics (Leicester) 1980.

**Ian Roger PAYNE** (Emanuel School) B Lambeth Hospital, Kennington 9/5/1958. RHB, RM. Debut 1977. Played in one John Player League match only in 1979. Did not play in 1980. HS: 29 v Kent (Oval) 1977. HSJPL: 20 v Kent (Maidstone) 1977. BBJPL: 4-31 v Northants (Guildford) 1977.

**Patrick Ian (Pat) POCOCK** (Wimbledon Technical School) B Bangor, Caernarvonshire 24/9/1946. RHB, OB. Debut 1964. Benefit (£18,500) in 1977. Played for Northern Transvaal in 1971-72 Currie Cup competition. Tests: 17 between 1967-68 and 1976. Tours: Pakistan 1966-67, West Indies 1967-68 and 1973-74, Ceylon and Pakistan 1968-69, India, Pakistan and Sri Lanka 1972-73. Took 112 wkts (av. 18.22) in 1967. Took 4 wkts in 4 balls, 5 in 6, 6 in 9, and 7 in 11 (the last two being first-class records) v Sussex (Eastbourne) 1972. Hat-tricks (2): as above and v Worcs (Guildford) 1971. Benson & Hedges Gold Awards: 2. HS: 75* v Notts (Oval) 1968. HSTC: 33 v Pakistan (Hyderabad) 1972-73. HSGC: 14 v Essex (Colchester) 1978. HSJPL: 22 v Notts (Nottingham) 1971. HSBH: 19 v Middlesex (Oval) 1972. BB: 9-57 v Glamorgan (Cardiff) 1979. BBTC: 6-79 v Australia (Manchester) 1968. BBGC: 3-34 v Somerset (Oval) 1975. BBJPL: 4-27 v Essex (Chelmsford) 1974. BBBH: 4-11 v Yorks (Barnsley) 1978.

**Clifton James (Jack) RICHARDS** (Humphrey Davy GS, Penzance) B Penzance 10/8/1958. RHB, WK. Debut 1976. Cap 1978. HS: 50 v Notts (Oval) 1978. HSGC: 14 v Essex (Colchester) 1978. HSJPL: 23* v Essex (Chelmsford) 1980. HSBH: 25* v Derbyshire (Derby) 1979.

**Graham Richard James ROOPE** (Bradfield College) B Fareham, Hants 12/7/1946. RHB, RM. Played for Public Schools XI v Comb. Services (Lord's) 1963 and 1964. Played for Berkshire 1963 scoring century against Wiltshire. Joined county staff and debut 1964. Cap 1969. Played for Griqualand West in 1973-74 Currie Cup competition. Benefit in 1980. Tests: 21 between 1972-73 and 1978. Tours: India, Pakistan and Sri Lanka 1972-73, Pakistan and New Zealand 1977-78.

1,000 runs (8) – 1,641 runs (av. 44.35) in 1971 best. Scored two centuries in match (109 and 103*) v Leics (Leicester) 1971. Held 59 catches in 1971. Benson & Hedges Gold Awards: 3. HS: 171 v Yorks (Oval) 1971. HSTC: 77 v Australia (Oval) 1975. HSGC: 66 v Somerset (Oval) 1975. HSJPL: 120* v Worcs (Byfleet) 1973. HSBH: 115* v Essex (Chelmsford) 1973. BB: 5-14 v West Indians (Oval) 1969. BBGC: 5-23 v Derbyshire (Oval) 1967. BBJPL: 4-31 v Glamorgan (Oval) 1974. BBBH: 3-31 v Essex (Chelmsford) 1978. Soccer (goalkeeper) for Corinthian Casuals and various Southern League sides.

**David Mark SMITH** (Battersea GS) B Balham 9/1/1956. LHB, RM. Played for 2nd XI in 1972. Debut 1973 aged 17 years 4 months, whilst still at school. Cap 1980. Benson & Hedges Gold Awards: 1. HS: 115 v Hants (Portsmouth) 1978. HSGC: 61 v Northants (Northampton) 1979. HSJPL: 87* v Hants (Oval) 1980. HSBH: 45* v Northants (Northampton) 1979 and 45* v Hants (Oval) 1980. BB: 3-40 v Sussex (Oval) 1976. BBGC: 3-39 v Derbyshire (Ilkeston) 1976. BBBH: 4-29 v Kent (Oval) 1980.

**David James THOMAS** (Licensed Victuallers School, Slough) B Solihull, Warwickshire 30/6/1959. LHB, LM. Debut 1977. HS: 43 v Kent (Oval) 1980. HSGC: 17 v Essex (Chelmsford) 1980. HSJPL: 56* v Leics (Oval) 1980. HSBH: 13 v Kent (Oval) 1980. BB: 6-84 v Derbyshire (Oval) 1979. BBJPL: 4-13 v Sussex (Oval) 1978.

**Peter Hugh L'Estrange WILSON** (Wellington College) B Guildford 17/8/1958. 6ft 5ins tall. RHB. RFM. Played for Hants 2nd XI 1976-77. Debut 1978. Played for Northern Transvaal in 1979-80 Currie Cup competition. HS: 29 Northern Transvaal v Transvaal (Pretoria) 1979-80. HSUK: 15 v Worcs (Guildford) 1979. HSJPL: 18* v Worcs (Oval) 1979. BB: 5-36 Northern Transvaal v Eastern Province (Pretoria) 1979-80. BBUK: 4-39 v Warwickshire (Oval) 1979. BBGC: 3-59 v Essex (Colchester) 1978. BBJPL: 4-32 v Middlesex (Oval) 1979. BBBH: 5-21 v Combined Universities (Oval) 1979.

NB. The following player whose particulars appeared in the 1980 Annual has been omitted: S. S. Surridge.

# County Averages

**Schweppes County Championship: Played 22, won 10, drawn 8, lost 4.**
**All first-class matches: Played 24, won 12, drawn 8, lost 4.**

## BATTING AND FIELDING

| Cap | | M | I | NO | Runs | HS | Avge | 100 | 50 | Ct | St |
|-----|---|---|---|----|------|-----|------|-----|----|----|----|
| 1975 | A.R. Butcher | 23 | 39 | 4 | 1679 | 216* | 47.97 | 3 | 12 | 29 | — |
| 1969 | G.R.J. Roope | 23 | 30 | 9 | 996 | 101 | 47.42 | 1 | 10 | 31 | — |
| 1978 | R.D.V. Knight | 24 | 37 | 7 | 1224 | 132 | 40.80 | 4 | 6 | 22 | — |
| 1980 | G.S. Clinton | 24 | 39 | 6 | 1240 | 120 | 37.57 | 1 | 8 | 3 | — |
| — | M.A. Lynch | 8 | 11 | 3 | 291 | 92 | 36.37 | — | 3 | 8 | — |
| 1980 | D.M. Smith | 22 | 31 | 9 | 771 | 104* | 35.04 | 1 | 4 | 18 | — |
| 1969 | Intikhab Alam | 11 | 10 | 3 | 212 | 57* | 30.28 | — | 1 | 1 | — |
| 1970 | R.D. Jackman | 23 | 24 | 8 | 363 | 47 | 22.68 | — | — | 14 | — |
| 1974 | G.P. Howarth | 11 | 17 | 2 | 332 | 66 | 22.13 | — | 3 | 3 | — |
| 1978 | C.J. Richards | 24 | 20 | 6 | 258 | 48 | 18.42 | — | — | 59 | 3 |
| — | D.B. Pauline | 8 | 11 | 1 | 162 | 46 | 16.20 | — | — | 1 | — |
| 1980 | S.T. Clarke | 21 | 18 | 1 | 248 | 55 | 14.58 | — | 1 | 8 | — |
| 1967 | P.I. Pocock | 23 | 16 | 6 | 97 | 20* | 9.70 | — | — | 9 | — |
| — | R.G.L. Cheatle | 14 | 10 | 6 | 29 | 9* | 7.25 | — | — | 8 | — |

*Played in three matches:* P.H.L. Wilson did not bat.
*Played in two matches:* D.J. Thomas 43.

## BOWLING

| | Type | O | M | R | W | Avge | Best | 5 wI | 10 wM |
|---|------|---|---|---|---|------|------|------|-------|
| D.J. Thomas | LM | 54.1 | 15 | 129 | 9 | 14.33 | 4-44 | — | — |
| R.D. Jackman | RFM | 745.2 | 220 | 1864 | 121 | 15.40 | 8-58 | 8 | 1 |
| S.T. Clarke | RF | 605.3 | 139 | 1700 | 79 | 21.51 | 6-73 | 4 | — |
| Intikhab Alam | LBG | 277.2 | 83 | 792 | 36 | 22.00 | 5-83 | 1 | — |
| R.D.V. Knight | RM | 307 | 74 | 838 | 34 | 24.64 | 4-9 | — | — |
| P.I. Pocock | OB | 565.4 | 155 | 1430 | 51 | 28.03 | 6-40 | 3 | — |
| R.G.L. Cheatle | SLA | 257.3 | 88 | 659 | 23 | 28.65 | 5-28 | 2 | — |
| P.H.L. Wilson | RFM | 81 | 21 | 174 | 6 | 29.00 | 2-31 | — | — |
| D.M. Smith | RM | 93 | 25 | 245 | 5 | 49.00 | 2-51 | — | — |

*Also bowled:* A.R. Butcher 25-7-58-1; G.S. Clinton 8-0-77-2; G.P. Howarth
20-2-102-1; M.A. Lynch 7-2-19-0; D.B. Pauline 3-0-5-0; G.R.J. Roope 17-3-63-1.

# County Records

### First-class cricket

| | | | |
|---|---|---|---|
| Highest innings<br>totals: | For | – 811 v Somerset (The Oval) | 1899 |
| | Agst | – 705-8d by Sussex (Hastings) | 1902 |
| Lowest innings<br>totals: | For | – 16 v Nottinghamshire (The Oval) | 1880 |
| | Agst | – 15 by MCC (Lord's) | 1839 |
| Highest Indi-<br>vidual innings: | For | – 357* R. Abel v Somerset (The Oval) | 1899 |
| | Agst | – 300* F. B. Watson for Lancashire (Manchester) | 1928 |
| | | – 300 R. Subba Row for Northants (The Oval) | 1958 |
| Best bowling<br>in an innings: | For | – 10-43 T. Rushby v Somerset (Taunton) | 1921 |
| | Agst | – 10-28 W. P. Howell for Australians (The Oval) | 1899 |
| Best bowling<br>in a match: | For | – 16-83 G. A. R. Lock v Kent (Blackheath) | 1956 |
| | Agst | – 15-57 W. P. Howell for Australians (The Oval) | 1899 |

| | | |
|---|---|---|
| Most runs in a season: | 3246 (av. 72.13) T. W. Hayward | 1906 |
| runs in a career: | 43554 (av. 49.72) J. B. Hobbs | 1905-1934 |
| 100s in a season: | 13 by T. W. Hayward and | 1906 |
| | J. B. Hobbs | 1925 |
| 100s in a career: | 144 by J. B. Hobbs | 1905-1934 |
| wickets in a season: | 250 (av. 14.06) T. Richardson | 1895 |
| wickets in a career: | 1775 (av. 17.88) T. Richardson | 1892-1905 |

## RECORD WICKET STANDS

| | | | |
|---|---|---|---|
| 1st | 428 | J. B. Hobbs & A. Sandham v Oxford U (The Oval) | 1926 |
| 2nd | 371 | J. B. Hobbs & E. G. Hayes v Hampshire (The Oval) | 1909 |
| 3rd | 353 | A. Ducat & E. G. Hayes v Hampshire (Southampton) | 1919 |
| 4th | 448 | R. Abel & T. W. Hayward v Yorkshire (The Oval) | 1899 |
| 5th | 308 | J. N. Crawford & F. C. Holland v Somerset (The Oval) | 1908 |
| 6th | 298 | A. Sandham & H. S. Harrison v Sussex (The Oval) | 1913 |
| 7th | 200 | T. F. Shepherd & J. W. Hitch v Kent (Blackheath) | 1921 |
| 8th | 204 | T. W. Hayward & L. C. Braund v Lancashire (The Oval) | 1898 |
| 9th | 168 | E. R. T. Holmes & E. W. J. Brooks v Hampshire (The Oval) | 1936 |
| 10th | 173 | A. Ducat & A. Sandham v Essex (Leyton) | 1921 |

### One-day cricket

| | | | |
|---|---|---|---|
| Highest innings<br>totals: | Gillette Cup | 280-5 v Middlesex (The Oval) | 1970 |
| | John Player League | 248-2 v Glos (The Oval) | 1976 |
| | Benson & Hedges Cup | 264 v Kent (The Oval) | 1976 |
| Lowest innings<br>totals: | Gillette Cup | 74 v Kent (The Oval) | 1967 |
| | John Player League | 64 v Worcs (Worcester) | 1978 |
| | Benson & Hedges Cup | 125 v Sussex (Hove) | 1972 |
| Highest indi-<br>vidual innings: | Gillette Cup | 101 M.J. Stewart v Durham<br>(Chester-le-Street) | 1972 |
| | John Player League | 122 G.P. Howarth v<br>Gloucestershire (The Oval) | 1976 |
| | Benson & Hedges Cup | 115 G.R.J. Roope v Essex<br>(Chelmsford) | 1973 |
| Best bowling<br>figures: | Gillette Cup | 7-33 R.D. Jackman v<br>Yorkshire (Harrogate) | 1970 |
| | John Player League | 6-25 Intikhab Alam v<br>Derbyshire (The Oval) | 1974 |
| | Benson & Hedges Cup | 5-21 P.H.L. Wilson v<br>Combined U. (The Oval) | 1979 |

# SUSSEX

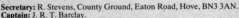

**Formation of present club:** 1839, reorganised 1857.
**Colours:** Dark blue, light blue, and gold.
**Badge:** County Arms of six martlets (in shape of
  inverted pyramid).
**County Championship Runners-up (6):** 1902,
  1903, 1932, 1933, 1934 and 1953.
**Gillette Cup Winners (3):** 1963, 1964, and 1978.
**Gillette Cup Finalists (3):** 1968, 1970, and 1973.
**John Player League Runners-up:** 1976.
**Benson & Hedges Cup Quarter-Finalists (3):** 1972,
  1977 and 1980.
**Gillette Man of the Match Awards:** 30.
**Benson & Hedges Gold Awards:** 22.

**Secretary:** R. Stevens, County Ground, Eaton Road, Hove, BN3 3AN.
**Captain:** J. R. T. Barclay.
**Prospects of Play Telephone No:** Hove (0273) 772766.

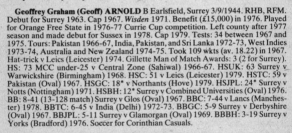

**Geoffrey Graham (Geoff) ARNOLD** B Earlsfield, Surrey 3/9/1944. RHB, RFM.
Debut for Surrey 1963. Cap 1967. *Wisden* 1971. Benefit (£15,000) in 1976. Played
for Orange Free State in 1976-77 Currie Cup competition. Left county after 1977
season and made debut for Sussex in 1978. Cap 1979. Tests: 34 between 1967 and
1975. Tours: Pakistan 1966-67, India, Pakistan, and Sri Lanka 1972-73, West Indies
1973-74, Australia and New Zealand 1974-75. Took 109 wkts (av. 18.22) in 1967.
Hat-trick v Leics (Leicester) 1974. Gillette Man of Match Awards: 3 (2 for Surrey).
HS: 73 MCC under-25 v Central Zone (Sahiwal) 1966-67. HSUK: 63 Surrey v
Warwickshire (Birmingham) 1968. HSC: 51 v Leics (Leicester) 1979. HSTC: 59 v
Pakistan (Oval) 1967. HSGC: 18* v Northants (Hove) 1979. HSJPL: 24* Surrey v
Notts (Nottingham) 1971. HSBH: 12* Surrey v Combined Universities (Oval) 1976.
BB: 8-41 (13-128 match) Surrey v Glos (Oval) 1967. BBC: 7-44 v Lancs (Manches-
ter) 1978. BBTC: 6-45 v India (Delhi) 1972-73. BBGC: 5-9 Surrey v Derbyshire
(Oval) 1967. BBJPL: 5-11 Surrey v Glamorgan (Oval) 1969. BBBH: 3-19 Surrey v
Yorks (Bradford) 1976. Soccer for Corinthian Casuals.

**John Robert Troutbeck BARCLAY** (Eton College) B Bonn, West Germany
22/1/1954. RHB, OB. Debut 1970 aged 16 years 205 days, whilst still at school. Was
in XI at school from age of 14 and scored the record number of runs for school in a
season in 1970. Played in MCC Schools matches at Lord's in 1969-71. Vice-captain
of England Schools Cricket Association team to India 1970-71. Captain of England
Young Cricketers team to West Indies 1972. Cap 1976. Played for Orange Free
State in 1978-79 Castle Bowl Competition. Appointed county captain for 1981.
1,000 runs (4) – 1,093 runs (av.32.14) in 1979 best. Benson & Hedges Gold Awards:
2. HS: 119 v Leics (Hove) 1980. HSGC: 44 v Derbyshire (Hove) 1977, and 44 v
Somerset (Lord's) 1978. HSJPL: 48 v Derbyshire (Derby) 1974. HSBH: 93* v
Surrey (Oval) 1976. BB: 6-61 v Sri Lankans (Horsham) 1979. BBGC: 3-27 v Lancs
(Hove) 1978. BBJPL: 3-11 v Worcs (Eastbourne) 1978. BBBH: 5-43 v Combined
Universities (Oxford) 1979.

**Timothy Douglas BOOTH JONES** (Hastings GS) B Dover 6/8/1952. RHB.
Played for 2nd XI in 1979. Debut 1980. HS: 89* v Cambridge U (Hastings) 1980.
HSJPL: 30 v Worcs (Horsham) 1980. Trained as a teacher at St. Luke's College of
Education, Exeter.

134

SUSSEX

**Ian James GOULD** B Slough, Bucks 19/8/1957. LHB, WK. Joined staff 1972. Debut for Middlesex 1975. Toured West Indies with England Young Cricketers 1976. Cap 1977. Played for Auckland in Shell Trophy in 1979-80. Left county after 1980 season and has joined Sussex for 1981. HS: 128 Middlesex v Worcs (Worcester) 1978. HSGC: 58 Middlesex v Derbyshire (Derby) 1978. HSJPL: 36* Middlesex v Yorks (Lord's) 1975. HSBH: 32 Middlesex v Notts (Nottingham) 1979.

**Allan Michael GREEN** (Brighton Sixth Form College) B Pulborough, Sussex 28/5/1960. RHB, RM. Joined staff 1979. Debut 1980. One match v Cambridge U (Hastings).

**Ian Alexander GREIG** (Queen's College, Queenstown and Cambridge) B Queenstown, South Africa 8/12/1955. RHB, RM. Younger brother of A.W. Greig. Debut for Border in 1974-75 Currie Cup competition. Played for Griqualand West in 1975-76. Has played for county 2nd XI since 1976. Debut for Cambridge U 1977. Blue 1977-78-79 (captain). Appeared in one John Player League match for county in 1979. Re-appeared for Border in 1979-80 Castle Bowl competition. Debut for county 1980 and is regarded as an English player for qualification purposes. HS: 96 Cambridge U v Kent (Canterbury) 1977. HSC: 53 v Somerset (Hove) 1980. HSGC: 17 v Middlesex (Hove) 1980. HSJPL: 30* v Essex (Hastings) 1980 and 30 v Middlesex (Hove) 1980. HSBH: 37 Combined Universities v Surrey (Oval) 1979. BB: 5-60 Border v Western Province B (Cape Town) 1979-80. BBUK: 4-76 Cambridge U v Glamorgan (Cambridge) 1977. BBC: 3-74 v Essex (Hove) 1980. BBBH: 3-51 Combined Universities v Glamorgan (Oxford) 1978. Blues for rugby 1977-78.

**Timothy John (Tim) HEAD** (Lancing College) B Hammersmith 22/9/1957. RHB, WK. Debut 1976. HS: 41 v Kent (Hove) 1980. HSJPL: 24 v Notts (Eastbourne) 1980. Held 7 catches in his debut match v Oxford U (Pagham).

**Jerry Richard Percy HEATH** (Imberhorne Comprehensive School, East Grinstead) B Turner's Hill, Sussex 26/4/1959. LHB. Debut 1980. One match v Yorks (Middlesbrough) and also played in two John Player League matches. HSJPL: 35 v Hants (Hove) 1980.

**IMRAN KHAN NIAZI** (Aitchison College and Cathedral School, Lahore, Worcester RGS and Oxford) B Lahore, Pakistan 25/11/1952. RHB, RF. Cousin of Majid Jahangir Khan. Debut for Lahore A 1969-70 and has played subsequently for various Lahore teams. Debut for Worcs 1971. Blue 1973-74-75 (capt. in 1974). Cap 1976. Left Worcs in 1977 and joined Sussex by special registration. Cap 1978. Tests: 29 for Pakistan between 1971 and 1979-80. Tours: Pakistan to England 1971 and 1974, Australia and West Indies 1976-77, New Zealand and Australia 1978-79, India 1979-80. 1,000 runs (3) – 1,339 runs (av. 41.84) in 1978 best. Scored two centuries in match (117* and 106), Oxford U v Notts (Oxford) 1974. Had match double of 111* and 13-99 (7-53 & 6-46) v Lancs (Worcester) 1976. Gillette Man of Match Awards: 4. (1 for Worcs). Benson & Hedges Gold Awards: 6. (1 for Oxford and Cambridge Universities, 1 for Worcs). HS: 170 Oxford U v Northants (Oxford) 1974. HSC: 167 v Glos (Hove) 1978. HSTC: 123 Pakistan v West Indies (Lahore) 1980-81. HSGC: 63* v Suffolk (Hove) 1980. HSJPL: 75 Worcs v Warwickshire (Worcester) 1976. HSBH: 72 Worcs v Warwickshire (Birmingham) 1976. BB: 7-52 v Glos (Bristol) 1978. BBTC: 6-63 (12-165 match) Pakistan v Australia (Sydney) 1976-77. BBGC: 4-27 v Staffs (Stone) 1978. BBJPL: 5-29 Worcs v Leics (Leicester) 1973. BBBH: 5-8 v Northants (Northampton) 1978.

**Garth Stirling LE ROUX** (Wynberg Boys High School) B Cape Town 4/9/1955.

135

## SUSSEX

6ft 3ins tall. RHB, RF. Debut for Western Province B in 1975-76 Currie Cup competition. Played for Derbyshire 2nd XI in 1977. Debut for county 1978. One match v New Zealanders (Hove). Joined staff in 1979. HS: 70* Western Province v Northern Transvaal (Cape Town) 1979-80. HSUK: 68* v Leics (Hove) 1980. HSJPL: 34 v Warwickshire (Birmingham) 1980. BB: 7-40 Western Province v Eastern Province (Port Elizabeth) 1977-78. BBUK: 6-84 v Essex (Hove) 1980. BBGC: 3-27 v Suffolk (Hove) 1980. BBJPL: 3-38 v Essex (Hastings) 1980.

**Gehan Dixon MENDIS** (St Thomas College, Colombo and Brighton, Hove and Sussex GS) B Colombo, Ceylon 20/4/1955. RHB, WK. Played for 2nd XI since 1971. Played in one John Player League match in 1973. Debut 1974. Cap 1980. Scored 1,437 runs (av. 35.04) in 1980. Gillette Man of Match Awards: 2. Benson & Hedges Gold Awards: 2. HS: 204 v Northants (Eastbourne) 1980. HSGC: 141* v Warwickshire (Hove) 1980. HSJPL: 70 v Hants (Hove) 1980. HSBH: 109 v Glos (Hove) 1980. Trained as a teacher at Bede College, Durham University.

**Paul William Giles PARKER** (Collyers' GS, Horsham and Cambridge) B Bulawayo, Rhodesia 15/1/1956. RHB, RM. Debut for both Cambridge U and county 1976. Blue 1976-77-78. University Secretary for 1977 and 1978. Cap 1979. Elected Best Young Cricketer for the Year in 1979 by Cricket Writers' Club. 1,000 runs (3) – 1,330 runs (av. 44.33) in 1979 best. Gillette Man of Match Awards: 2. HS: 215 Cambridge U v Essex (Cambridge) 1976. HSC: 122* v Northants (Eastbourne) 1980. HSGC: 69 v Lancs (Hove) 1978. HSJPL: 106* v Worcs (Horsham) 1980. HSBH: 59 v Middlesex (Lord's) 1980. Selected for University rugby match in 1977, but had to withdraw through injury.

**Christopher Paul PHILLIPSON** (Ardingly College) B Brindaban, India 10/2/1952. RHB, RM. Debut 1970. Cap 1980. Benson & Hedges Gold Awards: 1. HS: 87 v Hants (Hove) 1980. HSGC: 70* v Suffolk (Hove) 1980. HSJPL: 71 v Lancs (Hastings) 1979. HSBH: 38* v Essex (Chelmsford) 1979. BB: 6-56 v Notts (Hove) 1972. BBJPL: 4-25 v Middlesex (Eastbourne) 1972. BBBH: 5-32 v Combined Universities (Oxford) 1977. Trained as a teacher at Loughborough College of Education.

**Anthony Charles Shackleton (Tony) PIGOTT** (Harrow School) B London 4/6/1958. RHB, RFM. Played for 2nd XI since 1975. Debut 1978. Hat-trick v Surrey (Hove) 1978. HS: 55 v Yorks (Hove) 1979. HSGC: 30 v Northants (Hove) 1979. HSJPL: 49 v Warwickshire (Hove) 1979. BB: 4-40 v Cambridge U (Cambridge) 1979. BBGC: 3-43 v Notts (Hove) 1979. BBJPL: 3-29 v Middlesex (Hove) 1980. BBBH: 3-47 v Essex (Chelmsford) 1980.

**Christopher Edward (Chris) WALLER** B Guildford 3/10/1948. RHB, SLA. Debut for Surrey 1967. Cap 1972. Left staff after 1973 season and made debut for Sussex in 1974. Cap 1976. HS: 47 Surrey v Pakistanis (Oval) 1971. HSC: 38 v Worcs (Worcester) 1975. HSGC: 14* v Notts (Nottingham) 1975. HSJPL: 18* v Glamorgan (Hove) 1975. HSBH: 11* v Essex (Chelmsford) 1975. BB: 7-64 Surrey v Sussex (Oval) 1971. BBC: 6-40 v Surrey (Hove) 1975. BBJPL: 4-28 v Essex (Hove) 1976. BBBH: 4-25 v Minor Counties (South) (Hove) 1975.

**Colin Mark WELLS** (Tideway School, Newhaven) B Newhaven 3/3/1960. RHB, RM. Played in three John Player League matches in 1978. Debut 1979. Scored 1,024 runs (av. 44.52) in 1980. HS: 135 v Glamorgan (Swansea) 1980. HSGC: 23 v Middlesex (Hove) 1980. HSJPL: 65* v Essex (Hastings) 1980. BB: 4-23 v Oxford U (Pagham) 1979. BBBH: 4-21 v Middlesex (Lord's) 1980.

**Kepler Christoffel WESSELS** (Greys College, Bloemfontein) B Bloemfontein, South Africa 14/9/1957. LHB, OB. Debut for Orange Free State 1973-74 in Currie Cup competition, aged 16 years 4 months. Debut for county 1976. Cap 1977. Is now a naturalised Australian and is eligible to play for Australia. Has played for Queensland in Sheffield Shield competition since 1979-80. 1,000 runs (2) – 1,800 runs (av. 52.94) in 1979 best. Benson & Hedges Gold Awards: 2. HS: 254 v Middlesex (Hove) 1980. HSGC: 43 v Staffs (Stone) 1978. HSJPL: 88 v Notts (Nottingham) 1977. HSBH: 106 v Notts (Hove) 1977.

**Alan WILLOWS** (Portslade Community College and Sixth Form Centre) B Portslade, Sussex 24/4/1961. RHB, SLA. Played for 2nd XI in 1979. Debut 1980 (three matches). BB: 4-33 v Hants (Southampton) 1980.

NB. The following players whose particulars appeared in the 1980 Annual have been omitted: C.D.B. Fletcher (not re-engaged), P.J. Graves (retired), A. Long (retired) and J. Spencer (retired) who will have a benefit in 1981.

The career records of Graves, Long and Spencer will be found elsewhere in this annual.

# County Averages

**Schweppes County Championship: Played 22, won 4, drawn 15, lost 3.**
**All first-class matches: Played 24, won 4, drawn 17, lost 3.**

## BATTING AND FIELDING

| Cap | | M | I | NO | Runs | HS | Avge | 100 | 50 | Ct | St |
|---|---|---|---|---|---|---|---|---|---|---|---|
| 1977 | K.C. Wessels | 15 | 29 | 4 | 1562 | 254 | 65.08 | 2 | 11 | 13 | |
| — | C.M. Wells | 20 | 28 | 5 | 1024 | 135 | 44.52 | 1 | 6 | 6 | |
| 1976 | Imran Khan | 17 | 28 | 6 | 863 | 124 | 39.22 | 2 | 5 | 1 | |
| 1979 | P.W.G. Parker | 21 | 38 | 6 | 1167 | 122* | 36.46 | 4 | 3 | 15 | |
| 1980 | G.D. Mendis | 24 | 42 | 1 | 1437 | 204 | 35.04 | 1 | 8 | 6 | |
| 1976 | J.R.T. Barclay | 16 | 26 | 3 | 783 | 119 | 34.04 | 2 | 3 | 9 | |
| — | T.D. Booth Jones | 10 | 17 | 1 | 493 | 89* | 30.81 | — | 4 | 2 | |
| 1969 | P.J. Graves | 4 | 7 | 0 | 206 | 98 | 29.42 | — | 1 | 1 | |
| — | G.S. Le Roux | 15 | 20 | 5 | 431 | 68* | 28.73 | — | 3 | 3 | |
| — | I.A. Greig | 16 | 19 | 5 | 366 | 53 | 26.14 | — | 2 | 12 | |
| 1980 | C.P. Phillipson | 23 | 33 | 3 | 655 | 87 | 21.83 | — | 4 | 24 | |
| 1976 | A. Long | 16 | 15 | 5 | 165 | 31 | 16.50 | — | — | 31 | 1 |
| 1973 | J. Spencer | 8 | 9 | 4 | 66 | 14* | 13.20 | — | — | 3 | |
| 1976 | C.E. Waller | 20 | 17 | 11 | 79 | 15* | 13.16 | — | — | 7 | — |
| — | T.J. Head | 8 | 8 | 0 | 87 | 41 | 10.87 | — | — | 13 | 4 |
| — | A.C.S. Pigott | 5 | 7 | 2 | 52 | 17 | 10.40 | — | — | — | |
| 1979 | G.G. Arnold | 21 | 17 | 2 | 155 | 29* | 10.33 | — | — | 6 | — |
| — | A. Willows | 3 | 1 | 0 | 1 | 1 | 1.00 | — | — | — | |

*Played in one match:* A.M. Green 0; J.R.P. Heath 0.

## BOWLING

| | Type | O | M | R | W | Avge | Best | 5 wI | 10 wM |
|---|---|---|---|---|---|---|---|---|---|
| Imran Khan | RF | 402.5 | 109 | 967 | 54 | 17.90 | 6-80 | 2 | — |
| G.S. Le Roux | RFM | 281.3 | 84 | 780 | 33 | 23.63 | 6-84 | 2 | — |
| J.R.T. Barclay | OB | 274.5 | 77 | 718 | 30 | 23.93 | 5-58 | 1 | — |
| A. Willows | SLA | 82.2 | 26 | 203 | 8 | 25.37 | 4-33 | — | — |
| G.G. Arnold | RFM | 505.1 | 180 | 1220 | 47 | 25.95 | 5-29 | 1 | — |
| C.E. Waller | SLA | 480.4 | 128 | 1292 | 43 | 30.04 | 4-17 | — | — |
| A.C.S. Pigott | RFM | 62.1 | 4 | 250 | 7 | 35.71 | 4-65 | — | — |
| J. Spencer | RM | 194 | 53 | 537 | 14 | 38.35 | 5-97 | 1 | — |
| I.A. Greig | RM | 165.3 | 35 | 518 | 11 | 47.09 | 3-74 | — | — |
| C.M. Wells | RM | 226 | 39 | 733 | 9 | 81.44 | 2-53 | — | — |

*Also bowled:* P.W.G. Parker 1-0-12-0; C.P. Phillipson 42-5-142-1; K.C. Wessels 3-0-7-0.

# County Records

### First-class cricket

| | | |
|---|---|---|
| Highest innings totals: | For – 705-8d v Surrey (Hastings) | 1902 |
| | Agst – 726 by Nottinghamshire (Nottingham) | 1895 |
| Lowest innings totals: | For – 19 v Surrey (Godalming) | 1830 |
| | 19 v Nottinghamshire (Hove) | 1873 |
| | Agst – 18 by Kent (Gravesend) | 1867 |
| Highest individual innings | For – 333 K.S. Duleepsinhji v Northants (Hove) | 1930 |
| | Agst – 322 E. Paynter for Lancashire (Hove) | 1937 |
| Best bowling in an innings: | For – 10-48 C. H. G. Bland v Kent (Tonbridge) | 1899 |
| | Agst – 9-11 A. P. Freeman for Kent (Hove) | 1922 |
| Best bowling in a match: | For – 17-106 G.R. Cox v Warwickshire (Horsham) | 1926 |
| | Agst – 17-67 A. P. Freeman for Kent (Hove) | 1922 |

| | | |
|---|---|---|
| Most runs in a season: | 2850 (av. 64.77) John Langridge | 1949 |
| runs in a career: | 34152 (av. 37.69) John Langridge | 1928-1955 |
| 100s in a season: | 12 by John Langridge | 1949 |
| 100s in a career: | 76 by John Langridge | 1928-1955 |
| wickets in a season: | 198 (av. 13.45) M. W. Tate | 1925 |
| wickets in a career: | 2223 (av. 16.34) M. W. Tate | 1912-1937 |

## RECORD WICKET STANDS

| | | | |
|---|---|---|---|
| 1st | 490 | E. H. Bowley & John Langridge v Middlesex (Hove) | 1933 |
| 2nd | 385 | E. H. Bowley & M. W. Tate v Northamptonshire (Hove) | 1921 |
| 3rd | 298 | K. S. Ranjitsinhji & E. H. Killick v Lancashire (Hove) | 1901 |
| 4th | 326* | G. Cox & James Langridge v Yorkshire (Leeds) | 1949 |
| 5th | 297 | J. H. Parks & H. W. Parks v Hampshire (Portsmouth) | 1937 |
| 6th | 255 | K. S. Duleepsinhji & M. W. Tate v Northamptonshire (Hove) | 1930 |
| 7th | 344 | K. S. Ranjitsinhji & W. Newham v Essex (Leyton) | 1902 |
| 8th | 229* | C. L. A. Smith & G. Brann v Kent (Hove) | 1902 |
| 9th | 178 | H. W. Parks & A. F. Wensley v Derbyshire (Horsham) | 1930 |
| 10th | 156 | G. R. Cox & H. R. Butt v Cambridge U (Cambridge) | 1908 |

## One-day cricket

| | | | |
|---|---|---|---|
| Highest innings totals: | Gillette Cup | 314-7 v Kent (Tunbridge Wells) | 1963 |
| | John Player League | 293-4 v Worcestershire (Horsham) | 1980 |
| | Benson & Hedges Cup | 280-5 v Cambridge U (Hove) | 1974 |
| Lowest innings totals: | Gillette Cup | 49 v Derbyshire (Chesterfield) | 1969 |
| | John Player League | 61 v Derbyshire (Derby) | 1978 |
| | Benson & Hedges Cup | 61 v Middlesex (Hove) | 1978 |
| Highest individual innings: | Gillette Cup | 141* G. D. Mendis v Warwickshire (Hove) | 1980 |
| | John Player League | 129 A. W. Greig v Yorkshire (Scarborough) | 1976 |
| | Benson & Hedges Cup | 114* P. J. Graves v Cambridge U (Hove) | 1974 |
| Best bowling figures: | Gillette Cup | 6-30 D. L. Bates v Gloucestershire (Hove) | 1968 |
| | John Player League | 6-14 M. A. Buss v Lancashire (Hove) | 1973 |
| | Benson & Hedges Cup | 5-8 Imran Khan v Northamptonshire (Northampton) | 1978 |

# WARWICKSHIRE

**Formation of present club:** 1884.
**Colours:** Blue, gold, and silver.
**Badge:** Bear and ragged staff.
**County Champions (3):** 1911, 1951 and 1972.
**Gillette Cup Winners (2):** 1966 and 1968.
**Gillette Cup Finalists (2):** 1964 and 1972.
**John Player League Champions:** 1980.
**Benson & Hedges Cup Semi-Finalists (4):** 1972, 1975, 1976 and 1978.
**Gillette Man of the Match Awards:** 21.
**Benson & Hedges Gold Awards:** 23.

**Secretary:** A.C. Smith, County Ground, Edgbaston, Birmingham B5 7QU.
**Cricket Manager:** D.J. Brown.
**Captain:** R.G.D. Willis.
**Prospects of Play Telephone No:** (021) 440 3624.

**Dennis Leslie AMISS** B Birmingham 7/4/1943. RHB, SLC. Joined county staff 1958. Debut 1960. Cap 1965. *Wisden* 1974. Benefit (£34,947) in 1975. Tests: 50 between 1966 and 1977. Played in one match v Rest of World in 1970. Tours: Pakistan 1966-67, India, Pakistan, and Sri Lanka 1972-73, West Indies 1973-74, Australia and New Zealand 1974-75, India, Sri Lanka and Australia 1976-77. 1,000 runs (16) – 2,110 runs (av. 65.93) in 1976 best. Also scored 1,120 runs (av. 74.66) in West Indies 1973-74. Scored two centuries in match (155* and 112) v Worcs (Birmingham) 1978. Gillette Man of the Match Awards: 3. Benson & Hedges Gold Awards: 2. HS: 262* England v West Indies (Kingston) 1973-74. HSUK: 232* v Glos (Bristol) 1979. HSGC: 113 v Glamorgan (Swansea) 1966. HSJPL: 110 v Surrey (Birmingham) 1974. HSBH: 73* v Minor Counties (West) (Coventry) 1977. BB: 3-21 v Middlesex (Lord's) 1970.

**Neville John BULPITT** (Caludon Castle Comprehensive School, Coventry) B Coventry 15/4/1957. RHB, RM. Played for 2nd XI since 1975. Played in last three John Player League matches in 1979. Has yet to appear in first-class cricket. HSJPL: 11 v Yorks (Birmingham) 1979.

**Dilip Rasiklal DOSHI** (J.J. Ajmera High School and Calcutta University) B Rajkot, India 22/12/1947. LHB, SLA. Debut 1968-69 for Vazir Sultan Colts XI v State Bank of India in Moin-ud-Dowlah Tournament at Hyderabad and for Bengal in Ranji Trophy. Played for Sussex 2nd XI in 1972 and for Lancs and Notts 2nd XIs in 1973. Also played for Meltham in Huddersfield League in 1973. Debut for Notts 1973. Not re-engaged after 1974 season. Played for Hertfordshire in 1976. Rejoined Notts in 1977. Not re-engaged after 1978 season. Played for Northumberland in 1979. Debut for Warwickshire 1980. Cap 1980. Tests: 13 for India in 1979-80. Tour: Australia and New Zealand 1980-81. Took 101 wkts (av. 26.73) in 1980. Gillette Man of the Match Awards: 1 (for Herts). HS: 44 Bengal v Delhi (Delhi) 1979-80. HSUK: 23 Notts v Hants (Nottingham) 1978. HSC: 10* v Cambridge U (Cambridge) 1980. HSTC: 20 India v Pakistan (Kanpur) 1979-80. HSBH: 19* v Yorks (Leeds) 1980. BB: 7-29 Bengal v Assam (Nowgong) 1970-71. BBUK: 6-33 Notts v Cambridge U (Cambridge) 1978. BBC: 6-72 v Somerset (Taunton) 1980. BBTC: 6-103 India v Australia (Madras) on Test debut 1979-80. BBGC: 4-23 Herts v Essex (Hitchin) 1976. BBJPL: 3-32 v Worcs (Worcester) 1980.

**Anthonie Michal (Yogi) FERREIRA** (Hillview High School, Pretoria) B Pretoria 13/4/1955. 6ft 3ins tall. RHB, RM. Debut for Northern Transvaal 1974-75. Played for D.H. Robin's XI v both Oxford and Cambridge Universities at Eastbourne in 1978. Debut for county 1979. HS: 90 v Somerset (Taunton) 1980. HSGC: 14 v Oxfordshire (Birmingham) 1980. HSJPL: 37* v Glamorgan (Birmingham) 1980. HSBH: 29 v Northants (Birmingham) 1980. BB: 8-38 Northern Transvaal v Transvaal B (Pretoria) 1977-78. BBUK: 5-66 v Somerset (Birmingham) 1979. BBGC: 4-50 v Notts (Birmingham) 1979. BBJPL: 3-32 v Kent (Maidstone) 1979.

**David Charles HOPKINS** (Moseley GS) B Birmingham 11/2/1957. RHB, RM. 6ft 6½ins tall. Played for 2nd XI since 1975. Debut 1977. HS: 34* v Essex (Birmingham) 1979. HSJPL: 35* v Notts (Birmingham) 1980. BB: 6-67 v Somerset (Taunton) 1979. BBJPL: 3-26 v Lancs (Birmingham) 1979.

**Geoffrey William (Geoff) HUMPAGE** (Golden Hillock Comprehensive School, Birmingham) B Birmingham 24/4/1954. RHB, WK, RM. Debut 1974. Cap 1976. 1,000 runs (3) – 1,339 runs (av. 32.65) in 1980 best. HS: 125* v Sussex (Birmingham) 1976. HSGC: 58 v Somerset (Taunton) 1978. HSJPL: 108* v Middlesex (Birmingham) 1980. HSBH: 78 v Derbyshire (Derby) 1978. BBJPL: 4-53 v Glos (Moreton-in-Marsh) 1979.

**Alvin Isaac (Kalli) KALLICHARRAN** B Port Mourant, Berbice, Guyana 21/3/1949. LHB, OB. 5ft 4ins tall. Debut 1966-67 for Guyana in Shell Shield competition. Debut for county 1971. Cap 1972. Played for Queensland in 1977-78 Sheffield Shield competition. Tests: 62 for West Indies between 1971-72 and 1980 scoring 100* and 101 in first two innings in Tests v New Zealand and captaining country in 9 Tests. Tours: West Indies to England 1973 and 1976. India, Sri Lanka and Pakistan 1974-75, Australia 1975-76, India and Sri Lanka 1978-79 (captain), Australia and New Zealand 1979-80, Pakistan 1980-81. 1,000 runs (6) – 1,343 runs (av. 41.96) in 1977 best. Also scored 1,249 runs (av. 56.77) on 1974-75 tour. Benson & Hedges Gold Awards: 2. HS: 197 Guyana v Jamaica (Kingston) 1973-74. HSUK: 170* v Northants (Northampton) 1979. HSTC: 187 West Indies v India (Bombay) 1978-79. HSGC: 88 v Glamorgan (Birmingham) 1972. HSJPL: 101* v Derbyshire (Chesterfield) 1972 and 101 v Glos (Moreton-in-Marsh) 1979. HSBH: 109 v Glos (Bristol) 1978. BB: 4-48 v Derbyshire (Birmingham) 1978.

**Timothy Andrew (Andy) LLOYD** (Oswestry Boys' HS) B Oswestry, Shropshire 5/11/1956. LHB, RM. Played for both Shropshire and county 2nd XI in 1975. Appeared in one John Player League match in 1976 v Yorks (Leeds). Debut 1977. Played for Orange Free State in 1978-79 and 1979-80 Castle Bowl competitions. Cap 1980. Scored 1,423 runs (av. 36.48) in 1980. HS: 130* v Worcs (Birmingham) 1980. HSGC: 81 v Devon (Birmingham) 1980. HSJPL: 90 v Kent (Birmingham) 1980. HSBH: 47 v Northants (Birmingham) 1980.

**Gordon John LORD** (Warwick School) B Warwick 25/4/1961. LHB, SLA. Toured Australia 1979 and West Indies 1980 with England Young Cricketers. Joined staff in 1980. Has yet to appear in first-class cricket.

**Robert Keith MAGUIRE** (Smiths Wood School, Chelmsley Wood, Birmingham) B Birmingham 20/3/1961. RHB, RM. Joined staff in 1980. Has yet to appear in first-class cricket.

**Christopher (Chris) MAYNARD** (Bishop Vesey's GS, Sutton Coldfield) B Haslemere, Surrey 8/4/1958. RHB, WK. Played for 2nd XI since 1976. Debut 1978. HS: 85 v Kent (Birmingham) 1979. HSJPL: 35 v Essex (Birmingham) 1979. HSBH: 17* v Yorks (Leeds) 1980.

# WARWICKSHIRE

**Philip Robert OLIVER** B West Bromwich, Staffs 9/5/1956. RHB, OB. Played for Shropshire 1972-74. Debut 1975. HS: 83 v Yorks (Birmingham) 1979. HSGC: 32* v Oxfordshire (Birmingham) 1980. HSJPL: 78* v Hants (Southampton) 1978. HSBH: 46 v Essex (Chelmsford) 1979. BBJPL: 3-36 v Middlesex (Lord's) 1977. Has played soccer for Telford in Southern League.

**Stephen Peter (Steve) PERRYMAN** (Sheldon Heath Comprehensive School) B Yardley, Birmingham 22/10/1955. RHB, RM. Debut 1974. Cap 1977. Benson & Hedges Gold Awards: 1. HS: 43 v Somerset (Birmingham) 1977. HSJPL: 17* v Worcs (Birmingham) 1975. HSBH: 18 v Essex (Chelmsford) 1979. BB: 7-49 v Hants (Bournemouth) 1978. BBGC: 3-35 v Middlesex (Lord's) 1977. BBJPL: 4-19 v Surrey (Oval) 1975. BBBH: 4-17 v Minor Counties (West) (Birmingham) 1978.

**Stephen John (Mic) ROUSE** (Moseley County School) B Merthyr Tydfil, Glamorgan 20/1/1949. LHB, LFM. Debut 1970. Cap 1974. Benson & Hedges Gold Awards: 2. HS: 93 v Hants (Bournemouth) 1976. HSGC: 34 v Middlesex (Lord's) 1977. HSJPL: 38* v Surrey (Birmingham) 1980. HSBH: 34* v Glamorgan (Birmingham) 1978. BB: 6-34 v Leics (Leicester) 1976. BBGC: 4-27 v Sussex (Hove) 1976. BBJPL: 5-20 v Kent (Canterbury) 1976. BBBH: 5-21 v Worcs (Worcester) 1974.

**Gladstone Cleopthas SMALL** (Moseley School, Birmingham) B St. George, Barbados 18/10/1961. RHB, RFM. Played for 2nd XI in 1979. Toured New Zealand with D.H. Robins' XI in 1979-80 and made debut v Northern Districts (Hamilton). Debut for county 1980. HS: 16 v Northants (Northampton) 1980. HSJPL: 17 v Notts (Birmingham) 1980. BB: 3-42 v Worcs (Worcester) 1980. BBJPL: 3-9 v Sussex (Birmingham) 1980.

**Kenneth David SMITH** (Heaton GS, Newcastle-upon-Tyne) B Jesmond, Newcastle-upon-Tyne 9/7/1956. RHB. Son of Kenneth D. Smith, former Northumberland and Leics player. Played for 2nd XI 1972. Debut 1973. Cap 1978. 1,000 runs (3) – 1,582 runs (av. 36.79) in 1980 best. Benson & Hedges Gold Awards: 1. HS: 140 v Worcs (Worcester) 1980. HSGC: 64 v Sussex (Hove) 1980. HSJPL: 60 v Glamorgan (Swansea) 1979. HSBH: 84 v Worcs (Worcester) 1980.

**John Augustine SNOW** (Christ's Hospital, Horsham) B Peopleton, Worcs 13/10/1941. RHB, RFM. Debut for Sussex 1961. Cap 1964. *Wisden* 1972. Benefit (£18,000) in 1974. Not re-engaged after 1977 season. Played for county in John Player League and Gillette Cup in 1980. Tests: 49 between 1969 and 1976. Played in 5 matches v Rest of World 1970. Tours: West Indies 1967-68, Ceylon and Pakistan 1968-69, Australia 1970-71. 100 wkts (2) – 126 wkts (av. 19.09) in 1966 best. Gillette Man of the Match Awards: 1 (for Sussex). Benson & Hedges Gold Awards: 2 (for Sussex). HS: 73 England v India (Lord's) 1971 and 73* Sussex v Worcs (Worcester) 1977. HSGC: 19 Sussex v Worcs (Hove) 1974. HSJPL: 57 Sussex v Lancs (Horsham) 1977. HSBH: 25 Sussex v Essex (Chelmsford) 1977. BB: 8-87 Sussex v Middlesex (Lord's) 1975. BBTC: 7-40 v Australia (Sydney) 1970-71. BBGC: 4-35 Sussex v Surrey (Oval) 1970. BBJPL: 5-15 Sussex v Surrey (Hove) 1972. BBBH: 5-30 Sussex v Kent (Canterbury) 1974.

**Gary Philip THOMAS** (George Dixon GS, Birmingham) B Birmingham 8/11/1958. RHB, RM. Played for 2nd XI since 1975. Debut 1978. Played in one Championship match only in 1979. Did not play in 1980. HSJPL: 16 v Lancs (Manchester) 1978.

**Robert George Dylan (Bob) WILLIS** (Guildford RGS) B Sunderland 30/5/1949.

RHB, RF. Debut for Surrey 1969. Left staff after 1971 season and made debut for Warwickshire in 1972. Cap 1972. *Wisden* 1977. Appointed County Captain in 1980. Benefit in 1981. Tests: 57 between 1970-71 and 1980. Tours: Australia and New Zealand 1970-71 (flown out as replacement for A. Ward) and 1974-75, West Indies 1973-74 and 1980-81 (vice-captain), India, Sri Lanka and Australia 1976-77, Pakistan and New Zealand 1977-78, Australia 1978-79 (vice-captain), Australia and India 1979-80 (vice-captain). Hat-tricks (2) v Derbyshire (Birmingham) 1972 and v West Indians (Birmingham) 1976. Also in John Player League v Yorks (Birmingham) 1973. Gillette Man of the Match Awards: 1 (for Surrey). Benson & Hedges Gold Awards: 3. HS: 43 v Middlesex (Birmingham) 1976. HSTC: 24 v India (Manchester) 1974, 24* v Australia (Oval) 1977, 24 v Australia (Adelaide) 1978-79 and 24* v West Indies (Oval) 1980. HSGC: 12* Surrey v Sussex (Oval) 1970. HSJPL: 52* v Derbyshire (Birmingham) 1975. HSBH: 25* v Northants (Northampton) 1977. BB: 8-32 v Glos (Bristol) 1977. BBTC: 7-78 Australia (Lord's) 1977. BBGC: 6-49 Surrey v Middlesex (Oval) 1970. BBJPL: 4-12 v Middlesex (Lord's) 1973. BBBH: 5-27 v Lancs (Birmingham) 1976. Played soccer (goalkeeper) for Guildford City.

NB. The following players whose particulars appeared in the 1980 annual have been omitted: R.N. Abberley (not re-engaged), D.J. Brown (appointed Cricket Manager), J.A. Claughton (retired owing to injury), C.C. Clifford (not re-engaged), C.A. Sam (not re-engaged), R.L. Savage (not re-engaged), R.A. Smith (not re-engaged) and J. Whitehouse (retired).

The career records of Claughton, Clifford and Whitehouse will be found elsewhere in this annual.

# County Averages

**Schweppes County Championship: Played 22, won 3, drawn 15, lost 4.**
**All first-class matches: Played 25, won 4, drawn 17, lost 4.**

## BATTING AND FIELDING

| Cap | | M | I | NO | Runs | HS | Avge | 100 | 50 | Ct | St |
|---|---|---|---|---|---|---|---|---|---|---|---|
| 1973 | J. Whitehouse | 10 | 19 | 8 | 725 | 197 | 65.90 | 1 | 4 | 3 | — |
| 1965 | D.L. Amiss | 23 | 42 | 2 | 1686 | 117* | 42.15 | 1 | 12 | 11 | — |
| 1978 | K.D. Smith | 25 | 45 | 2 | 1582 | 140 | 36.79 | 2 | 12 | 14 | — |
| 1980 | T.A. Lloyd | 25 | 44 | 5 | 1423 | 130* | 36.48 | 2 | 10 | 12 | — |
| 1976 | G.W. Humpage | 25 | 43 | 2 | 1339 | 101 | 32.65 | 2 | 7 | 42 | 8 |
| — | P.R. Oliver | 22 | 35 | 7 | 772 | 76* | 27.57 | — | 4 | 14 | — |
| 1972 | A.I. Kallicharran | 5 | 9 | 0 | 223 | 52 | 24.77 | — | 1 | 1 | — |
| — | J.A. Claughton | 16 | 28 | 5 | 533 | 108* | 23.17 | 2 | — | 5 | — |
| — | A.M. Ferreira | 19 | 27 | 4 | 523 | 90 | 22.73 | — | 2 | 10 | — |
| — | D.C. Hopkins | 12 | 18 | 9 | 156 | 33 | 17.33 | — | — | — | — |
| 1974 | S.J. Rouse | 15 | 21 | 7 | 233 | 35 | 16.64 | — | — | 4 | — |
| — | C. Maynard | 6 | 8 | 1 | 91 | 30 | 13.00 | — | — | 3 | 3 |
| 1972 | R.G.D. Willis | 15 | 15 | 3 | 124 | 33 | 10.33 | — | — | 8 | — |
| — | G.C. Small | 15 | 15 | 4 | 64 | 16 | 5.81 | — | — | 3 | — |
| 1980 | D.R. Doshi | 25 | 23 | 7 | 81 | 10* | 5.06 | — | — | 3 | — |
| 1977 | S.P. Perryman | 12 | 8 | 4 | 16 | 5 | 4.00 | — | — | 8 | — |
| — | C.C. Clifford | 5 | 4 | 2 | 7 | 6 | 3.50 | — | — | — | — |

# WARWICKSHIRE

## BOWLING

| | Type | O | M | R | W | Avge | Best | 5 wI | 10 wM |
|---|---|---|---|---|---|---|---|---|---|
| D.R. Doshi | **SLA** | 961.2 | 70 | 2700 | 101 | 26.73 | 6-72 | 4 | 1 |
| R.G.D. Willis | **RF** | 347.1 | 91 | 959 | 35 | 27.40 | 4-87 | — | — |
| A.M. Ferreira | **RM** | 367.4 | 81 | 1166 | 40 | 29.15 | 4-75 | — | — |
| G.C. Small | **RFM** | 240 | 52 | 864 | 24 | 36.00 | 3-42 | — | — |
| D.C. Hopkins | **RM** | 208.3 | 50 | 615 | 16 | 38.43 | 4-20 | — | — |
| S.P. Perryman | **RM** | 279 | 64 | 836 | 21 | 39.80 | 4-20 | — | — |
| C.C. Clifford | **OB** | 191 | 41 | 688 | 13 | 52.92 | 4-110 | — | — |
| S.J. Rouse | **LFM** | 243.3 | 41 | 890 | 16 | 55.62 | 3-26 | — | — |
| P.R. Oliver | **OB** | 117 | 18 | 508 | 9 | 56.44 | 2-68 | — | — |

*Also bowled:* G.W. Humpage 12-4-34-3; A.I. Kallicharran 11-2-51-0; T.A. Lloyd 15-3-58-1; J. Whitehouse 1.3-0-12-0.

# County Records

### First-class cricket

| | | |
|---|---|---|
| Highest innings totals: | For – 657-6d v Hampshire (Birmingham) | 1899 |
| | Agst – 887 by Yorkshire (Birmingham) | 1896 |
| Lowest innings totals: | For – 16 v Kent (Tonbridge) | 1913 |
| | Agst – 15 by Hampshire (Birmingham) | 1922 |
| Highest individual innings: | For – 305* F.R. Foster v Worcestershire (Dudley) | 1914 |
| | Agst – 316 R.H. Moore for Hants (Bournemouth) | 1937 |
| Best bowling in an innings: | For – 10-41 J.D. Bannister v Combined Services (Birmingham) | 1959 |
| | Agst – 10-36 H Verity for Yorkshire (Leeds) | 1931 |
| Best bowling in a match: | For – 15-76 S. Hargreave v Surrey (The Oval) | 1903 |
| | Agst – 17-92 A.P. Freeman for Kent (Folkestone) | 1932 |
| Most runs in a season: | 2,417 (av. 60.42) M.J.K. Smith | 1959 |
| runs in a career: | 33,862 (av. 36.18) William Quaife | 1894-1928 |
| 100s in a season: | 8 by R.E.S. Wyatt | 1937 |
| | and R.B. Kanhai | 1972 |
| 100s in a career: | 71 by William Quaife | 1894-1928 |
| wickets in a season: | 180 (av. 15.13) W.E. Hollies | 1946 |
| wickets in a career: | 2,201 (av. 20.45) W.E. Hollies | 1932-1957 |

## RECORD WICKET STANDS

| | | | |
|---|---|---|---|
| 1st | 377* | N.F. Horner & K. Ibadulla v Surrey (The Oval) | 1960 |
| 2nd | 465* | J.A. Jameson & R.B. Kanhai v Gloucestershire (Birmingham) | 1974 |
| 3rd | 327 | S. Kinneir & William Quaife v Lancashire (Birmingham) | 1901 |
| 4th | 402 | R.B. Kanhai & K. Ibadulla v Notts (Nottingham) | 1968 |
| 5th | 268 | Walter Quaife & William Quaife v Essex (Leyton) | 1900 |
| 6th | 220 | H.E. Dollery & J. Buckingham v Derbyshire (Derby) | 1938 |
| 7th | 250 | H.E. Dollery & J.S. Ord v Kent (Maidstone) | 1953 |
| 8th | 228 | A.J.W. Croom & R.E.S. Wyatt v Worcestershire (Dudley) | 1925 |
| 9th | 154 | G.W. Stephens & A.J.W. Croom v Derbyshire (Birmingham) | 1925 |
| 10th | 128 | F.R. Santall & W. Sanders v Yorkshire (Birmingham) | 1930 |

**One-day cricket**

| | | | |
|---|---|---|---|
| Highest innings totals: | Gillette Cup | 314-6 v Oxfordshire (Birmingham) | 1980 |
| | John Player League | 265-5 v Northamptonshire (Northampton) | 1979 |
| | Benson & Hedges Cup | 269-9 v Worcestershire (Birmingham) | 1976 |
| | | 269-9 v Yorkshire (Leeds) | 1980 |
| Lowest innings totals: | Gillette Cup | 109 v Kent (Canterbury) | 1971 |
| | John Player League | 65 v Kent (Maidstone) | 1979 |
| | Benson & Hedges Cup | 96 v Leicestershire (Leicester) | 1972 |
| Highest individual innings | Gillette Cup | 126 R.B. Kanhai v Lincolnshire (Birmingham) | 1971 |
| | John Player League | 123* J.A. Jameson v Nottinghamshire (Nottingham) | 1973 |
| | Benson & Hedges Cup | 119* R.B. Kanhai v Northamptonshire (Northants) | 1975 |
| Best bowling figures: | Gillette Cup | 6-32 K. Ibadulla v Hants (Birmingham) | 1965 |
| | John Player League | 5-13 D.J. Brown v Worcestershire (Birmingham) | 1970 |
| | Benson & Hedges Cup | 5-21 S.J. Rouse v Worcestershire (Worcester) | 1974 |

# WORCESTERSHIRE

**Formation of present club:** 1865.
**Colours:** Dark Green and Black.
**Badge:** Shield, *Argent*, bearing *Fess* between three
*Pears Sable*.
**County Champions (3):** 1964, 1965 and 1974.
**Gillette Cup Finalists (2):** 1963 and 1966.
**John Player League Champions:** 1971.
**Benson & Hedges Cup Finalists (2):** 1973 and 1976.
**Gillette Man of the Match Awards:** 18.
**Benson & Hedges Gold Awards:** 25.

**Secretary:** M.D. Vockins, County Ground, New Road, Worcester WR2 4QQ.
**Captain:** G.M. Turner.
**Prospects of Play Telephone No:** (0905) 422011.

**Hartley Leroy ALLEYNE** B Bridgetown, Barbados 27/2/1957. RHB, RFM.
Debut for Barbados in one Shell Shield match in 1978-79. Played for Lincolnshire
and as a professional for Rochdale in Central Lancashire League in 1979. Debut for
county 1980. HS: 72 v Lancs (Stourport-on-Severn) 1980. HSGC: 19 v Somerset
(Taunton) 1980. HSJPL: 32 v Kent (Worcester) 1980. HSBH: 10 v Essex (Worcester) 1980. BB: 6-50 v Notts (Worcester) 1980. BBGC: 3-27 v Somerset (Taunton)
1980. BBJPL: 4-24 v Lancs (Worcester) 1980. BBBH: 3-39 v Lancs (Manchester)
1980.

**Jack BIRKENSHAW** (Rothwell GS) B Rothwell, Yorks 13/11/1940. LHB, OB.
Played for Yorks 1958 to 1960. Specially registered and made debut for Leics in
1961. Cap 1965. Benefit (£13,100) in 1974. Left county after 1980 season and has
joined Worcs for 1981. Tests: 5 in 1972-73 and 1973-74. Tours: India, Pakistan and
Sri Lanka 1972-73, West Indies 1973-74. 100 wkts: (2) – 111 wkts (av. 21.41) in
1967 best. Hat tricks: (2) Leics v Worcs (Worcester) 1967 and Leics v Cambridge U
(Cambridge) 1968. Shared in 7th wkt partnership record for Leics (206) with B.
Dudleston v Kent (Canterbury) 1969. Gillette Man of Match Awards: 1 (for Leics).
HS: 131 Leics v Surrey (Guildford) 1969. HSTC: 64 v India (Kanpur) 1972-73.
HSGC: 101* Leics v Hants (Leicester) 1976. HSJPL: 79 Leics v Yorks (Leicester)
1978. HSBH: 35* Leics v Worcs (Worcester) 1972. BB: 8-94 Leics v Somerset
(Taunton) 1972. BBGC: 3-19 Leics v Somerset (Leicester) 1968. BBJPL: 5-20
Leics v Essex (Leicester) 1975.

**James (Jimmy) CUMBES** (Didsbury Secondary Technical School) B East Didsbury, Lancs 4/5/1944. RHB, RFM. Brother-in-law of R. Collins, former Lancs
player. Debut for Lancs 1963. Not re-engaged at end of 1967 season and made debut
for Surrey in 1968. Not re-engaged after 1970 season and rejoined Lancs in 1971.
Made debut for Worcs in 1972 by special registration. Cap 1978. Hat-trick v
Northants (Worcester) 1977. HS: 43 v Sussex (Hove) 1980. HSJPL: 14* v Sussex
(Eastbourne) 1978. BB: 6-24 v Yorks (Worcester) 1977. BBGC: 4-23 v Sussex
(Hove) 1974. BBJPL: 3-13 v Middlesex (Worcester) 1978. BBBH: 3-34 v Somerset
(Taunton) 1978. Soccer (goalkeeper) for Tranmere Rovers, West Bromwich Albion, Aston Villa and Worcester City.

**Timothy Stephen CURTIS** (Worcester Royal GS) B Chislehurst, Kent 15/1/1960.
RHB, LB. Played for 2nd XI since 1976. Debut 1979. HS: 59* v Warwickshire
(Birmingham) 1980.

**Paul Bernard FISHER** (St. Ignatius College, Enfield and Oxford) B Edmonton 19/12/1954. RHB, WK. Debut for Oxford U 1974. Blue 1975-76-77-78. Played for Middlesex in one Fenner Trophy match and in last John Player League match in 1978. Debut for Middlesex in last two championship matches of 1979. Debut for Worcs 1980. HS: 42 Oxford U v Warwickshire (Oxford) 1975. HSC: 11 v Notts (Worcester) 1971. BBJPL: 4-42 v Essex (Worcester) 1971. Soccer for Shrewsbury Town, Sheffield United and Doncaster Rovers.

**Norman GIFFORD** B Ulverston, Lancs 30/3/1940. LHB, SLA. Joined staff 1958 and made debut 1960. Cap 1961. Appointed county captain in 1971 after being vice-captain since 1969. Relinquished captaincy after 1980. Benefit (£11,047) in 1974. *Wisden* 1974. Awarded MBE in 1978 Birthday Honours list. Second benefit in 1981. Tests: 15 between 1964 and 1973. Played in one match for Rest of World v Australia 1971-72. Tours: Rest of World to Australia 1971-72, India, Pakistan and Sri Lanka 1972-73. 100 wkts: (3) – 133 wkts (av. 19.66) in 1961 best. Hat-trick v Derbyshire (Chesterfield) 1965. Took 4 wkts in 6 balls v Cambridge U (Cambridge) 1972. Gillette Man of Match Awards: 1. Benson & Hedges Gold Awards: 2. HS: 89 v Oxford U (Oxford) 1963. HSTC: 25* v New Zealand (Nottingham) 1973. HSGC: 38 v Warwickshire (Lord's) 1966. HSJPL: 29 v Essex (Worcester) 1974. HSBH: 33 v Kent (Lord's) 1973. BB: 8-28 v Yorks (Sheffield) 1968. BBTC: 5-55 v Pakistan (Karachi) 1972-73. BBGC: 4-7 v Surrey (Worcester) 1972. BBJPL: 5-28 v Northants (Worcester) 1979. BBBH: 6-8 v Minor Counties (South) (High Wycombe) 1979.

**Edward John Orton (Ted) HEMSLEY** (Bridgnorth GS) B Norton, Stoke-on-Trent 1/9/1943. RHB, RM. Debut 1963. Cap 1969. Shared in 6th-wkt partnership record for county, 227 with D.N. Patel v Oxford U (Oxford) 1976. Scored 1,168 runs (av. 38.93) in 1978, Benson & Hedges Gold Awards: 3. HS: 176* v Lancs (Worcester) 1977. HSGC: 73 v Sussex (Hove) 1972. HSJPL: 75* v Glamorgan (Cardiff) 1979. HSBH: 95* v Warwickshire (Worcester) 1980. BB: 3-5 v Warwickshire (Worcester) 1971. BBJPL: 4-42 v Essex (Worcester) 1971. Soccer for Shrewsbury Town, Sheffield United and Doncaster Rovers.

**Stephen Peter HENDERSON** (Downside School) B Oxford 24/9/1958. Son of D. Henderson, former Oxford Blue. LHB, RM. Debut 1977. HS: 64 v Lancs (Stourport-on-Severn) 1980. HSGC: 33 v Glamorgan (Worcester) 1977. HSJPL: 28 v Warwickshire (Worcester) 1980. Studied at Durham University.

**David John HUMPHRIES** B Alveley, Shropshire 6/8/1953. LHB, WK. Played for Shropshire 1971-73. Debut for Leics 1974. Left county after 1976 season and made debut for Worcs in 1977. Cap 1978. Gillette Man of Match Awards: 1. HS: 111* v Warwickshire (Worcester) 1978. HSGC: 58 v Glamorgan (Worcester) 1977. HSJPL: 62 v Notts (Dudley) 1977. HSBH: 27 v Yorks (Worcester) 1980.

**John Darling INCHMORE** (Ashington GS) B Ashington, Northumberland 22/2/1949. RHB, RFM. Played for Northumberland in 1970. Played for both Warwickshire and Worcs 2nd XIs in 1972 and for Stourbridge in Birmingham League. Debut 1973. Cap 1976. Played for Northern Transvaal in 1976-77 Currie Cup competition. Benson & Hedges Gold Awards: 2. HS: 113* v Essex (Worcester) 1974. HSGC: 19* v Leics (Leicester) 1979. HSJPL: 30* v Essex (Dudley) 1976. HSBH: 49* v Somerset (Taunton) 1976. BB: 8-58 v Yorks (Worcester) 1977. BBGC: 3-11 v Essex (Worcester) 1975. BBJPL: 4-9 v Northants (Dudley) 1975. BBBH: 4-21 v Combined Universities (Cambridge) 1980.

# WORCESTERSHIRE

**Philip Anthony (Phil) NEALE** (Frederick Gough Comprehensive School, Bottesford and John Leggott Sixth Form College, Scunthorpe) B Scunthorpe, Lincs 5/6/1954. RHB, RM. Played for Lincolnshire 1973-74. Debut 1975. Cap 1978. 1,000 runs: (2) – 1,305 runs (av. 42.09) in 1979 best. HS: 163* v Notts (Worcester) 1979. HSGC: 68 v Glos (Bristol) 1976. HSJPL: 84 v Glos (Bristol) 1980. HSBH: 128 v Lancs (Manchester) 1980. Soccer for Lincoln City. Studied at Leeds University and obtained Degree in Russian.

**Joseph Alan ORMROD** (Kirkaldy HS) B Ramsbottom, Lancs 22/12/1942. RHB, OB. Debut 1962. Cap 1966. Benefit (£19,000) in 1977. Tour: Pakistan 1966-67. 1,000 runs: (12) – 1,535 runs (av. 45.14) in 1978 best. Scored two centuries in match (101 and 131*) v Somerset (Worcester) 1980. Shared in 4th wkt partnership record for county, 281 with Younis Ahmed v Notts (Nottingham) 1979. Benson & Hedges Gold Awards: 4. HS: 204* v Kent (Dartford) 1973. HSGC: 59 v Essex (Worcester) 1975. HSJPL: 110* v Kent (Canterbury) 1975. HSBH: 124* v Glos (Worcester) 1976. BB: 5-27 v Glos (Bristol) 1972. BBJPL: 3-51 v Hants (Worcester) 1972.

**Dipak Narshibhai PATEL** (George Salter Comprehensive School, West Bromwich) B Nairobi, Kenya 25/10/1958. Has lived in UK since 1967. RHB, OB. Debut 1976. Cap 1979. Shared in 6th wkt partnership record for county, 227 with E.J.O. Hemsley v Oxford U (Oxford) 1976. HS: 118* v Sri Lankans (Worcester) 1979. HSGC: 15 v Middlesex (Worcester) 1980. HSJPL: 40 v Glos (Worcester) 1979. HSBH: 39 v Glamorgan (Cardiff) 1979. BB: 6-47 v Oxford U (Oxford) 1980. BBJPL: 3-22 v Glos (Moreton-in-Marsh) 1978. BBBH: 3-42 v Yorks (Worcester) 1980.

**Alan Paul PRIDGEON** B Wall Heath, Staffs 22/2/1954. RHB, RM. 6ft 3ins tall. Joined staff 1971. Debut 1972. Cap 1980. HS: 32 v Yorks (Middlesbrough) 1978. HSGC: 13* v Somerset (Taunton) 1980. HSJPL: 16* v Essex (Dudley) 1976. HSBH: 10 v Leics (Leicester) 1976. BB: 7-35 v Oxford U (Oxford) 1976. BBGC: 3-25 v Somerset (Taunton) 1980. BBJPL: 6-26 v Surrey (Worcester) 1978. BBBH: 3-57 v Warwickshire (Birmingham) 1976. Soccer for Ledbury Town in West Midland League.

**Martyn SAUNDERS** B Worcester 16/5/1958. RHB, RFM. Debut 1980 (three matches). HS: 12 v Notts (Worcester) 1980. BB: 3-47 v Kent (Worcester) 1980.

**Glenn Maitland TURNER** (Otago Boys' HS) B Dunedin, New Zealand 26/5/1947. RHB, OB. Debut for Otago in Plunket Shield competition 1964-65 whilst still at school. Debut for county 1967. Cap 1968. Wisden 1970. Benefit (£21,103) in 1978. Appointed county captain for 1981. Tests: 39 for New Zealand between 1968-69 and 1976-77 captaining country in 10 Tests. Tours: New Zealand to England 1969 and 1973 (vice-captain), India and Pakistan 1969-70, Australia 1969-70 and 1973-74 (vice-captain), West Indies 1971-72, Pakistan and India 1976-77 (captain). 1,000 runs: (13) – 2,416 runs (av. 67.11) in 1973 best, including 1,018 runs (av. 78.30) by 31 May – the first occasion since 1938. Scored 1,284 runs (av. 85.60) in West Indies and Bermuda 1971-72. Scored 1,244 runs (av. 77.75) in 1975-76 – record aggregate for New Zealand season. Scored 10 centuries in 1970, a county record. Scored two centuries in match on four occasions (122 and 128*) v Warwickshire (Birmingham) 1972, (101 and 110*) New Zealand v Australia (Christchurch) 1973-74, (135 and 108) Otago v Northern Districts (Gisborne) 1974-75 and (105 and 186*) Otago v Central Districts (Dunedin) 1974-75. Scored 141* out of 169 – 83.4% of total – v Glamorgan (Swansea) 1977 – a record for first-class cricket. Gillette Man of Match Awards: 1. Benson & Hedges Gold Awards: 5. HS: 259 twice in successive innings, New Zealanders v Guyana and New

148

Zealand v West Indies (Georgetown) 1971-72. HSUK: 228* v Glos (Worcester) 1980. HSGC: 117* v Lancs (Worcester) 1971. HSJPL: 147 v Sussex (Horsham) 1980. HSBH: 143* v Warwickshire (Birmingham) 1976. BB: 3-18 v Pakistanis (Worcester) 1967. Has played hockey for Worcs and had trial for Midlands.

**Martin John WESTON** B Worcester 8/4/1959. RHB, RM. Played for 2nd XI since 1978. Debut 1979. HS: 43 v Sri Lankans (Worcester) 1979.

**Mohammad YOUNIS AHMED** (Moslem HS, Lahore) B Jullundur, Pakistan 20/10/1947. LHB, LM/SLA. Younger brother of Saeed Ahmed, Pakistan Test cricketer. Debut 1971-62 for Pakistan Inter Board Schools XI v South Zone at age of 14 years 4 months. Debut for Surrey 1965. Cap 1969. Played for South Australia in 1972-73 Sheffield Shield competition. Not re-engaged by county after 1978 season. Debut for Worcs and cap 1979. Is regarded as an English player for qualification purposes. Tests: 2 for Pakistan v New Zealand 1969-70. 1,000 runs: (9) – 1,760 runs (av. 47.56) in 1969 best. Shared in 4th wkt partnership record for county, 281 with J.A. Ormrod v Notts (Nottingham) 1979. Benson & Hedges Gold Awards: 3 (1 for Surrey). HS: 221* v Notts (Nottingham) 1979. HSTC: 62 Pakistan v New Zealand (Karachi) 1969-70. HSGC: 87 Surrey v Middlesex (Oval) 1970. HSJPL: 113 Surrey v Warwickshire (Birmingham) 1976 and 113 v Yorks (Worcester) 1979. HSBH: 115 v Yorks (Worcester) 1980. BB: 4-10 Surrey v Cambridge U (Cambridge) 1975. BBC: 3-33 v Oxford U (Oxford) 1979. BBJPL: 3-26 v Surrey (Oval) 1979. BBBH: 4-37 v Northants (Northampton) 1980.

NB. The following players whose particulars appeared in the 1980 Annual have been omitted: A. Brown (not re-engaged), V.A. Holder (left staff and will play for Shropshire in 1981) and B.J.R. Jones (not re-engaged). In addition, B.L. D'Oliveira who re-appeared in one match has not been included.
   The career records of Holder, Jones and D'Oliveira will be found elsewhere in this Annnual.

# County Averages

**Schweppes County Championship: Played 21, won 3, drawn 11, lost 7, abandoned 1.
All first-class matches: Played 23, won 3, drawn 12, lost 8, abandoned 1.**

## BATTING AND FIELDING

| Cap | | M | I | NO | Runs | HS | Avge | 100 | 50 | Ct | St |
|------|------|-----|-----|-----|------|------|------|-----|-----|-----|-----|
| 1968 | G.M. Turner | 21 | 35 | 4 | 1817 | 228* | 58.61 | 7 | 7 | 14 | — |
| 1966 | J.A. Ormrod | 22 | 35 | 3 | 1495 | 131* | 46.71 | 5 | 8 | 13 | — |
| 1979 | Younis Ahmed | 21 | 33 | 6 | 1018 | 121* | 37.70 | 2 | 7 | 17 | — |
| 1969 | E.J.O. Hemsley | 18 | 27 | 4 | 828 | 76 | 36.00 | — | 8 | 14 | — |
| 1978 | P.A. Neale | 20 | 33 | 3 | 933 | 123 | 31.10 | 1 | 6 | 4 | — |
| 1978 | D.J. Humphries | 16 | 21 | 3 | 518 | 108* | 28.77 | 1 | 1 | 28 | 3 |
| 1978 | J. Cumbes | 8 | 5 | 3 | 55 | 43 | 27.50 | — | — | — | — |
| 1979 | D.N. Patel | 13 | 18 | 4 | 360 | 74 | 25.71 | — | 3 | 9 | — |
| — | T.S. Curtis | 3 | 5 | 1 | 85 | 59* | 21.25 | — | 1 | — | — |
| 1961 | N. Gifford | 22 | 28 | 10 | 352 | 45 | 19.55 | — | — | 13 | — |
| — | S.P. Henderson | 6 | 8 | — | 147 | 64 | 18.37 | — | 1 | 6 | — |
| — | B.J.R. Jones | 10 | 17 | — | 227 | 49 | 13.35 | — | — | — | — |
| — | H.L. Alleyne | 17 | 19 | 2 | 225 | 72 | 13.23 | — | 1 | 4 | — |
| 1976 | J.D. Inchmore | 16 | 21 | 2 | 251 | 64 | 13.21 | — | 1 | 5 | — |
| 1970 | V.A. Holder | 6 | 8 | 1 | 78 | 34 | 11.14 | — | — | 4 | — |
| 1980 | A.P. Pridgeon | 21 | 22 | 11 | 118 | 28* | 10.72 | — | — | 8 | — |
| — | P.B. Fisher | 7 | 10 | 5 | 40 | 11 | 8.00 | — | — | 22 | 2 |
| — | M. Saunders | 3 | 2 | — | 12 | 12 | 6.00 | — | — | — | — |

*Played in two matches:* M.J. Weston 22, 3 (2 ct).
*Played in one match:* B.L. D'Oliveira 21, 16.

## BOWLING

| | Type | O | M | R | W | Avge | Best | 5 wI | 10 wM |
|------|------|-----|-----|-----|-----|------|------|------|-------|
| H.L. Alleyne | **RFM** | 521.1 | 100 | 1604 | 64 | 25.06 | 6-50 | 4 | 1 |
| N. Gifford | **SLA** | 727.1 | 204 | 1755 | 61 | 28.77 | 6-15 | 2 | 1 |
| V.A. Holder | **RFM** | 161.2 | 26 | 439 | 15 | 29.26 | 4-77 | — | — |
| A.P. Pridgeon | **RM** | 537 | 114 | 1614 | 51 | 31.64 | 5-50 | 1 | — |
| M. Saunders | **RFM** | 51 | 9 | 212 | 6 | 35.33 | 3-47 | — | — |
| J.D. Inchmore | **RFM** | 419.1 | 67 | 1419 | 40 | 35.47 | 6-107 | 2 | — |
| J. Cumbes | **RFM** | 186.4 | 38 | 558 | 15 | 37.20 | 4-124 | — | — |
| D.N. Patel | **OB** | 159.4 | 33 | 519 | 10 | 51.90 | 6-47 | 1 | — |

*Also bowled:* B.L. D'Oliveira 2-0-12-0; E.J.O. Hemsley 12.2-1-35-1; S.P. Henderson 2.4-0-16-0; P.A. Neale 3-1-6-0; Younis Ahmed 19-1-95-1; J.A. Ormrod 0.3-0-0-0.

# County Records

### First-class Cricket

| | | | |
|---|---|---|---|
| Highest innings totals: | For | – 633 v Warwickshire (Worcester) | 1906 |
| | Agst | – 701-4d by Leicestershire (Worcester) | 1906 |
| Lowest innings totals: | For | – 24 v Yorkshire (Huddersfield) | 1903 |
| | Agst | – 30 by Hampshire (Worcester) | 1903 |
| Highest individual innings: | For | – 276 F.L. Bowley v Hampshire (Dudley) | 1914 |
| | Agst | – 331* J.D.B. Robertson for Middlesex (Worcester) | 1949 |
| Best bowling in an innings: | For | – 9-23 C.F. Root v Lancashire (Worcester) | 1931 |
| | Agst | – 10-51 J. Mercer for Glamorgan (Worcester) | 1936 |
| Best bowling in a match: | For | – 15-87 A.J. Conway v Glos (Moreton-in-Marsh) | 1914 |
| | Agst | – 17-212 J.C. Clay for Glamorgan (Swansea) | 1937 |
| Most runs in a season: | | 2654 (av. 52.03) H.H.I. Gibbons | 1934 |
| runs in a career: | | 34490 (av. 34.04) D. Kenyon | 1946-1967 |
| 100s in a season: | | 10 by G.M. Turner | 1970 |
| 100s in a career: | | 70 by D. Kenyon | 1946-1967 |
| wickets in a season: | | 207 (av. 17.52) C.F. Root | 1925 |
| wickets in a career: | | 2143 (av. 23.73) R.T.D. Perks | 1930-1955 |

### RECORD WICKET STANDS

| | | | |
|---|---|---|---|
| 1st | 309 | F.L. Bowley & H.K. Foster v Derbyshire (Derby) | 1901 |
| 2nd | 274 | { H.H.I. Gibbons & Nawab of Pataudi v Kent (Worcester) | 1933 |
| | | { H.H.I. Gibbons & Nawab of Pataudi v Glam (Worcester) | 1934 |
| 3rd | 314 | M.J. Horton & T.W. Graveney v Somerset (Worcester) | 1962 |
| 4th | 281 | J.A. Ormrod & Younis Ahmed v Notts (Nottingham) | 1979 |
| 5th | 393 | E.G. Arnold & W.B. Burns v Warwickshire (Birmingham) | 1909 |
| 6th | 227 | E.J.O. Hemsley & D.N. Patel v Oxford U (Oxford) | 1976 |
| 7th | 197 | H.H.I. Gibbons & R. Howorth v Surrey (The Oval) | 1938 |
| 8th | 145* | F. Chester & W.H. Taylor v Essex (Worcester) | 1914 |
| 9th | 181 | J.A. Cuffe & R.D. Burrows v Gloucestershire (Worcester) | 1907 |
| 10th | 119 | W.B. Burns & G.A. Wilson v Somerset (Worcester) | 1906 |

### One-day Cricket

| | | | |
|---|---|---|---|
| Highest innings: | Gillette Cup | 265-9 v Lancashire (Worcester) | 1980 |
| | John Player League | 307-4 v Derbys (Worcester) | 1975 |
| | Benson & Hedges Cup | 314-5 v Lancs (Manchester) | 1980 |
| Lowest innings totals: | Gillette Cup | 98 v Durham (Chester-le-Street) | 1968 |
| | John Player League | 86 v Yorkshire (Leeds) | 1969 |
| | Benson & Hedges Cup | 92 v Oxford & Cambridge Universities (Cambridge) | 1975 |
| Highest individual innings: | Gillette Cup | 117* G.M. Turner v Lancashire (Worcester) | 1971 |
| | John Player League | 147 G.M. Turner v Sussex (Horsham) | 1980 |
| | Benson & Hedges Cup | 143* G.M. Turner v Warwickshire (Birmingham) | 1976 |
| Best bowling figures: | Gillette Cup | 6-14 J.A. Flavell v Lancashire (Worcester) | 1963 |
| | John Player League | 6-26 A.P. Pridgeon v Surrey (Worcester) | 1978 |
| | Benson & Hedges Cup | 6-8 N. Gifford v Minor Counties (South) (High Wycombe) | 1979 |

# YORKSHIRE

**Formation of present club:** 1863, reorganised 1891.
**Colours:** Oxford blue, Cambridge blue, and gold.
**Badge:** White rose.
**County Champions (31):** 1867, 1870, 1893, 1896,
1898, 1900, 1901, 1902, 1905, 1908, 1912,
1919, 1922, 1923, 1924, 1925, 1931, 1932,
1933, 1935, 1937, 1938, 1939, 1946, 1959,
1960, 1962, 1963, 1966, 1967, and 1968.
**Joint Champions (2):** 1869 and 1949.
**Gillette Cup Winners (2):** 1965 and 1969.
**John Player League runners-up:** 1973.
**Benson & Hedges Cup Finalists:** 1972.
**Fenner Trophy Winners (2):** 1972 and 1974.
**Gillette Man of the Match Awards:** 14.
**Benson & Hedges Gold Awards:** 22.

**Secretary:** J. Lister, Headingley Cricket Ground, Leeds LS6 3BU.
**Cricket Manager:** R. Illingworth, CBE.
**Captain:** C.M. Old.

   **Charles William Jeffrey (Bill) ATHEY** (Acklam Hall School, Middlesbrough) B
Middlesbrough 27/9/1957. RHB, RM. Toured West Indies with England Young
Cricketers 1976. Debut 1976. Cap 1980. Elected Best Young Cricketer of the Year
in 1980 by the Cricket Writers' Club. Tests: 1 in 1980. Scored 1,123 runs (av. 33.02)
in 1980. Gillette Man of Match Awards: 2. Benson & Hedges Gold Awards: 1. HS:
131* v Sussex (Leeds) 1976 and 131 v Somerset (Taunton) 1978. HSTC: 9 v
Australia (Lord's) 1980. HSGC: 115 v Kent (Leeds) 1980. HSJPL: 118 v Leics
(Leicester) 1978. HSBH: 74* v Combined Universities (Oxford) 1980. BB: 3-38 v
Surrey (Oval) 1978. BBJPL: 3-10 v Kent (Canterbury) 1978. BBBH: 3-32 v
Middlesex (Lord's) 1979.

   **David Leslie BAIRSTOW** (Hanson GS, Bradford) B Bradford 1/9/1951. RHB,
WK. Can bowl RM. Debut 1970 whilst still at school. Played for MCC Schools at
Lord's in 1970. Cap 1973. Played for Griqualand West in 1976-77 and 1977-78
(captain) Currie Cup and Castle Bowl competitions. Tests: 3 between 1979 and
1980. Tours: Australia 1978-79 (flown out as replacement for R.W. Tolchard),
Australia and India 1979-80, West Indies 1980-81. Dismissed 70 batsmen (64 ct 6
st) in 1971, including 9 in match and 6 in innings (all ct) v Lancs (Manchester).
Benson & Hedges Gold Awards: 4. HS: 145 v Middlesex (Scarborough) 1980.
HSTC: 59 v India (Oval) 1979. HSGC: 31* v Durham (Middlesbrough) 1978.
HSJPL: 76 v Sussex (Scarborough) 1976. HSBH: 35* v Essex (Middlesbrough)
1978. BB: 3-82 Griqualand West v Transvaal B (Johannesburg) 1976-77. Soccer for
Bradford City.

   **Geoffrey (Geoff) BOYCOTT** (Hemsworth GS) B Fitzwilliam, Yorks 21/10/1940.
RHB, RM. Plays in contact lenses. Debut 1962. Cap 1963. Elected Best Young
Cricketer of the Year in 1963 by the Cricket Writers' Club. *Wisden* 1964. County
captain from 1971 to 1978. Played for Northern Transvaal in 1971-72. Benefit
(£20,639) in 1974. Awarded OBE in 1980 Birthday Honours List. Tests: 94 between 1964 and 1980 captaining England in 4 Tests in 1977-78. Played in 2 matches
against Rest of World in 1970. Tours: South Africa 1964-65, Australia and New
Zealand 1965-66 and 1970-71 (returned home early through broken arm injury),

West Indies 1967-68, 1973-74 and 1980-81, Pakistan and New Zealand 1977-78 (vice captain), Australia 1978-79, Australia and India 1979-80. 1,000 runs (18) – 2,503 runs (av. 100.12) in 1971 best. Only English batsman ever to have an average of 100 for season and repeated the feat in 1979 with 1,538 runs (av. 102.53). Also scored 1,000 runs in South Africa 1964-65 (1,135 runs, av. 56.75), West Indies 1967-68 (1,154 runs, av. 82.42), Australia 1970-71 (1,535 runs, av. 95.93). Scored two centuries in match (103 and 105) v Notts (Sheffield) 1966 and (160* and 116) England v The Rest (Worcester) 1974. Completed 30,000 runs in 1977 and scored his 100th century in Leeds Test of that year – only player to have done so in a Test match. Scored 155 v India (Birmingham) 1979 to become the second batsman to have scored a century in a Test on all six grounds in this country. Gillette Man of Match Awards: 2. Benson & Hedges Gold Awards: 7. HS: 261* MCC v President's XI (Bridgetown) 1973-74. HSUK: 260* v Essex (Colchester) 1970. HSTC: 246* v India (Leeds) 1967. HSGC: 146 v Surrey (Lord's) 1965. HSJPL: 108* v Northants (Huddersfield) 1974. HSBH: 142 v Worcs (Worcester) 1980. BB: 4-14 v Lancs (Manchester) 1979. BBTC: 3-47 England v South Africa (Cape Town) 1964-65.

**Philip (Phil) CARRICK** B Armley, Leeds 16/7/1952. RHB, SLA. Debut 1970. Cap 1976. Played for Eastern Province in 1976-77 Currie Cup competition. HS: 131* v Northants (Northampton) 1980. HSGC: 19* v Kent (Leeds) 1980. HSJPL: 29 v Glamorgan (Swansea) 1980. HSBH: 19* v Notts (Bradford) 1979. BB: 8-33 v Cambridge U (Cambridge) 1973. BBJPL: 3-32 v Hants (Bournemouth) 1976 and 3-32 v Notts (Nottingham) 1980.

**Stephen Peter COVERDALE** (St. Peter's School, York) B York 20/11/1954. RHB, WK. Debut 1973 playing in one match through absence of D. L. Bairstow to play for Young England XI v West Indians. Debut for Cambridge U 1974. Blue 1974-75-76-77. Re-appeared in 1980 through absence of D.L. Bairstow in Test and Prudential Trophy matches. HS: 85 Cambridge U v Somerset (Cambridge) 1976. HSC: 18 v Northants (Northampton) 1980. HSJPL: 17* v Northants (Scarborough) 1980. HSBH: 79 Combined Universities v Sussex (Cambridge) 1976.

**Simon John DENNIS** (Scarborough College) B Scarborough 18/10/1960. Nephew of Sir Leonard Hutton and F. Dennis, former Yorkshire player. RHB, LFM. Played for 2nd XI since 1977. Toured Australia with England Young Cricketers in 1979. Debut 1980.

**John Harry HAMPSHIRE** (Oakwood Technical HS, Rotherham) B Thurnscoe, Yorks 10/2/1941. Son of J. Hampshire who played for Yorks in 1937. RHB, LB. Debut 1961. Cap 1963. Played for Tasmania in 1967-68, 1968-69, 1977-78 and 1978-79. Benefit (£28,425) in 1976. County captain in 1979 and 1980. Tests: 8 between 1969 and 1975. Scored 107 in his first Test v West Indies (Lord's) and is only English player to have scored a century on debut in Test cricket when this has occurred at Lord's. Tour: Australia and New Zealand 1970-71. 1,000 runs (13) – 1,596 runs (av. 53.20) in 1978 best. Gillette Man of Match Awards: 4. Benson & Hedges Gold Awards: 2. HS: 183* v Sussex (Hove) 1971. HSTC: 107 v West Indies (Lord's) 1969. HSGC: 110 v Durham (Middlesbrough) 1978. HSJPL: 119 v Leics (Hull) 1971. HSBH: 85* v Warwickshire (Leeds) 1980. BB: 7-52 v Glamorgan (Cardiff) 1963.

**Stuart Neil HARTLEY** (Beckfoot GS) B Shipley, Yorks 18/3/1956. RHB, RM. Played for 2nd XI since 1975. Debut 1978. HS: 72* v Somerset (Weston-super-Mare) 1980. HSGC: 23 v Surrey (Oval) 1980. HSJPL: 54* v Warwickshire (Birmingham) 1979. BB: 3-40 v Glos (Sheffield) 1980. BBJPL: 3-31 v Notts (Scarborough) 1980.

## YORKSHIRE

**Peter Geoffrey INGHAM** (Ashville College, Harrogate) B Sheffield 28/9/1956. RHB, RM. Played for 2nd XI since 1974. Debut 1979. HS: 64 v Northants (Leeds) 1980. HSJPL: 87* v Glos (Hull) 1980.

**James Derek (Jim) LOVE** B Leeds 22/4/1955. RHB, RM. Debut 1975. Cap 1980. HS: 170* v Worcs (Worcester) 1979. HSGC: 61* v Hants (Southampton) 1980. HSJPL: 90* v Derbyshire (Chesterfield) 1979. HSBH: 18 v Notts (Nottingham) 1978.

**Richard Graham LUMB** (Percy Jackson GS, Doncaster and Mexborough GS) B Doncaster 27/2/1950. 6ft 3ins tall. RHB, RM. Played in MCC Schools matches at Lord's 1968. Debut 1970 after playing in one John Player League match in 1969. Cap 1974. Appointed County vice-captain for 1981. 1,000 runs (5) – 1,532 runs (av. 41.40) in 1975 best. HS: 159 v Somerset (Harrogate) 1979. HSGC: 56 v Shropshire (Wellington) 1976. HSJPL: 101 v Notts (Scarborough) 1976. HSBH: 90 v Northants (Bradford) 1980.

**Martyn Douglas MOXON** (Holgate GS, Barnsley) B Barnsley 4/5/1960. RHB, RM. Played in two John Player League matches in 1980, without batting or bowling. Has yet to appear in first-class cricket.

**Christopher Middleton (Chris) OLD** (Acklam Hall Secondary GS, Middlesbrough) B Middlesbrough 22/12/1948. 6ft 3ins tall. LHB, RFM. Debut 1966. Cap 1969. Elected Best Young Cricketer of the Year in 1970 by the Cricket Writers' Club. Wisden 1978. Benefit (£32,916) in 1979. Appointed County Captain for 1981. Tests: 43 between 1972-73 and 1980. Played in 2 matches against Rest of World 1970. Tours: India, Pakistan and Sri Lanka 1972-73, West Indies 1973-74 and 1980-81, Australia and New Zealand 1974-75, India, Sri Lanka and Australia 1976-77, Pakistan and New Zealand 1977-78, Australia 1978-79. Scored century in 37 minutes v Warwickshire (Birmingham) 1977 – second fastest ever in first-class cricket. Took 4 wickets in 5 balls, England v Pakistan (Birmingham) 1978. Benson & Hedges Gold Awards: 3. HS: 116 v Indians (Bradford) 1974. HSTC: 65 v Pakistan (Oval) 1974. HSGC: 29 v Lancs (Leeds) 1974. HSJPL: 82 v Somerset (Bath) 1974 and 82* v Somerset (Glastonbury) 1976. HSBH: 72 v Sussex (Hove) 1976. BB: 7-20 v Glos (Middlesbrough) 1969. BBTC: 7-50 v Pakistan (Birmingham) 1978. BBGC: 4-9 v Durham (Middlesbrough) 1978. BBJPL: 5-53 v Sussex (Hove) 1971. BBBH: 4-17 v Derbyshire (Bradford) 1973.

**Alan RAMAGE** (Warsett School, Brotton) B Guisborough 29/11/1957. LHB, RFM. Played for 2nd XI since 1974 and in six Benson & Hedges Cup match and one Benson & Hedges Cup match between 1975 and 1977. Debut 1979. HS: 19 v Cambridge U (Cambridge) 1979. HSBH: 17* v Combined Universities (Barnsley) 1976. BB: 3-24 v Cambridge U (Cambridge) 1979. BBGC: 3-33 v Hants (Southampton) 1980. BBJPL: 3-51 v Kent (Canterbury) 1977. BBBH: 3-63 v Warwickshire (Leeds) 1980. Plays soccer for Middlesbrough.

**Kevin SHARP** (Abbey Grange C.E. High School, Leeds) B Leeds 6/4/1959. LHB, OB. Debut 1976. Captained England under-19 v West Indies under-19 in 1978 and scored 260* in match at Worcester. HS: 106 D.H. Robins XI v Northern Districts (Hamilton) 1979-80. HSUK: 100* v Middlesex (Lord's) 1980. HSGC: 25 v Middlesex (Lord's) 1979. HSJPL: 40 v Surrey (Oval) 1978. HSBH: 45 v Warwickshire (Leeds) 1980.

**Arnold SIDEBOTTOM** (Broadway GS, Barnsley) B Barnsley 1/4/1954. RHB, RFM. Played for 2nd XI since 1971 and in Schools matches at Lord's in that year.

154

Debut 1973. Cap 1980. HS: 124 v Glamorgan (Cardiff) 1977. HSGC: 45 v Hants (Bournemouth) 1977. HSJPL: 31 v Sussex (Hove) 1975 and 31 v Northants (Scarborough) 1980. HSBH: 15 v Notts (Bradford) 1979. BB: 7-18 v Oxford U (Oxford) 1980. BBGC: 4-35 v Kent (Leeds) 1980. BBJPL: 4-24 v Surrey (Scarborough) 1975. BBBH: 3-21 v Minor Counties (North) (Jesmond) 1979. Soccer for Manchester United, Huddersfield Town and Halifax Town.

**Graham Barry STEVENSON** (Minsthorpe GS) B Ackworth, Yorks 16/12/1955. RHB, RM. Played for 2nd XI in 1972. Debut 1973. Cap 1978. Tests: 1 in 1979-80. Tours: Australia and India 1979-80 (flown out as a replacement for M. Hendrick), West Indies 1980-81. HS: 111 v Derbyshire (Chesterfield) 1980. HSTC: 27* v India (Bombay) 1979-80. HSGC: 29 v Glos (Leeds) 1976. HSJPL: 43 v Derbyshire (Leeds) 1980. HSBH: 16 v Middlesex (Lord's) 1977. BB: 8-57 v Northants (Leeds) 1980. BBGC: 4-57 v Lancs (Leeds) 1974. BBJPL: 5-41 v Leics (Leicester) 1976. BBBH: 5-28 v Kent (Canterbury) 1978.

**John Peter WHITELEY** (Ashville College, Harrogate) B Otley, Yorks 28/2/1955. RHB, OB. Played for 2nd XI since 1972. Debut 1978. HS: 20 v Northants (Northampton) 1979. BB: 4-14 v Notts (Scarborough) 1978. Studied at Bristol University and obtained degree in Chemistry.

NB. The following players whose particulars appeared in the 1980 annual have been omitted: H.P. Cooper (not re-engaged), G.A. Cope (left staff), C. Johnson and S.Stuchbury.

The career records of Cope and Cooper will be found elsewhere in this annual.

## County Averages

**Schweppes County Championship: Played 22, won 4, drawn 15, lost 3.**
**All first-class matches: Played 24, won 5, drawn 15, lost 4.**

### BATTING AND FIELDING

| Cap | | M | I | NO | Runs | HS | Avge | 100 | 50 | Ct | St |
|-----|---|---|---|----|----|-----|------|-----|----|----|----|
| 1963 | J.H. Hampshire | 18 | 27 | 8 | 987 | 124 | 51.94 | 2 | 7 | 12 | |
| 1963 | G. Boycott | 11 | 16 | 2 | 706 | 154* | 50.42 | 2 | 4 | 14 | |
| 1969 | C.M. Old | 16 | 12 | 4 | 325 | 89 | 40.62 | — | 3 | 11 | |
| 1980 | J.D. Love | 20 | 32 | 7 | 917 | 105* | 36.68 | 2 | 4 | 9 | |
| 1974 | R.G. Lumb | 23 | 37 | 3 | 1223 | 129 | 35.97 | 3 | 8 | 7 | |
| 1973 | D.L. Bairstow | 19 | 21 | 5 | 569 | 145 | 35.56 | 1 | 2 | 39 | 2 |
| 1980 | C.W.J. Athey | 22 | 35 | 3 | 1113 | 125* | 34.78 | 2 | 6 | 25 | |
| 1978 | G.B. Stevenson | 22 | 29 | 9 | 668 | 111 | 33.40 | 1 | 3 | 10 | |
| 1976 | P. Carrick | 24 | 32 | 8 | 786 | 131* | 32.75 | 1 | 4 | 15 | |
| — | P.G. Ingham | 4 | 7 | 0 | 197 | 64 | 28.14 | — | 2 | — | |
| — | K. Sharp | 9 | 13 | 1 | 293 | 100* | 24.41 | 1 | — | 7 | 4 |
| 1980 | A. Sidebottom | 20 | 14 | 1 | 284 | 43 | 21.84 | — | — | 7 | |
| 1970 | G.A. Cope | 21 | 12 | 8 | 85 | 33 | 21.25 | — | — | 3 | |
| — | A. Ramage | 4 | 3 | 2 | 20 | 14* | 20.00 | — | — | 1 | |
| — | S.N. Hartley | 14 | 22 | 2 | 352 | 72* | 17.60 | — | 2 | 7 | |
| — | H.P. Cooper | 7 | 7 | 2 | 57 | 23 | 11.40 | — | — | 3 | |
| — | S.P. Coverdale | 5 | 3 | 0 | 31 | 18 | 10.33 | — | — | 9 | 3 |
| — | S.J. Dennis | 4 | 2 | 1 | 1 | 1* | 1.00 | — | — | 3 | |

*Played in one match:* H.P. Whiteley 1 (1 ct).

## BOWLING

| | Type | O | M | R | W | Avge | Best | 5 wI | 10 wM |
|---|---|---|---|---|---|---|---|---|---|
| C.M. Old | **RFM** | 419.1 | 136 | 957 | 47 | 20.36 | 6-44 | 2 | — |
| A. Sidebottom | **RFM** | 346.1 | 92 | 962 | 42 | 22.90 | 7-18 | 3 | 2 |
| G.B. Stevenson | **RM** | 602.1 | 164 | 1669 | 72 | 23.18 | 8-57 | 5 | 1 |
| S.N. Hartley | **RM** | 34.5 | 5 | 150 | 5 | 30.00 | 3-40 | — | — |
| P. Carrick | **SLA** | 608.5 | 189 | 1652 | 51 | 32.39 | 6-138 | 2 | — |
| G.A. Cope | **OB** | 584.3 | 175 | 1558 | 42 | 37.09 | 4-69 | — | — |
| H.P. Cooper | **RM** | 152 | 36 | 431 | 11 | 39.18 | 3-77 | — | — |
| S.J. Dennis | **LFM** | 70 | 10 | 237 | 6 | 39.50 | 2-38 | — | — |

*Also bowled:* C.W.J. Athey 18-2-82-2; G. Boycott 44-13-71-4; J.D. Love 3-0-22-0;
A. Ramage 66-10-225-4; K. Sharp 6-1-19-0; H.P. Whiteley 16-2-42-0.

# County Records

### First-class cricket

| | | | |
|---|---|---|---|
| Highest innings totals: | For | —887 v Warwickshire (Birmingham) | 1896 |
| | Agst | —630 by Somerset (Leeds) | 1901 |
| Lowest innings totals: | For | —23 v Hampshire (Middlesbrough) | 1965 |
| | Agst | —13 by Nottinghamshire (Nottingham) | 1901 |
| Highest individual innings: | For | —341 G.H. Hirst v Leicestershire (Leicester) | 1905 |
| | Agst | —318* W.G. Grace for Gloucestershire (Cheltenham) | 1876 |
| Best bowling in an innings: | For | —10-10 H. Verity v Nottinghamshire (Leeds) | 1932 |
| | Agst | —10-37 C.V. Grimmett for Australians (Sheffield) | 1930 |
| Best bowling in a match: | For | —17-91 H. Verity v Essex (Leyton) | 1933 |
| | Agst | —17-91 H. Dean for Lancashire (Liverpool) | 1913 |

| | | |
|---|---|---|
| runs in a career: | 38561 (av. 50.21) H. Sutcliffe | 1919-1945 |
| 100s in a season: | 12 by H. Sutcliffe | 1932 |
| 100s in a career: | 112 by H. Sutcliffe | 1919-1945 |
| wickets in a season: | 240 (av. 12.72) W. Rhodes | 1900 |
| wickets in a career: | 3608 (av. 16.00) W. Rhodes | 1898-1930 |

## RECORD WICKET STANDS

| | | | |
|---|---|---|---|
| 1st | 555 | P. Holmes & H. Sutcliffe v Essex (Leyton) | 1932 |
| 2nd | 346 | W. Barber & M. Leyland v Middlesex (Sheffield) | 1932 |
| 3rd | 323* | H. Sutcliffe & M. Leyland v Glamorgan (Huddersfield) | 1928 |
| 4th | 312 | G.H. Hirst & D. Denton v Hampshire (Southampton) | 1914 |
| 5th | 340 | E. Wainwright & G.H. Hirst v Surrey (The Oval) | 1899 |
| 6th | 276 | M. Leyland & E. Robinson v Glamorgan (Swansea) | 1926 |
| 7th | 254 | D.C.F. Burton & W. Rhodes v Hampshire (Dewsbury) | 1919 |
| 8th | 292 | Lord Hawke & R. Peel v Warwickshire (Birmingham) | 1896 |
| 9th | 192 | G.H. Hirst & S. Haigh v Surrey (Bradford) | 1898 |
| 10th | 148 | Lord Hawke & D. Hunter v Kent (Sheffield) | 1898 |

## One-day cricket

| Highest innings totals: | Gillette Cup | 317-4 v Surrey (Lord's) | 1965 |
|---|---|---|---|
| | John Player League | 248-5 v Derbyshire (Chesterfield) | 1979 |
| | Benson & Hedges Cup | 269-6 v Worcestershire (Worcester) | 1980 |
| Lowest innings totals: | Gillette Cup | 76 v Surrey (Harrogate) | 1970 |
| | John Player League | 74 v Warwickshire (Birmingham) | 1972 |
| | Benson & Hedges Cup | 114 v Kent (Canterbury) | 1978 |
| Highest individual innings: | Gillette Cup | 146 G. Boycott v Surrey (Lord's) | 1965 |
| | John Player League | 119 J.H. Hampshire v Leicestershire (Hull) | 1971 |
| | Benson & Hedges Cup | 142 G. Boycott v Worcestershire (Worcester) | 1980 |
| Best bowling figures: | Gillette Cup | 6-15 F.S. Trueman v Somerset (Taunton) | 1965 |
| | John Player League | 7-15 R.A. Hutton v Worcestershire (Leeds) | 1969 |
| | Benson & Hedges Cup | 6-27 A.G. Nicholson v Minor Counties (North) (Middlesbrough) | 1972 |

# CAMBRIDGE UNIVERSITY

**Captain:** I.G. Peck
**Secretary:** J.P.C. Mills

**Robin James BOYD-MOSS** (Bedford School and Magdalen College) B Hattoh, Ceylon (now Sri Lanka) 16/2/1959. RHB, SLA. Played for Bedfordshire 1977-79. Debut for University and also for Northants 1980, Blue 1980. HS: 71 v Middlesex (Cambridge) 1980. HSBH: 58 v Northants (Northampton) 1980. Rugby Blue 1980-81. Second year student, reading Land Economy.

**Neil Cameron CRAWFORD** (Shrewsbury School and Magdalen College) B Leeds 26/11/1958. Son of M.G. Crawford, Chairman of Yorkshire and former treasurer and 2nd XI captain. RHB, RM. Has played for Yorks 2nd XI. Debut 1978, Blue 1979-80. HS: 46 v Sussex (Cambridge) 1979. BB: 6-80 v Notts (Cambridge) 1979. Studied for Classics Degree. No longer in residence.

**Simon Jonathon Graham DOGGART** (Winchester College and Magdalen College) B Winchester 8/2/1961. Son of G.H.G. Doggart and grandson of A.G. Doggart, both former Cambridge Blues, father also played for Sussex and England. LHB, OB. Debut 1980, Blue 1980. HS: 43 v Surrey and 43 v Northants (Cambridge) 1980. BB: 3-54 v Oxford U (Lord's) 1980. Second year student, reading History.

**Philip David HEMSLEY** (Lewes Priory School and Clare College) B Buxted (Sussex) 23/11/1959. RHB, RM. Debut 1980. One match v Surrey. HS: 12* v Surrey (Cambridge) 1980. Third year student, reading Engineering.

**David Charles HOLLIDAY** (Oundle School and Christ's College) B Cambridge 20/12/1958. RHB, LB. Has played for Northants 2nd XI. Debut 1979, Blue 1979-80. Secretary in 1980. HS: 76* v Notts (Cambridge) 1980. Third year student, reading Engineering.

**Michael Gerald HOWAT** (Abingdon School and Magdalen College) B Tavistock (Devon) 2/3/1958. 6ft. 4in. tall. Son of writer, Gerald Howat. RHB, RM. Has played for Warwickshire and Gloucestershire 2nd XIs. debut 1977, Blue 1977 and 1980. HS: 32 v Middlesex (Cambridge) 1980. BB: 3-39 v Essex (Cambridge) 1977. Studied for History Degree and Certificate of Education. No longer in residence.

**John Peter Crispin MILLS** (Oundle School and Corpus Christi College) B Kettering (Northants) 6/12/1958. Son of J.M. Mills, former Cambridge captain. RHB, RM. Has played for Northants 2nd XI. Debut 1979, Blue 1979-80. Secretary for 1981. HS: 79 v Warwickshire (Cambridge) 1980. HSBH: 13 v Worcs (Cambridge) 1980. Third year student, reading History.

**Aziz Mohamed MUBARAK** (Royal College, Colombo, University of Sri Lanka and Christ's College) B Colombo, Ceylon (now Sri Lanka) 4/7/1951. RHB, RM/OB. Former captain of Sri Lanka University Club. Debut 1978. Blue 1978-79-80. HS: 105 v Warwickshire (Cambridge) 1980. HSBH: 39 v Sussex (Oxford) 1979. Studied for Doctor of Philosophy Degree. No longer in residence.

**André ODENDAAL** (Queen's College, Queenstown, Stellenbosch University and St. John's College) B Queenstown, South Africa 4/5/1954. RHB, OB. Debut 1980, Blue 1980. HS: 61 v Leics (Cambridge) 1980. HSBH: 74 v Warwickshire (Birmingham) 1980. Second year graduate student, reading for Doctor of Philosophy Degree. Has written books on South African cricket.

**Ian George PECK** (Bedford School and Magdalen College) B Great Staughton (Huntingdonshire) 18/10/1957. RHB, WK. Played for Bedfordshire 1976-79. Debut 1978 and for Northants 1980, Blue 1980 (Captain). Re-elected Captain for 1981. HS: 34 v Essex (Cambridge) 1980. HSBH: 31 v Worcs (Cambridge) 1980. Rugby Blue 1979-80. Appointed Captain for 1980-81, but had to withdraw from side through injury. Toured Japan, Fiji and Tonga with England team in 1979. Studied for Degree in Land Economy and is in fourth year on Certificate of Education course.

**Derek Raymond PRINGLE** (Felsted School and Fitzwilliam College) B Nairobi, Kenya 18/9/1958. 6ft. 4½in. tall. Son of late Donald Pringle who played for East Africa in 1975 Prudential Cup. Debut for University 1978. Debut for Essex 1978, Blue 1979-80. HS: 123 v Notts (Cambridge) 1980. HSBH: 58 v Essex (Cambridge) 1979. BB: 6-90 v Warwickshire (Cambridge) 1980. Third year student, reading Geography.

**Neil RUSSOM** (Huish's GS, Taunton and St. Catharine's College) B Finchley, London 3/12/1958. RHB, RM. Has played for Somerset 2nd XI since 1975. Played in one Fenner Trophy match in 1978. Debut 1979 and for Somerset 1980, Blue 1980. HS: 79* v Northants (Cambridge) 1980. HSBH: 16* v Worcs (Cambridge) 1980. BB: 4-84 v Leics (Cambridge) 1980. BBBH: 5-40 v Northants (Northampton) 1980. Third year student, reading Law.

## UNIVERSITY AVERAGES
All First-Class matches: Played 9, Won 0, Drawn 5, Lost 4.

### BATTING AND FIELDING

|  | M | I | NO | R | HS | Avge | 100 | 50 | Ct | St |
|---|---|---|---|---|---|---|---|---|---|---|
| †N. Russom | 9 | 12 | 8 | 226 | 79* | 56.50 | — | 2 | 2 | — |
| †D.R. Pringle | 9 | 14 | 3 | 604 | 123 | 54.90 | 2 | 3 | 10 | — |
| †J.P.C. Mills | 9 | 14 | 1 | 350 | 79 | 26.92 | — | 2 | 3 | — |
| †A.M. Mubarak | 9 | 14 | 0 | 359 | 105 | 25.64 | 1 | 2 | 5 | — |
| †R.J. Boyd-Moss | 9 | 13 | 0 | 320 | 71 | 24.61 | — | 3 | 4 | — |
| †A. Odendaal | 9 | 14 | 0 | 325 | 61 | 23.21 | — | 1 | 6 | — |
| †S.J.G. Doggart | 9 | 11 | 2 | 174 | 43 | 19.33 | — | — | 6 | — |
| †D.C. Holliday | 9 | 12 | 3 | 173 | 76* | 19.22 | — | 1 | 2 | — |
| †I.G. Peck | 9 | 12 | 2 | 147 | 34 | 14.70 | — | — | 6 | — |
| †N.C. Crawford | 8 | 7 | 1 | 84 | 28 | 14.00 | — | — | 2 | — |
| †M.G. Howat | 9 | 6 | 0 | 61 | 32 | 10.16 | — | — | 4 | — |

Played in one match: P.D. Hemsley 12*.

† Denotes played in University match.

### BOWLING

|  | O | M | R | W | Av | BB | 5wI | 10wM |
|---|---|---|---|---|---|---|---|---|
| D.R. Pringle | 241.1 | 57 | 652 | 24 | 27.16 | 6-90 | 1 | 1 |
| N.C. Crawford | 168.4 | 32 | 568 | 14 | 40.57 | 3-61 | — | — |
| S.J.G. Doggart | 153 | 43 | 392 | 9 | 43.55 | 3-54 | — | — |
| N. Russom | 253.3 | 52 | 810 | 18 | 45.00 | 4-84 | — | — |
| M.G. Howat | 185.2 | 34 | 679 | 8 | 84.87 | 2-61 | — | — |

Also bowled: R.J. Boyd-Moss 37-5-145-2; P.D. Hemsley 11-1-53-1; D.C. Holliday 37.5-9-123-1.

## UNIVERSITY RECORDS

| | | | |
|---|---|---|---|
| Highest Innings | For | 703-9d v Sussex (Hove) | 1890 |
| Totals: | Agst | 703-3d by West Indians (Cambridge) | 1950 |
| Lowest Innings | For | 30 v Yorkshire (Cambridge) | 1928 |
| Totals: | Agst | 32 by Oxford U (Lord's) | 1878 |
| Highest Indi- | For | 254* K.S. Duleepsinhji v Middlesex | |
| vidual Innings: | | (Cambridge) | 1927 |
| | Agst | 304* E.D. Weekes for West Indies | |
| | | (Cambridge) | 1950 |
| Best Bowling | For | 10-69 S.M.J. Woods v C.I. Thornton's XI | |
| in an Innings: | | (Cambridge) | 1890 |
| | Agst | 10-38 S.E. Butler for Oxford U (Lord's) | 1871 |
| Best Bowling | For | 15-88 S.M.J. Woods v C.I. Thornton's XI | |
| in a Match: | | (Cambridge) | 1890 |
| | Agst | 15-95 S.E. Butler for Oxford U (Lord's) | 1871 |
| Most runs in a season: | | 1581 (av. 79.05) D.S. Sheppard | 1952 |
| runs in a career: | | 4310 (av. 38.48) J.M. Brearley | 1961-1968 |
| 100s in a season: | | 7 by D.S. Sheppard | 1952 |
| 100s in a career: | | 14 by D.S. Sheppard | 1950-1952 |
| wickets in a season: | | 80 (av. 17.63) O.S. Wheatley | 1958 |

## RECORD WICKET STANDS

| | | | |
|---|---|---|---|
| 1st | 349 | J.G. Dewes & D.S. Sheppard v Sussex (Hove) | 1950 |
| 2nd | 429* | J.G. Dewes & G.H.G. Doggart v Essex (Cambridge) | 1949 |
| 3rd | 284 | E.T. Killick & G.C. Grant v Essex (Cambridge) | 1929 |
| 4th | 275 | R. de W.K. Winlaw & J.H. Human v Essex (Cambridge) | 1934 |
| 5th | 220 | R. Subba Row & F.C.M. Alexander v Nottinghamshire | |
| | | (Nottingham) | 1953 |
| 6th | 245 | J.L. Bryan & C.T. Ashton v Surrey (Oval) | 1921 |
| 7th | 289 | G. Goonesena & G.W. Cook v Oxford U (Lord's) | 1957 |
| 8th | 145 | H. Ashton & A.E.R. Gilligan v Free Foresters | |
| | | (Cambridge) | 1920 |
| 9th | 200 | G.W. Cook & C.S. Smith v Lancashire (Liverpool) | 1957 |
| 10th | 177 | A.E.R. Gilligan & J.H. Naumann v Sussex (Hove) | 1919 |

# OXFORD UNIVERSITY

**Captain:** R.P. Moulding
**Secretary:** S.P. Sutcliffe

**Thomas Edmund Oswell BURY** (Charterhouse School and St. Edmund Hall) B Chelmsford 14/5/1958. RHB, WK. Debut 1979, Blue 1980. HS: 22 v Worcs (Oxford) 1980. Studied for English Degree, no longer in residence.

**Ralph Stewart COWAN** (Lewes Priory School and Magdalen College) B Hamlin, West Germany 30/3/1960, 6ft. 4in. tall. RHB, RM. Has played for Sussex 2nd XI. Debut 1980, Blue 1980. HS: 63 v Lancs (Oxford) 1980. Soccer Blues 1979-80 and 1980-81. Second year student, reading Chemistry.

**Ian James CURTIS** (Whitgift School and Lincoln College) B Purley (Surrey) 13/5/1959, 6ft. 3¾in. tall. LHB, SLA/SLC. Has played for Surrey 2nd XI. Debut 1980, Blue 1980. HS: 9* v Hants (Oxford) and 9 v Worcs (Oxford) 1980. HSBH: 12* v Northants (Northampton) 1980. BB: 3-56 v Warwickshire (Oxford) 1980. Half-Blues for Rugby Fives 1978-79 and 1979-80. Third year student, reading Agricultural and Forest Sciences.

**John Philip DURACK** (Christ Church GS, Perth, University of Western Australia, Magdalen College) B Perth, Australia 18/5/1956. RHB, LB. Debut 1980. HS: 45 v Somerset (Oxford) 1980. Second year graduate student, reading for Civil Law Degree.

**Raymond Alan Bryan EZEKOWITZ** (Westville Boys High School, Durban, Cape Town University and Wolfson College) B Durban, South Africa 19/1/1954. RHB. Played in non-First Class matches for South African Universities. Debut 1980, Blue 1980. HS: 57 v Warwickshire (Oxford) 1980. HSBH: 26 v Warwickshire (Birmingham) 1980. Second year graduate student, reading for Doctor of Philosophy Degree.

**David Charles Geoffrey FOSTER** (Sutton Valence School and Christ Church College) B Holbeach (Lincolnshire) 19/9/1959. LHB, SLA. Debut 1980. HS: 67 v Lancs (Oxford) 1980. Third year student, reading Law.

**Simon John HALLIDAY** (Downside School and St. Benet's Hall) B Haverfordwest (Pembrokeshire) 13/7/1960. RHB, RM. Has played for Dorset. Debut 1980, Blue 1980. HS: 37 v Middlesex (Oxford) 1980. Rugby Blues 1979-80 and 1980-81. Third year student, reading Classics and Modern Languages.

**Kevin Anthony HAYES** (Queen Elizabeth's GS, Blackburn and Merton College) B Thurnscoe (Yorks) 26/9/1962. RHB, RM. Debut for Lancs 1980, one match v Oxford U (Oxford). Has not yet appeared for University. HS: 27 v Oxford U (Oxford) 1980. Soccer Blue 1980-81. First year student.

**Peter Nigel HUXFORD** (Richard Hale School, Hertford and Christ Church College) B Enfield (Middlesex) 17/2/1960. LHB, WK. Debut 1980 (two matches). Third year student, reading Modern History.

**John Mark KNIGHT** (Oundle School and Worcester College) B Oundle (Northants) 16/3/1958. RHB, RM. Has played for Wiltshire and Middlesex 2nd XI. Debut 1978, Blue 1979. Benson & Hedges Gold Awards: 1. HS: 20 v Sri Lankans (Guildford) 1979. HSBH: 54* v Northants (Cambridge) 1979. BB: 4-69 v Cambridge U (Lord's) 1979. Obtained Degree in Engineering and is in fourth year on Certificate of Education Course.

**Moray Charles Livingstone MACPHERSON** (Winchester College and Lincoln College) B Barton-on-Sea (Hants) 4/11/1959. Nephew of H.E. Webb, former Oxford Blue. RHB, WK. Debut 1980. HS: 22 v Hants (Oxford) 1980. Third year student, reading Law.

**Nicholas Vivian Haward MALLETT** (St. Andrew's College, Grahamstown, Cape Town University and University College) B Haileybury School (Herts) 30/10/1956. 6ft. 4in. tall. Son of A.W.H. Mallett, former Oxford Blue and Kent player. RHB, RM. Debut 1980. HS: 38 v Glos (Oxford) 1980. HSBH: 10* v Worcs (Cambridge) 1980. BB: 4-44 v Warwickshire (Oxford) 1980. Rugby Blue 1979-80. Appointed Captain for 1980-81, but had to withdraw from side through injury. Second year graduate student, reading for Doctor of Philosophy Degree.

**Robert MARSDEN** (Merchant Taylor's School, Northwood and Christ Church College) B Kensington, London 2/4/1959. RHB, OB. Debut 1979. HS: 50 v Worcs (Oxford) 1980. Third year student, reading History.

**Roger Peter MOULDING** (Haberdashers Aske's School, Elstree and Christ Church College) B Enfield (Middlesex) 3/1/1958. RHB, LB. Debut for Middlesex 1977. One match v Cambridge U (Cambridge). Debut for University 1978. Blues 1978-79-80. Secretary in 1979 and Captain for 1981. HS: 77* v Worcs (Worcester) 1978. HSBH: 27 v Somerset (Taunton) 1978. Fourth year student, reading Chemistry.

**Jonathan Oliver Darcy ORDERS** (Winchester College and Trinity College) B Beckenham (Kent) 12/8/1957. LHB, LM. Has played for Kent 2nd XI. Debut 1978. Blues 1978-79-80. HS: 79 v Worcs (Worcester) 1978. HSBH: 63 v Yorks (Oxford) 1980. Obtained Degree in History and is in fourth year on Certificate of Education course.

**John Lawrence (Lou) RAWLINSON** (Eton College and University College) B Edgware (Middlesex) 4/8/1959. 6ft. 3in. tall. RHB. Has played for Middlesex 2nd XI. Debut 1979. HS: 19 v Hants (Oxford) 1980. Third year student, reading History.

**James Julian ROGERS** (Sedbergh School and University College) B Kendal (Westmorland) 20/8/1958. RHB, OB/LB. Has played for Cumberland. Debut 1979, Blues 1979-80. HS: 53 v Somerset (Oxford) 1980. Half-Blue for rugby fives. Obtained Degree in History and is in fourth year on Certificate of Education course.

**Christopher Jonathan ROSS** (Wanganui Collegiate School, Wellington University and Magdalen College) B Warri, Nigeria 24/6/1954. RHB, RM. Debut 1975-76 for Wellington. Debut for University 1978. Blues 1978-79-80. Captain in 1980. HS: 23* v Cambridge U (Lord's) 1980. BB: 4-34 v Worcs (Worcester) 1978. Studied for Degree in Philosophy, Politics and Economics. No longer in residence.

**John Frederick Waley SANDERSON** (Westminster School and New College) B Highgate (Middlesex) 10/9/1954. 6ft. 6in. tall. RHB, RM. Debut 1979, Blue 1980. HS: 9 v Lancs (Oxford) 1980. BB: 6-67 v Middlesex (Oxford) 1980. Studied for Doctor of Philosophy Degree in French. No longer in residence.

**Simon Paul SUTCLIFFE** (King George V GS, Southport and Lincoln College) B Watford 22/5/1960. Son of Peter W. Sutcliffe, former National Coach. RHB, OB. Has played for Warwickshire 2nd XI. Debut 1980, Blue 1980. Secretary for 1981. HS: 16 v Somerset (Oxford) 1980. BB: 6-19 v Warwickshire (Oxford) 1980. Third year student, reading Modern History.

**Stephen Mark WOOKEY** (Malvern College, Emmanuel College, Cambridge University and Wycliffe Hall) B Upavon (Wilts) 2/9/1954. RHB, RM. Has played for Wiltshire. Debut for Cambridge U 1975, Blue 1975-76. Debut for Oxford U 1978, Blue 1978. Secretary in 1980. HS: 48 Cambridge U v Oxford U (Lord's) 1976. BB: 3-61 v Sussex (Oxford) 1978. Studied for Ordination into Church of England. No longer in residence.

### UNIVERSITY AVERAGES
All First-Class matches: Played 10, Won 0, Drawn 4, Lost 6.
#### BATTING AND FIELDING

| | M | I | NO | R | HS | Av | 100 | 50 | Ct | St |
|---|---|---|---|---|---|---|---|---|---|---|
| †J.O.D. Orders | 5 | 9 | 1 | 295 | 70* | 36.87 | — | 2 | 3 | — |
| †R.S. Cowan | 7 | 11 | 1 | 313 | 63 | 31.30 | — | 3 | 1 | — |
| D.C.G. Foster | 4 | 6 | 1 | 124 | 67 | 24.80 | — | 1 | — | — |
| †S.J. Halliday | 5 | 7 | 1 | 135 | 37 | 22.50 | — | — | 3 | — |
| †R.A.B. Ezekowitz | 10 | 17 | 1 | 340 | 57 | 21.25 | — | 2 | 7 | — |
| R. Marsden | 7 | 12 | 0 | 240 | 54 | 20.00 | — | 1 | 3 | — |
| †J.J. Rogers | 7 | 12 | 1 | 203 | 53 | 18.45 | — | 1 | 3 | — |
| N.V.H. Mallett | 4 | 8 | 0 | 98 | 38 | 12.25 | — | — | 1 | — |
| †T.E.O. Bury | 3 | 4 | 1 | 32 | 22 | 10.66 | — | — | 2 | — |
| S.M. Wookey | 3 | 3 | 1 | 21 | 10* | 10.50 | — | — | 1 | — |
| J.P. Durack | 7 | 13 | 0 | 136 | 45 | 10.46 | — | — | 1 | — |
| †R.P. Moulding | 3 | 5 | 0 | 47 | 24 | 9.40 | — | — | 3 | — |
| J.L. Rawlinson | 5 | 10 | 0 | 85 | 19 | 8.50 | — | — | 1 | — |
| †C.J. Ross | 8 | 13 | 2 | 64 | 23* | 5.81 | — | — | 2 | — |
| M.C.L. Macpherson | 5 | 10 | 1 | 52 | 22 | 5.77 | — | — | 8 | 1 |
| †I.J. Curtis | 9 | 12 | 7 | 27 | 9* | 5.40 | — | — | 1 | — |
| †J.F.W. Sanderson | 5 | 5 | 2 | 16 | 9 | 5.33 | — | — | 1 | — |
| †S.P. Sutcliffe | 10 | 13 | 0 | 57 | 16 | 4.38 | — | — | 1 | — |

Played in two matches: P.N. Huxford, 4. Played in one match: J.M. Knight, 4, 0.

† Denotes played in University match.

#### BOWLING

| | O | M | R | W | Av | BB | 5wI | 10wM |
|---|---|---|---|---|---|---|---|---|
| J.F.W. Sanderson | 84 | 25 | 216 | 8 | 27.00 | 6-67 | 1 | — |
| S.P. Sutcliffe | 252.3 | 61 | 749 | 24 | 31.20 | 6-19 | 1 | — |
| I.J. Curtis | 228 | 61 | 592 | 13 | 45.53 | 3-56 | — | — |
| N.V.H. Mallett | 94 | 11 | 386 | 8 | 48.25 | 4-44 | — | — |
| C.J. Ross | 162.4 | 27 | 589 | 12 | 49.08 | 4-76 | — | — |

Also bowled: R.S. Cowen 24-3-84-2; J.P. Durack 8.4-1-32-0; J.M. Knight 21-3-108-1; J.O.D. Orders 18-3-80-1; S.M. Wookey 40-8-108-2.

## OXFORD UNIVERSITY

### UNIVERSITY RECORDS

| | | | |
|---|---|---|---|
| Highest Innings | For | 651 v Sussex (Hove) | 1895 |
| Totals: | Agst | 679-6d by Australians (Oxford) | 1938 |
| Lowest Innings | For | 12 v MCC (Oxford) | 1877 |
| Totals: | Agst | 36 by MCC (Oxford) | 1867 |
| Highest Indi- | For | 281 K.J. Key v Middlesex (Chiswick) | 1887 |
| vidual Innings: | Agst | 338 W.W. Read for Surrey (Oval) | 1888 |
| Best Bowling | For | 10-38 S.E. Butler v Cambridge U (Lord's) | 1871 |
| in an Innings: | Agst | 10-49 W.G. Grace for MCC (Oxford) | 1886 |
| Best Bowling | For | 15-95 S.E. Butler v Cambridge U (Lord's) | 1871 |
| in a Match: | Agst | 16-225 J.E. Walsh for Leicestershire (Oxford) | 1953 |
| Most runs in a season: | | 1307 (av. 93.35) Nawab of Pataudi (Snr.) | 1931 |
| runs in a career: | | 3319 (av. 47.41) N.S. Mitchell-Innes | 1934-1937 |
| 100s in a season: | | 6 by Nawab of Pataudi (Snr.) | 1931 |
| 100s in a career: | | 9 by A.M. Crawley | 1927-1930 |
| | | Nawab of Pataudi (Snr.) | 1928-31 |
| | | N.S. Mitchell-Innes | 1934-37 |
| | | M.P. Donnelly | 1946-47 |
| wickets in a season: | | 70 (av. 18.15) I.A.R. Peebles | 1930 |

## RECORD WICKET STANDS

| | | | |
|---|---|---|---|
| 1st | 338 | T. Bowring & H. Teesdale v Gentlemen (Oxford) | 1908 |
| 2nd | 226 | W.G. Keighley & H.A. Pawson v Cambridge U (Lord's) | 1947 |
| 3rd | 273 | F.C. de Saram & N.S. Mitchell-Innes v Gloucestershire (Oxford) | 1934 |
| 4th | 276 | P.G.T. Kingsley & N.M. Ford v Surrey (Oval) | 1930 |
| 5th | 256* | A.A. Baig & C.A. Fry v Free Foresters (Oxford) | 1959 |
| 6th | 270 | D.R. Walsh & S.A. Westley v Warwickshire (Oxford) | 1969 |
| 7th | 340 | K.J. Key & H. Philipson v Middlesex (Chiswick) | 1887 |
| 8th | 133 | J.V. Richardson & T.B. Raikes v Free Foresters (Oxford) | 1924 |
| 9th | 160 | H. Philipson & A.C.M. Croome v MCC (Lord's) | 1889 |
| 10th | 149 | F.H. Hollins & B.A. Collins v MCC (Oxford) | 1901 |

# Disposable winner.

# THE FIRST-CLASS
# UMPIRES FOR 1981

*N.B. The abbreviations used below are as for 'The Counties and their Players'.*

**William Edward (Bill) ALLEY** B Sydney, Australia 3/2/1919. LHB, RM. Played for New South Wales 1945-46 to 1947-48. Subsequently came to England to play League cricket and then for Somerset from 1957 to 1968. *Wisden* 1961. Testimonial (£2,700) in 1961. Tours: India and Pakistan 1949-50, Pakistan 1963-64 with Commonwealth team. Scored 3,019 runs (av. 56.96) in 1961 including 2,761 runs and 10 centuries for county, both being records. Won Man of the Match Award in Gillette Cup Competition on three occasions. HS: 221* v Warwickshire (Nuneaton) 1961. BB: 8-65 v Surrey (Oval) 1962. Career record: 19,612 (av. 31.88), 31 centuries, 768 wkts (av. 22.68). Appointed 1969. Umpired in 9 Tests between 1974 and 1980.

**Ronald (Ron) ASPINALL** B Almondbury, Yorks 26/10/1918. RHB, RFM. Played for Yorkshire from 1946 to 1950 (retiring early through injury) and for Durham from 1951 to 1957. HS: 57* v Notts (Nottingham) 1948. BB: 8-42 v Northants (Rushden) 1949. Career record 763 runs (av. 19.07), 131 wkts (av. 20.38). Appointed 1960 (with A. Jepson is longest-serving umpire on list).

**Harold Denis BIRD** B Barnsley 19/4/1933. RHB, RM. Played for Yorks from 1956 to 1959 and for Leics from 1960 to 1964. Was subsequently professional at Paignton CC. HS: 181* Yorks v Glamorgan (Bradford) 1959. Career record: 3,315 runs (av. 20.71), 2 centuries. Appointed 1970. Umpired in 19 Tests between 1973 and 1980.

**William Lloyd BUDD** B Hawkley, Hants 25/10/1913. RHB, RFM. Played for Hampshire from 1934 to 1946. HS: 77* v Surrey (Oval) 1937. BB: 4-22 v Essex (Southend) 1937. Career record: 941 runs (av. 11.47), 64 wkts (av. 39.15). Was on Minor Counties list for some years. Appointed 1969. Umpired in 4 Tests between 1976 and 1978.

**David John CONSTANT** B Bradford-on-Avon, Wilts 9/11/1941. LHB, SLA. Played for Kent from 1961 to 1963 and for Leics from 1965 to 1968. HS: 80 v Glos (Bristol) 1966. Career record: 1,517 runs (av. 19.20), 1 wkt (36.00). Appointed 1969. Umpired in 20 Tests between 1971 and 1980.

**Cecil (Sam) COOK** B Tetbury, Glos 23/8/1921. RHB, SLA. Played for Gloucestershire from 1946 to 1964. Benefit (£3,067) in 1957. Took wicket with first ball in first-class cricket. Tests: 1 v SA 1947. HS: 35* v Sussex (Hove) 1957. BB: 9-42 v Yorks (Bristol) 1947. Career record: 1,964 runs (av. 5.39), 1,782 wkts (av. 20.52). Appointed 1971, after having withdrawn from appointment in 1966.

**Peter James EELE** B Taunton 27/1/1935. LHB, WK. Played for Somerset between 1958 and 1966. HS: 103* v Pakistan Eaglets (Taunton) 1963. Career record: 612 runs (av. 12.24), 1 century, 106 dismissals (87 ct, 19 st). Appointed 1981.

**David Gwilliam Lloyd EVANS** B Lambeth, London 27/7/1933. RHB, WK. Played for Glamorgan from 1956 to 1960. Benefit (£3,500) in 1969. HS: 46* v Oxford U (Oxford) 1961. Career record: 2,875 runs (av. 10.53), 558 dismissals (502 ct, 56 st). Appointed 1971.

**David John HALFYARD** B Winchmore Hill (Middlesex) 3/4/1931. RHB, RM. Played for Kent from 1956 to 1964 retiring through leg injury. Testimonial (£3,216) in 1965. Played for Notts from 1968 to 1970. Not re-engaged and has subsequently played in Minor Counties competition for Durham in 1971 and 1972, Northumberland in 1973 and Cornwall from 1974. HS: 79 Kent v Middlesex (Lord's) 1960. BB: 9-39 Kent v Glamorgan (Neath) 1957. Career record: 3,242 runs (av. 10.91), 963 wkts (av. 25.77). Appointed 1977, after having been on list in 1967.

**Robert Stephen (Bob) HERMAN** B Southampton 30/11/1946. Son of O.W. ('Lofty') Herman (former Hants player and first-class umpire). RHB, RFM. Played for Middlesex from 1965 to 1971 and for Hants from 1972 to 1977. Played for Dorset in 1978 and 1979. Won Benson & Hedges Gold Award on two occasions. HS: 56 v Worcs (Portsmouth) 1972. BB: 8-42 v Warwickshire (Portsmouth) 1972. Career record: 1,426 runs (av. 10.25), 506 wkts (av. 26.28). Appointed 1980.

**Arthur JEPSON** B Selston, Notts 12/7/1915. RHB, RFM. Played for Notts from 1938 to 1959. Benefit (£2,000) in 1951. HS: 130 v Worcs (Nottingham) 1950. BB: 8-45 v Leics (Nottingham) 1958. Career record: 6,369 runs (av. 14.31), 1 century, 1,051 wkts (av. 29.08). Soccer (goalkeeper) for Port Vale, Stoke City and Lincoln City. Appointed 1960 (with R. Aspinall is longest-serving umpire on list). Umpired in 4 Tests between 1966 and 1969.

**Raymond (Ray) JULIEN** B Cosby, Leics 23/8/1936. RHB, WK. Played for Leicestershire from 1953 (debut at age of 16) to 1971, but lost regular place in side to R.W. Tolchard in 1966. HS: 51 v Worcs (Worcester) 1962. Career record: 2,581 runs (av. 9.73), 421 dismissals (382 ct, 39 st). Appointed 1972.

**Barrie LEADBEATER** B Harehills, Leeds 14/8/1943. RHB, RM. Played for Yorkshire from 1966 to 1979. Joint benefit in 1980 with G.A. Cope. Won Man of the Match Award in 1969 Gillette Cup Final. HS: 140* v Hants (Portsmouth) 1976. Career record: 5,373 runs (av. 25.34), 1 century, 1 wkt (av. 5.00). Appointed 1981.

**Barrie John MEYER** B Bournemouth 21/8/1932. RHB, WK. Played for Gloucestershire from 1957 to 1971. Benefit 1971. HS: 63 v Indians (Cheltenham) 1959 v Oxford U (Bristol) 1962 and v Sussex (Bristol) 1964. Career record: 5,367 runs (av. 14.19), 826 dismissals (707 ct, 119 st). Soccer for Bristol Rovers, Plymouth Argyle, Newport County and Bristol City. Appointed 1973. Umpired in 6 Tests between 1978 and 1980.

**Donald Osmund OSLEAR** B Cleethorpes, Lincs 3/3/1929. Has not played first-class cricket. Played soccer for Grimsby Town, Hull City and Oldham Athletic. Also played ice hockey. Has umpired in county second XI matches since 1972. Appointed in 1975. Umpired in 2 Tests in 1980.

**Kenneth Ernest (Ken) PALMER** B Winchester 22/4/1937. RHB, RFM. Played for Somerset from 1955 to 1969. Testimonial (£4,000) in 1968. Tour: Pakistan with Commonwealth team 1963-64. Coached in Johannesburg 1964-65 and was called upon by MCC to play in final Test v South Africa owing to injuries to other bowlers. Tests: 1 v South Africa 1964-65. HS: 125* v Northants (Northampton) 1961. BB: 9-57 v Notts (Nottingham) 1963. Career record: 7,771 runs (av. 20.66), 2 centuries, 866 wkts (av. 21.34). Appointed 1972. Umpired in 6 Tests between 1978 and 1980.

**Roy PALMER** B Devizes, Wilts 12/7/1942. RHB, RFM. Younger brother of K.E. Palmer. Played for Somerset from 1965 to 1970. Won Man of the Match Award in Gillette Cup competition on two occasions. HS: 84 v Leics (Taunton) 1967. BB: 6-45 v Middlesex (Lord's) 1967. Career record: 1,037 runs (av. 13.29), 172 wkts (av. 31.62). Appointed 1980.

**Derek SHACKLETON** B Todmorden, Yorks 12/8/1924. RHB, RM. Played for Hampshire from 1948 to 1969. *Wisden* 1958. Benefit (£5,000) in 1958. Testimonial (£5,000) in 1967. Played for Dorset from 1971 to 1974. Tests: 7 between 1950 and 1963. Tours: India with Commonwealth XI 1950-51 and MCC 1952-53. Took 100 wkts in 20 consecutive seasons from 1949 to 1968, to create record. Only W. Rhodes has taken 100 wkts in more seasons (23). Took more wkts (2,669, av. 18.22) than any other Hants bowler. HS: 87* v Essex (Bournemouth) 1949. BB: 9-30 v Warwickshire (Portsmouth) 1960. Career record: 9,561 runs (av. 14.59), 2,857 wkts (av. 18.65), the eighth highest aggregate by a bowler in first-class cricket. Appointed 1979.

**David Robert SHEPHERD** B Bideford, Devon 27/12/1940. RHB, RM. Played for Gloucestershire from 1965 to 1979, scoring 108 in debut match v Oxford U. Joint benefit in 1978 with J. Davey. Won 1 Gillette Man of the Match Award and 1 Benson & Hedges Gold Award. HS: 153 v Middlesex (Bristol) 1968. Career record: 10,672 runs (av. 24.47), 12 centuries, 2 wkts (av. 53.00). Appointed 1981.

**Charles Terry SPENCER** B Leicester 18/8/1931. RHB, RFM. Played for Leicestershire from 1952 to 1974. Benefit (£3,500) in 1964. HS: 90 v Essex (Leicester) 1964. BB: 9-63 v Yorks (Huddersfield) 1954. Career record: 5,871 runs (av. 10.77), 1,367 wkts (av. 26.69). Appointed 1979.

**Peter Samuel George STEVENS** B Reading 27/7/1934. Has not played first-class cricket. Umpired in Minor Counties matches since 1975. Appointed 1980.

**Jack VAN GELOVEN** B Leeds 4/1/1934. RHB, RM. Played for Yorkshire in 1955 and for Leicestershire from 1956 to 1965. Subsequently played for Northumberland in Minor Counties competition from 1966 to 1973. HS: 157* v Somerset (Leicester) 1964. BB: 7-56 Hants (Leicester) 1959. Career record: 7,522 runs (av. 19.43), 5 centuries, 486 wkts (av. 28.62). Appointed 1977.

**Alan Geoffrey Thomas WHITEHEAD** B Butleigh, Somerset 28/10/1940. LHB, SLA. Played for Somerset from 1957 to 1961. HS: 15 v Hants (Southampton) 1959 and 15 v Leics (Leicester) 1960. BB: 6-74 v Sussex (Eastbourne) 1959. Career record: 137 runs (av. 5.70), 67 wkts (av. 34.41). Served on Minor Counties list in 1969. Appointed 1970.

**Peter Bernard WIGHT** B Georgetown, British Guiana 25/6/1930. RHB, OB. Played for British Guiana in 1950-51 and for Somerset from 1953 to 1965. Benefit (£5,000) in 1963. HS: 222* v Kent (Taunton) 1959. BB: 6-29 v Derbyshire (Chesterfield) 1957. Career record: 17,773 runs (av. 33.09), 28 centuries, 68 wkts (av. 32.26). Appointed 1966.

*NB. The Test match panel for 1981 is W.E. Alley, H.D. Bird, D.J. Constant, D.G.L. Evans, B.J. Meyer, D.O. Oslear and K.E. Palmer.*

# FIRST-CLASS AVERAGES
## 1980

The following averages include everyone who appeared in first-class cricket during the season.
†*Indicates left-handed batsman*

## Batting and fielding

| | Cap | M | I | NO | Runs | HS | Avge | 100 | 50 | Ct | St |
|---|---|---|---|---|---|---|---|---|---|---|---|
| †Abrahams, J. (La) | — | 9 | 14 | 0 | 191 | 59 | 13.64 | — | 2 | 3 | — |
| Acfield, D.L. (Ex) | 1970 | 20 | 19 | 8 | 83 | 26 | 7.54 | — | — | 4 | — |
| Agnew, J.P. (Le) | — | 15 | 13 | 0 | 98 | 31 | 7.53 | — | — | 5 | — |
| Allbrook, M.E. (Nt) | — | 3 | 1 | 1 | 0 | 0* | — | — | — | 1 | — |
| Alleyne, H.L. (Wo) | — | 17 | 19 | 2 | 225 | 72 | 13.23 | — | 1 | 4 | — |
| Allott, P.J.W. (La) | — | 11 | 11 | 4 | 72 | 30* | 10.28 | — | — | — | — |
| Amiss, D.L. (Wa) | 1965 | 23 | 42 | 2 | 1686 | 117* | 42.15 | 1 | 12 | 11 | — |
| Anderson, I.J. (Ire) | — | 1 | 2 | 1 | 35 | 22* | 35.00 | — | — | — | — |
| Anderson, I.S. (D) | — | 13 | 15 | 4 | 187 | 36 | 17.00 | — | — | 8 | — |
| Arnold, G.G. (Sx) | 1979 | 21 | 17 | 2 | 155 | 29* | 10.33 | — | — | 6 | — |
| Asif Iqbal (K) | 1968 | 9 | 16 | 2 | 208 | 41 | 14.85 | — | — | — | — |
| Athey, C.W.J. (E/Y) | 1980 | 23 | 37 | 3 | 1123 | 125* | 33.02 | 2 | 6 | 26 | — |
| | | | | | | | | | | | |
| Bacchus, S.F.A.F. (WI) | — | 15 | 23 | 2 | 710 | 164* | 33.80 | 1 | 4 | 14 | — |
| †Bailey, M.J. (H) | — | 5 | 9 | 5 | 82 | 24 | 20.50 | — | — | 1 | — |
| Bainbridge, P. (Gs) | — | 17 | 29 | 2 | 422 | 71 | 15.62 | — | 1 | 12 | — |
| Bairstow, D.L. (E/Y/MCC) | 1973 | 22 | 26 | 6 | 646 | 145 | 32.30 | 1 | 2 | 46 | 4 |
| Balderstone, J.C. (Le) | 1973 | 24 | 39 | 5 | 1472 | 158* | 43.29 | 2 | 9 | 17 | — |
| Barclay, J.R.T. (Sx) | 1976 | 16 | 26 | 3 | 783 | 119 | 34.04 | 2 | 3 | 9 | — |
| †Barlow, G.D. (M) | 1976 | 24 | 32 | 8 | 1002 | 128* | 41.75 | 3 | 4 | 11 | — |
| Barnett, K.J. (D) | — | 16 | 21 | 0 | 362 | 69 | 17.23 | — | 2 | 10 | — |
| Bell, D.L. (Sc) | — | 1 | 2 | 1 | 56 | 39 | 56.00 | — | — | 1 | — |
| †Benson, M.R. (K) | — | 9 | 13 | 2 | 248 | 58* | 22.54 | — | 2 | 2 | — |
| Birch, J.D. (Nt) | — | 18 | 27 | 5 | 632 | 105* | 28.72 | 1 | 3 | 20 | — |
| †Birkenshaw, J. (Le) | 1965 | 14 | 18 | 4 | 412 | 76 | 29.42 | — | 2 | 8 | — |
| Booden, C.D. (No) | — | 2 | 1 | 1 | 6 | 6* | — | — | — | 1 | — |
| Boon, T.J. (Le) | — | 8 | 12 | 1 | 253 | 53 | 23.00 | — | 1 | 3 | — |
| Booth, P. (Le) | 1976 | 4 | 3 | 1 | 49 | 41* | 24.50 | — | — | 1 | — |
| Booth Jones, T.D. (Sx) | — | 10 | 17 | 1 | 493 | 89* | 30.81 | — | 4 | 2 | — |
| †Border, A.R. (Aus) | — | 4 | 7 | 3 | 321 | 95 | 80.25 | — | 3 | 3 | — |
| Bore, M.K. (Nt) | 1980 | 16 | 16 | 7 | 63 | 24* | 7.00 | — | — | 2 | — |
| Borrington, A.J. (D) | 1977 | 6 | 10 | 1 | 93 | 36 | 10.33 | — | — | — | — |
| Botham, I.T. (E/So/MCC) | 1976 | 18 | 29 | 2 | 1149 | 228 | 42.55 | 2 | 6 | 24 | — |
| Boycott, G. (E/Y) | 1963 | 17 | 28 | 4 | 1264 | 154* | 52.66 | 3 | 8 | 14 | — |
| Boyd-Moss, R.J. (No/CU) | — | 16 | 23 | 1 | 426 | 71 | 19.36 | — | 4 | 7 | — |
| Brain, B.M. (Gs) | 1977 | 22 | 26 | 5 | 185 | 37* | 8.80 | — | — | 3 | — |
| Brassington, A.J. (Gs) | 1978 | 23 | 30 | 8 | 113 | 14* | 5.13 | — | — | 45 | 14 |
| †Breakwell, D. (So) | 1976 | 12 | 14 | 3 | 276 | 73* | 25.09 | — | 1 | 2 | — |
| Brearley, J.M. (M) | 1964 | 23 | 33 | 5 | 1335 | 134* | 47.67 | 5 | 5 | 18 | — |
| Briers, N.E. (Le) | — | 19 | 26 | 2 | 444 | 94 | 18.50 | — | 2 | 5 | — |
| Bright, R.J. (Aus) | — | 3 | 1 | 0 | 21 | 21 | 21.00 | — | — | 1 | — |
| †Broad, B.C. (Gs) | — | 20 | 35 | 1 | 961 | 120 | 28.26 | 3 | 3 | 7 | — |
| Brooks, K.G. (D) | — | 1 | 2 | 0 | 11 | 8 | 5.50 | — | — | 2 | — |
| Bury, T.E.O. (OU) | — | 3 | 4 | 1 | 32 | 22 | 10.66 | — | — | — | — |
| Bushe, E.A. (Ire) | — | 1 | 1 | 0 | 0 | 0* | — | — | — | 2 | — |

169

| | Cap | M | I | NO | Runs | HS | Avge | 100 | 50 | Ct | St |
|---|---|---|---|---|---|---|---|---|---|---|---|
| †Butcher, A.R. (Sy/MCC) | 1975 | 24 | 41 | 4 | 1713 | 216* | 46.29 | 3 | 12 | 19 | — |
| Butcher, I.P. (Le) | — | 1 | — | — | — | — | — | — | — | — | — |
| Butcher, R.O. (M) | 1979 | 16 | 22 | 2 | 792 | 179 | 39.60 | 2 | 3 | 16 | — |
| Carrick, P. (Y) | 1976 | 24 | 32 | 8 | 786 | 131* | 32.75 | 1 | 4 | 15 | — |
| Carter, R.M. (No) | — | 13 | 20 | 2 | 213 | 32 | 11.83 | — | — | 4 | — |
| Chappell, G.S. (Aus) | — | 4 | 6 | 0 | 303 | 101 | 50.50 | 1 | 2 | 4 | — |
| †Cheatle, R.G.L. (Sy) | — | 14 | 10 | 6 | 29 | 9* | 7.25 | — | — | 8 | — |
| †Childs, J.H. (Gs) | 1977 | 15 | 19 | 10 | 44 | 8* | 4.88 | — | — | 6 | — |
| Clark, J. (Sc) | — | 1 | 1 | 0 | 15 | 15 | 15.00 | — | — | — | — |
| Clarke, S.T. (Sy) | 1980 | 21 | 18 | 1 | 248 | 55 | 14.58 | — | 1 | 8 | — |
| Claughton, J.A. (Wa) | — | 16 | 28 | 5 | 533 | 108* | 23.17 | 2 | — | 5 | — |
| Clifford, C.C. (Wa) | — | 5 | 4 | 2 | 7 | 6 | 3.50 | — | — | — | — |
| Clift, P.B. (Le) | 1976 | 22 | 26 | 5 | 512 | 67 | 24.38 | — | 3 | 12 | — |
| †Clinton, G.S. (Sy) | 1980 | 24 | 39 | 6 | 1240 | 120 | 37.57 | 1 | 8 | 3 | — |
| Cobb, R.A. (Le) | — | 1 | — | — | — | — | — | — | — | — | — |
| Cockbain, I. (La) | — | 17 | 27 | 6 | 388 | 69* | 18.47 | — | 2 | 10 | — |
| Cohen, M.F. (Ire) | — | 1 | 1 | 0 | 0 | 0 | 0.00 | — | — | 1 | — |
| Cook, G. (No) | 1975 | 22 | 39 | 4 | 976 | 109 | 27.88 | 2 | 3 | 21 | — |
| Cook, N.G.B. (Le) | — | 25 | 24 | 9 | 180 | 75 | 12.00 | — | 1 | 13 | — |
| †Cooper, H.P. (Y) | — | 7 | 7 | 2 | 57 | 23 | 11.40 | — | — | 3 | — |
| †Cooper, K.E. (Nt) | 1980 | 15 | 15 | 4 | 93 | 35 | 8.45 | — | — | 3 | — |
| Cope, G.A. (Y) | 1970 | 21 | 12 | 8 | 85 | 33 | 21.25 | — | — | 3 | — |
| Cordle, A.E. (Gm) | 1967 | 5 | 4 | 1 | 17 | 6* | 5.66 | — | — | 2 | — |
| Corlett, S.C. (Ire) | — | 1 | 1 | 0 | 13 | 13 | 13.00 | — | — | 1 | — |
| Coverdale, S.P. (Y) | — | 5 | 3 | 0 | 31 | 18 | 10.33 | — | — | 9 | 3 |
| Cowan, R.S. (OU) | — | 7 | 11 | 1 | 313 | 63 | 31.30 | — | 3 | 1 | — |
| Cowans, N.G. (M) | — | 1 | 1 | 0 | 1 | 1 | 1.00 | — | — | — | — |
| Cowdrey, C.S. (K) | 1979 | 21 | 31 | 3 | 768 | 87 | 27.42 | — | 5 | 22 | — |
| Cowley, N.G. (H) | 1978 | 23 | 37 | 3 | 766 | 80* | 22.52 | — | 4 | 12 | — |
| Crawford, N.C. (CU) | — | 8 | 7 | 1 | 84 | 28 | 14.00 | — | — | 2 | — |
| Croft, C.E.H. (WI) | — | 9 | 4 | 3 | 8 | 7* | 8.00 | — | — | — | — |
| Cumbes, J. (Wo) | 1978 | 8 | 5 | 3 | 55 | 43 | 27.50 | — | — | — | — |
| †Curtis, I.T. (OU) | — | 9 | 12 | 7 | 27 | 9* | 5.40 | — | — | 1 | — |
| Curtis, T.S. (Wo) | — | 3 | 5 | 1 | 85 | 59* | 21.25 | — | 1 | — | — |
| Curzon, C.C. (Nt) | — | 10 | 13 | 1 | 192 | 45 | 16.00 | — | — | 26 | 1 |
| Daniel, W.W. (M) | 1977 | 19 | 12 | 4 | 56 | 15 | 7.00 | — | — | 3 | — |
| Davison, B.F. (Le) | 1971 | 21 | 32 | 4 | 1310 | 151 | 46.78 | 2 | 8 | 18 | — |
| Denness, M.H. (Ex) | 1977 | 18 | 30 | 4 | 805 | 87 | 30.96 | — | 8 | 7 | — |
| †Denning, P.W. (So) | 1973 | 23 | 34 | 2 | 1012 | 184 | 31.62 | 1 | 5 | 14 | — |
| Dennis, S.J. (Y) | — | 4 | 2 | 1 | 1 | 1* | 1.00 | — | — | 3 | — |
| Dexter, R.E. (Nt) | — | 5 | 8 | 1 | 83 | 32 | 11.85 | — | — | 7 | — |
| †Dilley, G.R. (E/K/MCC) | 1980 | 13 | 11 | 5 | 21 | 12* | 3.50 | — | — | 5 | — |
| †Doggart, S.J.G. (CU) | — | 9 | 11 | 2 | 174 | 43 | 19.33 | — | — | 6 | — |
| D'Oliveira, B.L. (Wo) | 1965 | 1 | 2 | 0 | 37 | 21 | 18.50 | — | — | — | — |
| Donald, W.A. (Sc) | — | 1 | 1 | 0 | 0 | 0 | 0.00 | — | — | — | — |
| †Doshi, D.R. (Wa) | 1980 | 25 | 23 | 7 | 81 | 10* | 5.06 | — | — | 3 | — |
| Downton, P.R. (M) | — | 9 | 15 | 2 | 521 | 90* | 40.07 | — | 4 | 26 | 3 |
| †Dredge, C.H. (So) | 1978 | 20 | 21 | 5 | 113 | 21* | 7.06 | — | — | 6 | — |
| Dudleston, B. (Le) | 1969 | 8 | 14 | 1 | 234 | 83 | 18.00 | — | 2 | 2 | — |
| Durack, J.P. (OU) | — | 7 | 13 | 0 | 136 | 45 | 10.46 | — | — | 3 | — |
| †Dymock, G. (Aus) | — | 2 | 1 | 0 | 37 | 37 | 37.00 | — | — | — | — |
| Dyson, J. (Aus) | — | 3 | 6 | 1 | 66 | 33 | 13.20 | — | — | — | — |
| Ealham, A.G.E. (K) | 1970 | 20 | 29 | 2 | 801 | 145 | 29.66 | 1 | 4 | 5 | — |

| | Cap | M | I | NO | Runs | HS | Avge | 100 | 50 | Ct | St |
|---|---|---|---|---|---|---|---|---|---|---|---|
| East, R.E. (Ex) | 1967 | 20 | 25 | 4 | 361 | 47 | 17.19 | — | — | 7 | — |
| Edmonds, P.H. (M/MCC) | 1974 | 16 | 13 | 2 | 208 | 52 | 18.90 | — | 1 | 6 | — |
| Elder, J.W.G. (Ire) | — | 1 | 1 | 0 | 6 | 6 | 6.00 | — | — | — | — |
| Emburey, J.E. (E/M) | 1977 | 21 | 19 | 5 | 300 | 43* | 21.42 | — | — | 20 | — |
| Ezekowitz, R.A.B. (OU) | — | 10 | 17 | 1 | 340 | 57 | 21.25 | — | 2 | 7 | — |
| | | | | | | | | | | | |
| Featherstone, N.G. (Gm) | 1980 | 22 | 34 | 6 | 1015 | 107 | 36.25 | 1 | 8 | 11 | — |
| Ferreria, A.M. (Wa) | — | 19 | 27 | 4 | 523 | 90 | 22.73 | — | 2 | 10 | — |
| Fisher, P.B. (Wo) | — | 7 | 10 | 5 | 40 | 11 | 8.00 | — | — | 22 | 2 |
| Fletcher, K.W.R. (Ex) | 1963 | 24 | 38 | 4 | 1349 | 122* | 39.67 | 1 | 9 | 23 | — |
| †Forster, G. (No) | — | 1 | — | — | — | — | — | — | — | 1 | — |
| †Foster, D.C.G. (OU) | — | 4 | 6 | 1 | 124 | 67 | 24.80 | — | 1 | — | — |
| Foster, N.A. (Ex) | — | 1 | 1 | 1 | 8 | 8* | — | — | — | — | — |
| †Fowler, G. (La) | — | 10 | 12 | 1 | 262 | 106* | 23.81 | 1 | — | 7 | 2 |
| Francis, D.A. (Gm) | — | 9 | 14 | 3 | 276 | 78* | 25.09 | — | 2 | 2 | — |
| French, B.N. (Nt) | 1980 | 15 | 20 | 4 | 317 | 70* | 19.81 | — | 1 | 38 | 6 |
| | | | | | | | | | | | |
| Gard, T. (So) | — | 3 | 2 | 0 | 41 | 22 | 20.50 | — | — | 4 | 1 |
| Garner, J. (WI) | — | 11 | 10 | 0 | 206 | 104 | 20.60 | 1 | — | 8 | — |
| Garnham, M.A. (Le) | — | 2 | 1 | 0 | 14 | 14 | 14.00 | — | — | 2 | — |
| Gatting, M.W. (E/M) | 1977 | 19 | 25 | 4 | 880 | 136 | 41.90 | 2 | 4 | 17 | — |
| Gavaskar, S.M. (So) | 1980 | 15 | 23 | 3 | 686 | 155* | 34.30 | 2 | 2 | 5 | — |
| †Gifford, N. (Wo) | 1961 | 22 | 28 | 10 | 352 | 45 | 19.55 | — | — | 13 | — |
| Goddard, G.F. (Sl) | — | 1 | 1 | 1 | 14 | 14* | — | — | — | 1 | — |
| Gooch, G.A. (E/Ex) | 1975 | 19 | 35 | 5 | 1437 | 205 | 47.90 | 6 | 2 | 17 | — |
| Gore, H.E.I. (So) | — | 11 | 11 | 5 | 48 | 22* | 8.00 | — | — | 3 | — |
| †Gould, I.J. (M) | 1977 | 15 | 16 | 4 | 388 | 57 | 32.33 | — | 3 | 36 | 7 |
| †Gower, D.I. (E/Le) | 1977 | 24 | 36 | 1 | 1142 | 138 | 32.62 | 2 | 3 | 16 | — |
| †Graf, S.F. (H) | — | 15 | 19 | 5 | 284 | 57* | 20.28 | — | 1 | 9 | — |
| Graveney, D.A. (Gs) | 1976 | 21 | 31 | 7 | 513 | 119 | 21.37 | 1 | 2 | 8 | — |
| †Graves, P.J. (Sx) | 1969 | 4 | 7 | 0 | 206 | 98 | 29.42 | — | 1 | 1 | — |
| Green, A.M. (Sx) | — | 1 | 1 | 0 | 0 | 0 | 0.00 | — | — | — | — |
| Greenidge, C.G. (WI/H) | 1972 | 16 | 24 | 2 | 744 | 165 | 33.81 | 1 | 3 | 6 | — |
| Greig, I.A. (Sx) | — | 16 | 19 | 5 | 366 | 53 | 26.14 | — | 2 | 12 | — |
| Griffiths, B.J. (No) | 1978 | 22 | 16 | 1 | 35 | 10 | 2.33 | — | — | 5 | — |
| | | | | | | | | | | | |
| Hacker, P.J. (Nt) | 1980 | 17 | 18 | 7 | 69 | 12 | 6.27 | — | — | 3 | — |
| †Hadlee, R.J. (Nt) | 1978 | 8 | 9 | 1 | 231 | 68 | 28.87 | — | 1 | 4 | — |
| Halliday, M. (Ire) | — | 1 | 1 | 0 | 0 | 0 | 0.00 | — | — | 1 | — |
| Halliday, S.J. (OU) | — | 5 | 7 | 1 | 135 | 37 | 22.50 | — | — | 3 | — |
| Hampshire, J.H. (Y) | 1963 | 18 | 27 | 6 | 987 | 124 | 51.94 | 2 | 7 | 12 | — |
| Hardie, B.R. (Ex) | 1974 | 24 | 36 | 4 | 1084 | 95 | 33.87 | — | 6 | 21 | — |
| Harpur, T. (Ire) | — | 1 | 1 | 0 | 4 | 4 | 4.00 | — | — | 1 | — |
| Harris, M.J. (Nt) | 1970 | 12 | 20 | 2 | 289 | 65 | 16.05 | — | 2 | 11 | — |
| Hartley, S.N. (Y) | — | 14 | 22 | 2 | 352 | 72* | 17.60 | — | 2 | 7 | — |
| Hassan, S.B. (Nt) | 1970 | 16 | 27 | 3 | 720 | 91 | 30.00 | — | 5 | 19 | — |
| Hayes, F.C. (La) | 1972 | 21 | 33 | 6 | 1117 | 102* | 41.37 | 1 | 9 | 6 | — |
| Hayes, K.A. (La) | — | 1 | 1 | 0 | 27 | 27 | 27.00 | — | — | 1 | — |
| Haynes, D.L. (WI) | — | 14 | 22 | 3 | 874 | 184 | 46.00 | 1 | 6 | 2 | — |
| Hays, D.L. (Sc) | — | 1 | 2 | 0 | 22 | 14 | 11.00 | — | — | 1 | — |
| Head, T.J. (Sx) | — | 8 | 8 | 0 | 87 | 41 | 10.87 | — | — | 13 | 4 |
| †Heath, J.R.P. (Sx) | — | 1 | 1 | 0 | 0 | 0 | 0.00 | — | — | — | — |
| Hemmings, E.E. (Nt) | 1980 | 24 | 28 | 4 | 496 | 86 | 20.66 | — | 1 | 11 | — |
| Hemsley, E.J.O. (Wo) | 1969 | 18 | 27 | 4 | 828 | 76 | 36.00 | — | 8 | 14 | — |
| Hemsley, P.D. (CU) | — | 1 | 1 | 1 | 12 | 12* | — | — | — | — | — |
| †Henderson, S.P. (Wo) | — | 6 | 8 | 0 | 147 | 64 | 18.37 | — | 1 | 6 | — |

171

| | Cap | M | I | NO | Runs | HS | Avge | 100 | 50 | Ct | St |
|---|---|---|---|---|---|---|---|---|---|---|---|
| Hendrick, M. (E/D) | 1972 | 15 | 17 | 8 | 122 | 33 | 13.55 | — | — | 9 | — |
| Herbert, R. (Ex) | — | 3 | 4 | 1 | 29 | 14* | 9.66 | — | — | 3 | — |
| †Higgs, K. (Le) | 1972 | 3 | 2 | 2 | 9 | 7* | — | — | — | 2 | — |
| Hignell, A.J. (Gs) | 1977 | 15 | 23 | 5 | 630 | 100* | 35.00 | 1 | 3 | 11 | — |
| Hill, A. (D) | 1976 | 2 | 4 | 0 | 14 | 7 | 3.50 | — | — | 1 | — |
| Hills, R.W. (K) | 1977 | 11 | 16 | 4 | 82 | 12 | 6.83 | — | — | 11 | — |
| Hobbs, R.N.S. (Gm) | 1979 | 7 | 8 | 2 | 34 | 14 | 5.66 | — | — | 1 | — |
| Hogg, W. (La) | — | 15 | 13 | 5 | 18 | 5* | 2.25 | — | — | 2 | — |
| Holder, V.A. (Wo) | 1970 | 6 | 8 | 1 | 78 | 34 | 11.14 | — | — | 4 | — |
| Holding, M.A. (WI) | — | 11 | 11 | 6 | 99 | 35 | 19.80 | — | — | 2 | — |
| Holliday, D.C. (CU) | — | 9 | 12 | 3 | 173 | 76* | 19.22 | — | 1 | 3 | — |
| Holmes, G.C. (Gm) | — | 18 | 28 | 6 | 393 | 40* | 17.86 | — | — | 8 | — |
| Hopkins, D.C. (Wa) | — | 12 | 18 | 9 | 156 | 33 | 17.33 | — | — | — | — |
| Hopkins, J.A. (Gm) | 1977 | 22 | 39 | 1 | 1123 | 112 | 29.55 | 2 | 5 | 21 | — |
| Howarth, G.P. (Sy) | 1974 | 11 | 17 | 2 | 332 | 66 | 22.13 | — | 3 | 3 | — |
| Howat, M.G. (CU) | — | 9 | 6 | 0 | 61 | 32 | 10.16 | — | — | 4 | — |
| Hughes, D.P. (La) | 1970 | 18 | 21 | 6 | 405 | 66* | 27.00 | — | 2 | 18 | — |
| Hughes, K.J. (Aus) | — | 5 | 9 | 1 | 249 | 117 | 31.12 | 1 | 1 | 3 | — |
| Hughes, S.P. (M) | — | 5 | 4 | 2 | 0 | 0* | 0.00 | — | — | 3 | — |
| Humpage, G.W. (Wa) | 1976 | 25 | 43 | 2 | 1339 | 101 | 32.65 | 2 | 7 | 42 | 8 |
| †Humphries, D.J. (Wo) | 1978 | 16 | 21 | 3 | 518 | 108* | 28.77 | 1 | 1 | 28 | — |
| †Huxford, P.N. (OU) | — | 2 | 1 | 0 | 4 | 4 | 4.00 | — | — | — | — |
| Imran Khan (Sx) | 1978 | 17 | 28 | 6 | 863 | 124 | 39.22 | 2 | 5 | 1 | — |
| Inchmore, J.D. (Wo) | 1976 | 16 | 21 | 2 | 251 | 64 | 13.21 | — | 1 | 5 | — |
| Ingham, P.G. (Y) | — | 4 | 7 | 0 | 197 | 64 | 28.14 | — | 2 | — | — |
| Intikhab Alam (Sy) | 1969 | 11 | 10 | 3 | 212 | 57* | 30.28 | — | 1 | 1 | — |
| Jackman, R.D. (Sy) | 1970 | 23 | 24 | 8 | 363 | 47 | 22.68 | — | — | 14 | — |
| †James, K.D. (M) | — | 1 | 1 | 0 | 16 | 16 | 16.00 | — | — | — | — |
| Jarvis, K.B.S. (K) | 1977 | 18 | 11 | 4 | 12 | 4 | 1.71 | — | — | 2 | — |
| Javed Miandad (Gm) | 1980 | 20 | 32 | 5 | 1460 | 181 | 54.07 | 3 | 6 | 7 | — |
| Jennings, K.F. (So) | 1978 | 11 | 10 | 4 | 104 | 21* | 17.33 | — | — | 13 | — |
| Jesty, T.E. (H) | 1971 | 16 | 25 | 3 | 522 | 114* | 23.72 | 1 | 2 | 6 | — |
| Johnson, G.W. (K) | 1970 | 21 | 29 | 5 | 509 | 84 | 21.20 | — | 2 | 10 | — |
| †Jones, A. (Gm) | 1962 | 21 | 37 | 4 | 1393 | 204* | 42.21 | 2 | 7 | 5 | — |
| Jones, A.A. (Gm) | — | 16 | 14 | 3 | 50 | 12 | 4.54 | — | — | 4 | — |
| †Jones, A.L. (Gm) | — | 3 | 5 | 0 | 47 | 22 | 9.40 | — | — | 3 | — |
| †Jones, B.J.R. (Wo) | — | 10 | 17 | 0 | 227 | 49 | 13.35 | — | — | 4 | — |
| Jones, E.W. (Gm) | 1967 | 22 | 29 | 5 | 465 | 67 | 19.37 | — | 3 | 43 | 2 |
| †Kallicharran, A.I. (WI/Wa) | 1972 | 20 | 28 | 1 | 876 | 90 | 32.44 | — | 6 | 15 | — |
| Kemp, N.J. (K) | — | 5 | 5 | 0 | 48 | 23 | 9.60 | — | — | 2 | — |
| †Kennedy, A. (La) | 1975 | 22 | 38 | 3 | 1194 | 169* | 34.11 | 1 | 7 | 12 | — |
| King, C.L. (WI) | — | 9 | 11 | 2 | 86 | 26* | 9.55 | — | — | 4 | — |
| Kirsten, P.N. (D) | 1978 | 21 | 36 | 6 | 1895 | 213* | 63.16 | 6 | 8 | 12 | — |
| Knight, J.M. (OU) | — | 1 | 2 | 0 | 4 | 4 | 2.00 | — | — | 1 | — |
| †Knight, R.D.V. (Sy) | 1978 | 24 | 37 | 7 | 1224 | 132 | 40.80 | 4 | 6 | 22 | — |
| Knott, A.P.E. (E/K) | 1965 | 20 | 28 | 4 | 540 | 85* | 22.50 | — | 1 | 39 | 3 |
| Laird, B.M. (Aus) | — | 5 | 9 | 1 | 240 | 85 | 30.00 | — | 3 | 3 | — |
| Lamb, A.J. (No) | 1978 | 23 | 39 | 12 | 1797 | 152 | 66.55 | 5 | 6 | 11 | — |
| Lamb, T.M. (No) | 1978 | 24 | 21 | 12 | 108 | 13* | 12.00 | — | — | 8 | — |
| Larkins, W. (E/No) | 1976 | 23 | 42 | 3 | 1772 | 156 | 45.43 | 4 | 8 | 9 | — |
| Lee, P.G. (La) | 1972 | 1 | 2 | 1 | 0 | 0* | 0.00 | — | — | — | — |
| Le Roux, G.S. (Sx) | — | 15 | 20 | 5 | 431 | 68* | 28.73 | — | 3 | 3 | — |

172

| | Cap | M | I | NO | Runs | HS | Avge | 100 | 50 | Ct | St |
|---|---|---|---|---|---|---|---|---|---|---|---|
| Lever, J.K. (E/Ex) | 1970 | 21 | 21 | 10 | 123 | 18* | 11.18 | — | — | 6 | — |
| Lillee, D.K. (Aus) | — | 4 | 4 | 1 | 81 | 33 | 27.00 | — | — | — | — |
| Lilley, A.W. (Ex) | — | 1 | 2 | 0 | 15 | 9 | 7.50 | — | — | — | — |
| †Llewellyn, M.J. (Gm) | 1977 | 14 | 19 | 5 | 395 | 69 | 28.21 | — | 2 | 4 | — |
| Lloyd, B.J. (Gm) | — | 12 | 14 | 7 | 140 | 30 | 20.00 | — | — | 5 | — |
| †Lloyd, C.H. (WI/La) | 1969 | 14 | 15 | 2 | 621 | 116 | 47.76 | 4 | 1 | 9 | — |
| †Lloyd, D. (La) | 1968 | 19 | 30 | 6 | 827 | 112* | 34.45 | 1 | 3 | 11 | — |
| †Lloyd, T.A. (Wa) | 1980 | 25 | 44 | 5 | 1423 | 130* | 36.48 | 2 | 10 | 12 | — |
| †Lloyds, J.W. (So) | — | 11 | 16 | 3 | 388 | 70 | 29.84 | — | 4 | 7 | — |
| †Long, A. (Sx) | 1976 | 16 | 15 | 5 | 165 | 31 | 16.50 | — | — | 31 | 1 |
| Love, J.D. (Y) | 1980 | 20 | 32 | 7 | 917 | 105* | 36.68 | 2 | 4 | 9 | — |
| Lumb, R.G. (Y/MCC) | 1974 | 24 | 39 | 3 | 1223 | 129 | 33.97 | 3 | 8 | 7 | — |
| Lynch, M.A. (Sy) | — | 8 | 11 | 3 | 291 | 92 | 36.37 | — | 3 | 8 | — |
| | | | | | | | | | | | |
| McEvoy, M.S.A. (Ex) | — | 16 | 29 | 0 | 600 | 65 | 20.68 | — | 2 | 14 | — |
| McEwan, K.S. (Ex) | 1974 | 23 | 38 | 6 | 1217 | 140* | 38.03 | 2 | 8 | 16 | — |
| †Mack, A.J. (Gm) | — | 8 | 7 | 4 | 17 | 6 | 5.66 | — | — | — | — |
| Mackintosh, K.S. (Nt) | — | 4 | 5 | 3 | 46 | 16* | 23.00 | — | — | 1 | — |
| Macpherson, M.C.L. (OU) | — | 5 | 10 | 1 | 52 | 22 | 5.77 | — | — | 8 | 1 |
| Mallender, N.A. (No) | — | 5 | 6 | 3 | 4 | 2* | 1.33 | — | — | 1 | — |
| Mallett, A.A. (Aus) | — | 4 | 3 | 1 | 49 | 30* | 24.50 | — | — | 4 | — |
| Mallett, N.V.H. (OU) | — | 4 | 8 | 0 | 98 | 38 | 12.25 | — | — | 1 | — |
| Malone, M.F. (La) | — | 16 | 14 | 3 | 181 | 38 | 16.45 | — | — | 1 | — |
| Malone, S.J. (H) | — | 7 | 11 | 5 | 70 | 20 | 11.66 | — | — | 1 | — |
| Marks, V.J. (So) | 1979 | 22 | 32 | 7 | 765 | 82 | 30.60 | — | 5 | 11 | — |
| Marsden, R. (OU) | — | 7 | 12 | 0 | 240 | 50 | 20.00 | — | 1 | 3 | — |
| †Marsh, R.W. (Aus) | — | 5 | 7 | 4 | 172 | 56 | 57.33 | — | 2 | 11 | — |
| Marshall, M.D. (WI/H) | — | 17 | 22 | 3 | 462 | 72* | 24.31 | — | 3 | 6 | — |
| Maru, R.J. (M) | — | 9 | 7 | 1 | 49 | 13 | 8.16 | — | — | 8 | — |
| Maynard, C. (Wa) | — | 6 | 8 | 1 | 91 | 30 | 13.00 | — | — | 3 | 3 |
| Mellor, A.J. (D) | — | 1 | 2 | 0 | 0 | 0 | 0.00 | — | — | — | — |
| Mendis, G.D. (Sx) | 1980 | 24 | 42 | 1 | 1437 | 204 | 35.04 | 1 | 8 | 6 | — |
| Merry, W.G. (M) | — | 5 | 11 | 6 | 6 | 6* | — | — | — | — | — |
| Miller, G. (D/MCC) | 1976 | 21 | 29 | 5 | 693 | 78* | 28.87 | — | 6 | 22 | — |
| Mills, J.P.C. (CU) | — | 9 | 14 | 1 | 350 | 79 | 26.92 | — | 2 | 3 | — |
| †Mohamed, T. (WI) | — | 1 | 2 | 0 | 47 | 45 | 23.50 | — | — | — | — |
| Moir, D.G. (Sc) | — | 1 | 2 | 0 | 70 | 44 | 35.00 | — | — | 1 | — |
| Monteith, J.D. (Ire) | — | 1 | 1 | 0 | 6 | 6 | 6.00 | — | — | — | — |
| Moseley, E.A. (Gm) | — | 14 | 16 | 6 | 294 | 70* | 29.40 | — | 2 | 2 | — |
| Moseley, H.R. (So) | 1972 | 17 | 9 | 4 | 55 | 16 | 11.00 | — | — | 5 | — |
| Moulding, R.P. (OU) | — | 3 | 5 | 0 | 47 | 24 | 9.40 | — | — | 1 | — |
| Muburak, A.M. (CU) | — | 9 | 14 | 0 | 359 | 105 | 25.64 | 1 | 2 | 5 | — |
| Murray, D.A. (WI) | — | 6 | 8 | 2 | 161 | 49 | 26.83 | — | — | 16 | 1 |
| Murry, D.L. (WI) | — | 12 | 14 | 2 | 315 | 64 | 26.25 | — | 2 | 33 | 2 |
| | | | | | | | | | | | |
| Nanan, N. (Nt) | — | 2 | 4 | 0 | 26 | 11 | 6.50 | — | — | — | — |
| †Nash, M.A. (Gm) | 1969 | 18 | 24 | 2 | 342 | 49* | 15.54 | — | — | 8 | — |
| Neale, P.A. (Wo) | 1978 | 20 | 33 | 3 | 933 | 123 | 31.10 | 1 | 6 | 4 | — |
| Newman, P.G. (D) | — | 3 | 4 | 3 | 60 | 29* | 60.00 | — | — | 1 | — |
| Nicholas, M.C.J. (H) | — | 18 | 31 | 1 | 783 | 112 | 26.10 | 1 | 3 | 9 | — |
| | | | | | | | | | | | |
| O'Brien, B.A. (Ire) | — | 1 | 2 | 0 | 36 | 33 | 18.00 | — | — | — | — |
| Odenaal, A. (CU) | — | 9 | 14 | 0 | 325 | 61 | 23.21 | — | 1 | 6 | — |
| †Old, C.M. (E/Y) | 1969 | 18 | 14 | 5 | 355 | 89 | 39.44 | — | 3 | 11 | — |
| Oldham, S. (D) | 1980 | 19 | 10 | 4 | 11 | 7 | 1.83 | — | — | 7 | — |
| Olive, M. (So) | — | 9 | 17 | 1 | 290 | 50 | 18.12 | — | 1 | 4 | — |

| | Cap | M | I | NO | Runs | HS | Avge | 100 | 50 | Ct | St |
|---|---|---|---|---|---|---|---|---|---|---|---|
| Oliver, P.R. (Wa) | — | 22 | 35 | 7 | 772 | 76* | 27.57 | — | 4 | 14 | — |
| Ontong, R.C. (Gm) | 1979 | 5 | 7 | 1 | 110 | 52 | 18.33 | — | 1 | 1 | — |
| †Orders, J.O.D. (OU) | — | 5 | 9 | 1 | 295 | 70* | 36.87 | — | 2 | 3 | — |
| Ormrod, J.A. (Wo) | 1966 | 22 | 35 | 3 | 1495 | 131* | 46.71 | 5 | 8 | 13 | — |
| O'Shaughnessy, S.J. (La) | — | 4 | 5 | 2 | 91 | 50* | 30.33 | — | 1 | 2 | — |
| Parker, P.W.G. (Sx/MCC) | 1979 | 22 | 40 | 6 | 1200 | 122* | 35.29 | 4 | 3 | 16 | — |
| Parks, R.J. (H) | — | 7 | 13 | 3 | 233 | 64* | 23.30 | — | 2 | 12 | 5 |
| Parry, D.R. (WI) | — | 11 | 13 | 8 | 103 | 26* | 20.60 | — | — | 2 | — |
| †Parsons, G.J. (Le) | — | 14 | 13 | 4 | 106 | 25* | 11.77 | — | — | 8 | — |
| Partridge, M.D. (Gs) | — | 11 | 18 | 6 | 286 | 48 | 28.83 | — | — | 4 | — |
| Pascoe, L.S. (Aus) | — | 4 | 3 | 1 | 8 | 6 | 4.00 | — | — | 1 | — |
| Patel, D.N. (Wo) | 1979 | 18 | 18 | 4 | 360 | 74 | 25.71 | — | 3 | 9 | — |
| Pauline, D.B. (Sy) | — | 8 | 11 | 1 | 162 | 46 | 16.20 | — | — | 1 | — |
| Peck, I.G. (No/CU) | — | 10 | 13 | 2 | 151 | 34 | 13.72 | — | — | 6 | — |
| Perry, N.J. (Gm) | — | 6 | 5 | 1 | 11 | 6 | 2.75 | — | — | 7 | — |
| Perryman, S.P. (Wa) | 1977 | 12 | 8 | 4 | 16 | 5 | 4.00 | — | — | 8 | — |
| Phillip, N. (Ex) | 1978 | 20 | 24 | 4 | 376 | 77* | 18.80 | — | 2 | 5 | — |
| Phillipson, C.P. (Sx) | 1980 | 23 | 33 | 3 | 655 | 87 | 21.83 | — | 4 | 24 | — |
| Pigott, A.C.S. (Sx) | — | 5 | 7 | 2 | 52 | 17 | 10.40 | — | — | — | — |
| Pilling, H. (La) | 1965 | 3 | 6 | 1 | 80 | 56* | 16.00 | — | 1 | 1 | — |
| Pocock, N.E.J. (H) | 1980 | 24 | 40 | 3 | 874 | 66 | 23.62 | — | 5 | 27 | — |
| Pocock, P.I. (Sy) | 1967 | 23 | 16 | 6 | 97 | 20* | 9.70 | — | — | 9 | — |
| Pont, K.R. (Ex) | 1976 | 12 | 17 | 2 | 210 | 36 | 14.00 | — | — | 5 | — |
| Popplewell, N.F.M. (So) | — | 14 | 20 | 6 | 445 | 135* | 31.78 | 1 | 1 | 17 | — |
| Pridgeon, A.P. (Wo) | 1980 | 21 | 22 | 11 | 118 | 28* | 10.72 | — | — | 8 | — |
| Pringle, D.R. (Ex/CU) | — | 17 | 24 | 4 | 713 | 123 | 35.65 | 2 | 3 | 14 | — |
| Proctor, M.J. (Gs) | 1968 | 19 | 33 | 2 | 1081 | 134* | 34.87 | 1 | 7 | 17 | — |
| Racionzer, T.B. (Sc) | — | 1 | 2 | 0 | 81 | 61 | 40.50 | — | 1 | — | — |
| Radford, N.V. (La) | — | 4 | 7 | 0 | 115 | 34 | 16.42 | — | — | 2 | — |
| Radley, C.T. (M) | 1967 | 24 | 34 | 8 | 1491 | 136* | 57.34 | 5 | 5 | 18 | — |
| †Ramage, A. (Y) | — | 4 | 3 | 2 | 20 | 14* | 20.00 | — | — | 1 | — |
| Randall, D.W. (Nt) | 1973 | 22 | 37 | 1 | 1361 | 170 | 37.80 | 2 | 8 | 15 | — |
| Ratcliffe, R.M. (La) | 1976 | 4 | 3 | 0 | 38 | 26 | 12.66 | — | — | 1 | — |
| Rawlinson, J.L. (OU) | — | 5 | 10 | 0 | 85 | 19 | 8.50 | — | — | 3 | — |
| †Reidy, B.W. (La) | 1980 | 16 | 27 | 5 | 671 | 110* | 30.50 | 1 | 4 | 9 | — |
| †Reith, M.S. (Ire) | — | 1 | 2 | 0 | 63 | 59 | 31.50 | — | 1 | — | — |
| Rice, C.E.B. (Nt) | 1975 | 23 | 36 | 9 | 1448 | 131* | 53.62 | 5 | 7 | 16 | — |
| Rice, J.M. (H) | 1975 | 9 | 16 | 0 | 171 | 30 | 10.68 | — | — | 6 | — |
| Richards, C.J. (Sy) | 1978 | 24 | 20 | 6 | 258 | 48 | 18.42 | — | — | 59 | 3 |
| Richards, I.V.A. (WI/So) | 1974 | 17 | 25 | 1 | 1217 | 170 | 50.70 | 5 | 5 | 19 | — |
| Roberts, A.M.E. (WI) | — | 9 | 10 | 1 | 114 | 31 | 12.66 | — | — | 4 | — |
| Robertson, F. (Sc) | — | 1 | 1 | 0 | 0 | 0 | 0.00 | — | — | — | — |
| Robinson, R.T. (Nt) | — | 15 | 26 | 3 | 765 | 138 | 33.26 | 1 | 3 | 7 | — |
| Roebuck, P.M. (So/MCC) | 1978 | 23 | 37 | 3 | 885 | 101 | 26.02 | 1 | 3 | 11 | — |
| Rogers, J.J. (OU) | — | 7 | 12 | 1 | 203 | 53 | 18.45 | — | 1 | 3 | — |
| Roope, G.R.J. (Sy) | 1969 | 23 | 30 | 9 | 996 | 101 | 47.42 | 1 | 10 | 31 | — |
| †Rose, B.C. (E/So) | 1975 | 17 | 26 | 4 | 1084 | 150* | 49.27 | 2 | 5 | 6 | — |
| Ross, C.J. (OU) | — | 8 | 13 | 2 | 64 | 23* | 5.81 | — | — | 2 | — |
| †Rouse, S.J. (Wa) | 1974 | 15 | 21 | 7 | 233 | 35 | 16.64 | — | — | 4 | — |
| Rowe, C.J.C. (K) | 1977 | 15 | 24 | 2 | 539 | 109 | 24.50 | 1 | 2 | 8 | — |
| Rowe, L.G. (WI) | — | 3 | 2 | 0 | 13 | 13 | 6.50 | — | — | 2 | — |
| Russom, N. (So/CU) | — | 10 | 13 | 8 | 235 | 79* | 47.00 | — | 2 | 2 | — |
| †Sadiq Mohammad (Gs) | 1973 | 22 | 40 | 4 | 1172 | 92 | 32.55 | — | 10 | 27 | — |

| | Cap | M | I | NO | Runs | HS | Avge | 100 | 50 | Ct | St |
|---|---|---|---|---|---|---|---|---|---|---|---|
| Sainsbury, G.E. (Ex) | — | 2 | 2 | 2 | 2 | 2* | — | — | — | — | — |
| Sanderson, J.F.W. (OU) | — | 5 | 5 | 2 | 16 | 9 | 5.33 | — | — | 1 | — |
| Sarfraz Nawaz (No) | 1975 | 17 | 16 | 5 | 324 | 50 | 29.45 | — | 1 | 14 | — |
| Saunders, M. (Wo) | — | 3 | 2 | 0 | 12 | 12 | 6.00 | — | — | — | — |
| Saxelby, K. (Nt) | — | 2 | 2 | 0 | 15 | 15 | 7.50 | — | — | 1 | — |
| Schepens, M. (Le) | — | 1 | 2 | 0 | 8 | 8 | 4.00 | — | — | — | — |
| †Scott, C.J. (La) | — | 17 | 18 | 5 | 75 | 14 | 5.76 | — | — | 41 | 2 |
| Selvey, M.W.W. (M) | 1973 | 21 | 17 | 4 | 322 | 40* | 24.76 | — | — | 3 | — |
| Sharp, G. (No) | 1973 | 23 | 28 | 8 | 562 | 94 | 28.10 | — | 3 | 39 | 3 |
| †Sharp, K. (Y) | — | 9 | 13 | 1 | 293 | 100* | 24.41 | 1 | — | 4 | — |
| Shepherd, J.N. (K) | 1967 | 20 | 23 | 8 | 428 | 100 | 28.53 | 1 | 1 | 8 | — |
| Short, J.F. (Ire) | — | 1 | 2 | 1 | 45 | 44* | 45.00 | — | — | 2 | — |
| Shuttleworth, K. (Le) | 1977 | 3 | 2 | 0 | 6 | 6 | 3.00 | — | — | 1 | — |
| Sidebottom, A. (Y) | 1980 | 20 | 14 | 1 | 284 | 43 | 21.84 | — | — | 7 | — |
| Simmons, J. (La) | 1971 | 21 | 30 | 6 | 682 | 96 | 28.41 | — | 5 | 20 | — |
| †Slack, W.N. (M) | — | 10 | 13 | 0 | 276 | 47 | 21.23 | — | — | 1 | — |
| Slocombe, P.A. (So) | 1978 | 13 | 18 | 2 | 256 | 114 | 16.00 | 1 | — | 2 | — |
| Small, G.C. (Wa) | — | 15 | 15 | 4 | 64 | 16 | 5.81 | — | — | 3 | — |
| Smith, C.L. (H) | — | 20 | 35 | 2 | 1048 | 130 | 31.75 | 3 | 3 | 11 | — |
| †Smith, D.M. (Sy) | 1980 | 22 | 31 | 9 | 771 | 104* | 35.04 | 1 | 4 | 18 | — |
| Smith, K.D. (Wa) | 1978 | 25 | 45 | 2 | 1582 | 140 | 36.79 | 2 | 12 | 14 | — |
| Smith, M.J. (M) | 1967 | 5 | 6 | 0 | 83 | 24 | 13.83 | — | — | 1 | — |
| Smith, N. (Ex) | 1975 | 21 | 25 | 5 | 290 | 63* | 14.50 | — | 1 | 39 | 2 |
| Southern, J.W. (H) | 1978 | 22 | 25 | 7 | 282 | 46* | 15.66 | — | — | 11 | — |
| †Spelman, G.D. (K) | — | 6 | 7 | 1 | 9 | 4 | 1.50 | — | — | 2 | — |
| Spencer, J. (Sx) | 1973 | 8 | 9 | 4 | 66 | 14* | 13.20 | — | — | 3 | — |
| Steele, A. (Sc) | — | 1 | 1 | 0 | 4 | 4 | 4.00 | — | — | — | — |
| Steele, D.S. (D) | 1979 | 20 | 31 | 7 | 698 | 86 | 29.08 | — | 3 | 19 | — |
| Steele, J.F. (Le) | 1971 | 22 | 37 | 4 | 979 | 118 | 29.66 | 2 | 4 | 16 | — |
| Stephenson, G.R. (H) | 1969 | 17 | 23 | 5 | 304 | 65 | 16.88 | — | 1 | 19 | 1 |
| Stevenson, G.B. (Y) | 1978 | 22 | 29 | 9 | 668 | 111 | 33.40 | 1 | 3 | 11 | — |
| Stevenson, K. (H) | 1979 | 23 | 26 | 8 | 156 | 25 | 8.66 | — | — | 9 | — |
| Stovold, A.W. (Gs) | 1976 | 22 | 39 | 2 | 958 | 89 | 25.89 | — | 6 | 10 | — |
| †Stovold, M.W. (Gs) | — | 5 | 8 | 2 | 137 | 75* | 22.83 | — | 1 | — | — |
| Surridge, D. (Gs) | — | 5 | 1 | — | — | — | — | — | — | — | — |
| Sutcliffe, S.P. (OU) | — | 10 | 13 | 0 | 57 | 16 | 4.38 | — | — | 1 | — |
| Swan, R.G. (Sc) | — | 1 | 2 | 0 | 5 | 5 | 2.50 | — | — | 1 | — |
| Tavare, C.J. (E/K/MCC) | 1978 | 22 | 37 | 5 | 1339 | 144* | 41.84 | 5 | 5 | 23 | — |
| Taylor, D.J.S. (So) | 1971 | 20 | 26 | 9 | 743 | 59 | 43.70 | — | 5 | 33 | 4 |
| Taylor, L.B. (Le) | — | 19 | 14 | 8 | 28 | 8 | 4.66 | — | — | 7 | — |
| Taylor, M.N.S. (H) | 1973 | 10 | 15 | 2 | 279 | 58 | 21.46 | — | 1 | 3 | — |
| Taylor, N.R. (K) | — | 10 | 17 | 4 | 396 | 63 | 30.46 | — | 1 | 5 | — |
| Taylor, R.W. (D) | 1962 | 21 | 23 | 6 | 241 | 75 | 14.17 | — | 1 | 35 | 7 |
| Terry, V.P. (H) | — | 3 | 6 | 0 | 87 | 31 | 14.50 | — | — | — | — |
| †Thomas, D.J. (Sy) | — | 2 | 1 | 0 | 43 | 43 | 43.00 | — | — | 3 | — |
| Thomson, J.R. (Aus) | — | 3 | 4 | 0 | 42 | 33 | 10.50 | — | — | 3 | — |
| †Tindall, R.M. (No) | — | 8 | 14 | 3 | 204 | 60* | 18.54 | — | 1 | 3 | — |
| Titmus, F.J. (M) | 1953 | 5 | 6 | 3 | 23 | 10* | 7.66 | — | — | 2 | — |
| Todd, P.A. (Nt) | 1977 | 19 | 35 | 3 | 874 | 71 | 27.31 | — | 8 | 8 | — |
| Tolchard, R.W. (Le) | 1966 | 23 | 34 | 8 | 898 | 109 | 34.53 | 1 | 6 | 43 | 6 |
| Tomlins, K.P. (M) | — | 6 | 8 | 1 | 169 | 55 | 24.14 | — | 1 | 2 | — |
| Tremlett, T.M. (H) | — | 17 | 30 | 4 | 717 | 84 | 27.57 | — | 7 | 4 | — |
| Trim, G.E. (La) | — | 5 | 8 | 0 | 105 | 31 | 13.12 | — | — | 1 | — |
| Tunnicliffe, C.J. (D) | 1977 | 20 | 24 | 7 | 264 | 56* | 15.52 | — | 1 | 14 | — |
| Tunnicliffe, H.T. (Nt) | — | 10 | 17 | 3 | 296 | 100* | 21.14 | 1 | 1 | 7 | — |

175

| | Cap | M | I | NO | Runs | HS | Avge | 100 | 50 | Ct | St |
|---|---|---|---|---|---|---|---|---|---|---|---|
| †Turner, D.R. (H) | 1970 | 20 | 35 | 3 | 925 | 115* | 28.90 | 1 | 4 | 7 | — |
| Turner, G.M. (Wo) | 1968 | 21 | 35 | 4 | 1817 | 228* | 58.61 | 7 | 7 | 14 | — |
| Turner, S. (Ex) | 1970 | 18 | 28 | 7 | 662 | 83* | 31.52 | — | 4 | 7 | — |
| Underwood, D.L. (E/K) | 1964 | 21 | 16 | 6 | 47 | 11* | 4.70 | — | — | 4 | — |
| Van der Bijl, V.A.P. (M) | 1980 | 20 | 16 | 3 | 331 | 76 | 25.46 | — | 1 | 5 | — |
| Waller, C.E. (Sx) | 1976 | 20 | 17 | 11 | 79 | 15* | 13.16 | — | — | 7 | — |
| †Walters, J. (D) | — | 17 | 26 | 4 | 460 | 72 | 20.90 | — | 2 | 16 | — |
| †Warner, C.J. (Sc) | — | 1 | 2 | 0 | 51 | 48 | 25.50 | — | — | 2 | — |
| Waterton, S.N.V. (K) | — | 7 | 9 | 1 | 110 | 40* | 13.75 | — | — | 11 | 1 |
| Watson, W.K. (Nt) | — | 6 | 9 | 3 | 85 | 44 | 14.16 | — | — | — | — |
| †Watts, P.J. (No) | 1962 | 14 | 15 | 3 | 220 | 37* | 18.33 | — | — | 11 | — |
| Wells, C.M. (Sx) | — | 20 | 28 | 5 | 1024 | 135 | 44.52 | 1 | 6 | 6 | — |
| Wenlock, D.A. (Le) | — | 4 | 5 | 3 | 30 | 13* | 15.00 | — | — | 1 | — |
| †Wessels, K.C. (Sx) | 1977 | 15 | 29 | 5 | 1562 | 254 | 65.08 | 2 | 11 | 13 | — |
| Weston, M.J. (Wo) | — | 2 | 2 | 0 | 25 | 22 | 12.50 | — | — | 2 | — |
| †White, R.A. (Nt) | 1966 | 2 | 3 | 0 | 10 | 6 | 3.33 | — | — | 1 | — |
| Whitehouse, J. (Wa) | 1973 | 10 | 19 | 8 | 725 | 197 | 65.90 | 1 | 4 | 3 | — |
| Whiteley, J.P. (Y) | — | 1 | 1 | 0 | 1 | 1 | 1.00 | — | — | 1 | — |
| †Wild, D.J. (No) | — | 1 | 2 | 0 | 22 | 22 | 11.00 | — | — | 1 | — |
| Wilkins, A.H. (Gs) | — | 19 | 24 | 3 | 262 | 44 | 12.47 | — | — | 8 | — |
| Willey, P. (E/No) | 1971 | 19 | 29 | 4 | 572 | 100* | 22.88 | 1 | 3 | 3 | — |
| Williams, R.G. (No) | 1979 | 24 | 41 | 4 | 1262 | 175* | 34.10 | 2 | 6 | 8 | — |
| Willis, R.G.D. (E/Wa) | 1972 | 19 | 21 | 6 | 185 | 33 | 12.33 | — | — | 8 | — |
| Willows, A. (Sx) | — | 3 | 1 | 0 | 1 | 1 | 1.00 | — | — | — | — |
| Wilson, P.H.L. (Sy/MCC) | — | 4 | — | — | — | — | — | — | — | — | — |
| †Wincer, R.C. (D) | — | 2 | — | — | — | — | — | — | — | — | — |
| Windaybank, S.J. (Gs) | — | 1 | 2 | 0 | 63 | 43 | 31.50 | — | — | 1 | — |
| Wood, B. (D) | 1980 | 17 | 30 | 3 | 880 | 113 | 32.59 | 2 | 2 | 24 | — |
| †Wood, G.M. (Aus) | — | 4 | 7 | 1 | 282 | 112 | 47.00 | 1 | 1 | 4 | — |
| Wookey, S.M. (OU) | — | 3 | 3 | 1 | 21 | 10* | 10.50 | — | — | 1 | — |
| Woolmer, R.A. (E/K) | 1970 | 19 | 32 | 2 | 948 | 171 | 31.60 | 2 | 3 | 12 | 1 |
| †Wright, J.G. (D) | 1977 | 20 | 36 | 5 | 1504 | 166* | 48.51 | 3 | 10 | 9 | — |
| Yallop, G.N. (Aus) | — | 5 | 7 | 1 | 108 | 45 | 18.00 | — | — | 5 | — |
| †Yardley, T.J. (No) | 1978 | 24 | 31 | 5 | 685 | 100* | 26.34 | 1 | 4 | 21 | — |
| †Younis, Ahmed, (Wo) | 1979 | 21 | 33 | 6 | 1018 | 121* | 37.70 | 2 | 7 | 17 | — |
| Zaheer Abbas (Gs) | 1975 | 20 | 35 | 1 | 1296 | 173 | 38.11 | 2 | 7 | 4 | — |

# Bowling

| | Type | O | M | R | W | Avge | Best | 5 wI | 10 wM |
|---|---|---|---|---|---|---|---|---|---|
| †Abrahams, J. (La) | OB | 14 | 5 | 48 | 0 | — | — | — | — |
| Acfield, D.L. (Ex) | OB | 553.5 | 171 | 1210 | 47 | 25.74 | 6-37 | 2 | — |
| Agnew, J.P. (Le) | RF | 247.4 | 52 | 880 | 31 | 28.38 | 4-36 | — | — |
| Allbrook, M.E. (Nt) | OB | 40 | 6 | 131 | 1 | 131.00 | 1-32 | — | — |
| Alleyne, H.L. (Wo) | RFM | 521.1 | 100 | 1604 | 64 | 25.06 | 6-50 | 4 | 1 |
| Allott, P.J.W. (La) | RFM | 183 | 47 | 473 | 23 | 20.56 | 4-30 | — | — |
| Anderson, I.J. (Ire) | OB | 10 | 2 | 21 | 0 | — | — | — | — |
| Anderson, I.S. (D) | OB | 23 | 2 | 94 | 0 | — | — | — | — |
| Arnold, G.G. (Sx) | RFM | 505.1 | 180 | 1220 | 47 | 25.95 | 5-29 | 1 | — |
| Asif Iqbal (K) | RM | 7 | 3 | 13 | 0 | — | — | — | — |
| Athey, C.W.J. (E/Y) | RM | 18 | 2 | 82 | 2 | 41.00 | 1-13 | — | — |
| | | | | | | | | | |
| Bacchus, S.F.A.F. (WI) | RM | 2 | 0 | 11 | 0 | — | — | — | — |
| †Bailey, M.J. (H) | OB | 83 | 14 | 280 | 5 | 56.00 | 5-89 | 1 | — |
| Bainbridge, P. (Gs) | RM | 144.4 | 23 | 504 | 15 | 33.60 | 4-48 | — | — |
| Balderstone, J.C. (Le) | SLA | 129.4 | 37 | 368 | 8 | 46.00 | 2-17 | — | — |
| Barclay, J.R.T. (Sx) | OB | 274.5 | 77 | 718 | 30 | 23.93 | 5-58 | 1 | — |
| †Barlow, G.D. (M) | RM | 8 | 0 | 31 | 2 | 15.50 | 1-10 | — | — |
| Barnett, K.J. (D) | LB | 55.3 | 13 | 230 | 7 | 32.85 | 4-76 | — | — |
| Birch, J.D. (Nt) | RM | 4 | 0 | 24 | 1 | 24.00 | 1-24 | — | — |
| †Birkenshaw, J. (Le) | OB | 135.4 | 35 | 374 | 12 | 31.16 | 4-34 | — | — |
| Booden, C.D. (No) | RM | 34 | 1 | 111 | 0 | — | — | — | — |
| Boon, T.J. (Le) | RM | 13 | 5 | 50 | 0 | — | — | — | — |
| Booth, P. (Le) | RFM | 71 | 19 | 217 | 5 | 43.40 | 3-49 | — | — |
| Bore, M.K. (Nt) | LM | 389.2 | 126 | 970 | 32 | 30.31 | 4-24 | — | — |
| Botham, I.T. (E/So/MCC) | RFM | 453.3 | 122 | 1387 | 40 | 34.67 | 4-38 | — | — |
| Boycott, G. (E/Y) | RM | 51 | 15 | 82 | 4 | 20.50 | 2-10 | — | — |
| Boyd-Moss, R.J. (No/CU) | SLA | 74 | 9 | 275 | 3 | 91.66 | 1-10 | — | — |
| Brain, B.M. (Gs) | RFM | 525.5 | 104 | 1609 | 57 | 28.22 | 6-68 | 3 | — |
| Breakwell, D. (So) | SLA | 330 | 101 | 910 | 18 | 50.55 | 4-80 | — | — |
| Brearley, J.M. (M) | RM | 16.4 | 3 | 70 | 0 | — | — | — | — |
| Briers, N.E. (Le) | RM | 13 | 2 | 36 | 0 | — | — | — | — |
| Bright, R.J. (Aus) | SLA | 105.1 | 40 | 292 | 7 | 41.71 | 3-20 | — | — |
| Broad, B.C. (Gs) | RM | 28 | 8 | 109 | 3 | 36.33 | 2-14 | — | — |
| Butcher, A.R. (Sy/MCC) | SLA | 28 | 8 | 69 | 1 | 69.00 | 1-37 | — | — |
| | | | | | | | | | |
| Carrick, P. (Y) | SLA | 608.5 | 189 | 1652 | 51 | 32.39 | 6-138 | 2 | — |
| Carter, R.M. (No) | RM | 77.2 | 12 | 312 | 10 | 31.20 | 4-27 | — | — |
| Chappell, G.S. (Aus) | RM | 16 | 4 | 51 | 2 | 25.50 | 2-32 | — | — |
| Cheatle, R.G.L. (Sy) | SLA | 257.3 | 88 | 659 | 23 | 28.65 | 5-28 | 2 | — |
| Childs, J.H. (Gs) | SLA | 373.4 | 98 | 1034 | 43 | 24.04 | 6-90 | 2 | — |
| Clark, J. (Sc) | RM | 28 | 10 | 42 | 6 | 7.00 | 4-29 | — | — |
| Clarke, S.T. (Sy) | RF | 605.3 | 139 | 1700 | 79 | 21.51 | 6-73 | 4 | — |
| Clifford, C.C. (Wa) | OB | 191 | 40 | 688 | 13 | 52.92 | 4-110 | — | — |
| Clift, P.B. (Le) | RM | 551.3 | 172 | 1282 | 56 | 22.89 | 5-43 | 2 | — |
| Clinton, G.S. (Sy) | RM | 8 | 0 | 77 | 2 | 38.50 | 2-77 | — | — |
| Cook, G. (No) | SLA | 3 | 0 | 11 | 0 | — | — | — | — |
| Cook, N.G.B. (Le) | SLA | 754.1 | 237 | 1856 | 75 | 24.74 | 5-17 | 5 | — |
| Cooper, H.P. (Y) | RM | 152 | 36 | 431 | 11 | 39.18 | 3-77 | — | — |
| Cooper, K.E. (Nt) | RFM | 353.3 | 93 | 985 | 31 | 31.77 | 5-31 | 1 | — |
| Cope, G.A. (Y) | OB | 584.3 | 175 | 1558 | 42 | 37.09 | 4-69 | — | — |
| | | | | | | | | | |
| Cordle, A.E. (Gm) | RFM | 162 | 56 | 370 | 8 | 46.25 | 3-84 | — | — |
| Corlett, S.C. (Ire) | RM | 30.3 | 10 | 64 | 5 | 12.80 | 5-32 | 1 | — |

| | Type | O | M | R | W | Avge | Best | 5 wI | 10 wM |
|---|---|---|---|---|---|---|---|---|---|
| Cowan, R.S. (OU) | RM | 24 | 3 | 84 | 2 | 42.00 | 1-40 | — | — |
| Cowans, N.G. (M) | RFM | 16 | 4 | 42 | 1 | 42.00 | 1-32 | — | — |
| Cowdrey, C.S. (K) | RM | 53.3 | 8 | 188 | 6 | 31.33 | 3-17 | — | — |
| Cowley, N.G. (H) | OB | 458.4 | 125 | 1271 | 40 | 31.77 | 4-47 | — | — |
| Crawford, N.C. (CU) | RM | 168.4 | 32 | 568 | 14 | 40.57 | 3-61 | — | — |
| Croft, C.E.H. (WI) | RF | 230.3 | 54 | 690 | 25 | 27.60 | 6-80 | 1 | — |
| Cumbes, J. (Wo) | RFM | 186.4 | 38 | 558 | 15 | 37.20 | 4-124 | — | — |
| Curtis, I.T. (OU) | SLA/SLC | 228 | 61 | 592 | 13 | 45.53 | 3.56 | — | — |
| | | | | | | | | | |
| Daniel, W.W. (M) | RF | 492.5 | 112 | 1454 | 67 | 21.70 | 5.32 | 1 | — |
| Davison, B.F. (Le) | RM | 13.4 | 2 | 56 | 1 | 56.00 | 1.18 | — | — |
| †Denning, P.W. (So) | OB | 1.5 | 0 | 8 | 0 | — | — | — | — |
| Dennis, S.J. (Y) | LFM | 70 | 10 | 237 | 6 | 39.50 | 2.38 | — | — |
| †Dilley, G.R. (E/K/MCC) | RF | 292.5 | 68 | 861 | 37 | 23.27 | 5.94 | 1 | — |
| †Doggart, S.J.G. (CU) | OB | 153 | 43 | 392 | 9 | 43.55 | 3.54 | — | — |
| D'Oliveira, B.L. (Wo) | RM/OB | 2 | 0 | 12 | 0 | — | — | — | — |
| †Doshi, D.R. (Wa) | SLA | 961.2 | 268 | 2700 | 101 | 26.73 | 6-72 | 4 | 1 |
| †Dredge, C.H. (So) | RM | 571.2 | 136 | 1600 | 63 | 25.39 | 6-57 | 5 | — |
| Dudleston, B. (Le) | SLA | 9 | 4 | 11 | 2 | 5.50 | 2-8 | — | — |
| Durack, J.P. (OU) | LB | 8.4 | 1 | 32 | 0 | — | — | — | — |
| †Dymock, G. (Aus) | LFM | 42 | 6 | 184 | 2 | 92.00 | 1-35 | — | — |
| | | | | | | | | | |
| Ealham, A.G.E. (K) | OB | 5 | 0 | 42 | 0 | — | — | — | — |
| East, R.E. (Ex) | SLA | 530.2 | 135 | 1494 | 61 | 24.49 | 6-56 | 5 | 2 |
| Edmonds, P.H. (M/MCC) | SLA | 473 | 141 | 1125 | 38 | 29.60 | 5-94 | 1 | — |
| Elder, J.W.G. (Ire) | RFM | 33 | 8 | 78 | 1 | 78.00 | 1-36 | — | — |
| Emburey, J.E. (E/M) | OB | 735.2 | 243 | 1518 | 75 | 20.24 | 6-31 | 5 | 1 |
| | | | | | | | | | |
| Featherstone, N.G. (Gm) | OB | 154 | 40 | 487 | 11 | 44.27 | 5-90 | 1 | — |
| Ferreira, A.M. (Wa) | RM | 367.4 | 80 | 1166 | 40 | 29.15 | 4-75 | — | — |
| Fletcher, K.W.R. (Ex) | LB | 33.2 | 2 | 246 | 5 | 49.20 | 1-13 | — | — |
| †Forster, G. (No) | OB | 30 | 5 | 100 | 3 | 33.33 | 2-30 | — | — |
| Foster, N.A. (Ex) | RFM | 25 | 5 | 80 | 3 | 26.66 | 3-51 | — | — |
| | | | | | | | | | |
| Garner, J. (WI) | RFM | 351 | 123 | 683 | 49 | 13.93 | 5-22 | 1 | — |
| Gatting, M.W. (E/M) | RM | 61.4 | 9 | 192 | 6 | 32.00 | 2-3 | — | — |
| Gavaskar, S.M. (So) | RM | 14.2 | 2 | 69 | 0 | — | — | — | — |
| †Gifford, N. (Wo) | SLA | 727.1 | 204 | 1755 | 61 | 28.77 | 6-15 | 2 | 1 |
| Goddard, G.F. (Sc) | OB | 20 | 3 | 44 | 0 | — | — | — | — |
| Gooch, G.A. (E/Ex) | RM | 144 | 38 | 367 | 15 | 24.46 | 3-57 | — | — |
| Gore, H.E.I. (So) | LFM | 253.5 | 66 | 669 | 14 | 47.78 | 5-66 | 1 | — |
| †Gould, I.J. (M) | — | 2 | 1 | 1 | 0 | — | — | — | — |
| †Gower, D.I. (E/Le) | OB | 2 | 1 | 1 | 0 | — | — | — | — |
| †Graf, S.F. (H) | RFM | 313.5 | 72 | 889 | 20 | 44.45 | 2-24 | — | — |
| Graveney, D.A. (Gs) | SLA | 554.4 | 152 | 1598 | 55 | 29.05 | 6-49 | 4 | — |
| Greenidge, C.G. (WI/H) | RM | 6 | 3 | 6 | 0 | — | — | — | — |
| Greig, I.A. (Sx) | RM | 165.3 | 35 | 518 | 11 | 47.09 | 3-74 | — | — |
| Griffiths, B.J. (No) | RFM | 564.3 | 143 | 1612 | 51 | 31.60 | 7-52 | 2 | — |
| | | | | | | | | | |
| Hacker, P.J. (Nt) | LFM | 379.2 | 99 | 1092 | 52 | 21.00 | 6-35 | 2 | — |
| Hadlee, R.J. (Nt) | RFM | 222.1 | 82 | 410 | 29 | 14.13 | 5-32 | 1 | — |
| Halliday, M. (Ire) | OB | 39 | 19 | 66 | 4 | 16.50 | 4-66 | — | — |
| Harris, M.J. (Nt) | LBG | 11 | 4 | 36 | 0 | — | — | — | — |
| Hartley, S.N. (Y) | RM | 34.4 | 5 | 150 | 5 | 30.00 | 3-40 | — | — |
| Haynes, D.L. (WI) | RM | 1 | 0 | 2 | 0 | — | — | — | — |

178

| | Type | O | M | R | W | Avge | Best | 5 wI | 10 wM |
|---|---|---|---|---|---|---|---|---|---|
| Hemmings, E.E. (Nt) | OB | 622.5 | 171 | 1700 | 77 | 22.07 | 7-62 | 4 | 1 |
| Hemsley, E.J.O. (Wo) | RM | 12.2 | 1 | 35 | 1 | 35.00 | 1-18 | — | — |
| Hemsley, P.D. (CU) | RM | 11 | 1 | 53 | 1 | 53.00 | 1-4 | — | — |
| Henderson, S.P. (Wo) | RM | 2.4 | 0 | 16 | 0 | | | — | — |
| Hendrick, M. (E/D) | RFM | 444.5 | 128 | 980 | 55 | 17.81 | 7-19 | 4 | — |
| Herbert, R. (Ex) | OB | 36.4 | 3 | 148 | 3 | 49.33 | 3-64 | — | — |
| Higgs, K. (Le) | RM | 96.5 | 30 | 222 | 6 | 37.00 | 3-80 | — | — |
| Hignell, A.J. (Gs) | LB | 2 | 1 | 3 | 1 | 3.00 | 1-3 | — | — |
| Hills, R.W. (K) | RM | 197 | 54 | 524 | 16 | 32.75 | 3-27 | — | — |
| Hobbs, R.N.S. (Gm) | LBG | 113.3 | 27 | 414 | 8 | 51.75 | 2-58 | — | — |
| Hogg, W. (La) | RFM | 340.1 | 69 | 1114 | 51 | 21.84 | 6-45 | 2 | 1 |
| Holder, V.A. (Wo) | RFM | 161.2 | 26 | 439 | 15 | 29.26 | 4-77 | — | — |
| Holding, M.A. (WI) | RF | 392.1 | 96 | 1096 | 44 | 24.90 | 6-67 | 2 | — |
| Holliday, D.C. (CU) | LB | 37.5 | 9 | 123 | 1 | 123.00 | 1-40 | — | — |
| Holmes, G.C. (Gm) | RM | 149 | 29 | 522 | 12 | 43.50 | 5-86 | 1 | — |
| Hopkins, D.C. (Wa) | RM | 208.3 | 50 | 615 | 16 | 38.43 | 4-20 | — | — |
| Howarth, G.P. (Sy) | OB | 20 | 2 | 102 | 1 | 102.00 | 1-93 | — | — |
| Howat, M.G. (CU) | RFM | 185.2 | 34 | 679 | 8 | 84.87 | 2-61 | — | — |
| Hughes, D.P. (La) | SLA | 336.1 | 96 | 861 | 26 | 33.11 | 5-40 | 1 | — |
| Hughes, S.P. (M) | RFM | 110.4 | 25 | 352 | 18 | 19.55 | 4-36 | — | — |
| Humpage, G.W. (Wa) | RM | 12 | 4 | 34 | 3 | 11.33 | 2-13 | — | — |
| Imran Khan (Sx) | RF | 402.5 | 109 | 967 | 54 | 17.90 | 6-80 | 2 | — |
| Inchmore, J.D. (Wo) | RFM | 419.1 | 67 | 1419 | 40 | 35.47 | 6-107 | 1 | — |
| Intikhab Alam (Sy) | LBG | 277.2 | 83 | 792 | 36 | 22.00 | 5-83 | 1 | — |
| Jackman, R.D. (Sy) | RFM | 745.2 | 220 | 1864 | 121 | 15.40 | 8-58 | 8 | 1 |
| James, K.D. (M) | LFM | 15 | 6 | 29 | 4 | 7.25 | 3-14 | — | — |
| Jarvis, K.B.S. (K) | RFM | 384.3 | 86 | 1209 | 53 | 22.81 | 6-100 | 2 | — |
| Javed Miandad (Gm) | LBG | 34 | 8 | 132 | 2 | 66.00 | 2-25 | — | — |
| Jennings, K.F. (So) | RM | 225.2 | 53 | 615 | 14 | 43.92 | 4-87 | — | — |
| Jesty, T.E. (H) | RM | 205.2 | 56 | 584 | 14 | 41.71 | 3-11 | — | — |
| Johnson, G.W. (K) | OB | 351.1 | 95 | 959 | 42 | 22.83 | 5-41 | 4 | 1 |
| Jones, A.A. (Gm) | RFM | 445 | 76 | 1604 | 41 | 39.12 | 5-51 | 1 | — |
| Kallicharran, A.I. (WI/Wa) | OB | 26 | 5 | 106 | 2 | 53.00 | 1-1 | — | — |
| Kemp, N.J. (K) | RM | 80.5 | 5 | 348 | 7 | 49.71 | 6-119 | 1 | — |
| Kennedy, A. (La) | RM | 63 | 17 | 209 | 5 | 41.80 | 3-58 | — | — |
| King, C.L. (WI) | RM | 98 | 24 | 301 | 7 | 43.00 | 4-46 | — | — |
| Kirsten, P.N. (D) | OB | 28.5 | 8 | 90 | 1 | 90.00 | 1-44 | — | — |
| Knight, J.M. (OU) | RM | 21 | 3 | 108 | 1 | 108.00 | 1-77 | — | — |
| Knight, R.D.V. (Sy) | RM | 307 | 74 | 838 | 34 | 24.64 | 4-9 | — | — |
| Knott, A.P.E. (E/K) | OB | 1 | 0 | 5 | 1 | 5.00 | 1-5 | — | — |
| Lamb, A.J. (No) | RM | 5 | 0 | 27 | 1 | 27.00 | 1-26 | — | — |
| Lamb, T.M. (No) | RM | 627 | 162 | 1725 | 66 | 26.13 | 7-56 | 2 | — |
| Larkins, W. (E/No) | RM | 42 | 3 | 181 | 2 | 90.50 | 1-27 | — | — |
| Lee, P.G. (La) | RFM | 193.1 | 56 | 512 | 18 | 28.44 | 8-34 | 1 | — |
| Le Roux, G.S. (Sx) | RFM | 281.3 | 34 | 780 | 33 | 23.63 | 6-84 | 2 | — |
| Lever, J.K. (E/Ex) | LFM | 591 | 123 | 1703 | 60 | 28.38 | 6-121 | 3 | — |
| Lillee, D.K. (Aus) | RF | 116.2 | 25 | 391 | 20 | 19.55 | 6-133 | 1 | — |
| Lloyd, B.J. (Gm) | OB | 208.1 | 57 | 679 | 11 | 61.72 | 4-95 | — | — |
| Lloyd, C.H. (WI/La) | RM | 1 | 0 | 1 | 0 | | — | — | — |
| Lloyd, D. (La) | SLA | 167 | 35 | 515 | 16 | 32.18 | 4-39 | — | — |
| Lloyd, T.A. (Wa) | RM | 15 | 3 | 58 | 1 | 58.00 | 1-23 | — | — |

| | Type | O | M | R | W | Avge | Best | 5 wI | 10 wM |
|---|---|---|---|---|---|---|---|---|---|
| Lloyds, J.W. (So) | OB | 264 | 55 | 899 | 28 | 32.10 | 6-61 | 2 | 1 |
| Love, J.D. (Y) | RM | 3 | 0 | 22 | 0 | — | — | — | — |
| Lynch, M.A. (Sy) | RM/OB | 7 | 2 | 19 | 0 | — | — | — | — |
| | | | | | | | | | |
| Mack, A.J. (Gm) | LM | 98 | 16 | 362 | 7 | 51.71 | 3-32 | — | — |
| Mackintosh, K.S. (Nt) | RM | 78 | 15 | 241 | 7 | 34.42 | 3-36 | — | — |
| Mallender, N.A. (No) | RFM | 114.4 | 21 | 393 | 7 | 56.14 | 3-29 | — | — |
| Mallett, A.A. (Aus) | OB | 77.2 | 16 | 282 | 5 | 56.40 | 2-69 | — | — |
| Mallett, N.V.H. (OU) | RM | 94 | 11 | 386 | 8 | 48.25 | 4-44 | — | — |
| Malone, M.F. (La) | RFM | 466 | 131 | 1191 | 45 | 26.46 | 5-57 | 2 | — |
| Malone, S.J. (H) | RM | 140.1 | 27 | 457 | 13 | 35.15 | 3-56 | — | — |
| Marks, V.J. (So) | OB | 766.1 | 196 | 2157 | 46 | 46.89 | 5-77 | 2 | — |
| Marshall, M.D. (WI/H) | RFM | 477.3 | 128 | 1170 | 66 | 17.72 | 7-56 | 3 | — |
| Maru, R.J. (M) | SLA | 140.4 | 36 | 412 | 12 | 34.33 | 3-29 | — | — |
| Mellor, A.J. (D) | SLA | 6 | 1 | 37 | 0 | — | — | — | — |
| Merry, W.G. (M) | RM | 96 | 21 | 300 | 15 | 20.00 | 4-24 | — | — |
| Miller, G. (D/MCC) | OB | 576.2 | 182 | 1446 | 56 | 25.82 | 5-52 | 2 | — |
| Moir, D.G. (Sc) | SLA | 34 | 9 | 78 | 4 | 19.50 | 4-43 | — | — |
| Monteith, J.D. (Ire) | SLA | 42.5 | 15 | 81 | 5 | 16.20 | 5-81 | 1 | — |
| Moseley, E.A. (Gm) | RFM | 430 | 94 | 1340 | 51 | 26.27 | 6-41 | 2 | — |
| Moseley, H.R. (So) | RFM | 470.5 | 115 | 1193 | 40 | 29.82 | 6-58 | 2 | — |
| Murray, D.A. (WI) | — | 1 | 0 | 1 | 0 | — | — | — | — |
| | | | | | | | | | |
| Nash, M.A. (Gm) | LM | 611.4 | 196 | 1723 | 74 | 23.28 | 7-79 | 4 | 2 |
| Neale, P.A. (Wo) | RM | 3 | 1 | 6 | 0 | — | — | — | — |
| Newman, P.G. (D) | RFM | 40.2 | 7 | 143 | 4 | 35.75 | 2-41 | — | — |
| Nicholas, M.C.J. (H) | RM | 16.2 | 0 | 67 | 0 | — | — | — | — |
| | | | | | | | | | |
| Old, C.M. (E/Y) | RFM | 503 | 160 | 1159 | 55 | 21.07 | 6-44 | 2 | — |
| Oldham, S. (D) | RFM | 460.2 | 102 | 1381 | 41 | 33.68 | 4-41 | — | — |
| Oliver, P.R. (Wa) | RM | 117 | 18 | 508 | 9 | 56.44 | 2-68 | — | — |
| Ontong, R.C. (Gm) | RFM | 73 | 12 | 289 | 4 | 72.25 | 1-23 | — | — |
| Orders, J.O.D. (OU) | LM | 18 | 3 | 80 | 1 | 80.00 | 1-44 | — | — |
| Ormrod, J.A. (Wo) | OB | 0.3 | 0 | 0 | 0 | — | — | — | — |
| O'Shaughnessy, S.J. (La) | RM | 27 | 6 | 70 | 1 | 70.00 | 1-16 | — | — |
| | | | | | | | | | |
| Parker, P.W.G. (Sx/MCC) | RM | 1 | 0 | 12 | 0 | — | — | — | — |
| Parry, D.R. (WI) | OB | 303.1 | 93 | 800 | 40 | 20.00 | 5-83 | 1 | — |
| Parsons, G.J. (Le) | RM | 206 | 40 | 722 | 24 | 30.08 | 4-38 | — | — |
| Partridge, M.D. (Gs) | RM | 161.5 | 36 | 572 | 11 | 52.00 | 3-18 | — | — |
| Pascoe, L.S. (Aus) | RF | 114.1 | 14 | 445 | 17 | 26.17 | 5-59 | 2 | — |
| Patel, D.N. (Wo) | OB | 159.4 | 33 | 519 | 10 | 51.90 | 6-47 | 1 | — |
| Pauline, D.B. (Sy) | RM | 3 | 0 | 5 | 0 | — | — | — | — |
| Perry, N.J. (Gm) | SLA | 88.5 | 33 | 268 | 6 | 44.66 | 2-13 | — | — |
| Perryman, S.P. (Wa) | RM | 279 | 64 | 836 | 21 | 39.80 | 4-20 | — | — |
| Phillip, N. (Ex) | RFM | 412.2 | 59 | 1412 | 40 | 35.30 | 6-47 | 1 | — |
| Phillipson, C.P. (Sx) | RM | 42 | 5 | 142 | 1 | 142.00 | 1-36 | — | — |
| Pigott, A.C.S. (Sx) | RFM | 62.1 | 4 | 250 | 7 | 35.71 | 4-65 | — | — |
| Pocock, H.J. (H) | LM | 1 | 0 | 8 | 0 | — | — | — | — |
| Pocock, P.I. (Sy) | OB | 565.4 | 155 | 1430 | 51 | 28.03 | 6-40 | 3 | — |
| Pont, K.R. (Ex) | RM | 124.4 | 27 | 306 | 11 | 27.81 | 5-33 | 1 | — |
| Popplewell, N.F.M. (So) | RM | 186.5 | 46 | 587 | 17 | 34.52 | 3-54 | — | — |
| Pridgeon, A.P. (Wo) | RM | 537 | 114 | 1614 | 51 | 31.64 | 5-50 | 1 | — |
| Pringle, D.R. (Ex/CU) | RM | 352.2 | 82 | 976 | 34 | 28.70 | 6-90 | 1 | 1 |
| Procter, M.J. (Gs) | RF/OB | 372.1 | 102 | 931 | 51 | 18.25 | 7-16 | 3 | 1 |

| | Type | O | M | R | W | Avge | Best | 5 wI | 10 wM |
|---|------|---|---|---|---|------|------|------|-------|
| Radford, N.V. (La) | RF | 48.5 | 11 | 176 | 2 | 88.00 | 1-6 | — | — |
| Radley, C.T. (M) | LB | 8 | 2 | 23 | 3 | 7.66 | 1-0 | — | — |
| Ramage, A. (Y) | RM | 66 | 10 | 225 | 4 | 56.25 | 1-16 | — | — |
| Randall, D.W. (Nt) | RM | 5 | 0 | 23 | 0 | — | — | — | — |
| Ratcliffe, R.M. (La) | RM | 88.1 | 30 | 238 | 2 | 119.00 | 2-48 | — | — |
| Reidy, B.W. (La) | LM | 188.2 | 46 | 543 | 19 | 28.57 | 4-24 | — | — |
| Reith, M.S. (Ire) | RM | 3 | 1 | 8 | 0 | — | — | — | — |
| Rice, C.E.B. (Nt) | RFM | 329.4 | 91 | 859 | 39 | 22.02 | 5-25 | 2 | — |
| Rice, J.M. (H) | RM | 94 | 20 | 269 | 3 | 89.66 | 1-17 | — | — |
| Richards, I.V.A. (WI/So) | OB | 98 | 23 | 287 | 4 | 71.75 | 3-12 | — | — |
| Roberts, A.M.E. (WI) | RF | 234.2 | 57 | 657 | 27 | 24.33 | 5-72 | 1 | — |
| Robertson, F. (Sc) | RM | 17 | 3 | 44 | 1 | 44.00 | 1-32 | — | — |
| Robinson, R.T. (Nt) | RM | 6 | 0 | 47 | 1 | 47.00 | 1-47 | — | — |
| Roebuck, P.M. (So/MCC) | OB | 24.2 | 2 | 113 | 2 | 56.50 | 2-43 | — | — |
| Roope, G.R.J. (Sy) | RM | 17 | 3 | 63 | 1 | 63.00 | 1-32 | — | — |
| Rose, B.C. (E/So) | LM | 5 | 0 | 25 | 0 | — | — | — | — |
| Ross, C.J. (OU) | RM | 162.4 | 27 | 589 | 12 | 49.08 | 4-76 | — | — |
| Rouse, S.J. (Wa) | LFM | 243.3 | 41 | 890 | 16 | 55.62 | 3-26 | — | — |
| Rowe, C.J.C. (K) | OB | 48 | 12 | 132 | 4 | 33.00 | 2-31 | — | — |
| Russom, N. (So/CU) | RM | 272.3 | 59 | 864 | 18 | 48.00 | 4-84 | — | — |
| | | | | | | | | | |
| Sadiq Mohammad (Gs) | LBG | 54.5 | 5 | 252 | 1 | 252.00 | 1-56 | — | — |
| Sainsbury, G.E. (Ex) | LM | 57 | 10 | 189 | 7 | 27.00 | 4-85 | — | — |
| Sanderson, J.F.W. (OU) | RM | 84 | 25 | 216 | 8 | 27.00 | 6-67 | 1 | — |
| Sarfraz Nawaz (No) | RFM | 408.1 | 114 | 1104 | 36 | 30.66 | 6-49 | 3 | — |
| Saunders, M. (Wo) | RFM | 51 | 9 | 212 | 6 | 35.33 | 3-47 | — | — |
| Saxelby, K. (Nt) | RM | 21 | 2 | 79 | 1 | 79.00 | 1-29 | — | — |
| Selvey, M.W.W. (M) | RFM | 487.3 | 155 | 1188 | 37 | 32.10 | 5-42 | 2 | — |
| Sharp, G. (No) | SLA | 13 | 2 | 47 | 1 | 47.00 | 1-47 | — | — |
| Sharp, K. (Y) | OB | 6 | 1 | 19 | 0 | — | — | — | — |
| Shepherd, J.N. (K) | RM | 473.1 | 118 | 1220 | 44 | 27.72 | 5-40 | 1 | — |
| Shuttleworth, K. (Le) | RFM | 52 | 9 | 140 | 1 | 140.00 | 1-57 | — | — |
| Sidebottom, A. (Y) | RFM | 346.1 | 92 | 962 | 42 | 22.90 | 7-18 | 3 | 2 |
| Simmons, J. (La) | OB | 398.3 | 110 | 988 | 24 | 41.16 | 4-43 | — | — |
| Slocombe, P.A. (So) | RM | 3 | 0 | 18 | 2 | 9.00 | 1-5 | — | — |
| Small, G.C. (Wa) | RFM | 240 | 52 | 864 | 24 | 36.00 | 3-42 | — | — |
| Smith, C.L. (H) | OB | 26 | 7 | 61 | 0 | — | — | — | — |
| Smith, D.M. (Sy) | RM | 93 | 25 | 245 | 5 | 49.00 | 2-51 | — | — |
| Southern, J.W. (H) | SLA | 556.1 | 143 | 1530 | 51 | 30.00 | 6-109 | 2 | — |
| Spelman, G.D. (K) | RM | 98.1 | 23 | 291 | 7 | 41.57 | 2-27 | — | — |
| Spencer, J. (Sx) | RM | 194 | 53 | 537 | 14 | 38.35 | 5-97 | 1 | — |
| Steele, D.S. (D) | SLA | 430 | 123 | 1221 | 54 | 22.61 | 7-133 | 4 | 1 |
| Steele, J.F. (Le) | SLA | 347.5 | 139 | 704 | 40 | 17.60 | 7-29 | 1 | — |
| Stephenson, G.R. (H) | RFM | 1 | 1 | 0 | 0 | — | — | — | — |
| Stevenson, G.B. (Y) | RM | 602.1 | 164 | 1669 | 72 | 23.18 | 8-57 | 5 | 1 |
| Stevenson, K. (H) | RFM | 493.4 | 105 | 1588 | 53 | 29.96 | 5-66 | 2 | — |
| Stovold, A.W. (Gs) | OB | 4.4 | 0 | 24 | 0 | — | — | — | — |
| Surridge, D. (Gs) | RFM | 21 | 11 | 33 | 4 | 8.25 | 3-25 | — | — |
| Sutcliffe, S.P. (OU) | OB | 252.3 | 61 | 749 | 24 | 31.20 | 6-19 | 1 | — |
| | | | | | | | | | |
| Tavare, C.J. (E/K/MCC) | RM | 14.3 | 2 | 71 | 0 | — | — | — | — |
| Taylor, D.J.S. (So) | RM | 2 | 1 | 1 | 0 | — | — | — | — |
| Taylor, L.B. (Le) | RFM | 385.5 | 83 | 1164 | 30 | 38.80 | 4-59 | — | — |
| Taylor, M.N.S. (H) | RM | 89.5 | 17 | 261 | 9 | 29.00 | 4-46 | — | — |
| Taylor, N.R. (K) | OB | 9 | 2 | 20 | 0 | — | — | — | — |

181

| | Type | O | M | R | W | Avge | Best | 5 wI | 10 wM |
|---|---|---|---|---|---|---|---|---|---|
| Thomas, D.J. (Sy) | LM | 54.1 | 15 | 129 | 9 | 14.33 | 4-44 | — | — |
| Thomson, J.R. (Aus) | RF | 68 | 15 | 265 | 6 | 44.16 | 2-45 | — | — |
| Tindall, R.M. (No) | SLA | 32.4 | 2 | 162 | 2 | 81.00 | 2-60 | — | — |
| Titmus, F.J. (M) | OB | 149.2 | 38 | 313 | 12 | 26.08 | 3-55 | — | — |
| Tomlins, K.P. (M) | RM | 31 | 8 | 103 | 0 | — | — | — | — |
| Tremlett, T.M. (H) | RM | 178.2 | 32 | 579 | 17 | 34.05 | 5-30 | 1 | — |
| Tunnicliffe, C.J. (D) | LFM | 427.5 | 89 | 1244 | 47 | 26.46 | 7-36 | 2 | — |
| Tunnicliffe, H.T. (Nt) | RM | 85 | 27 | 187 | 9 | 20.77 | 3-55 | — | — |
| Turner, D.R. (H) | RM | 7.1 | 1 | 33 | 0 | — | — | — | — |
| Turner, S. (Ex) | RFM | 481.4 | 94 | 1343 | 45 | 29.84 | 6-69 | 2 | — |
| Underwood, D.L. (E/K) | LM | 585.1 | 208 | 1418 | 61 | 23.24 | 7-75 | 4 | 2 |
| Van der Bijl, V.A.P. (M) | RFM | 642.3 | 213 | 1252 | 85 | 14.72 | 6-47 | 5 | 1 |
| Waller, C.E. (Sx) | SLA | 480.4 | 128 | 1292 | 43 | 30.04 | 4-17 | — | — |
| Walters, J. (D) | RM | 35.4 | 1 | 130 | 1 | 130.00 | 1-70 | — | — |
| Watson, W.K. (Nt) | RFM | 124.3 | 23 | 463 | 17 | 27.23 | 5-57 | 1 | — |
| Watts, P.J. (No) | RM | 8 | 0 | 54 | 0 | — | — | — | — |
| Wells, C.M. (Sx) | RM | 226 | 39 | 733 | 9 | 81.44 | 2-53 | — | — |
| Wenlock, D.A. (Le) | RM | 27.5 | 4 | 89 | 2 | 44.50 | 2-23 | — | — |
| Wessels, K.C. (Sx) | OB | 3 | 0 | 7 | 0 | — | — | — | — |
| White, R.A. (Nt) | OB | 48 | 16 | 85 | 11 | 7.72 | 6-24 | 1 | 1 |
| Whitehouse, J. (Wa) | OB | 1.3 | 0 | 12 | 0 | — | — | — | — |
| Whiteley, J.P. (Y) | OB | 16 | 2 | 42 | 0 | — | — | — | — |
| Wilkins, A.H. (Gs) | LM | 393.5 | 86 | 1245 | 52 | 23.94 | 5-50 | 2 | — |
| Willey, P. (E/No) | OB | 447.5 | 123 | 1056 | 28 | 37.71 | 5-85 | 1 | — |
| Williams, R.G. (No) | OB | 535.5 | 100 | 1611 | 48 | 33.56 | 7-73 | 3 | — |
| Willis, R.G.D. (E/Wa) | RF | 457.2 | 118 | 1366 | 49 | 27.87 | 5-65 | 1 | — |
| Willows, A. (Sx) | SLA | 82.2 | 26 | 203 | 8 | 25.37 | 4-33 | — | — |
| Wilson, P.H.L. (Sy/MCC) | RFM | 104 | 25 | 246 | 11 | 22.36 | 3-23 | — | — |
| Wincer, R.C. (D) | RFM | 27 | 5 | 109 | 3 | 36.33 | 1-18 | — | — |
| Wood, B. (D) | RM | 142 | 29 | 364 | 10 | 36.40 | 3-22 | — | — |
| Wookey, S.M. (OU) | RM | 40 | 8 | 108 | 2 | 54.00 | 1-28 | — | — |
| Woolmer, R.A. (E/K) | RM | 54 | 15 | 154 | 5 | 30.80 | 2-12 | — | — |
| Wright, J.G. (D) | RM | 0.4 | 0 | 4 | 1 | 4.00 | 1-4 | — | — |
| Yardley, T.J. (No) | RM | 3 | 0 | 14 | 0 | — | — | — | — |
| Younis Ahmed, (Wo) | LM | 19 | 1 | 95 | 1 | 95.00 | 1-37 | — | — |
| Zaheer Abbas (Gs) | OB | 11 | 3 | 46 | 2 | 23.00 | 1-17 | — | — |

# The Winners.

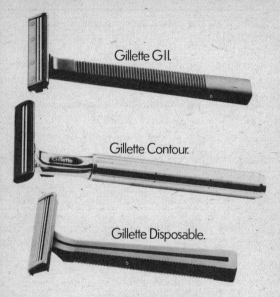

Gillette G II.

Gillette Contour.

Gillette Disposable.

# CAREER FIGURES FOR THE LEADING PLAYERS

The following are the abbreviated figures of the leading batsmen and bowlers based on their career averages, and fielders and wicket-keepers based on the number of their catches and dismissals. The figures are complete to the end of the 1980 season and the full career records will be found in the main tables on pages 185 to 201. qualification for inclusion for batsmen and bowlers are 100 innings and 100 wickets respectively.

Only those players likely to play first-class county cricket in 1981 have been included.

## BATTING AND FIELDING

| BATSMEN | Runs | Avge | 100s | BOWLERS | Wkts | Avge |
|---|---|---|---|---|---|---|
| G. Boycott | 37,624 | 56.74 | 120 | J. Garner | 292 | 17.80 |
| A.J. Lamb | 7,057 | 50.76 | 15 | M.D. Marshall | 219 | 18.69 |
| C.H. Lloyd | 23,440 | 49.14 | 65 | M.J. Procter | 1,327 | 19.06 |
| Zaheer Abbas | 24,570 | 49.04 | 73 | W.W. Daniel | 359 | 19.40 |
| Javed Miandad | 11,797 | 48.74 | 31 | D.L. Underwood | 1,926 | 19.48 |
| G.M. Turner | 30,941 | 48.72 | 89 | M. Hendrick | 630 | 20.55 |
| I.V.A. Richards | 16,082 | 48.00 | 45 | G.S. Le Roux | 202 | 20.58 |
| K.C. Wessels | 6,710 | 47.58 | 12 | G.G. Arnold | 1,084 | 21.72 |
| D.L. Amiss | 31,724 | 43.45 | 75 | C.M. Old | 816 | 21.85 |
| P.N. Kirsten | 8,403 | 43.09 | 22 | N. Gifford | 1,626 | 21.94 |
| A.I. Kallicharran | 18,799 | 42.62 | 43 | R.J. Hadlee | 481 | 22.01 |
| C.G. Greenidge | 18,056 | 42.28 | 40 | C.E.B. Rice | 543 | 22.16 |
| C.E.B. Rice | 12,053 | 39.91 | 18 | R.D. Jackman | 1,248 | 22.41 |
| K.W.R. Fletcher | 29,870 | 38.44 | 49 | S.T. Clarke | 214 | 22.53 |
| K.S. McEwan | 13,225 | 38.44 | 31 | J.E. Emburey | 373 | 22.86 |

| FIELDERS | Ct | WICKET-KEEPERS | Total | Ct | St |
|---|---|---|---|---|---|
| G.R.J. Roope | 542 | R.W. Taylor | 1,388 | 1,238 | 150 |
| K.W.R. Fletcher | 510 | A.P.E. Knott | 1,090 | 982 | 108 |
| D.S. Steele | 448 | R.W. Tolchard | 906 | 800 | 106 |
| C.T. Radley | 401 | E.W. Jones | 811 | 733 | 78 |
| J.H. Hampshire | 388 | D.L. Bairstow | 665 | 576 | 89 |
| J.M. Brearley | 385 | D.J.S. Taylor | 599 | 525 | 74 |
| G.M. Turner | 376 | G. Sharp | 471 | 400 | 71 |
| J.A. Ormrod | 365 | N. Smith | 419 | 372 | 47 |
| K. Higgs | 311 | G.W. Humpage | 253 | 231 | 22 |
| D.L. Amiss | 310 | A.J. Brassington | 205 | 167 | 38 |
| J. Birkenshaw | 308 | I.J. Gould | 199 | 170 | 29 |
| D. Lloyd | 303 | C.J. Richards | 185 | 160 | 25 |
| M.J. Procter | 300 | D.J. Humphries | 183 | 158 | 25 |
| Asif Iqbal | 292 | A.W. Stovold | 178 | 153 | 25 |
| J.F. Steele | 291 | B.N. French | 163 | 141 | 22 |
| | | P.R. Downton | 155 | 140 | 15 |

# CAREER RECORDS

## Compiled by Michael Fordham

The following career records are for all players appearing in first-class cricket in the 1980 season.

A few cricketers who did not re-appear for their counties in 1980, but who may do so in 1981, as well as others who appeared only in John Player League and other one-day matches are also included.

Aggregates of 1,000 runs overseas are preceded by a + sign, e.g. D.L. Amiss 16 + 1.

### BATTING AND FIELDING

| | M | I | NO | Runs | HS | Avge | 100s | 1000 runs in season | Ct | St |
|---|---|---|---|---|---|---|---|---|---|---|
| Abrahams, J. | 107 | 162 | 18 | 3365 | 126 | 23.36 | 2 | — | 65 | — |
| Acfield, D.L. | 287 | 297 | 144 | 1367 | 42 | 8.93 | — | — | 96 | — |
| Agnew, J.P. | 22 | 16 | 0 | 109 | 31 | 6.81 | — | — | 5 | — |
| Allbrook, M.E. | 47 | 56 | 19 | 320 | 39 | 8.64 | — | — | 15 | — |
| Alleyne, H.L. | 18 | 20 | 3 | 233 | 72 | 13.70 | — | — | 4 | — |
| Allott, P.J.W. | 27 | 19 | 7 | 92 | 30* | 7.66 | — | — | 5 | — |
| Amiss, D.L. | 482 | 825 | 95 | 31724 | 262* | 43.45 | 75 | 16 + 1 | 310 | — |
| Anderson, I.J. | 17 | 30 | 8 | 836 | 147 | 38.00 | 3 | — | 9 | — |
| Anderson, I.S. | 24 | 34 | 8 | 425 | 75 | 16.34 | — | — | 12 | — |
| Arnold, G.G. | 344 | 357 | 79 | 3761 | 73 | 13.52 | — | — | 115 | — |
| Asif Iqbal | 411 | 655 | 71 | 21565 | 196 | 36.92 | 42 | 6 + 2 | 292 | — |
| Athey, C.W.J. | 95 | 150 | 11 | 3655 | 131* | 26.29 | 6 | 1 | 91 | 2 |
| | | | | | | | | | | |
| Bacchus, S.F.A.F. | 59 | 92 | 6 | 3022 | 250 | 35.13 | 5 | — | 41 | — |
| Bailey, M.J. | 9 | 15 | 6 | 158 | 24 | 17.55 | — | — | 2 | — |
| Bainbridge, P. | 36 | 59 | 6 | 1015 | 81* | 19.15 | — | — | 20 | — |
| Bairstow, D.L. | 261 | 372 | 64 | 6646 | 145 | 21.57 | 3 | — | 576 | 89 |
| Balderstone, J.C. | 257 | 393 | 43 | 11665 | 178* | 33.32 | 16 | 6 | 133 | — |
| Barclay, J.R.T. | 158 | 271 | 21 | 6245 | 119 | 24.98 | 7 | 4 | 112 | — |
| Barlow, G.D. | 155 | 241 | 37 | 6890 | 160* | 33.77 | 11 | 4 | 82 | — |
| Barnett, K.J. | 41 | 59 | 6 | 1163 | 96 | 21.94 | — | — | 23 | — |
| Bell, D.L. | 6 | 11 | 2 | 144 | 39 | 16.00 | — | — | 3 | — |
| Benson, M.R. | 9 | 13 | 2 | 248 | 58* | 22.54 | — | — | 2 | — |
| Birch, J.D. | 80 | 119 | 19 | 2097 | 105* | 20.97 | 1 | — | 60 | — |
| Birkenshaw, J. | 480 | 655 | 123 | 12615 | 131* | 23.71 | 4 | — | 308 | — |
| Booden, C.D. | 2 | 1 | 1 | 6 | 6* | — | — | — | 1 | — |
| Boon, T.J. | 8 | 12 | 1 | 253 | 53* | 23.00 | — | — | 2 | — |
| Booth, P. | 83 | 71 | 20 | 625 | 58* | 12.25 | — | — | 26 | — |
| Booth Jones, T.D. | 10 | 17 | 1 | 493 | 89* | 30.81 | — | — | 2 | — |
| Border, A.R. | 56 | 101 | 13 | 4289 | 200 | 48.73 | 11 | 0 + 2 | 43 | — |
| Bore, M.K. | 112 | 111 | 36 | 589 | 37* | 7.85 | — | — | 34 | — |
| Borrington, A.J. | 122 | 203 | 24 | 4230 | 137 | 23.63 | 3 | — | 57 | — |
| Botham, I.T. | 151 | 230 | 21 | 6292 | 228 | 30.10 | 12 | 2 | 146 | — |
| Boycott, G. | 474 | 782 | 119 | 37624 | 261* | 56.74 | 120 | 18 + 3 | 198 | — |
| Boyd-Moss, R.J. | 16 | 23 | 1 | 426 | 71 | 19.36 | — | — | 7 | — |
| Brain, B.M. | 250 | 265 | 66 | 1669 | 57 | 8.26 | — | — | 47 | — |

| | M | I | NO | Runs | HS | Avge | 100s | 1000 runs in season | Ct | St |
|---|---|---|---|---|---|---|---|---|---|---|
| Brassington, A.J. | 98 | 127 | 37 | 705 | 28 | 7.83 | — | — | 167 | 38 |
| Breakwell, D. | 217 | 290 | 61 | 4436 | 100* | 19.37 | 1 | — | 79 | — |
| Brearley, J.M. | 413 | 698 | 92 | 22515 | 312* | 37.15 | 36 | 9 | 385 | 12 |
| Briers, N.E. | 70 | 112 | 9 | 2318 | 119 | 22.50 | 4 | — | 24 | — |
| Bright, R.J. | 73 | 102 | 23 | 1582 | 67 | 20.02 | — | — | 54 | — |
| Broad, B.C | 29 | 51 | 3 | 1473 | 129 | 30.68 | 4 | — | 10 | — |
| Brooks, K.G. | 1 | 2 | 0 | 11 | 8 | 5.50 | — | — | 2 | — |
| Bury, T.E.O. | 4 | 4 | 1 | 32 | 22 | 10.66 | — | — | 2 | — |
| Bushe, E.A. | 2 | 2 | 1 | 14 | 14 | 14.00 | — | — | 7 | 1 |
| Butcher, A.R. | 155 | 251 | 22 | 6950 | 216* | 30.34 | 11 | 2 | 60 | — |
| Butcher, I.P. | 1 | — | — | — | — | — | — | — | — | — |
| Butcher, R.O. | 71 | 113 | 5 | 3004 | 179 | 27.81 | 4 | — | 75 | — |
| | | | | | | | | | | |
| Carrick, P. | 171 | 214 | 44 | 3964 | 131* | 23.31 | 3 | — | 96 | — |
| Carter, R.M. | 25 | 31 | 6 | 315 | 32 | 12.60 | — | — | 8 | — |
| Chappell, G.S. | 265 | 455 | 62 | 20435 | 247* | 51.99 | 60 | 4 + 7 | 300 | — |
| Cheatle, R.G.L. | 54 | 41 | 15 | 305 | 49 | 11.73 | — | — | 51 | — |
| Childs, J.H. | 95 | 88 | 53 | 189 | 12 | 5.40 | — | — | 36 | — |
| Clark, J. | 11 | 14 | 3 | 79 | 29 | 7.18 | — | — | 12 | — |
| Clarke, S.T. | 56 | 59 | 12 | 593 | 55 | 12.61 | — | — | 26 | — |
| Claughton, J.A. | 55 | 96 | 7 | 1910 | 130 | 21.46 | 4 | — | 21 | — |
| Clifford, C.C. | 47 | 45 | 16 | 210 | 26 | 7.24 | — | — | 16 | — |
| Clift, P.B. | 175 | 254 | 60 | 4416 | 88* | 22.76 | — | — | 89 | — |
| Clinton, G.S. | 82 | 135 | 14 | 3602 | 134 | 29.76 | 3 | 2 | 28 | — |
| Cobb, R.A. | 1 | — | — | — | — | — | — | — | — | — |
| Cockbain, I. | 18 | 28 | 6 | 411 | 69* | 18.68 | — | — | 10 | — |
| Cohen, M.F. | 1 | 1 | 0 | 0 | 0 | 00.00 | — | — | 0 | — |
| Cook, G. | 226 | 396 | 29 | 10358 | 172 | 28.22 | 13 | 5 | 232 | — |
| Cook, N.G.B. | 43 | 40 | 16 | 295 | 75 | 12.29 | — | — | 20 | — |
| Cooper, H.P. | 101 | 113 | 30 | 1191 | 56 | 14.34 | — | — | 61 | — |
| Cooper, K.E. | 71 | 65 | 16 | 363 | 35 | 7.40 | — | — | 22 | — |
| Cope, G.A. | 246 | 261 | 93 | 2383 | 78 | 14.18 | — | — | 71 | — |
| Cordle, A.E. | 312 | 433 | 76 | 5239 | 81 | 14.67 | — | — | 141 | — |
| Corlett, S.C. | 26 | 37 | 6 | 462 | 60 | 14.90 | — | — | 23 | — |
| Coverdale, S.P. | 45 | 75 | 6 | 1245 | 85 | 18.04 | — | — | 41 | 10 |
| Cowan, R.S. | 7 | 11 | 1 | 313 | 63 | 31.30 | — | — | 1 | — |
| Cowans, N.G. | 1 | 1 | 0 | 1 | 1 | 1.00 | — | — | — | — |
| Cowdrey, C.S. | 77 | 101 | 16 | 2209 | 101* | 25.98 | 1 | — | 55 | — |
| Cowley, N.G. | 113 | 180 | 27 | 3339 | 109* | 21.82 | 1 | — | 52 | — |
| Crawford, N.C. | 22 | 22 | 2 | 262 | 46* | 13.10 | — | — | 5 | — |
| Croft, C.E.H. | 83 | 88 | 34 | 533 | 46* | 9.87 | — | — | 16 | — |
| Cumbes, J. | 137 | 110 | 56 | 416 | 43 | 7.70 | — | — | 28 | — |
| Curtis, I.J. | 9 | 12 | 7 | 27 | 9* | 5.40 | — | — | 1 | — |
| Curtis, T.S. | 4 | 7 | 1 | 127 | 59* | 21.16 | — | — | 1 | — |
| Curzon, C.C. | 17 | 21 | 4 | 254 | 45 | 14.94 | — | — | 31 | 3 |
| | | | | | | | | | | |
| Daniel, W.W. | 106 | 88 | 38 | 535 | 53* | 10.70 | — | — | 20 | — |
| Davies, T. | 1 | — | — | — | — | — | — | — | 3 | — |
| Davison, B.F. | 331 | 542 | 47 | 18972 | 189 | 38.32 | 33 | 10 | 250 | — |
| Denness, M.H. | 501 | 838 | 65 | 25886 | 195 | 33.48 | 33 | 14 + 1 | 411 | — |
| Denning, P.W. | 205 | 345 | 31 | 8835 | 184 | 28.13 | 7 | 5 | 103 | — |
| Dennis, S.J. | 4 | 2 | 1 | 1 | 1* | 1.00 | — | — | 3 | — |
| Dexter, R.E. | 14 | 22 | 3 | 255 | 48 | 13.42 | — | — | 10 | — |

186

| | M | I | NO | Runs | HS | Avge | 100s | 1000 runs in season | Ct | St |
|---|---|---|---|---|---|---|---|---|---|---|
| Dilley, G.R. | 44 | 46 | 20 | 426 | 81 | 16.38 | — | — | 26 | — |
| Doggart, S.J.G. | 9 | 11 | 2 | 174 | 43 | 19.33 | — | — | 6 | — |
| D'Oliveira, B.L. | 362 | 566 | 88 | 18919 | 227 | 39.57 | 43 | 9 | 211 | — |
| Donald, W.A. | 2 | 2 | 0 | 0 | 0 | 00.00 | — | — | — | — |
| Doshi, D.R. | 163 | 169 | 40 | 1015 | 44 | 7.86 | — | — | 42 | — |
| Downton, P.R. | 61 | 63 | 12 | 926 | 90* | 18.15 | — | — | 140 | 15 |
| Dredge, C.H. | 78 | 90 | 27 | 871 | 56* | 13.82 | — | — | 30 | — |
| Dudleston, B. | 286 | 485 | 45 | 14217 | 202 | 32.31 | 31 | 8 | 226 | 7 |
| Durack, J.P. | 7 | 13 | 0 | 136 | 45 | 10.46 | — | — | 3 | — |
| Dymock, G. | 104 | 133 | 47 | 1172 | 67 | 13.62 | — | — | 34 | — |
| Dyson, J. | 43 | 81 | 7 | 2443 | 197 | 33.01 | 4 | — | 18 | — |
| | | | | | | | | | | |
| Ealham, A.G.E. | 301 | 459 | 67 | 10808 | 153 | 27.57 | 7 | 3 | 173 | — |
| East, R.E. | 343 | 438 | 101 | 6004 | 113 | 17.81 | 1 | — | 211 | — |
| Edmonds, P.H. | 219 | 295 | 50 | 4862 | 141* | 19.84 | 2 | — | 220 | — |
| Elder, J.W.G. | 8 | 8 | 2 | 25 | 7 | 4.16 | — | — | 6 | — |
| Emburey, J.E. | 115 | 134 | 40 | 1694 | 91* | 18.02 | — | — | 118 | — |
| Ezekowitz, R.A.B. | 10 | 17 | 1 | 340 | 57 | 21.25 | — | — | 7 | — |
| | | | | | | | | | | |
| Featherstone, N.G. | 299 | 476 | 49 | 12593 | 147 | 29.49 | 10 | 3 | 242 | — |
| Ferreira, A.M. | 54 | 73 | 14 | 1629 | 90 | 27.61 | — | — | 32 | — |
| Fisher, P.B. | 50 | 77 | 11 | 580 | 42 | 8.78 | — | — | 87 | 11 |
| Fletcher, K.W.R. | 546 | 906 | 129 | 29870 | 228* | 38.44 | 49 | 16 | 510 | — |
| Forster, G. | 1 | — | — | — | — | — | — | — | 1 | — |
| Foster, D.C.G. | 4 | 6 | 1 | 124 | 67 | 24.80 | — | — | — | — |
| Foster, N.A. | 1 | 1 | 1 | 8 | 8* | — | — | — | — | — |
| Fowler, G. | 12 | 16 | 1 | 286 | 106* | 19.06 | 1 | — | 7 | 2 |
| Francis, D.A. | 91 | 157 | 26 | 2865 | 110 | 21.87 | 1 | — | 43 | — |
| French, B.N. | 77 | 94 | 28 | 994 | 70* | 15.06 | — | — | 141 | 22 |
| | | | | | | | | | | |
| Gard, T. | 12 | 11 | 5 | 124 | 51* | 20.66 | — | — | 17 | 5 |
| Garner, J. | 64 | 68 | 16 | 1011 | 104 | 19.44 | 1 | — | 44 | — |
| Garnham, M.A. | 5 | 5 | 2 | 64 | 21 | 21.33 | — | — | 4 | 2 |
| Gatting, M.W. | 112 | 167 | 26 | 4435 | 136 | 31.45 | 4 | 2 | 97 | — |
| Gavaskar, S.M. | 234 | 388 | 40 | 17712 | 282 | 50.89 | 57 | 2 + 7 | 210 | — |
| Gifford, N. | 532 | 632 | 195 | 5863 | 89 | 13.41 | — | — | 268 | — |
| Goddard, G.F. | 22 | 33 | 5 | 371 | 39 | 13.25 | — | — | 8 | — |
| Gooch, G.A. | 161 | 269 | 27 | 8594 | 205 | 35.51 | 16 | 4 | 139 | — |
| Gore, H.E.I. | 32 | 41 | 12 | 382 | 67 | 13.17 | — | — | 14 | — |
| Gould, I.J. | 92 | 122 | 18 | 2142 | 128 | 20.59 | 1 | — | 170 | 29 |
| Gower, D.I. | 120 | 183 | 16 | 5383 | 200* | 32.23 | 8 | 2 | 57 | — |
| Graf, S.F. | 21 | 26 | 7 | 419 | 58* | 22.05 | — | — | 11 | — |
| Graveney, D.A. | 174 | 245 | 56 | 3314 | 119 | 17.53 | 1 | — | 77 | — |
| Graves, P.J. | 292 | 502 | 51 | 12076 | 145* | 26.77 | 14 | 5 | 223 | — |
| Green, A.M. | 1 | 1 | 0 | 0 | 0 | 00.00 | — | — | — | — |
| Greenidge, C.G. | 262 | 455 | 28 | 18056 | 273* | 42.28 | 40 | 9 | 278 | — |
| Greig, I.A. | 44 | 59 | 8 | 1184 | 96 | 23.21 | — | — | 24 | — |
| Griffiths, B.J. | 72 | 62 | 24 | 111 | 11 | 2.92 | — | — | 16 | — |
| | | | | | | | | | | |
| Hacker, P.J. | 56 | 68 | 24 | 409 | 35 | 9.29 | — | — | 11 | — |
| Hadlee, R.J. | 123 | 170 | 32 | 3131 | 103 | 22.68 | 2 | — | 53 | — |
| Halliday, M. | 7 | 5 | 2 | 35 | 13* | 11.66 | — | — | 3 | — |
| Halliday, S.J. | 5 | 7 | 1 | 135 | 37 | 22.50 | — | — | 3 | — |

187

|  | M | I | NO | Runs | HS | Avge | 100s | 1000 runs in season | Ct | St |
|---|---|---|---|---|---|---|---|---|---|---|
| Hampshire, J.H. | 496 | 792 | 95 | 23731 | 183* | 34.04 | 36 | 13 | 388 | — |
| Hardie, B.R. | 162 | 268 | 33 | 7689 | 162 | 32.71 | 9 | 5 | 152 | — |
| Harpur, T. | 1 | 1 | 0 | 4 | 4 | 4.00 | — | — | 1 | — |
| Harris, M.J. | 334 | 568 | 52 | 18919 | 201* | 36.66 | 41 | 11 | 279 | 14 |
| Hartley, S.N. | 18 | 29 | 3 | 509 | 72* | 19.57 | — | — | 8 | — |
| Hassan, S.B. | 259 | 429 | 39 | 11285 | 182* | 28.93 | 13 | 5 | 231 | 1 |
| Hayes, F.C. | 233 | 362 | 53 | 11430 | 187 | 36.99 | 19 | 6 | 158 | — |
| Hayes, K.A. | 1 | 1 | 0 | 27 | 27 | 27.00 | — | — | 1 | — |
| Haynes, D.L. | 42 | 72 | 8 | 2805 | 184 | 43.82 | 5 | — | 20 | — |
| Hays, D.L. | 25 | 47 | 1 | 751 | 72 | 16.32 | — | — | 26 | 2 |
| Head, T.J. | 20 | 22 | 5 | 262 | 41 | 15.41 | — | — | 48 | 6 |
| Heath, J.R.P. | 1 | 1 | 0 | 0 | 0 | 00.00 | — | — | — | — |
| Hemmings, E.E. | 224 | 316 | 69 | 5255 | 86 | 21.27 | — | — | 107 | — |
| Hemsley, E.J.O. | 207 | 335 | 51 | 8807 | 176* | 31.01 | 8 | 1 | 161 | — |
| Hemsley, P.D. | 1 | 1 | 1 | 12 | 12* | — | — | — | — | — |
| Henderson, S.P. | 18 | 27 | 3 | 384 | 64 | 16.00 | — | — | 12 | — |
| Hendrick, M. | 218 | 217 | 85 | 1332 | 46 | 10.09 | — | — | 141 | — |
| Herbert, R. | 6 | 9 | 1 | 62 | 14* | 7.75 | — | — | 5 | — |
| Higgs, K. | 508 | 528 | 206 | 3637 | 98 | 11.29 | — | — | 311 | — |
| Hignell, A.J. | 113 | 191 | 19 | 4772 | 149* | 27.74 | 8 | 2 | 115 | — |
| Hill, A. | 146 | 263 | 19 | 6763 | 160* | 27.71 | 7 | 2 | 58 | — |
| Hills, R.W. | 85 | 95 | 25 | 995 | 45 | 14.21 | — | — | 33 | — |
| Hobbs, R.N.S. | 425 | 531 | 128 | 4839 | 100 | 12.00 | 2 | — | 287 | — |
| Hogg, W. | 45 | 41 | 13 | 120 | 19 | 4.28 | — | — | 9 | — |
| Holder, V.A. | 311 | 354 | 81 | 3559 | 122 | 13.03 | 1 | — | 98 | — |
| Holding, M.A. | 57 | 78 | 15 | 780 | 62 | 12.38 | — | — | 23 | — |
| Holliday, D.C. | 19 | 26 | 6 | 318 | 76* | 15.90 | — | — | 9 | — |
| Holmes, G.C. | 30 | 46 | 11 | 676 | 100* | 19.31 | 1 | — | 10 | — |
| Hopkins, D.C. | 35 | 43 | 12 | 315 | 34* | 10.16 | — | — | 7 | — |
| Hopkins, J.A. | 137 | 242 | 14 | 6368 | 230 | 27.92 | 7 | 4 | 105 | 1 |
| Howarth, G.P. | 213 | 374 | 27 | 11286 | 183 | 32.52 | 21 | 3 | — | — |
| Howat, M.G. | 26 | 22 | 3 | 194 | 32 | 10.21 | — | — | 7 | — |
| Hughes, D.P. | 259 | 312 | 65 | 4668 | 101 | 18.89 | 1 | — | 169 | — |
| Hughes, K.J. | 83 | 143 | 7 | 4693 | 137* | 34.50 | 9 | 0 + 1 | 59 | — |
| Hughes, S.P. | 5 | 4 | 2 | 0 | 0* | 00.00 | — | — | 3 | — |
| Humpage, G.W. | 120 | 188 | 20 | 5551 | 125* | 33.04 | 6 | 3 | 231 | 22 |
| Humphries, D.J. | 89 | 124 | 20 | 2423 | 111* | 23.29 | 2 | — | 158 | 25 |
| Huxford, P.N. | 2 | 1 | 0 | 4 | 4 | 4.00 | — | — | — | — |
| Imran Khan | 214 | 343 | 47 | 9484 | 170 | 32.04 | 16 | 3 | 71 | — |
| Inchmore, J.D. | 116 | 139 | 32 | 1588 | 113 | 14.84 | 1 | — | 42 | — |
| Ingham, P.G. | 6 | 10 | 0 | 229 | 64 | 22.90 | — | — | — | — |
| Intikhab Alam | 471 | 692 | 75 | 13858 | 182 | 22.46 | 9 | — | 226 | — |
| Jackman, R.D. | 350 | 418 | 135 | 4785 | 92* | 16.90 | — | — | 164 | — |
| James, K.D. | 1 | 1 | 0 | 16 | 16 | 16.00 | — | — | — | — |
| Jarvis, K.B.S. | 115 | 79 | 38 | 130 | 12* | 3.17 | — | — | 29 | — |
| Javed Miandad | 178 | 292 | 50 | 11797 | 311 | 48.74 | 31 | 2 + 4 | 174 | 3 |
| Jennings, K.F. | 66 | 72 | 24 | 517 | 49 | 10.77 | — | — | 46 | — |
| Jesty, T.E. | 269 | 428 | 52 | 10408 | 159* | 27.68 | 13 | 4 | 156 | 1 |
| Johnson, G.W. | 277 | 440 | 40 | 10121 | 168 | 25.30 | 10 | 3 | 215 | — |
| Jones, A. | 575 | 1043 | 63 | 32307 | 204* | 32.96 | 50 | 20 | 272 | — |
| Jones, A.A. | 211 | 213 | 66 | 785 | 33 | 5.34 | — | — | 51 | — |

188

| | M | I | NO | Runs | HS | Avge | 100s | 1000 runs in season | Ct | St |
|---|---|---|---|---|---|---|---|---|---|---|
| Jones, A.L. | 50 | 89 | 6 | 1532 | 83 | 18.45 | — | — | 25 | — |
| Jones, B.J.R. | 46 | 81 | 3 | 1076 | 65 | 13.79 | — | — | 19 | — |
| Jones, E.W. | 352 | 521 | 109 | 7585 | 146* | 18.41 | 3 | — | 733 | 78 |
| | | | | | | | | | | |
| Kallicharran, A.I. | 298 | 486 | 45 | 18799 | 197 | 42.62 | 43 | 7 + 1 | 209 | — |
| Kemp, N.J. | 12 | 12 | 1 | 84 | 23 | 7.63 | — | — | 3 | — |
| Kennedy, A. | 117 | 189 | 19 | 5012 | 176* | 29.48 | 5 | 2 | 73 | — |
| King, C.L. | 83 | 136 | 21 | 4518 | 163 | 39.28 | 11 | 1 | 79 | — |
| Kirsten, P.N. | 123 | 215 | 20 | 8403 | 213* | 43.09 | 22 | 3 + 1 | 80 | — |
| Knight, J.M. | 18 | 26 | 1 | 182 | 20 | 7.28 | — | — | 2 | — |
| Knight, R.D.V. | 292 | 511 | 45 | 14836 | 165* | 31.83 | 25 | 9 | 221 | — |
| Knott, A.P.E. | 409 | 599 | 108 | 14783 | 156 | 30.10 | 16 | 2 | 982 | 108 |
| | | | | | | | | | | |
| Laird, B.M. | 55 | 102 | 6 | 3298 | 171 | 34.35 | 6 | — | 33 | — |
| Lamb, A.J. | 105 | 176 | 37 | 7057 | 178 | 50.76 | 15 | 2 | 70 | — |
| Lamb, T.M. | 114 | 119 | 44 | 941 | 77 | 12.54 | — | — | 31 | — |
| Larkins, W. | 148 | 249 | 20 | 6884 | 170* | 30.06 | 15 | 3 | 75 | — |
| Lee, P.G. | 186 | 149 | 64 | 715 | 26 | 8.41 | — | — | 29 | — |
| Le Roux, G.S. | 51 | 66 | 28 | 947 | 70* | 24.92 | — | — | 22 | — |
| Lever, J.K. | 339 | 351 | 149 | 2194 | 91 | 10.86 | — | — | 138 | — |
| Lillee, D.K. | 128 | 154 | 45 | 1483 | 73* | 13.60 | — | — | 41 | — |
| Lilley, A.W. | 6 | 9 | 1 | 213 | 100* | 26.62 | 1 | — | 1 | — |
| Llewellyn, M.J. | 127 | 202 | 28 | 4157 | 129* | 23.89 | 3 | — | 78 | — |
| Lloyd, B.J. | 86 | 112 | 35 | 936 | 45* | 12.15 | — | — | 50 | — |
| Lloyd, C.H. | 365 | 554 | 77 | 23440 | 242* | 49.14 | 65 | 8 + 3 | 263 | — |
| Lloyd, D. | 353 | 566 | 66 | 16269 | 214* | 32.53 | 29 | 9 | 303 | — |
| Lloyd, T.A. | 67 | 115 | 18 | 3225 | 130* | 33.24 | 3 | 1 | 49 | — |
| Lloyds, J.W. | 15 | 23 | 3 | 505 | 70 | 25.25 | — | — | 9 | — |
| Long, A. | 452 | 537 | 131 | 6801 | 92 | 16.75 | — | — | 922 | 124 |
| Love, J.D. | 79 | 129 | 19 | 3305 | 170* | 30.04 | 6 | — | 45 | — |
| Lumb, R.G. | 190 | 316 | 25 | 9311 | 159 | 31.99 | 19 | 5 | 113 | — |
| Lynch, M.A. | 34 | 57 | 5 | 1065 | 101 | 20.48 | 1 | — | 18 | — |
| | | | | | | | | | | |
| McEvoy, M.S.A. | 32 | 55 | 1 | 1004 | 67* | 18.59 | — | — | 32 | — |
| McEwan, K.S. | 222 | 376 | 32 | 13225 | 218 | 38.44 | 31 | 7 | 214 | 7 |
| Mack, A.J. | 31 | 32 | 10 | 102 | 18 | 4.63 | — | — | 4 | — |
| Mackintosh, K.S. | 19 | 21 | 8 | 186 | 23* | 14.30 | — | — | 9 | — |
| MacPherson, M.C.L. | 5 | 10 | 1 | 52 | 22 | 5.77 | — | — | 8 | 1 |
| Mallender, N.A. | 5 | 6 | 3 | 4 | 2* | 1.33 | — | — | 1 | — |
| Mallett, A.A. | 174 | 216 | 57 | 2248 | 92 | 14.13 | — | — | 99 | — |
| Mallett, N.V.H. | 4 | 8 | 0 | 98 | 38 | 12.25 | — | — | 1 | — |
| Malone, M.F. | 60 | 65 | 18 | 735 | 46 | 15.63 | — | — | 25 | — |
| Malone, S.J. | 9 | 11 | 5 | 70 | 20 | 11.66 | — | — | 1 | — |
| Marks, V.J. | 112 | 178 | 23 | 4473 | 105 | 28.85 | 1 | — | 49 | — |
| Marsden, R. | 8 | 13 | 0 | 243 | 50 | 18.69 | — | — | 5 | — |
| Marsh, R.W. | 189 | 295 | 33 | 8592 | 236 | 32.79 | 10 | 0 + 1 | 555 | 54 |
| Marshall, M.D. | 60 | 78 | 11 | 1058 | 72* | 15.79 | — | — | 29 | — |
| Maru, R.J. | 9 | 7 | 1 | 49 | 13 | 8.16 | — | — | 8 | — |
| Maynard, C. | 23 | 25 | 6 | 475 | 85 | 25.00 | — | — | 34 | 4 |
| Mellor, A.J. | 13 | 15 | 6 | 26 | 10* | 2.88 | — | — | 4 | — |
| Mendis, G.D. | 85 | 149 | 13 | 4054 | 204 | 29.80 | 5 | 1 | 53 | 1 |
| Merry, W.G. | 14 | 8 | 6 | 13 | 6* | 6.50 | — | — | 1 | — |
| Miller, G. | 178 | 259 | 37 | 5857 | 98* | 26.38 | — | — | 112 | — |

| | M | I | NO | Runs | HS | Avge | 100s | 1000 runs in season | Ct | St |
|---|---|---|---|---|---|---|---|---|---|---|
| Mills, J.P.C. | 19 | 27 | 1 | 548 | 79 | 21.07 | — | — | 7 | — |
| Mohamed, T. | 13 | 19 | 3 | 665 | 193 | 41.56 | 3 | — | 5 | — |
| Moir, D.G. | 1 | 2 | 0 | 70 | 44 | 35.00 | — | — | 1 | — |
| Monteith, J.D. | 16 | 22 | 3 | 277 | 78 | 14.57 | — | — | 11 | — |
| Moseley, E.A. | 14 | 16 | 6 | 294 | 70* | 29.40 | — | — | 2 | — |
| Moseley, H.R. | 175 | 177 | 73 | 1258 | 67 | 12.09 | — | — | 63 | — |
| Moulding, R.P. | 20 | 30 | 4 | 495 | 77* | 19.03 | — | — | 10 | — |
| Mubarak, A.M. | 24 | 38 | 2 | 765 | 105 | 21.25 | 1 | — | 14 | — |
| Murray, D.A. | 81 | 126 | 21 | 3431 | 206* | 32.67 | 7 | — | 183 | 30 |
| Murray, D.L. | 362 | 549 | 85 | 13092 | 166* | 28.21 | 10 | 3 | 735 | 104 |
| | | | | | | | | | | |
| Nanan, N. | 34 | 62 | 5 | 900 | 72 | 15.78 | — | — | 22 | — |
| Nash, M.A. | 292 | 416 | 60 | 6602 | 130 | 18.54 | 2 | — | 123 | — |
| Neale, P.A. | 100 | 173 | 18 | 5034 | 163* | 32.47 | 8 | 2 | 43 | — |
| Needham, A. | 13 | 13 | 1 | 83 | 21 | 6.91 | — | — | 5 | — |
| Newman, P.G. | 3 | 4 | 3 | 60 | 29* | 60.00 | — | — | 1 | — |
| Nicholas, M.C.J. | 25 | 43 | 4 | 993 | 112 | 25.46 | 2 | — | 12 | — |
| | | | | | | | | | | |
| O'Brien, B.A. | 10 | 16 | 1 | 280 | 45* | 18.66 | — | — | 5 | — |
| Odendaal, A. | 9 | 14 | 0 | 325 | 61 | 23.21 | — | — | 6 | — |
| Old, C.M. | 280 | 344 | 70 | 6130 | 116 | 22.37 | 6 | — | 174 | — |
| Oldham, S. | 68 | 41 | 18 | 130 | 50 | 5.65 | — | — | 22 | — |
| Olive, M. | 14 | 26 | 2 | 395 | 50 | 16.45 | — | — | 8 | — |
| Oliver, P.R. | 74 | 105 | 17 | 1982 | 83 | 22.52 | — | — | 40 | — |
| Ontong, R.C. | 114 | 188 | 17 | 4381 | 135* | 25.61 | 6 | 1 | 50 | — |
| Orders, J.O.D. | 18 | 32 | 2 | 831 | 79 | 27.70 | — | — | 6 | — |
| Ormrod, J.A. | 424 | 714 | 84 | 19725 | 204* | 31.30 | 29 | 12 | 365 | — |
| O'Shaughnessy, S.J. | 4 | 5 | 2 | 91 | 50* | 30.33 | — | — | 2 | — |
| | | | | | | | | | | |
| Parker, P.W.G. | 105 | 181 | 22 | 5523 | 215 | 34.73 | 13 | 4 | 61 | — |
| Parks, R.J. | 7 | 13 | 3 | 233 | 64* | 23.30 | — | — | 12 | 5 |
| Parry, D.R. | 57 | 84 | 17 | 1813 | 96 | 27.05 | — | — | 32 | — |
| Parsons, G.J. | 19 | 19 | 5 | 137 | 25* | 9.78 | — | — | 8 | — |
| Partridge, M.D. | 46 | 66 | 21 | 1202 | 90 | 26.71 | — | — | 16 | — |
| Pascoe, L.S. | 45 | 47 | 17 | 255 | 51* | 8.50 | — | — | 13 | — |
| Patel, D.N. | 90 | 128 | 11 | 2641 | 118* | 22.57 | 5 | — | 57 | — |
| Pauline, D.B. | 9 | 11 | 1 | 162 | 46 | 16.20 | — | — | 2 | — |
| Payne, I.R. | 12 | 15 | 1 | 96 | 29 | 6.85 | — | — | 10 | — |
| Peck, I.G. | 16 | 21 | 2 | 177 | 34 | 9.31 | — | — | 7 | — |
| Perry, N.J. | 12 | 11 | 4 | 19 | 6 | 2.71 | — | — | 8 | — |
| Perryman, S.P. | 115 | 109 | 43 | 647 | 43 | 9.80 | — | — | 44 | — |
| Phillip, N. | 128 | 187 | 27 | 3983 | 134 | 24.89 | 1 | — | 38 | — |
| Phillipson, C.P. | 128 | 170 | 48 | 2218 | 87 | 18.18 | — | — | 82 | — |
| Pigott, A.C.S. | 27 | 35 | 5 | 422 | 55 | 14.06 | — | — | 8 | — |
| Pilling, H. | 333 | 542 | 68 | 15279 | 149* | 32.23 | 25 | 8 | 89 | — |
| Pocock, C.D. | 51 | 88 | 9 | 1712 | 143* | 21.67 | 1 | — | 51 | — |
| Pocock, P.I. | 433 | 469 | 113 | 4135 | 75* | 11.61 | — | — | 149 | — |
| Pont, K.R. | 126 | 196 | 26 | 3880 | 113 | 22.82 | 5 | — | 67 | — |
| Popplewell, N.F.M. | 46 | 60 | 13 | 1040 | 135* | 22.12 | 1 | — | 24 | — |
| Pridgeon, A.P. | 97 | 92 | 43 | 395 | 32 | 8.06 | — | — | 28 | — |
| Pringle, D.R. | 31 | 42 | 8 | 1177 | 123 | 34.61 | 3 | — | 22 | — |
| Procter, M.J. | 366 | 615 | 54 | 20825 | 254 | 37.12 | 47 | 9 | 300 | — |

190

| | M | I | NO | Runs | HS | Avge | 100s | 1000 runs in season | Ct | St |
|---|---|---|---|---|---|---|---|---|---|---|
| Racionzer, T.B. | 43 | 76 | 9 | 1376 | 91 | 20.53 | — | | 35 | — |
| Radford, N.V. | 15 | 21 | 4 | 293 | 38* | 17.23 | — | | 5 | — |
| Radley, C.T. | 402 | 646 | 90 | 19795 | 171 | 35.60 | 35 | 13 | 401 | — |
| Ramage, A. | 9 | 8 | 5 | 53 | 19 | 17.66 | — | | 1 | — |
| Randall, D.W. | 226 | 389 | 31 | 12325 | 209 | 34.42 | 18 | 6 | 130 | — |
| Ratcliffe, R.M. | 82 | 84 | 22 | 1022 | 101* | 16.48 | 1 | | 23 | — |
| Rawlinson, J.L. | 9 | 16 | 2 | 112 | 19 | 8.00 | — | | 5 | — |
| Reidy, B.W. | 83 | 126 | 22 | 2818 | 131* | 27.09 | 2 | | 42 | — |
| Reith, M.S. | 9 | 16 | 0 | 346 | 82 | 21.62 | — | | 5 | — |
| Rice, C.E.B. | 217 | 359 | 57 | 12053 | 246 | 39.91 | 18 | 6 | 154 | — |
| Rice, J.M. | 134 | 208 | 15 | 3675 | 96* | 19.04 | — | | 120 | — |
| Richards, C.J. | 85 | 86 | 21 | 908 | 50 | 13.96 | — | | 160 | 25 |
| Richards, I.V.A. | 213 | 357 | 22 | 16082 | 291 | 48.00 | 45 | 7 + 2 | 203 | 1 |
| Roberts, A.M.E. | 153 | 187 | 49 | 1856 | 62 | 13.44 | — | | 31 | — |
| Robertson, F. | 11 | 16 | 1 | 151 | 51 | 10.06 | — | | 3 | — |
| Robinson, R.T. | 17 | 30 | 4 | 869 | 138 | 33.42 | 1 | | 4 | — |
| Roebuck, P.M. | 115 | 193 | 32 | 5038 | 158 | 31.29 | 5 | 1 | 66 | — |
| Rogers, J.J. | 18 | 31 | 3 | 440 | 53 | 15.71 | — | | 6 | — |
| Roope, G.R.J. | 367 | 582 | 118 | 17648 | 171 | 38.03 | 25 | 8 | 542 | 1 |
| Rose, B.C. | 173 | 294 | 28 | 8992 | 205 | 33.80 | 19 | 6 | 80 | — |
| Ross, C.J. | 31 | 41 | 13 | 132 | 23* | 4.71 | — | | 8 | — |
| Rouse, S.J. | 124 | 152 | 33 | 1836 | 93 | 15.42 | — | | 54 | — |
| Rowe, C.J.C. | 117 | 184 | 33 | 4084 | 147* | 27.04 | 5 | 1 | 41 | — |
| Rowe, L.G. | 129 | 211 | 11 | 7766 | 302 | 38.83 | 16 | | 98 | — |
| Russell, P.E. | 167 | 207 | 44 | 2015 | 72 | 12.36 | — | | 124 | — |
| Russom, N. | 13 | 16 | 9 | 267 | 79* | 38.14 | — | | 2 | — |
| Sadiq Mohammad | 317 | 552 | 33 | 19505 | 184* | 37.58 | 41 | 7 + 2 | 259 | — |
| Sainsbury, G.E. | 3 | 2 | 2 | 2 | 2* | — | — | | 1 | — |
| Sanderson, J.F.W. | 6 | 6 | 2 | 18 | 9 | 4.50 | — | | 2 | — |
| Sarfraz Nawaz | 241 | 302 | 63 | 4657 | 86 | 19.48 | — | | 137 | — |
| Saunders, M. | 3 | 2 | 0 | 12 | 12 | 6.00 | — | | — | — |
| Saxelby, K. | 4 | 5 | 1 | 18 | 15 | 4.50 | — | | 2 | — |
| Schepens, M. | 19 | 28 | 5 | 407 | 57 | 17.69 | — | | 12 | — |
| Scott, C.J. | 25 | 27 | 7 | 124 | 16 | 6.20 | — | | 57 | 5 |
| Selvey, M.W.W. | 208 | 204 | 73 | 1497 | 45 | 11.42 | — | | 55 | — |
| Sharp, G. | 215 | 292 | 60 | 4494 | 94 | 19.37 | — | | 400 | 71 |
| Sharp, K. | 55 | 87 | 10 | 2071 | 106 | 26.89 | 2 | | 17 | — |
| Shepherd, J.N. | 337 | 484 | 78 | 10544 | 170 | 25.97 | 8 | 1 | 244 | — |
| Short, J.F. | 8 | 13 | 2 | 438 | 114 | 39.81 | 1 | | 6 | — |
| Shuttleworth, K. | 239 | 241 | 85 | 2589 | 71 | 16.59 | — | | 128 | — |
| Sidebottom, A. | 68 | 72 | 12 | 1114 | 124 | 18.56 | 1 | | 22 | — |
| Simmons, J. | 286 | 344 | 92 | 5644 | 112 | 22.39 | 3 | | 225 | — |
| Slack, W.N. | 29 | 46 | 1 | 845 | 66 | 18.77 | — | | 10 | — |
| Slocombe, P.A. | 111 | 187 | 24 | 4664 | 132 | 28.61 | 7 | 2 | 50 | — |
| Small, G.C. | 16 | 15 | 4 | 64 | 16 | 5.81 | — | | 3 | — |
| Smith, C.L. | 29 | 51 | 8 | 1502 | 130 | 34.93 | 5 | 1 | 15 | — |
| Smith, D.M. | 97 | 138 | 36 | 2723 | 115 | 26.69 | 3 | | 54 | — |
| Smith, K.D. | 108 | 188 | 14 | 5329 | 140 | 30.62 | 7 | 3 | 39 | — |
| Smith, M.J. | 422 | 704 | 78 | 19814 | 181 | 31.65 | 40 | 11 | 217 | — |
| Smith, N. | 177 | 227 | 49 | 3145 | 126 | 17.66 | — | | 372 | 47 |
| Southern, J.W. | 117 | 132 | 53 | 977 | 61* | 12.36 | — | | 38 | — |
| Spelman, G.D. | 6 | 7 | 1 | 9 | 4 | 1.50 | — | | 2 | — |

|  | M | I | NO | Runs | HS | Avge | 100s | 1000 runs in season | Ct | St |
|---|---|---|---|---|---|---|---|---|---|---|
| Spencer, J. | 215 | 286 | 80 | 2787 | 79 | 13.52 | — | — | 75 | — |
| Steele, A. | 14 | 25 | 0 | 621 | 97 | 24.84 | — | — | 12 | 1 |
| Steele, D.S. | 401 | 668 | 89 | 19263 | 140* | 33.26 | 29 | 10 | 448 | — |
| Steele, J.F. | 268 | 446 | 48 | 12026 | 195 | 30.21 | 19 | 6 | 291 | — |
| Stephenson, G.R. | 272 | 357 | 66 | 4781 | 100* | 16.42 | 1 | — | 584 | 77 |
| Stevenson, G.B. | 106 | 129 | 25 | 2513 | 111 | 24.16 | 1 | — | 49 | — |
| Stevenson, K. | 114 | 135 | 46 | 737 | 33 | 8.28 | — | — | 38 | — |
| Stovold, A.W. | 157 | 281 | 13 | 7820 | 196 | 29.17 | 6 | 3 | 153 | 25 |
| Stovold, M.W. | 12 | 18 | 3 | 221 | 75* | 14.73 | — | — | 1 | — |
| Surridge, D. | 10 | 8 | 6 | 40 | 14* | 20.00 | — | — | 3 | — |
| Sutcliffe, S.P. | 10 | 13 | 0 | 57 | 16 | 4.38 | — | — | 1 | — |
| Swan, R.G. | 1 | 2 | 0 | 5 | 5 | 2.50 | — | — | 1 | — |
|  |  |  |  |  |  |  |  |  |  |  |
| Tavare, C.J. | 121 | 201 | 27 | 6486 | 150* | 37.27 | 13 | 4 | 137 | — |
| Taylor, D.J.S. | 261 | 366 | 83 | 6700 | 179 | 23.67 | 4 | 1 | 525 | 74 |
| Taylor, L.B. | 48 | 31 | 16 | 82 | 15 | 5.46 | — | — | 14 | — |
| Taylor, M.N.S. | 375 | 518 | 116 | 8031 | 105 | 19.97 | 3 | — | 214 | — |
| Taylor, N.R. | 11 | 19 | 4 | 517 | 110 | 34.46 | 1 | — | 9 | — |
| Taylor, R.W. | 532 | 738 | 136 | 10290 | 97 | 17.09 | — | — | 1238 | 150 |
| Terry, V.P. | 10 | 16 | 0 | 189 | 31 | 11.81 | — | — | 4 | — |
| Thomas, D.J. | 25 | 28 | 6 | 175 | 43 | 7.95 | — | — | 7 | — |
| Thomas, G.P. | 2 | 3 | 0 | 14 | 9 | 4.66 | — | — | — | — |
| Thomas, J.G. | 1 | 1 | 0 | 34 | 34 | 34.00 | — | — | — | — |
| Thomson, J.R. | 96 | 121 | 30 | 1231 | 61 | 13.52 | — | — | 38 | — |
| Tindall, R.M. | 8 | 14 | 3 | 204 | 60* | 18.54 | — | — | 3 | — |
| Titmus, F.J. | 791 | 1141 | 207 | 21587 | 137* | 23.11 | 6 | 8 | 474 | — |
| Todd, P.A. | 123 | 218 | 10 | 5808 | 178 | 27.92 | 5 | 3 | 85 | — |
| Tolchard, R.W. | 413 | 575 | 165 | 12920 | 126* | 31.51 | 11 | — | 800 | 106 |
| Tomlins, K.P. | 21 | 28 | 3 | 469 | 94 | 18.76 | — | — | 12 | — |
| Tremlett, T.M. | 31 | 54 | 9 | 970 | 84 | 21.55 | — | — | 9 | — |
| Trim, G.E. | 15 | 25 | 0 | 399 | 91 | 15.96 | — | — | 10 | — |
| Tunnicliffe, C.J. | 96 | 107 | 27 | 1112 | 82* | 13.90 | — | — | 45 | — |
| Tunnicliffe, H.T. | 65 | 110 | 27 | 2116 | 100* | 25.49 | 1 | — | 37 | — |
| Turner, D.R. | 283 | 476 | 39 | 12309 | 181* | 28.16 | 19 | 6 | 152 | — |
| Turner, G.M. | 419 | 729 | 94 | 30941 | 259 | 48.72 | 89 | 13 + 3 | 376 | — |
| Turner, S. | 284 | 412 | 79 | 7426 | 121 | 22.30 | 4 | — | 185 | — |
|  |  |  |  |  |  |  |  |  |  |  |
| Underwood, D.L. | 497 | 530 | 136 | 3611 | 80 | 9.16 | — | — | 217 | — |
|  |  |  |  |  |  |  |  |  |  |  |
| Van der Bijl, V.A.P. | 125 | 158 | 37 | 1920 | 87 | 15.86 | — | — | 48 | — |
|  |  |  |  |  |  |  |  |  |  |  |
| Waller, C.E. | 162 | 171 | 65 | 959 | 47 | 9.04 | — | — | 84 | — |
| Walters, J. | 58 | 80 | 15 | 1296 | 90 | 19.93 | — | — | 26 | — |
| Warner, C.J. | 4 | 7 | 1 | 131 | 48 | 21.83 | — | — | 3 | — |
| Waterton, S.N.V. | 7 | 9 | 1 | 110 | 40* | 13.75 | — | — | 11 | 1 |
| Watson, W.K. | 62 | 76 | 30 | 593 | 44 | 12.89 | — | — | 22 | — |
| Watts, P.J. | 375 | 607 | 90 | 14449 | 145 | 27.94 | 10 | 7 | 277 | — |
| Wells, C.M. | 25 | 34 | 6 | 1084 | 135 | 38.71 | 1 | 1 | 7 | — |
| Wenlock, D.A. | 4 | 5 | 3 | 30 | 13* | 15.00 | — | — | 1 | — |
| Wessels, K.C. | 90 | 160 | 19 | 6710 | 254 | 47.58 | 12 | 2 | 63 | — |
| Weston, M.J. | 3 | 4 | 0 | 84 | 43 | 21.00 | — | — | 2 | — |
| White, R.A. | 413 | 642 | 105 | 12452 | 116* | 23.18 | 5 | 1 | 189 | — |
| Whitehouse, J. | 180 | 309 | 38 | 8693 | 197 | 32.07 | 15 | 3 | 120 | — |

|  | M | I | NO | Runs | HS | Avge | 100s | 1000 runs in season | Ct | St |
|---|---|---|---|---|---|---|---|---|---|---|
| Whiteley, J.P. | 22 | 13 | 5 | 61 | 20 | 7.62 | — | — | 10 | — |
| Wild, D.J. | 1 | 2 | — | 22 | 22 | 11.00 | — | — | 1 | — |
| Wilkins, A.H. | 70 | 82 | 22 | 579 | 70 | 9.65 | — | — | 24 | — |
| Willey, P. | 288 | 468 | 70 | 10534 | 227 | 26.46 | 14 | 2 | 118 | — |
| Williams, R.G. | 89 | 142 | 16 | 3329 | 175* | 26.42 | 6 | 2 | 35 | — |
| Willis, R.G.D. | 228 | 238 | 106 | 1832 | 43 | 13.87 | — | — | 100 | — |
| Willows, A. | 3 | 1 | 0 | 1 | 1 | 1.00 | — | — | — | — |
| Wilson, P.H.L. | 38 | 29 | 14 | 178 | 29 | 11.86 | — | — | 5 | — |
| Wincer, R.C. | 23 | 21 | 8 | 131 | 26 | 10.07 | — | — | 8 | — |
| Windaybank, S.J. | 3 | 5 | 0 | 164 | 53 | 32.80 | — | — | 1 | — |
| Wood, B. | 311 | 514 | 65 | 15141 | 198 | 33.72 | 26 | 7 | 250 | — |
| Wood, G.M. | 49 | 89 | 5 | 2938 | 126 | 34.97 | 6 | 0+1 | 43 | — |
| Wookey, S.M. | 19 | 27 | 6 | 260 | 48 | 12.38 | — | — | 5 | — |
| Woolmer, R.A. | 287 | 436 | 66 | 12358 | 171 | 33.40 | 25 | 5 | 195 | 1 |
| Wright, J.G. | 123 | 223 | 17 | 7650 | 166* | 37.13 | 13 | 3 | 76 | — |
| Yallop, G.N. | 85 | 149 | 17 | 5493 | 172 | 41.61 | 14 | 0+2 | 64 | 1 |
| Yardley, T.J. | 233 | 348 | 60 | 7373 | 135 | 25.60 | 5 | 1 | 205 | 2 |
| Younis Ahmed | 350 | 588 | 84 | 18824 | 221* | 37.34 | 29 | 9 | 196 | — |
| Zaheer Abbas | 326 | 555 | 54 | 24570 | 274 | 49.04 | 73 | 9+4 | 218 | — |

## BOWLING

|  | Runs | Wkts | Avge | BB | 5 wI | 10 wM | 100 wkts in season |
|---|---|---|---|---|---|---|---|
| Abrahams, J. | 79 | 0 | — | — | — | — | — |
| Acfield, D.L. | 18573 | 666 | 27.88 | 7-36 | 24 | 2 | — |
| Agnew, J.P. | 1294 | 44 | 29.40 | 4-36 | — | — | — |
| Allbrook, M.E. | 3504 | 76 | 46.10 | 7-79 | 2 | — | — |
| Alleyne, H.L. | 1645 | 66 | 24.92 | 6-50 | 4 | 1 | — |
| Allott, P.J.W. | 1538 | 50 | 30.76 | 5-39 | 2 | — | — |
| Amiss, D.L. | 700 | 18 | 38.88 | 3-21 | — | — | — |
| Anderson, I.J. | 217 | 16 | 13.56 | 5-21 | 1 | — | — |
| Anderson, I.S. | 257 | 2 | 128.50 | 1-24 | — | — | — |
| Arnold, G.G. | 23551 | 1084 | 21.72 | 8-41 | 45 | 3 | 1 |
| Asif Iqbal | 8715 | 290 | 30.05 | 6-45 | 5 | — | — |
| Athey, C.W.J. | 741 | 16 | 46.31 | 3-38 | — | — | — |
| Bacchus, S.F.A.F. | 25 | 0 | — | — | — | — | — |
| Bailey, M.J. | 431 | 8 | 53.87 | 5-89 | 1 | — | — |
| Bainbridge, P. | 803 | 22 | 36.50 | 4-48 | — | — | — |
| Bairstow, D.L. | 167 | 5 | 33.40 | 3-82 | — | — | — |
| Balderstone, J.C. | 7054 | 276 | 25.55 | 6-25 | 5 | — | — |
| Barclay, J.R.T. | 5490 | 192 | 28.59 | 6-61 | 7 | 1 | — |
| Barlow, G.D. | 45 | 3 | 15.00 | 1-6 | — | — | — |
| Barnett, K.J. | 756 | 14 | 54.00 | 4-76 | — | — | — |
| Bell, D.L. | — | — | — | — | — | — | — |
| Benson, M.R. | — | — | — | — | — | — | — |
| Birch, J.D. | 1816 | 37 | 49.08 | 6-64 | 1 | — | — |

| | Runs | Wkts | Avge | BB | 5 wI | 10 wM | 100 wkts in season |
|---|---|---|---|---|---|---|---|
| Birkenshaw, J. | 28632 | 1062 | 26.96 | 8-94 | 44 | 4 | 2 |
| Booden, C.D. | 111 | 0 | — | — | — | — | — |
| Boon, T.J. | 50 | 0 | — | — | — | — | — |
| Booth, P. | 4224 | 148 | 28.54 | 6-93 | 1 | — | — |
| Booth Jones, T.D. | — | — | — | — | — | — | — |
| Border, A.R. | 1053 | 30 | 35.10 | 3-32 | — | — | — |
| Bore, M.K. | 7721 | 255 | 30.27 | 8-89 | 7 | — | — |
| Borrington, A.J. | 19 | 0 | — | — | — | — | — |
| Botham, I.T. | 12722 | 545 | 23.34 | 8-34 | 34 | 6 | 1 |
| Boycott, G. | 1215 | 36 | 33.75 | 4-14 | — | — | — |
| Boyd-Moss, R.J. | 275 | 3 | 91.66 | 1-10 | — | — | — |
| Brain, B.M. | 19585 | 808 | 24.23 | 8-55 | 33 | 6 | — |
| Brassington, A.J. | 10 | 0 | — | — | — | — | — |
| Breakwell, D. | 12168 | 399 | 30.49 | 8-39 | 11 | 1 | — |
| Brearley, J.M. | 173 | 1 | 173.00 | 1-21 | — | — | — |
| Briers, N.E. | 77 | 1 | 77.00 | 1-22 | — | — | — |
| Bright, R.J. | 5443 | 205 | 26.55 | 7-87 | 12 | 2 | — |
| Broad, B.C. | 109 | 3 | 36.33 | 2-14 | — | — | — |
| Brooks, K.G. | — | — | — | — | — | — | — |
| Bury, T.E.O. | — | — | — | — | — | — | — |
| Bushe, E.A. | — | — | — | — | — | — | — |
| Butcher, A.R. | 3045 | 79 | 38.54 | 6-48 | 1 | — | — |
| Butcher, I.P. | — | — | — | — | — | — | — |
| Butcher, R.O. | 34 | 0 | — | — | — | — | — |
| | | | | | | | |
| Carrick, P. | 12711 | 461 | 27.57 | 8-33 | 23 | 2 | — |
| Carter, R.M. | 671 | 18 | 37.27 | 4-27 | — | — | — |
| Chappell, G.S. | 7324 | 255 | 28.72 | 7-40 | 5 | — | — |
| Cheatle, R.G.L. | 3068 | 100 | 30.68 | 6-32 | 6 | — | — |
| Childs, J.H. | 7324 | 245 | 29.89 | 8-34 | 11 | 2 | — |
| Clark, J. | 652 | 33 | 19.75 | 4-10 | — | — | — |
| Clarke, S.T. | 4823 | 214 | 22.53 | 6-39 | 10 | 1 | — |
| Claughton, J.A. | 4 | 0 | — | — | — | — | — |
| Clifford, C.C. | 4740 | 126 | 37.61 | 6-89 | 6 | — | — |
| Clift, P.B. | 11931 | 480 | 24.85 | 8-17 | 15 | — | — |
| Clinton, G.S. | 86 | 4 | 21.50 | 2-8 | — | — | — |
| Cobb, R.A. | — | — | — | — | — | — | — |
| Cockbain, I. | — | — | — | — | — | — | — |
| Cohen, M.F. | — | — | — | — | — | — | — |
| Cook, G. | 147 | 1 | 147.00 | 1-12 | — | — | — |
| Cook, N.G.B. | 2985 | 122 | 24.46 | 6-57 | 6 | — | — |
| Cooper, H.P. | 6529 | 233 | 28.02 | 8-62 | 4 | 1 | — |
| Cooper, K.E. | 4527 | 152 | 29.78 | 6-32 | 4 | — | — |
| Cope, G.A. | 16948 | 686 | 24.70 | 8-73 | 35 | 6 | — |
| Cordle, A.E. | 19281 | 701 | 27.50 | 9-49 | 19 | 2 | — |
| Corlett, S.C. | 1722 | 50 | 34.44 | 5-32 | 2 | — | — |
| Coverdale, S.P. | 0 | 1 | 00.00 | 1-0 | — | — | — |
| Cowan, R.S. | 84 | 2 | 42.00 | 1-40 | — | — | — |
| Cowans, N.G. | 42 | 1 | 42.00 | 1-32 | — | — | — |
| Cowdrey, C.S. | 406 | 13 | 31.23 | 3-17 | — | — | — |
| Cowley, N.G. | 6231 | 179 | 34.81 | 5-44 | 3 | — | — |
| Crawford, N.C. | 1030 | 32 | 32.18 | 6-80 | 1 | — | — |
| Croft, C.E.H. | 7122 | 289 | 24.64 | 8-29 | 12 | 1 | — |

|  | Runs | Wkts | Avge | BB | 5 wI | 10 wM | 100 wkts in season |
|---|---|---|---|---|---|---|---|
| Cumbes, J. | 9606 | 330 | 29.10 | 6-24 | 12 | — | — |
| Curtis, I.J. | 592 | 13 | 45.53 | 3-56 | — | — | — |
| Curtis, T.S. | 2 | 0 | — | — | — | — | — |
| Curzon, C.C. | — | — | — | — | — | — | — |
| | | | | | | | |
| Daniel, W.W. | 6967 | 359 | 19.40 | 7-95 | 16 | 4 | — |
| Davies, T. | — | — | — | — | — | — | — |
| Davison, B.F. | 2617 | 82 | 31.91 | 5-52 | 1 | — | — |
| Denness, M.H. | 62 | 2 | 31.00 | 1-7 | — | — | — |
| Denning, P.W. | 78 | 1 | 78.00 | 1-4 | — | — | — |
| Dennis, S.J. | 237 | 6 | 39.50 | 2-38 | — | — | — |
| Dexter, R.E. | — | — | — | — | — | — | — |
| Dilley, G.R. | 2475 | 101 | 24.50 | 6-66 | 3 | — | — |
| Doggart, S.J.G. | 392 | 9 | 43.55 | 3-54 | — | — | — |
| D'Oliveira, B.L. | 15021 | 548 | 27.41 | 6-29 | 17 | 2 | — |
| Donald, W.A. | — | — | — | — | — | — | — |
| Doshi, D.R. | 15244 | 644 | 23.67 | 7-29 | 29 | 4 | 1 |
| Downton, P.R. | — | — | — | — | — | — | — |
| Dredge, C.H. | 5676 | 190 | 29.87 | 6-57 | 7 | — | — |
| Dudleston, B. | 1063 | 40 | 26.57 | 4-6 | — | — | — |
| Durack, J.P. | 32 | 0 | — | — | — | — | — |
| Dymock, G. | 9410 | 370 | 25.43 | 7-67 | 11 | 1 | — |
| Dyson, J. | 0 | 0 | — | — | — | — | — |
| | | | | | | | |
| Ealham, A.G.E. | 189 | 3 | 63.00 | 1-1 | — | — | — |
| East, R.E. | 22133 | 884 | 25.03 | 8-30 | 43 | 9 | — |
| Edmonds, P.H. | 17596 | 699 | 25.17 | 8-132 | 28 | 4 | — |
| Elder, J.W.G. | 310 | 12 | 25.83 | 3-56 | — | — | — |
| Emburey, J.E. | 8529 | 373 | 22.86 | 7-36 | 19 | 4 | — |
| Ezekowitz, R.A.B. | — | — | — | — | — | — | — |
| | | | | | | | |
| Featherstone, N.G. | 4921 | 180 | 27.33 | 5-32 | 4 | — | — |
| Ferreira, A.M. | 4054 | 142 | 28.54 | 8-38 | 7 | 1 | — |
| Fisher, P.B. | — | — | — | — | — | — | — |
| Fletcher, K.W.R. | 1890 | 46 | 41.08 | 5-41 | 1 | — | — |
| Forster, G. | 100 | 3 | 33.33 | 2-30 | — | — | — |
| Foster, D.C.G. | — | — | — | — | — | — | — |
| Foster, N.A. | 80 | 3 | 26.66 | 3-51 | — | — | — |
| Fowler, G. | — | — | — | — | — | — | — |
| Francis, D.A. | 6 | 0 | — | — | — | — | — |
| French, B.N. | — | — | — | — | — | — | — |
| | | | | | | | |
| Gard, T. | — | — | — | — | — | — | — |
| Garner, J. | 5198 | 292 | 17.90 | 8-31 | 15 | — | — |
| Garnham, M.A. | — | — | — | — | — | — | — |
| Gatting, M.W. | 1631 | 62 | 26.30 | 5-59 | 1 | — | — |
| Gavaskar, S.M. | 1017 | 21 | 48.42 | 3-43 | — | — | — |
| Gifford, N. | 35688 | 1626 | 21.94 | 8-28 | 77 | 12 | 3 |
| Goddard, G.F. | 1094 | 41 | 26.68 | 8-34 | 2 | 1 | — |
| Gooch, G.A. | 1796 | 48 | 37.41 | 5-40 | 1 | — | — |
| Gore, H.E.I. | 1917 | 57 | 33.63 | 5-66 | 1 | — | — |
| Gould, I.J. | 1 | 0 | — | — | — | — | — |
| Gower, D.I. | 62 | 3 | 20.66 | 3-47 | — | — | — |

| | Runs | Wkts | Avge | BB | 5 wI | 10 wM | 100 wkts in season |
|---|---|---|---|---|---|---|---|
| Graf, S.F. | 1363 | 37 | 36.83 | 4-71 | — | — | — |
| Graveney, D.A. | 12044 | 411 | 29.30 | 8-85 | 19 | 3 | — |
| Graves, P.J. | 797 | 15 | 53.13 | 3-69 | — | — | — |
| Green, A.M. | — | — | — | — | — | — | — |
| Greenidge, C.G. | 437 | 16 | 27.31 | 5-49 | 1 | — | — |
| Greig, I.A. | 2026 | 53 | 38.22 | 5-60 | 1 | — | — |
| Griffiths, B.J. | 5443 | 182 | 29.90 | 7-52 | 5 | — | — |
| | | | | | | | |
| Hacker, P.J. | 3669 | 105 | 34.94 | 6-35 | 2 | — | — |
| Hadlee, R.J. | 10589 | 481 | 22.01 | 7-23 | 24 | 5 | — |
| Halliday, M. | 369 | 18 | 20.50 | 5-39 | 1 | — | — |
| Halliday, S.J. | — | — | — | — | — | — | — |
| Hampshire, J.H. | 1585 | 29 | 54.65 | 7-52 | 2 | — | — |
| Hardie, B.R. | 60 | 2 | 30.00 | 2-39 | — | — | — |
| Harpur, T. | — | — | — | — | — | — | — |
| Harris, M.J. | 3420 | 79 | 43.29 | 4-16 | — | — | — |
| Hartley, S.N. | 156 | 5 | 31.20 | 3-40 | — | — | — |
| Hassan, S.B. | 407 | 6 | 67.83 | 3-33 | — | — | — |
| Hayes, F.C. | 15 | 0 | — | — | — | — | — |
| Hayes, K.A. | — | — | — | — | — | — | — |
| Haynes, D.L. | 2 | 0 | — | — | — | — | — |
| Hays, D.L. | 5 | 0 | — | — | — | — | — |
| Head, T.J. | — | — | — | — | — | — | — |
| Heath, J.R.P. | — | — | — | — | — | — | — |
| Hemmings, E.E. | 17667 | 584 | 30.25 | 7-33 | 25 | 6 | — |
| Hemsley, E.J.O. | 2340 | 69 | 33.91 | 3-5 | — | — | — |
| Hemsley, P.D. | 53 | 1 | 53.00 | 1-4 | — | — | — |
| Henderson, S.P. | 46 | 0 | — | — | — | — | — |
| Hendrick, M. | 12947 | 630 | 20.55 | 8-45 | 23 | 3 | — |
| Herbert, R. | 148 | 3 | 49.33 | 3-64 | — | — | — |
| Higgs, K. | 36132 | 1530 | 23.61 | 7-19 | 49 | 5 | 5 |
| Hignell, A.J. | 161 | 1 | 161.00 | 1-3 | — | — | — |
| Hill, A. | 128 | 5 | 25.60 | 3-5 | — | — | — |
| Hills, R.W. | 4494 | 161 | 27.91 | 6-64 | 2 | — | — |
| Hobbs, R.N.S. | 28625 | 1064 | 26.90 | 8-63 | 48 | 8 | 2 |
| Hogg, W. | 3047 | 124 | 24.57 | 7-84 | 5 | 1 | — |
| Holder, V.A. | 23183 | 947 | 24.48 | 7-40 | 38 | 3 | — |
| Holding, M.A. | 4858 | 192 | 25.30 | 8-92 | 7 | 1 | — |
| Holliday, D.C. | 304 | 5 | 60.80 | 2-23 | — | — | — |
| Holmes, G.C. | 764 | 19 | 40.21 | 5-86 | 1 | — | — |
| Hopkins, D.C. | 1986 | 53 | 37.47 | 6-67 | 1 | — | — |
| Hopkins, J.A. | 27 | 0 | — | — | — | — | — |
| Howarth, G.P. | 3064 | 102 | 30.03 | 5-32 | 1 | — | — |
| Howat, M.G. | 1560 | 26 | 60.00 | 3-39 | — | — | — |
| Hughes, D.P. | 16168 | 551 | 29.34 | 7-24 | 20 | 2 | — |
| Hughes, K.J. | 29 | 1 | 29.00 | 1-0 | — | — | — |
| Hughes, S.P. | — | — | — | — | — | — | — |
| Humpage, G.W. | 130 | 3 | 43.33 | 2-13 | — | — | — |
| Humphries, D.J. | — | — | — | — | — | — | — |
| Huxford, P.N. | — | — | — | — | — | — | — |
| | | | | | | | |
| Imran Khan | 17334 | 736 | 23.55 | 7-52 | 43 | 7 | — |
| Inchmore, J.D. | 8631 | 308 | 28.02 | 8-58 | 12 | 1 | — |

196

| | Runs | Wkts | Avge | BB | 5 wI | 10 wM | 100 wkts in season |
|---|---|---|---|---|---|---|---|
| Ingham, P.G. | — | — | — | — | — | — | — |
| Intikhab Alam | 41870 | 1505 | 27.82 | 8-54 | 82 | 13 | 1 |
| | | | | | | | |
| Jackman, R.D. | 27969 | 1248 | 22.41 | 8-40 | 61 | 8 | 1 |
| James, K.D. | 29 | 4 | 7.25 | 3-14 | — | — | — |
| Jarvis, K.B.S. | 8343 | 306 | 27.26 | 8-97 | 8 | 1 | — |
| Javed Miandad | 5118 | 157 | 32.59 | 6-93 | 5 | — | — |
| Jennings, K.F. | 3329 | 92 | 36.18 | 5-18 | 1 | — | — |
| Jesty, T.E. | 11437 | 397 | 28.80 | 7-75 | 12 | — | — |
| Johnson, G.W. | 11652 | 382 | 30.50 | 6-32 | 13 | 2 | — |
| Jones, A. | 329 | 3 | 109.66 | 1-24 | — | — | — |
| Jones, A.A. | 15177 | 541 | 28.05 | 9-51 | 23 | 3 | — |
| Jones, A.L. | 17 | 0 | — | — | — | — | — |
| Jones, B.J.R. | — | — | — | — | — | — | — |
| Jones, E.W. | 5 | 0 | — | — | — | — | — |
| | | | | | | | |
| Kallicharran, A.I. | 1663 | 34 | 48.91 | 4-48 | — | — | — |
| Kemp, N.J. | 589 | 12 | 49.08 | 6-119 | 1 | — | — |
| Kennedy, A. | 268 | 7 | 38.28 | 3-58 | — | — | — |
| King, C.L. | 3318 | 107 | 31.00 | 5-91 | 1 | — | — |
| Kirsten, P.N. | 1826 | 49 | 37.26 | 4-44 | — | — | — |
| Knight, J.M. | 1140 | 28 | 40.71 | 4-69 | — | — | — |
| Knight, R.D.V. | 10080 | 294 | 34.28 | 6-44 | 4 | — | — |
| Knott, A.P.E. | 82 | 2 | 41.00 | 1-5 | — | — | — |
| | | | | | | | |
| Laird, B.M. | 54 | 0 | — | — | — | — | — |
| Lamb, A.J. | 55 | 4 | 13.75 | 1-1 | — | — | — |
| Lamb, T.M. | 7492 | 261 | 28.70 | 7-56 | 9 | — | — |
| Larkins, W. | 867 | 21 | 41.28 | 3-34 | — | — | — |
| Lee, P.G. | 14422 | 572 | 25.21 | 8-34 | 27 | 6 | 2 |
| Le Roux, G.S. | 4159 | 202 | 20.58 | 7-40 | 11 | 1 | — |
| Lever, J.K. | 24340 | 1026 | 23.72 | 8-49 | 45 | 4 | 2 |
| Lillee, D.K. | 13226 | 587 | 22.53 | 8-29 | 36 | 11 | — |
| Lilley, A.W. | — | — | — | — | — | — | — |
| Llewellyn, M.J. | 615 | 23 | 26.73 | 4-35 | — | — | — |
| Lloyd, B.J. | 5339 | 118 | 45.24 | 4-49 | — | — | — |
| Lloyd, C.H. | 4104 | 114 | 36.00 | 4-48 | — | — | — |
| Lloyd, D. | 5385 | 187 | 28.79 | 7-38 | 4 | 1 | — |
| Lloyd, T.A. | 197 | 3 | 65.66 | 1-14 | — | — | — |
| Lloyds, J.W. | 913 | 28 | 32.60 | 6-61 | 2 | 1 | — |
| Long, A. | 2 | 0 | — | — | — | — | — |
| Love, J.D. | 73 | 0 | — | — | — | — | — |
| Lumb, R.G. | — | — | — | — | — | — | — |
| Lynch, M.A. | 78 | 2 | 39.00 | 1-14 | — | — | — |
| | | | | | | | |
| McEvoy, M.S.A. | 4 | 0 | — | — | — | — | — |
| McEwan, K.S. | 95 | 2 | 47.50 | 1-0 | — | — | — |
| Mack, A.J. | 1889 | 44 | 42.93 | 4-28 | — | — | — |
| Mackintosh, K.S. | 957 | 23 | 41.60 | 4-49 | — | — | — |
| MacPherson, M.C.L. | — | — | — | — | — | — | — |
| Mallender, N.A. | 393 | 7 | 56.14 | 3-29 | — | — | — |
| Mallett, A.A. | 17285 | 666 | 25.95 | 8-59 | 31 | 5 | — |
| Mallett, N.V.H. | 386 | 8 | 48.25 | 4-44 | — | — | — |

| | Runs | Wkts | Avge | BB | 5 wI | 10 wM | 100 wkts in season |
|---|---|---|---|---|---|---|---|
| Malone, M.F. | 5215 | 227 | 22.97 | 7-88 | 13 | 1 | — |
| Malone, S.J. | 558 | 15 | 37.20 | 3-56 | — | — | — |
| Marks, V.J. | 7810 | 222 | 35.18 | 6-33 | 8 | — | — |
| Marsden, R. | — | — | — | — | — | — | — |
| Marsh, R.W. | 74 | 0 | — | — | — | — | — |
| Marshall, M.D. | 4095 | 219 | 18.69 | 7-56 | 12 | 1 | — |
| Maru, R.J. | 412 | 12 | 34.33 | 3-29 | — | — | — |
| Maynard, C. | — | — | — | — | — | — | — |
| Mellor, A.J. | 653 | 17 | 38.41 | 5-52 | 1 | — | — |
| Mendis, G.D. | 9 | 0 | — | — | — | — | — |
| Merry, W.G. | 838 | 29 | 28.89 | 4-24 | — | — | — |
| Miller, G. | 10859 | 460 | 23.60 | 7-54 | 23 | 5 | — |
| Mills, J.P.C. | 5 | 0 | — | — | — | — | — |
| Mohamed, T. | 20 | 0 | — | — | — | — | — |
| Moir, D.G. | 78 | 4 | 19.50 | 4-43 | — | — | — |
| Monteith, J.D. | 1048 | 65 | 16.12 | 7-38 | 5 | 1 | — |
| Moseley, E.A. | 1340 | 51 | 26.27 | 6-41 | 2 | — | — |
| Moseley, H.R. | 11392 | 473 | 24.08 | 6-34 | 14 | 1 | — |
| Moulding, R.P. | — | — | — | — | — | — | — |
| Mubarak, A.M. | 6 | 0 | — | — | — | — | — |
| Murray, D.A. | 11 | 0 | — | — | — | — | — |
| Murray, D.L. | 367 | 5 | 73.40 | 2-50 | — | — | — |
| | | | | | | | |
| Nanan, N. | 322 | 9 | 35.77 | 3-12 | — | — | — |
| Nash, M.A. | 22444 | 880 | 25.50 | 9-56 | 42 | 5 | — |
| Neale, P.A. | 72 | 1 | 72.00 | 1-15 | — | — | — |
| Needham, A. | 441 | 9 | 49.00 | 3-25 | — | — | — |
| Newman, P.G. | 143 | 4 | 35.75 | 2-41 | — | — | — |
| Nicholas, M.C.J. | 68 | 0 | — | — | — | — | — |
| | | | | | | | |
| O'Brien, B.A. | — | — | — | — | — | — | — |
| Odendaal, A. | — | — | — | — | — | — | — |
| Old, C.M. | 17830 | 816 | 21.85 | 7-20 | 31 | 1 | — |
| Oldham, S. | 4425 | 149 | 29.69 | 5-40 | 2 | — | — |
| Olive, M. | — | — | — | — | — | — | — |
| Oliver, P.R. | 2115 | 27 | 78.33 | 2-28 | — | — | — |
| Ontong, R.C. | 6618 | 213 | 31.07 | 7-60 | 8 | — | — |
| Orders, J.O.D. | 428 | 7 | 61.14 | 2-16 | — | — | — |
| Ormrod, J.A. | 1089 | 25 | 43.56 | 5-27 | 1 | — | — |
| O'Shaughnessy, S.J. | 70 | 1 | 70.00 | 1-16 | — | — | — |
| | | | | | | | |
| Parker, P.W.G. | 432 | 8 | 54.00 | 2-23 | — | — | — |
| Parks, R.J. | — | — | — | — | — | — | — |
| Parry, D.R. | 5284 | 192 | 27.52 | 9-76 | 10 | 1 | — |
| Parsons, G.J. | 979 | 33 | 29.66 | 4-38 | — | — | — |
| Partridge, M.D. | 2076 | 41 | 50.63 | 5-29 | 1 | — | — |
| Pascoe, L.S. | 4336 | 173 | 25.06 | 7-18 | 7 | 1 | — |
| Patel, D.N. | 3625 | 97 | 37.37 | 6-47 | 4 | — | — |
| Pauline, D.B. | 5 | 0 | — | — | — | — | — |
| Payne, I.R. | 325 | 3 | 108.33 | 2-41 | — | — | — |
| Peck, I.G. | — | — | — | — | — | — | — |
| Perry, N.J. | 831 | 19 | 43.73 | 3-51 | — | — | — |

| | Runs | Wkts | Avge | BB | 5 wI | 10 wM | 100 wkts in season |
|---|---|---|---|---|---|---|---|
| Perryman, S.P. | 8325 | 285 | 29.21 | 7-49 | 15 | 3 | — |
| Phillip, N. | 9262 | 376 | 24.63 | 6-33 | 13 | 1 | — |
| Phillipson, C.P. | 5141 | 152 | 33.82 | 6-56 | 4 | — | — |
| Pigott, A.C.S. | 1575 | 46 | 34.23 | 4-40 | — | — | — |
| Pilling, H. | 195 | 1 | 195.00 | 1-42 | — | — | — |
| Pocock, N.E.J. | 106 | 2 | 53.00 | 1-4 | — | — | — |
| Pocock, P.I. | 33451 | 1308 | 25.57 | 9-57 | 51 | 6 | 1 |
| Pont, K.R. | 2183 | 67 | 32.58 | 5-33 | 1 | — | — |
| Popplewell, N.F.M. | 2210 | 48 | 46.04 | 3-18 | — | — | — |
| Pridgeon, A.P. | 7137 | 191 | 37.36 | 7-35 | 3 | 1 | — |
| Pringle, D.R. | 1636 | 57 | 28.70 | 6-90 | 1 | 1 | — |
| Procter, M.J. | 25302 | 1327 | 19.06 | 9-71 | 67 | 14 | 2 |
| | | | | | | | |
| Racionzer, T.B. | 5 | 0 | — | — | — | — | — |
| Radford, N.V. | 1168 | 37 | 31.56 | 5-47 | 2 | — | — |
| Radley, C.T. | 60 | 6 | 10.00 | 1-0 | — | — | — |
| Ramage, A. | 573 | 19 | 30.15 | 3-24 | — | — | — |
| Randall, D.W. | 123 | 0 | — | — | — | — | — |
| Ratcliffe, R.M. | 5411 | 205 | 26.39 | 7-58 | 15 | 2 | — |
| Rawlinson, J.L. | — | — | — | — | — | — | — |
| Reidy, B.W. | 1615 | 42 | 38.45 | 5-61 | 1 | — | — |
| Reith, M.S. | 56 | 1 | 56.00 | 1-24 | — | — | — |
| Rice, C.E.B. | 12034 | 543 | 22.16 | 7-62 | 16 | 1 | — |
| Rice, J.M. | 7209 | 222 | 32.47 | 7-48 | 3 | — | — |
| Richards, C.J. | — | — | — | — | — | — | — |
| Richards, I.V.A. | 3133 | 76 | 41.22 | 3-12 | — | — | — |
| Roberts, A.M.E. | 12514 | 590 | 21.21 | 8-47 | 27 | 2 | 1 |
| Robertson, F. | 626 | 33 | 18.96 | 6-58 | 2 | — | — |
| Robinson, R.T. | 47 | 1 | 47.00 | 1-47 | — | — | — |
| Roebuck, P.M. | 1870 | 41 | 45.60 | 6-50 | 1 | — | — |
| Rogers, J.J. | 39 | 1 | 39.00 | 1-24 | — | — | — |
| Roope, G.R.J. | 8209 | 218 | 37.65 | 5-14 | 4 | — | — |
| Rose, B.C. | 204 | 6 | 34.00 | 3-9 | — | — | — |
| Ross, C.J. | 1938 | 55 | 35.23 | 4-34 | — | — | — |
| Rouse, S.J. | 8143 | 268 | 30.38 | 6-34 | 5 | — | — |
| Rowe, C.J.C. | 2212 | 59 | 37.49 | 6-46 | 3 | 1 | — |
| Rowe, L.G. | 215 | 2 | 107.50 | 1-19 | — | — | — |
| Russell, P.E. | 10108 | 535 | 30.17 | 7-46 | 5 | — | — |
| Russom, N. | 952 | 20 | 47.60 | 4-84 | — | — | — |
| | | | | | | | |
| Sadiq Mohammad | 6318 | 201 | 31.43 | 7-34 | 7 | — | — |
| Sainsbury, G.E. | 268 | 8 | 33.50 | 4-85 | — | — | — |
| Sanderson, J.F.W. | 282 | 10 | 28.20 | 6-67 | 1 | — | — |
| Sarfraz Nawaz | 20073 | 848 | 23.67 | 9-86 | 44 | 4 | 1 |
| Saunders, M. | 212 | 6 | 35.33 | 3-47 | — | — | — |
| Saxelby, K. | 202 | 2 | 101.00 | 1-29 | — | — | — |
| Schepens, M. | 13 | 0 | — | — | — | — | — |
| Scott, C.J. | — | — | — | — | — | — | — |
| Selvey, M.W.W. | 15654 | 619 | 25.28 | 7-20 | 31 | 4 | 1 |
| Sharp, G. | 49 | 1 | 49.00 | 1-47 | — | — | — |
| Sharp, K. | 41 | 0 | — | — | — | — | — |
| Shepherd, J.N. | 24501 | 925 | 26.48 | 8-40 | 46 | 2 | — |
| Short, J.F. | — | — | — | — | — | — | — |

|  | Runs | Wkts | Avge | BB | 5 wI | 10 wM | 100 wkts in season |
|---|---|---|---|---|---|---|---|
| Shuttleworth, K. | 15270 | 623 | 24.51 | 7-41 | 21 | 1 | — |
| Sidebottom, A. | 3232 | 118 | 27.38 | 7-18 | 3 | 2 | — |
| Simmons, J. | 16883 | 611 | 27.63 | 7-59 | 18 | 2 | — |
| Slack, W.N. | 3 | 0 | — | — | — | — | — |
| Slocombe, P.A. | 43 | 2 | 21.50 | 1-5 | — | — | — |
| Small, G.C. | 914 | 24 | 38.08 | 3-42 | — | — | — |
| Smith, C.L. | 61 | 0 | — | — | — | — | — |
| Smith, D.M. | 1405 | 26 | 54.03 | 3-40 | — | — | — |
| Smith, K.D. | 3 | 0 | — | — | — | — | — |
| Smith, M.J. | 1866 | 57 | 32.73 | 4-13 | — | — | — |
| Smith, N. | — | — | — | — | — | — | — |
| Southern, J.W. | 9051 | 310 | 29.19 | 6-46 | 12 | — | — |
| Spelman, G.D. | 291 | 7 | 41.57 | 2-27 | — | — | — |
| Spencer, J. | 14622 | 554 | 26.39 | 6-19 | 21 | 1 | — |
| Steele, A. | — | — | — | — | — | — | — |
| Steele, D.S. | 9007 | 374 | 24.08 | 8-29 | 12 | 2 | — |
| Steele, J.F. | 9620 | 377 | 25.51 | 7-29 | 9 | — | — |
| Stephenson, G.R. | 39 | 0 | — | — | — | — | — |
| Stevenson, G.B. | 7721 | 288 | 26.80 | 8-57 | 11 | 2 | — |
| Stevenson, K. | 7858 | 276 | 28.47 | 7-22 | 12 | — | — |
| Stovold, A.W. | 86 | 2 | 43.00 | 1-0 | — | — | — |
| Stovold, M.W. | — | — | — | — | — | — | — |
| Surridge, D. | 616 | 31 | 19.87 | 4-22 | — | — | — |
| Sutcliffe, S.P. | 749 | 24 | 31.20 | 6-19 | 1 | — | — |
| Swan, R.G. | — | — | — | — | — | — | — |
| Tavare, C.J. | 158 | 2 | 79.00 | 1-20 | — | — | — |
| Taylor, D.J.S. | 15 | 0 | — | — | — | — | — |
| Taylor, L.B. | 3302 | 117 | 28.22 | 6-61 | 2 | — | — |
| Taylor, M.N.S. | 22016 | 830 | 26.52 | 7-23 | 24 | — | — |
| Taylor, N.R. | 20 | 0 | — | — | — | — | — |
| Taylor, R.W. | 46 | 0 | — | — | — | — | — |
| Terry, V.P. | — | — | — | — | — | — | — |
| Thomas, D.J. | 1709 | 43 | 39.74 | 6-84 | 1 | — | — |
| Thomas, G.P. | — | — | — | — | — | — | — |
| Thomas, J.G. | 132 | 1 | 132.00 | 1-65 | — | — | — |
| Thomson, J.R. | 9180 | 383 | 23.96 | 7-33 | 19 | 3 | — |
| Tindall, R.M. | 162 | 2 | 81.00 | 2-60 | — | — | — |
| Titmus, F.J. | 63221 | 2827 | 22.36 | 9-52 | 168 | 26 | 16 |
| Todd, P.A. | 3 | 0 | — | — | — | — | — |
| Tolchard, R.W. | 20 | 1 | 20.00 | 1-4 | — | — | — |
| Tomlins, K.P. | 132 | 0 | — | — | — | — | — |
| Tremlett, T.M. | 1092 | 34 | 32.11 | 5-30 | 1 | — | — |
| Trim, G.E. | 13 | 0 | — | — | — | — | — |
| Tunnicliffe, C.J. | 6117 | 201 | 30.43 | 7-36 | 2 | — | — |
| Tunnicliffe, H.T. | 1601 | 42 | 38.11 | 4-30 | — | — | — |
| Turner, D.R. | 234 | 5 | 46.80 | 1-1 | — | — | — |
| Turner, G.M. | 189 | 5 | 37.80 | 3-18 | — | — | — |
| Turner, S. | 17368 | 686 | 25.31 | 6-26 | 25 | 1 | — |
| Underwood, D.L. | 37519 | 1926 | 19.48 | 9-28 | 126 | 39 | 9 |
| Van der Bijl, V.A.P. | 10046 | 585 | 17.17 | 8-35 | 32 | 7 | — |

| | Runs | Wkts | Avge | BB | 5 wI | 10 wM | 100 wkts in season |
|---|---|---|---|---|---|---|---|
| Waller, C.E. | 11317 | 405 | 27.94 | 7-64 | 15 | 1 | — |
| Walters, J. | 1935 | 47 | 41.17 | 4-100 | — | — | — |
| Warner, C.J. | — | — | — | — | — | — | — |
| Waterton, S.N.V. | — | — | — | — | — | — | — |
| Watson, W.K. | 5148 | 200 | 25.74 | 6-51 | 7 | — | — |
| Watts, P.J. | 8710 | 333 | 26.15 | 6-18 | 7 | — | — |
| Wells, C.M. | 870 | 19 | 45.78 | 4-23 | — | — | — |
| Wenlock, D.A. | 89 | 2 | 44.50 | 2-23 | — | — | — |
| Wessels, K.C. | 90 | 3 | 30.00 | 1-4 | — | — | — |
| Weston, M.J. | — | — | — | — | — | — | — |
| White, R.A. | 21138 | 693 | 30.50 | 7-41 | 28 | 4 | — |
| Whitehouse, J. | 471 | 6 | 78.50 | 2-55 | — | — | — |
| Whiteley, J.P. | 1063 | 32 | 33.21 | 4-14 | — | — | — |
| Wild, D.J. | — | — | — | — | — | — | — |
| Wilkins, A.H. | 4629 | 175 | 26.45 | 6-79 | 8 | — | — |
| Willey, P. | 11988 | 410 | 29.23 | 7-37 | 17 | 2 | — |
| Williams, R.G. | 3408 | 98 | 34.77 | 7-73 | 4 | — | — |
| Willis, R.G.D. | 16344 | 679 | 24.07 | 8-32 | 28 | 2 | — |
| Willows, A. | 203 | 8 | 25.37 | 4-33 | — | — | — |
| Wilson, P.H.L. | 1957 | 72 | 27.18 | 5-36 | 1 | — | — |
| Wincer, R.C. | 1653 | 46 | 35.93 | 4-42 | — | — | — |
| Windaybank, S.J. | — | — | — | — | — | — | — |
| Wood, B. | 7581 | 271 | 27.97 | 7-52 | 8 | — | — |
| Wood, G.M. | 111 | 5 | 22.20 | 3-18 | — | — | — |
| Wookey, S.M. | 1158 | 28 | 41.35 | 3-61 | — | — | — |
| Woolmer, R.A. | 10289 | 393 | 26.18 | 7-47 | 12 | 1 | — |
| Wright, J.G. | 4 | 1 | 4.00 | 1-4 | — | — | — |
| | | | | | | | |
| Yallop, G.N. | 296 | 1 | 296.00 | 1-21 | — | — | — |
| Yardley, T.J. | 35 | 0 | — | — | — | — | — |
| Younis Ahmed | 1408 | 36 | 39.11 | 4-10 | — | — | — |
| | | | | | | | |
| Zaheer Abbas | 753 | 22 | 34.22 | 5-15 | 1 | — | — |

# FIRST-CLASS CRICKET RECORDS

## COMPLETE TO END OF 1980 SEASON

### Highest Innings Totals

| | | |
|---|---|---|
| 1107 | Victoria v New South Wales (Melbourne) | 1926-27 |
| 1059 | Victoria v Tasmania (Melbourne) | 1922-23 |
| 951-7d | Sind v Baluchistan (Karachi) | 1973-74 |
| 918 | New South Wales v South Australia (Sydney) | 1900-01 |
| 912-8d | Holkar v Mysore (Indore) | 1945-46 |
| 910-6d | Railways v Dera Ismail Khan (Lahore) | 1964-65 |
| 903-7d | England v Australia (Oval) | 1938 |
| 887 | Yorkshire v Warwickshire (Birmingham) | 1896 |
| 849 | England v West Indies (Kingston) | 1929-30 |

*NB. There are 22 instances of a side making 800 or more in an innings, the last occasion being 951-7 declared by Sind as above.*

### Lowest Innings Totals

| | | |
|---|---|---|
| 12* | Oxford University v MCC and Ground (Oxford) | 1877 |
| 12 | Northamptonshire v Gloucestershire (Gloucester) | 1907 |
| 13 | Wellington v Nelson (Nelson) | 1862-63 |
| 13 | Auckland v Canterbury (Auckland) | 1877-78 |
| 13 | Nottinghamshire v Yorkshire (Nottingham) | 1901 |
| 15 | MCC v Surrey (Lord's) | 1839 |
| 15* | Victoria v MCC (Melbourne) | 1903-04 |
| 15* | Northamptonshire v Yorkshire (Northampton) | 1908 |
| 15 | Hampshire v Warwickshire (Birmingham) | 1922 |
| 16 | MCC and Ground v Surrey (Lord's) | 1872 |
| 16 | Derbyshire v Nottinghamshire (Nottingham) | 1879 |
| 16 | Surrey v Nottinghamshire (Oval) | 1880 |
| 16 | Warwickshire v Kent (Tonbridge) | 1913 |
| 16 | Trinidad v Barbados (Bridgetown) | 1941-42 |
| 16 | Border v Natal (East London) | 1959-60 |

*\*Batted one man short*

*NB. There are 26 instances of a side making less than 20 in an innings, the last occasion being 16 and 18 by Border v Natal at East London in 1959-60. The total of 34 is the lowest by one side in a match.*

### Highest Aggregates in a Match

| | | | |
|---|---|---|---|
| 2376 | (38) | Bombay v Maharashtra (Poona) | 1948-49 |
| 2078 | (40) | Bombay v Holkar (Bombay) | 1944-45 |
| 1981 | (35) | England v South Africa (Durban) | 1938-39 |
| 1929 | (39) | New South Wales v South Australia (Sydney) | 1925-26 |
| 1911 | (34) | New South Wales v Victoria (Sydney) | 1908-09 |
| 1905 | (40) | Otago v Wellington (Dunedin) | 1923-24 |

## In England the highest are:

| | | | |
|---|---|---|---|
| 1723 | (34) | England v Australia (Leeds) 5 day match | 1948 |
| 1601 | (29) | England v Australia (Lord's) 4 day match | 1930 |
| 1507 | (28) | England v West Indies (Oval) 5 day match | 1976 |
| 1502 | (28) | MCC v New Zealanders | 1927 |
| 1499 | (31) | T.N. Pearce's XI v Australians (Scarborough) | 1961 |
| 1496 | (24) | England v Australia (Nottingham) 4 day match | 1938 |
| 1494 | (37) | England v Australia (Oval) 4 day match | 1934 |
| 1492 | (33) | Worcestershire v Oxford U (Worcester) | 1904 |
| 1477 | (32) | Hampshire v Oxford U (Southampton) | 1913 |
| 1477 | (33) | England v South Africa (Oval) 4 day match | 1947 |
| 1475 | (27) | Northamptonshire v Surrey (Northampton) | 1920 |

## Lowest Aggregates in a Match

| | | | |
|---|---|---|---|
| 105 | (31) | MCC v Australia (Lord's) | 1878 |
| 134 | (30) | England v The B's (Lord's) | 1831 |
| 147 | (40) | Kent v Sussex (Sevenoaks) | 1828 |
| 149 | (30) | England v Kent (Lord's) | 1858 |
| 151 | (30) | Canterbury v Otago (Christchurch) | 1866-67 |
| 153 | (37) | MCC v Sussex (Lord's) | 1843 |
| 153 | (31) | Otago v Canterbury (Dunedin) | 1896-97 |
| 156 | (30) | Nelson v Wellington (Nelson) | 1885-86 |
| 158 | (22) | Surrey v Worcestershire (Oval) | 1954 |

*Wickets that fell are given in parentheses.*

## Tie Matches

Due to the change of law made in 1948 for tie matches, a tie is now a rarity. The law states that only if the match is played out and the scores are equal is the result a tie.

The most recent tied matches are as follows:

| | |
|---|---|
| Yorkshire (351-4d & 113) v Leicestershire (328 & 136) at Huddersfield | 1954 |
| Sussex (172 & 120) v Hampshire (153 & 139) at Eastbourne | 1955 |
| Victoria (244 & 197) v New South Wales (281 & 160) at Melbourne (St. Kilda) | 1956-57 |
| (The first tie in Sheffield Shield cricket) | |
| T.N. Pearce's XI (313-7d & 258) v New Zealanders (268 & 303-8d) at Scarborough | 1958 |
| Essex (364-6d & 176-8d) v Gloucestershire (329 & 211) at Leyton | 1959 |
| Australia (505 & 232) v West Indies (453 & 284) at Brisbane | 1960-61 |
| (The first tie in Test cricket) | |
| Bahawalpur (123 & 282) v Lahore B (127 & 278) at Bahawalpur | 1961-62 |
| Middlesex (327-5d & 123-9d) v Hampshire (277 & 173) at Portsmouth | 1967 |
| England XI (312-8d & 190-3d) v England Under-25 XI (320-9d & 182) at Scarborough | 1968 |
| Yorkshire (106-9d & 207) v Middlesex (102 & 211) at Bradford | 1973 |
| Sussex (245 & 173-5d) v Essex (200-8d & 218) at Hove | 1974 |
| South Australia (431 & 171-7d) v Queensland (340-8d & 262) at Adelaide | 1976-77 |
| England XI (296-6d & 104) v Central Districts (198 & 202) at New Plymouth | 1977-78 |
| Habib Bank (240 & 87) v Peshawar (139 & 188) at Peshawar | 1979-80 |

## Highest Individual Scores

| | | |
|---|---|---|
| 499 | Hanif Mohammad, Karachi v Bahawalpur (Karachi) | 1958-59 |
| 452* | D.G. Bradman, New South Wales v Queensland (Sydney) | 1929-30 |
| 443* | B.B. Nimbalkar, Maharashtra v Kathiawar (Poona) | 1948-49 |
| 437 | W.H. Ponsford, Victoria v Queensland (Melbourne) | 1927-28 |
| 429 | W.H. Ponsford, Victoria v Tasmania (Melbourne) | 1922-23 |
| 428 | Aftab Baloch, Sind v Baluchistan (Karachi) | 1973-74 |
| 424 | A.C. MacLaren, Lancashire v Somerset (Taunton) | 1895 |
| 385 | B. Sutcliffe, Otago v Canterbury (Christchurch) | 1952-53 |
| 383 | C.W. Gregory, New South Wales v Queensland (Brisbane) | 1906-07 |
| 369 | D.G. Bradman, South Australia v Tasmania (Adelaide) | 1935-36 |
| 365* | C. Hill, South Australia v New South Wales (Adelaide) | 1900-01 |
| 365* | G.S. Sobers, West Indies v Pakistan (Kingston) | 1957-58 |
| 364 | L. Hutton, England v Australia (Oval) | 1938 |
| 359* | V.M. Merchant, Bombay v Maharashtra (Bombay) | 1943-44 |
| 359 | R.B. Simpson, New South Wales v Queensland (Brisbane) | 1963-64 |
| 357* | R. Abel, Surrey v Somerset (Oval) | 1899 |
| 357 | D.G. Bradman, South Australia v Victoria (Melbourne) | 1935-36 |
| 356 | B.A. Richards, South Australia v Western Australia (Perth) | 1970-71 |
| 355 | B. Sutcliffe, Otago v Auckland (Dunedin) | 1949-50 |
| 352 | W.H. Ponsford, Victoria v New South Wales (Melbourne) | 1926-27 |
| 350 | Rashid Israr, National Bank v Habib Bank (Lahore) | 1976-77 |

NB. *There are 91 instances of a batsman scoring 300 or more in an innings, the last occasion being 350 by Rashid Israr as above.*

## Most Centuries in a Season

| | | |
|---|---|---|
| 18 | D.C.S. Compton | 1947 |
| 16 | J.B. Hobbs | 1925 |
| 15 | W.R. Hammond | 1938 |
| 14 | H. Sutcliffe | 1932 |

## Most Centuries in an Innings

| | | |
|---|---|---|
| 6 | for Holkar v Mysore (Indore) | 1945-46 |
| 5 | for New South Wales v South Australia (Sydney) | 1900-01 |
| 5 | for Australia v West Indies (Kingston) | 1954-55 |

## Most Centuries in Successive Innings

| | | |
|---|---|---|
| 6 | C.B. Fry | 1901 |
| 6 | D.G. Bradman | 1938-39 |
| 6 | M.J. Procter | 1970-71 |
| 5 | E.D. Weekes | 1955-56 |

NB. *The feat of scoring 4 centuries in successive innings has been achieved on 31 occasions.*

## Most Centuries in Succession in Test Matches

| | | |
|---|---|---|
| 5 | E.D. Weekes, West Indies | 1947-48 and 1948-49 |
| 4 | J.H.W. Fingleton, Australia | 1935-36 and 1936-37 |
| 4 | A. Melville, South Africa | 1938-39 and 1947 |

## Two Double Centuries in a Match

A.E. Fagg, 244 and 202* for Kent v Essex (Colchester)     1938

### A Double Century and a Century in a Match

C.B. Fry, 125 and 229, Sussex v Surrey (Hove)     1900
W.W. Armstrong, 157* and 245, Victoria v South Australia (Melbourne)   1920-21
H.T.W. Hardinge, 207 and 102* for Kent v Surrey (Blackheath)     1921
C.P. Mead, 113 and 224, Hampshire v Sussex (Horsham)     1921
K.S. Duleepsinhji, 115 and 246, Sussex v Kent (Hastings)     1929
D.G. Bradman, 124 and 225, Woodfull's XI v Ryder's XI (Sydney)     1929-30
B. Sutcliffe, 243 and 100*, New Zealanders v England (Southend)     1949
M.R. Hallam, 210* and 157, Leicestershire v Glamorgan (Leicester)     1959
M.R. Hallam, 203* and 143* Leicestershire v Sussex (Worthing)     1961
Hanumant Singh, 109 and 213*, Rajasthan v Bombay (Bombay)     1966-67
Salahuddin, 256 and 102*, Karachi v East Pakistan (Karachi)     1968-69
K.D. Walters, 242 and 103, Australia v West Indies (Sydney)     1968-69
S.M. Gavaskar, 124 and 220, India v West Indies (P. of Spain)     1970-71
L.G. Rowe, 214 and 100*, West Indies v New Zealand (Kingston)     1971-72
G.S. Chappell, 247* and 133, Australia v New Zealand (Wellington)     1973-74
L. Baichan, 216* and 102, Berbice v Demerara (Georgetown)     1973-74
Zaheer Abbas, 216* and 156*, Gloucestershire v Surrey (Oval)     1976
Zaheer Abbas, 230* and 104*, Gloucestershire v Kent (Canterbury)     1976
Zaheer Abbas, 205* and 108*, Gloucestershire v Sussex (Cheltenham)     1977
Saadat Ali, 141 and 222, Income Tax v Multan (Multan)     1977-78
Talat Ali, 214* and 104, Pakistan International Airways v Punjab (Lahore)   1978-79
Shafiq Ahmed, 129 and 217*, National Bank v Muslim Commercial Bank
(Karachi)     1978-79
D.W. Randall, 209 and 146, Nottinghamshire v Middlesex (Nottingham)     1979

### Two Centuries in a Match on Most Occasions

7   W.R. Hammond     6   J.B. Hobbs     5   C.B. Fry

*NB. 12 Batsmen have achieved the feat on four occasions, 23 batsmen on three occasions and 39 batsmen on two occasions.*

### Most Centuries

J.B. Hobbs, 197 (175 in England); E.H. Hendren, 170 (151); W.R. Hammond, 167 (134); C.P. Mead, 153 (145); H. Sutcliffe, 149 (135); F.E. Woolley, 145 (135); L. Hutton, 129 (105); W.G. Grace, 124 (123); D.C.S. Compton, 123 (92); T.W. Graveney, 122 (91); G. Boycott, 120 (96); D.G. Bradman, 117 (41); M.C. Cowdrey, 107 (80); A. Sandham, 107 (87); T.W. Hayward, 104 (100); J.H. Edrich, 103 (90); L.E.G. Ames, 102 (89); G.E. Tyldesley, 102 (94).

### Highest Individual Batting Aggregate in a Season

| | | Season | M | Innings | NO | HS | Avge | 100s |
|---|---|---|---|---|---|---|---|---|
| 3,816 | D.C.S. Compton | 1947 | 30 | 50 | 8 | 246 | 90.85 | 18 |
| 3,539 | W.J. Edrich | 1947 | 30 | 52 | 8 | 267* | 80.43 | 12 |

*NB. The feat of scoring 3,000 runs in a season has been achieved on 28 occasions, the last instance being by W.E. Alley (3,019 runs, av. 59.96) in 1961.*
*Since the reduction of the matches in the County Championship in 1969, the highest aggregate in a season is 2,554 runs (av. 75.11) by Zaheer Abbas in 1976.*

## Partnerships for First Wicket

| | | |
|---|---|---|
| 561 | Waheed Mirza and Mansoor Akhtar, Karachi Whites v Quetta (Karachi) | 1976-77 |
| 555 | H. Sutcliffe and P. Holmes, Yorkshire v Essex (Leyton) | 1932 |
| 554 | J.T. Brown and J. Tunnicliffe, Yorkshire v Derbyshire (Chesterfield) | 1898 |
| 490 | E.H. Bowley and J.G. Langridge, Sussex v Middlesex (Hove) | 1933 |
| 456 | W.H. Ponsford and E.R. Mayne, Victoria v Queensland (Melbourne) | 1923-24 |
| 451* | S. Desai and R. Binny, Karnataka v Kerala (Chikmalagalor) | 1977-78 |
| 428 | J.B. Hobbs and A. Sandham, Surrey v Oxford U (Oval) | 1926 |
| 424 | J.F.W. Nicholson and I.J. Siedle, Natal v Orange Free State (Bloemfontein) | 1926-27 |
| 413 | V.M.H. Mankad and P. Roy, India v New Zealand (Madras) | 1955-56 |
| 405 | C.P.S. Chauban and M. Gupte, Maharashtra v Vidarbha (Poona) | 1972-73 |

## Partnerships for Second Wicket

| | | |
|---|---|---|
| 465* | J.A. Jameson and R.B. Kanhai, Warwickshire v Gloucestershire (Birmingham) | 1974 |
| 455 | K.V. Bhandarkar and B.B. Nimbalkar, Maharashtra v Kathiawar (Poonah) | 1948-49 |
| 451 | D.G. Bradman and W.H. Ponsford, Australia v England (Oval) | 1934 |
| 446 | C.C. Hunte and G.S. Sobers, West Indies v Pakistan (Kingston) | 1957-58 |
| 429* | J.G. Dewes and G.H.G. Doggart, Cambridge U v Essex (Cambridge) | 1949 |
| 426 | Arshad Pervez and Mohsin Khan, Habib Bank v Income Tax Department (Lahore) | 1977-78 |
| 398 | W. Gunn and A. Shrewsbury, Nottinghamshire v Sussex (Nottingham) | 1890 |

## Partnerships for Third Wicket

| | | |
|---|---|---|
| 456 | Aslam Ali and Khalid Irtiza, United Bank v Multan (Karachi) | 1975-76 |
| 445 | P.E. Whitelaw and W.N. Carson, Auckland v Otago (Dunedin) | 1936-37 |
| 434 | J.B. Stollmeyer and G.E. Gomez, Trinidad v British Guiana (Port of Spain) | 1946-47 |
| 424* | W.J. Edrich and D.C.S. Compton, Middlesex v Somerset (Lord's) | 1948 |
| 410 | R.S. Modi and L. Armanath, India v Rest (Calcutta) | 1946-47 |
| 399 | R.T. Simpson and D.C.S. Compton, MCC v NE Transvaal (Benoni) | 1948-49 |

## Partnerships for Fourth Wicket

| | | |
|---|---|---|
| 577 | Gul Mahomed and V.S. Hazare, Baroda v Holkar (Baroda) | 1946-47 |
| 574* | C.L. Walcott and F.M.M. Worrell, Barbados v Trinidad (Port of Spain) | 1945-46 |
| 502* | F.M.M. Worrell and J.D.C. Goddard, Barbados v Trinidad (Bridgetown) | 1943-44 |
| 448 | R. Abel and T.W. Hayward, Surrey v Yorkshire (Oval) | 1899 |
| 424 | I.S. Lee and S.O. Quin, Victoria v Tasmania (Melbourne) | 1933-34 |
| 411 | P.B.H. May and M.C. Cowdrey, England v West Indies (Birmingham) | 1957 |
| 410 | G. Abraham and B. Pandit, Kerala v Andhra (Pulghat) | 1959-60 |
| 402 | W. Watson and T.W. Graveney, MCC v British Guiana (Georgetown) | 1953-54 |
| 402 | R.B. Kanhai and K. Ibadulla, Warwickshire v Nottinghamshire (Nottingham) | 1968 |

## Partnerships for Fifth Wicket

| | | |
|---|---|---|
| 405 | D.G. Bradman and S.G. Barnes, Australia v England (Sydney) | 1946-47 |
| 397 | W. Bardsley and C. Kellaway, New South Wales v South Australia (Sydney) | 1920-21 |
| 393 | E.G. Arnold and W.B. Burns, Worcestershire v Warwickshire (Birmingham) | 1909 |
| 360 | V.M. Merchant and M.N. Raiji, Bombay v Hyderabad (Bombay) | 1947-48 |
| 347 | D. Brookes and D.W. Barrick, Northamptonshire v Essex (Northampton) | 1952 |

## Partnerships for Sixth Wicket

| | | |
|---|---|---|
| 487* | G.A. Headley and C.C. Passailaigue, Jamaica v Lord Tennyson's XI (Kingston) | 1931-32 |
| 428 | W.W. Armstrong and M.A. Noble, Australians v Sussex (Hove) | 1902 |
| 411 | R.M. Poore and E.G. Wynyard, Hampshire v Somerset (Taunton) | 1899 |
| 376 | R. Subba Row and A. Lightfoot, Northamptonshire v Surrey (Oval) | 1958 |
| 371 | V.M. Merchant and R.S. Modi, Bombay v Maharashtra (Bombay) | 1943-44 |

## Partnerships for Seventh Wicket

| | | |
|---|---|---|
| 347 | D.S. Atkinson and C.C. Depeiza, West Indies v Australia (Bridgetown) | 1954-55 |
| 344 | K.S. Ranjitsinjhi and W. Newham, Sussex v Essex (Leyton) | 1902 |
| 340 | K.J. Key and H. Philipson, Oxford U v Middlesex (Chiswick Park) | 1887 |
| 336 | F.C.W. Newman and C.R. Maxwell, Cahn's XI v Leicestershire (Nottingham) | 1935 |
| 335 | C.W. Andrews and E.C. Bensted, Queensland v New South Wales (Sydney) | 1934-35 |

## Partnerships for Eighth Wicket

| | | |
|---|---|---|
| 433 | V.T. Trumper and A. Sims, Australians v Canterbury (Christchurch) | 1913-14 |
| 292 | R. Peel and Lord Hawke, Yorkshire v Warwickshire (Birmingham) | 1896 |
| 270 | V.T. Trumper and E.P. Barbour, New South Wales v Victoria (Sydney) | 1912-13 |
| 263 | D.R. Wilcox and R.M. Taylor, Essex v Warwickshire (Southend) | 1946 |
| 255 | E.A.V. Williams and E.A. Martindale, Barbados v Trinidad (Bridgetown) | 1935-36 |

## Partnerships for Ninth Wicket

| | | |
|---|---|---|
| 283 | A.R. Warren and J. Chapman, Derbyshire v Warwickshire (Blackwell) | 1910 |
| 251 | J.W.H.T. Douglas and S.N. Hare, Essex v Derbyshire (Leyton) | 1921 |
| 245 | V.S. Hazare and N.D. Nagarwalla, Maharashtra v Baroda (Poona) | 1939-40 |
| 239 | H.B. Cave and I.B. Leggat, Central Districts v Otago (Dunedin) | 1952-53 |
| 232 | C. Hill and E. Walkley, South Australia v New South Wales (Adelaide) | 1900-01 |

## Partnerships for Tenth Wicket

| | | |
|---|---|---:|
| 307 | A.F. Kippax and J.E.H. Hooker, New South Wales v Victoria (Melbourne) | 1928-29 |
| 249 | C.T. Sarwate and S.N. Bannerjee, Indians v Surrey (Oval) | 1946 |
| 235 | F.E. Woolley and A. Fielder, Kent v Worcestershire (Stourbridge) | 1909 |
| 230 | R.W. Nicholls and W. Roche, Middlesex v Kent (Lord's) | 1899 |
| 228 | R. Illingworth and K. Higgs, Leicestershire v Northamptonshire (Leicester) | 1977 |
| 218 | F.H. Vigar and T.P.B. Smith, Essex v Derbyshire (Chesterfield) | 1947 |

## BOWLING
### Most Wickets in a Season

| W | | Season | M | O | M | R | Avge |
|---|---|---|---|---|---|---|---|
| 304 | A.P. Freeman | 1928 | 37 | 1976.1 | 432 | 5489 | 18.05 |
| 298 | A.P. Freeman | 1933 | 33 | 2039 | 651 | 4549 | 15.26 |

*NB.  The feat of taking 250 wickets in a season has been achieved on 12 occasions, the last instance being by A.P. Freeman in 1933 as above. 200 or more wickets in a season have been taken on 59 occasions, the last instance being by G.A.R. Lock (212 wkts, avge 12.02) in 1957.*

The most wickets taken in a season since the reduction of County Championship matches in 1969 are as follows.

| W | | Season | M | O | M | R | Avge |
|---|---|---|---|---|---|---|---|
| 131 | L.R. Gibbs | 1971 | 23 | 1024.1 | 295 | 2475 | 18.89 |
| 121 | R.D. Jackman | 1980 | 23 | 746.2 | 220 | 1864 | 15.40 |
| 119 | A.M.E. Roberts | 1974 | 21 | 727.4 | 198 | 1621 | 13.62 |

*NB.   100 wickets in a season have been taken on 29 occasions since 1969.*

### All Ten Wickets in an Innings

The feat has been achieved on 69 occasions.
On three occasions: A.P. Freeman, 1929, 1930 and 1931.
On two occasions: J.C.Laker, 1956, H. Verity, 1931 and 1932, V.E. Walker, 1859 and 1865.
Instances since the war:
W.E. Hollies, Warwickshire v Nottinghamshire (Birmingham) 1946; J.M. Sims of Middlesex playing for East v West (Kingston) 1948; J.K.R. Graveney, Gloucestershire v Derbyshire (Chesterfield) 1949; T.E. Bailey, Essex v Lancashire (Clacton) 1949; R. Berry, Lancashire v Worcestershire (Blackpool) 1953; S.P. Gupte, Bombay v Pakistan Services (Bombay), 1954-55; J.C. Laker, Surrey v Australians (Oval) 1956; J.C. Laker, England v Australia (Manchester) 1956; G.A.R. Lock, Surrey v Kent (Blackheath) 1956; K. Smales, Nottinghamshire v Gloucestershire (Stroud) 1956; P. Chatterjee, Bengal v Assam (Jorhat) 1956-57; J.D. Bannister, Warwickshire v Combined Services (Birmingham) 1959; A.J.G. Pearson, Cambridge U v Leicestershire (Loughborough) 1961; N.I. Thompson, Sussex v Warwickshire (Worthing) 1964; P.J. Allan, Queensland v Victoria (Melbourne) 1965-66; I. Brayshaw, Western Australia v Victoria (Perth) 1967-78; Shahid Mahmood, Karachi Whites v Khairpur (Karachi) 1969-70.

### Nineteen Wickets in a Match

J.C. Laker 19-90 (9-37 and 10-53), England v Australia (Manchester) 1956.

### Eighteen Wickets in a Match

H.A. Arkwright 18-96 (9-43 and 9-53), MCC v Gentlemen of Kent (Canterbury) 1861, (twelve-a-side match).

## Seventeen Wickets in a Match

The feat has been achieved on 18 occasions.
Instances between the two wars were: A.P. Freeman (for 67 runs), Kent v Sussex (Hove) 1922; F.C.L. Matthews (89 runs), Nottinghamshire v Northamptonshire (Nottingham) 1923; C.W.L. Parker (56 runs), Gloucestershire v Essex (Gloucester) 1925; G.R. Cox (106 runs), Sussex v Warwickshire (Horsham) 1926; A.P. Freeman (92 runs), Kent v Warwickshire (Folkestone) 1932; H. Verity (91 runs), Yorkshire v Essex (Leyton) 1933; J.C. Clay (212 runs), Glamorgan v Worcestershire (Swansea) 1937; T.W.J. Goddard (106 runs), Gloucestershire v Kent (Bristol) 1939. There has been no instance since the last war.

## Most Hat-tricks in a Career

7  D.V.P. Wright.
6  T.W.J. Goddard, C.W.L. Parker.
5  S. Haigh, V.W.C. Jupp, A.E.G. Rhodes, F.A. Tarrant.
*NB. Nine bowlers have achieved the feat on four occasions and 24 bowlers on three occasions.*

## The 'Double' Event

3,000 runs and 100 wickets: J.H. Parks, 1937.
2,000 runs and 200 wickets: H.G. Hirst, 1906.
2,000 runs and 100 wickets: F.E. Woolley (4), J.W. Hearne (3), G.H. Hirst (2), W. Rhodes (2), T.E. Bailey, D.E. Davies, W.G. Grace, G.L. Jessop, V.W.C. Jupp, James Langridge, F.A. Tarrant, C.L. Townsend, L.F. Townsend.
1,000 runs and 200 wickets: M.W. Tate (3), A.E. Trott (2), A.S. Kennedy.
Most 'Doubles': W. Rhodes (16), G.H. Hirst (14), V.W.C. Jupp (10).
'Double' in first season: D.B. Close, 1949. *At the age of 18, Close is the youngest player ever to perform this feat.*
*The feat of scoring 1,000 runs and taking 100 wickets has been achieved on 302 occasions, the last instance being F.J. Titmus in 1967.*

## FIELDING

| Most catches in a season: | 78  W.R. Hammond | 1928 |
| | 77  M.J. Stewart | 1957 |
| Most catches in a match: | 10  W.R. Hammond, Gloucestershire | |
| | v Surrey (Cheltenham) | 1928 |
| Most catches in an innings: | 7  M.J. Stewart, Surrey v | |
| | Northamptonshire (Northampton) | 1957 |
| | 7  A.S. Brown, Gloucestershire v | |
| | Nottinghamshire (Nottingham) | 1966 |

## WICKET-KEEPING

| Most dismissals in a season: | 127 (79ct, 48st), L.E.G. Ames | 1929 |

*NB. The feat of making 100 dismissals in a season has been achieved on 12 occasions, the last instance being by R. Booth (100 dismissals–91 ct, 9st) in 1964.*

| Most dismissals in a match: | 12  E. Pooley (8 ct, 4 st) Surrey v | |
| | Sussex (Oval) | 1868 |
| | 12  D. Tallon (9 ct, 3 st), Queensland | |
| | v New South Wales (Sydney) | 1938-39 |
| | 12  H.B. Taber (9 ct, 3 st), New | |
| | South Wales v South Australia | |
| | (Adelaide) | 1968-69 |
| Most catches in a match: | 11  A. Long, Surrey v Sussex (Hove) | 1964 |
| | 11  R.W. Marsh, Western Australia | |
| | v Victoria (Perth) | 1975-76 |
| Most dismissals in an innings: | 8  A.T.W. Grout (8 ct), Queensland | |
| | v W. Australia (Brisbane) | 1959-60 |

# TEST CRICKET RECORDS

**COMPLETE TO END OF VARIOUS SERIES**
**IN AUSTRALIA AND PAKISTAN v WEST INDIES**

Matches between England and Rest of the World 1970 and between Australia and
Rest of the World 1971-72 are excluded.

## HIGHEST INNINGS TOTALS

| | | |
|---|---|---|
| 903-7d | England v Australia (Oval) | 1938 |
| 849 | England v West Indies (Kingston) | 1929-30 |
| 790-3d | West Indies v Pakistan (Kingston) | 1957-58 |
| 758-8d | Australia v West Indies (Kingston) | 1954-55 |
| 729-6d | Australia v England (Lord's) | 1930 |
| 701 | Australia v England (Oval) | 1934 |
| 695 | Australia v England (Oval) | 1930 |
| 687-8d | West Indies v England (Oval) | 1976 |
| 681-8d | West Indies v England (Port of Spain) | 1953-54 |
| 674 | Australia v India (Adelaide) | 1947-48 |
| 668 | Australia v West Indies (Bridgetown) | 1954-55 |
| 659-8d | Australia v England (Sydney) | 1946-47 |
| 658-8d | England v Australia (Nottingham) | 1938 |
| 657-8d | Pakistan v West Indies (Bridgetown) | 1957-58 |
| 656-8d | Australia v England (Manchester) | 1964 |
| 654-5d | England v South Africa (Durban) | 1938-39 |
| 652-8d | West Indies v England (Lord's) | 1973 |
| 650-6d | Australia v West Indies (Bridgetown) | 1964-65 |

**The highest innings for the countries not mentioned above are:**

| | | |
|---|---|---|
| 644-7d | India v West Indies (Kanpur) | 1978-79 |
| 622-9d | South Africa v Australia (Durban) | 1969-70 |
| 551-9d | New Zealand v England (Lord's) | 1973 |

*NB. There are 44 instances of a side making 600 or more in an innings in a Test
Match.*

## LOWEST INNINGS TOTALS

| | | |
|---|---|---|
| 26 | New Zealand v England (Auckland) | 1954-55 |
| 30 | South Africa v England (Port Elizabeth) | 1895-96 |
| 30 | South Africa v England (Birmingham) | 1924 |
| 35 | South Africa v England (Cape Town) | 1898-99 |
| 36 | Australia v England (Birmingham) | 1902 |
| 36 | South Africa v Australia (Melbourne) | 1931-32 |
| 42 | Australia v England (Sydney) | 1887-88 |
| 42 | New Zealand v Australia (Wellington) | 1945-46 |
| 42† | India v England (Lord's) | 1974 |
| 43 | South Africa v England (Cape Town) | 1888-89 |
| 44 | Australia v England (Oval) | 1896 |
| 45 | England v Australia (Sydney) | 1886-87 |
| 45 | South Africa v Australia (Melbourne) | 1931-32 |
| 47 | South Africa v England (Cape Town) | 1888-89 |
| 47 | New Zealand v England (Lord's) | 1958 |

*†Batted one man short*

**The lowest innings for the countries not mentioned above are:**

| | | |
|---|---|---|
| 76 | West Indies v Pakistan (Dacca) | 1958-59 |
| 87 | Pakistan v England (Lord's) | 1954 |

## HIGHEST INDIVIDUAL INNINGS

| | | |
|---|---|---|
| 365* | G.S. Sobers, West Indies v Pakistan (Kingston) | 1957-58 |
| 364 | L. Hutton, England v Australia (Oval) | 1938 |
| 337 | Hanif Mohammad, Pakistan v West Indies (Bridgetown) | 1957-58 |
| 336* | W.R. Hammond, England v New Zealand (Auckland) | 1932-33 |
| 334 | D.G. Bradman, Australia v England (Leeds) | 1930 |
| 325 | A. Sandham, England v West Indies (Kingston) | 1929-30 |
| 311 | R.B. Simpson, Australia v England (Manchester) | 1964 |
| 310* | J.H. Edrich, England v New Zealand (Leeds) | 1965 |
| 307 | R.M. Cowper, Australia v England (Melbourne) | 1965-66 |
| 304 | D.G. Bradman, Australia v England (Leeds) | 1934 |
| 302 | L.G. Rowe, West Indies v England (Bridgetown) | 1973-74 |
| 299* | D.G. Bradman, Australia v South Africa (Adelaide) | 1931-32 |
| 291 | I.V.A. Richards, West Indies v England (Oval) | 1976 |
| 287 | R.E. Foster, England v Australia (Sydney) | 1903-04 |
| 285* | P.B.H. May, England v West Indies (Birmingham) | 1957 |
| 278 | D.C.S. Compton, England v Pakistan (Nottingham) | 1954 |
| 274 | R.G. Pollock, South Africa v Australia (Durban) | 1969-70 |
| 274 | Zaheer Abbas, Pakistan v England (Birmingham) | 1971 |
| 270* | G.A. Headley, West Indies v England (Kingston) | 1934-35 |
| 270 | D.G. Bradman, Australia v England (Melbourne) | 1936-37 |
| 266 | W.H. Ponsford, Australia v England (Oval) | 1934 |
| 262* | D.L. Amiss, England v West Indies (Kingston) | 1973-74 |
| 261 | F.M.M. Worrell, West Indies v England (Nottingham) | 1950 |
| 260 | C.C. Hunte, West Indies v Pakistan (Kingston) | 1957-58 |
| 259 | G.M. Turner, New Zealand v West Indies (Georgetown) | 1971-72 |
| 258 | T.W. Graveney, England v West Indies (Nottingham) | 1957 |
| 258 | S.M. Nurse, West Indies v New Zealand (Christchurch) | 1968-69 |
| 256 | R.B. Kanhai, West Indies v India (Calcutta) | 1958-59 |
| 256 | K.F. Barrington, England v Australia (Manchester) | 1964 |
| 255* | D.J. McGlew, South Africa v New Zealand (Wellington) | 1952-53 |
| 254 | D.G. Bradman, Australia v England (Leeds) | 1930 |
| 251 | W.R. Hammond, England v Australia (Sydney) | 1928-29 |
| 250 | K.D. Walters, Australia v New Zealand (Christchurch) | 1976-77 |
| 250 | S.F.A.F. Bacchus, West Indies v India (Kanpur) | 1978-79 |

### The highest individual innings for India is:

| | | |
|---|---|---|
| 231 | V.M.H. Mankad, India v New Zealand (Madras) | 1955-56 |

*NB. There are 120 instances of a double-century being scored in a Test Match.*

## HIGHEST RUN AGGREGATES IN A TEST RUBBER

| R | | Season | T | I | NO | HS | Avge | 100s | 50s |
|---|---|---|---|---|---|---|---|---|---|
| 974 | D.G. Bradman (A v E) | 1930 | 5 | 7 | 0 | 334 | 139.14 | 4 | — |
| 905 | W.R. Hammond (E v A) | 1928-29 | 5 | 9 | 1 | 251 | 113.12 | 4 | — |
| 834 | R.N. Harvey (A v SA) | 1952-53 | 5 | 9 | 0 | 205 | 92.66 | 4 | 3 |
| 829 | I.V.A. Richards (WI v E) | 1976 | 4 | 7 | 0 | 291 | 118.42 | 3 | 2 |
| 827 | C.L. Walcott (WI v A) | 1954-55 | 5 | 10 | 0 | 155 | 82.70 | 5 | 2 |
| 824 | G.S. Sobers (WI v P) | 1957-58 | 5 | 8 | 2 | 365* | 137.33 | 3 | 3 |
| 810 | D.G. Bradman (A v SA) | 1936-37 | 5 | 9 | 0 | 270 | 90.00 | 3 | 1 |
| 806 | D.G. Bradman (A v SA) | 1931-32 | 5 | 5 | 1 | 299* | 201.50 | 4 | — |
| 779 | E.D. Weekes (WI v I) | 1948-49 | 5 | 7 | 0 | 194 | 111.28 | 4 | 2 |
| 774 | S.M. Gavaskar (I v WI) | 1970-71 | 4 | 8 | 3 | 220 | 154.80 | 4 | 3 |
| 758 | D.G. Bradman (A v E) | 1934 | 5 | 8 | 0 | 304 | 94.75 | 2 | 1 |
| 753 | D.C.S. Compton (E v SA) | 1947 | 5 | 8 | 0 | 208 | 94.12 | 4 | 2 |

## RECORD WICKET PARTNERSHIPS—ALL TEST CRICKET

| | | | |
|---|---|---|---|
| 1st | 413 | V.M.H. Mankad & P. Roy, I v NZ (Madras) | 1955-56 |
| 2nd | 451 | W.H. Ponsford & D.G. Bradman, A v E (Oval) | 1934 |
| 3rd | 370 | W.J. Edrich & D.C.S. Compton, E v SA (Lord's) | 1947 |
| 4th | 411 | P.B.H. May & M.C. Cowdrey, E v WI (Birmingham) | 1957 |
| 5th | 405 | S.G. Barnes & D.G. Bradman, A v E (Sydney) | 1946-47 |
| 6th | 346 | J.H.W. Fingleton & D.G. Bradman, A v E (Melbourne) | 1936-37 |
| 7th | 347 | D.S. Atkinson & C.C. Depeiza, WI v A (Bridgetown) | 1954-55 |
| 8th | 246 | L.E.G. Ames & G.O.B. Allen, E v NZ (Lord's) | 1931 |
| 9th | 190 | Asif Iqbal & Intikhab Alam, P v E (Oval) | 1967 |
| 10th | 151 | B.F. Hastings & R.O. Collinge, NZ v P (Auckland) | 1972-73 |

## WICKET PARTNERSHIPS OF OVER 300

| | | |
|---|---|---|
| 451 | 2nd W.H. Ponsford & D.G. Bradman, A v E (Oval) | 1934 |
| 446 | 2nd C.C. Hunte & G.S. Sobers, WI v P (Kingston) | 1957-58 |
| 413 | 1st V.M.H. Mankad & P. Roy, I v NZ (Madras) | 1955-56 |
| 411 | 4th P.B.H. May & M.C. Cowdrey, E v WI (Birmingham) | 1957 |
| 405 | 5th S.G. Barnes & D.B. Bradman, A v E (Sydney) | 1946-47 |
| 399 | 4th G.S. Sobers & F.M.M. Worrell, WI v E (Bridgetown) | 1959-60 |
| 388 | 4th W.H. Ponsford & D.G. Bradman, A v E (Leeds) | 1934 |
| 387 | 1st G.M. Turner & T.W Jarvis, NZ v WI (Georgetown) | 1971-72 |
| 382 | 2nd L. Hutton & M. Leyland, E v A (Oval) | 1938 |
| 382 | 1st W.M. Lawry & R.B. Simpson, A v WI (Bridgetown) | 1964-65 |
| 370 | 3rd W.J. Edrich & D.C.S. Compton, E v SA (Lord's) | 1947 |
| 369 | 2nd J.H. Edrich & K.F. Barrington, E v NZ (Leeds) | 1965 |
| 359 | 1st L. Hutton & C. Washbrook, E v SA (Johannesburg) | 1948-49 |
| 350 | 4th Mushtaq Mohammad & Asif Iqbal, P v NZ (Dunedin) | 1972-73 |
| 347 | 7th D.S. Atkinson & C.C. Depeiza, WI v A (Bridgetown) | 1954-55 |
| 346 | 6th J.H.W. Fingleton & D.G. Bradman, A v E (Melbourne) | 1936-37 |
| 344* | 2nd S.M. Gavaskar & D.B. Vengsarkar, I v WI (Calcutta) | 1978-79 |
| 341 | 3rd E.J. Barlow & R.G. Pollock, SA v A (Adelaide) | 1963-64 |
| 338 | 3rd E.D. Weekes & F.M.M. Worrell, WI v E (Port of Spain) | 1953-54 |
| 336 | 4th W.M. Lawry & K.D. Walters, A v WI (Sydney) | 1968-69 |
| 323 | 1st J.B. Hobbs & W. Rhodes, E v A (Melbourne) | 1911-12 |
| 319 | 3rd A. Melville & A.D. Nourse, SA v E (Nottingham) | 1947 |
| 308 | 7th Waqar Hasan & Imtiaz Ahmed, P v NZ (Lahore) | 1955-56 |
| 303 | 3rd I.V.A. Richards & A.I. Kallicharran, WI v E (Nottingham) | 1976 |
| 301 | 2nd A.R. Morris & D.G. Bradman, A v E (Leeds) | 1948 |

## HAT-TRICKS

| | | |
|---|---|---|
| F.R. Spofforth | Australia v England (Melbourne) | 1878-79 |
| W. Bates | England v Australia (Melbourne) | 1882-83 |
| J. Briggs | England v Australia (Sydney) | 1891-92 |
| G.A. Lohmann | England v South Africa (Port Elizabeth) | 1895-96 |
| J.T. Hearne | England v Australia (Leeds) | 1899 |
| H. Trumble | Australia v England (Melbourne) | 1901-02 |
| H. Trumble | Australia v England (Melbourne) | 1903-04 |
| T.J. Matthews (2)* | Australia v South Africa (Manchester) | 1912 |
| M.J.C. Allom† | England v New Zealand (Christchurch) | 1929-30 |
| T.W.J. Goddard | England v South Africa (Johannesburg) | 1938-39 |
| P.J. Loader | England v West Indies (Leeds) | 1957 |
| L.F. Kline | Australia v South Africa (Cape Town) | 1957-58 |
| W.W. Hall | West Indies v Pakistan (Lahore) | 1958-59 |
| G.M. Griffin | South Africa v England (Lord's) | 1960 |
| L.R. Gibbs | West Indies v Australia (Adelaide) | 1960-61 |
| P.J. Petherick | New Zealand v Pakistan (Lahore) | 1976-77 |

*In each innings    †Four wickets in five balls

## NINE OR TEN WICKETS IN AN INNINGS

| | | |
|---|---|---|
| 10-53 | J.C. Laker, England v Australia (Manchester) | 1956 |
| 9-28 | G.A. Lohmann, England v South Africa (Johannesburg) | 1895-96 |
| 9-37 | J.C. Laker, England v Australia (Manchester) | 1956 |
| 9-69 | J.M. Patel, India v Australia (Kanpur) | 1959-60 |
| 9-86 | Sarfraz Nawaz, Pakistan v Australia (Melbourne) | 1978-79 |
| 9-95 | J.M. Noreiga, West Indies v India (Port of Spain) | 1970-71 |
| 9-102 | S.P. Gupte, India v West Indies (Kanpur) | 1958-59 |
| 9-103 | S.F. Barnes, England v South Africa (Johannesburg) | 1913-14 |
| 9-113 | H.J. Tayfield, South Africa v England (Johannesburg) | 1956-57 |
| 9-121 | A.A. Mailey, Australia v England (Melbourne) | 1920-21 |

*NB.   There are 39 instances of a bowler taking 8 wickets in an innings in a Test Match.*

## FIFTEEN OR MORE WICKETS IN A MATCH

| | | |
|---|---|---|
| 19-90 | J.C. Laker, England v Australia (Manchester) | 1956 |
| 17-159 | S.F. Barnes, England v South Africa (Johannesburg) | 1913-14 |
| 16-137 | R.A.L. Massie, Australia v England (Lord's) | 1972 |
| 15-28 | J. Briggs, England v South Africa (Cape Town) | 1888-89 |
| 15-45 | G.A. Lohmann, England v South Africa (Port Elizabeth) | 1895-96 |
| 15-99 | C. Blythe, England v South Africa (Leeds) | 1907 |
| 15-104 | H. Verity, England v Australia (Lord's) | 1934 |
| 15-124 | W. Rhodes, England v Australia (Melbourne) | 1903-04 |

*NB.   There are 7 instances of a bowler taking 14 wickets in a Test Match.*

## HIGHEST WICKET AGGREGATES IN A TEST RUBBER

| Wkts | | Season | Tests | Balls | Mdns | Runs | Avge | 5 wI | 10 M |
|---|---|---|---|---|---|---|---|---|---|
| 49 | S.F. Barnes (E v SA) | 1913-14 | 4 | 1356 | 56 | 536 | 10.93 | 7 | 3 |
| 46 | J.C. Laker (E v A) | 1956 | 5 | 1703 | 127 | 442 | 9.60 | 4 | 2 |
| 44 | C.V. Grimmett (A v SA) | 1935-36 | 5 | 2077 | 140 | 642 | 14.59 | 5 | 3 |
| 41 | R.M. Hogg (A v E) | 1978-79 | 5 | 1740 | 60 | 527 | 12.85 | 5 | 2 |
| 39 | A.V. Bedser (E v A) | 1953 | 5 | 1591 | 48 | 682 | 17.48 | 5 | 1 |
| 38 | M.W. Tate (E v A) | 1924-25 | 5 | 2528 | 62 | 881 | 23.18 | 5 | 1 |
| 37 | W.J. Whitty (A v SA) | 1910-11 | 5 | 1395 | 55 | 632 | 17.08 | 2 | — |
| 37 | H.J. Tayfield (SA v E) | 1956-57 | 5 | 2280 | 105 | 636 | 17.18 | 4 | 1 |
| 36 | A.E.E. Vogler (SA v E) | 1909-10 | 5 | 1349 | 33 | 783 | 21.75 | 4 | 1 |
| 36 | A.A. Mailey (A v E) | 1920-21 | 5 | 1463 | 27 | 946 | 26.27 | 4 | 2 |
| 35 | G.A. Lohmann (E v SA) | 1895-96 | 3 | 520 | 38 | 203 | 5.80 | 4 | 2 |
| 35 | B.S. Chandrasekhar (I v E) | 1972-73 | 5 | 1747 | 83 | 662 | 18.91 | 4 | — |

## MOST WICKET-KEEPING DISMISSALS IN AN INNINGS

| | | |
|---|---|---|
| 7 (7 ct) | Wasim Bari, Pakistan v New Zealand (Auckland) | 1978-79 |
| 7 (7 ct) | R.W. Taylor, England v India (Bombay) | 1979-80 |
| 6 (6 ct) | A.T.W. Grout, Australia v South Africa (Johannesburg) | 1957-58 |
| 6 (6 ct) | D.T. Lindsay, South Africa v Australia (Johannesburg) | 1966-67 |
| 6 (6 ct) | J.T. Murray, England v India (Lord's) | 1967 |
| 6 (5 ct, 1 st) | S.M.H. Kirmani, India v New Zealand (Christchurch) | 1975-76 |

## MOST WICKET-KEEPING DISMISSALS IN A MATCH

| | | |
|---|---|---|
| 10 (10 ct) | R.W. Taylor, England v India (Bombay) | 1979-80 |

## MOST WICKET-KEEPING DISMISSALS IN A SERIES

| | | |
|---|---|---|
| 26 (23 ct, 3 st) | J.H.B. Waite, South Africa v New Zealand | 1961-62 |
| 26 (26 ct) | R.W. Marsh, Australia v West Indies | 1975-76 |
| 24 (22 ct, 2 st) | D.L. Murray, West Indies v England | 1963 |
| 24 (24 ct) | D.T. Lindsay, South Africa v Australia | 1966-67 |
| 24 (21 ct, 3 st) | A.P.E. Knott, England v Australia | 1970-71 |

## HIGHEST WICKET-KEEPING DISMISSAL AGGREGATES

| Total | | Tests | Ct | St |
|---|---|---|---|---|
| 263 | A.P.E. Knott (E) | 93 | 244 | 19 |
| 253 | R.W. Marsh (A) | 68 | 242 | 11 |
| 219 | T.G. Evans (E) | 91 | 173 | 46 |
| 189 | D.L. Murray (WI) | 62 | 181 | 8 |
| 187 | A.T.W. Grout (A) | 51 | 163 | 24 |
| 156 | Wasim Bari (P) | 58 | 137 | 19 |
| 141 | J.H.B. Waite (SA) | 50 | 124 | 17 |
| 130 | W.A.S. Oldfield (A) | 54 | 78 | 52 |
| 114 | J.M. Parks (E) | 46 | 103 | 11 |
| 110 | S.M.H. Kirmani (I) | 45 | 84 | 26 |

*NB. Parks' figures include 2 catches as a fielder.*

## HIGHEST RUN AGGREGATES

| Runs | | | Tests | Inns | NO | HS | Avge | 100s | 50s |
|---|---|---|---|---|---|---|---|---|---|
| 8032 | G.S. Sobers | (WI) | 93 | 160 | 21 | 365* | 57.78 | 26 | 30 |
| 7624 | M.C. Cowdrey | (E) | 114 | 188 | 15 | 182 | 44.06 | 22 | 38 |
| 7249 | W.R. Hammond | (E) | 85 | 140 | 16 | 336* | 58.45 | 22 | 24 |
| 7115 | G. Boycott | (E) | 94 | 165 | 21 | 246* | 49.40 | 19 | 38 |
| 6996 | D.G. Bradman | (A) | 52 | 80 | 10 | 334 | 99.94 | 29 | 13 |
| 6971 | L. Hutton | (E) | 79 | 138 | 15 | 364 | 56.67 | 19 | 33 |
| 6806 | K.F. Barrington | (E) | 82 | 131 | 15 | 256 | 58.67 | 20 | 35 |
| 6227 | R.B. Kanhai | (WI) | 79 | 137 | 6 | 256 | 47.53 | 15 | 28 |
| 6149 | R.N. Harvey | (A) | 79 | 137 | 10 | 205 | 48.41 | 21 | 24 |
| 6092 | S.M. Gavaskar | (I) | 66 | 120 | 8 | 22 | 54.39 | 23 | 26 |
| 5807 | D.C.S. Compton | (E) | 78 | 131 | 15 | 278 | 50.06 | 17 | 28 |
| 5719 | G.S. Chappell | (A) | 67 | 119 | 15 | 247* | 54.99 | 18 | 28 |
| 5410 | J.B. Hobbs | (E) | 61 | 102 | 7 | 211 | 56.94 | 15 | 28 |
| 5357 | K.D. Walters | (A) | 74 | 125 | 14 | 250 | 48.26 | 15 | 33 |
| 5345 | I.M. Chappell | (A) | 75 | 136 | 10 | 196 | 42.42 | 14 | 26 |
| 5234 | W.M. Lawry | (A) | 67 | 123 | 12 | 210 | 47.15 | 13 | 27 |
| 5216 | G.R. Viswanath | (I) | 72 | 127 | 9 | 179 | 44.20 | 12 | 30 |
| 5173 | C.H. Lloyd | (WI) | 78 | 132 | 9 | 242* | 42.05 | 13 | 23 |
| 5138 | J.H. Edrich | (E) | 77 | 127 | 9 | 310* | 43.54 | 12 | 24 |
| 4882 | T.W. Graveney | (E) | 79 | 123 | 13 | 258 | 44.38 | 11 | 20 |
| 4869 | R.B. Simpson | (A) | 62 | 111 | 7 | 311 | 46.81 | 10 | 27 |
| 4737 | I.R. Redpath | (A) | 66 | 120 | 11 | 171 | 43.45 | 8 | 31 |
| 4555 | H. Sutcliffe | (E) | 54 | 84 | 9 | 194 | 60.73 | 16 | 23 |
| 4537 | P.B.H. May | (E) | 56 | 106 | 9 | 285* | 46.77 | 13 | 22 |
| 4502 | E.R. Dexter | (E) | 62 | 102 | 8 | 205 | 47.89 | 9 | 27 |
| 4455 | E.D. Weekes | (WI) | 48 | 81 | 5 | 207 | 58.61 | 15 | 19 |
| 4399 | A.I. Kallicharran | (WI) | 66 | 109 | 10 | 187 | 44.43 | 12 | 21 |
| 4334 | R.C. Fredericks | (WI) | 59 | 109 | 7 | 169 | 42.49 | 8 | 26 |
| 4211 | A.P.E. Knott | (E) | 93 | 145 | 14 | 135 | 32.14 | 5 | 28 |
| 3915 | Hanif Mohammad | (P) | 55 | 97 | 8 | 337 | 43.98 | 12 | 15 |
| 3860 | F.M.M. Worrell | (WI) | 51 | 87 | 9 | 261 | 49.48 | 9 | 22 |
| 3798 | C.L. Walcott | (WI) | 44 | 74 | 7 | 220 | 56.68 | 15 | 14 |
| 3716 | Majid Khan | (P) | 57 | 97 | 5 | 167 | 40.39 | 8 | 17 |
| 3643 | Mushtaq Mohammad | (P) | 57 | 100 | 7 | 201 | 39.17 | 10 | 19 |
| 3631 | P.R. Umrigar | (I) | 59 | 94 | 8 | 223 | 42.22 | 12 | 14 |
| 3629 | I.V.A. Richards | (WI) | 40 | 63 | 3 | 291 | 60.48 | 11 | 16 |
| 3612 | D.L. Amiss | (E) | 50 | 88 | 10 | 262* | 46.30 | 11 | 11 |

214

| Runs | | | Tests | Inns | NO | HS | Avge | 100s | 50s |
|---|---|---|---|---|---|---|---|---|---|
| 3599 | A.W. Greig | (E) | 58 | 93 | 4 | 148 | 40.43 | 8 | 20 |
| 3575 | Asif Iqbal | (P) | 58 | 99 | 7 | 175 | 38.85 | 11 | 12 |
| 3533 | A.R. Morris | (A) | 46 | 79 | 3 | 206 | 46.48 | 12 | 12 |
| 3525 | E.H. Hendren | (E) | 51 | 83 | 9 | 205* | 47.63 | 7 | 21 |
| 3471 | B. Mitchell | (SA) | 42 | 80 | 9 | 189* | 48.88 | 8 | 21 |
| 3448 | B.E. Congdon | (NZ) | 61 | 114 | 7 | 176 | 32.22 | 7 | 19 |
| 3428 | J.R. Reid | (NZ) | 58 | 108 | 5 | 142 | 33.28 | 6 | 22 |
| 3412 | C. Hill | (A) | 49 | 89 | 2 | 191 | 39.21 | 7 | 19 |
| 3283 | F.E. Woolley | (E) | 64 | 98 | 7 | 154 | 36.07 | 5 | 23 |
| 3245 | C.C. Hunte | (WI) | 44 | 78 | 6 | 260 | 45.06 | 8 | 13 |
| 3208 | V.L. Manjrekar | (I) | 55 | 92 | 10 | 189* | 39.12 | 7 | 15 |
| 3163 | V.T. Trumper | (A) | 48 | 89 | 8 | 214* | 39.04 | 8 | 13 |
| 3106 | C.C. McDonald | (A) | 47 | 83 | 4 | 170 | 39.31 | 5 | 17 |
| 3104 | B.F. Butcher | (WI) | 44 | 78 | 6 | 209* | 43.11 | 7 | 16 |
| 3073 | A.L. Hassett | (A) | 43 | 69 | 3 | 198* | 46.56 | 10 | 11 |
| 3061 | C.G. Borde | (I) | 55 | 97 | 11 | 177* | 35.59 | 5 | 18 |

## HIGHEST WICKET AGGREGATES

| Wkts | | | Tests | Balls | Mdns | Runs | Avge | 5 wI | 10 wM |
|---|---|---|---|---|---|---|---|---|---|
| 309 | L.R. Gibbs | (WI) | 79 | 27115 | 1313 | 8989 | 29.09 | 18 | 2 |
| 307 | F.S. Trueman | (E) | 67 | 15178 | 522 | 6625 | 21.57 | 17 | 3 |
| 279 | D.L. Underwood | (E) | 79 | 20159 | 1119 | 7141 | 25.59 | 16 | 6 |
| 266 | B.S. Bedi | (I) | 67 | 21364 | 1096 | 7637 | 28.71 | 14 | 1 |
| 252 | J.B. Statham | (E) | 70 | 16056 | 595 | 6261 | 24.84 | 9 | 1 |
| 251 | D.K. Lillee | (A) | 48 | 12778 | 418 | 5866 | 23.37 | 17 | 5 |
| 248 | R. Benaud | (A) | 63 | 19090 | 805 | 6704 | 27.03 | 16 | 1 |
| 246 | G.D. McKenzie | (A) | 60 | 17681 | 547 | 7238 | 29.78 | 16 | 3 |
| 242 | B.S. Chandrasekhar | (I) | 58 | 15963 | 584 | 7199 | 29.74 | 16 | 2 |
| 236 | A.V. Bedser | (E) | 51 | 15923 | 572 | 5876 | 24.89 | 15 | 5 |
| 235 | G.S. Sobers | (WI) | 93 | 21599 | 995 | 7999 | 34.03 | 6 | — |
| 228 | R.R. Lindwall | (A) | 61 | 13666 | 418 | 5257 | 23.05 | 12 | — |
| 216 | C.V. Grimmett | (A) | 37 | 14513 | 735 | 5231 | 24.21 | 21 | 7 |
| 202 | J.A. Snow | (E) | 49 | 12021 | 415 | 5387 | 26.66 | 8 | 1 |
| 198 | R.G.D. Willis | (E) | 57 | 10871 | 319 | 5043 | 25.46 | 12 | — |
| 193 | J.C. Laker | (E) | 46 | 12009 | 673 | 4099 | 21.23 | 9 | 3 |
| 192 | W.W. Hall | (WI) | 48 | 10415 | 312 | 5066 | 26.38 | 9 | 1 |
| 189 | S.F. Barnes | (E) | 27 | 7873 | 356 | 3106 | 16.43 | 24 | 7 |
| 189 | E.A.S. Prasanna | (I) | 49 | 14353 | 602 | 5742 | 30.38 | 10 | 2 |
| 186 | A.K. Davidson | (A) | 44 | 11665 | 432 | 3838 | 20.58 | 14 | 2 |
| 174 | G.A.R. Lock | (E) | 49 | 13147 | 819 | 4451 | 25.58 | 9 | 3 |
| 170 | K.R. Miller | (A) | 55 | 10474 | 338 | 3905 | 22.97 | 7 | 1 |
| 170 | H.J. Tayfield | (SA) | 37 | 13568 | 602 | 4405 | 25.91 | 14 | 2 |
| 162 | V.M.H. Mankad | (I) | 44 | 14686 | 777 | 5235 | 32.31 | 8 | 2 |
| 160 | W.A. Johnston | (A) | 40 | 11048 | 370 | 3825 | 23.90 | 7 | — |
| 159 | A.M.E. Roberts | (WI) | 35 | 8594 | 280 | 4052 | 25.48 | 10 | 2 |
| 158 | S. Ramadhin | (WI) | 43 | 13939 | 813 | 4579 | 28.98 | 10 | 1 |
| 155 | M.W. Tate | (E) | 39 | 12523 | 581 | 4055 | 26.16 | 7 | 1 |
| 153 | I.T. Botham | (E) | 31 | 7202 | 288 | 3092 | 20.20 | 14 | 3 |
| 153 | F.J. Titmus | (E) | 53 | 15118 | 777 | 4931 | 32.22 | 7 | — |
| 152 | J.R. Thomson | (A) | 34 | 7512 | 210 | 3892 | 25.60 | 6 | — |

# MOST TEST APPEARANCES FOR EACH COUNTRY

*NB. The abandoned match at Melbourne in 1970-71 is excluded from these figures.*

| England | | Australia | |
|---|---|---|---|
| M.C. Cowdrey | 114 | R.N. Harvey | 79 |
| G. Boycott | 94 | I.M. Chappell | 75 |
| A.P.E. Knott | 93 | K.D. Walters | 74 |
| T.G. Evans | 91 | R.W. Marsh | 68 |
| W.R. Hammond | 85 | G.S. Chappell | 67 |
| K.F. Barrington | 82 | W.M. Lawry | 67 |
| T.W. Graveney | 79 | I.R. Redpath | 66 |
| L. Hutton | 79 | R. Benaud | 63 |
| D.L. Underwood | 79 | R.B. Simpson | 62 |
| D.C.S. Compton | 78 | R.R. Lindwall | 61 |
| J.H. Edrich | 77 | G.D. McKenzie | 60 |
| J.B. Statham | 70 | S.E. Gregory | 58 |
| F.S. Trueman | 67 | K.R. Miller | 55 |
| P.B.H. May | 66 | W.A.S. Oldfield | 54 |
| F.E. Woolley | 64 | D.G. Bradman | 52 |
| E.R. Dexter | 62 | A.T.W. Grout | 51 |
| T.E. Bailey | 61 | W.W. Armstrong | 50 |
| J.B. Hobbs | 61 | | |
| R. Illingworth | 61 | | |

| South Africa | | West Indies | |
|---|---|---|---|
| J.H.B. Waite | 50 | G.S. Sobers | 93 |
| A.W. Nourse | 45 | L.R. Gibbs | 79 |
| B. Mitchell | 42 | R.B. Kanhai | 79 |
| H.W. Taylor | 42 | C.H. Lloyd | 78 |
| T.L. Goddard | 41 | A.I. Kallicharran | 66 |
| R.A. McLean | 40 | D.L. Murray | 62 |
| H.J. Tayfield | 37 | R.C. Fredericks | 59 |
| D.J. McGlew | 34 | F.M.M. Worrell | 51 |
| A.D. Nourse | 34 | W.W. Hall | 48 |
| E.J. Barlow | 30 | E.D. Weekes | 48 |
| W.R. Endean | 28 | B.F. Butcher | 44 |
| P.M. Pollock | 28 | C.C. Hunte | 44 |
| K.G. Viljoen | 27 | C.L. Walcott | 44 |
| H.B. Cameron | 26 | S. Ramadhin | 43 |
| E.A.B. Rowan | 26 | V.A. Holder | 40 |
| S.J. Snooke | 26 | I.V.A. Richards | 40 |

| New Zealand | | India | |
|---|---|---|---|
| B.E. Congdon | 61 | G.R. Viswanath | 72 |
| J.R. Reid | 58 | B.S. Bedi | 67 |
| M.G. Burgess | 50 | S.M. Gavaskar | 66 |
| B. Sutcliffe | 42 | P.R. Umrigar | 59 |
| G.T. Dowling | 39 | B.S. Chandrasekhar | 58 |
| G.M. Turner | 39 | C.G. Borde | 55 |
| J.M. Parker | 36 | V.L. Manjrekar | 55 |
| R.O. Collinge | 35 | S. Venkataraghavan | 50 |
| K.J. Wadsworth | 33 | E.A.S. Prasanna | 49 |
| R.J. Hadlee | 32 | F.M. Engineer | 46 |
| R.C. Motz | 32 | M.A.K. Pataudi | 46 |
| V. Pollard | 32 | S.M.H. Kirmani | 45 |
| B.F. Hastings | 31 | V.M.H. Mankad | 44 |
| H.J. Howarth | 30 | P. Roy | 43 |
| B.R. Taylor | 30 | R.G. Nadkarni | 41 |

| Pakistan | |
|---|---|
| Asif Iqbal | 58 |
| Wasim Bari | 58 |
| Majid Khan | 57 |
| Mushtaq Mohammad | 57 |
| Hanif Mohammad | 55 |
| Intikhab Alam | 47 |
| Zaheer Abbas | 43 |
| Imtiaz Ahmed | 41 |
| Sadiq Mohammad | 41 |
| Saeed Ahmed | 41 |
| Sarfraz Nawaz | 39 |
| Wasim Raja | 37 |
| Fazal Mahmood | 34 |
| Javed Miandad | 34 |
| Imran Khan | 33 |

# Twin blade winner.

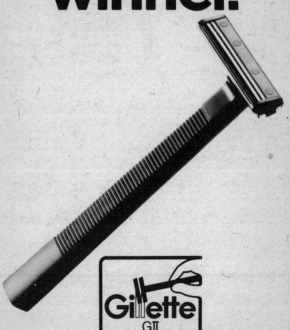

Gillette
G II

# TEST CAREER RECORDS

### (including Australia v New Zealand and India and Pakistan v West Indies in 1980-81)

## compiled by Barry McCaully

## ENGLAND

**BATTING AND FIELDING**

| | M | I | NO | Runs | HS | Avge | 100 | 50 | Ct | St |
|---|---|---|---|---|---|---|---|---|---|---|
| C.W.J. Athey | 1 | 2 | 0 | 10 | 9 | 5.00 | — | — | 1 | — |
| D.L. Amiss | 50 | 88 | 10 | 3612 | 262* | 46.30 | 11 | 11 | 24 | — |
| D.L. Bairstow | 3 | 5 | 1 | 123 | 59 | 30.75 | — | 1 | 7 | 1 |
| J.C. Balderstone | 2 | 4 | 0 | 39 | 35 | 9.75 | — | — | 1 | — |
| G.D. Barlow | 3 | 5 | 1 | 17 | 7* | 4.25 | — | — | — | — |
| I.T. Botham | 31 | 45 | 2 | 1505 | 137 | 35.00 | 6 | 4 | 38 | — |
| G. Boycott | 94 | 165 | 21 | 7115 | 246* | 49.40 | 19 | 38 | 27 | — |
| J.M. Brearley | 35 | 58 | 3 | 1301 | 91 | 23.65 | — | 8 | 48 | — |
| A.R. Butcher | 1 | 2 | 0 | 34 | 20 | 17.00 | — | — | — | — |
| G.A. Cope | 3 | 3 | 0 | 40 | 22 | 13.33 | — | — | 1 | — |
| G.R. Dilley | 5 | 8 | 2 | 82 | 38* | 13.66 | — | — | 2 | — |
| P.H. Edmonds | 18 | 21 | 5 | 277 | 50 | 17.31 | — | 1 | 21 | — |
| J.E. Emburey | 10 | 15 | 3 | 150 | 42 | 12.50 | — | — | 10 | — |
| K.W.R. Fletcher | 52 | 85 | 11 | 2975 | 216 | 40.20 | 7 | 16 | 46 | — |
| M.W. Gatting | 7 | 12 | 1 | 246 | 56 | 22.36 | — | 2 | 5 | — |
| G.A. Gooch | 26 | 45 | 3 | 1401 | 123 | 33.35 | 1 | 10 | 27 | — |
| D.I. Gower | 22 | 35 | 3 | 1416 | 200* | 44.25 | 3 | 6 | 10 | — |
| F.C. Hayes | 9 | 17 | 1 | 244 | 106* | 15.25 | 1 | — | 7 | — |
| M. Hendrick | 28 | 32 | 12 | 122 | 15 | 6.10 | — | — | 25 | — |
| A.P.E. Knott | 93 | 145 | 14 | 4211 | 135 | 32.14 | 5 | 28 | 244 | 19 |
| W. Larkins | 5 | 9 | 0 | 118 | 33 | 13.11 | — | — | 3 | — |
| J.K. Lever | 18 | 27 | 4 | 303 | 53 | 13.17 | — | 1 | 11 | — |
| G. Miller | 24 | 32 | 3 | 817 | 98* | 28.17 | — | 5 | 10 | — |
| C.M. Old | 43 | 60 | 8 | 781 | 65 | 15.01 | — | 2 | 22 | — |
| P.I. Pocock | 17 | 27 | 2 | 165 | 33 | 6.60 | — | — | 13 | — |
| C.T. Radley | 8 | 10 | 0 | 481 | 158 | 48.10 | 2 | 2 | 4 | — |
| D.W. Randall | 27 | 45 | 4 | 1125 | 174 | 27.43 | 2 | 6 | 18 | — |
| G.R.J. Roope | 21 | 32 | 4 | 860 | 77 | 30.71 | — | 7 | 35 | — |
| B.C. Rose | 8 | 14 | 2 | 343 | 70 | 28.58 | — | 2 | 4 | — |
| M.W.W. Selvey | 3 | 5 | 3 | 15 | 5* | 7.50 | — | — | 1 | — |
| D.S. Steele | 8 | 16 | 0 | 673 | 106 | 42.06 | 1 | 5 | 7 | — |
| G.B. Stevenson | 1 | 1 | 1 | 27 | 27* | — | — | — | — | — |
| C.J. Tavare | 2 | 4 | 0 | 65 | 42 | 16.25 | — | — | 2 | — |
| R.W. Taylor | 26 | 33 | 3 | 620 | 97 | 20.66 | — | 2 | 79 | 6 |
| R.W. Tolchard | 4 | 7 | 2 | 129 | 67 | 25.80 | — | 1 | 5 | — |
| D.L. Underwood | 79 | 108 | 31 | 899 | 45* | 11.67 | — | — | 43 | — |
| P. Willey | 12 | 22 | 2 | 500 | 100* | 25.00 | 1 | 2 | 3 | — |
| R.G.D. Willis | 57 | 80 | 38 | 512 | 24* | 12.19 | — | — | 22 | — |
| B. Wood | 12 | 21 | 0 | 454 | 90 | 21.61 | — | 2 | 6 | — |
| R.A. Woolmer | 17 | 30 | 2 | 1029 | 149 | 36.75 | 3 | 2 | 8 | — |

| | Balls | Runs | Wkts | Avge | Best | 5 wI | 10 wM |
|---|---|---|---|---|---|---|---|
| J.C. Balderstone | 96 | 80 | 1 | 80.00 | 1-80 | — | — |
| I.T. Botham | 7202 | 3092 | 153 | 20.20 | 8-34 | 14 | 3 |
| G. Boycott | 908 | 375 | 7 | 53.57 | 3-47 | — | — |
| A.R. Butcher | 12 | 9 | 0 | — | — | — | — |
| G.A. Cope | 864 | 277 | 8 | 34.62 | 3-102 | — | — |
| G.R. Dilley | 762 | 326 | 14 | 23.28 | 4-57 | — | — |
| P.H. Edmonds | 4083 | 1251 | 49 | 25.53 | 7-66 | 2 | — |
| J.E. Emburey | 1850 | 568 | 25 | 22.72 | 4-46 | — | — |
| K.W.R. Fletcher | 249 | 173 | 1 | 173.00 | 1-48 | — | — |
| M.W. Gatting | 8 | 1 | 0 | — | — | — | — |
| G.A. Gooch | 594 | 207 | 6 | 34.50 | 2-16 | — | — |
| M. Hendrick | 5606 | 2027 | 81 | 25.02 | 4-28 | — | — |
| J.K. Lever | 3677 | 1581 | 60 | 26.35 | 7-46 | 2 | 1 |
| G. Miller | 3693 | 1200 | 42 | 28.57 | 5-44 | 1 | — |
| C.M. Old | 8258 | 3796 | 137 | 27.70 | 7-50 | 4 | — |
| P.I. Pocock | 4482 | 2023 | 47 | 43.04 | 6-79 | 3 | — |
| D.W. Randall | 16 | 3 | 0 | — | — | — | — |
| G.R.J. Roope | 172 | 76 | 0 | — | — | — | — |
| M.W.W. Selvey | 492 | 343 | 6 | 57.16 | 4-41 | — | — |
| D.S. Steele | 88 | 39 | 2 | 19.50 | 1-1 | — | — |
| G.B. Stevenson | 114 | 72 | 2 | 36.00 | 2-59 | — | — |
| D.L. Underwood | 20159 | 7141 | 279 | 25.59 | 8-51 | 16 | 6 |
| P. Willey | 689 | 295 | 4 | 73.75 | 2-73 | — | — |
| R.G.D. Willis | 10871 | 5043 | 198 | 25.46 | 7-78 | 12 | — |
| B. Wood | 98 | 50 | 0 | — | — | — | — |
| R.A. Woolmer | 546 | 299 | 4 | 74.75 | 1-8 | — | — |

# AUSTRALIA

## BATTING AND FIELDING

| | M | I | NO | Runs | HS | Avge | 100 | 50 | Ct | St |
|---|---|---|---|---|---|---|---|---|---|---|
| G.R. Beard | 3 | 5 | — | 114 | 49 | 22.80 | — | — | — | — |
| A.R. Boarder | 27 | 49 | 8 | 2060 | 162 | 50.24 | 6 | 11 | 29 | — |
| R.J. Bright | 9 | 14 | 4 | 142 | 26* | 14.20 | — | — | 3 | — |
| G.S. Chappell | 67 | 119 | 15 | 5719 | 247* | 54.99 | 18 | 28 | 97 | — |
| W.M. Darling | 14 | 27 | 1 | 697 | 91 | 26.80 | — | 6 | 5 | — |
| G. Dymock | 21 | 32 | 7 | 236 | 31* | 9.44 | — | — | 1 | — |
| J. Dyson | 9 | 17 | 2 | 314 | 53 | 20.93 | — | 1 | 1 | — |
| J.D. Higgs | 22 | 36 | 16 | 111 | 16 | 5.55 | — | — | 3 | — |
| A.M.J. Hilditch | 9 | 18 | 0 | 452 | 85 | 25.11 | — | 4 | 9 | — |
| R.M. Hogg | 20 | 33 | 3 | 246 | 36 | 8.20 | — | — | 4 | — |
| D.W. Hookes | 8 | 15 | 0 | 436 | 85 | 29.06 | — | 3 | 2 | — |
| K.J. Hughes | 33 | 60 | 4 | 2373 | 213 | 42.37 | 5 | 13 | 28 | — |
| A.G. Hurst | 12 | 20 | 3 | 102 | 26 | 6.00 | — | — | 3 | — |

| | M | I | NO | Runs | HS | Avge | 100 | 50 | Ct | St |
|---|---|---|---|---|---|---|---|---|---|---|
| B.M. Laird | 9 | 17 | 0 | 611 | 92 | 35.94 | — | 6 | 3 | — |
| G.F. Lawson | 1 | 1 | 0 | 16 | 16 | 16.00 | — | — | — | — |
| D.K. Lillee | 48 | 62 | 17 | 651 | 73* | 14.46 | — | 1 | 13 | — |
| R.B. McCosker | 25 | 46 | 5 | 1622 | 127 | 39.56 | 4 | 9 | 21 | — |
| A.A. Mallett | 38 | 50 | 13 | 430 | 43* | 11.62 | — | — | 30 | — |
| R.W. Marsh | 68 | 107 | 11 | 2828 | 132 | 29.45 | 3 | 14 | 242 | 11 |
| L.S. Pascoe | 13 | 17 | 8 | 96 | 30* | 10.66 | — | — | 2 | — |
| S.J. Rixon | 10 | 19 | 3 | 341 | 54 | 21.31 | — | 2 | 31 | 4 |
| P.R. Sleep | 3 | 6 | 0 | 95 | 64 | 15.83 | — | 1 | — | — |
| J.R. Thomson | 34 | 46 | 9 | 433 | 49 | 11.70 | — | 14 | — | — |
| P.M. Toohey | 15 | 29 | 1 | 893 | 122 | 31.89 | 1 | 7 | 9 | — |
| M.H.N. Walker | 34 | 43 | 13 | 586 | 78* | 19.53 | — | 1 | 12 | — |
| K.D. Walters | 74 | 125 | 14 | 5357 | 250 | 48.26 | 15 | 33 | 43 | — |
| D.F. Whatmore | 7 | 13 | 0 | 293 | 77 | 22.53 | — | 2 | 13 | — |
| J.M. Wiener | 6 | 11 | 0 | 281 | 93 | 25.54 | — | 2 | 4 | — |
| G.M. Wood | 22 | 43 | 2 | 1394 | 126 | 34.00 | 5 | 5 | 21 | — |
| K.J. Wright | 10 | 18 | 5 | 219 | 55* | 16.84 | — | 1 | 31 | 4 |
| G.N. Yallop | 25 | 47 | 3 | 1727 | 172 | 39.25 | 5 | 6 | 9 | — |
| B. Yardley | 16 | 30 | 4 | 597 | 74 | 22.96 | — | 3 | 14 | — |

## BOWLING

| | Balls | Runs | Wkts | Avge | Best | 5 wI | 10 wM |
|---|---|---|---|---|---|---|---|
| G.R. Beard | 259 | 109 | 1 | 109.00 | 1-26 | — | — |
| A.R. Border | 938 | 298 | 8 | 37.25 | 2-35 | — | — |
| R.J. Bright | 1956 | 736 | 22 | 33.45 | 7-87 | 2 | 1 |
| G.S. Chappell | 4580 | 1638 | 43 | 38.09 | 5-61 | 1 | — |
| G. Dymock | 5545 | 2116 | 78 | 27.12 | 7-67 | 5 | 1 |
| J.D. Higgs | 4752 | 2057 | 66 | 31.16 | 7-143 | 2 | — |
| R.M. Hogg | 4408 | 1814 | 78 | 23.25 | 6-74 | 5 | 2 |
| D.W. Hookes | 30 | 15 | 0 | — | — | — | — |
| K.J. Hughes | 66 | 20 | 0 | — | — | — | — |
| A.G. Hurst | 3054 | 1200 | 43 | 27.90 | 5-28 | 2 | — |
| B.M. Laird | 12 | 3 | 0 | — | — | — | — |
| G.F. Lawson | 120 | 65 | 3 | 21.66 | 2-26 | — | — |
| D.K. Lillee | 12778 | 5866 | 251 | 23.37 | 6-26 | 17 | 5 |
| A.A. Mallett | 9990 | 3940 | 132 | 29.84 | 8-59 | 6 | 1 |
| R.W. Marsh | 60 | 51 | 0 | — | — | — | — |
| L.S. Pascoe | 3091 | 1490 | 60 | 24.83 | 5-59 | 1 | — |
| P.R. Sleep | 373 | 223 | 2 | 111.50 | 1-16 | — | — |
| J.R. Thomson | 7512 | 3892 | 152 | 25.60 | 6-46 | 6 | — |
| P.M. Toohey | 2 | 4 | 0 | — | — | — | — |
| M.H.N. Walker | 10094 | 3792 | 138 | 27.47 | 8-143 | 6 | — |
| K.D. Walters | 3295 | 1425 | 49 | 29.08 | 5-66 | 1 | — |
| D.F. Whatmore | 30 | 11 | 0 | — | — | — | — |
| J.M. Wiener | 78 | 41 | 0 | — | — | — | — |
| G.N. Yallop | 144 | 99 | 1 | 99.00 | 1-21 | — | — |
| B. Yardley | 4207 | 1662 | 44 | 37.77 | 4-35 | — | — |

# WEST INDIES

## BATTING AND FIELDING

| | M | I | NO | Runs | HS | Avge | 100 | 50 | Ct | St |
|---|---|---|---|---|---|---|---|---|---|---|
| Imtiaz Ali | 1 | 1 | 1 | 1* | | | — | — | — | — |
| Inshan Ali | 12 | 18 | 2 | 172 | 25 | 10.75 | — | — | 7 | — |
| R.A. Austin | 2 | 2 | 0 | 22 | 20 | 11.00 | — | — | 2 | — |
| S.F.A.F. Bacchus | 17 | 26 | 0 | 754 | 250 | 29.00 | 1 | 3 | 15 | — |
| L. Baichan | 3 | 6 | 2 | 184 | 105* | 46.00 | 1 | — | 2 | — |
| H.S. Chang | 1 | 2 | 0 | 8 | 6 | 4.00 | — | — | — | — |
| S.T. Clarke | 10 | 14 | 5 | 153 | 35* | 17.00 | — | — | 2 | — |
| C.E.H. Croft | 20 | 27 | 16 | 100 | 23* | 9.09 | — | — | 7 | — |
| W.W. Daniel | 5 | 5 | 2 | 29 | 11 | 9.66 | — | — | 2 | — |
| J. Garner | 21 | 27 | 2 | 296 | 60 | 11.84 | — | 1 | 15 | — |
| H.A. Gomes | 15 | 24 | 0 | 826 | 115 | 34.41 | 2 | 5 | 2 | — |
| A.T. Greenidge | 6 | 10 | 0 | 222 | 69 | 22.20 | — | 2 | 5 | — |
| C.G. Greenidge | 30 | 54 | 3 | 2212 | 134 | 43.37 | 5 | 14 | 32 | — |
| D.L. Haynes | 17 | 27 | 1 | 1072 | 184 | 41.23 | 3 | 5 | 9 | — |
| M.A. Holding | 24 | 35 | 7 | 324 | 55 | 11.57 | — | 1 | 6 | — |
| R.R. Jumadeen | 12 | 14 | 10 | 84 | 56 | 21.00 | — | 1 | 4 | — |
| A.I. Kallicharran | 66 | 109 | 10 | 4399 | 187 | 44.43 | 12 | 21 | 51 | — |
| C.L. King | 9 | 16 | 3 | 418 | 100* | 32.15 | 1 | 2 | 5 | — |
| C.H. Lloyd | 78 | 132 | 9 | 5173 | 242* | 42.05 | 13 | 23 | 55 | — |
| M.D. Marshall | 11 | 15 | 1 | 111 | 45 | 7.92 | — | — | 4 | — |
| D.A. Murray | 13 | 22 | 1 | 470 | 84 | 22.38 | — | 3 | 32 | 5 |
| D.L. Murray | 62 | 96 | 9 | 1993 | 91 | 22.90 | — | 11 | 181 | 8 |
| R. Nanan | 1 | 2 | 0 | 16 | 8 | 8.00 | — | — | 2 | — |
| A.L. Padmore | 2 | 2 | 1 | 8 | 8* | 8.00 | — | — | — | — |
| D.R. Parry | 12 | 20 | 3 | 381 | 65 | 22.41 | — | 3 | 4 | — |
| N. Phillip | 9 | 15 | 5 | 297 | 47 | 29.70 | — | — | 5 | — |
| I.V.A. Richards | 40 | 63 | 3 | 3629 | 291 | 60.48 | 11 | 16 | 44 | — |
| A.M.E. Roberts | 35 | 47 | 8 | 463 | 54 | 11.87 | — | 1 | 7 | — |
| L.G. Rowe | 30 | 49 | 2 | 2047 | 302 | 43.55 | 7 | 7 | 47 | — |
| I.T. Shillingford | 4 | 7 | 0 | 218 | 120 | 31.14 | 1 | — | 1 | — |
| S. Shivnarine | 8 | 14 | 1 | 379 | 63 | 29.15 | — | 4 | 6 | — |
| A.B. Williams | 7 | 12 | 0 | 469 | 111 | 39.08 | 2 | 1 | 5 | — |

## BOWLING

| | Balls | Runs | Wkts | Avge | Best | 5 wI | 10 wM |
|---|---|---|---|---|---|---|---|
| Imtiaz Ali | 204 | 89 | 2 | 44.50 | 2-37 | — | — |
| Inshan Ali | 3718 | 1621 | 34 | 47.67 | 5-59 | 1 | — |
| R.A. Austin | 6 | 5 | 0 | | | — | — |
| S.F.A.F. Bacchus | 6 | 3 | 0 | | | — | — |
| S.T. Clarke | 2285 | 1095 | 41 | 26.70 | 5-126 | 1 | — |
| C.E.H. Croft | 4389 | 2097 | 94 | 22.30 | 8-29 | 1 | — |
| W.W. Daniel | 788 | 381 | 15 | 25.44 | 4-53 | — | — |
| J. Garner | 5008 | 1982 | 102 | 19.43 | 6-56 | 1 | — |
| H.A. Gomes | 252 | 122 | 1 | 122.00 | 1-54 | — | — |
| C.G. Greenidge | 26 | 4 | 0 | | | — | — |

| | Balls | Runs | Wkts | Avge | Best | 5 wI | 10 wM |
|---|---|---|---|---|---|---|---|
| D.L. Haynes | 12 | 4 | 1 | 4.00 | 1-2 | — | — |
| M.A. Holding | 5525 | 2535 | 98 | 25.86 | 8-92 | 5 | 1 |
| R.R. Jumadeen | 3140 | 1141 | 29 | 39.34 | 4-72 | — | — |
| A.I. Kallicharran | 406 | 158 | 4 | 39.50 | 2-16 | — | — |
| C.L. King | 582 | 282 | 3 | 94.00 | 1-30 | — | — |
| C.H. Llyod | 1716 | 622 | 10 | 62.20 | 2-13 | — | — |
| M.D. Marshall | 2094 | 1019 | 31 | 32.87 | 4-25 | — | — |
| R. Nanan | 216 | 91 | 4 | 22.75 | 2-37 | — | — |
| A.L. Padmore | 474 | 135 | 1 | 135.00 | 1-36 | — | — |
| D.R. Parry | 1909 | 936 | 23 | 40.69 | 5-15 | 1 | — |
| N. Phillip | 1820 | 1041 | 28 | 37.17 | 4-48 | — | — |
| I.V.A. Richards | 1030 | 388 | 8 | 48.50 | 2-20 | — | — |
| A.M.E. Roberts | 8594 | 4052 | 159 | 25.48 | 7-54 | 10 | 2 |
| L.G. Rowe | 86 | 44 | 0 | | | — | — |
| S. Shivnarine | 336 | 167 | 1 | 167.00 | 1-13 | — | — |

## NEW ZEALAND

### BATTING AND FIELDING

| | M | I | NO | Runs | HS | Avge | 100 | 50 | Ct | St |
|---|---|---|---|---|---|---|---|---|---|---|
| R.W. Anderson | 9 | 18 | 0 | 423 | 92 | 23.50 | — | 3 | 1 | — |
| S.L. Boock | 12 | 19 | 6 | 37 | 8 | 2.84 | — | — | 8 | — |
| B.P. Bracewell | 5 | 10 | 2 | 17 | 8 | 2.12 | — | — | 1 | — |
| J.G. Bracewell | 3 | 5 | 1 | 28 | 16 | 7.00 | — | — | 2 | — |
| M.G. Burgess | 50 | 92 | 6 | 2684 | 119* | 31.20 | 5 | 14 | 34 | — |
| B.L. Cairns | 20 | 34 | 5 | 435 | 52* | 15.00 | — | 1 | 14 | — |
| E.J. Chatfield | 4 | 7 | 3 | 31 | 13* | 7.75 | — | — | 2 | — |
| J.V. Coney | 12 | 21 | 3 | 634 | 82 | 35.22 | — | 5 | 15 | — |
| B.A. Edgar | 12 | 22 | 1 | 654 | 129 | 31.14 | 2 | 3 | 8 | — |
| G.N. Edwards | 5 | 10 | 0 | 244 | 55 | 24.40 | — | 3 | 7 | — |
| D.R. Hadlee | 26 | 42 | 5 | 530 | 56 | 14.32 | — | 1 | 8 | — |
| R.J. Hadlee | 32 | 57 | 7 | 1120 | 103 | 22.40 | 1 | 5 | 16 | — |
| G.P. Howarth | 22 | 41 | 3 | 1433 | 147 | 37.71 | 5 | 5 | 11 | — |
| W.K. Lees | 17 | 31 | 3 | 642 | 152 | 22.92 | 1 | — | 35 | 7 |
| P.E.McEwan | 3 | 6 | 0 | 56 | 21 | 9.33 | — | — | 2 | — |
| J.F.M. Morrison | 14 | 24 | 0 | 610 | 117 | 25.41 | 1 | 3 | 9 | — |
| D.R. O'Sullivan | 11 | 21 | 4 | 158 | 23* | 9.29 | — | — | 2 | — |
| J.M. Parker | 36 | 63 | 2 | 1498 | 121 | 24.56 | 3 | 5 | 30 | — |
| N.M. Parker | 3 | 6 | 0 | 89 | 40 | 14.83 | — | — | 2 | — |
| P.J. Petherick | 6 | 11 | 4 | 34 | 13 | 4.85 | — | — | 4 | — |
| J.F. Reid | 1 | 2 | 0 | 19 | 19 | 9.50 | — | — | — | — |
| A.D.G. Roberts | 7 | 12 | 1 | 254 | 84* | 23.09 | — | 1 | 4 | — |
| I.D.S. Smith | 1 | 2 | 0 | 14 | 7 | 7.00 | — | — | — | — |
| G.B. Troup | 8 | 10 | 4 | 31 | 13* | 5.16 | — | — | 2 | — |
| G.M. Turner | 39 | 70 | 6 | 2920 | 259 | 45.62 | 7 | 14 | 40 | — |
| P.N. Webb | 2 | 3 | 0 | 11 | 5 | 3.66 | — | — | 2 | — |
| J.G. Wright | 14 | 26 | 0 | 575 | 88 | 22.11 | — | 3 | 6 | — |

## BOWLING

| | Balls | Runs | Wkts | Avge | Best | 5 wI | 10 wM |
|---|---|---|---|---|---|---|---|
| S.L. Boock | 2107 | 706 | 19 | 37.15 | 5-67 | 1 | — |
| B.P. Bracewell | 838 | 456 | 10 | 45.60 | 3-110 | — | — |
| J.G. Bracewell | 336 | 154 | 2 | 77.00 | 1-22 | — | — |
| M.G. Burgess | 498 | 212 | 6 | 35.33 | 3-23 | — | — |
| B.L. Cairns | 5110 | 2029 | 54 | 37.57 | 6-85 | 3 | — |
| E.J. Chatfield | 1054 | 485 | 8 | 60.62 | 4-100 | — | — |
| J.V. Coney | 873 | 299 | 7 | 42.71 | 3-28 | — | — |
| D.R. Hadlee | 4883 | 2389 | 71 | 33.64 | 4-30 | — | — |
| R.J. Hadlee | 8230 | 3950 | 145 | 27.24 | 7-23 | 10 | 3 |
| G.P. Howarth | 398 | 199 | 3 | 66.33 | 1-13 | — | — |
| W.K. Lees | 5 | 4 | 0 | — | — | — | — |
| J.F.M. Morrison | 24 | 9 | 0 | — | — | — | — |
| D.R. O'Sullivan | 2739 | 1221 | 18 | 67.83 | 5-148 | 1 | — |
| J.M. Parker | 40 | 24 | 1 | 24.00 | 1-24 | — | — |
| P.J. Petherick | 1305 | 685 | 16 | 42.81 | 3-90 | — | — |
| A.D.G. Roberts | 440 | 182 | 4 | 45.50 | 1-12 | — | — |
| G.B. Troup | 1998 | 811 | 24 | 33.79 | 6-95 | 1 | 1 |
| G.M. Turner | 12 | 5 | 0 | — | — | — | — |

# INDIA

## BATTING AND FIELDING

| | M | I | NO | Runs | HS | Avge | 100 | 50 | Ct | St |
|---|---|---|---|---|---|---|---|---|---|---|
| R.M.H. Binny | 8 | 13 | 1 | 161 | 46 | 13.41 | — | — | 6 | — |
| C.P.S. Chauhan | 37 | 63 | 2 | 1945 | 97 | 31.88 | — | 15 | 35 | — |
| D.R. Doshi | 16 | 19 | 4 | 80 | 20 | 5.33 | — | — | 8 | — |
| S.M. Gavaskar | 66 | 120 | 8 | 6092 | 221 | 54.39 | 23 | 26 | 55 | — |
| K.D. Ghavri | 38 | 56 | 14 | 896 | 86 | 21.33 | — | 2 | 16 | — |
| Kapil Dev | 29 | 42 | 4 | 1123 | 126* | 29.55 | 1 | 6 | 12 | — |
| S.M.H. Kirmani | 45 | 68 | 11 | 1563 | 101* | 27.42 | 1 | 6 | 84 | 26 |
| S.M. Patil | 6 | 11 | 1 | 449 | 174 | 44.90 | 1 | 2 | 3 | — |
| B. Reddy | 4 | 5 | 1 | 38 | 21 | 9.50 | — | — | 9 | 2 |
| D.B. Vengsarkar | 39 | 65 | 6 | 2206 | 157* | 37.38 | 5 | 10 | 34 | — |
| G.R. Viswanath | 72 | 127 | 9 | 5216 | 179 | 44.20 | 12 | 30 | 52 | — |
| N.S. Yadav | 13 | 16 | 6 | 158 | 29* | 15.80 | — | — | 3 | — |
| Yashpal Sharma | 19 | 30 | 4 | 851 | 100* | 32.73 | 1 | 5 | 3 | — |

## BOWLING

| | Balls | Runs | Wkts | Avge | Best | 5 wI | 10 wM |
|---|---|---|---|---|---|---|---|
| R.M.H. Binny | 929 | 539 | 12 | 44.91 | 3-53 | — | — |
| C.P.S. Chauhan | 132 | 90 | 1 | 90.00 | 1-11 | — | — |
| D.R. Doshi | 4607 | 1643 | 57 | 28.82 | 6-103 | 2 | — |
| S.M. Gavaskar | 262 | 138 | 1 | 138.00 | 1-34 | — | — |
| K.D. Ghavri | 6982 | 3623 | 108 | 33.54 | 5-33 | 4 | — |
| Kapil Dev | 6236 | 3091 | 117 | 26.41 | 7-56 | 8 | 1 |
| S.M. Patil | 105 | 41 | 2 | 20.50 | 2-28 | — | — |
| D.B. Vengsarkar | 11 | 10 | 0 | — | — | — | — |
| G.R. Viswanath | 70 | 46 | 1 | 46.00 | 1-11 | — | — |
| N.S. Yadav | 2753 | 1285 | 40 | 32.12 | 4.35 | — | — |

# PAKISTAN

## BATTING AND FIELDING

| | M | I | NO | Runs | HS | Avge | 100 | 50 | Ct | St |
|---|---|---|---|---|---|---|---|---|---|---|
| Abdul Qadir | 8 | 12 | 2 | 131 | 29* | 13.10 | — | — | 5 | — |
| Asif Iqbal | 58 | 99 | 7 | 3575 | 175 | 38.85 | 11 | 12 | 36 | — |
| Azhar Khan | 1 | 1 | 0 | 14 | 14 | 14.00 | — | — | — | — |
| Azmat Rana | 1 | 1 | 0 | 49 | 49 | 49.00 | — | — | — | — |
| Ehteshamuddin | 4 | 1 | 0 | 2 | 2 | 2.00 | — | — | 2 | — |
| Ejaz Faqih | 1 | 2 | 0 | 8 | 8 | 4.00 | — | — | — | — |
| Haroon Rashid | 16 | 28 | 1 | 890 | 122 | 32.96 | 2 | 3 | 7 | — |
| Imran Khan | 33 | 54 | 6 | 1183 | 123 | 24.64 | 1 | 2 | 5 | — |
| Iqbal Qasim | 27 | 33 | 10 | 180 | 32 | 7.82 | — | — | 22 | — |
| Javed Miandad | 34 | 58 | 12 | 2663 | 206 | 57.89 | 7 | 15 | 34 | 1 |
| Majid Khan | 57 | 97 | 5 | 3716 | 167 | 40.39 | 8 | 17 | 65 | — |
| Mansoor Akhtar | 2 | 4 | 0 | 36 | 16 | 9.00 | — | — | 2 | — |
| Mohammed Nazir | 8 | 11 | 7 | 89 | 29* | 22.25 | — | — | 2 | — |
| Mudassar Nazar | 19 | 30 | 1 | 888 | 126 | 30.62 | 2 | 4 | 11 | — |
| Sadiq Mohammad | 41 | 74 | 2 | 2579 | 166 | 35.81 | 5 | 10 | 28 | — |
| Sarfraz Nawaz | 39 | 52 | 8 | 708 | 55 | 16.09 | — | 3 | 22 | — |
| Shafiq Ahmed | 6 | 10 | 1 | 99 | 27* | 11.00 | — | — | — | — |
| Sikander Bakht | 20 | 26 | 8 | 115 | 22* | 6.38 | — | — | 6 | — |
| Taslim Arif | 6 | 10 | 2 | 501 | 210* | 62.62 | 1 | 2 | 6 | 3 |
| Tausif Ahmed | 3 | 1 | 0 | 0 | 0 | 0.00 | — | — | — | — |
| Wasim Bari | 58 | 86 | 21 | 1069 | 85 | 16.44 | — | 5 | 137 | 19 |
| Wasim Raja | 37 | 61 | 11 | 2022 | 117* | 40.44 | 2 | 15 | 11 | — |
| Zaheer Abbas | 43 | 76 | 6 | 2719 | 274 | 38.84 | 6 | 9 | 24 | — |

## BOWLING

| | Balls | Runs | Wkts | Avge | Best | 5 wI | 10 wM |
|---|---|---|---|---|---|---|---|
| Abdul Qadir | 1855 | 703 | 22 | 31.95 | 6-44 | 1 | — |
| Asif Iqbal | 3864 | 1502 | 53 | 28.33 | 5-48 | 2 | — |
| Azhar Khan | 18 | 2 | 1 | 2.00 | 1-1 | — | — |
| Ehteshamuddin | 856 | 329 | 15 | 21.93 | 5-47 | 1 | — |
| Ejaz Faqih | 24 | 9 | 0 | | | | |
| Haroon Rashid | 8 | 3 | 0 | | | | |
| Imran Khan | 8313 | 3769 | 128 | 29.44 | 6-63 | 8 | 1 |
| Iqbal Qasim | 6714 | 2509 | 79 | 31.75 | 7-49 | 3 | 2 |
| Javed Miandad | 1308 | 591 | 17 | 34.76 | 3-74 | — | — |
| Majid Khan | 3482 | 1416 | 27 | 52.44 | 4-45 | — | — |
| Mohammed Nazir | 1798 | 635 | 26 | 24.42 | 7-99 | 2 | — |
| Mudassar Nazar | 1085 | 465 | 11 | 42.27 | 3-48 | — | — |
| Sadiq Mohammad | 199 | 98 | 0 | | | | |
| Sarfraz Nawaz | 9651 | 4003 | 124 | 32.28 | 9-86 | 4 | 1 |
| Shafiq Ahmed | 8 | 1 | 0 | | | | |
| Sikander Bakht | 3862 | 1909 | 58 | 32.91 | 8-69 | 3 | 1 |
| Taslim Arif | 30 | 28 | 1 | 28.00 | 1-28 | — | — |
| Tausif Ahmed | 866 | 356 | 12 | 29.66 | 4-64 | — | — |
| Wasim Bari | 8 | 2 | 0 | | | | |
| Wasim Raja | 2242 | 1062 | 31 | 34.25 | 4-68 | — | — |
| Zaheer Abbas | 20 | 2 | 0 | | | | |

# MINOR COUNTIES
## FINAL TABLE

|  | P | W | L | D | NR | Pts | Avge |
|---|---|---|---|---|---|---|---|
| Durham | 10 | 7 | 0 | 2 | 1 | 74 | 7.40 |
| Hertfordshire | 10 | 6 | 1 | 3 | 0 | 70 | 7.00 |
| Somerset II | 8 | 4 | 0 | 2 | 2 | 50 | 6.25 |
| Cheshire | 10 | 4 | 1 | 4 | 1 | 52 | 5.20 |
| Suffolk | 10 | 4 | 2 | 4 | 0 | 50 | 5.00 |
| Oxfordshire | 10 | 3 | 1 | 5 | 1 | 48 | 4.80 |
| Norfolk | 10 | 3 | 2 | 4 | 0 | 46 | 4.60 |
| Devon | 10 | 3 | 1 | 4 | 2 | 40 | 4.00 |
| Berkshire | 10 | 3 | 5 | 2 | 0 | 39 | 3.90 |
| Dorset | 10 | 2 | 3 | 3 | 2 | 39 | 3.90 |
| Shropshire | 10 | 2 | 4 | 2 | 2 | 36 | 3.60 |
| Northumberland | 12 | 3 | 3 | 5 | 1 | 41 | 3.41 |
| Lancashire II | 8 | 2 | 4 | 1 | 1 | 26 | 3.25 |
| Lincolnshire | 10 | 1 | 1 | 7 | 1 | 27 | 2.70 |
| Buckinghamshire | 12 | 1 | 5 | 5 | 1 | 32 | 2.66 |
| Staffordshire | 10 | 1 | 3 | 5 | 1 | 26 | 2.60 |
| Bedfordshire | 10 | 2 | 4 | 3 | 1 | 25 | 2.50 |
| Cornwall | 8 | 1 | 3 | 3 | 1 | 19 | 2.37 |
| Wiltshire | 8 | 1 | 3 | 4 | 0 | 17 | 2.12 |
| Cambridgeshire | 10 | 0 | 4 | 6 | 0 | 12 | 1.20 |
| Cumberland | 8 | 0 | 4 | 2 | 2 | 6 | 0.75 |

# MINOR COUNTIES FIXTURES

**MAY**
| Sun | 24 | Lincolnshire v Cambridgeshire: Sleaford |
| Wed | 27 | Cheshire v Durham: Alderley Edge |
| Sun | 31 | Northumberland v Lincolnshire: Jesmond |

**JUNE**
| Wed | 3 | Staffordshire v Shropshire: Burton-on-Trent (Bass) |
| Mon | 8 | Lancashire II v Cheshire: Heywood |
| Tues | 9 | Hertfordshire v Norfolk: Watford |
| Sun | 14 | Cheshire v Staffordshire: Nantwich |
|  |  | Cumberland v Lincolnshire: Carlisle |
| Mon | 15 | Lancashire II v Northumberland: Lytham |
|  |  | Durham v Shropshire: Sunderland |
| Wed | 17 | Cambridgeshire v Norfolk: Wisbech |
| Sun | 21 | Cumberland v Northumberland: Netherfield |
|  |  | Lincolnshire v Staffordshire: Cleethorpes |
| Wed | 24 | Hertfordshire v Cambridgeshire: Hitchin |
| Sat | 27 | Oxfordshire v Buckinghamshire: Oxford (Christ Church) |
| Sun | 28 | Lincolnshire v Norfolk: Grimsby (Ross) |
|  |  | Shropshire v Cheshire: St. Georges (Telford) |
|  |  | Cumberland v Durham: Penrith |
| Tues | 30 | Staffordshire v Durham: Longton |

## JULY

| | | |
|---|---|---|
| Sat | 4 | Hertfordshire v Bedfordshire: St. Albans (Clarence Park) |
| Sun | 5 | Durham v Northumberland: Durham City |
| | | Staffordshire v Cheshire: Stone |
| | | Bucks v Berkshire: Slough |
| | | Cornwall v Somerset II: Falmouth |
| Wed | 8 | Cambridgeshire v Lincolnshire: Papworth |
| Sun | 12 | Lincolnshire v Northumberland: Stamford (Burghley Park) |
| | | Berkshire v Buckinghamshire: Maidenhead (Boyne Hill) |
| | | Cornwall v Devon: Truro |
| Mon | 13 | Shropshire v Staffordshire: Wellington |
| Sat | 18 | Bedfordshire v Buckinghamshire: Bedford School |
| Sun | 19 | Northumberland v Cumberland: Jesmond |
| | | Cornwall v Berkshire: Penzance |
| Mon | 20 | Wiltshire v Oxfordshire: Devizes |
| | | Cambridgeshire v Suffolk: Fenners |
| Tues | 21 | Devon v Berkshire: Sidmouth |
| Wed | 22 | Wiltshire v Somerset II: Trowbridge |
| Fri | 24 | Oxfordshire v Berkshire: Morris Motors |
| Sat | 25 | Bedfordshire v Cambridgeshire: Bedford (Goldington Bury) |
| Sun | 26 | Cornwall v Dorset: Camborne |
| | | Hertfordshire v Buckinghamshire: Hertfordshire (Balls Park) |
| | | Cheshire v Shropshire: Wallasey |
| Mon | 27 | Staffordshire v Northumberland: Brewood |
| | | Berkshire v Wiltshire: Reading (Ibis C.C.) |
| | | Lancashire II v Cumberland: Lancaster |
| | | Norfolk v Cambridgeshire: Lakenham |
| Tues | 28 | Devon v Dorset: Exmouth |
| Wed | 29 | Cheshire v Northumberland: Bowdon |
| | | Berkshire v Oxfordshire: Reading (Courage C.C.) |
| | | Norfolk v Lincolnshire: Lakenham |
| | | Somerset II v Wiltshire: Keynsham |

## AUG

| | | |
|---|---|---|
| Sat | 1 | Oxfordshire v Dorset: Oxford (St. Edward's) |
| | | Suffolk v Buckinghamshire: Ipswich (G.R.E.) |
| Sun | 2 | Northumberland v Durham: Jesmond |
| | | Berkshire v Cornwall: Hungerford |
| | | Shropshire v Bedfordshire: Shrewsbury (London Rd.) |
| | | Cumberland v Lancashire II: Millom |
| Mon | 3 | Dorset v Somerset II: Weymouth |
| | | Norfolk v Bucks: Lakenham |
| | | Suffolk v Hertfordshire: Ipswich (Ransomes) |
| Tues | 4 | Wiltshire v Cornwall: Salisbury |
| Wed | 5 | Staffordshire v Lincolnshire: Walsall |
| | | Devon v Somerset II: Torquay |
| | | Norfolk v Hertfordshire: Lakenham |
| Thurs | 6 | Dorset v Cornwall: Weymouth |
| | | Wiltshire v Berkshire: Swindon |
| Fri | 7 | Bucks v Oxfordshire: Marlow |
| | | Bedfordshire v Hertfordshire: Henlow |
| | | Norfolk v Suffolk: Lakenham |
| Sun | 9 | Northumberland v Cheshire: Jesmond |
| | | Bucks v Suffolk: Chesham |

| Mon | 10 | Wiltshire v Dorset: Chippenham |
| | | Shropshire v Lancashire II: Bridgnorth |
| | | Oxfordshire v Devon: Abingdon School |
| Tues | 11 | Bedfordshire v Suffolk: Dunstable |
| | | Durham v Cheshire: Chester-le-Street |
| Wed | 12 | Berkshire v Devon: Reading |
| Thurs | 13 | Cambridgeshire v Bedfordshire: March |
| Fri | 14 | Dorset v Devon: Bournemouth |
| | | Oxfordshire v Wiltshire: Shipton-u-Wychwood |
| Sat | 15 | Buckinghamshire v Bedfordshire: Stowe School (Buckingham) |
| | | Hertfordshire v Suffolk: Bishops Stortford |
| Sun | 16 | Lincolnshire v Cumberland: Lincoln |
| Mon | 17 | Durham v Staffordshire: Hartlepool |
| | | Somerset II v Cornwall: Taunton School |
| Tues | 18 | Dorset v Wiltshire: Blandford |
| | | Bedfordshire v Shropshire: Luton (Wardown Park) |
| | | Suffolk v Norfolk: Felixstowe |
| Wed | 19 | Northumberland v Staffordshire: Jesmond |
| | | Cheshire v Lancashire II: Neston |
| | | Devon v Cornwall: Exeter |
| Thurs | 20 | Somerset II v Dorset: Weston (Westlands) |
| | | Suffolk v Cambridgeshire: Bury St. Edmunds |
| Sun | 23 | Buckinghamshire v Norfolk: High Wycombe |
| | | Durham v Cumberland: Stockton-on-Tees |
| | | Cornwall v Wiltshire: Wadebridge |
| Mon | 24 | Northumberland v Lancashire II: Jesmond |
| | | Devon v Oxfordshire: Bovey Tracey |
| Wed | 26 | Dorset v Oxfordshire: Poole Park |
| | | Shropshire v Durham: Newport |
| Thurs | 27 | Cambridgeshire v Hertfordshire: Fenners |
| | | Somerset II v Devon: Taunton |
| Sun | 30 | Buckinghamshire v Hertfordshire: Amersham |
| | | Suffolk v Bedfordshire: Ipswich (Ransomes) |
| Mon | 31 | Lancashire II v Shropshire: Old Trafford |

# Swivel head winner.

# YOUNG CRICKETER OF THE YEAR

At the end of each season the members of the Cricket Writers' Club select by ballot the player they consider the best young cricketer of the season.

C.W.J. Athey (Yorkshire) was elected last year.

The selections to date are:

| | |
|---|---|
| 1950 R. Tattersall (Lancashire) | 1965 A.P.E. Knott (Kent) |
| 1951 P.B.H. May (Surrey) | 1966 D.L. Underwood (Kent) |
| 1952 F.S. Trueman (Yorkshire) | 1967 A.W. Greig (Sussex) |
| 1953 M.C. Cowdrey (Kent) | 1968 R.H.M. Cottam (Hampshire) |
| 1954 P.J. Loader (Surrey) | 1969 A. Ward (Derbyshire) |
| 1955 K.F. Barrington (Surrey) | 1970 C.M. Old (Yorkshire) |
| 1956 B. Taylor (Essex) | 1971 J. Whitehouse (Warwickshire) |
| 1957 M.J. Stewart (Surrey) | 1972 D.R. Owen-Thomas (Surrey) |
| 1958 A.C.D. Ingleby-Mackenzie (Hampshire) | 1973 M. Hendrick (Derbyshire) |
| | 1974 P.H. Edmonds (Middlesex) |
| 1959 G. Pullar (Lancashire) | 1975 A. Kennedy (Lancashire) |
| 1960 D.A. Allen (Gloucestershire) | 1976 G. Miller (Derbyshire) |
| 1961 P.H. Parfitt (Middlesex) | 1977 I.T. Botham (Somerset) |
| 1962 P.J. Sharpe (Yorkshire) | 1978 D.I. Gower (Leicestershire) |
| 1963 G. Boycott (Yorkshire) | 1979 P.W.G. Parker (Sussex) |
| 1964 J.M. Brearley (Middlesex) | 1980 C.W.J. Athey (Yorkshire) |

# SCORING OF POINTS IN THE SCHWEPPES CHAMPIONSHIP

The scheme is as follows:

(a) For a win, 16 points, plus any points scored in the first innings.

(b) In a tie, each side to score 8 points, plus any points scored in the first innings.

(c) If the scores are equal in a drawn match, the side batting in the fourth innings to score 8 points, plus any points scored in the first innings.

(d) First innings points (awarded only for performances in the first 100 overs of each innings and retained whatever the result of the match).

(i) A maximum of 4 batting points to be available as follows: 150 to 199 runs—1 point; 200 to 249 runs—2 points; 250 to 299 runs—3 points; 300 runs or over—4 points.

(ii) A maximum of 4 bowling points to be available as follows: 3-4 wickets taken—1 point; 5-6 wickets taken—2 points; 7-8 wickets taken—3 points; 9-10 wickets taken—4 points.

(e) If play starts when less than eight hours playing time remains and a one innings match is played, no first innings points shall be scored. The side winning on the one innings to score 12 points.

(f) The side which has the highest aggregate of points gained at the end of the season shall be the Champion County. Should any sides in the Schweppes Championship Table be equal on points, the side with most wins will have priority.

# PRINCIPAL FIXTURES 1981

*Including play on Sunday*

**Wednesday 22 April**

Cambridge: Cambridge U v Essex

**Saturday 25 April**

*Cambridge: Cambridge U v Hants
Oxford: Oxford U v Glam

**Wednesday 29 April**

Lord's: MCC v Middx (three days)
Cambridge: Cambridge U v Northants
Oxford: Oxford U v Somerset

**Saturday 2 May**

Cambridge: Cambridge U v Lancs
Oxford: Oxford U v Yorks

**Wednesday 6 May**

Cardiff: Glam v Glos
Southampton: Hants v Somerset
Canterbury: Kent v Notts
Leicester: Leics v Derbys
Lord's: Middx v Essex
Northampton: Northants v Lancs
Edgbaston: Warwicks v Yorks
Worcester: Worcs v Sussex
Cambridge: Cambridge U v Surrey

**Saturday 9 May**

*Benson & Hedges Cup*
Derby: Derbys v Yorks
Swansea: Glam v Essex
Old Trafford: Lancs v Warwicks
Leicester: Leics v Glos
Lord's: Middx v Hants
Northampton: Northants v Notts

**Sunday 10 May**

*John Player League*
Abergavenny: Glam v Worcs
Moreton-in-Marsh: Glos v Leics
Old Trafford: Lancs v Derbys
Lord's: Middx v Hants
Northampton: Northants v Notts
Taunton: Somerset v Essex
Hove: Sussex v Surrey
Edgbaston: Warwicks v Yorks

**Monday 11 May**

*Benson & Hedges Cup*
Canterbury: Kent v Combined U
Hove: Sussex v Surrey

**Wednesday 13 May**

Old Trafford: Lancs v Somerset
Trent Bridge: Notts v Leics
The Oval: Surrey v Derbys
Hove: Sussex v Glam
Nuneaton (Griff & Coton): Warwicks v
  Kent
Headingley: Yorks v Middx
Cambridge: Cambridge U v Worcs
Oxford: Oxford U v Glos
*Benson & Hedges Cup*
Southampton: Hants v Minor Counties

**Saturday 16 May**

Arundel: Lavinia, Duchess of Norfolk's
  XI v Australia (one day)
*Benson & Hedges Cup*
Oxford: Combined U v Glam
Chelmsford: Essex v Somerset
Bristol: Glos v Northants
Bournemouth: Hants v Surrey
Slough: Minor Counties v Middx
Trent Bridge: Notts v Worcs
Glasgow (Titwood): Scotland v Lancs
Edgbaston: Warwicks v Derbys

**Sunday 17 May**

*John Player League*
Bournemouth: Hants v Glam
Milton Keynes: Northants v Glos
Trent Bridge: Notts v Somerset
The Oval: Surrey v Middx
Worcester: Worcs v Sussex
Huddersfield: Yorks v Kent
Edgbaston: Warwicks v Leics

**Tuesday 19 May**

*Benson & Hedges Cup*
Cambridge: Combined U v Somerset
Derby: Derbys v Scotland
Cardiff: Glam v Kent
Lord's: Middx v Sussex
Northampton: Northants v Leics
Edgbaston: Warwicks v Yorks
Worcester: Worcs v Glos

231

### Wednesday 20 May

*Holt Products Trophy*
Southampton: Hants v Australia

### Thursday 21 May

*Benson & Hedges Cup*
Chelmsford: Essex v Combined U
Bristol: Glos v Notts
Old Trafford: Lancs v Derbys
Leicester: Leics v Worcs
Slough: Minor Counties v Sussex
Taunton: Somerset v Kent
The Oval: Surrey v Middx
Bradford: Yorks v Scotland

### Saturday 23 May

Derby: Derbys v Notts
Chelmsford: Essex v Glos
Cardiff: Glam v Kent
Old Trafford: Lancs v Yorks
Lord's: Middx v Sussex
Northampton: Northants v Leics
The Oval: Surrey v Hants
Edgbaston: Warwicks v Worcs
Oxford: Oxford U v Free Foresters
 (three days)
*Holt Products Trophy*
*Taunton: Somerset v Australia

### Sunday 24 May

*John Player League*
Derby: Derbys v Notts
Chelmsford: Essex v Glos
Cardiff: Glam v Kent
Old Trafford: Lancs v Northants
Lord's: Middx v Sussex
Edgbaston: Warwicks v Worcs
Headingley: Yorks v Leics

### Wednesday 27 May

Chelmsford: Essex v Surrey
Bristol: Glos v Sussex
Dartford: Kent v Yorks
Leicester: Leics v Hants
Uxbridge: Middx v Notts
Northampton: Northants v Derbys
Worcester: Worcs v Lancs
Oxford: Oxford U v Warwicks
*Holt Products Trophy*
Swansea: Glam v Australia

### Saturday 30 May

*Benson & Hedges Cup*
Dartford: Kent v Essex
Trent Bridge: Notts v Leics
Glasgow (Titwood): Scotland v Warwicks
Taunton: Somerset v Glam
The Oval: Surrey v Minor Counties
Hove: Sussex v Hants
Worcester: Worcs v Northants
Headingley: Yorks v Lancs
*Holt Products Trophy*
*Bristol: Glos v Australia

### Sunday 31 May

*John Player League*
Chelmsford: Essex v Kent
Basingstoke: Hants v Sussex
Old Trafford: Lancs v Somerset
Northampton: Northants v Leics
The Oval: Surrey v Derbys
Bradford: Yorks v Middx

### Wednesday 3 June

Basingstoke: Hants v Middx
Old Trafford: Lancs v Surrey
Trent Bridge: Notts v Glos
Hove: Sussex v Somerset
Edgbaston: Warwicks v Northants
Hereford: Worcs v Glam
Headingley: Yorks v Essex
Oxford: Oxford U v Leics

### Thursday 4 June

**PRUDENTIAL TROPHY
LORD'S:
ENGLAND v AUSTRALIA
(first one-day international match)**

### Saturday 6 June

**PRUDENTIAL TROPHY
EDGBASTON:
ENGLAND v AUSTRALIA
(second one-day international match)**

Derby: Derbys v Warwicks
Swansea: Glam v Surrey
Bristol: Glos v Yorks
Lord's: Middx v Somerset
Northampton: Northants v Kent
Hove: Sussex v Lancs
Worcester: Worcs v Essex
Cambridge: Cambridge U v Notts
Oxford: Oxford U v MCC (three days)

**Sunday 7 June**

*John Player League*
Swansea: Glam v Surrey
Bristol: Glos v Yorks
Maidstone: Kent v Northants
Lord's: Middx v Somerset
Trent Bridge: Notts v Essex
Hove: Sussex v Lancs

**Monday 8 June**

**PRUDENTIAL TROPHY
HEADINGLEY:
ENGLAND v AUSTRALIA
(third one-day international match)**

**Wednesday 10 June**

Bristol: Glos v Northants
Bournemouth: Hants v Glam
Tunbridge Wells: Kent v Leics
Old Trafford: Lancs v Warwicks
The Oval: Surrey v Worcs
Cambridge: Cambridge U v Sussex
Oxford: Oxford U v Middx
*Holt Products Trophy*
Derby: Derbys v Australia

**Saturday 13 June**

Derby: Derbys v Essex
Tunbridge Wells: Kent v Sussex
Leicester: Leics v Glam
Bath: Somerset v Glos
Stourport: Worcs v Hants
Bradford: Yorks v Notts
Oxford: Combined U v Sri Lanka
*Holt Products Trophy*
*Lord's: Middx v Australia

**Sunday 14 June**

*John Player League*
Derby: Derbys v Hants
Leicester: Leics v Glam
Bath: Somerset v Glos
The Oval: Surrey v Northants
Worcester: Worcs v Essex

**Wednesday 17 June**

Ilford: Essex v Middx
Cardiff: Glam v Warwicks
Northampton: Northants v Sussex
Bath: Somerset v Notts
The Oval: Surrey v Lancs
Sheffield: Yorks v Derbys
Bristol: Glos v Sri Lanka

Leicester: Leics v Cambridge U
Oxford: Oxford U v Kent

**Thursday 18 June**

• **TRENT BRIDGE: ENGLAND v
AUSTRALIA
(First Cornhill Insurance Test match)**

**Saturday 20 June**

Derby: Derbys v Northants
Ilford: Essex v Sussex
Southampton: Hants v Glos
Liverpool: Lancs v Notts
Worcester: Worcs v Somerset
Lord's: Oxford v Cambridge (three days)
Edgbaston: Warwicks v Sri Lanka

**Sunday 21 June**

*John Player League*
Ilford: Essex v Sussex
Portsmouth: Hants v Glos
Old Trafford: Lancs v Notts
Lord's: Middx v Leics
Bath: Somerset v Kent
Edgbaston: Warwicks v Derbys
Worcester: Worcs v Northants
Hull: Yorks v Glam

**Wednesday 24 June**

*Benson & Hedges Cup Quarter-Finals*
County not in B & H Quarter-Final v
   Sri Lanka

**Thursday 25 June**

County not in B & H Quarter-Final v
   Australia (one day)

**Saturday 27 June**

Swansea: Glam v Somerset
Gloucester: Glos v Warwicks
Old Trafford: Lancs v Hants
Leicester: Leics v Essex
Trent Bridge: Notts v Middx
The Oval: Surrey v Northants
Worcester: Worcs v Yorks
Hastings: Sussex v Sri Lanka
*Holt Products Trophy*
*Canterbury: Kent v Australia

**Sunday 28 June**

*John Player League*
Swansea: Glam v Warwicks
Gloucester: Glos v Derbys

235

Old Trafford: Lancs v Hants
Leicester: Leics v Essex
Trent Bridge: Notts v Middx
Hastings: Sussex v Northants
Worcester: Worcs v Yorks

## Wednesday 1 July

Derby: Derbys v Lancs
Chelmsford: Essex v Notts
Swansea: Glam v Hants
Maidstone: Kent v Middx
Northampton: Northants v Glos
Taunton: Somerset v Surrey
Bradford: Yorks v Leics
Worcester: Worcs v Sri Lanka

## Thursday 2 July

**LORD'S: ENGLAND v AUSTRALIA
(Second Cornhill Insurance Test match)**

## Saturday 4 July

Derby: Derbys v Worcester
Bournemouth: Hants v Notts
Maidstone: Kent v Lancs
Leicester: Leics v Somerset
Northampton: Northants v Glam
Hove: Sussex v Glos
Edgbaston: Warwicks v Essex
Harrogate: Yorks v Surrey

## Sunday 5 July

*John Player League*
Derby: Derbys v Worcester
Portsmouth: Hants v Notts
Maidstone: Kent v Lancs
Leicester: Leics v Somerset
Luton: Northants v Glam
Hove: Sussex v Glos
Edgbaston: Warwicks v Essex
Scarborough: Yorks v Surrey

## Wednesday 8 July

*Benson & Hedges Cup Semi-Finals*
Trent Bridge (or Derby): A
representative XI v Sri Lanka
Harrogate: Tilcon Trophy (three days)

## Thursday 9 July

County not in B & H Semi-Final v
Australia (one day)

## Saturday 11 July

Trent Bridge: Notts v Worcs
Taunton: Somerset v Sussex
Oval: Surrey v Warwicks
*Leicester: Leics v Sri Lanka
*Holt Products Trophy*
*Northampton: Northants v Australia
*NatWest Bank Trophy First Round*
Southampton: Hants v Cheshire -
Hitchin: Herts v Essex
Dublin (Clontarf): Ireland v Glos
Canterbury: Kent v Yorks
Old Trafford: Lancs v Durham
Oxford (Christ Church): Oxford v Glam
Bury St. Edmunds: Suffolk v Derbys

## Sunday 12 July

*John Player League*
Canterbury: Kent v Notts
Old Trafford: Lancs v Middx
Taunton: Somerset v Sussex
The Oval: Surrey v Warwicks
Worcester: Worcs v Hants

## Wednesday 15 July

Southend: Essex v Northants
Cardiff: Glam v Yorks
Bristol: Glos v Worcs
Portsmouth: Hants v Derbys
Lord's: Middx v Kent
Hove: Sussex v Surrey
Coventry (Courtaulds): Warwicks v Leics
Old Trafford: Lancs v Sri Lanka

## Thursday 16 July

**HEADINGLEY: ENGLAND v
AUSTRALIA
(Third Cornhill Insurance Test match)**

## Saturday 18 July

Southend: Essex v Lancs
Bristol: Glos v Glam
Portsmouth: Hampshire v Surrey
Leicester: Leics v Kent
Lord's: Middx v Worcs
Worksop: Notts v Yorks
Taunton: Somerset v Derbys
Hove: Sussex v Warwicks
*Northampton: Northants v Sri Lanka

**Sunday 19 July**

*John Player League*
Southend: Essex v Lancs
Bristol: Glos v Glam
Southampton: Hants v Surrey
Leicester: Leics v Kent
Lord's: Middx v Worcs
Trent Bridge: Notts v Yorks
Taunton: Somerset v Derbys
Horsham: Sussex v Warwicks

**Wednesday 22 July**

*NatWest Bank Trophy Second Round*
Chester-le-Street or Old Trafford: Durham or Lancs v Middx
Cardiff or Oxford (Christ Church): Glam or Oxford v Cheshire or Hants
Bristol or Belfast (Ormeau): Glos or Ireland v Essex or Herts
Canterbury or Headingley: Kent or Yorks v Notts
Northampton: Northants v Somerset
The Oval: Surrey v Leics
Edgbaston: Warwicks v Sussex
Worcester: Worcs v Derbys or Suffolk
*Other match*
Canterbury or Sheffield: Kent or Yorks v Sri Lanka, whichever county not in NWBT second round; two day match only if either county in B & H Final

**Thursday 23 July**

Glasgow (Titwood): Scotland v Australia (one day)

**Saturday 25 July**

**LORD'S: BENSON & HEDGES CUP FINAL**
Derby: Derbys v Kent (or 9, 10, 11 Sept. if either County in B&H Final)
Trent Bridge: Notts v Lancs (or 12, 13, 14 Aug. if either County in B&H Final)
The Oval (or Taunton): Surrey (or Somerset if Surrey in B&H Final) v Sri Lanka
*Dublin (Clontarf): Ireland v Scotland (three days)
*Holt Products Trophy*
*Worcester: Worcs (provided not in B&H Final) v Australia

**Sunday 26 July**

*John Player League*
Derby: Derbys v Kent
Chelmsford: Essex v Yorks
Ebbw Vale: Glam v Sussex
Leicester: Leics v Notts
Tring: Northants v Middx
The Oval: Surrey v Lancs
Edgbaston: Warwicks v Hants

**Wednesday 29 July**

Derby: Derbys v Gloucs
Canterbury: Kent v Essex
Southport: Lancs v Middx
Hinckley: Leics v Notts
Taunton: Somerset v Glam
Guildford: Surrey v Sussex
Stourbridge: Worcs v Northants
Scarborough: Yorks v Warwicks
Bournemouth: Hants v Sri Lanka

**Thursday 30 July**

*EDGBASTON: ENGLAND v AUSTRALIA
(Fourth Cornhill Insurance Test match)

**Saturday 1 August**

Chelmsford: Essex v Derbys
Canterbury: Kent v Hants
Old Trafford: Lancs v Worcs
Leicester: Leics v Sussex
Lord's: Middx v Glos
Northampton: Northants v Warwicks
Trent Bridge: Notts v Surrey
Sheffield: Yorks v Somerset
*Cardiff: Glam v Sri Lanka

**Sunday 2 August**

*John Player League*
Chelmsford: Essex v Derbys
Canterbury: Kent v Hants
Old Trafford: Lancs v Worcs
Leicester: Leics v Sussex
Lord's: Middx v Glos
Northampton: Northants v Warwicks
Trent Bridge: Notts v Surrey
Scarborough: Yorks v Somerset

**Tuesday 4 August**

Reading: Minor Counties v Sri Lanka

237

**Wednesday 5 August**

*NatWest Bank Trophy Quarter-finals*
Scotland v MCC (three days)

**Thursday 6 August**

County not in NWBT Quarter-finals v
    Australia (one day)

**Saturday 8 August**

Derby: Derbys v Leics
Cardiff: Glam v Lancs
Cheltenham: Glos v Surrey
Lord's: Middx v Warwicks
Weston-s-Mare: Somerset v Northants
Eastbourne: Sussex v Kent
Worcester: Worcs v Notts
Middlesbrough: Yorks v Hants
*Holt Products Trophy*
*Chelmsford: Essex v Australia

**Sunday 9 August**

*John Player League*
Derby: Derbys v Leics
Cardiff: Glam v Lancs
Cheltenham: Glos v Surrey
Lord's: Middx v Warwicks
Weston-s-Mare: Somerset v Northants
Eastbourne: Sussex v Kent
Worcester: Worcs v Notts
Middlesbrough: Yorks v Hants

**Wednesday 12 August**

Chelmsford: Essex v Kent
Cheltenham: Glos v Hants
Northampton: Northants v Middx
Trent Bridge: Notts v Lancs (if not played
    on 25, 27, 28 July)
Weston-s-Mare: Somerset v Worcs
The Oval: Surrey v Leics
Eastbourne: Sussex v Derbys
Edgbaston: Warwicks v Glam

**Thursday 13 August**

*OLD TRAFFORD: ENGLAND v
AUSTRALIA
(Fifth Cornhill Insurance Test match)

**Saturday 15 August**

Swansea: Glam v Derbys
Cheltenham: Glos v Kent
Southampton: Hants v Essex
Leicester: Leics v Worcs

Wellingborough: Northants v Yorks
Trent Bridge: Notts v Sussex
The Oval: Surrey v Middx
Edgbaston: Warwicks v Lancs

**Sunday 16 August**

Pontardulais: Wales v Ireland (three days)
Warwickshire Under-25 Competition
    Semi-finals (one day)
*John Player League*
Swansea: Glam v Derbys
Cheltenham: Glos v Kent
Southampton: Hants v Essex
Leicester: Leics v Worcs
Wellingborough: Northants v Yorks
Trent Bridge: Notts v Sussex
The Oval: Surrey v Somerset
Edgbaston: Warwicks v Lancs

**Wednesday 19 August**

*NatWest Bank Trophy Semi-finals*

**Thursday 20 August**

County not in NWBT Semi-finals v
    Australia (one day)

**Saturday 22 August**

Derby: Derbys v Yorks
Folkestone: Kent v Surrey
Old Trafford: Lancs v Leics
Lord's: Middx v Glam
Northampton: Northants v Essex
Taunton: Somerset v Hants
Edgbaston: Warwicks v Notts
Worcester: Worcs v Glos
*Holt Products Trophy*
*Hove: Sussex v Australia

**Sunday 23 August**

*John Player League*
Derby: Derbys v Yorks
Folkestone: Kent v Surrey
Old Trafford: Lancs v Leics
Lord's: Middx v Glam
Northampton: Northants v Essex
Taunton: Somerset v Hants
Edgbaston: Warwicks v Notts
Worcester: Worcs v Glos
Warwickshire Under-25 Competition
    Semi-finals (one day)

**Wednesday 26 August**

Colchester: Essex v Leics
Swansea: Glam v Worcs
Bournemouth: Hants v Sussex
Folkestone: Kent v Somerset
Blackpool: Lancs v Derbys
Lord's: Middx v Yorks
Cleethorpes: Notts v Northants

**Thursday 27 August**

**THE OVAL: ENGLAND v
AUSTRALIA
(Sixth Cornhill Insurance Test match)**

**Saturday 29 August**

Colchester: Essex v Glam
Bristol: Glos v Somerset
Bournemouth: Hants v Kent
Leicester: Leics v Northants
Trent Bridge: Notts v Derbys
Hove: Sussex v Middx
Worcester: Worcs v Warwicks
Headingley: Yorks v Lancs

**Sunday 30 August**

*John Player League*
Derby: Derbys v Northants
Colchester: Essex v Glam
Bristol: Glos v Warwicks
Canterbury: Kent v Middx
Leicester: Leics v Surrey
Worcester: Worcs v Somerset
Headingley: Yorks v Lancs
Edgbaston: Warwickshire Under-25
  Competition Final (one day)

**Wednesday 2 September**

Leicester: Leics v Middx
The Oval: Surrey v Kent
Hove: Sussex v Hants
Edgbaston: Warwicks v Somerset
Scarborough: Fenner Trophy KO
  Competition (three days)

**Saturday 5 September**

**LORD'S: NATWEST BANK TROPHY
  FINAL**

**Sunday 6 September**

*John Player League*
Chelmsford: Essex v Middx
Cardiff: Glam v Somerset

Bournemouth: Hants v Leics
Canterbury: Kent v Warwicks
Trent Bridge: Notts v Glos
The Oval: Surrey v Worcs
Hove: Sussex v Derbys

**Wednesday 9 September**

Derby: Derbys v Kent (if not played on
  25, 27, 28 July)
Cardiff: Glam v Leics
Old Trafford: Lancs v Glos
Lord's or Uxbridge: Middx v Surrey
Taunton: Somerset v Essex
Edgbaston: Warwicks v Hants
Scarborough: Yorks v Northants

**Saturday 12 September**

Derby: Derbys v Middx
Bristol: Glos v Leics
Southampton: Hants v Northants
Canterbury: Kent v Worcs
Trent Bridge: Notts v Glam
Taunton: Somerset v Warwicks
The Oval: Surrey v Essex
Hove: Sussex v Yorks

**Sunday 13 September**

*John Player League*
Derby: Derbys v Middx
Bristol: Glos v Lancs
Southampton: Hants v Northants
Canterbury: Kent v Worcs
Trent Bridge: Notts v Glam
Taunton: Somerset v Warwicks
The Oval: Surrey v Essex
Hove: Sussex v Yorks

## PROPOSED FUTURE CRICKET TOURS

**TO ENGLAND**
1982 India and Pakistan
1983 World Cup and New Zealand
1984 West Indies

**ENGLAND TOURS OVERSEAS**
1981-82 India
1982-83 Australia
1983-84 Pakistan and New Zealand

### OTHER TOURS

1981-82 Pakistan to Australia
West Indies to Australia
Australia to New Zealand
New Zealand to West Indies
1982-83 India to Pakistan
Pakistan to New Zealand and West Indies
1983-84 Australia to West Indies

ISBN 0362 02030 2

© 1981 Queen Anne Press

Published in 1981 by
Queen Anne Press
Macdonald Futura Publishers
Paulton House, 8 Shepherdess Walk,
London N1

Typeset by SIOS Limited, London
Printed and bound in Great Britain
by Richard Clay (The Chaucer Press),
Bungay and London